College Basketball Prospectus 2012-13

THE ESSENTIAL GUIDE TO THE MEN'S COLLEGE BASKETBALL SEASON
Featuring Tempo-Free Analysis of all D-I Teams

Joey Berlin • Drew Cannon • John Ezekowitz
Asher Fusco • Matt Giles • Jeff Haley
Dan Hanner • C.J. Moore • Jeff Nusser
Kevin Pelton • Ken Pomeroy • Mike Portscheller
Craig Powers • Josh Reed • Nic Reiner
Eddie Roach • Corey Schmidt • John Templon

Foreword by John Calipari
Edited by John Gasaway

Copyright 2012 Prospectus Entertainment Ventures LLC
ISBN 1480284394
All rights reserved
Without limiting the rights under copyright reserved above, no part of this publication may be reproduced, stored in or introduced into a retrieval system, or transmitted, in any form, or by any means (electronic, mechanical, photocopying, recording, or otherwise), without the prior written permission of both the copyright owner and the above publisher of this book.

Cover by Amanda Bonner
Layout by Bryan Davidson
and Jon Franke

FOREWORD 5
JOHN CALIPARI

INTRODUCTION 7
JOHN GASAWAY

TERMS USED IN THIS BOOK 9

Thoughts for a New Season

LINEUP-DERIVED TEAM PROJECTIONS 13
DAN HANNER

EVALUATING NBA DRAFTS BEFORE THEY HAPPEN 33
KEVIN PELTON

TRANSFERRING UP OR DOWN 39
JOHN TEMPLON

THE NEW POWER STRUCTURE 43
DREW CANNON

BREAKING DOWN THE SOPHOMORE BREAKOUT 45
JOSH REED

THE RPI IS NOT DYING FAST ENOUGH 47
JOHN GASAWAY

Previewing the Conferences

THE MAJORS

ACC 57
DREW CANNON

BIG 12 83
C.J. MOORE

BIG EAST 107
JOHN GASAWAY

BIG TEN 143
MIKE PORTSCHELLER AND JOSH REED

PAC-12 175
KEVIN PELTON

SEC 207
JOHN EZEKOWITZ

THE "HIGH-MIDS"

ATLANTIC 10 241
MATT GILES

CAA 255
CRAIG POWERS

CONFERENCE USA 265
JOEY BERLIN

HORIZON 275
JEFF HALEY

MISSOURI VALLEY 283
MATT GILES

MOUNTAIN WEST 293
JEFF NUSSER

WAC 303
ASHER FUSCO

WEST COAST 313
NIC REINER

THE MID-MAJORS

America East 323
Matt Giles

Atlantic Sun 331
Craig Powers

Big Sky 339
Ken Pomeroy

Big South 347
Mike Portscheller

Big West 355
Eddie Roach

Great West 363
John Gasaway

Independents 367
John Templon

Ivy 369
John Ezekowitz

MAAC 377
John Templon

MAC 385
Jeff Haley

MEAC 393
Craig Powers

Northeast 403
John Templon

Ohio Valley 411
Corey Schmidt

Patriot 419
Asher Fusco

Southern 427
Joey Berlin

Southland 435
Nic Reiner

Summit 441
Corey Schmidt

Sun Belt 447
Nic Reiner

SWAC 455
Jeff Haley

AUTHOR BIOS 463

Foreword

One of the things we talk about when we look back at what we accomplished this past season—and I haven't spent a whole lot of time looking back because I'm always looking forward—is how we did it by putting our players first. We were the best team in the country because we played to our strengths, everyone played for each other, and everyone sacrificed for the good of the team.

When the No. 1 draft pick in the NBA (Anthony Davis) takes the fourth-most shots on your team, leads the nation in blocked shots, and is a great rebounder, you have a chance to win the whole thing. When the No. 2 pick in the draft (Michael Kidd-Gilchrist) takes the fifth-most shots on your team, absolutely plays with the highest motor, and guarded three different positions, you really have a chance to win. Lastly, when your senior captain who started the year before, was the MVP of the Southeastern Conference Tournament, and led his team to the Final Four accepts that it's the best thing for our team to be the sixth starter, you start having a good feeling that we may win this whole thing.

We had two players return in Terrence Jones and Doron Lamb who could have easily put their names in the draft, yet they blended with the team. We had a point guard in Marquis Teague who grew all year and learned from day one until the last day of the year. Our seventh man, Kyle Wiltjer, could have started on 95 percent of the teams in the country, yet he accepted 15 minutes a game knowing it was what was best for our team.

At the end of the day, the term we used was shared sacrifice. Everyone gave up a little of their game so that our team could move forward. We had seven different players lead us in scoring. We were one of the most efficient teams on offense, on defense, and after timeouts. What I'm saying is that while we were very talented, we were a special group that truly became their brother's keeper. Each individual sacrificed something for the betterment of the team.

As I look forward to this year's team, I must put last year's team out of my mind. We are not defending the national title. That's already in the trophy case. We are trying to become the best team that we can be this year. Our goal will be as it is every year: Let's get better day to day, week to week, and month to month, and at the end of the year we want to be the team that's fresh, mentally and physically, and having a ball playing basketball together.

How we will get there with this team, I don't really know at this point. The staples of our program—playing fast, playing great team defense, being a great rebounding and shot-blocking team, being an attacking team on offense and running the Dribble Drive Motion Offense—will remain the same, yet how we get into those things changes each year. Who will play in what spot—wings or trailers, guards or forwards—we don't know yet. Who can guard what positions, we don't know yet. It's been this way for the last four to five years in that we've had a brand new team every year.

I'm excited about our team and our young talent, yet I'm guarded against thinking just because you're wearing a Kentucky uniform you're going to win. You win because you're a better team who has better players. You must be both.

Everyone knows that Kentucky is a players-first program. If we continue to care about our players, if we continue to put them first, if we continue to make every decision with them in mind, they will continue to drag us where we want to go. At the end of the day, as they reach their dreams, they help us reach our dreams.

I've stated many times that my dream is to coach a team that goes 40-0. My other dream would be to have six first-round draft picks. We had five in 2010 and we had six draft picks overall—four in the first round—last year. People say it can't be done and I say why not. Let's have a ball and go for it.

John Calipari
University of Kentucky Head Coach

Introduction

Former North Carolina head coach Dean Smith formulated the precepts of reliable basketball analysis more than 50 years ago, but the dispersion of that information has charted an exceptionally strange course. Usually things that are clearly superior to the alternative are adopted immediately. But, for whatever reason, I for one had no idea Smith's vein of basketball analysis existed until 2004 (by which time Dean Oliver and Ken Pomeroy, among others, were already all over it). It would be like learning smart phones and HDTVs have been available since the Eisenhower administration.

The good news is reliable basketball information has crossed a few frontiers in the eight years since I first encountered it. Such information is now acknowledged and passed along by most national content providers, it informs the comments uttered by a growing number of analysts on telecasts, and, at the risk of highlighting the obvious, you're reading the introduction to a fifth annual preview book saturated with this stuff.

But there's still work to be done. Just last season an esteemed national writer snuck into the Museum of Hoops Antiquities after hours to borrow the desiccated fossil known as rebound margin. When he was promptly and roundly abused on Twitter, he responded with more justice than irritation that if rebound percentages were really so very useful we'd be able to find the damn things in box scores.

That's an excellent point. I think the continuing sub rosa tinge attached to Smith's handiwork is fueled by two allied misunderstandings. Reliable basketball information's misperceived as an esoteric retrofitting of stats that are misperceived to be basically satisfactory and more easily created.

In fact in many of its most illuminating manifestations there's nothing at all esoteric about this stuff. It can be just as easy to create as what everyone's using now, and anyway what everyone's using now can on occasion look us straight in the eye and lie to us. The same math that brings field goal percentages to our box scores can also give us rebound percentages. The issue's not simplicity. (Division is simple.) The issue is habit, and this book comprises an annual 400-some-page attempt to nudge habits along.

Previewing every Division I team in said book with some degree of insight requires a substantial amount of work. To get all that work done we've called upon no fewer than 20 contributors. Every year the best thing about editing this book is being the first reader to see what some of the nation's sharpest hoops minds have come up with. I'm yet to be disappointed.

Speaking of sharp hoops minds, John Calipari thrilled us all when he agreed to contribute this year's Foreword. We can be here a long time arguing about who's the game's "best" coach, but at a minimum it's true that no other coach has been to the last seven Sweet 16s, a remarkable run capped off, of course, by the 2012 national championship. For years Coach Cal's been a one-man refutation of the lazy conventional wisdom that says top players don't play defense "anymore." We like that kind of iconoclasm at Prospectus, and we're honored to have the coach along with us for the ride this year.

John Wooden once said basketball's not a complicated game, "but we coaches complicate it." I hope this book clears up any needless confusion and brings some clarity to the game that, apparently, you love as much as we do.

Enjoy.

John Gasaway
November 2012

Terms Used in this Book

Here it is 2012 and what we said in our first College Basketball Prospectus four years ago is still true today: The language we use is a little different than what you'll see in any other preview. If you're a regular visitor to the site, you should be familiar with this language. If not, don't fret. Here's what you need to know.

We judge a team's offense and defense in terms of their **points scored or allowed per possession**. In this way, we remove the corrupting influence of a team's pace from our judgment of their skills. We'll call these stats **offensive and defensive efficiency** from time to time. We tend to focus on how these measures look during regular-season conference games only in order to get the best estimate of how a team stacks up to its conference brethren in a setting that equalizes home and road games.

Occasionally, though, we'll refer to **adjusted efficiencies** which includes all games played and accounts for schedule strength, among other things, to provide an estimate of how a team stacks up nationally.

We're also big believers in Dean Oliver's Four Factors. For the uninitiated, nearly all of a team's offensive and defensive efficiency can be explained by its performance in four areas: Shooting, rebounding, turnovers, and free throws.

For shooting, we use **effective field goal percentage** (typically shortened to **eFG**) in lieu of traditional field goal percentage. The version we use gives 50 percent more credit for a made three-pointer, just like the scoreboard does. Thus, a player going 4-for-10 from the field while making all of his shots from beyond the arc would have an eFG of 60 percent. His two-point making counterpart would have an eFG of just 40 percent.

In the rebounding department, we also use a percentage. In this case, the number of rebounding opportunities is the divisor. When we talk about a **defensive rebounding percentage**, we mean the percentage of rebounds a defense grabbed among those available. The same principle applies for **offensive rebounding percentage**.

With ball security, we use **turnover percentage**. (Sensing a theme here?) This is just the percentage of possessions where a team commits or forces a turnover.

Finally, for free throws we'll refer to something called **free throw rate** which is just free throw attempts divided by field goal attempts.

We use similar measures to define a player's ability. Additional terms on the personal level you should acquaint yourself with are **offensive rating**, which is just the player version of offensive efficiency, and **usage** or **possessions used**, which described how often a player did something statistically on the offensive end. This helps us distinguish the go-to guy from the screen-setter.

Thoughts For a New Season

Lineup-Derived Team Projections

BY DAN HANNER

The College Basketball Prospectus book has always used player-level data to project team performance. But ever since I joined the book's writing team in 2009-10, I've hoped we would be able to develop a comprehensive model that made lineup-based team projections.

Unfortunately, in 2009 no one had taken the time to code multiple years of tempo-free player stats for every Division I team. Other key pieces of information such as the head coach, recruiting rankings, and data on transfers was not typically merged to player data either. But over the last few years I've pulled this data together, and combined with the insights of numerous other basketball analysts, this has allowed me to model the college basketball season from the ground up. Today, in my fourth contribution to this publication, comprehensive history-based lineup-derived team predictions are here.

The NBA may have its PER ratings, but college basketball has always preferred a few more descriptive statistics for its players. While offensive rating (ORtg) may measure a players points scored per 100 possessions, it is only useful when you know the context of how often that player shoots. And thus each player's percentage of possessions used is critical. But neither value matters if the player doesn't see the floor, and thus percentage of minutes is also vital. Other factors matter, but for the most part these three simple numbers form the basis for the team level predictions. If your team is ranked somewhere you did not expect, this player data is where to start.

Looking at the player data, a few results have struck me as counter-intuitive, but here's the logic behind them:

HOW CAN ALEX ORIAKHI'S EFFICIENCY PREDICTION BE SO HIGH?

After all, his ORtg was only 98.2 at Connecticut last year. What's going on here? Part of this is an adjustment based on the quality of his new Missouri teammates, Frank Haith's success at developing offensive players, and Oriakhi's high upside as a former elite recruit. But the point I want to emphasize is that college basketball has a small sample-size problem. When we predict the season, we often look back at only one year's past data. But my model uses all past seasons of player data. Oriakhi was dominant two years ago, and that's a strong predictor of a bounce-back season in 2013. Wild swings in ORtg are even more common for players who rely on their three-point shooting. If you see a player who seems to have a surprisingly high or low efficiency rating, look back more than one season and you may find the explanation.

WHY ARE THERE SUCH HIGH ORTGS FOR KENTUCKY'S FRESHMEN?

UK is in a bit of a good situation because most of the players in its lineup project to be aggressive shooters. But since everyone can't use 24 percent of the possessions, we expect that, on average, John Calipari's freshmen should have higher efficiency and lower aggressiveness than is typical for elite prospects. And if the Wildcats' freshmen do shoot more, the efficiency of other players (like Kyle Wiltjer) should go up further, meaning the team-level evaluation stays the same. Kentucky lost an immense amount of production this off-season, but when you keep adding super-elite talent under a super-elite coach, the expectations are always high.

HOW CAN KYLE WILTJER'S PLAYING TIME PROJECTION BE SO LOW?

One thing my model tries to account for is unexpected playing time deviations. Wiltjer was a top-20 recruit and a very effective scorer last year. And yet he saw the court less than 30 percent of the time. Yes, Kentucky had a national championship-caliber lineup, but the Wildcats only played a six-player rotation for much of the year. With Wiltjer unable to earn playing time as the seventh man in the rotation, the model has a significant flag for his defense. Perhaps Calipari will always be a little concerned that Wiltjer doesn't have the strength to defend the post or the quickness to defend the perimeter. Or maybe last year was a fluke. But the model sees some information in Wiltjer's lack of playing time last year.

WHY ISN'T RICARDO GATHERS PROJECTED TO PLAY MORE MINUTES AT BAYLOR?

Related: DeAndre Daniels was inefficient (and basically invisible) last season for Connecticut, so why is he projected to get so much more playing time? Coincidentally both of these guys rated out as the No. 32 recruit in the nation in their respective years, and freshman recruits outside the top 20 are not sure things. In fact for such freshmen logging around 50 percent of the available minutes is typical. But many of these same players do indeed develop into stars later in their careers. Which brings me back to Daniels, who is now a sophomore. Our memory of him as a non-factor last season taints our perception, because the reality is that a former highly-ranked recruit is a solid candidate for a breakout season. As for Gathers, he's joining a deep Baylor team where playing time may be at more of a premium.

At the team level, most of the counter-intuitive results are due to the defensive projections. Given how little predictive power the defensive statistics have, I believe incorporating coach-level defensive effects is important. But I will readily admit the defensive model is not perfect. Michigan is almost certainly too low in my prediction, but I have yet to devise a way to use historic data to generate a higher ranking for the Wolverines. John Beilein has never had a top-25 defense, and a team of newcomers is not the situation where a coach typically has his best defensive season. All the experts say this is the most athletic team Beilein has ever had in Ann Arbor, so I am willing to believe Michigan's defense will be better than what is projected here. But I have yet to come up with a way to project that using data.

Despite these nuances, most of the rankings are intuitive and easy to follow if you have reviewed last year's tempo-free stats. What follows are predictions for the 2012-13 season.

TEAM TEMPO-FREE PREDICTIONS

Rank	Team	Conf	Pred CW	Pred CL	Last Off	Last Def	Pred Off	Pred Def	Pred Pyth
1	Indiana	B10	14	4	120.6	95.3	124.9	93.8	0.949
2	Kentucky	SEC	15	3	122.9	88.2	119.8	90.8	0.945
3	UCLA	P12	15	3	107.3	93	119.5	91.2	0.941
4	Kansas	B12	13	5	114.2	86	110.7	86.2	0.928
5	Michigan St.	B10	13	5	115.2	85.8	113.9	89.1	0.926
6	Florida	SEC	14	4	121.1	95.9	120.0	94.0	0.924
7	Duke	ACC	14	4	116.1	95.8	116.9	91.6	0.924
8	Ohio St.	B10	13	5	117.4	85.2	111.4	87.6	0.921
9	Arizona	P12	14	4	106.8	93.8	117.2	92.6	0.918
10	Louisville	BE	13	5	105	84	105.2	83.2	0.917
11	Syracuse	BE	13	5	118.1	90.3	116.7	92.5	0.916
12	NC State	ACC	13	5	111	95.4	116.9	94.3	0.900
13	Gonzaga	WCC	14	2	111.7	92.9	115.3	93.7	0.894
14	UNLV	MWC	12	4	107.4	92.9	111.4	90.6	0.893
15	New Mexico	MWC	11	5	111	89.7	112.6	91.7	0.892
16	Missouri	SEC	12	6	125.4	98.4	119.6	97.7	0.888
17	Tennessee	SEC	12	6	104.8	93.3	111.8	91.4	0.887
18	Memphis	CUSA	14	2	113.2	88.7	113.1	92.6	0.886
19	Pittsburgh	BE	11	7	112.5	100.3	117.4	96.1	0.886
20	Texas	B12	11	7	111.4	94.1	112.5	92.2	0.886
21	Marquette	BE	11	7	110.9	89.2	111.4	91.5	0.883
22	Notre Dame	BE	11	7	109.7	95	113.1	93.2	0.879
23	Minnesota	B10	11	7	107.9	94.4	111.9	92.6	0.875
24	Creighton	MVC	15	3	118.5	101.8	117.8	97.6	0.873
25	Baylor	B12	11	7	116.2	93.4	115.1	95.4	0.873
26	North Carolina	ACC	12	6	114.7	88.6	110.1	91.5	0.870
27	Georgetown	BE	11	7	110.7	87.8	109.4	90.9	0.869
28	Alabama	SEC	11	7	104.4	87.9	108.0	89.9	0.868
29	Kansas St.	B12	11	7	109	91.1	108.6	90.4	0.868
30	Iowa St.	B12	11	7	112.9	94.9	113.5	94.5	0.867
31	Stanford	P12	11	7	106.6	90.6	111.4	92.8	0.867
32	St. Louis	A10	12	4	110.8	88.3	107.2	89.3	0.866
33	Wisconsin	B10	10	8	114.3	87.1	104.1	86.8	0.865
34	Miami FL	ACC	12	6	109.9	96.1	113.6	94.7	0.865
35	Arkansas	SEC	11	7	104.6	101.3	116.1	97.1	0.862
36	Butler	A10	12	4	98	92.5	109.5	91.7	0.860
37	Saint Joseph's	A10	12	4	109.2	98	113.9	95.5	0.859

Lineup-Derived Team Projections

Rank	Team	Conf	Pred CW	Pred CL	Last Off	Last Def	Pred Off	Pred Def	Pred Pyth
38	Florida St.	ACC	11	7	107	89.3	110.3	92.6	0.857
39	Temple	A10	12	4	112	97.4	111.6	94.1	0.852
40	California	P12	11	7	109.6	92.1	110.7	93.7	0.848
41	San Diego St.	MWC	10	6	105.4	94.7	109.5	92.9	0.844
42	Ohio	MAC	14	2	105.2	93.7	108.2	92.2	0.838
43	Rutgers	BE	10	8	100.8	95.7	109.9	93.9	0.835
44	Michigan	B10	9	9	113	95.1	110.7	94.5	0.834
45	USC	P12	10	8	87.6	94.4	105.6	90.3	0.832
46	Northern Iowa	MVC	14	4	105	96.5	112.3	96.1	0.831
47	Oklahoma St.	B12	9	9	105.9	98.1	109.2	93.9	0.825
48	VCU	A10	11	5	105.3	91.2	106.3	91.7	0.819
49	Murray St.	OVC	14	2	105.7	91.8	107.8	93.2	0.817
50	St. Mary's	WCC	12	4	112.2	97.2	113.2	98.1	0.814
51	Davidson	SC	16	2	110.4	98.9	112.5	97.4	0.814
52	Cincinnati	BE	9	9	109.6	91.8	106.1	92.0	0.812
53	Oklahoma	B12	9	9	103.1	97.2	112.2	97.3	0.812
54	Illinois	B10	9	9	103.3	93.3	108.7	94.4	0.810
55	West Virginia	B12	9	9	109.8	96.5	107.1	93.3	0.805
56	Mississippi	SEC	9	9	104.1	95.7	109.5	95.9	0.796
57	Akron	MAC	13	3	106.5	97.1	108.4	95.2	0.792
58	Wyoming	MWC	8	8	99.2	92.5	101.3	89.1	0.790
59	Villanova	BE	8	10	107.8	98.4	106.9	94.2	0.784
60	BYU	WCC	12	4	104.1	91.7	104.8	92.4	0.783
61	Robert Morris	NEC	15	3	104.2	99.7	109.8	97.0	0.781
62	Bucknell	Pat	12	2	105.4	97.5	110.5	97.8	0.779
63	Virginia	ACC	9	9	102.9	87.7	103.5	91.8	0.774
64	Drexel	CAA	14	4	109.7	95.1	105.9	94.0	0.774
65	Iowa	B10	7	11	110.9	101.9	110.8	98.6	0.766
66	Colorado	P12	9	9	103	93.2	106.1	94.6	0.764
67	Washington	P12	8	10	108.4	95.2	106.8	95.6	0.756
68	Virginia Tech	ACC	9	9	105.3	97.1	107.4	96.3	0.755
69	Seton Hall	BE	7	11	104.8	92.8	102.8	92.2	0.751
70	Colorado St.	MWC	7	9	109.3	101.5	110.3	99.1	0.748
71	South Florida	BE	7	11	101.7	88.9	103.8	93.4	0.748
72	LSU	SEC	8	10	99.6	92.8	103.9	93.4	0.748
73	Purdue	B10	7	11	116.7	97.1	103.3	93.1	0.744
74	Belmont	OVC	13	3	116.3	97	110.0	99.6	0.734
75	Massachusetts	A10	9	7	105.4	95.3	106.2	96.2	0.734
76	St. John's	BE	7	11	102.3	101.3	107.2	97.1	0.734
77	South Dakota St.	Sum	13	3	111.4	98.9	112.9	102.2	0.734

Lineup-Derived Team Projections

Rank	Team	Conf	Pred CW	Pred CL	Last Off	Last Def	Pred Off	Pred Def	Pred Pyth
78	Boise St.	MWC	7	9	102.7	102.5	110.7	100.6	0.728
79	Lehigh	Pat	12	2	106.2	97.2	108.5	98.7	0.724
80	College of Charleston	SC	15	3	99.7	99.8	105.1	95.9	0.719
81	Washington St.	P12	7	11	108.6	99.8	108.1	98.7	0.718
82	Central Florida	CUSA	10	6	104.4	98.4	107.2	98.0	0.715
83	Oregon St.	P12	7	11	109.6	100.7	108.4	99.1	0.715
84	Manhattan	MAAC	14	4	101.6	97.2	105.8	96.9	0.713
85	South Carolina	SEC	8	10	101.6	101	105.8	96.8	0.712
86	Fresno St.	MWC	7	9	98.9	101.3	107.5	98.4	0.712
87	Detroit	Horz	12	4	106.1	101	109.9	100.6	0.712
88	Penn St.	B10	6	12	100.8	97.3	104.1	95.3	0.711
89	Vermont	AE	14	2	102.9	97.6	104.0	95.3	0.710
90	Clemson	ACC	8	10	104	94.6	101.9	93.5	0.708
91	North Dakota St.	Sum	13	3	104.1	105.5	110.5	101.3	0.708
92	Illinois St.	MVC	11	7	107.8	98.6	105.9	97.4	0.702
93	North Texas	SB	15	5	98.5	98.2	105.2	96.8	0.701
94	Dayton	A10	9	7	111.8	99.9	107.4	98.9	0.700
95	Princeton	Ivy	11	3	106.6	98.6	104.1	95.9	0.699
96	East Carolina	CUSA	10	6	102.9	99.5	109.0	100.5	0.696
97	Richmond	A10	8	8	107.5	100.8	110.3	101.8	0.694
98	Middle Tennessee	SB	15	5	106.5	94.6	105.6	97.8	0.687
99	Oregon	P12	7	11	115.4	101	107.0	99.3	0.683
100	Marshall	CUSA	10	6	108.7	99.3	104.7	97.4	0.678
101	Auburn	SEC	7	11	96.1	95.4	104.3	97.1	0.676
102	UTEP	CUSA	10	6	99.5	97.6	101.7	94.7	0.674
103	Northwestern	B10	6	12	113.6	102.2	108.4	101.0	0.673
104	Wagner	NEC	14	4	102.4	96.9	101.8	94.9	0.671
105	Long Beach St.	BW	14	4	108.7	93.7	105.3	98.5	0.665
106	DePaul	BE	6	12	106.7	105	111.1	103.9	0.664
107	Valparaiso	Horz	11	5	102.9	101.4	106.0	99.3	0.660
108	Connecticut	BE	6	12	109.8	94.8	103.4	97.0	0.659
109	Utah St.	WAC	13	5	106.1	102	106.7	100.1	0.658
110	Tennessee St.	OVC	12	4	98.4	99.6	104.4	98.2	0.653
111	Maryland	ACC	7	11	104.4	101.2	104.5	98.3	0.652
112	Texas A&M	SEC	7	11	99.9	94.7	101.7	95.7	0.650
113	SC Upstate	ASun	13	5	100.9	97.6	103.7	97.7	0.650
114	Nevada	MWC	6	10	103.9	98.2	106.5	100.3	0.650
115	Green Bay	Horz	10	6	99	101.4	105.0	99.2	0.641
116	Georgia	SEC	6	12	102.1	96.9	101.1	95.7	0.638
117	Xavier	A10	8	8	108.3	94.8	102.1	96.6	0.637

Lineup-Derived Team Projections

Rank	Team	Conf	Pred CW	Pred CL	Last Off	Last Def	Pred Off	Pred Def	Pred Pyth
118	La Salle	A10	8	8	106.2	94.7	105.3	99.8	0.635
119	Mercer	ASun	13	5	103.9	95.9	105.0	99.6	0.633
120	Old Dominion	CAA	11	7	101.1	94.3	100.6	95.5	0.630
121	St. Bonaventure	A10	7	9	110.5	97.1	106.2	100.9	0.629
122	Providence	BE	5	13	108.3	103.8	107.4	102.2	0.626
123	Florida Gulf Coast	ASun	13	5	103.5	105.1	108.1	103.0	0.622
124	Georgia St.	CAA	11	7	100.4	90.6	99.4	95.1	0.612
125	Northeastern	CAA	11	7	98.8	101.4	105.3	101.2	0.600
126	Tulane	CUSA	9	7	96.7	100.2	102.8	98.9	0.599
127	Wichita St.	MVC	8	10	115.4	90.6	99.3	95.9	0.588
128	Georgia Tech	ACC	5	13	95.8	98.1	100.5	97.2	0.585
129	Evansville	MVC	8	10	108.7	103.9	105.2	102.0	0.579
130	Arizona St.	P12	5	13	98.4	104.9	103.7	100.7	0.576
131	Texas Tech	B12	4	14	91.9	100.2	103.5	100.4	0.575
132	Columbia	Ivy	10	4	100.4	103.3	104.6	101.6	0.574
133	Iona	MAAC	12	6	114.5	101.7	105.4	102.5	0.570
134	South Alabama	SB	13	7	98.2	103.9	104.8	102.1	0.565
135	Indiana St.	MVC	8	10	99.2	97.6	99.1	96.7	0.562
136	St. Francis NY	NEC	12	6	95	100.1	101.5	99.1	0.562
137	Delaware	CAA	10	8	102	103.1	104.9	102.4	0.561
138	Southern Illinois	MVC	8	10	96.3	103.4	101.5	99.2	0.557
139	George Mason	CAA	10	8	102.5	96.5	98.5	96.4	0.555
140	Montana	BSky	15	5	101.3	95	102.2	100.1	0.554
141	Cleveland St.	Horz	9	7	104.2	95.4	99.5	97.6	0.550
142	Idaho	WAC	11	7	104.3	104.4	103.9	102.2	0.543
143	Air Force	MWC	4	12	97.5	101.4	102.3	101.2	0.530
144	Long Island	NEC	12	6	107.1	107.5	107.2	106.0	0.527
145	Oral Roberts	SInd	14	4	108.9	102.7	102.9	102.0	0.523
146	Santa Clara	WCC	8	8	101.5	113.1	109.9	108.9	0.523
147	Quinnipiac	NEC	12	6	102.9	100.7	102.3	101.5	0.519
148	George Washington	A10	6	10	99.7	101.3	101.2	100.5	0.517
149	James Madison	CAA	9	9	99.5	107.5	104.6	104.1	0.511
150	Hawaii	BW	11	7	101.1	106.6	102.7	102.4	0.509
151	Nebraska	B10	3	15	100.2	99.9	101.1	100.8	0.508
152	New Mexico St.	WAC	10	8	107.4	96.1	98.7	98.6	0.505
153	Texas Arlington	WAC	10	8	103.5	98.1	99.3	99.1	0.505
154	Western Kentucky	SB	12	8	96.5	99.1	96.8	96.7	0.504
155	Harvard	Ivy	9	5	107.4	93.3	101.0	100.9	0.504
156	Niagara	MAAC	10	8	101.2	109.2	105.1	105.0	0.503
157	Fairfield	MAAC	10	8	99.1	92.6	94.8	94.8	0.501

Lineup-Derived Team Projections

Rank	Team	Conf	Pred CW	Pred CL	Last Off	Last Def	Pred Off	Pred Def	Pred Pyth
158	Denver	WAC	10	8	108.8	99.4	100.1	100.3	0.495
159	Louisiana Tech	WAC	10	8	100.2	102.9	100.0	100.2	0.494
160	San Diego	WCC	7	9	100	104.8	100.4	100.6	0.494
161	Kent St.	MAC	10	6	103.1	99.7	101.6	101.9	0.493
162	Utah	P12	4	14	89.6	105.7	103.1	103.4	0.491
163	NC Wilmington	CAA	9	9	97.4	105.6	101.9	102.3	0.490
164	Southern Miss	CUSA	7	9	109.3	99.3	100.5	101.0	0.486
165	Portland	WCC	7	9	95.8	107.9	103.2	103.9	0.483
166	Youngstown St.	Horz	8	8	104.3	104.7	102.9	103.6	0.482
167	Wake Forest	ACC	4	14	99.8	104.8	106.6	107.4	0.480
168	Drake	MVC	7	11	98.4	96.9	99.3	100.1	0.479
169	Loyola MD	MAAC	10	8	102.3	98.5	101.7	102.7	0.474
170	Stephen F. Austin	Slnd	13	5	95.8	94.3	95.6	96.7	0.469
171	Boston College	ACC	4	14	92.6	102.4	100.5	102.0	0.464
172	Missouri St.	MVC	6	12	103.3	96.7	97.3	98.8	0.461
173	Houston	CUSA	7	9	102.7	106.1	103.0	104.6	0.460
174	SMU	CUSA	7	9	94.9	98.9	95.9	97.5	0.458
175	Jacksonville St.	OVC	10	6	97.2	101	100.5	102.3	0.456
176	Sacred Heart	NEC	11	7	99.8	107.6	103.9	105.8	0.454
177	Toledo	MAC	9	7	100.8	105.7	101.6	103.5	0.452
178	Buffalo	MAC	9	7	106.1	99.2	97.6	99.5	0.451
179	Weber St.	BSky	14	6	107.2	105.8	102.6	104.7	0.449
180	Pacific	BW	10	8	94.7	107.6	101.8	104.0	0.446
181	Vanderbilt	SEC	4	14	115.7	92.7	94.2	96.4	0.442
182	UC Irvine	BW	10	8	94.8	104.1	99.8	102.2	0.440
183	Arkansas St.	SB	10	10	101.1	105.3	99.3	101.9	0.435
184	Texas Southern	SWAC	16	2	89.2	101.4	99.6	102.3	0.431
185	Elon	SC	11	7	95.3	105.1	100.6	103.3	0.430
186	Stetson	ASun	10	8	99.1	107.4	102.2	105.2	0.426
187	Northern Colorado	BSky	13	7	102.3	112.4	105.1	108.4	0.421
188	Morehead St.	OVC	9	7	98	101.4	95.1	98.2	0.419
189	TCU	B12	2	16	105.1	104.6	97.2	100.4	0.418
190	Cal Poly	BW	10	8	102.7	103.7	100.8	104.1	0.416
191	UAB	CUSA	6	10	99.7	96.7	98.1	101.4	0.416
192	Louisiana Lafayette	SB	10	10	91.4	96.4	94.6	97.9	0.413
193	Florida Atlantic	SB	10	10	98.4	103.1	102.0	105.6	0.410
194	Bowling Green	MAC	8	8	101.6	98.8	97.8	101.5	0.406
195	North Dakota	BSky	13	7	93.4	103.7	98.2	101.9	0.406
196	Cornell	Ivy	7	7	95.8	100.5	95.6	99.3	0.405
197	Savannah St.	MEAC	12	4	92.6	94.5	93.6	97.2	0.403

Lineup-Derived Team Projections

Rank	Team	Conf	Pred CW	Pred CL	Last Off	Last Def	Pred Off	Pred Def	Pred Pyth
198	Western Illinois	Sum	9	7	94.8	97.6	95.8	99.5	0.402
199	Marist	MAAC	9	9	96.1	105.1	99.2	103.2	0.399
200	Loyola Marymount	WCC	6	10	100.2	98.5	96.9	101.0	0.397
201	Milwaukee	Horz	6	10	98.5	97.4	96.0	100.1	0.395
202	Hofstra	CAA	7	11	96.7	102.4	98.5	102.8	0.393
203	Loyola Chicago	Horz	6	10	93.4	105.7	99.3	103.7	0.392
204	North Florida	ASun	9	9	100	103.7	99.9	104.4	0.389
205	Cal St. Fullerton	BW	9	9	106.7	108.3	102.3	107.5	0.377
206	Bradley	MVC	5	13	90.8	101.9	96.3	101.2	0.374
207	American	Pat	8	6	99.1	100.9	97.1	102.1	0.374
208	Duquesne	A10	4	12	104.7	101.2	96.9	102.0	0.371
209	Wright St.	Horz	6	10	92.6	98.5	93.3	98.5	0.365
210	NC Asheville	BSth	11	5	108.4	102.8	99.6	105.2	0.364
211	SE Missouri St.	OVC	8	8	103	110.1	102.8	108.6	0.362
212	Canisius	MAAC	8	10	93.7	113	104.3	110.5	0.355
213	Albany	AE	10	6	106.6	110.8	101.4	107.7	0.352
214	Seattle	WAC	7	11	96.5	102.6	96.4	102.4	0.350
215	Arkansas Little Rock	SB	9	11	96.1	98.4	93.0	98.9	0.348
216	Oakland	Sum	8	8	112.4	111.2	102.8	109.4	0.344
217	Gardner Webb	BSth	11	5	92.8	103.2	95.3	101.7	0.340
218	Western Michigan	MAC	7	9	102.9	105.5	97.2	103.9	0.336
219	Stony Brook	AE	9	7	102.1	99.3	94.1	100.7	0.333
220	Army	Pat	7	7	91.1	105.6	95.9	102.7	0.331
221	Southern Utah	BSky	11	9	95.6	103.1	97.0	104.0	0.329
222	UC Davis	BW	8	10	90.2	112.7	104.2	111.9	0.326
223	Fordham	A10	4	12	92.9	104.1	98.9	106.3	0.324
224	Florida International	SB	8	12	97.3	104.4	94.0	101.1	0.322
225	IPFW	Sum	7	9	95.2	106.9	98.5	106.0	0.320
226	Mississippi St.	SEC	2	16	109.9	101.3	92.3	99.5	0.316
227	Texas St.	WAC	7	11	97.1	108.1	98.3	106.2	0.311
228	UC Santa Barbara	BW	7	11	109.8	102.8	94.7	102.4	0.308
229	Charlotte	A10	3	13	98.4	97.7	90.0	97.5	0.305
230	Coastal Carolina	BSth	10	6	101.2	104.4	97.4	105.5	0.304
231	Texas San Antonio	WAC	6	12	101.4	103.5	96.5	104.8	0.301
232	NC Greensboro	SC	9	9	95.5	106.7	97.1	105.5	0.300
233	Lipscomb	ASun	7	11	98.9	103.4	97.6	106.0	0.300
234	Miami OH	MAC	7	9	100	104.1	95.0	103.2	0.299
235	Ball St.	MAC	7	9	97.5	102.9	93.9	102.1	0.297
236	Delaware St.	MEAC	11	5	98.9	108.3	100.1	108.9	0.297
237	William & Mary	CAA	6	12	95.9	109	97.9	106.5	0.296

Lineup-Derived Team Projections

Rank	Team	Conf	Pred CW	Pred CL	Last Off	Last Def	Pred Off	Pred Def	Pred Pyth
238	San Jose St.	WAC	6	12	97.1	108.7	97.2	105.8	0.295
239	Liberty	BSth	10	6	98.6	110.1	97.8	106.5	0.295
240	East Tennessee St.	ASun	7	11	99.8	97.9	93.5	101.9	0.293
241	Siena	MAAC	6	12	95.5	102.1	95.1	103.7	0.292
242	Cal St. Bakersfield	ind			98.6	107.9	99.6	108.6	0.291
243	Mount St. Mary's	NEC	8	10	91.1	105.1	95.9	104.8	0.287
244	Eastern Kentucky	OVC	7	9	98.3	110.1	99.8	109.3	0.284
245	Utah Valley	GWC	6	2	96.8	105	95.5	104.5	0.283
246	Sam Houston St.	SInd	10	8	86.8	99.9	92.0	100.9	0.281
247	Chattanooga	SC	8	10	95.4	105.3	95.8	105.1	0.280
248	Eastern Michigan	MAC	6	10	87.8	99.3	89.0	97.7	0.278
249	SE Louisiana	SInd	10	8	83.7	99.6	92.6	102.0	0.272
250	Campbell	BSth	9	7	100.7	109.1	98.4	108.4	0.271
251	Yale	Ivy	5	9	98.8	98.5	94.8	104.5	0.269
252	Charleston Southern	BSth	9	7	101.9	104	98.9	109.2	0.266
253	VMI	BSth	9	7	99.7	109.9	101.5	112.1	0.265
254	Rhode Island	A10	3	13	101	105.6	97.4	107.7	0.264
255	Maine	AE	8	8	94	105	94.1	104.0	0.264
256	Montana St.	BSky	10	10	93.5	108.8	98.3	108.6	0.264
257	UMKC	Sum	6	10	96.5	110.2	95.9	106.0	0.263
258	Cal St. Northridge	BW	6	12	95.8	112.4	97.6	108.2	0.259
259	Western Carolina	SC	8	10	99.1	106.6	94.8	105.1	0.257
260	Furman	SC	8	10	95.5	103.5	93.5	103.8	0.255
261	Jacksonville	ASun	6	12	97.7	104.6	94.8	105.3	0.255
262	Rider	MAAC	6	12	102.2	106.5	96.7	107.5	0.252
263	Georgia Southern	SC	8	10	95.4	103.3	93.5	104.0	0.251
264	Tennessee Tech	OVC	6	10	100.2	104.8	96.6	107.5	0.249
265	Morgan St.	MEAC	10	6	95.8	107	93.4	104.2	0.247
266	Austin Peay	OVC	6	10	99.7	105.6	96.0	107.3	0.241
267	IUPUI	Sum	6	10	105.6	110.2	99.4	111.2	0.241
268	Dartmouth	Ivy	5	9	88.9	103	91.7	102.6	0.240
269	Wofford	SC	8	10	100	104	94.2	105.5	0.239
270	North Carolina A&T	MEAC	10	6	91.3	106.7	93.4	104.7	0.237
271	Bethune Cookman	MEAC	10	6	99.4	110.8	99.8	111.9	0.236
272	Illinois Chicago	Horz	4	12	94.8	108.6	95.3	107.0	0.235
273	Boston University	AE	7	9	97.2	99.3	89.5	100.5	0.235
274	Tulsa	CUSA	3	13	105	97	90.0	101.0	0.234
275	San Francisco	WCC	3	13	107.5	105.4	93.3	104.8	0.232
276	Jackson St.	SWAC	13	5	85	109.6	94.2	106.1	0.227
277	Northwestern St.	SInd	9	9	94.5	101.7	93.4	105.3	0.226

Lineup-Derived Team Projections

Rank	Team	Conf	Pred CW	Pred CL	Last Off	Last Def	Pred Off	Pred Def	Pred Pyth
278	Rice	CUSA	3	13	99	97.8	92.3	104.1	0.226
279	Brown	Ivy	5	9	91.9	110.1	97.6	110.1	0.225
280	South Dakota	Sum	6	10	96.2	109.1	98.5	111.4	0.221
281	New Hampshire	AE	7	9	89.3	102.4	91.5	103.7	0.218
282	Monmouth	NEC	6	12	95.5	107.3	93.8	106.3	0.217
283	Eastern Washington	BSky	8	12	98.8	104.7	96.7	109.6	0.216
284	Holy Cross	Pat	5	9	95.8	102.5	92.8	105.3	0.215
285	Pennsylvania	Ivy	4	10	101.9	99.1	89.7	102.0	0.213
286	St. Peter's	MAAC	5	13	86.4	105.7	89.3	101.5	0.212
287	Troy	SB	5	15	101.9	113.4	97.3	110.6	0.212
288	McNeese St.	SInd	8	10	99.3	106.1	93.7	106.6	0.211
289	Sacramento St.	BSky	8	12	95.8	110.1	95.3	109.2	0.198
290	UMBC	AE	6	10	88.2	114.8	96.4	110.7	0.194
291	Central Connecticut	NEC	6	12	97.8	102.7	91.5	105.2	0.193
292	The Citadel	SC	6	12	89.7	109.2	95.7	110.1	0.192
293	UC Riverside	BW	5	13	87.6	99.5	89.7	103.5	0.188
294	Texas A&M CC	SInd	8	10	87.1	105.3	89.5	103.4	0.185
295	Tennessee Martin	OVC	5	11	90.5	115.6	96.4	111.4	0.184
296	Hartford	AE	6	10	89.4	105.1	90.4	104.8	0.179
297	Pepperdine	WCC	3	13	91.7	104.8	89.7	104.1	0.179
298	North Carolina Central	MEAC	8	8	95.4	99.9	89.7	104.3	0.176
299	Idaho St.	BSky	7	13	93.7	111.3	94.9	110.8	0.171
300	Lafayette	Pat	5	9	103	110.9	95.4	111.6	0.167
301	Navy	Pat	4	10	89.2	110.1	93.0	108.9	0.166
302	Samford	SC	6	12	100.2	112	96.7	113.3	0.164
303	Lamar	SInd	7	11	105.8	100.2	85.2	100.0	0.163
304	Howard	MEAC	8	8	86.7	106.4	90.3	106.5	0.156
305	Nebraska Omaha	Sum	4	12	94	117.8	98.7	116.4	0.155
306	Southern	SWAC	11	7	86.8	107.8	91.5	108.2	0.151
307	Bryant	NEC	5	13	91	115.9	96.7	114.5	0.151
308	Appalachian St.	SC	5	13	98.1	107.4	91.9	108.7	0.151
309	Radford	BSth	6	10	87.9	105.7	87.8	104.1	0.148
310	Houston Baptist	GWC	4	4	90.2	110.6	94.3	112.0	0.146
311	Prairie View A&M	SWAC	11	7	83	104.5	87.5	104.0	0.145
312	Hampton	MEAC	8	8	89.8	101.8	86.6	102.9	0.145
313	Portland St.	BSky	6	14	105.2	110.6	96.2	114.5	0.144
314	Presbyterian	BSth	6	10	99.8	109.1	90.8	108.7	0.136
315	Nicholls St.	SInd	6	12	94	119.4	96.1	115.2	0.135
316	Northern Arizona	BSky	5	15	86.9	113.3	93.9	113.1	0.130
317	Binghamton	AE	5	11	85.3	112.4	94.3	113.6	0.129

Lineup-Derived Team Projections

Rank	Team	Conf	Pred CW	Pred CL	Last Off	Last Def	Pred Off	Pred Def	Pred Pyth
318	Winthrop	BSth	6	10	92.7	102.2	87.0	104.9	0.129
319	High Point	BSth	6	10	103.5	110.9	91.2	109.9	0.128
320	Texas Pan American	GWC	4	4	89.5	108.7	90.1	108.9	0.125
321	Northern Illinois	MAC	3	13	87	109.9	88.1	106.7	0.123
322	NJIT	GWC	4	4	94.3	109.6	89.4	108.3	0.123
323	Florida A&M	MEAC	7	9	90.8	110.7	92.3	112.0	0.121
324	Central Michigan	MAC	3	13	94.9	106	89.1	108.3	0.119
325	SIU Edwardsville	OVC	4	12	92.5	110.1	89.9	109.3	0.118
326	Central Arkansas	Slnd	5	13	89.6	111.9	90.6	110.8	0.113
327	Norfolk St.	MEAC	6	10	97.7	102.1	87.5	107.1	0.112
328	Kennesaw St.	ASun	3	15	94.4	114.5	91.7	112.7	0.108
329	Louisiana Monroe	SB	3	17	93.4	112.6	93.2	114.6	0.108
330	St. Francis PA	NEC	4	14	91.3	109.2	88.9	109.9	0.102
331	Maryland Eastern Shore	MEAC	6	10	83.9	106.5	87.4	108.5	0.098
332	Fairleigh Dickinson	NEC	3	15	86.1	108.3	87.9	109.4	0.096
333	Colgate	Pat	3	11	95.1	115.8	92.5	115.2	0.095
334	Arkansas Pine Bluff	SWAC	8	10	90.3	112.8	87.1	108.6	0.095
335	Alcorn St.	SWAC	8	10	85	109.7	86.4	107.8	0.094
336	Alabama St.	SWAC	8	10	84.3	105.2	83.9	105.5	0.087
337	Towson	CAA	1	17	83.8	108.5	85.2	107.5	0.085
338	South Carolina St.	MEAC	5	11	88.4	117	88.4	113.3	0.073
339	Chicago St.	GWC	2	6	85.3	109.6	85.9	111.0	0.067
340	Alabama A&M	SWAC	7	11	87.1	113.6	87.5	113.6	0.064
341	Mississippi Valley St.	SWAC	6	12	94.2	103.9	82.0	108.0	0.056
342	Longwood	BSth	3	13	93.9	122.6	90.5	119.3	0.056
343	Eastern Illinois	OVC	2	14	94	110.7	86.2	114.3	0.053
344	Coppin St.	MEAC	3	13	103.8	117	84.4	112.8	0.049
345	Grambling	SWAC	2	16	80.2	116.8	78.4	118.7	0.014

INDIVIDUAL PLAYER PROJECTIONS

And here are individual player projections for the top 30 teams. RSCI refers to a top-100 player's ranking coming out of high school. "SOSmod" is an adjustment for strength of schedule. Everything else should be familiar—if not see "Terms Used in this Book."

1. INDIANA

	RSCI Rank	Class	Pred ORtg	Pred Min	Pred Poss
Cody Zeller	10	So	132.2	78%	23%
Jordan Hulls	74	Sr	128.0	72%	17%
Christian Watford	45	Sr	119.8	69%	22%
Maurice Creek	58	Jr	120.3	58%	21%
Victor Oladipo		Jr	115.6	50%	21%
Will Sheehey		Jr	115.8	42%	19%
Kevin Yogi Ferrell	25	Fr	108.9	40%	18%
Jeremy Hollowell	45	Fr	108.8	31%	18%
Derek Elston		Sr	114.8	30%	17%
Hanner Perea	50	Fr	108.8	30%	18%
		SOSmod	1.039		
		Pred Off	124.9		

3. UCLA

	RSCI Rank	Class	Pred ORtg	Pred Min	Pred Poss
Shabazz Muhammad	1	Fr	119.4	69%	21%
Kyle Anderson	3	Fr	119.4	67%	21%
Travis Wear	38	Jr	123	64%	20%
Joshua Smith	18	Jr	119.4	55%	28%
Larry Drew	44	Sr	113	52%	18%
David Wear	37	Jr	120.5	51%	17%
Tyler Lamb	39	Jr	105.8	47%	18%
Tony Parker	24	Fr	109	35%	18%
Norman Powell	53	So	112.4	35%	16%
Jordan Adams	59	Fr	106.5	27%	17%
		SOSmod	1.025		
		Pred Off	119.5		

2. KENTUCKY

	RSCI Rank	Class	Pred ORtg	Pred Min	Pred Poss
Nerlens Noel	2	Fr	118.7	82%	21%
Alex Poythress	8	Fr	118.7	82%	21%
Archie Goodwin	10	Fr	118.7	80%	21%
Ryan Harrow	22	So	113.2	66%	21%
Kyle Wiltjer	19	So	119.6	54%	20%
Julius Mays		Sr	109.8	52%	20%
Willie Cauley	38	Fr	108.4	51%	17%
Jon Hood	64	Sr	100.7	34%	16%
		SOSmod	1.039		
		Pred Off	119.8		

4. KANSAS

	RSCI Rank	Class	Pred ORtg	Pred Min	Pred Poss
Elijah Johnson	25	Sr	112.6	83%	20%
Travis Releford	49	Sr	116.5	81%	18%
Jeff Withey	27	Sr	111.4	69%	22%
Perry Ellis	31	Fr	100.1	51%	21%
Ben McLemore	41	Fr	100.0	49%	21%
Kevin Young		Sr	105.5	43%	21%
Andrew White	52	Fr	97.8	43%	20%
Landen Lucas		Fr	93.5	30%	19%
Zach Peters		Fr	93.5	28%	19%
Naadir Tharpe	91	So	88.2	23%	20%
		SOSmod	1.051		
		Pred Off	110.7		

Lineup-Derived Team Projections

5. MICHIGAN STATE

	RSCI Rank	Class	Pred ORtg	Pred Min	Pred Poss
Keith Appling	34	Jr	113.7	83%	21%
Branden Dawson	17	So	114.1	69%	22%
Adreian Payne	27	Jr	113.3	65%	20%
Gary Harris	16	Fr	108.6	56%	21%
Derrick Nix	88	Sr	109.4	54%	23%
Travis Trice		So	102.6	48%	17%
Matt Costello	87	Fr	101.4	40%	18%
Russell Byrd	92	So	103.9	31%	19%
Denzel Valentine	89	Fr	101.3	30%	18%
Kenny Kaminski	98	Fr	101.3	22%	18%
		SOSmod	1.045		
		Pred Off	113.9		

7. DUKE

	RSCI Rank	Class	Pred ORtg	Pred Min	Pred Poss
Ryan Kelly	14	Sr	122.4	71%	21%
Mason Plumlee	18	Sr	110.1	68%	22%
Seth Curry		Sr	120.0	67%	21%
Quinn Cook	31	So	119.7	58%	22%
Rasheed Sulaimon	12	Fr	107.9	53%	21%
Tyler Thornton		Jr	114.0	48%	13%
Amile Jefferson	21	Fr	103.1	44%	20%
Alex Murphy	49	Fr	103.0	36%	20%
Marshall Plumlee	61	Fr	100.6	28%	18%
Josh Hairston	32	Jr	101.2	27%	20%
		SOSmod	1.039		
		Pred Off	116.9		

6. FLORIDA

	RSCI Rank	Class	Pred ORtg	Pred Min	Pred Poss
Kenny Boynton	9	Sr	123.5	84%	25%
Patric Young	19	Jr	122.6	84%	20%
Erik Murphy	43	Sr	120.4	78%	20%
Mike Rosario	31	Sr	108.9	47%	25%
Scottie Wilbekin		Jr	118.8	47%	12%
Will Yeguete		Jr	113.0	38%	15%
Braxton Ogbueze	54	Fr	101.6	38%	19%
Michael Frazier	86	Fr	101.5	31%	19%
Cody Larson	88	So	95.5	30%	19%
Casey Prather	52	Jr	93.3	22%	20%
		SOSmod	1.048		
		Pred Off	120.0		

8. OHIO STATE

	RSCI Rank	Class	Pred ORtg	Pred Min	Pred Poss
Deshaun Thomas	17	Jr	123.3	81%	26%
Aaron Craft		Jr	113.0	75%	18%
Lenzelle Smith, Jr.		Jr	111.4	66%	18%
Evan Ravenel		Sr	105.8	50%	20%
LaQuinton Ross	44	So	96.9	50%	20%
Amir Williams	50	So	103.3	48%	20%
Sam Thompson	46	So	105.1	43%	17%
Amedeo Della Valle		Fr	95.8	30%	19%
Trey McDonald		So	88.1	29%	19%
Shannon Scott	32	So	86.6	28%	19%
		SOSmod	1.038		
		Pred Off	111.4		

Lineup-Derived Team Projections

9. ARIZONA

	RSCI Rank	Class	Pred ORtg	Pred Min	Pred Poss
Kaleb Tarczewski	7	Fr	119.5	73%	22%
Solomon Hill	56	Sr	121.0	71%	21%
Nick Johnson	22	So	113.0	62%	20%
Grant Jerrett	11	Fr	114.1	53%	20%
Mark Lyons		Sr	112.7	51%	23%
Brandon Ashley	15	Fr	114.1	51%	20%
Kevin Parrom		Sr	122.2	48%	19%
Gabe York	47	Fr	109.0	37%	18%
Angelo Chol	59	So	112.8	27%	15%
Jordin Mayes		Jr	109.7	26%	17%
		SOSmod	1.012		
		Pred Off	117.2		

11. SYRACUSE

12. Syracuse	RSCI Rank	Class	Pred ORtg	Pred Min	Pred Poss
Brandon Triche		Sr	114.5	76%	24%
C.J. Fair	96	Jr	119.8	76%	19%
DaJuan Coleman	18	Fr	108.9	71%	22%
James Southerland		Sr	120.7	59%	19%
Michael Carter-Williams	25	So	109.9	51%	21%
Jerami Grant	41	Fr	104.1	51%	21%
Rakeem Christmas	21	So	111.4	48%	18%
Trevor Cooney	79	Fr	101.6	35%	19%
Baye Moussa Keita		Jr	117.5	34%	11%
		SOSmod	1.037		
		Pred Off	116.7		

10. LOUISVILLE

	RSCI Rank	Class	Pred ORtg	Pred Min	Pred Poss
Gorgui Dieng	69	Jr	112.5	85%	16%
Peyton Siva	27	Sr	100.6	72%	21%
Chane Behanan	24	So	110.6	71%	20%
Luke Hancock		Jr	107.4	54%	20%
Wayne Blackshear	26	So	97.7	47%	21%
Russ Smith		Jr	94.6	47%	29%
Montrezl Harrell	85	Fr	98.2	40%	17%
Zach Price	58	So	92.5	32%	17%
Stephan Van Treese		Sr	90.6	27%	16%
Kevin Ware	74	So	80.1	25%	23%
		SOSmod	1.042		
		Pred Off	105.2		

12. NC STATE

	RSCI Rank	Class	Pred ORtg	Pred Min	Pred Poss
Lorenzo Brown	56	Jr	113.6	79%	22%
Scott Wood		Sr	131.7	79%	14%
C.J. Leslie	12	Jr	113.6	76%	26%
Richard Howell	60	Sr	115.3	62%	23%
Rodney Purvis	17	Fr	112.1	58%	20%
T.J. Warren	27	Fr	107.2	49%	19%
Tyler Lewis	43	Fr	107.2	49%	19%
Jordan Vandenberg		Jr	101.2	29%	15%
Thomas De Thaey		So	94.8	19%	18%
		SOSmod	1.031		
		Pred Off	116.9		

13. GONZAGA

	RSCI Rank	Class	Pred ORtg	Pred Min	Pred Poss
Gary Bell, Jr.	77	So	125.2	76%	18%
Elias Harris		Sr	120.6	75%	23%
Kevin Pangos		So	121.8	74%	20%
Sam Dower		Jr	119.9	56%	23%
David Stockton		Jr	107.4	46%	17%
Kelly Olynyk		Sr	110.1	46%	19%
Guy Edi		Sr	108.5	40%	18%
Drew Barham		Sr	103.4	32%	20%
Przemek Karnowski		Fr	104.1	28%	18%
Kyle Dranginis		Fr	104.0	27%	18%
		SOSmod	0.996		
		Pred Off	115.3		

15. NEW MEXICO

	RSCI Rank	Class	Pred ORtg	Pred Min	Pred Poss
Kendall Williams		Jr	118.6	74%	23%
Tony Snell		Jr	117.3	62%	19%
Alex Kirk	98	So	111.7	59%	20%
Jamal Fenton		Sr	113.2	57%	21%
Cameron Bairstow		Jr	108.7	51%	17%
Hugh Greenwood		So	115.4	47%	17%
Demetrius Walker		Jr	104.0	46%	26%
Chad Adams		Sr	113.4	36%	17%
Nick Banyard		Fr	101.1	34%	19%
Devon Williams		Fr	101.1	33%	19%
		SOSmod	1.009		
		Pred Off	112.6		

14. UNLV

	RSCI Rank	Class	Pred ORtg	Pred Min	Pred Poss
Anthony Bennett	6	Fr	115.6	77%	22%
Anthony Marshall	82	Sr	107.8	71%	22%
Mike Moser	57	Jr	101.6	61%	24%
Justin Hawkins		Sr	116.1	53%	15%
Quintrell Thomas	90	Sr	119.9	50%	19%
Katin Reinhardt	36	Fr	105.8	46%	18%
Khem Birch	11	So	110.2	39%	18%
Carlos Lopez		Jr	115.4	38%	21%
Bryce Jones	82	So	101.4	37%	21%
Savon Goodman	82	Fr	103.3	29%	17%
		SOSmod	1.014		
		Pred Off	111.4		

16. MISSOURI

	RSCI Rank	Class	Pred ORtg	Pred Min	Pred Poss
Phil Pressey	41	Jr	117.3	77%	21%
Alex Oriakhi	16	Sr	121.9	73%	18%
Mike Dixon		Sr	125.4	72%	23%
Keion Bell		Sr	115.7	54%	23%
Laurence Bowers		Sr	117.8	50%	19%
Earnest Ross		Jr	115.5	47%	20%
Jabari Brown	16	So	115.1	40%	19%
Tony Criswell		Jr	108.0	33%	18%
Stefan Jankovic		Fr	103.2	28%	17%
Ryan Rosburg		Fr	103.2	27%	17%
		SOSmod	1.023		
		Pred Off	119.6		

Lineup-Derived Team Projections

17. TENNESSEE

	RSCI Rank	Class	Pred ORtg	Pred Min	Pred Poss
Trae Golden	86	Jr	114.3	81%	23%
Jeronne Maymon	73	Sr	107.5	67%	24%
Jordan McRae	40	Jr	106.3	66%	21%
Jarnell Stokes	14	So	109.9	66%	23%
Kenny Hall	62	Sr	109.4	53%	18%
Skylar McBee		Sr	117.4	53%	14%
D'montre Edwards		Jr	103.6	34%	18%
Yemi Makanjuola		So	110.3	32%	16%
Dwight Miller		Sr	105.3	28%	17%
Derek Reese		Fr	99.1	20%	17%
		SOSmod	1.023		
		Pred Off	111.8		

19. PITTSBURGH

	RSCI Rank	Class	Pred ORtg	Pred Min	Pred Poss
Dante Taylor	13	Sr	124.8	69%	17%
Steven Adams	5	Fr	116.6	67%	22%
Travon Woodall		Sr	115.5	66%	22%
Lamar Patterson		Sr	116.6	53%	18%
Talib Zanna	87	Jr	122.7	53%	17%
Trey Zeigler	29	Jr	104.4	53%	29%
J.J. Moore	67	Jr	116.8	50%	21%
John Johnson		So	110.5	33%	16%
James Robinson	63	Fr	103.8	30%	17%
Malcolm Gilbert	74	So	97.8	27%	17%
		SOSmod	1.028		
		Pred Off	117.4		

18. MEMPHIS

	RSCI Rank	Class	Pred ORtg	Pred Min	Pred Poss
Joe Jackson	16	Jr	110.3	82%	27%
Tarik Black	59	Jr	120.5	71%	20%
Adonis Thomas	9	So	110.8	70%	22%
Chris Crawford		Jr	105.1	53%	20%
Antonio Barton		Jr	112.3	52%	17%
William Goodwin	35	Fr	104.3	47%	20%
D.J. Stephens		Sr	121.2	41%	13%
Damien Wilson		Fr	99.8	31%	18%
Anthony Cole		Fr	99.8	28%	18%
Ferrakohn Hall		Sr	101.3	26%	16%
		SOSmod	1.028		
		Pred Off	113.1		

20. TEXAS

	RSCI Rank	Class	Pred ORtg	Pred Min	Pred Poss
Myck Kabongo	13	So	109.9	79%	24%
Cameron Ridley	14	Fr	108.5	73%	21%
Sheldon McClellan	48	So	122.6	70%	21%
Jonathan Holmes	70	So	116.1	53%	19%
Julien Lewis	68	So	105.1	52%	19%
Prince Ibeh	62	Fr	101.3	45%	19%
Javan Felix	80	Fr	101.2	38%	19%
Jaylen Bond		So	110.2	32%	15%
Connor Lammert		Fr	96.9	30%	18%
Danny Newsome		Fr	96.9	30%	18%
		SOSmod	1.033		
		Pred Off	112.5		

Lineup-Derived Team Projections

21. MARQUETTE

	RSCI Rank	Class	Pred ORtg	Pred Min	Pred Poss
Jamil Wilson	40	Jr	112.2	66%	17%
Vander Blue	48	Jr	103.2	65%	21%
Davante Gardner		Jr	120.3	64%	23%
Trent Lockett		Sr	109.4	63%	23%
Junior Cadougan	47	Sr	97.9	50%	19%
Jake Thomas		Jr	106.3	48%	19%
Todd Mayo		So	104.6	43%	20%
Chris Otule		Sr	98.2	38%	17%
Steve Taylor	83	Fr	100.7	35%	18%
Juan Anderson	81	So	94.6	28%	19%
	SOSmod		1.045		
	Pred Off		111.4		

23. MINNESOTA

	RSCI Rank	Class	Pred ORtg	Pred Min	Pred Poss
Trevor Mbakwe	91	Sr	111.8	78%	25%
Rodney Williams	46	Sr	117.2	74%	19%
Austin Hollins		Jr	113.1	61%	17%
Julian Welch		Sr	108.9	52%	21%
Andre Hollins		So	106.9	47%	22%
Maurice Walker		So	101.2	46%	21%
Joe Coleman		So	104.3	43%	19%
Elliot Eliason		So	105.4	37%	15%
Maverick Ahanmisi		Jr	100.3	32%	16%
Oto Osenieks		So	97.6	29%	19%
	SOSmod		1.032		
	Pred Off		111.9		

22. NOTRE DAME

	RSCI Rank	Class	Pred ORtg	Pred Min	Pred Poss
Jerian Grant		Jr	113.5	82%	21%
Eric Atkins		Jr	110.5	75%	20%
Jack Cooley		Sr	124.9	73%	22%
Scott Martin	41	Sr	102.9	59%	20%
Pat Connaughton		So	110.8	50%	17%
Cameron Biedscheid	46	Fr	103.8	49%	20%
Garrick Sherman		Sr	107.7	46%	18%
Joey Brooks		Sr	97.6	25%	21%
Mike Broghammer		Sr	98.5	22%	21%
Tom Knight		Sr	97.9	19%	21%
	SOSmod		1.030		
	Pred Off		113.1		

24. CREIGHTON

	RSCI Rank	Class	Pred ORtg	Pred Min	Pred Poss
Doug McDermott		Jr	120.0	80%	28%
Gregory Echenique	94	Sr	122.8	77%	23%
Grant Gibbs		Sr	112.1	71%	17%
Jahenns Manigat		Jr	124.6	54%	14%
Ethan Wragge		Sr	123.9	53%	18%
Josh Jones		Sr	112.2	50%	18%
Geoff Groselle		Fr	102.9	35%	18%
Nevin Johnson		Fr	102.8	28%	18%
Avery Dingman		So	107.7	28%	18%
Will Artino		So	102.9	24%	20%
	SOSmod		1.014		
	Pred Off		117.8		

Lineup-Derived Team Projections

25. BAYLOR

	RSCI Rank	Class	Pred ORtg	Pred Min	Pred Poss
Pierre Jackson		Sr	113.3	78%	24%
Isaiah Austin	4	Fr	115.5	77%	24%
Brady Heslip		Jr	133.2	72%	15%
Ricardo Gathers	32	Fr	105.7	48%	20%
Cory Jefferson	92	Jr	113.5	46%	18%
Deuce Bello	56	So	105.8	43%	21%
J'mison Morgan	25	Sr	101.3	43%	20%
L.J. Rose	66	Fr	103.3	35%	19%
A.J. Walton		Sr	96.3	32%	18%
Gary Franklin, Jr.	57	Jr	100.6	26%	18%
		SOSmod	1.035		
		Pred Off	115.1		

27. GEORGETOWN

	RSCI Rank	Class	Pred ORtg	Pred Min	Pred Poss
Otto Porter	34	So	118.3	82%	22%
Nate Lubick	42	Jr	113.9	76%	18%
Markel Starks	94	Jr	104.9	64%	18%
D'Vauntes Smith-Rivera	37	Fr	101.2	53%	21%
Greg Whittington		So	99.9	45%	17%
Jabril Trawick		So	105.6	44%	19%
Mikael Hopkins	98	So	101.9	44%	25%
Tyler Adams	80	So	95.7	36%	20%
Bradley Hayes		Fr	91.6	28%	20%
Brandon Bolden		Fr	91.6	27%	20%
		SOSmod	1.038		
		Pred Off	109.4		

26. NORTH CAROLINA

	RSCI Rank	Class	Pred ORtg	Pred Min	Pred Poss
James McAdoo	6	So	108.3	87%	23%
Reggie Bullock	15	Jr	120.8	73%	18%
Dexter Strickland	24	Sr	112.2	64%	17%
P.J. Hairston	11	So	108.4	53%	23%
Brice Johnson	40	Fr	101.9	52%	20%
Marcus Paige	28	Fr	101.9	52%	20%
Leslie McDonald	44	Jr	100.9	47%	21%
Joel James	58	Fr	99.4	33%	19%
J.P. Tokoto	57	Fr	99.4	33%	19%
Desmond Hubert		So	91.2	8%	16%
		SOSmod	1.029		
		Pred Off	110.1		

28. ALABAMA

	RSCI Rank	Class	Pred ORtg	Pred Min	Pred Poss
Trevor Releford	60	Jr	112.9	77%	23%
Trevor Lacey	36	So	107.1	72%	21%
Levi Randolph	29	So	107.2	72%	19%
Devonte Pollard	22	Fr	101.8	59%	21%
Andrew Steele		Sr	110.8	55%	17%
Rodney Cooper	90	So	103.5	52%	21%
Nick Jacobs		So	101.0	52%	20%
Retin Obasohan		Fr	92.9	31%	19%
Carl Engstrom		Jr	94.3	29%	15%
		SOSmod	1.025		
		Pred Off	108.0		

29. KANSAS STATE

	RSCI Rank	Class	Pred ORtg	Pred Min	Pred Poss
Rodney McGruder		Sr	121.4	78%	21%
Will Spradling		Jr	112.8	72%	17%
Angel Rodriguez		So	97.9	65%	25%
Jordan Henriguez-Roberts		Sr	105.2	59%	21%
Thomas Gipson		So	100.6	47%	23%
Martavious Irving		Sr	107.0	44%	16%
DJ Johnson		Fr	97.8	44%	19%
Adrian Diaz		So	95.7	34%	21%
Shane Southwell		Jr	95.6	29%	16%
Michael Orris		Fr	97.7	28%	19%
	SOSmod	1.033			
	Pred Off	108.6			

30. IOWA STATE

	RSCI Rank	Class	Pred ORtg	Pred Min	Pred Poss
Korie Lucious	87	Sr	110.6	72%	22%
Chris Babb		Sr	114.6	71%	15%
Melvin Ejim		Jr	112.7	66%	23%
Will Clyburn		Sr	114.2	56%	21%
Tyrus McGee		Sr	117.1	52%	20%
Anthony Booker	83	Sr	107.9	50%	20%
Georges Niang	71	Fr	103.4	44%	20%
Percy Gibson		So	107.5	32%	20%
Kerwin Okoro		Fr	101.3	29%	19%
Sherron Dorsey-Walker		Fr	101.3	28%	19%
	SOSmod	1.029			
	Pred Off	113.5			

Evaluating NBA Drafts Before They Happen

BY KEVIN PELTON

Don't stay in school, kids. That was the message sent by NBA teams last season. Likely because of the then-looming lockout, four of the top freshmen from 2010-11 returned for a second year on campus: North Carolina's Harrison Barnes, Kentucky's Terrence Jones, Baylor's Perry Jones III, and Ohio State's Jared Sullinger. They made up four of the top five consensus returning prospects in this chapter in last year's book, yet all four of them were drafted lower than projected entering the season.

Barnes still went in the lottery and Terrence Jones didn't slip too far from his preseason ranking, but the other two players, PJIII and Sullinger, tumbled on draft night. Because of concerns about his size and his back, Sullinger went from a preseason lottery ranking (his average projection was between the fifth and the sixth picks) to the 21st overall selection by Boston. Perry Jones was also pegged between the fifth and the sixth picks in the preseason, and his tumble was even more dramatic. Knee issues helped push Jones nearly out of the first round before he was taken 28th overall by Oklahoma City.

The crop of elite freshmen that we saw in 2011-12, however, did not make the same mistake. Of the freshmen featured in last year's top five, four entered the draft. One-and-done players made up the top three picks, five of the top 10, and eight total first-round picks. After Shabazz Muhammad and Nerlens Noel, this year's newcomers aren't quite as talented, but expect something similar next June.

For returning players, Basketball Prospectus has lent a level of statistical sophistication to the scouting process by translating college stats to their NBA equivalents. Our translations utilize a database of more than 200 players from the 2000-2008 NBA drafts, to model how players' tempo-free statistics have carried over from their final season in the NCAA to their first in the NBA, accounting for strength of schedule (as measured by Ken Pomeroy's SOS ratings).

To represent the scouting perspective, we've used the 2013 mock draft from DraftExpress.com (DX) and Chad Ford's Top 100 list (ESPN) to rank both the consensus top 10 returning prospects and the five incoming freshmen with the highest draft stock. To highlight the places where the scouts apparently disagree with the stats, we also look at five players rated more highly by the numbers and five players projected to go earlier than their performance would suggest.

For each returning player, we've listed some key translated statistics. Most notable is TW%, the estimated winning percentage of a team made up of the player in question and four average NBA teammates. Also note that "BS%" is the player's combined block and steal percentages.

THE CONSENSUS TOP 10 RETURNING PROSPECTS

1. Cody Zeller, C, Indiana

DX	Ford 100	Avg	TW%	TS%	Usg	Reb%	Ast%	BS%
3	2	2.5	.482	.566	.178	.127	.020	.030

The youngest of the Zeller brothers has proven to be the most talented member of the family. As a freshman, Cody emerged as the go-to guy for a much improved Indiana team. Had Zeller joined older brother Tyler in the draft, he could have been a top-five pick. As it is, Zeller will need to fall on his face as a sophomore to drop out of the 2013 top five. A skilled big man, Zeller proved highly efficient as a scorer last season.

2. James McAdoo, PF, North Carolina

DX	Ford 100	Avg	TW%	TS%	Usg	Reb%	Ast%	BS%
5	4	4.5	.289	.398	.149	.109	.007	.025

At this point, McAdoo's top-five draft status is based much more on potential than production. Playing behind first-round picks Tyler Zeller and John Henson in the Tar Heel frontcourt, McAdoo was inconsistent as a freshman and was particularly disappointing on the glass. He becomes the featured player up front for North Carolina this season and will have the chance to prove he's a future NBA star. Otherwise, he could be this year's equivalent to Perry Jones III.

3. Tony Mitchell, PF, North Texas

DX	Ford 100	Avg	TW%	TS%	Usg	Reb%	Ast%	BS%
8	5	6.5	.413	.512	.153	.139	.021	.037

Not to be confused with Alabama's Tony Mitchell, who went undrafted after his junior season and joined the Sacramento Kings for training camp, this Mitchell is sure to become the first NBA player ever from North Texas. In his first year on campus, he averaged a double-double with nearly three blocks per game. While the strength-of-schedule adjustment tones down his numbers somewhat, Mitchell still appears ready to step into the NBA at age 20. Asked about his athleticism by ESPNDallas.com, anonymous NBA scouts made comparisons to Blake Griffin, Shawn Marion, and Dominique Wilkins.

4. Mason Plumlee, PF, Duke

DX	Ford 100	Avg	TW%	TS%	Usg	Reb%	Ast%	BS%
12	15	13.5	.402	.487	.155	.161	.025	.027

Speaking of basketball families from the state of Indiana, Plumlee will join brother Miles in the NBA next season. Mason was the more productive of the two players last season, suggesting he should go higher than his brother did (26th overall pick by the Indiana Pacers). This Plumlee is more skilled at creating his own shot. He's also a fine passer for his size.

5. Adonis Thomas, SF, Memphis

DX	Ford 100	Avg	TW%	TS%	Usg	Reb%	Ast%	BS%
16	13	14.5	.274	.449	.142	.066	.015	.018

Consider Thomas the type of sophomore who is in danger of sliding down draft boards with a poor season. At this point, scouts are giving Thomas the benefit of the doubt based on the potential he demonstrated coming out of high school. As a freshman battling an ankle injury, Thomas played a limited role on a deep Tigers squad. With Wesley Witherspoon graduating and Will Barton leaving early for the NBA, the opportunity is there for Thomas. He will have to contribute more on the glass.

6. B.J. Young, SG, Arkansas

DX	Ford 100	Avg	TW%	TS%	Usg	Reb%	Ast%	BS%
17	14	15.5	.339	.487	.200	.056	.037	.019

Young put his name in the draft before withdrawing, a good sign that he's headed to the NBA after this season. As a freshman he impressed scouts with his ability to create offense. A combo guard whose size is better suited for the point, Young could help his stock considerably by demonstrating growth as a playmaker.

7. C.J. Leslie, SF, North Carolina State

DX	Ford 100	Avg	TW%	TS%	Usg	Reb%	Ast%	BS%
11	22	16.5	.337	.460	.194	.122	.016	.029

Despite the progress Leslie made in his second season on campus, he continues to divide experts, as demonstrated by the gulf between his ranking on DraftExpress and in Chad Ford's Top 100. Leslie improved his two-point percentage considerably but will have to continue to make strides to develop into an efficient NBA scorer.

8. Alex Len, C, Maryland

DX	Ford 100	Avg	TW%	TS%	Usg	Reb%	Ast%	BS%
13	21	17.0	.294	.470	.114	.122	.012	.032

The 7-1 Len had a difficult transition to the NCAA last season. Because he played for a pro team in his native Ukraine, he was suspended for the Terrapins' first 10 games. He had to blend in midseason while also learning English. Len's stats might understate his ability because he didn't get the benefit of facing easier non-conference opponents. To justify being a first-round pick, Len will have to be more of a presence on the glass and a bigger part of the Maryland offense.

9. Otto Porter, SF, Georgetown

DX	Ford 100	Avg	TW%	TS%	Usg	Reb%	Ast%	BS%
24	12	18.0	.417	.494	.127	.122	.024	.024

Because he didn't play AAU basketball, Porter was something of an unknown quantity before an impressive debut season at Georgetown. He did a little of everything for John Thompson III, including making 61 percent of his two-point attempts. Look for Porter to play a bigger role on offense with the departure of Henry Sims and Hollis Thompson. Ford's rankings tend to hew more toward production rather than potential, which favors Porter over Len and Leslie.

10. Myck Kabongo, PG, Texas

DX	Ford 100	Avg	TW%	TS%	Usg	Reb%	Ast%	BS%
20	17	18.5	.318	.437	.147	.051	.073	.017

The electrifying Kabongo could extend a two-year streak of Canadians being drafted in the first round (Tristan Thompson and Corey Joseph in 2011, followed by Andrew Nicholson last June). Kabongo must improve his shooting, having made just 43 percent of his two-point attempts and 32 percent of his threes as a freshman. Still, NBA teams will hope that Kabongo's ability to penetrate will be even more dangerous with better floor spacing in the pro game.

THE STATS LIKE...

Pierre Jackson, PG, Baylor

DX	Ford 100	Avg	TW%	TS%	Usg	Reb%	Ast%	BS%
54	77	65.5	.420	.494	.180	.049	.082	.023

The nation's best JC transfer, Jackson had an incredible junior season to help Baylor to the Elite Eight. NBA teams will rightfully be concerned about drafting a sub-six-footer, but Jackson's translated statistics are solid. He's got more than enough playmaking chops to run an offense and can put points on the board as a backup.

Arsalan Kazemi, SF, Oregon

DX	Ford 100	Avg	TW%	TS%	Usg	Reb%	Ast%	BS%
-	113	113	.462	.518	.135	.155	.030	.034

Kazemi repeats in this spot, but with a new school. He announced late in the summer that he would leave Rice and chose Oregon, a popular destination for transfers under Dana Altman. If Kazemi can maintain his elite rebounding and show improvement as an outside shooter against Pac-12 foes, he's got a chance to sneak into the second round and become the first Iranian player ever drafted.

Phil Pressey, PG, Missouri

DX	Ford 100	Avg	TW%	TS%	Usg	Reb%	Ast%	BS%
28	50	39.0	.426	.455	.137	.052	.089	.026

Pressey did a terrific job at the controls of the nation's best offense, setting up the Tigers' fleet of shooters. While not as accurate himself, particularly from deep, he maintained solid efficiency thanks to his ability to get to the free throw line. Pressey's size is a concern on defense, but the son of long-time NBA wing Paul Pressey (now an assistant for the Cavaliers) will follow his dad to the pros soon.

Andre Roberson, PF, Colorado

DX	Ford 100	Avg	TW%	TS%	Usg	Reb%	Ast%	BS%
23	32	27.5	.472	.473	.151	.179	.017	.034

After posting intriguing numbers in a limited role as a freshman, Roberson broke out last season as the leader of a Colorado team that exceeded expectations to win a game in the NCAA tournament. The nation's third-best translated rebounder (after NBA-bound Thomas Robinson and Colorado State's Pierce Hornung), Roberson also racked up blocks and steals. He's got some offensive skill—he made 19 three-pointers—and profiles as a lesser version of Kenneth Faried as a pro.

Jeff Withey, C, Kansas

DX	Ford 100	Avg	TW%	TS%	Usg	Reb%	Ast%	BS%
22	33	27.5	.469	.526	.130	.129	.013	.052

The Arizona transfer likely played himself into the first round during his first year as a regular, but Withey still might not be getting enough credit. It was Withey, not Anthony Davis, who led the nation in block percentage. He is also efficient offensively because of his fine free throw shooting. Withey's translated winning percentage ranks behind only Cody Zeller's among projected lottery picks.

THE SCOUTS LIKE...

Le'Bryan Nash, SF, Oklahoma State

DX	Ford 100	Avg	TW%	TS%	Usg	Reb%	Ast%	BS%
14	26	20.0	.217	.404	.218	.087	.023	.012

DraftExpress puts Nash in the last lottery spot, but during his freshman season in Stillwater, he wasn't nearly efficient enough to justify that kind of investment. Nash made just 44 percent of his twos and 24 percent of his threes, numbers that would translate into ghastly performance against pros. So far, creating shots and getting to the free throw line are the only things Nash does at NBA caliber.

Joshua Smith, C, UCLA

DX	Ford 100	Avg	TW%	TS%	Usg	Reb%	Ast%	BS%
21	35	28.0	.310	.489	.221	.146	.011	.025

Surprisingly, Smith hasn't been dinged much for his poor sophomore campaign, with DraftExpress projecting him in the first round and Ford putting him just outside that group. Smith rated well as a freshman, but last season his turnover problems and middling free throw shooting limited his productivity. So far, Smith hasn't demonstrated he'll be able to defend NBA opponents without fouling.

Patric Young, C, Florida

DX	Ford 100	Avg	TW%	TS%	Usg	Reb%	Ast%	BS%
19	31	25.0	.344	.517	.141	.129	.019	.016

While Young still made this list, the gulf between scouts and stats on his performance isn't nearly what it was a year ago. As a sophomore, Young made huge strides forward in his development into an offensive threat. Few players surpassed his 61.8 percent shooting from the field, and Young's ability in the pick-and-roll at both ends will serve him well in the NBA. Still, Young doesn't rebound or block shots at the rates his athletic prowess would suggest.

TOP FIVE FRESHMEN

1. Nerlens Noel, C, Kentucky

DX	Ford 100	Avg
2	1	1.5

Hmm. A skinny shot-blocker with excellent athleticism to his size headed to Lexington. Where have we heard this one before? If Noel is compared to Davis, who submitted one of the best freshman seasons in NCAA history, he will inevitably fall short. If judged on his own merits, Noel has a chance to help as much as any newcomer in the country, especially on defense. Such performance would assure him of the top spot next June.

2. Shabazz Muhammad, G/F, UCLA

DX	Ford 100	Avg
1	3	2.0

Assuming Muhammad's eligilbity is cleared up, he is likely to be the most polished freshman in the NCAA ranks. With a strong, compact frame, he looks a little like a smaller version of LeBron James. A natural scorer with playmaking chops, Muhammad is at his best operating from midrange with a smooth lefty stroke.

3. Isaiah Austin, C, Baylor

DX	Ford 100	Avg
6	6	6.0

A versatile big man with the ability to step away from the basket on offense, Austin could fade in and out of the Baylor attack not unlike Perry Jones last season. He's likely to make more of an impact at the defensive end, where his 9-3 standing reach translates into major shot-blocking potential.

4. Alex Poythress, F, Kentucky

DX	Ford 100	Avg
7	7	7.0

The second of three one-and-done candidates recruited by John Calipari (the last is shooting guard Archie Goodwin, who finished just outside these rankings), Poythress figures to step in for Terrence Jones as a face-up four man. In AAU ball, he showed range all the way to the three-point line. Poythress also has defensive potential at either forward spot thanks to his quickness and size.

5. Steven Adams, C, Pittsburgh

DX (2014)	Ford 100	Avg
7	9	8.0

With all due respect to the great Sean Marks, Adams is the most talented player ever to come from New Zealand. The 6-11 Kiwi figures to take some time to adapt to the American game, which explains why DraftExpress doesn't have him declaring next June. When he does catch on, Adams has a high ceiling thanks to his size and skills.

Transferring Up or Down

BY JOHN TEMPLON

When first-team All-Horizon League member Brandon Wood elected to transfer to Michigan State over Purdue and Tennessee in March 2011, he changed the face of the Big Ten race. Expectations were high, but Valparaiso's 1,000-point scorer flourished against major-conference foes. As Wood poured in 21 points during a 68-64 victory over Ohio State in the Big Ten tournament finale, it was obvious that Tom Izzo's one-season gamble had paid off.

While programs such as Michigan State are finding key contributors for one season, other institutions are using transfers to build programs. Between 450 and 500 players transfer each season, because of coaching changes, over-recruiting, academics, or a bad fit. That hasn't changed in years.

MOVING ON UP

What has changed, as Luke Winn astutely pointed out this summer, is that more players are transferring "up." The past two seasons have seen a definitive upward trend in the number of players leaving the mid-major ranks and heading to major conferences. The most notable examples are Wood, Seth Curry (Liberty to Duke), and Arnett Moultrie (UTEP to Mississippi State). All of those transfers made an impact last season.

Wood is part of a related trend, one where transfers receive a waiver from the NCAA and don't take a year off before joining their new team. For instance Wood's waiver was granted because he'd finished his studies at Valparaiso. Five other players jumped from the mid-major to major-conference ranks through waivers last season, and nine will do so this season. That includes guys like Mark Lyons (Xavier to Arizona), Julius Mays (Wright State to Kentucky) and Logan Aronhalt (Albany to Maryland). And while nine might not seem like a significant number in the grand scheme of things, in 2007-08 there were just six players total transferring up from a mid-major to a major-conference school.

That being said, the bigger question is what impact are these players making? Are they worth taking on? Do their skills translate when moving up a level?

The short answer is, "It depends." If you're desperately searching for a go-to superstar, the mid-major ranks probably aren't the right place to look. But if you need a solid contributor, you've come to the right place.

I looked at 50 players who transferred up from a mid-major to a major-conference team over the past five seasons. On average here's what happens to their numbers:

Stat	Impact of Moving from Mid-Major to Major
Offensive Rating	+7.7%
Possession Percentage	-19.5%
Effective Field Goal Percentage	+8.2%
Offensive Rebound Percentage	+7.5%
Defensive Rebound Percentage	-8.0%
Assist Rate	-13.1%
Turnover Rate	-7.8%
Free Throw Rate	-11.1%

Only about a quarter of up-transfers during this time period saw their offensive rating decrease. That's not because playing major-conference basketball is easier, it's because those players were consistently asked to do less in their new setting. Just one player out of 50, Bryce Cartwright, who went from Fresno State to Iowa with a stop at junior college in between, saw his possession percentage increase by more than four percent. Cartwright and Moultrie are the two biggest outliers in the entire data set. Both saw their minutes, possessions and offensive rating increase while playing against tougher competition. It's also worth noting that in general there's no tangible difference in performance at the BCS level between an up-transfer that takes a year off or one on a waiver that is eligible to play immediately.

With that in mind, let's check out how a few important players might fare this season.

Trey Zeigler
Pitt from Central Michigan

Zeigler lifted a heavy load last season while playing for his father, Ernie Zeigler, with the Chippewas. He probably won't have to use 31.6 percent of his team's possessions this season with the Panthers, nor will Jamie Dixon let him. Zeigler should provide a solid option for Pitt on the perimeter to help ease the departure of Ashton Gibbs.

Mark Lyons
Arizona from Xavier

While not the entire focal point of the offense, Lyons' numbers at Xavier suggest he's more than capable of becoming a key cog alongside Solomon Hill and Kyle Fogg. In fact Lyons could be the most efficient scorer on the Wildcats this season. Considering the decrease in assist rate most players have when going up a level, however, he's not the answer for the departure of the mercurial Josiah Turner at point guard.

Julius Mays
Kentucky from Wright State

Much like his Horizon League counterpart Wood, Mays looks primed to become an excellent off-ball option for a title contender. In fact, given Mays' numbers last season with Wright State, he can be expected to provide a perfect complement to Nerlens Noel and the other incoming freshmen at Kentucky. Mays might not shoot 42 percent on his threes like he did last season, but he'll certainly be able to space the floor and give John Calipari another weapon on offense.

Aaric Murray
West Virginia from La Salle

The Mountaineers will actually be relying on two up-transfers this season, as Juwan Staten is coming from Dayton. I'm more concerned about Murray because of how difficult it is for defensive rebounding to translate when moving up in competition. Also, while up-transfers as a group have seen their block rates rise, that's not the case for players who were prolific shot blockers at the mid-major level. The 6-10 forward has some question marks to answer coming into this season.

Glen Dean
Utah from Eastern Washington

The former Big Sky Freshman of the Year should give Utah a lift on the offensive end, meaning his three-point shooting is likely to be a skill that will translate to the Pac-12. On the other hand, it'll be interesting to see if the 5-10 point guard's assist rate, which was among the best in the nation, holds up moving forward.

DOWN TRANSFERS: AN OLD STORY

Of course "up" transfers only tell half the story. Almost three times as many players transfer "down," from a major-conference program to a mid-major. With their big-school pedigrees, those players often come with increased expectations, but the fact is most won't live up to the hype. On average, no more than five of these down transfers will hit all of the following (relatively modest) goals in their first season: play more than 65 percent of their team's minutes; have an offensive rating over 100; and post a usage rate above 22 percent.

Those five or so players are the ones mid-major fans think about when they hear the words "major-conference transfer." The success of Xavier Silas (Northern Illinois), Rakim Sanders (Fairfield), Lamont Jones (Iona) and Armon Bassett (Ohio) makes fans think that happiness is just one transfer away. Unfortunately that's not the case. The 27 players who fit those criteria make up just 11.6 percent of the total number of down transfers the past five seasons.

Of course there's one way to hedge your bets. Most down transfers are moving on because of a lack of playing time. The unique players are ones like Silas, Sanders, Jones and Bassett. What all four of them have in common is that they played more than 50 percent of the minutes for their major-conference team in their final season before transferring down. Here's a look at a few transfers who fit that criterion this season.

Rotnei Clarke
Butler from Arkansas

There's nothing from Clarke's time at Arkansas to suggest that he won't be one of the best players in the Atlantic 10 from day one. An elite shooter with the Razorbacks, Clarke will slide over to point guard. His 120.8 offensive rating in 2010-11 with Arkansas, along with his 20.1 percent possession usage, suggest that a high-possession, high-impact weapon is about to be unleashed by Brad Stevens. Due to his move to point guard, Clarke might see his assist rate go up even more than the one-fifth that is typical.

Malcolm Armstead
Wichita State from Oregon

Armstead started 52 games at Oregon before transferring to WSU and, while he probably won't need to make a huge contribution on offense for the Shockers to be successful, his athleticism will make him a terror in the Missouri Valley Conference. Armstead was ninth in the nation in steal percentage in 2010-11. Not surprisingly, that's a skill that tends to translate—and even rise slightly—when moving down a level. Expect Armstead to be a key contributor for a WSU team that's thinking NCAA tournament again.

Tony Freeland
Long Beach State from DePaul

Freeland won't be eligible until December after leaving DePaul at mid-season, but once he gets on the court there's a chance the 6-6 forward's game could take off. While he sometimes struggled against the taller frontcourt players in the Big East, his knack for offensive rebounding should continue to make a difference for LBSU. Freeland is one player who could see his usage decrease at the mid-major level, and that'd probably be a good thing for him and the 49ers.

Overall, players transferring down do pretty well for themselves. Almost all find increased playing time and get the ball more often. Most impressively, on average every aspect of a down transfer's game improves at the mid-major level. The smallest gains are made in offensive rebounding.

The average down transfer plays 52 percent of his team's minutes, with an offensive rating around 99.4 while using 21.2 percent of his new team's possessions. Not a savior, but certainly a useful player nonetheless.

If you find the right player for your system, getting a transfer continues to be a viable way to quickly restock or bolster a program with veterans.

Thanks to Dan Hanner, whose initial set of data on players moving between schools was invaluable.

The New Power Structure

BY DREW CANNON

If you pay attention to college basketball even a little bit, you hear the term "mid-major" thrown around a lot. Recruiting analysts like to toss "low-major" at you, as well—it's great to be able to discuss the quality of a prospect (and the type of school he should eventually attend) in that kind of quick generality. Traditionally, "mid-major" in the media is much like the term "non-BCS." The breakdown goes like this:

High majors: ACC, Big 12, Big East, Big Ten, Pac-12, SEC
Mid-majors: A-10, CAA, C-USA, Horizon, MVC, MWC, WAC, WCC
Low mid-majors: Everyone else

For the past seven years, Ken Pomeroy's conference ratings have named the six high-major conferences the top six conferences nationally, with the single exception that the Atlantic 10 was rated above the Pac-12 in 2012.

Similarly, the eight mid-major conferences have been rated Nos. 7 through 14 for the past seven years, except that 1) the Atlantic Sun placed above the Horizon League in 2012, 2) the Mid-American rated above the Western Athletic in 2008, 3) the Mid-American ranked above the Colonial Athletic in 2007, and 4) the Metro Atlantic Athletic finished ahead of the Horizon League in 2006.

The average men's basketball budgets of the high-major conferences ranged from five to seven million dollars, of the mid-major conferences from 1.6 to 2.8 million dollars, and of the low-major conferences from 0.6 to 1.6 million dollars.

In case you haven't noticed, though, the conferences are changing quite a bit. If each league had been populated all those years by the teams they have now, in 2012-13, the table shows where each conference would have ranked in average KenPom ranking (weighted a little for recency) from 2004-12.

Conf	2004	'05	'06	'07	'08	'09	'10	'11	'12
ACC	1	1	3	1	1	1	1	3	5
Big East	2	3	1	4	5	5	4	2	2
Big Ten	5	5	4	3	6	3	5	1	1
Big 12	4	2	5	5	2	2	2	4	3
SEC	3	4	2	2	4	6	3	6	4
Pac-12	7	6	6	7	3	4	6	5	7
Mtn. West	6	8	7	8	9	9	10	7	8
MVC	9	7	8	6	7	10	8	11	9
A-10	8	12	10	9	8	7	7	9	6
C-USA	10	11	13	10	10	8	9	8	10
WCC	11	10	9	11	11	11	11	10	11
MAC	12	9	12	12	12	18	16	18	16
Horizon	13	13	16	13	13	12	12	12	15
CAA	14	16	11	14	16	14	13	13	14
MAAC	17	18	15	20	15	15	15	15	17
Big West	16	14	14	16	17	16	18	17	21
WAC	18	17	17	25	22	13	14	16	12
Sun Belt	15	15	19	21	14	19	19	26	18
SoCon	19	22	23	15	18	24	17	21	25
Southland	27	19	18	17	19	17	22	25	26
Ivy	21	20	22	19	26	26	20	14	13
OVC	20	24	25	28	29	21	21	20	20
Summit	24	26	28	24	20	22	25	19	22
Am. East	25	21	21	22	24	20	24	29	27
Big Sky	22	27	20	23	23	23	23	23	28
Patriot	26	23	27	18	21	25	27	22	23
NEC	28	28	26	29	28	28	29	24	24
Big South	31	29	24	26	27	29	28	28	29
A-Sun	29	31	32	30	30	27	26	27	19
Ind.	23	25	29	31	25	30	31	32	31
Grt West	30	30	30	27	31	31	33	31	32
MEAC	32	32	33	32	32	32	30	30	30
SWAC	33	33	31	33	33	33	32	33	33

The dividing lines aren't quite as definitive as they once were, but there are clearly five levels now, rather than three. (The Sun Belt's kind of up for grabs.) Below is how the conferences will rate out based on their membership as far into the future as we can see (for instance with Notre Dame in the ACC).

So going forward, and beginning this season, the new power structure has five levels. (See table.)

Conf	2004	'05	'06	'07	'08	'09	'10	'11	'12
ACC	1	1	1	1	1	1	1	2	5
Big Ten	4	4	3	3	5	3	4	1	1
Big 12	3	2	5	4	2	2	2	3	2
SEC	2	3	2	2	4	5	3	6	3
Big East	5	6	4	7	6	6	5	5	4
Pac-12	6	5	6	6	3	4	6	4	7
A-10	8	12	10	9	8	7	7	8	6
MVC	9	7	8	5	7	8	8	10	8
Mtn. West	7	8	7	8	9	9	9	7	9
WCC	10	9	9	10	10	10	10	11	12
C-USA	11	11	14	14	12	11	10	11	10
Horizon	13	13	16	12	13	12	13	12	14
MAC	12	10	12	11	11	16	15	17	15
CAA	17	15	11	13	17	15	14	13	19
Big West	14	14	13	15	14	14	16	14	16
MAAC	15	16	15	19	16	13	12	16	18
Ivy	20	18	19	18	25	26	20	15	13
WAC	21	24	22	21	24	18	18	22	11
Sun Belt	16	17	17	25	15	17	19	26	17
SoCon	18	20	23	16	18	25	17	20	25
OVC	19	23	26	27	28	19	21	19	22
Patriot	24	19	21	17	21	24	24	21	20
Summit	23	25	28	24	19	21	23	18	23
Big Sky	22	26	18	22	22	22	22	23	26
Am. East	26	21	25	23	23	20	27	28	28
Southland	25	22	20	20	20	23	26	29	29
A-Sun	29	30	30	30	29	27	25	25	21
NEC	27	27	27	28	27	28	29	24	24
Big South	30	28	24	26	26	29	28	27	27
MEAC	31	31	32	31	30	30	30	30	30
Grt West	28	29	31	29	31	32	32	32	31
SWAC	32	32	29	32	32	31	31	31	32
Ind.	-	-	-	-	-	-	-	-	-

High majors: ACC, Big 12, Big East, Big Ten, Pac-12, SEC
High mid-majors: A-10, C-USA, MVC, MWC, WCC
Mid-majors: Big West, CAA, Horizon, MAAC, MAC, WAC
Low mid-majors: America East, A-Sun, Big Sky, Big South, Ivy, NEC, OVC, Patriot, SoCon, Southland, Sun Belt
Fringe mid-majors: MEAC, SWAC, Great West, Ind.

This assumes the WAC continues to exist. Right now the 2014 conference has six teams, and Idaho's been in talks with the Big Sky.

Then again it's better to classify teams rather than conferences. So here are the top and bottom five programs at each level, meaning had these levels existed at the time a case could have been made over the past few years that these teams should have been pushed up or pulled down a peg. Again, these rankings are based on historical (2004-12) KenPom ratings, and are in no way meant to suggest that Rutgers should be booted out of the Big East:

High majors
Top: Kansas, Duke, North Carolina, Wisconsin, Kentucky
Bottom: Rutgers, UCF, Oregon State, TCU, SMU
High mid-majors
Top: Gonzaga, Xavier, BYU, UNLV, New Mexico
Bottom: Fordham, Pepperdine, San Jose State, UTSA, Florida International
Mid-majors
Top: San Diego State, Kent State, George Mason, Akron, Ohio
Bottom: Canisius, Towson, Seattle, UC Riverside, UC Davis
Low mid-majors
Top: Oral Roberts, Davidson, Murray State, Western Kentucky, Belmont
Bottom: Omaha, Houston Baptist, SIU Edwardsville, Bryant, Longwood
Fringe mid-majors
Top: Utah Valley, Morgan State, New Orleans, Hampton, Delaware State
Bottom: Howard, NJIT, Grambling, Alcorn State, Maryland Eastern Shore

Breaking Down the Sophomore Breakout

BY JOSH REED

"The best thing about freshmen is that they become sophomores."

Al McGuire said that, and he was absolutely right. The vast majority of freshmen are not very good. The centers can't convert in the paint, the wings can't shoot threes, and the point guards pass the ball to the other team nearly as often as they pass it to a teammate. If the fate of your team resides in the hands of a freshman that was not invited to a national All-Star game or two as a high school senior, chances are your team is in trouble.

But, as it turns out, freshmen improve quite a bit over their first offseason, and by the time they're sophomores, they're largely unrecognizable. (In my experience this holds true for freshmen that didn't play college basketball as well. My freshman Winamp playlist was downright embarrassing.) Indeed, the improvement that the average sophomore shows from his freshman season is about equal to the jumps we see in the subsequent two offseasons—combined.

Still, not every freshman blossoms as a sophomore, and even among those that do, there are jumps and then there are leaps. Over my offseason, I looked at what predicts a sophomore leap, other than being named "John Jenkins."

But before we get to that, let me offer an explanation on what exactly was measured. The sample of players were those from power conference teams, in the high school classes of 2006 through 2010 (Greg Oden through Harrison Barnes). The only numbers I used were conference numbers, and because the goal was to measure freshman-to-sophomore improvement, that means players who didn't play enough in either season were excluded. So, one-and-dones are out (sorry, Greg Oden), as are sophomores that come from out of nowhere.

GOOD FRESHMEN MAKE FOR GOOD SOPHOMORES

Yes, good players tend to stay that way. Film at 11. But while this axiom holds true for every subcategory of freshman I looked at, the effect was definitely stronger for some than others.

And towering above them all was short players. The catch-all statistic we'll use is Drew Cannon's Four Pettinella Score, or "PET," unadjusted for schedule (though by looking at conference-only data, we've minimized any inaccuracies that would arise). PET is a rate statistic, like free throw percentage, but we can convert it to a counting statistic by adjusting it by minutes (or "PETMin").

Players that stand 6-2 or under show about twice as much correlation from freshmen to sophomore PETMin as everyone else. Stated differently, this means that short freshmen who play well are about twice as likely to hold onto those gains as sophomores than are their taller teammates. I wish I could tell you why this happens, but alas, it remains a mystery. But I can rule out at least one theory.

"DON'T PUT ME IN, COACH"

A comment one hears frequently is that big men tend to be "projects," while smaller guys are more ready to play. But, as best as I can tell, the only thing true about that comment is that coaches seem to believe it.

Freshmen	PET	Percentage of Minutes Played
6-2 and Under	18.48	49.69
6-5 and Under	18.47	47.85
Between 6-3 and 6-7	18.58	46.20
6-6 and Taller	18.34	41.58
6-8 and Taller	18.11	38.96
6-10 and Taller	17.66	36.90

Generally speaking, shorter freshmen aren't any more ready to play than any other group. While the taller guys do lag the field, the difference is still much smaller than the minutes distribution would indicate. What seems to be happening is that smaller players are thrown into the deep end as freshmen, while post players are slowly introduced to the college game.

That said, keep in mind that this study only observes offense, and it ignores defense entirely. Defending the paint is much more important than defending the perimeter, and it's quite possible, if not likely, that big men sit on the bench until they're strong enough to defend (or defend without hacking).

But for our purposes, it's still a notable result, coupled with the finding that the percentage of minutes one plays as a freshman actually correlates negatively with sophomore improvement. This does not mean that hiding a freshman on the bench is a good strategy for developing impact sophomores. Playing time, after all, is partly a function of how good a player is, but it's also a function of how good his teammates are. So the fact that we see a negative correlation here probably only indicates that roster turnover exists. But although the effect isn't particularly strong, it's there, and it's sufficient to rule out the notion that putting a freshman on the court for longer stretches counts as some sort of investment.

LISTEN TO WHAT DAVE TELEP SAYS, BECAUSE IT MATTERS

A few years ago, I studied how freshmen performed against their high school ranking. One of the things that came from that study was that outside of the top 20 or so, it's a crapshoot. It doesn't really matter whether a freshman is ranked at No. 40 or 90, either way he had about an equal chance to be an impact performer.

This pattern is repeated when we look at sophomore improvement. The change in PETMin from freshman to sophomore seasons is virtually identical for players ranked in the top 50 as for those ranked in the bottom 50. However, it's important to keep in mind that one-and-done freshmen are excluded from this study, and those guys tend to dominate the top 50. Nonetheless, there's no correlation between a player's ranking and his sophomore performance or improvement.

Of course that doesn't mean rankings are unimportant. As a group, players that are ranked not only perform better as freshmen, but they also show about a 25 percent greater improvement in sophomore PETMin. Thus, while it doesn't matter whether a player is ranked No. 40 or 90, it does matter whether he's ranked at all, and this effect outlasts how they perform as freshmen. In fact, the average unranked sophomore is about as good as a freshman ranked in the bottom 50. Ranked players start out well ahead, and that gap only increases.

THIS IS AARON WHITE'S WORLD, AND WE'RE ALL JUST LIVING IN IT

Finally, there's one more freshman statistic that seems to matter—and matter quite a bit—in terms of sophomore improvement. The unfortunate thing is that it only reveals itself for a certain category of player. Specifically, for freshmen who stand at 6-8 or taller, the number of three-pointers they attempt shows a strong correlation for both sophomore improvement and sophomore performance.

It doesn't matter if they make them. And it doesn't seem to be any stronger for players who are predominantly three-point shooters. If anything, those actually tend to be negative. What matters is that a taller player has some three-point confidence. In fact, there was no stronger correlator of sophomore improvement, in any subgroup, than three-point attempts for tall players. What this means is that guys like Brandon Mobley, Ryan Anderson, and yes, Aaron White figure to be pretty good this season.

Credit to Drew Cannon for his help in unraveling the data.

The RPI Is Not Dying Fast Enough

BY JOHN GASAWAY

Tom Hagen: "His medical condition is reported as terminal. He's only gonna live another six months anyway."

Michael Corleone: "He's been dying of the same heart attack for 20 years."

A couple years ago I started asking people in basketball if they could tell me who invented the Ratings Percentage Index. Invariably the answer I received was "the NCAA," but the NCAA's not a person. I wanted a name.

No one knew that name, and, for one of the few times in my adult life, Google and Wikipedia were no help either. So I looked into the question myself, and learned that an NCAA staffer named Jim Van Valkenburg formulated the RPI in the fall of 1980. Last February, after I attended the NCAA's annual mock selection exercise in Indianapolis, I wrote about Van Valkenburg's creation in a piece I titled, "The RPI's Birth, Triumph, and Encirclement."

By "triumph" I meant not merely that the RPI has survived far longer than one might have expected. I meant additionally that the original impetus behind the RPI—giving the committee the knowledge it needs, even if that means inventing something entirely new—required vision, a truly open institutional mind, and an extraordinary amount of effort.

At a time when very few games were televised and college basketball fans had little to go by other than final scores, the NCAA unquestionably advanced the committee's knowledge through the creation of the RPI. That time, however, has long since passed. The problem with the NCAA isn't that it invented the RPI. The problem with the NCAA is that it stopped doing things like inventing the RPI.

Van Valkenburg passed away in 1995, but I was able to meet with his son:

"If your dad were sitting here right now," I say, "and I told him his RPI is still being used in 2012 even though a goodly number of outside observers think there are better metrics, what would he say?" Van Valkenburg's son doesn't hesitate. "Dad was a realist. I think he'd say, 'If there's something better, use it.'"

There's something better, but it would be a mistake to classify this as merely a question of competing rating systems. We do the game no great favors if we replace an untrustworthy rating system that plays too large a role in college basketball with a trustworthy rating system that plays too large a role in college basketball. It would be better to unseat the hegemonic and flawed rating system we have, shrink the job description, and create an index comprised of several reliable and mutually correcting rating systems. Out with the erratic and mercurial Czar, in with a newly constituted cabinet populated by steady, boring, straight-arrow types.

That a rating system should measure performance with reasonable accuracy, that we should be most suspicious precisely when that system's outputs veer wildly from those of other systems, that programs should be evaluated on basketball performance and not on some intrinsically unstable compound of performance plus schedule-based happenstance—such assertions are surely innocuous to the point of banality. And while it's true the NCAA has on occasion viewed innocuous banalities as radical notions, I am cautiously optimistic that better and more accurate days lie ahead for college hoops. I have my reasons.

STRANGE BEDFELLOWS AND ENCOURAGING SIGNS

For many years and indeed continuing well into the present century, the most common criticism of the RPI was not that is was some pitiably crude antique but rather the opposite, that it was just some weird number cooked up in a lab somewhere by a bunch of NCAA brainiacs who probably didn't know anything about "real" basketball. One or two prominent commentators still speak of the RPI in this manner, and if sports were as important as politics these commentators would doubtless be labeled paleos. So it is that today the NCAA's besieged metric is encircled by an unusual alliance, one forged between paleos who think evaluating teams should be more or less stat-free and those of us who think the process should simply be informed by better stats.

Thus far the NCAA has pleased neither camp, of course, but there are at long last some hopeful straws in the wind coming from Indy. This summer the NCAA had talks with at least one purveyor of a superior metric, discussions that included analysis of said metric's predictive capability in NCAA tournament games. Nothing has come of those talks yet, and maybe in the end nothing will issue directly from this particular event. Nevertheless, this is precisely the kind of discussion the NCAA should be open to.

In addition, the NCAA is now at least saying some of the right things. "The committee does reference other computer rankings," NCAA associate director of men's basketball David Worlock remarked last February, "and it is noted when there are significant discrepancies between the RPI and other rankings." The part about noting significant discrepancies, if true, would be fantastic, and indeed would be the next best thing to retiring the RPI altogether.

Call it lip service if you wish, but saying the right things is important. It's often the penultimate step before doing the right things, and in the NCAA's case saying the right things constitutes a new development. For years the things the NCAA said about their RPI were arguably worse than the metric's actual impact on the selection and seeding of the tournament field. The official version long promulgated from HQ held that the NCAA was truly "open" to other metrics but, lo and behold, the RPI had managed to go 32-0 in a free and unbiased annual competition where all possible analytic measures were considered.

Instead the NCAA could have spent those years saying, "Look, we have the Internet in Indianapolis too. Enough already. We understand the RPI's inferior to other rating systems. But what you have to understand is that performance isn't our only criterion. The RPI is ours. We're proud of it, we're comfortable with it, and over the course of three decades we've learned how to work around it and still craft brackets that even the RPI's critics admit are by and large pretty well constructed."

If the NCAA had said words to this effect, their stance would be no less questionable in terms of basketball analysis, but their credibility as an organization would most certainly have improved. Even today it's commonly assumed by the hoops fan in the street that if the NCAA's still using the RPI it must be because they don't understand there's a problem.

Nothing could be further from the truth. NCAA staffers are well aware of the RPI's deficiencies, and on occasion they can take pugnacious delight in deploying their best forensic weapons on behalf of their beleaguered metric. Call me a dreamer, but I'm chalking that up as still another good sign. Such a stance is far more pliant than either simple incomprehension or blind faith would be. It suggests maybe we'll all be chuckling about this in the past tense over a beer sometime soon.

Then again last March the committee gave at-large bids to Southern Miss and Colorado State, teams that, as we'll see, occasioned two of the largest rating-system "discrepancies" that the NCAA says it's now noting. So, no, don't pour that beer just yet.

RATING SPORTS TEAMS AND RATING BASKETBALL TEAMS

Last spring Nate Silver wrote about the NCAA's use of the RPI, and somewhere at the New York Times there's an editor who deserves a big pat on the back for coming up with this headline: "NCAA Builds Solid Brackets from a Shaky Foundation."

That about sums it up. The committee that selects and seeds the field will always be second-guessed, because the essentials of the situation are impossible. Staff the committee any way you choose, with philosopher-kings/queens, Bill Raftery alone, or the first 10 names in the Indy phone book, and those essentials won't change. The difference between the verdicts handed out by the committee—teams are either in the field or they're not—will always be orders of magnitude greater than the difference in actual performance between the last team in and the best team left out.

To its credit the NCAA has met this impossible situation with unfailing diligence and a proper regard for the impact their decisions will have. So what's the problem?

Though Van Valkenburg was tasked with creating a rating system expressly for use by the men's basketball committee, the RPI is not a basketball metric. It is instead an opponent- and venue-adjusted winning percentage applicable to any team sport. As such it can be quite handy, of course, and today the NCAA uses it in no fewer than 11 Division I sports.

But, irony of ironies, the sport that Van Valkenburg had in mind at the RPI's birth is one that can be captured with much greater detail. The RPI's limitation is that it can do nothing more than treat basketball as just another sport where games produce outcomes. Conversely metrics that treat basketball as basketball yield information that is, not surprisingly, superior.

How do we know the information produced by these basketball-based metrics is so very superior? The intuitive answer is that the resulting information is way better than the RPI at predicting outcomes. (As Nate has put it, "Over the long run, the RPI has predicted the outcome of NCAA games more poorly than almost any other system.") That answer, however, tends to upset a few observers. Such people will tell you that the NCAA isn't trying to predict anything with their selection and seeding of the NCAA tournament field, and that the committee is or should be in the business of simply and explicitly rewarding past performance.

Which is why the intuitive answer has always required clarification. Why are basketball-centered metrics so good at predicting future outcomes? Because they bring accuracy to bear on past performance.

Wherever the RPI is defended, you may hear this issue rendered as prediction (boo) versus past performance (yay). Actually there's no need to traffic in verb tenses. The choice lies instead between a reliable measure of past basketball performance and an unreliable measure of past generic sports team performance.

If we observe hundreds of Division I coaches using basketball-specific metrics, if we grant that none of them are trying to win their office pool, and if we remark that no coach uses the RPI as a basketball performance measure, we can state the case plainly. To reward past performance you will want to measure it, and no one but the NCAA tries to measure past basketball performance with the RPI.

Naturally "past performance" is never a perfectly clear construct, no matter how accurately it's measured. In basketball, as in all sports except perhaps bowling, "best performance" and "most wins" will never be totally synonymous.

It's this synapse which has led to claims that these fancy-pants new metrics will subvert the importance of good old-fashioned wins. It's said that, by adding reliable performance measures to the discussion, basketball-based metrics will move the focus of interest and decision from the hardwood to the hard drive.

This vein of worry echoes the dire forecasts issued nearly three decades ago, when all manner of terrible things were said to be imminent because the college game was about to adopt the shot clock. The fears may well prove equally groundless in this instance. For one thing, the NCAA and its committee have been subverting good old-fashioned wins for years, very often correctly and with the RPI's blessing, and I haven't noticed any Occupy Indy outrage in response. To take just one example close at hand, Washington won the Pac-12 regular season championship outright in 2012, yet the Huskies did not receive an invitation to play in the NCAA tournament.

Second, if the RPI were reliably favoring teams that "just go out and win their games," it would actually be a far more lovable metric. Instead it's been known to develop fevered and reckless analytic crushes on the likes of Colorado State. Last year the Rams went 8-6 in the weakest Mountain West we've seen since 2006. Meanwhile Drexel won 19 consecutive games between January and March. CSU was given a No. 11 seed, and the Dragons were sent to the NIT. The RPI values teams that just go out and win their games? If only.

Lastly, this professed fear of accuracy fails to acknowledge how all of us evaluate actual basketball teams. If someday the NCAA does make the jump to basketball-specific performance measures, I seriously doubt the committee's members will become unquestioning puppets at the ends of new statistical strings. The point is simply to help those committee members ground their discussions on premises that are finally in accord with observed basketball occurrences.

As it stands currently, those discussions can in a small number of instances be preempted by an RPI so erroneously high that no one dares to stand in the way. On Selection Sunday last year, Southern Miss had an RPI of 21, while Colorado State clocked in at No. 24. By contrast the consensus of multiple independently designed basketball-specific metrics pegged those teams in the low 70s and high 90s, respectively. Maybe there were legitimate cases to be made for both teams, but, with the RPI inflating both beyond all recognition, there was no occasion or wish to find out.

THE RPI AS MID-MAJOR POWER-UP

In its past two end-of-year top 100s, the RPI has included 25 teams that Ken Pomeroy didn't have in his top 100s, and 24 of those 25 programs are mid-majors. And in the same population of teams over the same time period, if you look at the 20 largest discrepancies between the two rating systems in cases where the RPI liked a team more than Ken's system did, you'll find that all 20 are mid-majors.

This does not mean the RPI "overrates mid-majors." Belmont in particular will be forgiven if they laugh out loud at that sequence of words. In fact major-conference powers dominate the top of the RPI just like they dominate the top of the polls, the basketball-specific metrics, and pretty much everything else. What it does mean is that the teams in the vicinity of the bubble who have been most egregiously overrated by the RPI the past two years been drawn exclusively from the ranks of the mid-majors. It need hardly be added that the teams who are bumped out of the field of 68 by these RPI-fueled competitors may very well be fellow mid-majors, as we saw this past season with a near miss like Drexel.

Of course in cases where an overrated team wins its league's automatic bid, the harm done here is negligible. (See Long Island in both 2011 and 2012.) But where the team in question doesn't have an autobid in its pocket, the potential for selection malpractice is high. And the capacity of the RPI to act as a mid-major power-up was displayed unmistakably by Southern Miss and Colorado State in 2012.

My point isn't that these two teams should not have received bids. Merely that, particularly in the case of Southern Miss, I suspect there was little opportunity for or inclination on the part of committee members to look more closely at the question. And, as things stand now, I don't blame the committee one bit.

The truth is it would have required something bordering on real courage for the committee not to give a bid to Southern Miss. Basketball-specific metrics may have pegged the Golden Eagles as merely the 70-somethingth best team in the country, but a substantial and lovingly catalogued body of custom and tradition going back decades states that a team with an RPI this high will almost certainly get a bid. For weeks prior to Selection Sunday, the mock brackets crafted by reputable and widely read analysts showed Southern Miss safely in the field of 68.

Suffice it to say if for some strange reason the committee had revealed on Selection Sunday that they'd excluded Southern Miss, they would have been instantly criticized from all directions. The first question put to the committee chair that night by Jim Nantz would have been about Southern Miss. Larry Eustachy would have popped up on a live feed from Hattiesburg looking shocked and dejected. After all, his team had gathered to watch the bracket show thinking they'd learn where they'd be playing. Analysts had been unanimous in saying that Southern Miss was "in," not one had them on the bubble or anywhere close to it. So what happened? What in the world was the committee thinking?

Perhaps 2013 will be quiet on this front (2011 was, by chance), but if not we already know the specific contours of the challenge that will arise. The committee can't jettison all that custom and tradition without giving prior warning to the outside world. They'd be savaged if they did and, anyway, the last project they have time to undertake in February and March is a fresh look at something as exhaustively discussed as the Ratings Percentage Index.

Our fatigue with regard to the RPI as a topic is cumulative, and we've long since reached the point where everyone is not just tired but tired of being tired of this discussion. The NCAA most certainly is tired of being asked about the RPI, and I'm tired of seeing it calculated four places to the right of the decimal as if it actually signifies anything remotely so precise. By the same token with each passing year the NCAA becomes a little more adept at addressing this topic that both they and their interlocutors have grown so very weary of. Think of those two quantities—topical fatigue and the NCAA's discursive chops on this topic—as steadily increasing over time.

The actual mischief visited upon the selection process by the RPI, conversely, fluctuates year to year, and it does so for reasons substantially outside the committee's control. Any committee that inherits the RPI and is presented with at-large candidates enhanced by mid-major power-ups is virtually guaranteed to wreak evaluative havoc on a line or two. It's an accident waiting to happen, so please stop yelling at that year's committee chair. You're yelling at a person who can cite chapter and verse from Bart Simpson: "It was like that when I got here."

DOCTORS BURY MISTAKES, LAWYERS HANG THEM, AND THE RPI GIVES THEM BIDS

The NCAA has long displayed laudable consistency in specifying they want to select the "best" teams for their tournament. In basketball the best teams score points and prevent opponents from scoring, and the best way of measuring that is to track a large body of possessions. Drill down into those possessions, pull up a core sample of basketball performance, make due allowance for strength of schedule, and you'll have a good departure point for discussion.

At least that's how the process has played out for me as I've analyzed teams under the RPI dynasty's sun. If on the other hand the NCAA announces tomorrow that they're going to start using basketball-specific metrics more extensively, I suppose there's a chance the ensuing full moon could awaken the werewolf inside every head coach and teams will promptly start running up the score at every opportunity.

I'm just not sure that chance is a large one. Happily this is not September-variety college football, so the following reassurances apply: 1) Running up the score is rare in college basketball; 2) If a team does run up the score it doesn't help their numbers as much as commonly thought (last year in conference play Kentucky built perhaps the best basketball-specific numbers I've ever seen less by blowing out opponents than by never losing to them); and 3) If a team does run up the score—or, what's more likely, if they're simply on the scene when the opponent happens to implode completely—it's simple enough to adjust the resulting numbers to something more descriptive of their actual ability.

If you want to make sure teams aren't rewarded for running up the score, don't reward teams for running up the score. Look at a trusty measure of team performance and filter out any funky scoring distributions.

A similar filter for the RPI, one that would make its raw outputs reliably congruent with team performance, would make life far easier for the men's basketball committee. But there is no such filter, and it's likely there can't be one, for the simple reason that the RPI is erratic. My comparison of the ratings produced by different systems for 100-plus teams pulled from the top of D-I in each of the last two seasons turned up multiple instances where the RPI likely underrated or overrated teams by 50, 60, or even 70 spots in a 345-team population.

These are extreme cases, to be sure. In the sample I pulled together the RPI sported a degree of evaluative uniqueness greater than 50 spots seven percent of the time. But it's precisely these exceptionally divergent days for the RPI that can lift a team into tournament consideration and indeed a bid. As it stands now, being the team that the RPI really screws up on can be the best thing that happens to a coach. Of the 225 ratings I looked at where the RPI assessed teams in the tournament discussion over the past two seasons, the rating given to Colorado State last season ranked No. 221 in its congruence with basketball-specific metrics. That is, there were only four ratings over the past two years in this sample that were even more aberrant.

In September Luke Winn detailed how then-Colorado State coach Tim Miles, with the help of then-athletic director Paul Kowalczyk, set out to bend the RPI's eccentricities in the Rams' favor by scheduling what the two men hoped would be high-RPI but relatively low-basketball-performance opponents. Hopes can be dashed, of course. Those opponents don't always turn out the way you think they will, but in this case CSU caught all the breaks. Give Miles credit. The way the NCAA sets up its game, a coach would be negligent if he didn't indulge in this kind of reconnaissance. But is such recon really germane to the question of which teams should play in the tournament?

Granted, there are instances where the long belittled RPI eagerly joins the chorus being sung by those snooty basketball-specific metrics. Last year teams like Kentucky (obviously), Michigan State, Indiana, Georgetown, Vanderbilt, NC State, Washington, and VCU all had RPI's that corresponded quite well with their actual levels of performance. It's possible for the RPI to be correct with respect to a given team, but "possible" isn't good enough to earn our trust, for a basketball metric or anything else.

THE PALEOS HAVE A POINT

If the RPI were a window air conditioner, for example, the stereotypical view of the NCAA's metric as merely an antiquated relic would hold that the stupid thing would just sit there in your window, rusting and inoperable. But the reality's a bit more schizophrenic. Some of the time your RPI-brand air conditioner will in fact work perfectly. Then again some of the time it will work pretty well but not as well as you'd like. Some of the time it will function, quixotically enough, as a heater. And on some admittedly rare but nevertheless memorable occasions, it will turn into a blowtorch.

That actually puts the best face on the RPI, for the NCAA's metric is at its most benign when it's attempting to rate just one team. A single rating may turn out to be more or less correct, and even when it's not there's a chance the error won't have tangible consequences, whether because the team has an automatic bid or because they're not even in the tournament picture.

But as we pull back from that close-up and consider the RPI in relation to teams, plural, and indeed to college basketball as a whole, the picture changes. Even a team that the RPI happens to rate correctly will arrive at Selection Sunday having played, say, 25 different opponents, and the chances are good that the RPI will have badly mischaracterized a significant minority of those teams. For example, any team that was lucky enough to have Southern Miss or Colorado State on their schedule last year had an excellent chance to earn credit for a "top-50 win." Indeed part of the Golden Eagles' hypnotic power over the RPI was due to the fact that they went to Fort Collins on November 19 and beat putatively mighty CSU.

By definition the men's basketball committee traffics in close calls. Should this team be given a No. 1 or No. 2 seed? Should we give the last at-large bid to Team X or Team Y? In such cases having one or two additional top-50 wins can be huge. With the RPI's erratic assessments functioning as the mortar for all this intricate brickwork, it's fairly amazing the committee has done as well as they have.

The men's basketball committee may manage to wriggle free of the RPI on occasion, but the metric has succeeded in tying up the entirety of D-I when it comes to scheduling. The careful research that coaching staffs devote to cobbling together an RPI-kosher slate of opponents, the consultants advising mid-major league offices on the metric's intricacies, the willingness of major-conference programs to record their early-season wins against off-the-RPI-radar Division II opponents—maybe it's all an invitation for us to see what is in front of one's nose.

Somewhere along the line an idea was accepted and institutionalized, and it still frankly surprises me. It's the idea that the NCAA should be in the business of explicitly *favoring* some schedules at the expense of others, as opposed to simply *measuring* strength of schedule as one discrete variable incidental to rating teams. Last March, for example, Jeff Hathaway, the chair of the men's basketball committee, said teams "have to be aggressive in their [non-conference] scheduling." Hathaway was just voicing the conventional wisdom, of course, but how did this come to be regarded as either conventional or wise?

Naturally as a fan I love aggressive non-conference scheduling. It's more fun to watch two good teams play each other in November or December than it is to watch a game with just one good team or none. I also recognize, however, that a team's ability to achieve the highest level of performance in basketball is independent of its coach's ability to achieve the highest level of performance in scheduling to the NCAA's liking.

In a normal evaluative world that still had conference play, we would surely tell every coach, "Go Izzo or go cupcake, we don't care. Play the non-conference schedule you want to play and don't worry about it. Our rating systems will do their thing, and the committee will watch your games. We'll know how well you've played regardless." But the famously schedule-myopic RPI can't say that. In effect the NCAA, whether unintentionally or ingeniously, has recast a mathematical shortcoming as a settled matter of policy on the plane of The Good of the Game. If you want to improve your standing in our rating, the NCAA says with a straight face, you must excel not only at basketball but at scheduling. It would have required less effort and been far more just to simply address the mathematical shortcoming.

No wonder the paleos are suspicious of statistics. The first stat they saw roll down the pike was the RPI, and it reordered a good deal of the sport by its own capricious and ambitious lights. I'd be suspicious too.

The RPI was created to give the men's basketball committee information it could not otherwise have, and in its early years that's precisely what Jim Van Valkenburg's metric did. But the value of the RPI has always been contextual and not intrinsic. In those early years it was worth consulting because there was little or nothing else available under the category of comprehensive rating systems for all of D-I. Now, three decades later, the world that has grown up around the RPI has effectively transformed Van Valkenburg's creation into the exact opposite of what it was meant to be. It is now a hindrance to good information, something the committee must work around.

For all the derision directed the RPI's way for predating the Commodore 64, the issue here is only partly one of age. Actually, basketball-specific metrics are based on insights formulated by Dean Smith a good 20 years before the RPI was even a gleam in the NCAA's eye. The core issue is one of performance, and on that criterion the RPI would be found lacking even if it had been invented late yesterday afternoon.

Perhaps a better day is coming. Maybe someday soon the NCAA will be guided by an index comprised of several independently designed basketball-specific metrics. Maybe said index will be respectfully silent on the issue of how a coach should go about creating his team's schedule. Maybe someday the subjective preferences shown by the committee will be sanctioned by accuracy and thus acquire a clarity and weight they've never had before.

Maybe someday, but not just yet. Tomorrow the RPI will still be here, and you and I will still be fans of college basketball. This is the business we've chosen.

Previewing the Major Conferences

ACC

BY DREW CANNON

The ACC no longer seems like the dominant league it was five years ago. Every school but Duke, North Carolina, and Florida State has changed coaches since the end of the 2009 season. A lot of teams cycled down simultaneously, and the new wave of coaches is still getting their teams on the floor. It's kind of amazing, actually, how many teams are trending up.

There are really just three teams who both (1) seem to be headed for a worse season this year than last year, and (2) didn't just clean house with a new coach. And two of those three schools are Florida State and North Carolina, neither of which a sane person could call an unhealthy program. The only team that's left is Clemson, and it's not like they're in any real trouble at this point.

In a few years, when Pittsburgh, Syracuse, and Notre Dame are fully ingrained in the conference and it looks like the ACC is back to glory, there will be plenty of stories considering the former Big East schools the catalyst. In reality, there are a bunch of teams right now who look like they'll be awfully good in 2015.

There aren't many surefire NCAA tournament teams in the 2013 ACC, and there weren't many in 2011 or 2012, either. Consider that span the transition between the old guard and new guard of head coaches. It wasn't that the programs were in trouble nearly so much as it was that the programs were changing—and at least a few of these programs will find themselves in a much better place in 2016 than they were in 2006.

The ACC wasn't down, and it isn't down. It's rebuilding, using the actual definition of that word rather than as a euphemism for "bad." By 2015, people will forget other conferences ever challenged for the crown.

DREW'S PRESEASON ALL-ACC TEAMS

First Team
Lorenzo Brown (NC State)
C.J. Leslie (NC State)
James Michael McAdoo (North Carolina)
Mason Plumlee (Duke)
Michael Snaer (Florida State)

Second Team
Reggie Bullock (North Carolina)
Seth Curry (Duke)
Reggie Johnson (Miami)
Ryan Kelly (Duke)
Rodney Purvis (NC State)

Third Team
Erick Green (Virginia Tech)
C.J. Harris (Wake Forest)
Richard Howell (NC State)
Kenny Kadji (Miami)
Alex Len (Maryland)

DREW'S 2013 STANDINGS

	2012 Record	Returning Poss (%)	Returning Min (%)	2013 Prediction
Duke	13-3	61	61	14-4
NC State	9-7	68	63	13-5
North Carolina	14-2	31	35	13-5
Miami	9-7	78	80	11-7
Florida State	12-4	41	39	9-9
Maryland	6-10	41	41	9-9
Virginia	9-7	54	59	8-10
Wake Forest	4-12	55	50	7-11
Boston College	4-12	74	71	7-11
Clemson	8-8	56	54	6-12
Virginia Tech	4-12	60	61	6-12
Georgia Tech	4-12	82	81	5-13

BOSTON COLLEGE

2012: 9-22 (4-12 ACC); Lost to NC State 78-57, ACC first round
In-conference offense: 0.88 points per possession (12th)
In-conference defense: 1.05 points allowed per possession (10th)

What BC did well: *Not finish alone in last.*

BC lost just about everyone from a middle-of-the-pack ACC team in 2011, bringing in a class of newcomers that absolutely merited respect but by no means suggested instant impact. They had zero business, talent-wise, winning four ACC basketball games (and one over NCAA tournament No. 3 seed Florida State). And while win total landed them in a four-way tie in the conference cellar, we should all consider that a nice year for the Eagles.

What we learned in 2012: *Steve Donahue isn't a real-life wizard.*

Donahue's last five teams, which included the previous year's squad at BC and four years of evolving personnel at Cornell, all finished in the top 35 nationally in effective field goal percentage, including three seasons in the top 10. Last year's Eagles finished No. 201. Don't get me wrong—this was still a really strong coaching job by Donahue—but what he had been doing was just ridiculous.

What's in store for 2013: Respectability. Ryan Anderson and Dennis Clifford plan on being perfectly solid ACC big men in 2013, and they're surrounded by some high-potential teammates, particularly Patrick Heckmann. Donahue doesn't need much to get his team scoring, and the Eagles should start finding the basket again this season. While they'll improve on the other side of the ball, I'm sure, it's hard to project anything too incredible for the defense.

MEET THE EAGLES

Ryan Anderson (6-8, 220, So.): Anderson had a really nice season in 2012, but I think it was a bit overhyped. He was the best player on his team and a freshman, which will always earn a little extra buzz in a major-conference program. Anderson is a solid scorer (and could probably move up to "good" if he didn't shoot 27 percent on threes) and an excellent rebounder. He's not a serious threat for All-ACC, standing where we are preseason, but he is only a sophomore.

Patrick Heckmann (6-5, 205, So.): Heckmann's season was derailed by a bout with mononucleosis, but he was very good while on the floor, with one glaring exception: A sky-high 31 percent turnover rate. But he contributed on the glass, shot 52/35/72 with plenty of trips to the line, and trailed only 5-8 Jordan Daniels for the team lead in assist rate. If he can cut down on the sloppiness with the ball, don't be surprised if he explodes.

Dennis Clifford (7-0, 250, So.): Clifford was a good, solid big man with a flaw last season. He scored a little, blocked a few shots, grabbed a few rebounds, and got to the free throw line. His turnover rate was too high, though, at 27 percent.

Lonnie Jackson (6-3, 175, So.): Jackson was a highly effective deep threat for the 2012 Eagles, and one who spent more time in the lane than a typical spot-up shooter. I like that he's getting to the stripe; I don't like that he's shooting 39 percent inside the arc when he doesn't draw the foul.

Jordan Daniels (5-8, 155, So.): For a freshman point guard put in charge of a team of fellow newcomers, Daniels certainly could have been worse. He posted ugly though not horrific numbers in the turnover, two-point, and free throw rate departments, but he moved the ball around well and demanded respect from three-point range.

Olivier Hanlan (6-4, 190, Fr.): Hanlan is a strong, smart guard who has the passing skills to spell Daniels and Rahon at the point. In the 2011 EYBL, he shot 57/40/69 at an 18 percent usage rate.

KC Caudill (6-11, 275, So.): Caudill really struggled as a freshman, running into serious turnover and foul problems and shooting a shrug-inducing 49 percent from the field. He didn't rebound like someone pushing 300 pounds, either. That said, I don't think it's out of the realm of possibility that Caudill is a perfectly fine backup this season.

Joe Rahon (6-2, 195, Fr.): A shooter first, Rahon's other skills should push him above Rubin on the depth chart. It remains to be seen whether he'll be responsible for backing up Daniels at point guard or whether Hanlan will. Both options have pros and cons.

Danny Rubin (6-6, 190, Jr.): The squad's most seasoned veteran, Rubin played just over 10 percent of the team's minutes last year without making a two-pointer or attempting a free throw—no easy task. Rubin's an extra shooter in case Donahue needs one.

Eddie Odio (6-7, 205, So.): Odio played about half as many minutes as Caudill off the bench last season. He was a better rebounder than Caudill and didn't have the same turnover issues, but made just eight field goals on the season.

Prospectus says: The Eagles are trending back upwards. "Bottoming out" didn't turn out to be as bad as expected, and now the Boston College roster is still extraordinarily young and reasonably promising. If Heckmann blows up, this is a team that could push for an NCAA tournament bid. Either way, last place shouldn't be a fear for a team whose eight best players are freshmen and sophomores. That's a good place to be.

CLEMSON

2012: 16-15 (8-8 ACC); Lost to Virginia Tech 68-63, ACC first round
In-conference offense: 1.02 points per possession (6th)
In-conference defense: 0.98 points allowed per possession (4th)

What Clemson did well: *Promote new leaders.*

In 2011, Clemson's stars were Demontez Stitt and Jerai Grant. They both graduated, and last season Tanner Smith and Andre Young demonstrated that they were up to the task of carrying the Tigers. Smith became both an elite passer and an elite rebounder, while Young was much improved attacking the basket. Now that Smith and Young are gone, Devin Booker and Milton Jennings will have to pick up the torch.

What we learned in 2012: *If you wait long enough, highly-touted high schoolers tend to be worth having.*

It took years, but as a senior Catalin Baciu, once named a top-100 high school senior nationally by Scout.com, became a very good fourth big man for the Tigers. He hit 58 percent of his field goal attempts, contributed on the glass, and swatted a few shots. Not many top-100 kids truly, truly fail, even when it looks like they already have.

What's in store for 2013: Unless you're Kentucky, you don't run through two sets of dynamic duos in two years without a hitch. This year may well be the hitch.

Devin Booker and Milton Jennings are both good players who could be even better, but, despite the last two paragraphs, I'm not comfortable declaring them 2013 superstars. There's a lot of potential on this roster, though. Bernard Sullivan can be a lot better than he showed last season. K.J. McDaniels is progressing and fast. And BYU transfer Damarcus Harrison is a high-potential scorer, even if he didn't blow anyone away last year. There are a lot of ifs—I'm not ready to buy in just yet.

MEET THE TIGERS

Devin Booker (6-8, 250, Sr.): Clemson's best shot to not miss a beat would be another improvement from Booker. He is already an outstanding rebounder and a solid scoring option. Last season, he shot 48/22/70 (with less than 10 percent of his attempts coming from deep) at a 23 percent usage rate. Which is fine. But Clemson is going to need more than fine from Booker—as a scorer—if they're going to force their way into the postseason.

Milton Jennings (6-9, 225, Sr.): Every year I expect Jennings to find that killer instinct and start destroying people, because he absolutely has the tools to be an All-ACC type player. I'm accepting, this year, that this is just who Milton Jennings is, which is still a pretty good player. That said, if he fulfills his potential Clemson is a completely different team.

K.J. McDaniels (6-6, 195, So.): We knew McDaniels was an athlete, but I don't think anybody expected him to block shots like that. His block percentage was the second-highest in the country for someone his size or smaller, trailing only Memphis's D.J. Stephens. He ranked eighth of the same group nationally in offensive rebounding percentage, though his defensive rebounding was remarkably pedestrian by comparison—only Campbell's Jihad Wright and Samford's Brandon Hayman had larger differences in their rebounding rates (in that direction). McDaniels can score a little bit and rarely turns the ball over; I expect good things from him in 2013 and monstrous things in 2014.

Jaron Blossomgame (6-7, 190, Fr.): Blossomgame suffered a broken leg last April, and word is he may redshirt this season. But if Blossomgame's healthy, I can't imagine Clemson could roll out a starting lineup including Booker, Jennings, McDaniels, and Blossomgame, and that's really a shame because those are probably their four best players. Blossomgame's EYBL numbers suggest that he was underrated by recruiting gurus. He shot 65 percent on twos (at a 22 percent usage rate), never turned the ball over, and rebounded like a true big man.

Rod Hall (6-1, 210, So.): Hall's no offensive threat, but he is a nasty defender. Nasty. He also has the highest assist rate of any returning Tiger. Right now I'd consider Hall the favorite to start at point guard, which isn't something I'd be comfortable with as a Clemson fan.

Damarcus Harrison (6-4, 195, So.): A highly regarded prospect out of high school, Harrison spent his freshman season at BYU before transferring to Clemson due to a mix-up regarding his Mormon mission. He missed a lot of shots as a Cougar, with percentages of 40/27/53, but on a Clemson team without much guaranteed backcourt scoring, Harrison could get a long leash to fix those issues.

T.J. Sapp (6-2, 195, So.): Sapp is a serviceable shooter on a team in need of serviceable shooters. Oddly, he made less than half his free throws (though he shot 7-of-16, so it's tough to read too much into it).

Bernard Sullivan (6-7, 230, So.): Sullivan is likely to be buried after a disappointing freshman campaign. There's a bear of a player in there, though. He should be just fine moving into the rotation when Booker and Jennings graduate.

Landry Nnoko (6-10, 240, Fr.),
Josh Smith (6-8, 255, Fr.): Nnoko's raw, and the plan on the large majority of teams wouldn't be for him to see serious playing time as a freshman. Smith is a pretty good player who's just getting crowded out.

Adonis Filer (6-2, 185, Fr.),
Jordan Roper (5-11, 155, Fr.): Both are score-first point guards, and I would be unsurprised if either breaks into the starting lineup. They could also be the fourth and fifth guards—tough to read at this juncture.

Prospectus says: I think the Tigers take a step back this season, but whether that happens rests entirely on the shoulders of Jennings and Booker. This is a team with a loaded frontcourt and a backcourt that struggles to put points on the board. They really need their top forwards to be productive if they're going to win games. We'll know quickly if this team was underrated in the preseason.

DUKE

2012: 27-7 (13-3 ACC); Lost to Lehigh 75-70, NCAA round of 64
In-conference offense: 1.11 points per possession (1st)
In-conference defense: 1.01 points allowed per possession (7th)

What Duke did well: *Score.*

Duke's defense in 2012 was not up to typical Duke standards (see below), but that doesn't mean their offense wasn't outstanding. They boasted five regular three-point shooters who broke 35 percent on the season, three guys who shot better than 55 percent on twos, and three players who picked up over 100 points from the free throw line. They grabbed offensive rebounds and avoided turnovers. Offense was not a problem in Durham.

What we learned in 2012: *The Duke defensive system can falter.*

In the last ten years the Blue Devils have finished outside the top 20 nationally in adjusted defensive efficiency just once. It happened last season, and they finished No. 70.

A large portion of this blame was laid at the feet of Andre Dawkins, Seth Curry, and (for far too long) Austin Rivers. I disagree with this assessment, mostly with regard to early-season Rivers but also with regard to Curry. By this I mean that they were not problem defenders—they just also weren't dominant ballhawks in the mold of Nolan Smith and Sean Dockery, which is why the Blue Devils' defensive turnover percentage was by far the worst of the KenPom era.

But it's not like they were leaving shooters open. Duke allowed the third-fewest three-point attempts per field goal attempt in the country (which, to be fair, is not atypical for a Krzyzewski team). The problem was an exceedingly mediocre two-point defense. True, that could have been caused by guards consistently blowing by their Blue Devil defenders, but to my eyes that was only part of the problem.

What's in store for 2013: The round of 64 loss to Lehigh, coming from a team already (rightfully) considered overrated, means that the 2012 Blue Devils are largely being dismissed.

Still, that overrated team was without a doubt a top-20 team, and likely better than that. There's reasonable concern over the departure of Austin Rivers as "the only Blue Devil who could create his own shot," but, looking at the 2013 roster, I see Quinn Cook, Alex Murphy, and Rasheed Sulaimon. Mason Plumlee and Ryan Kelly are slowly moving from "underrated" to "criminally underrated," and Duke may carry the three most intriguing bench players in the league in Cook, Sulaimon, and Amile Jefferson. Meanwhile, there's quite a bit of respect being shown to a team (NC State) who was not a top-20 team last season, with a coach who's never placed a defense better than No. 50 nationally, and who seem to only have two big men. And there's quite a bit of respect being shown to a North Carolina team whose projected star shot 43 percent from the floor last year, whose point guard is a freshman, and who seem to have only one surefire big man. Now, both of those teams should be perfectly fine, don't get me wrong. From where I sit, though, Duke's potential problems aren't as harrowing, and I don't understand why the Blue Devils are being written so consistently into the third slot of preseason conference projections.

MEET THE BLUE DEVILS

Mason Plumlee (6-10, 235, Sr.): Mason Plumlee is still widely considered a player who hasn't lived up to his potential, and that's becoming increasingly unfair. KenPom lists his most similar player as 2011 Trevor Mbakwe, who deservedly got no end of positive publicity. Last season Plumlee was one of the best rebounders on both ends of the floor in the ACC. He shot 57 percent from the floor at a 23 percent usage rate. He swatted his fair share of shots while continuing to see his fouls trend downward. The only real issue in his game is that he spends so much of his time on the foul line, a place where he hits just 53 percent of his tries. If he can get out of his own head and get more comfortable from the stripe, the sky's the limit. Actually the sky might be the limit, regardless.

Ryan Kelly (6-11, 230, Sr.): Kelly must now be considered a truly dangerous offensive player. He shot 47/41/81 (with nearly 100 three-point attempts and 140 free throws) at a 22 percent usage rate. This is interesting most of all because, in 2011, he shot 64 percent on twos while attempting just 41 free throws in reasonably similar minutes. He forced considerably more contact, with the tradeoff that his un-whistled shots are considerably more difficult.

Seth Curry (6-2, 185, Sr.): With Cook ready to play a larger role, and Thornton likely reprising his outsize role from 2012, Curry won't have to be responsible for running much point anymore. And, while he did an admirable job of maintaining order offensively a year ago, few would disagree that it's better for him to put his full focus into being a scorer. Last season he shot 46/38/87 at a 22 percent usage rate. If he can continue shooting like that and get off 100 twos, threes, and free throws again, Duke will be in good shape.

Alex Murphy (6-8, 220, Fr.): Murphy graduated high school a year early to join the Blue Devils, and now an injury redshirt has put him back on the same track as his original Class of 2012 mates. There aren't a lot of true small forwards in college basketball, and Murphy is one. He should contribute immediately and in a way that nobody on last year's team could.

Quinn Cook (6-1, 175, So.): Cook may have posted the most impressive advanced statistics of any player in the country limited by playing time. His assist rate almost doubled the second-best number on the squad, while his turnover rate was as low as anyone's. When looking for his own scoring opportunities, he shot 55/25/78 at a 22 percent usage rate. As a defender, he was the most widely praised of the Duke guards with the possible exception of Tyler Thornton. I have very high expectations of Cook this year, though it doesn't appear set in stone, just yet, that he'll be the opening day starter..

Rasheed Sulaimon (6-4, 185, Fr.): Sulaimon takes pride in his defense and is a legitimate ballhawk right now. His AAU stats were merely very good. He poured in three-pointers and rarely turned the ball over, but shot just 40 percent inside the arc without many trips to the foul line.

Tyler Thornton (6-1, 190, Jr.): Thornton has proven himself to be a better shooter than Cook, and it's true that he has a better feel for the offense. Cook's upside is just much, much higher. It's rare for players who use as few possessions as Thornton did in 2012 to develop into legitimate offensive threats.

Amile Jefferson (6-8, 195, Fr.): There may not have been a high school senior in the country last season who made scoring 20 points look easier. Jefferson just found gap after gap in the defense. That said, he's 195 pounds and without much of a jump shot. It's entirely possible that his brand of sneaky continues to be unstoppable or that he can't do anything against college athletes.

Josh Hairston (6-7, 240, Jr.): If it does turn out that Jefferson just isn't ready for college basketball yet, physically, Hairston becomes the team's third big man. His best attribute last season was that he hit the offensive boards like a Plumlee. His worst was that he hit the defensive boards like Andre Dawkins.

Marshall Plumlee (6-11, 235, Fr.): The youngest Plumlee suffered a broken foot the first week of practice and will be sidelined six to eight weeks.

Prospectus says: People are sleeping on this Duke team, but they shouldn't be. Cook, Sulaimon, and Murphy will provide quite the infusion of defense. And there should be no doubt that this team can score. A good 2012 was overshadowed by an ugly performance against Lehigh. Everyone remembers that game, rightly, and now there's a good chance Duke reminds the conference of the "overshadowed" part.

FLORIDA STATE

2012: 25-10 (12-4 ACC); Lost to Cincinnati 62-56, NCAA round of 32
In-conference offense: 1.02 points per possession (5th)
In-conference defense: 0.95 points allowed per possession (3rd)

What Florida State did well: *Defend the interior.*

Thanks largely to the departed trio of Bernard James, Xavier Gibson, and Jon Kreft, Florida State ranked fifth nationally in block rate and tenth nationally in opponents' two-point percentage. That performance is even more impressive when you realize how few two-pointers the Seminoles allowed their opponents to even attempt. Repeating this triumph will be awfully difficult, though. Okaro White and Terrance Shannon are the only returning rotation members bigger than Mike Snaer.

What we learned in 2012: *Be cautious of hot streaks.*

The prevailing wisdom as the 2012 NCAA tournament began was that Florida State was on a dominant tear after beating Duke and North Carolina in the final two rounds of the ACC tournament. The Seminoles, winners of their last two games of the regular season, were heavy favorites to reach the Sweet 16 as a No. 3 seed and a popular sleeper pick for the Final Four. What happened instead was a narrowly avoided upset (66-63) against St. Bonaventure before a loss at the hands of Cincinnati in the round of 32. FSU's hot streak doesn't look quite so mind-blowing in retrospect, and maybe we should remember that more often in the future.

What's in store for 2013: Leonard Hamilton seems to think that his team is again as good as any in the conference, so maybe I'm way off here, but I see the Seminoles taking a step back in 2013. Michael Snaer is, until further notice, a member of the All-ACC first team and the ACC Defensive Player of the Year. And Okaro White and Ian Miller are proven commodities. There's a real question mark at center, though, and nobody else has demonstrated an ability to score from the wing. I'm sure that, as always, the Florida State defense will be strong, but I think that the offense may be more like it was in 2010 or 2011. Without the actual best defense in the country, that could mean a year closer to the middle of the league than the top.

MEET THE SEMINOLES

Michael Snaer (6-5, 200, Sr.): It's not easy to cultivate a great defensive reputation without outrageous steal numbers on the perimeter, but Snaer has accomplished just that. Last year, he combined that with a breakout offensive season. While increasing his usage from 19 percent to 23 percent, he went from shooting 43/37/78 as a sophomore to 46/40/85 as a junior. Even more importantly, he cut his turnovers down drastically, from 27 percent of his possessions to 18. We always knew Snaer had potential. Last year he produced.

Ian Miller (6-3, 185, Jr.): Like Snaer, Miller really improved offensively last season, cutting turnovers from 23 percent to 14 percent. Luke Loucks and Jeff Peterson were the point guards in 2011-12, but that role is indisputably Miller's to lose this season. I think he's ready.

Okaro White (6-8, 205, Jr.): White is not a 5, whether as a defender or a rebounder. And that's fine, but it means that one of the other four bigs listed below is going to have to really step up. White shot 51/33/75 last year with many free throws. His biggest issue, for now, is avoiding foul trouble.

Terrance Shannon (6-8, 240, Jr.): Shannon will likely be forced into the starting center role, and I can't tell if he's ready. He played in seven games last season before an injury forced him to redshirt, and he played very well. Shannon made his shots, defended, and rebounded against admittedly mediocre competition. I tend to think he'll be just fine as the fourth offensive option, but I'd like to see more of him first.

Terry Whisnant (6-3, 185, So.): Whisnant has been known as an elite shooter for a few years now, but he didn't show it in his first taste of college, hitting 11-of-40 threes. He'll get a real chance to break out this season, and he'll stay in the lineup if he hits.

Montay Brandon (6-7, 215, Fr.): Brandon really struggled in the EYBL as compared to other top-100-type talents. He played just over 200 minutes, so the sample size is small, but he shot just 49/18/73 at a 16 percent usage rate. Brandon looked like a different player in December than he did over the summer in the EYBL, though, so I'd be surprised if he has this much trouble. If he does end up having some issues early on, it will be because his style works a lot better when he can overpower his defenders.

Aaron Thomas (6-5, 195, Fr.): Thomas is the type of offense-first slashing wing that Florida State didn't really have last year. He's a well-rounded player, and one who's perfectly capable of beating out Brandon and Whisnant for more playing time.

Devon Bookert (6-3, 180, Fr.): Bookert was rounding into a steady point guard as he finished his high school career. That would be really valuable for a team like Florida State, where Ian Miller is the only guy who's played any point guard before.

Boris Bojanovsky (7-3, 240, Fr.),
Robert Gilchrist (6-9, 220, Jr.),
Michael Ojo (7-1, 290, Fr.): I know almost nothing about any of these three, but one of them will almost certainly see some playing time eventually, unless Shannon and White are playing 40 minutes a game or Snaer or Brandon is ready to see a bunch of time at the 4.

Prospectus says: Florida State's defense should be perfectly fine. I trust Leonard Hamilton to morph one of those unknown bigs into a terror on the defensive end. But offensively I'm not sold. Snaer must be respected as an offensive player, but everyone else presents pretty significant reasons to doubt their 2013 performance (though White is also largely excepted here). The offense doesn't have to be great for FSU to be good, but it does have to be at least decent. I think it'll be just decent, and therefore Florida State will be as good as anyone outside the Triangle and Miami.

GEORGIA TECH

2012: 11-20 (4-12 ACC); Lost to Miami 54-36, ACC first round
In-conference offense: 0.94 points per possession (11th)
In-conference defense: 1.05 points allowed per possession (11th)

What Georgia Tech did well: *Protect the basket.*

Last year's Yellow Jacket defense was no dominant force, but it was considerably better than their offense largely due to its ability to force misses inside. Daniel Miller led the way, finishing No. 34 nationally in block rate, but Nate Hicks swatted a few shots in limited time and so did now-departed wing Glen Rice. The team block rate, which placed No. 15 in the country, was a big part of holding opponents to 43 percent two-point shooting.

What we learned in 2012: *Brian Gregory continues to value integrity over talent.*

It always seemed that way at Dayton, but you never can tell what a coach will tolerate with the increased pressure of a high-major job. Gregory made a major statement about what kind of program Georgia Tech will be going forward in March, when he dismissed his best player, Glen Rice, from the team. I have no idea whether Rice deserved it, obviously, but I do respect Gregory's willingness to face a larger challenge in 2013 in order to have the type of program he wants going forward.

What's in store for 2013: Georgia Tech is starting to get the wheels of the train rolling, but this is a 4-12 team who lost their best player. The two newcomers, Robert Carter and Stacey Poole, are capable and project to be very good down the line, but Carter is raw and Poole, who shows up at the semester break, has scored four points in his collegiate career.

Any of the starting five could start at other ACC schools, but no one would have to take on such a large offensive role. Kammeon Holsey can score a little bit, but I don't know where the rest of their points will come from. (Editor's note: Current 2013 recruit Solomon Poole is a high-volume scorer who may reclassify and enroll at the semester break.)

MEET THE YELLOW JACKETS

Daniel Miller (6-11, 255, Jr.): Miller is the leading returning shot blocker in the ACC, and he was no slouch on the glass, either. The success of his season depends on his offense. As a freshman, Miller was a nonfactor offensively, while last year he was a reasonable third or fourth option. His quickest path to improvement is to draw more contact. He shot 50 percent from the field on over 200 shots but took just 42 free throws.

Kammeon Holsey (6-8, 230, Jr.): Holsey is without a doubt the Jackets' most productive returning offensive player. He shot 59 percent from the floor at a 23 percent usage rate while successfully amassing offensive rebounds. His issues are twofold: Holsey turned the ball over on 25 percent of his possessions, and shot just 53 percent from the free throw line.

Mfon Udofia (6-2, 195, Sr.): Udofia still isn't the point guard Georgia Tech thought they were getting out of high school. He's an adequate passer who can hit the open three-pointer, but he struggled with turnovers and finishing inside. Sometimes it all comes together for point guards as seniors, but more likely Udofia will continue to have too much responsibility thrust upon him.

Jason Morris (6-5, 225, Jr.): There's always potential for more from anyone with Morris's athleticism. Last season, though, he shot 38/29/71 without too many free throws, and he was using 22 percent of the Yellow Jackets' possessions. That needs to change, somehow, for Georgia Tech to be successful going forward.

Brandon Reed (6-3, 180, Jr.): Like Morris, Reed struggled from the field and made his free throws, but took quite a few shots from the floor and not many from the stripe. Percentages of 41/28/73 are a little unnerving at a 21 percent usage rate.

Robert Carter (6-8, 245, Fr.): Carter is the best prospect on this team, but I doubt he makes a massive offensive impact from the outset. He'll perform well on the glass, though, and he should make his shots. The fear with Carter going forward is he gets away from his natural interior skills and starts to float away from the basket.

Julian Royal (6-7, 245, So.): Royal really struggled with some traditional big man tasks. He trailed Udofia and Reed in defensive rebounding rate, shot just 45 percent on twos, and spent little time at the free throw line. He did shoot 38 percent on 29 three-point attempts, and his offensive rebounding was impressive. Royal had a reasonable freshman season, but he's going to need to start performing some of those other duties if he's going to be a big man in this league.

Stacey Poole (6-4, 185, So.): Poole was buried at Kentucky for all of his freshman year and the first few games of his sophomore year before transferring. High school Poole showed the ability to be a passable high-volume scorer, something that would be of immense value to the Yellow Jackets if it turns out to still be true today.

Marcus Georges-Hunt (6-5, 220, Fr.): Georges-Hunt's AAU numbers weren't bad, per se, but they were unimpressive, which isn't typical of top-100 seniors. He is a big athletic guard at 6-6, which will certainly come in handy for Georgia Tech more than once. But I'd be surprised if he makes much of an impact before next season.

Chris Bolden (6-3, 210, Fr.): Bolden isn't quite ready to take on the ACC, but the Yellow Jackets are a little guard-thin before Stacey Poole shows up.

Prospectus says: Georgia Tech is already recruiting again at a level Atlanta hasn't seen since Derrick Favors showed up on campus. Combining that with a coach who considers the long term more important than the short term is encouraging. This isn't the Yellow Jackets' year, though. This is a year for enjoying Kammeon Holsey, progressing the freshmen, teaching shot selection, and finding a replacement for Udofia. I preach patience.

MARYLAND

2012: 17-15 (6-10 ACC); Lost to North Carolina 85-69, ACC quarterfinals
In-conference offense: 0.98 points per possession (8th)
In-conference defense: 1.04 points allowed per possession (9th)

What Maryland did well: *Get to the free throw line.*

For the fourth consecutive year, a Mark Turgeon-coached team placed in the top 15 nationally in offensive free throw rate. The key is that, while big men traditionally spend plenty of time at the free throw line, Turgeon's guards join the bigs on a consistent basis. Sean Mosley and Nick Faust both took over 100 shots from the line, and Terrell Stoglin took over 200.

What we learned in 2012: *Mark Turgeon can get some interesting players on campus.*

I didn't want to just flatly say, "Mark Turgeon can recruit," because that's only part of the story here. He beat out some legitimate competition for Shaq Cleare, who was always considered a top-50-type player. He got in early on late bloomer Jake Layman and stole him. He beat out some tough opponents for Seth Allen, who was a top-100 threat at one point but leveled off. He got Alex Len on the Maryland campus, and he grabbed a solid piece from Albany in grad transfer Logan Aronhalt. His combination of finding diamonds in the rough and yet being able to fight it out with the big boys is extremely useful.

What's in store for 2013: Maryland has a bunch of good players but no star. For all Terrell Stoglin's flaws, he could put point after point on the scoreboard, and that can erase a lot of everyone else's flaws. So now we have a ragtag group of high-potential options who haven't really put it all together before. It wouldn't be hard to track down someone who thinks Nick Faust or Alex Len or Shaq Cleare is in for a truly dominant season offensively, and it wouldn't be hard to find someone who thinks James Padgett or Pe'Shon Howard or Logan Aronhalt or Jake Layman can be one heck of a second banana. Until it happens, though, tread carefully when predicting the Terrapins' future success. The potential solution may already be on campus. Dez Wells, a Xavier transfer, may have his redshirt season waived by the NCAA, and he's probably more ready than any of the above to take on a scorer's role.

MEET THE TERRAPINS

Nick Faust (6-6, 175, So.): Faust really struggled to put the ball in the basket last year (his effective field goal percentage was among the lowest in the conference), and he ran into some turnover problems. Faust's numbers should improve dramatically this year, but probably not as dramatically as expected by many. He was really starting to roll when the season ended, though.

Alex Len (7-1, 225, So.): Alex Len has a chance to be a pretty incredible player, but understand that he's still unproven. Last year in limited time, Len was a strong rebounder and shot blocker who shot 56 percent from the floor. That's a really good start. You'd like to see him hit a few more of his free throws, or turn the ball over a little less, or be a little more involved in the offense, though, before we anoint him All-ACC.

James Padgett (6-8, 225, Sr.): Padgett is an offensive rebounding force. Last season, he grabbed 16 percent of available offensive rebounds against just 12 percent of available defensive rebounds. However the way projecting offensive rebounding works going forward (essentially it varies more year-to-year than defensive rebounding) I've got him down for a 12/15 rebounding season in 2013. That being said, Padgett may be the most proven offensive player on the squad. Last year he hit 52 percent of his attempts at a 22 percent usage rate, and shot a ton of free throws without turning the ball over much.

Pe'Shon Howard (6-3, 195, Jr.): Howard had a rough sophomore campaign after a promising freshman season. He really struggled with turnovers and shot 45/27/66 as a role scorer. He's not the best returning point guard in the country, but I think a lot of his perceived issues had more to do with injury and small sample size than deteriorating abilities.

Shaq Cleare (6-9, 270, Fr.): Cleare is in his internship year for the title of Wide Load of the ACC. Once Reggie Johnson graduates at Miami, Cleare will be the most immovable object in the conference. Sometimes guys like that walk out for their first collegiate game and are immediately dominant. Other times they struggle to adapt to the speed of the game on both ends of the floor. Cleare is a skilled big man, and I would be very surprised if he isn't an effective offensive player right away. In fact if he doesn't steal the starting job from Padgett, consider that a sign of confidence in Padgett rather than a lack of confidence in Cleare. He'll be a force in this league eventually, and he might be one right now.

Jake Layman (6-8, 190, Fr.): Layman is long and thin and sneaky-effective. He's an astute reader of passing lanes who causes no end of problems on the defensive end. Plus he's extraordinarily efficient. In the EYBL, he shot 73/41/69 at a 22 percent usage rate. This is not a player prone to making mistakes.

Logan Aronhalt (6-3, 210, Sr.): Aronhalt was a good player at Albany, which by itself is unlikely to make him a good player in the ACC. Still, he's the only player on the roster who's a proven shooter, with percentages of 45/36/89 last season (about half his field goals came from beyond the arc). Aronhalt did a little bit of rebounding and kept turnovers down, but his assist rate was unusually low for someone his size. I'm tempted to chalk that specific issue up to the shot-jacking stylings of the Great Danes' leading scorer, Gerardo Suero.

Seth Allen (6-1, 190, Fr.): Allen is a scorer first, which is a skill desperately needed by this team. He's just not quite ready to unleash that skill on the ACC. He'll be a nice source of pop off the bench, though.

Charles Mitchell (6-8, 260, Fr.): Mitchell is a grounded big who has some post moves and skill with the ball. His services shouldn't be needed extensively, but he's nice to have in a pinch.

Prospectus says: Like so many ACC teams with relatively new coaches, Maryland is tracking nicely. This is a team that should be better next year than this year, and better again the year after that. Even so, there are a lot of really interesting pieces here. If somebody is ready to step up and be King of the Hill, the Terps could be really competitive.

MIAMI

2012: 20-13 (9-7 ACC); Lost to Minnesota 78-60, NIT second round
In-conference offense: 1.05 points per possession (3rd)
In-conference defense: 0.98 points allowed per possession (5th)

What Miami did well: *Spread out the scoring.*

The Hurricanes had five players last season (Durand Scott, Malcolm Grant, Kenny Kadji, Reggie Johnson, and Rion Brown) who could carry the team offensively for stretches. Depth will again be a major strength for Miami, as they carry ten guys who would be rotation players for just about anyone in the conference. And scoring will again be spread. Four of those five guys are back, and Shane Larkin, Trey McKinney Jones, and Garrius Adams could all join their number by season's end.

What we learned in 2012: *Three-point percentage is really hard to predict.*

In Malcolm Grant's first three seasons in college basketball, he shot 189-443 (43 percent) from behind the arc. In Kenny Kadji's first two, he shot 0-for-1. Grant hit 33 percent of his 206 three-point attempts last year, while Kadji hit 42 percent of his 67 tries. Now, Grant was still worth more as a shooter, though people who stick just to three-point percentage may argue. Even so, it's shocking that it was that close.

What's in store for 2013: Miami returns Kadji, who was a third-team All-ACC selection last year, Johnson, who likely would have received a similar honor had he been healthy, and Scott, who hasn't been far off two years in a row. Add in three guys who have already proven to be solid players in Larkin, Brown, and McKinney Jones, and three who could blow up at any moment in Adams, Jekiri, and Daniels, and there's a lot of potential without too much risk here. Miami is a good, solid basketball team in a year without too many good, solid basketball teams in the ACC.

MEET THE HURRICANES

Reggie Johnson (6-10, 290, Sr.): Johnson's impending 2012 explosion was postponed by injury, then erased from memory by solid but unspectacular performance once he hit the floor. He was still an excellent rebounder, but not the overwhelming one from 2011. Johnson hit half his shots and got to the free throw line, but in neither case was he as impressive as he was the season before. I say give Johnson a full offseason to get into game shape, and he'll be back to annihilating opponents in 2013.

Durand Scott (6-5, 205, Sr.): Scott cut down on his turnovers and maintained his strong scoring from 2011. We know who he is at this point. If it turns out he's got another production leap, he's a no-doubt All-ACC guy. If not, he'll hover around honorable mention like he's been doing.

Kenny Kadji (6-11, 240, Sr.): I realize Kadji was the award-getter last season, but I'd expect him to be the third-best player on the 2013 edition of the Hurricanes. I think his newness to the league and low preseason expectations contributed to his award as much as his success (which was near All-ACC level). Kadji was a good all-around big with no dominant characteristics. His next step is to become a real force on the glass, or start hitting all his free throws, or get involved as a passer. Add a luxury skill.

Shane Larkin (5-11, 175, So.): Though he is very much the Miami point guard, Larkin's assist rate is actually lower than Scott's. Larkin wasn't asked to be much of a scorer last year, but he may find his role expanded. He shot 39/32/86, which means he's entirely capable of taking the open shots that Grant had a year ago. It also means he probably shouldn't venture inside as often as he did.

Rion Brown (6-6, 200, Jr.): After a so-so freshman campaign, Brown was a highly efficient role player for the 'Canes in 2012. He shot 48/39/77 (with 60 percent of his field goal attempts coming from deep) while turning the ball over on just 12 percent of his possessions.

Trey McKinney Jones (6-5, 220, Sr.): McKinney Jones's shooting percentages look outstanding: 60/37/72. And he was a solid player for Miami, no doubt. But a below-average turnover rate, a low usage rate, and a low free throw rate combine to explain why he was merely a solid role player.

Garrius Adams (6-6, 195, Sr.): Adams's numbers were eerily similar to McKinney Jones's, with the exceptions of free throw percentage (Adams shot 55 percent) and turnover percentage (Adams at 17 percent while TMJ was at 21 percent).

Tonye Jekiri (7-0, 225, Fr.): Jekiri has a high ceiling, and some think he's a future NBA player. He's a rebounder and shot blocker today, but he's still really raw offensively.

Julian Gamble (6-10, 250, Sr.): Gamble spent last season as a redshirt, and he's a perfectly acceptable rotation big. He's listed behind Jekiri because, while I could see Jekiri explode, it's tougher to picture that with Gamble.

Bishop Daniels (6-3, 175, Fr.): Like Gamble, Daniels is coming off a redshirt season. He's a big-time athlete who might find himself buried on the bench assuming the team stays healthy.

Raphael Akpejiori (6-10, 235, Jr.),
Erik Swoope (6-6, 235, Jr.): Swoope and Akpejiori both got a decent number of minutes last season, but with the injuries healed and new blood infused, there shouldn't be as many minutes available for these two.

Prospectus says: I'd be disappointed with falling short of the NCAA tournament were I a Miami fan. One player from the Kadji-Johnson-Scott trio needs to be a star all season long, but that's not an unreasonable need. Larkin needs to be steady, and the defense needs to be at least fairly good, but neither of those are unreasonable needs, either. There are just so many pieces here for the Hurricanes. Enough of them will fall into place to push Miami in the right direction.

NORTH CAROLINA

2012: 32-6 (14-2 ACC); Lost to Kansas 80-67, Elite Eight
In-conference offense: 1.10 points per possession (2nd)
In-conference defense: 0.93 points allowed per possession (2nd)

What North Carolina did well: *Play together.*

Four Tar Heels were drafted in 2012 (Harrison Barnes, Kendall Marshall, John Henson, and Tyler Zeller), a group that James Michael McAdoo will join whenever he so chooses and that Reggie Bullock and P.J. Hairston could both sneak into. There was no talk of alpha-dog chaos in the Tar Heel locker room. Roy Williams collected an amazing amount of talent, and then they just went out there and played basketball. As long as that happened, North Carolina would win quite a few games, but that lack of pandemonium was by no means a lock.

What we learned in 2012: *High-potential freshmen who struggle can still become stars.*

Of those four draft picks, zero had freshman seasons free of doubt. Zeller barely played. Henson struggled to score. Barnes failed, loudly, to meet expectations, and even Marshall had distinct (if quieter) turnover issues. Yes, this is a section about McAdoo and his 43 percent two-point shooting as a freshman.

What's in store for 2013: This is a very different North Carolina team than any we've seen recently. The Tar Heels' frontcourt is as weak as its been since at least 2006. They have zero guaranteed volume scorers, although it's also true they have five or so who could be very good in that capacity. There are actually a lot of similarities between this team and 2006—with McAdoo as Tyler Hansbrough, Bullock as Reyshawn Terry, and filling in the rest of the rotation with solid role guys. The comparison isn't perfect, but I do think that team is a good expectations benchmark. This is no dominant team. Grabbing a No. 3 seed should be considered a great season, as it was then.

MEET THE TAR HEELS

James Michael McAdoo (6-9, 230, So.): McAdoo is being touted as an All-ACC pick this season, and I agree, but it needs to be recognized that there's a lot of room between there and McAdoo's freshman performance. He rebounded well and didn't turn the ball over, but really struggled when it came to actually putting the ball in the basket. At a 20 percent usage rate, McAdoo shot an unimpressive 43/0/64. He also posted one of the lowest assist rates in the league.

Reggie Bullock (6-7, 205, Jr.): There was some fear that Bullock just wasn't the type of shooter he was once touted to be, but a 71-of-186 (38 percent) season from deep silenced those doubts. Bullock was an excellent role scorer last season, shooting 51/38/73 at a 15 percent usage rate. His free throw rate was extraordinarily low, as he attempted just 22 free throws but nearly 300 field goals (and over 100 two-pointers, a rate only matched in the league by Georgia Tech's Daniel Miller).

P.J. Hairston (6-5, 220, So.): Hairston was pouring in three-pointers early in the season, but a cold finish left him with season shooting percentages of 39/27/84. I'd be floored if he repeated that performance, but I do think the low two-point percentage should be taken more seriously than it has been. I expect Hairston to be the Heels' third-best player, but his lagging defense could mean he starts below McDonald and Strickland on the depth chart, and a poor-shooting start to the season could mean he stays there.

Dexter Strickland (6-3, 180, Sr.): Before his injury Strickland's shooting was trending nicely. He'd cut out the three-point shots that he'd never consistently hit, and he was making 58 percent of his twos (compared to 49 percent the previous two years). The tradeoff was that his free throw rate was way down.

Marcus Paige (6-1, 155, Fr.): Where Kendall Marshall was a high-risk, high-reward passer, Paige is low-risk and low-reward. His assist numbers won't wow you, but he won't turn the ball over. In the EYBL, Paige shot 52/34/83, with about a third of his field goals coming from deep and very few shots coming from the free throw line. Paige shouldn't explode on the scene so much as make it seem as if he's been the point guard forever.

Brice Johnson (6-9, 190, Fr.): In the summer of 2011 Johnson posted arguably the best AAU numbers of anyone outside current Tennessee sophomore Jarnell Stokes. He finished sixth in the league in defensive rebounding percentage and fourth in block rate while shooting 74/67/68 (with three three-point attempts). Johnson wasn't the center of the offense, posting a 19 percent usage rate, and he ran into foul trouble, but he took advantage of his opportunities and never took anything off the table. In addition to shooting such high percentages, he turned the ball over on less than 10 percent of his possessions. Johnson is really thin, though, so it's unlikely he can step in and play the 5 alongside McAdoo. Carolina will either be taking a polish hit at the center spot game-long, or else the polished likes of Johnson and McAdoo are going to see more time at the 5 than any similar Tar Heels in recent memory.

Leslie McDonald (6-5, 215, Jr.): McDonald returns after a 2012 redshirt season. Two years ago, he shot 38 percent from deep but just 39 percent inside the arc, numbers that, if repeated, could push McDonald to the fourth wing option.

Desmond Hubert (6-9, 220, So.): The dearth of viable bigs on the roster will push Hubert into the spotlight. It's entirely possible that Hubert starts, although it's also possible that McAdoo, Johnson, and Joel James take the great majority of the frontcourt minutes.

Joel James (6-10, 260, Fr.): James has size and intensity, and can't be left alone in the midrange. But he's no block scorer, at least not yet. James is the only true center on the squad, which means at the very least he'll be seeing time against Miami and Reggie Johnson.

J.P. Tokoto (6-5, 185, Fr.),
Jackson Simmons (6-7, 220, So.): These two are unlikely to see too much court time, but they're next in line if injuries crop up. Tokoto was once considered a top-5 talent in his class.

Prospectus says: North Carolina is in a trickier situation than you may have been led to believe. There are a lot of players here that would be exciting pieces on most teams nationally, but nobody has had to carry any real load before. McAdoo and Hairston both struggled last season, and nobody else's style really lends itself to ball dominance. There are only three locks in the starting lineup at this point (McAdoo, Bullock, Paige), and there are significant issues with all the options available to fill the two remaining spots. I can't imagine the Tar Heels will be bad, per se, but this feels like a fringe top-25 team to me. And if McAdoo doesn't have his expected explosion, they could be in real trouble.

NC STATE

2012: 24-13 (9-7 ACC); Lost to Kansas 60-57, Sweet 16
In-conference offense: 1.04 points per possession (4th)
In-conference defense: 1.01 points allowed per possession (6th)

What NC State did well: *Win again.*

After five consecutive seasons in the NCAA tournament under Herb Sendek, the Wolfpack faithful ran Sendek out of town in favor of former basketball hero Sidney Lowe. Then, after five years of watching the NCAA hold its tournament without the Wolfpack, it was time for another change. Mark Gottfried came into a potentially treacherous situation and led NC State to an NCAA tournament appearance and then the Sweet 16. Now four starters are back, and a huge in-state recruiting class has been signed. Expectations for the Wolfpack are again sky-high.

What we learned in 2012: *Depth is overrated.*

One of the greatest fears with NC State going into last season was that, while they appeared to have three potentially excellent players and three solid role players, the cupboard seemed unusually bare after that. Gottfried played those six plus transfer Alex Johnson, and that was really it. It worked out just fine. The seniors and transfer Deshawn Painter were ushered out, they've been replaced by three stud freshmen, and it's entirely possible we'll see a similar usage pattern this season. If we do, remember not to panic.

What's in store for 2013: Agreed, there's a pretty amazing amount of talent on the Wolfpack roster. No fewer than six guys on this team could end the season superstars. My fear, though, is that all seven definite rotation members are considerably better on the offensive end than the defensive end. Repeat, all of them (though Richard Howell isn't that far off). If this isn't an elite offensive team, that's on Gottfried. But it's entirely possible that, defensively, this team falls below average in the conference. You can have good teams like that (naming these two teams will create an unintended narrative, but Duke and Missouri both did fine last season), but you don't like your conference favorite to look this questionable on one side of the ball in October. Which is why the Wolfpack aren't my conference favorite.

MEET THE WOLFPACK

C.J. Leslie (6-9, 200, Jr.): There were two major changes in Leslie's line from 2011 to 2012. His offensive rebounding went from excellent to normal, and he started hitting 53 percent of his twos instead of 45 percent. Now his biggest statistical flaw is 60 percent free throw shooting. Everything is really just "good;" he hasn't really taken any facet of his game and destroyed people with it. And he can.

Lorenzo Brown (6-5, 185, Jr.): Brown advanced himself some as a scorer (went from shooting 45/30/71 to 48/35/73 while expanding his role), but quite a bit more as a playmaker. It's not a stretch to consider him a legitimate point guard, whereas at this point last season that was up for grabs. What's really nice is that, anytime Tyler Lewis is on the floor, Brown can shift over to the 2-guard slot and be a pure scorer, which would be a pretty outstanding offensive lineup.

Richard Howell (6-8, 250, Sr.): Howell was one of the better rebounders in the country last season, posting fantastic offensive/defensive rebounding percentages of 16/23. He was a solid scorer as well, hitting about half his shots and making a reasonable number of free throws on a reasonable number of attempts. This is generally a solid player whose rebounding is otherworldly. If Howell makes a jump of any kind offensively the Wolfpack offense can contend for the best in the nation.

Rodney Purvis (6-3, 195, Fr.): Everybody in Wolfpack Nation (and everyone in College Basketball Nation who was paying attention) breathed a sigh of relief when Purvis was belatedly declared eligible by the NCAA in September. Make no mistake, Rodney Purvis is a high-major scorer. Few disagree with that assessment. In the EYBL, he shot 53/38/68 (with about one in eight shots coming from beyond the arc) at a 30 percent usage rate. But what shocks recruiting analysts is the fact that Purvis finished fourth in the league in assist rate. He's no point guard, and he earned his reputation as a volume shooter, but his vision should not be ignored as an asset.

Scott Wood (6-6, 170, Sr.): Wood is a very good role player, shooting 47/41/91 (with three-fourths of his field goal attempts coming from deep) and rarely turning the ball over. Although Warren, Purvis, Lewis, and Brown will all have good nights shooting the ball, Wood is the only no-doubt deep threat on a team that needs one. Call him Mike Miller.

T.J. Warren (6-8, 235, Fr.): Warren is another guy capable of being a volume scorer—that's at least four now if you're keeping track, and five if you count Howell. He's one of the bigger guys in this recruiting class nationally athletic enough to be called a wing, and his game is attacking the basket and drawing fouls. Warren should hit some free throws but the three-point shot doesn't appear to be all there just yet.

Tyler Lewis (5-11, 155, Fr.): Lewis will probably be famous by December. If you're not careful you'll assume he's a team manager, but he's an utterly electric passer and is slowly coming along as a scorer. He throws passes that make Kendall Marshall look cautious. Defense will be a problem, but the offense will absolutely change when he's on the floor. So long as turnovers don't become an issue and Lewis doesn't feel the need to be a scorer, it will change for the better.

Thomas de Thaey (6-8, 245, So.): Gottfried didn't feel the need to play de Thaey as an eighth man last season, so who knows whether he'll feel the need to do so this year. But de Thaey is a year better and, instead of Deshawn Painter, Warren is probably the team's third big out of the top seven. I'd expect de Thaey to get some more run than previously.

Jordan Vandenberg (7-1, 265, Jr.): If Howell gets hurt or in foul trouble against a man of extreme size (like Reggie Johnson, for instance), Vandenberg will be the solution.

Prospectus says: NC State will be plenty good this season. They may end up even better than the 2005 team that made the Sweet 16. But NC State fans are easily excited and easily disgusted, and I fear they will be both if they continue to consider the Wolfpack the best team in the ACC. This is a top-25 team, and a top-5 most exciting team in the nation. The ACC title is certainly within reach, though considerably less likely than a coin flip.

VIRGINIA

2012: 22-10 (9-7 ACC); Lost to Florida 71-45, NCAA round of 64
In-conference offense: 0.99 points per possession (7th)
In-conference defense: 0.92 points allowed per possession (1st)

What Virginia did well: *Defend.*

Virginia had one of the best defenses in the country last season, bar none. They were extraordinary on the defensive glass and held opponents to just 29 percent three-point shooting. There really weren't any weaknesses. They defended well enough that they won even though nobody but Mike Scott and Joe Harris ever seemed to make any shots on the offensive end.

What we learned in 2012: *Never fear pre-redshirt numbers.*

Mike Scott was a good, solid player in 2010. But in the first few games of 2011, Scott was absolutely extraordinary before an injury forced him to redshirt. The fear was that the small sample size was reflective more of random variation and early-season scheduling than improvement. As it turned out, 2012 Scott was even better than absolutely extraordinary.

What's in store for 2013: Tony Bennett is too good a defensive coach for the Cavalier defense to fall too far, but the already tenuous offense loses perhaps the most irreplaceable offensive player in the conference. Among returnees only Harris used more than 15 percent of the Cavaliers' possessions last season and posted an offensive rating above 100. And of the newcomers, only Justin Anderson is really a high-volume scorer. This could be a tough year for the Virginia offense.

MEET THE CAVALIERS

Joe Harris (6-6, 210, Jr.): Harris is suddenly responsible for determining how far this offense can go. Last year, he was a respectable second offensive option to Scott, shooting 50/38/77 without turning the ball over. But Harris's 21 percent usage rate is the highest of anyone coming back, and that means everyone will have to take more shots. He's not ready to be the featured scorer on an ACC team, but he's more ready than any other Cavalier.

Jontel Evans (5-11, 190, Sr.): Evans is an outstanding defender and a solid, if sometimes sloppy, passer. He could do with cutting down on his turnovers, but so long as he can hit a few more shots this season than last, point guard play shouldn't be Virginia's problem. Note however that foot surgery put Evans on the sidelines for preseason practice, and he's likely to be out for the start of the season.

Justin Anderson (6-6, 225, Fr.): Anderson is probably the key to Virginia's season. I said above that Harris is more ready than any other Cavalier to be the featured scorer on an ACC team. In actuality, it's probably Anderson. In the EYBL he was responsible for 26 percent of Boo Williams's possessions, and he shot 55/37/61. He racked up some assists and some rebounds with few turnovers. No incoming ACC freshman put up similarly efficient, high-volume EYBL numbers, and only NC State's Rodney Purvis really came close.

Darion Atkins (6-8, 220, So.): Atkins is a big man who made sure to take nothing off the table in 2012. He shot 58 percent from the field and turned the ball over on less than 10 percent of his possessions. Atkins rebounded and blocked shots, as well, though he committed over seven fouls per 40 minutes. A role expansion is probably in order, considering his high efficiency and the high availability of shots on this team. He's likely to start alongside Akil Mitchell in the frontcourt.

Malcolm Brogdon (6-5, 215, So.): Brogdon was just a bit lacking across the board last season on the offensive end. He shot 45/32/80 with a turnover rate just a bit too high for comfort. He was only a freshman, though.

Akil Mitchell (6-8, 235, Jr.): Mitchell earned his minutes through defense and rebounding. Offensively, he doesn't cause any problems but doesn't strike any fear into the hearts of opponents, either.

Paul Jesperson (6-6, 195, So.): When a shooter doesn't hit his shots, his numbers can look really ugly. That's what happened to Jesperson. Even so, you really should take at least one free throw if you're on the floor for 200 minutes.

Mike Tobey (6-11, 225, Fr.): The third big until further notice, Tobey put up fantastic numbers in a smallish sample size in the 2011 EYBL. He could reasonably be called the best senior rebounder in the league, grabbing 13 percent of available offensive boards and 26 percent of possible defensive rebounds. He swatted more than his share of shots, as well, even if they came with more than his share of fouls. I'm less certain that he's ready to contribute on the offensive end, where Tobey shot 56 percent but spent very little time at the free throw line.

Evan Nolte (6-8, 205, Fr.): Nolte is a smart, high-feel wing who could absolutely pass Brogdon and Jesperson by opening day. His EYBL numbers were solid but unspectacular, shooting 46/32/66 at a 23 percent usage rate, though with the low turnover rate you'd expect.

Teven Jones (6-0, 180, Fr.): Jones enrolled for the spring semester of 2012 and redshirted. He's the backup to Evans at point guard. It sounds like he was really rounding into shape during his prep year before heading to college early. He's suspended for the regular season opener, and, with Evans out as well, Harris is the likely lead guard.

Prospectus says: Virginia is another entry on the list of solid but flawed ACC teams for 2013. Their offense could really struggle if Anderson isn't hugely productive immediately. There are multiple ACC All-Defense candidates on this team, and they'll keep Virginia from anything approaching "bad," but the lack of proven offense means an NCAA tournament bid should be considered a very successful year.

VIRGINIA TECH

2012: 16-17 (4-12 ACC); Lost to Duke 60-56, ACC quarterfinals
In-conference offense: 0.96 points per possession (9th)
In-conference defense: 1.03 points allowed per possession (8th)

What Virginia Tech did well: *Defend the three-point line.*

The Hokies finished second in the country in three-point percentage defense at 28 percent. There's been debate lately about how much that actually means, but it remains true that nobody seemed to be able to hit threes against Virginia Tech in 2012.

What we learned in 2012: *The ACC coaching carousel hadn't quite finished turning yet.*

In my ACC preview for the book last year, I pointed out that just four of the league's coaches had been in their current jobs for longer than Tony Bennett's (then) two years. That's still true, but now one of the veterans is Tony Bennett: Only Mike Krzyzewski, Roy Williams, and Leonard Hamilton held ACC head coaching jobs before 2010. At the other end of that spectrum is the conference's newest coach, Virginia Tech's James Johnson.

What's in store for 2013: This year won't be pretty in Blacksburg, but it could certainly be worse. The Hokies have just eight eligible scholarship players, which makes things tough, but at least they return All-ACC selection Erick Green and rotation members Jarell Eddie, Cadarian Raines, and Robert Brown. Tech went 4-12 in conference, lost two starters and a rotation big, and forced an unrepeatable number of three-point misses. There are enough winnable games in this conference that the Hokies won't be miserable, not with Green at the helm, but this isn't a very good basketball team.

MEET THE HOKIES

Erick Green (6-3, 185, Sr.): Green is an extraordinarily low-turnover point guard who is entirely capable of scoring on his own. Last season, he shot 46/38/83 at a 24 percent usage rate. He's an All-ACC type player, no doubt.

Jarell Eddie (6-7, 220, Jr.): Eddie has developed into an unusual type of player, a combination outstanding shooter (44 percent on 122 three-point attempts) and defensive rebounder (19 percent). He shot just 40 percent from inside the arc, but he's otherwise effective enough that he's still a very efficient role scorer. Eddie sometimes has trouble with fouls, however.

Cadarian Raines (6-9, 240, Jr.): Raines's best qualities are excellent offensive rebounding and turnover prevention. You'd like to see someone with his rebounding tools performing better on the defensive boards, though. As a scorer, he makes a solid 52 percent of his field goal attempts, but also just 52 percent of his free throws. Fouls can be a problem for him.

C.J. Barksdale (6-8, 230, So.): Barksdale is a good rebounder and defender, but offensively he's a role player who isn't very efficient. He doesn't turn the ball over, but last season he shot just 42/0/75 despite a small (16 percent) usage rate.

Robert Brown (6-5, 190, So.): Brown's 2012 season wasn't very efficient, but he's close to being effective in many ways. He shot 41/32/62, with a few too many turnovers and not quite enough free throw attempts. He may be ready to be the Hokies' second scoring option by opening day.

Marquis Rankin (6-1, 170, So.): Rankin hit 39 percent of his 23 three-point attempts, but he shot just 31 percent inside the arc and had major turnover problems. He'll have an expanded role this year, and I don't see any reason why he wouldn't be able to handle it.

Marshall Wood (6-8, 210, Fr.): With the Hokies so thin, Wood could end up seeing quite a bit of time backing up Jarell Eddie at the 3 as well as C.J. Barksdale at the 4. Wood is an excellent rebounder for his weight class and is capable of stepping out behind the arc a few times a game.

Joey van Zegeren (6-10, 225, Fr.): Van Zegeren will become most necessary whenever Raines gets in foul trouble. (Barksdale at the 5 won't work against some opponents.) The Dutch forward spent last season as a redshirt.

Prospectus says: New coach Johnson has a tough season ahead, and more could follow if he doesn't recruit well right off the bat. Green will be one of the best players in the conference, but there just isn't enough talent on the rest of the roster to hang with most of the ACC on a game-by-game basis. And with just eight scholarship players, any injuries whatsoever would be devastating.

WAKE FOREST

2012: 13-18 (4-12 ACC); Lost to Maryland 82-60, ACC first round
In-conference offense: 0.95 points per possession (10th)
In-conference defense: 1.08 points allowed per possession (12th)

What Wake Forest did well: *Form a dynamic duo.*

C.J. Harris had a really ugly 2011, but he broke out as a junior. Now Wake Forest has two big-time ACC scorers, something not even half the teams in the league can currently say with confidence. Both Harris and Travis McKie are using at least 24 percent of the Deacons' possessions and shooting at least 51/38/74. Last year Wake struggled to fill in the gaps left by those two, but it's certainly an easier task than, say, Mark Turgeon is being forced to address at Maryland.

What we learned in 2012: *A tough transition can make anybody look bad.*

When I started thinking about Wake for this season, I was coming from the perspective that Jeff Bzdelik really needs to get this team in gear if he wants to keep his job. That's what was just floating in my head about Bzdelik's work at Wake Forest. But once I actually looked at it again, that's totally unfair. Bzdelik's first squad brought three rotation guys back from a 9-7 ACC team, and they understandably went 8-24. Then, despite losing two starters, his second team improved to 13-18. Now, he's got a team that doesn't look too great, but he has just two upperclassmen and one senior. It feels like this is slow going, and it is, but that's mostly a result of the construction of the roster Bzdelik was originally handed. Sometimes it only takes two years to figure out where a coach can take a program. That's very much untrue in this case.

What's in store for 2013: This is the year that the Demon Deacons climb out of the cellar. They will still have problems, certainly, chief among them finding a true center on the roster, but their problems going into the season do not compare to those of Georgia Tech and Virginia Tech. Again, Bzdelik has two proven ACC scorers on the roster, and that's more than a bunch of coaches in this league can say. If Codi Miller-McIntyre can run the show—and I think he can—just sticking Chase Fischer in a corner should mean there are three legitimate scoring threats on the floor at all times. This team will go as far as their defense will let them.

MEET THE DEMON DEACONS

C.J. Harris (6-3, 190, Sr.): After shooting 40/34/82 with a 27 percent turnover rate as a sophomore, Harris expanded his role and shot 51/42/84 with a 17 percent turnover rate as a junior. Harris's most unique skill is his ability to get to the free throw line from the wing—few pick up so many points at the stripe.

Travis McKie (6-7, 220, Jr.): McKie didn't quite have the explosion I thought possible, but he made a distinct improvement over his freshman season. He increased his usage rate from 22 percent to 25 percent, while shooting 38 percent from behind the three-point line rather than the 30 percent he shot as a freshman.

Chase Fischer (6-3, 195, So.): Fischer is a deadeye deep threat, but he was just OK from three-point range as a freshman, making 32 percent of his attempts. He will almost certainly improve on that as a sophomore, and if he could expand his game to get to the free throw line more often on the drive, that would be a bonus.

Codi Miller-McIntyre (6-3, 195, Fr.): Miller-McIntyre will be handed the ball from day one as the Wake Forest point guard. He's a good passer and a good scorer. The keys here will be consistency and ball protection.

Arnaud William Adala Moto (6-6, 225, Fr.)
Moto was a supremely efficient role player for an excellent Team Takeover squad in the EYBL. His usage rate was just 17 percent, but he shot 54/50/76 (with about 20 percent of his field goal attempts coming from beyond the arc) and spent a ton of time at the free throw line. He really attacked the defensive boards and rarely turned the ball over.

Tyler Cavanaugh (6-9, 230, Fr.): Cavanaugh was a solid big for the Albany City Rocks in the EYBL. He shot 57/30/70 at an 18 percent usage rate. He may end up starting at the 5 for the Deacons.

Aaron Rountree (6-8, 190, Fr.): Rountree is a surprisingly good passer for a freshman with ACC-level size.

Devin Thomas (6-9, 240, Fr.): A high-motor forward, Thomas could steal minutes if effort ever becomes a problem for this team. He's a rebounder and opportunistic interior scorer—not really a skill set any of his teammates have.

Madison Jones (6-1, 160, Fr.): Jones's EYBL numbers are really ugly. He used 15 percent of his team's possessions, and he wasn't bad attacking the basket. He really struggled from beyond the arc (4-of-26, 15 percent) and didn't help himself from the free throw line (55 percent) or with turnovers (24 percent TO rate).

Andre Washington (7-0, 220, Fr.): Washington has size only Green can match, and his physical tools don't trail too far behind. A good fall could put him in the rotation.

Prospectus says: This isn't a team to be excited about, but it's no longer a team to be excited about playing, either. Harris and McKie will score, Fischer will spread the floor, and Miller-McIntyre will distribute. Regardless of who plays at center, the Deacons won't have too much trouble putting the ball in the basket. Defense could still be a problem, though. Last year, Wake finished outside the top 200 nationally in opponents' effective field goal percentage, defensive rebounding percentage, and opponents' turnover percentage. And their two most capable interior stoppers, Carson Desrosiers and Ty Walker, have left the program. The offense will be fine, but the defense will be the difference maker.

Big 12

BY C.J. MOORE

A year ago Bill Self sat in front of a group of reporters at Big 12 media day and said he had a point guard (Tyshawn Taylor) and an anchor (Thomas Robinson), and a lot of teams would like to start with that. Self almost seemed like he was trying to convince himself, for his fear and the belief of many was that he had his worst team since he had arrived at Kansas in 2003.

Six months later Self was a few Anthony Davis swats away from winning his second national championship. He won the Big 12 for an eighth straight year, and very nearly got a No. 1 seed for the fifth season in six years. By reaching the Final Four, the Jayhawks recorded more wins in six years (197) than any program in NCAA history.

This year marks Self's tenth season in the Big 12, and with it comes a "six degrees of Kevin Bacon" transition year for the conference. Self left Illinois in 2003 to come to Kansas, and Illinois hired Bruce Weber. In Weber's first season in Champaign, he held a mock funeral for Self to try to get his players to move on. That didn't exactly sit well with Self, and the Illini never really did move on. Whatever Weber accomplished, it was never enough. Yeah, he took the Illini to the national title game in 2005, but that was with Self's players.

What a natural hire Weber was for Kansas State when Frank Martin went the way of the Missouri Tigers and bolted to the SEC. Weber is used to hearing all about Self, and now he gets to coach the school that by default becomes the Jayhawks' biggest conference rival. He inherits a team that has made three straight NCAA tournaments and returns four of five starters.

Weber takes over for Martin, who came to Manhattan with Bob Huggins and took over for Huggins when he left for his alma mater West Virginia in 2007. And just as soon as Martin exits, Huggy Bear returns to the Big 12. Huggins is trying to pull an Iowa State this season, hoping to win with a trio of talented transfers that includes former La Salle big man Aaric Murray, a player Self tried to convince to come to Kansas.

Huggins took over at West Virginia for John Beilein, who left for Michigan in 2007 to take over for Tommy Amaker, the former Duke guard. A fellow Duke guard Jeff Capel was the head man at Oklahoma until he was let go in 2011, and Lon Kruger, a Kansas State grad, took over. Kruger has the Big 12's most experienced team this year, returning five senior starters. Last season the Sooners showed some potential—they beat K-State twice—but they lacked depth. Kruger fixed that by adding three freshmen to the backcourt, plus Wyoming transfer Amath M'Baye, the Big 12 preseason newcomer of the year.

C.J.'S 2013 STANDINGS

	2012 Record	Returning Poss (%)	Returning Min (%)	2013 Prediction
Kansas	16-2	45	56	15-3
Baylor	12-6	49	51	14-4
Iowa State	12-6	44	53	12-6
Kansas State	10-8	83	83	11-7
Oklahoma State	7-11	66	69	10-8
West Virginia	9-9*	53	60	9-9
Texas	9-9	55	58	9-9
Oklahoma	5-13	86	83	8-10
Texas Tech	1-17	54	52	1-17
TCU	7-7**	55	59	1-17
* Big East				
** Mountain West				

Kruger came to Oklahoma from UNLV, where he coached from 2004 to 2011. Before that, he was at Illinois. His replacement: Self.

When Self arrived at Illinois he brought along an up and coming assistant named Billy Gillispie. Self was one of the few to come out in defense of Gillispie in September when word out of Lubbock was that he was mistreating his players. Gillispie was forced to resign and the next head coach at Texas Tech is one of the big question marks coming into this season. Possibly Doc Sadler? He was fired in March by Nebraska—formerly of the Big 12, of course—and naturally landed on Self's staff at Kansas. If interim coach Chris Walker is unable to win the job, whoever lands at Tech will take over a program that is still in major rebuilding mode.

The two-week Gillispie fiasco in Lubbock was exhausting, a story that seemed to drag on almost as long as conference realignment. Unlike Gillispie, however, the Big 12 is finally stable. We think.

Conference realignment left us as dizzy and confused as the annual coaching carousel. Speaking of which, TCU enters the Big 12 after a short fling with the Big East and with new coach Trent Johnson, formerly of LSU, Stanford and Nevada. Johnson went from nine wins in his first year at Nevada to 25 in the fifth and final year, taking the Wolf Pack to the NCAA tournament. Getting TCU to the tourney could be an even tougher task. The Horned Frogs have made one NCAA tournament in the last 23 years. It was in 1998 when they were led by former OU coach Billy Tubbs.

Johnson need look no further than Waco for proof that it's possible to build something out of nothing in the Big 12. He'll likely have his eye on the Bears anyway, or at least one Bear, freshman forward Rico Gathers. Gathers, who's from Louisiana, was quoted as saying that Johnson "didn't work hard enough" recruiting him to LSU, which Johnson said was "comical." Now he gets to face Gathers twice a year.

It's not much fun recruiting against Scott Drew. His staff has turned Baylor into one of the most talented teams year in and year out in the Big 12. It's an impressive feat, considering Drew took over a program on probation and five years later was in the NCAA tournament. The next step for the Bears is to win a Big 12 title, and they might be the biggest challenger to Self's Jayhawks. The Bears return Big 12 preseason player of the year Pierre Jackson, and Drew also signed yet another top recruiting class, which includes Isaiah Austin, a top-five recruit.

The only other Big 12 school with a top-10 recruit is Oklahoma State, courtesy of incoming freshman guard Marcus Smart. Travis Ford has the most stacked backcourt in the Big 12, pairing Smart with Markel Brown and Le'Bryan Nash, who was expected to be a one-and-done player. If one of their big men can be productive, the Cowboys could be a smart sleeper pick to finish near the top of the Big 12.

Last year's Big 12 sleeper was Iowa State, coached by native son Fred Hoiberg, who might be the only coach in this league not somehow connected to a fellow program or coach. His players, however, have plenty of connections. Hoiberg has two new transfers, former Michigan State point guard Korie Lucious and former Utah guard Will Clyburn. It will be difficult to try to duplicate the success of last year's transfer-heavy tourney team without Royce White, who would have been the best player in the Big 12 had he returned to school.

The team that is thought to be the other legitimate challenger to Kansas is Texas. Barnes is the only current coach to win the Big 12 since Self arrived in Lawrence. Oklahoma State and Eddie Sutton won the Big 12 in 2004. Barnes shared the conference crown with KU in 2006 and 2008.

The Longhorns lose KU killer and last year's Big 12 leading scorer J'Covan Brown, but they return six talented freshmen, who are now sophomores, led by point guard Mych Kabongo. Kabongo is probably the fastest player in the Big 12, but he will need to address his tendency to give the ball to the other team. That is assuming he plays. As this book goes to press the NCAA is investigating Kabongo's relationship with a professional agent. With or (especially) without Kabongo, replacing Brown's scoring will be a challenge.

And that brings us back to the Jayhawks, who are the favorites to win the conference until someone knocks them off their perch. They also have their question marks. Will they be able to replace All-American big man Thomas Robinson and the leadership of point guard Tyshawn Taylor? Of course, what has made the Jayhawks consistently successful is their ability to lose players to the NBA and simply plug in guys who have been around for a few years in much smaller roles. The Jayhawks will be led by veteran point guard Elijah Johnson and a new anchor, Jeff Withey.

And you better believe there are a lot of teams that would like to start with that.

BAYLOR

2012: 30-8 (12-6 Big 12); Lost to Kentucky 82-70, Elite Eight
In-conference offense: 1.09 points per possession (3rd)
In-conference defense: 1.01 points allowed per possession (4th)

What Baylor did well: *Balanced scoring.*

LaceDaruis Dunn is Baylor's all-time scorer, and the Bears were much better off without him last season. Dunn never saw a shot he didn't like—he took more than 33 percent of the shots when he was on the court in 2010-11—and his graduation was a big reason why Baylor's offense went from No. 92 in the country to No. 10 last year.

The biggest difference was Scott Drew's new backcourt. The previous year A.J. Walton had run the point, and not only was he not a good playmaker, he turned the ball over way too often. Pierre Jackson took over in 2011-12, and though he had a fairly high turnover rate (26 percent), he was a superior playmaker and his penetration opened up shots for teammates. Dunn's replacement Brady Heslip was the anti-Dunn, a low-usage, high-efficiency shooter. Heslip made better than 45 percent of his threes, and he led the nation in points per used possession (1.39).

All five of the Bears' starters led the team in scoring at some point. Perry Jones III took the most shots, and he was scrutinized for not being aggressive enough.

What we learned in 2012: *Baylor's defense needs to improve.*

Drew has leaned heavily on a zone defense the last couple years, and, against inferior opponents, it works. Conversely Baylor's toughest opponents often carve that zone up. In six of the Bears' eight losses, they allowed more than 1.14 points per possession.

To his credit, Drew decided to scrap the zone during Baylor's Big 12 tournament game against Kansas State. That helped the Bears knock off Kansas the next day for the first time since 2009. Drew stuck to mostly man throughout the NCAA tournament and the Bears made it to the Elite Eight.

The best Baylor's defense has ranked nationally in Drew's nine seasons was No. 34 in 2010, and the coach had Ekpe Udoh to thank partly for that. With the level of athletes Drew has been able to recruit, Baylor should be better defensively. Until he figures out the solution, it will be difficult for the Bears to win a Big 12 title.

What's in store for 2013: Baylor returns Jackson, Heslip, Walton, and its top reserves in the backcourt. The Bears are starting over in the frontcourt with the loss of Jones and Quincy Acy. Thanks to another banner year in recruiting, they start over with top-five recruit Isaiah Austin and a top-50 talent in Rico Gathers.

MEET THE BEARS

Pierre Jackson (5-10, 180, Sr.): Jackson has the speed, strength and handle to get to the rim pretty much whenever he wants, and he's a good enough shooter that his defender can't sag off of him. He also creates for teammates. Jackson led the Bears in scoring last season and he has the potential to be one of the Big 12's top scorers this year. If Drew has had one player who deserved to dominate the ball like Dunn, it's Jackson.

Brady Heslip (6-2, 180, Jr.): Heslip is one of the best catch-and-shoot shooters in the country. He also has the ability to come off screens and shoot on the run. Other than that, there is not a lot to his game. He rarely makes mistakes and he shoots when he has space. Defensively, he rarely fouls and is not a great on-ball defender.

A.J. Walton (6-1, 185, Sr.): Drew would be well served to find someone other than Walton to handle the ball when Jackson is off the court. Walton makes poor decisions, is not a good ball-handler, and is and a below-average shooter. Walton earns his playing time because he's Baylor's best perimeter defender. He's ranked in the top 60 nationally in steal percentage in all three of his seasons so far at Baylor.

Isaiah Austin (7-1, 220, Fr.): Is Austin the next PJ3? Like Jones, Austin is extremely gifted offensively. He has range out to the perimeter, a good handle for a big man, nice touch around the rim and moves really well for his height. But a look at his numbers as a high school senior—15 points, 11 rebounds and five blocks per game—raises a question. Is Austin too passive to dominate?

Rico Gathers (6-8, 260, Fr.): Gathers will not look like a college freshman. He is a built to be a physical player, and he plays that way. Gathers attacks the rim well and will be a good replacement for Acy, who was Baylor's most physical player. Look for Gathers to be the team's best rebounder right away if he's able to beat out Cory Jefferson at the 4.

Duece Bello (6-4, 185, So.): Bello rarely played meaningful minutes in 2011-12 until the postseason. In Baylor's final two Big 12 tournament games and in the NCAA tournament, he averaged 16 minutes per game. For some reason, he had earned Drew's trust at the end of the year. Bello does bring something off the bench. He's Baylor's best athlete on the wing and also rebounds well from the perimeter. His jumper is suspect, however.

L.J. Rose (6-4, 190, Fr.): Rose is a solid playmaker, ranked No. 74 in his class by Rivals.com. He's not an elite athlete, but he has good body control and can also knock down jumpers. Rose could be the best option as Baylor's backup point guard, enabling Walton to play off the ball when Jackson is on the bench.

Cory Jefferson (6-9, 210, Jr.): Jefferson played limited minutes last season, but when he did play he was his team's best defensive rebounder and shot blocker. His advanced numbers are similar to Acy, only he's Acy without the motor and not as good a finisher.

J'Mison Morgan (6-11, 275, Sr.): Baylor redshirted Morgan last season, probably to try to find some potential in his big body. Once a highly-recruited player, the UCLA transfer is simply a big body who takes up space. Anything more will qualify as a new development.

Prospectus says: Jones was an amazing talent but he left everyone wanting more. It might be a lot to ask Austin to be his equal, but that feels like a wash. The player the Bears will miss the most is Acy, who brought a Kevin Garnett-like intensity, was a great finisher around the rim, and an efficient scorer. On a team full of nice guys, Acy had a mean streak. Jackson might be the favorite to win Big 12 player of the year, and Heslip is such a good shooter it's doubtful his production will decrease. Baylor will be able to out-talent almost everyone in the Big 12, but until Drew proves he can win a Big 12 title and get his Bears to play championship-level defense, he's always going to be the preseason runner-up, no matter how much talent he has lured to Waco.

IOWA STATE

2012: 23-11 (12-6 Big 12); Lost to Kentucky 87-71, round of 32
In-conference offense: 1.07 points per possession (4th)
In-conference defense: 0.99 points allowed per possession (3rd)

What Iowa State did well: *Play through Royce White.*

It was weird to see a 6-8, 250-pound power forward bring the ball up the floor, but that typically was the case for the Cyclones last season. White was a rare breed, from his personality to his point-forward game.

Fred Hoiberg was innovative in how he used White. Sometimes White would get the ball isolated on the perimeter. Other times Hoiberg would post his star on the block or 15 feet away from the basket, sort of like an NBA set. The coach then surrounded White with three or four shooters, and Iowa State had the best three-point shooting team in the Big 12. The Cyclones shot 38 percent from the perimeter in conference play and 38 percent of their points came from behind the three-point line.

ISU's defense was also unique in that White was their biggest defender and they played 6-6 Melvin Ejim next to him. Ejim is more of a wing than a post player, and the Cyclones' interior defense and first-shot D was not great. But when opponents did miss, the Cyclones were the best defensive rebounding team in the conference. Whether they were on defense or offense, the goal was to get the ball to White and let him make decisions from there.

What we learned in 2012: *Transfer-ball works.*

Out of Iowa State's top seven 2011-12 rotation players, only Ejim and Scott Christopherson played for the team the previous season. The rest were transfers. (Tyrus McGee was a juco transfer; the rest were Division I transfers.)

Many questioned Hoiberg's idea of rebuilding through retreads, but it worked beautifully. Then again White had a lot to do with that, and he'll be the most difficult player to replace in the Big 12 this season. No player did more things for his team, not even Thomas Robinson at Kansas.

No worries in Ames, though. Hoiberg has two more transfers who could be the team's best players this season. Michigan State transfer Korie Lucious gives the Cyclones a true point guard and will take over ball-handling responsibilities from White. Utah transfer guard Will Clyburn will likely take over star responsibilities. The 6-7 shooting guard was Utah's best player in 2011 and should lead the Cyclones in scoring.

It worked in 2012. Who is to say it won't work in 2013?

What's in store for 2013: The Cyclones will rely heavily on three-point shooting again. Clyburn was a 40 percent perimeter shooter at Utah, and the Cyclones also return shooters Chris Babb and Tyrus McGee on the perimeter. Even interior-oriented Anthony Booker made 16 of 38 threes last year. ISU will be able to spread the floor and allow Lucious to penetrate and kick, a role similar to Diante Garrett's two seasons ago. True big man Percy Gibson gives the Cyclones a back-to-the-basket player.

MEET THE CYCLONES

Will Clyburn (6-7, 210, Sr.): Remember former Iowa State/Syracuse star Wesley Johnson? Clyburn's game is similar. He's a tall shooting guard with good range. Clyburn can shoot both off the dribble or the catch. Like Johnson, he's rangy and can finish at the rim. Instead of losing players like Johnson, Hoiberg is now bringing them to Ames.

Korie Lucious (5-11, 170, Sr.): In 2010, Lucious averaged nine points per game in Michigan State's Final Four run. In other words, he should adapt to the Big 12 just fine. Lucious is a pass-first point guard who can also create his own shot if need be. Look for Hoiberg to run more pick-and-rolls this season similar to two years ago with Garrett. This is Lucious' team and his offense to run.

Melvin Ejim (6-6, 230, Jr.): Two seasons ago as a freshman Ejim averaged double figures, but last year he averaged a point less per game. Why? For one, there was more talent around him, and he played fewer minutes. But the other factor was the graduation of Garrett. As a freshman Ejim was often on the receiving end of a nice dish from Garrett. Ejim is a great athlete, rebounder, and finisher, and he will be happy to have Lucious feed him around the rim.

Chris Babb (6-5, 225, Sr.): Babb fits the Iowa State offense perfectly because he has one role: spot-up shooter. Last season he attempted 195 threes and only 48 twos. He doesn't try to do much other than shoot, and in this offense, that's perfectly acceptable.

Anthony Booker (6-9, 255, Sr.): Booker likes to float to the perimeter and if he shoots like he did last season (14 of 29 from distance in Big 12 play), Hoiberg should be fine with him floating. He's the perfect candidate to play a two-man pick-and-pop game with Lucious. He's also good on the boards and will battle more traditional big man Percy Gibson for the final starting job.

Percy Gibson (6-9, 260, So.): Gibson's advanced numbers as a freshman suggest he could be a productive big man. He shot 66 percent and took 21 percent of Iowa State's shots when he was on the court. The lefty finishes well in the paint and is the team's biggest player.

Tyrus McGee (6-2, 205, Sr.): Sorry if this is repetitive, but McGee is yet another Cyclone spot-up shooter. He attempted more than twice as many threes as twos last season. McGee came off the bench and wasn't afraid to shoot. He got up 20 percent of ISU's shots when he was on the court, and should play a similar role this season.

Georges Niang (6-7, 245, Fr.): Niang, who was Rivals.com's No. 69 player in his class, can play with his back to the basket and also knock down a three. He finishes well with both hands and has nice footwork in the post. Niang played alongside Kentucky freshman Nerlens Noel in high school, and it was Niang who was the team's leading scorer. He's not a great athlete, but he makes up for it with his footwork and positioning.

Prospectus says: It's going to be difficult for Clyburn to be as great as White was last year, but Hoiberg has proven his transfer model works and that will help this team know it can succeed right away. Lucious played on two Final Four teams at Michigan State and he should have instant credibility with his teammates. Plus, he's been around for a year so they know his game. Hoiberg has a good mind when it comes to offense, and he's shown he can play a style that fits his talent. If he can mold this team like he did last year's squad, the Cyclones will return to the tourney and finish with a winning record in the Big 12.

KANSAS

2012: 32-7 (16-2 Big 12); Lost to Kentucky 67-59, National Championship Game
In-conference offense: 1.11 points per possession (2nd)
In-conference defense: 0.93 points allowed per possession (1st)

What Kansas did well: *Get stops.*

The Jayhawks' path to the NCAA title game was pretty remarkable. From the round of 32 on, they trailed in the second half of every game. They made only 24 percent of their threes in the first five games of the tournament. They beat NC State in the Sweet 16 despite making only two shots outside of six feet.

Before 2012, Bill Self's teams were 0-9 in the NCAA tournament when trailing at the half. Last year's team went 3-0 until they ran into Kentucky. So how did it happen?

It helped that this Kansas team never panicked when it was down. But what made all of those comebacks possible was KU's ability to get stops when they needed them most, and that's a staple of Self's teams.

Kansas has finished in the top nine nationally in defensive efficiency for seven straight years. The formula is usually allowing almost nothing in the paint and making opponents take guarded shots. This team did just that, and if the defense broke down, the Jayhawks still had Jeff Withey protecting the paint.

What we learned in 2012: *The Jayhawks will always score enough.*

Last year's team was the worst shooting Kansas squad since 2004, Self's first year at KU. The Jayhawks still managed to score 1.14 points per possession and were the second-most efficient team in the Big 12.

Chalk that up to the fact that Self's teams always take good shots and have a purpose offensively. The purpose last year was to play through Robinson or let Tyshawn Taylor use his speed to get to the basket. In the tournament, the team also leaned heavily on Elijah Johnson to take the big shots. Self's teams always have defined roles, with no confusion on who is supposed to do what.

The concern heading into this season would be that the Jayhawks do not exactly have the players to slide into some of those roles. Mainly, most years the Jayhawks have a scoring big man (Wayne Simien, Darrell Arthur, Cole Aldrich, the Morris twins, and Robinson). Last season, Robinson emerged from backup to star. This season the Jayhawks have star potential in Withey, but that's for his defense. He is likely to improve offensively, but it might be asking too much to build the offense around him. Freshman Perry Ellis has potential as a scorer, but the Jayhawks have never had to rely on a freshman to be the go-to big man inside.

To keep KU's concerns in perspective, last year the thought was Self had his worst team at Kansas and that team managed to win an eighth straight Big 12 title and make the national championship game. So the smart money says Self will figure out a way to make the offense efficient enough.

What's in store for 2013: Since the Jayhawks are missing a big-time scorer in the post after losing Robinson, this team will rely heavily on its perimeter players. Johnson will likely be the go-to guy, taking over Taylor's ball-handling and play-making responsibilities. Travis Releford is a steady fifth-year senior who is great in transition and picks his spots to attack on offense. The wildcard is Ben McLemore, who was forced to redshirt last season. Self's staff was convinced McLemore was the best NBA prospect on the roster in 2012 and that included Robinson. Look for Self to run an offense similar to the 2008 championship team, which used a lot of ball screens to free its perimeter players.

MEET THE JAYHAWKS

Elijah Johnson (6-4, 195, Sr.): Johnson relied on his outside shot too often last season. He was on the court more than 80 percent of the time and shot just 46 free throws, the only starter to shoot less than 100. He has the athleticism to get to the basket and KU will need more of that from him this year. He struggled with his outside shot in KU's first 30 games when he made just

30 percent of his threes. Self encouraged Johnson to keep shooting and it paid off. Johnson shot 47 percent from outside in KU's final nine games, and he made several big shots in key moments during the tournament. His tourney performance suggests he's ready to take over the role as KU's go-to scorer as long as he's willing to do more than settle for outside shots.

Jeff Withey (7-0, 235, Sr.): During the final practice before KU's trip overseas this summer, Withey shot everything with his left hand. That was an emphasis this summer, as was expanding his repertoire of post moves. Most of his points last season were created by teammates, and KU needs him to be able to score more with his back to the basket. As a defender early last year Withey could be bullied and buried under the goal. But by the end of the season he was holding his ground. Withey held Jared Sullinger in check (13 points, 5-of-19 shooting) and shut down Anthony Davis (six points, 1-of-10 shooting). Withey has great timing and moves his feet well for his size. Expect him to lead the nation in block percentage again.

Travis Releford (6-6, 210, Sr.): Releford has an old man's game. He works angles and is a sneaky scorer. He's also efficient and knows his limitations—he's not going to try to take his man one-on-one in the halfcourt. A lot of his points come in transition, where he excels. Defensively, he's the team's best on-ball defender and typically draws the opponent's best perimeter player.

Ben McLemore (6-5, 195, Fr.): McLemore is a great athlete with a picture-perfect jump shot. If KU has one player who is destined to improve dramatically throughout the year, it's McLemore. His biggest weakness is his ball-handling and the fact that he's still trying to figure out where he's supposed to be on both ends. Once he finds his place, he should be one of KU's top scorers. He also has the tools to be a really good defender.

Perry Ellis (6-8, 225, Fr.): Ellis has the misfortune of replacing Robinson, but he's a much different player. He's smooth and much more similar to former Jayhawk Marcus Morris. Ellis' go-to move is a baseline spin and he finishes pretty well around the rim. He also has a reliable jump shot from 15 to 17 feet. One area where he struggled during KU's Europe trip was turning the ball over. Once he catches up to the speed of the game, he should improve in that area.

Andrew White (6-6, 210, Fr.): White is KU's best outside shooter. Self was already running sets to get White shots this summer. He will step into Conner Teahan's role as KU's shooter off the bench. Like Teahan, the one area where he could struggle is defending the perimeter.

Naadir Tharpe (5-11, 170, So.): Tharpe had a rough freshman year. He played only 11 percent of available minutes, and when he played, he was a turnover machine (39.9 turnover rate). But consider Tharpe the next KU player who struggles to get on the floor as a freshman and then becomes a solid rotation player the next season. He has a good feel for how to play point guard and set up teammates, and he is KU's only true point.

Kevin Young (6-8, 190, Sr.): Young broke a bone in his hand in October, but reportedly will be back no later than December. Assuming he's healthy, he's a guy that you have to play because of his energy and ability to get to loose balls. Young was KU's best offensive rebounder and was a spark plug off the bench during the tournament. He should be KU's first big man off the bench.

Jamari Traylor (6-8, 220, Fr.), Justin Wesley (6-9, 220, Jr.), Zach Peters (6-9, 240, Fr.): These three players will battle for KU's other backup big man spot.

Prospectus says: The missing piece is a dominant inside scorer. The Jayhawks will go through stretches where they struggle to score, similar to stretches they had in the NCAA tourney. The difference, as it was last season, is this team will be incredibly tough to score against with Withey protecting the rim. He's able to take away another team's best post player and also provides great help-side defense. Turnovers could be a bugaboo, but the same could have been said last year with Taylor at the point. A ninth straight Big 12 title is the expectation and this team is capable of another deep tourney run.

KANSAS STATE

2012: 22-11 (10-8 Big 12); Lost to Syracuse 75-59, NCAA round of 32
In-conference offense: 1.02 points per possession (6th)
In-conference defense: 0.97 points allowed per possession (2nd)

What Kansas State did well: *Force bad offense.*

Frank Martin made you uncomfortable, and that's how his teams played defense. Martin's in-your-face persona was reflected in his team's aggressive D. The Wildcats were the best Big 12 team at forcing turnovers. In four of Martin's five seasons as head coach in Manhattan, K-State finished in the top two in defensive turnover percentage during conference play.

What this team did better than any of Martin's previous teams was defend inside the three-point line. The Wildcats could gamble because they had Jordan Henriquez protecting the rim. Henriquez was one of the best shot blockers in the nation. He had an eight-game stretch near the end of the year when he blocked 34 shots.

Since the Wildcats could apply so much pressure, it was difficult to have a good offensive flow. They could push you off your spots. The good teams like Kansas would use their pressure against them, but most opponents got out of their flow and forced too many bad shots.

What we learned in 2012: *Martin's model works.*

The Wildcats leaned heavily on Jacob Pullen in his final few years in Manhattan, and where the points would come from when Pullen graduated was a huge question mark. Rodney McGruder slid into the role as the go-to Wildcat, and although he did not dominate the ball as much as Pullen, he was effective.

What we figured out was one player didn't make Martin succeed; it was his system. Martin wanted his teams to get up a shot and then fight to get the rebound. In his five years in Manhattan, K-State finished in the top six in offensive rebounding percentage every year.

Martin also proved that he could adapt. In Pullen's senior year when the offense was struggling, Martin installed Johnny Orr's pinch-post offense. The Cats continued to use Orr's offense periodically last season.

That scheme should help ease the transition into the Bruce Weber era. When Martin wasn't running Orr's offense, he wanted his players driving hard to the basket or pounding it in the post and drawing fouls. Weber runs a five-man motion with much more passing and cutting, and his teams do not get to the line nearly as often.

Weber was unable to sustain his early success at Illinois and he made only two NCAA tournaments in his final five years in Champaign. Then again Weber did have his best years with someone else's recruits (Bill Self's), so there's hope he can win right away with players who are used to winning.

What's in store for 2013: K-State returns four of five starters, led by McGruder and sophomore point guard Angel Rodriguez. Rodriguez played out of control too often as a freshman, but he could also get hot and score in spurts. McGruder and Will Spradling should be good fits in Weber's system. Both are better-suited for a motion offense. Rodriguez may have the biggest learning curve. Inside, Henriquez was K-State's most improved player last year. Space-eater Thomas Gipson will likely start next to Henriquez, giving K-State a big frontline and putting the team's best rebounders from a year ago on the court together. The Wildcats will be less aggressive defensively under Weber, but with Gipson and Henriquez on the back line, they should be a better defensive rebounding team, one area where they were below average last year.

MEET THE WILDCATS

Rodney McGruder (6-4, 205, Sr.): McGruder usually gets his points quietly. His game is simple and efficient. He's a great mid-range shooter and can also knock down the three consistently. McGruder has improved throughout his career at being able to score and shoot off the dribble. He rarely creates for others, but you can bank on him making good decisions and taking good shots.

Angel Rodriguez (5-11, 180, So.): Rodriguez is extremely fast with the basketball, which can be good and bad. When he's good, he's hitting floaters in the lane and creating for his teammates. When he's bad, he makes careless decisions and lets one bad turnover snowball into a series of mistakes. But Rodriguez keeps attacking. He's a gambler on both ends of the court.

Jordan Henriquez (6-11, 250, Sr.): Henriquez has gotten stronger over the years and that's the major reason why he's improved every season. Like a shooter, he developed more and more confidence on the defensive end last season the more blocks he got. Offensively, he has developed a jump hook that is not pretty but fairly effective. Henriquez has improved finishing at the rim because of his increased strength. He's never going to be a great scorer, but he doesn't hurt his team offensively.

Will Spradling (6-2, 180, Jr.): Spradling's shooting numbers were not as good last season. His freshman year he could come off the bench and take open shots. Last season he had to create more for himself and was a bigger part of the offense. Spradling is capable of creating offense for himself, and like McGruder, he can knock down the mid-range jumper and the three. He's just not as talented as McGruder, and is better suited as a complementary piece.

Thomas Gipson (6-7, 275, So.): Good luck moving this dude. Gipson is a load inside. He's physical and uses his wide frame to his advantage. He has a simple post game. Gipson usually goes over his right shoulder to his dominant left hand, but since most players are not used to guarding lefties, he can be tricky to defend.

Martavious Irving (6-1, 210, Sr.): Irving is a good energy man off the bench. Offensively, he's a decent shooter and can create off the dribble. His main value is his defense and ability to guard multiple positions on the perimeter.

Shane Southwell (6-6, 210, Jr.): See Irving's description. Southwell is a similar player, but with more size and a less reliable jump shot.

Adrian Diaz (6-10, 225, So.): Diaz will back up Henriquez, which makes sense because he's a very similar player. He has potential to be a good shot-blocker, but needs to add some muscle first. After a year in the program, Diaz should be improved this season.

Prospectus says: The Wildcats were always willing to be coached under Martin and this is a good team to inherit. They are not the Big 12's most talented group, but they're the only team that has both experienced success and returns almost all the key pieces from last season. Weber is a good defensive coach, although his defense is not as aggressive. His teams force fewer turnovers and foul much less. With Henriquez protecting the rim, that model should work. If Weber can get this team to run his offense, there's no reason K-State should not get back to the NCAA tournament.

OKLAHOMA

2012: 15-16 (5-13 Big 12); Lost to Texas A&M 62-53, Big 12 first round
In-conference offense: 0.97 points per possession (8th)
In-conference defense: 1.07 points allowed per possession (8th)

What Oklahoma did well: *Play good basketball for a half.*

Had games ended at halftime, the Sooners would have been an NCAA tournament bubble team. In the regular season they outscored opponents by 103 points in the first half but came up 78 points short in the second half. They led at halftime in nine of their Big 12 games—including against KU at home and on the road at Baylor, both losses—and were outscored by 129 in the second half in conference play.

The explanation is simple. The Sooners did not have any depth and their starters would tire out in the second half. Those starters, all of whom return this season, accounted for 70 percent of the team's points.

The nice thing for Lon Kruger is he wasn't trying to fit a square peg in a round hole with his starters. Each player fit a specific role. Kruger had a point guard, Sam Grooms, who distributed the ball well and ranked third in the Big 12 with a 33.5 assist rate. Steven Pledger provided scoring on the wing and also made 42 percent of his threes. Cameron Clark supplied athleticism and rebounding. Big men Andrew Fitzgerald and Romero Osby both averaged double figures and made OU the best rebounding team Kruger has coached in years.

For a half, that was typically enough to stick with Big 12 competition.

What we learned in 2012: *The Sooners need depth to play Kruger's style.*

Kruger's teams have traditionally limited their own turnovers while forcing opponents to commit them, but last season was the exception to that rule. The Sooners gave the ball away on 19 percent of their possessions in Big 12 play, which ranked fourth in the league. So far, so good. However, they forced a turnover on just 19 percent of their defensive possessions in conference play. As a reference point, Kruger's last three teams at UNLV all forced turnovers on more than 23 percent of their defensive possessions.

To apply the kind of ball pressure that Kruger wants, he needed to go out and add some depth, particularly on the perimeter. He did that by adding nine new players, including three freshman guards (Buddy Hield, Je'lon Hornbeak and Isaiah Cousins) who should all play right away. He also added a scorer in Wyoming transfer Amath M'Baye, a 6-9 forward who averaged 12 points per game in his sophomore season.

The Sooners typically won the games they should have won last year. Their only bad loss was at Texas Tech, and they went 11-3 against teams outside of Ken Pomeroy's top 100. They also showed their top-end potential by sweeping Kansas State. But when they played top-tier teams like Baylor and KU close for a half, they lost in double digits both times.

What's in store for 2013: The Sooners need to find another shooter to go along with Pledger. They have the pieces inside for a nice frontline and the freshmen provide depth in the backcourt. This might not be the ideal Kruger team (his teams are usually more perimeter-oriented) but a second year under the respected coach could make a big difference for the Sooners.

MEET THE SOONERS

Steven Pledger (6-4, 220, Sr.): Pledger's three-point shooting numbers have gone up every season. Last year he was fourth in the Big 12 in both makes (72) and percentage (41.6). He's not just a long-range gunner either. For the first time in his career, Pledger attempted more twos (197) than threes (172), showing an ability to go to the basket if a defender closed on him. He's the Big 12's top returning scorer, and if his production/usage goes up, as it has each year, he could lead the conference in scoring.

Romero Osby (6-8, 230, Sr.): Osby became more of a low-post threat last season than he had been in his first two years at Mississippi State. He was the best Sooner at getting to the line (drawing nearly five fouls per 40 minutes) and shot a respectable 72 percent at the line. Osby was also OU's best rebounder, gobbling up 18 percent of opponents' misses during his minutes.

Andrew Fitzgerald (6-8, 240, Sr.): Fitzgerald has one of the best mid-range jumpers in the Big 12 and consistently knocks down the 14- to 17-footer. Surprisingly, he never drifts to the three-point line: Fitzgerald has never attempted a three. He shot the worst percentage of his career in 2011-12 (47) but he raised his offensive rating by lowering his turnover rate from 19.0 to 12.1. He did not rebound as well on the defensive end as he had his sophomore season, but that was likely because he had Osby playing next to him. Both players will have to battle M'Baye to hold on to their starting spots.

Sam Grooms (6-1, 205, Sr.): Grooms would be well served to stick to passing. He made just 39 percent of his twos and was 8-of-40 from distance. On the other hand Grooms did a nice job distributing the ball. With more shooters and another scorer (M'Baye) in the rotation, Grooms should have more weapons to work with.

Cameron Clark (6-6, 210, Jr.): Clark performed better than expected as a freshman but saw his production drop as a sophomore. His two-point accuracy dropped from 51 to 42 percent and he was less of a threat from deep, going just 5-of-18. Clark did improve on the defensive end, and his athleticism and size gives OU a college basketball rarity, a true 3.

Amath M'Baye (6-9, 210, Jr.): Kruger went up against M'Baye for two years in the Mountain West and must have liked what he saw. M'Baye was an efficient inside scorer as a sophomore and also his team's best rebounder. The one area where he struggled was from the perimeter (8-of-49), so he spent much of last year working on his outside shot and ball handling. The expectation is that he'll compete for a starting role and perhaps displace Fitzgerald. If M'Baye meets expectations, the Sooners could have the Big 12's best scoring frontline.

Tyler Neal (6-7, 230, Jr.): Neal only played 33 percent of available minutes, but he made the second-most threes (23, on 68 attempts) on the team. That shows how limited the Sooners were on the perimeter. Neal should once again provide some outside shooting in limited minutes.

Buddy Hield (6-3, 200, Fr.),
Je'lon Hornbeak (6-3, 180, Fr.),
Isaiah Cousins (6-3, 180, Fr.): Hield, a shooting guard, was rated the No. 86 prospect by Rivals.com and Hornbeak, a combo guard, was ranked No. 102. Cousins, a combo guard, was a three-star recruit. All three should have a chance to play right away, as Carl Blair, OU's top guard off the bench in 2012, transferred to Prairie View.

Prospectus says: Kruger made the NCAA tournament in four of his last five years at UNLV, but it did take him three seasons to get there. All five of his returning starters are upperclassmen and four are seniors, so he has the experience to make some noise in the Big 12. How much noise could depend on how much of an impact M'Baye makes and how well the freshman guards play. If the newcomers pan out, the Sooners could turn last year's first-half results into actual ones and become a bubble team.

OKLAHOMA STATE

2012: 15-18 (7-11 Big 12); Lost to Missouri 88-70, Big 12 second round
In-conference offense: 1.00 points per possession (7th)
In-conference defense: 1.07 points allowed per possession (9th)

What Oklahoma State did well: *Get shots up.*

The Cowboys had the second-lowest turnover rate (18 percent) in the Big 12 during conference games. Part of that was an offensive philosophy of letting Keiton Page chuck it whenever he could see the rim. The offense was geared toward getting shots for Page, particularly late in the season when injuries left Travis Ford with limited options offensively. And Page, who also handled the ball a lot, rarely turned it over.

Page was definitely important to the OSU offense, but he typically got his numbers win or lose. The player who the Cowboys' success was tied to the most was Le'Bryan Nash. In OSU's Big 12 wins, Nash averaged 20 points while taking 26 percent of the team's shots during his minutes. In the conference losses he averaged just 10 points and took 22 percent of the shots.

The other area where the Cowboys excelled was defending the three-point line, which is hardly surprising given the number of athletic wings on the roster. Nash, Markel Brown, Jean-Paul Olukemi (before he was injured) and Brian Williams—they're all good athletes who are 6-3 or taller.

What we learned in 2012: *The Cowboys need big men.*

Oklahoma State was the worst rebounding team in the Big 12 on both ends. One issue was a lack of talent in the post, forcing Ford to go small. Freshman Michael Cobbins was the only true interior player to log more than 50 percent of available minutes.

If Ford would have been willing to sacrifice scoring for rebounding and defense, he would have played Philip Jurick more. Now Jurick might not be available. The team's best rebounder enters this season suspended indefinitely after pleading guilty in September to misdemeanor counts of possession of marijuana and drug paraphernalia from an August arrest. Jurick played 17 minutes per game last year but missed the final six games with a torn Achilles.

Ford did sign 6-8 forward Kamari Murphy to help his inside depth. Murphy, who spent a post-grad year at IMG Academy in Florida, averaged seven rebounds during a foreign tour of Spain this summer.

What's in store for 2013: Brian Williams is out for the year after fracturing his left wrist during the first week of practice. Yet somehow the Cowboys are still stacked on the wing. Not only do Brown, Nash, and Olukemi return, 6-4 freshman guard Marcus Smart could potentially be OSU's best player. Smart is expected to start at point guard, but he's more naturally a wing. The Cowboys will miss Page's three-point shooting but they could be better off with a more balanced attack. Look for Brown to take on more of the scoring and Smart to take a leadership role right away.

MEET THE COWBOYS

Le'Bryan Nash (6-7, 230, So.): Nash was thought to be a one-and-done player, so the fact that he's still here speaks to his inconsistencies as a freshman. He had stretches where he was dominant (he scored 27 points in an upset of Missouri) only to disappear at other times. Nash's biggest issue was inefficiency. He made just 24 percent of his threes and shot 44 percent inside the arc. Basically Nash left everyone wanting more, but that's not to say he won't deliver as a sophomore.

Markel Brown (6-3, 190, Jr.): Brown made a name last season with his highlight-reel dunks. Players talk about momentum changing in games because of big dunks, and Brown was that kind of dunker. He started the Missouri game off by nearly jumping over Kim English, setting the tone for an upset victory. Brown played more minutes than any other Cowboy other than Page last year, and he could take over Page's scoring role this season. He led the Cowboys in scoring during their trip to Spain, averaging 18 points per game. His one area where he needs to improve is his outside shot: he made just 32 percent of his threes last year.

Marcus Smart (6-4, 225, Fr.): Smart will play point guard, but he could probably go inside if the Cowboys wanted him there. He's a banger, who can post up, rebound, and get to the rim from the perimeter. Smart led USA's U-18 national team to a gold medal in the FIBA Americas Championships this summer, and left Billy Donovan telling anyone who asked how awesome Smart was. He's expected to be a leader right away in Stillwater.

Jean-Paul Olukemi (6-6, 215, Sr.): If Olukemi were three inches shorter or Brown three inches taller, they would essentially be the same player. Their advanced numbers almost mirror each other. The Cowboys missed Olukemi after he was lost for the season after 13 games, but they did have a replica in Brown. Olukemi was the team's second-best returning player last year after Page. He could be the odd wing out of the starting lineup, but he's an asset because of his ability to get to the free throw line. If Olukemi doesn't start, he'll likely be the sixth man.

Michael Cobbins (6-8, 220, So.): Ford seems to like uber-athletic players, and Cobbins fits the mold. He's not gifted offensively, but he's a good rebounder and shot blocker. The Cowboys will have to use their wings to score and attack, and Cobbins' role offensively will be to set screens and hit the offensive glass since he's not your typical back-to-the-basket post player.

Kamari Murphy (6-8, 210, Fr.): Murphy is a great athlete and should be another highlight waiting to happen, joining Brown and the Cowboys' other gifted dunkers. He has the ability to face up and hit the mid-range jumper as well.

Philip Jurick (6-11, 260, Sr.): Similar to Cobbins, Jurick is a low-usage big man who does all the dirty work. He was the team's best rebounder and shot blocker, but not much of a threat to score. Jurick's status is up in the air, but the Cowboys could certainly use him as they don't have much depth in the post.

Kirby Gardner (6-2, 200, Jr.): The Cowboys lost point guard Cezar Guerrero, who transferred this summer to Fresno State. That leaves Gardner as the only true point guard on the team. The late signee averaged 17 points and four assists last season at San Bernardino Valley College. If Ford decides Smart is better suited on the wing, Gardner could become the starter at the point.

Phil Forte (5-11, 195, Fr.): Forte was Smart's teammate in high school, and while Smart could fill Page's role as OSU's leader, Forte is likely the Cowboys' next dead-eye shooter. Like Page, he's not an intimidating figure but he can stroke it from all over the court.

Prospectus says: Two years ago the Cowboys made the NIT with a scoring big man in Marshall Moses. Before that, in 2009 and 2010, the Cowboys made the NCAA tournament in large part because of James Anderson, a first-round draft pick. Ford has yet to replace Moses' production and Nash did not play like a first-round talent last year. But this team has too much talent to miss the NCAA tournament for a third straight year.

TEXAS

2012: 20-14 (9-9 Big 12), lost to Cincinnati 65-59, round of 64
In-conference offense: 1.04 points per possession (5th)
In-conference defense: 1.03 points allowed per possession (5th)

What Texas did well: *Let J'Covan Brown do his thing.*

Texas making the NCAA tournament with only one returning starter last season was a testament to the talents of J'Covan Brown.

Brown was the focus of every opponent's defense and he still found a way to lead the Big 12 in scoring while posting his most efficient season as a Longhorn. The guy was built to be a high-volume shooter. He liked the ball in his hands and he liked finding creative ways to get up shots. Rick Barnes was smart to let him do his thing, because the Horns didn't really have many other options offensively.

Myck Kabongo was the second option and he had a so-so year, making just 43 percent of his twos and 32 percent from beyond the arc. When he didn't turn the ball over Kabongo did a good job penetrating and either setting up teammates or drawing fouls. But he was too erratic to dominate the ball, and the Longhorns were lucky to have a combo guard like Brown who could take some of the pressure off Kabongo.

What we learned in 2012: *Barnes deserves more credit than he gets.*

This team relied heavily on five freshmen and still made the NCAA tournament. Sure Kentucky won the title leaning on some talented freshmen, but Barnes' class was simply solid and not overly talented. Sheldon McClellan was better than expected and Kabongo had moments where he looked like he could one day be a star, but the Longhorns didn't win simply because they could out-talent everyone.

Barnes catches a lot of flack for not doing more with the talent he has had. He's made only one Final Four in 14 seasons at Texas, and he's coached six NBA lottery picks, including Kevin Durant.

What last year proved was that Barnes deserves some credit for how consistent Texas has been through the years, even in down years. He's never missed an NCAA tournament at UT and his offense is typically one of the most efficient in the country. With Brown and not a lot else last season, the Longhorns still ranked No. 31 nationally in offensive efficiency. If you want to say Brown does less with more, that's fine. But in the next breath you should say when he has less, he does more.

What's in store for 2013: One reason Texas had less talent last season was that Barnes probably didn't anticipate Tristan Thompson leaving after one season. He didn't have time to make up for the loss of Thompson in recruiting last year, but he did bring in a reliable big man this year in Cameron Ridley, ranked the No. 7 center in his class by Rivals.com. Kabongo (if he's eligible) and McClellan will have to do more with the loss of Brown. They'll be joined in the rotation by fellow sophomores Julien Lewis, Jonathan Holmes and Jaylen Bond, who should all be improved.

MEET THE LONGHORNS

Myck Kabongo (6-1, 180, So.): As this book goes to press Kabongo is under investigation, as the NCAA looks into his relationship with agent Rich Paul. Assuming he plays, his best attribute as a freshman was his ability to get to the free throw line. Only one player in the country shorter than 6-5 (Butler's Ronald Nored) ranked ahead of Kabongo in free throw rate. If Kabongo can learn how to play more in the half-court and improve his pick-and-roll game (Barnes likes running ball screens for his lead guard) he could put up big numbers.

Sheldon McClellan (6-4, 200, So.): McClellan has a nice mid-range game and was the Longhorns' most efficient scorer. His game has some similarities to Kansas State's Rodney McGruder. He shoots well off the catch and off the dribble. McClellan rarely made a mistake and took good shots within the flow of the offense. He'll need to take on an increased role with Brown gone.

Julien Lewis (6-3, 190, So.): Like Kabongo, Lewis struggled with his shot as a freshman. He was either on or way off. Lewis does have a nice looking jumper, so there's hope that his shooting numbers could go up.

Cameron Ridley (6-9, 270, Fr.): Remember Dexter Pittman? Ridley is similar. Big body, soft hands, and a nice touch around the basket. Ridley also seems to have a good understanding for how to use his big body to establish position. The one concern might be that he doesn't have enough lift to score over some of the Big 12's top shot blockers.

Jonathan Holmes (6-7, 240, So.): Holmes is another Longhorn who thrived getting to the free throw line. He is one of Barnes' best athletes and a good finisher around the rim.

Jaylen Bond (6-7, 225, So.): In the minutes he played as a freshman, Bond was UT's best defensive rebounder. He's an athlete who can also finish at the basket.

Prince Ibeh (6-10, 245, Fr.): The Big 12 is full of talented shot blockers and Ibeh could be next in line. He's quick off his feet and averaged nearly five blocks a game as a senior in high school. Offensively Ibeh doesn't have much game yet, but he should earn some playing time.

Javan Felix (5-10, 190, Fr.): Felix will back up Kabongo. He's a more under-control, pass-first point guard in the mold of D.J. Augustin, who helped convince Felix to go to Texas. Felix could allow Barnes to move Kabongo off the ball occasionally.

Prospectus says: Most observers believe Texas will work its way back toward the top of the Big 12 standings this year, but it's difficult to buy into the fact that they'll be better without Brown. Ridley should be able to provide more scoring inside than the Horns had last year, and a year of experience will go a long way for all of the sophomores. But Brown could bail Texas out when nothing else was working, and unless Kabongo is not only cleared by the NCAA but also emerges as one of the top guards in the country, I'm not sold on Texas as one of the Big 12's top teams. I see the Horns returning to the bubble again this year and finishing around .500 in conference play.

TCU

2012: 18-15 (7-7 Mountain West); Lost to Oregon State 101-81, CBI second round
In-conference offense: 1.05 points per possession (2nd, MWC)
In-conference defense: 1.08 points allowed per possession (8th, MWC)

What TCU did well: *Make threes during conference play.*

One of the head-scratcher wins of 2012 was TCU's overtime victory against UNLV. In that game the Horned Frogs trailed by 18 in the second half and they had already lost to UNLV earlier in the season by 23. Ken Pomeroy estimated that when UNLV led by 18, TCU had less than a one percent chance of winning the game.

That night the Horned Frogs made a season-high 14 of their 32 threes. If there was ever a team that, excuse the cliché, lived and died by the three, it was TCU last season. They lost against Norfolk State by going 1-of-18 from the perimeter, nearly knocked off a solid Colorado State team in double-OT by going 12-of-31, beat CSU at home by going 12-of-27 and finally got blown out by the Rams in the Mountain West tournament by going 2-of-20.

How a team that shot pretty well from the perimeter most nights could go so cold is a mystery. The Horned Frogs made a Mountain West-best 38 percent of their threes during conference play, but shot just 33 percent outside the arc in all other games.

It was pretty simple. When the Frogs were making shots, they could beat almost anyone in the MWC because they rarely turned the ball over. When they weren't hitting, they were a below average team.

What we learned in 2012: *TCU's defense is not Big 12 caliber.*

Texas Tech allowed 1.09 points per possession during Big 12 play last year and won one game. TCU let Mountain West teams score 1.08 points per possession. And that was against Mountain West offenses.

TCU allowed conference opponents to shoot an effective FG percentage of 54.6. Only eight teams in the country had a better effective FG percentage than 54.6. So when you played TCU, you became one of the best shooting teams in the country.

As the Horned Frogs enter the Big 12, it's clear they need to drastically improve defensively to be able to compete. That's why hiring Trent Johnson looks like a wise move. Johnson's teams have traditionally been solid defensively. He had two really bad years at LSU, but last season it looked like the program was beginning to turn things around and his defense ranked No. 32 in the nation in efficiency.

Former TCU coach Jim Christian had bad defenses for three straight years, so it wasn't a one-year issue. It might take a few years for Johnson to get his own players, but on the surface it looks like Johnson was a wise choice to help TCU compete in the Big 12.

What's in store for 2013: TCU will miss do-everything point guard Hank Thorns, and in his place steps Mountain West freshman of the year Kyan Anderson, who was second to Thorns in assists and third in made threes. MWC sixth man of the year Amric Fields will likely move into the starting lineup with Anderson and Garlon Green, the team's leading returning scorer. Adrick McKinney came off the bench last season and was one of the team's best rebounders. The Frogs also return rotation players Nate Butler and Connell Crossland. In the backcourt TCU signed two three-star guards, Charles Hill, Jr., and Clyde Smith III.

MEET THE HORNED FROGS

Kyan Anderson (5-11, 175, So.): Anderson will need to take over point guard responsibilities for Thorns, and his performance as a freshman suggests he should do well in that position. He had good assist numbers and also showed an ability to knock down the open jump shot.

Garlon Green (6-7, 210, Sr.): Green is an athletic wing who can play both inside and out. He was TCU's streakiest scorer a year ago. Some nights he'll go off for 20 and then he had eight games where he scored five points or less.

Amric Fields (6-9, 210, Jr.): Fields is a stretch 4 who finishes well around the basket and made 62 percent of his twos last season. He was the team's best shot blocker, though that's not saying a lot, and the one knock on his game is that he did a poor job rebounding for his size.

Devonta Abron (6-8, 255, So.): After playing last season for Arkansas, Abron was granted a transfer eligibility waiver in September and should compete for a starting job in Fort Worth. He's a good athlete who posted both the Razorbacks' best offensive rebound percentage and the best steal rate. Considering Mike Anderson's style, that's an impressive feat.

Adrick McKinney (6-8, 250, Sr.): McKinney is a physical player and did a good job getting to the line last year. He shot poorly from the field but earned his playing time by rebounding well and taking up space inside.

Nate Butler Lind (6-6, 200, Sr.): Butler Lind's role was to come off the bench and shoot from outside, but he struggled to hit shots most the season. He did knock down 3-of-4 threes in a win against Wisconsin Milwaukee in the first round of the CBI.

Connell Crossland (6-7, 190, Sr.): In limited minutes last season, Crossland was TCU's best rebounder. He also made 7-of-18 threes. If there was one reason he didn't play more, it's that he turned the ball over too often.

Charles Hill, Jr. (6-2, 180, Fr.): Hill was one of the best high school players in the Fort Worth area. He's a good slasher with big-time hops.

Clyde Smith III (6-2, 185, Fr.): Smith was a top-50 point guard prospect and could allow Anderson to continue playing off the ball. Smith has a nice handle and can score off the dribble.

Prospectus says: It's difficult to see this team finishing anywhere above ninth in the Big 12. The Frogs might be able to sneak out a couple wins if they catch fire from the perimeter, but their talent is not on par with the rest of the conference. They are clearly one of the Big 12's two worst teams.

TEXAS TECH

2012: 8-23 (1-17 Big 12); Lost to Oklahoma State 76-60, Big 12 first round
In-conference offense: 0.84 points per possession (10th)
In-conference defense: 1.09 points allowed per possession (10th)

What Texas Tech did well: *Get to the free throw line.*

It's difficult to say the Red Raiders did anything well last season. Billy Gillispie had cleaned house and was trying to build the program from scratch. The Raiders simply weren't talented enough to compete in the Big 12, a fact that was reflected in pretty much every advanced statistical measure.

Leading scorers Jordan Tolbert and Jaye Crockett were two players who could compete and they did a good job getting to the line. Tolbert drew six fouls per 40 minutes and Crockett also had a high free throw rate. Other than Ty Nurse's outside shooting, Texas Tech did not have a lot else going on offensively.

What we learned in 2012: *Texas Tech has a long way to go.*

Gillispie had a heck of a challenge in front of him. Now interim head coach Chris Walker has an impossible mission. It's doubtful he can win enough games with this group to go from acting to permanent head coach.

Texas Tech had maybe four players who should have been playing serious minutes in the Big 12: Tolbert, Nurse, Crockett, and former Red Raider Robert Lewandowski. Other than that, Tech didn't have the shooters or the athletes to win in this league.

What's in store for 2013: Before he resigned, Gillispie signed four junior college players, a Canadian transfer, and three freshmen. Unfortunately, the most-heralded freshman, Aaron Ross, is out for the season with an ACL tear. Tolbert, Crockett and Nurse will be relied upon to carry the load offensively. Tolbert, who was undoubtedly Tech's go-to player, played just 59 percent percent of the team's minutes last season. Expect him to play a lot more as a sophomore.

MEET THE RED RAIDERS

Jordan Tolbert (6-7, 220, So.): Tolbert is a tough cover for opposing post players because of his ability to attack off the dribble. His quickness allowed him to drive past bigger players and get to the foul line. His numbers as a freshman were respectable, especially considering the fact that he had to be the Red Raiders' go-to scorer.

Jaye Crockett (6-7, 200, Jr.): Crockett is undersized to play down low, but like Tolbert, he can use his quickness to get to the basket. He's a good athlete and gets off the floor quickly, which made him Tech's best defensive rebounder.

Ty Nurse (6-1, 185, Sr.): Nurse did a good job in pick-and-roll situations and could shoot off the dribble or catch. He's not super quick but has a good understanding of how to get himself open in the half-court.

Josh Gray (6-1, 175, Fr.): Gray will likely start at point guard, and is Tech's top incoming freshman now that Ross is out for the season. He was ranked as the No. 107 prospect by Rivals.com. Gray put up impressive numbers in high school in the Houston area, and is extremely quick off the dribble.

Toddrick Gotcher (6-3, 195, Fr.): Gotcher got off to a nice start as a freshman until injuring his foot, which forced him to miss the rest of the season and take a medical redshirt. He started eight of nine games and shot the ball well.

Trency Jackson (6-2, 185, So.): Jackson originally signed with Southern Miss out of high school but didn't qualify. He was ranked as the No. 13 junior college prospect and played on the NJCAA title team last season. Jackson is a physical guard who should provide some highlight-reel dunks.

Dejan Kravic (6-11, 230, Jr.): Kravic is a skilled big man who dominated at York College in Canada. He averaged 16 points and 10 rebounds and was second in the country in blocks.

Prospectus says: Tolbert, Crockett, and Nurse at least have some Big 12 experience, and if a couple of the newcomers pan out, the Red Raiders could compete with TCU for the ninth spot in the Big 12. A few of the newcomers are intriguing, so the talent could at least be better than last year. Still, it's a tough situation to inherit for Walker.

WEST VIRGINIA

2012: 19-14 (9-9 Big East); Lost to Gonzaga 77-54, round of 64
In-conference offense: 1.06 points per possession (3rd, Big East)
In-conference defense: 1.03 points allowed per possession (11th, Big East)

What West Virginia did well: *Offensive rebounds.*

Not surprisingly the philosophies of Bob Huggins and Frank Martin are similar. Both want their teams to hit the offensive glass hard.

The Mountaineers got better than 40 percent of their misses back, and that was a good thing because they had a lot of misses. They shot a dreadful 30 percent from beyond the arc and were also bad from the free throw line (67 percent).

Kevin Jones was the team's best offensive rebounder, and he will be missed. Jones was the Mountaineers' most consistent player, and one of the most efficient scorers in the country. He made 59 percent of his twos and rarely turned it over.

What we learned in 2012: *This was Huggins' worst team at West Virginia.*

The Mountaineers were inconsistent, and that's not shocking considering Jones, Darryl Bryant and Deniz Kilicli were joined in WVU's rotation by four freshmen. They could never put together more than two wins in a row in Big East play and had a stretch where they went 2-7.

Huggins managed to get enough from his offense because of Jones and the team's ability to get second shots, but defensively the Mountaineers struggled more than any of Huggins' past teams. Big East opponents shot better than 52 percent inside the arc and the Mountaineers were one of the conference's worst teams at creating turnovers.

Help is on the way in transfer Aaric Murray, who broke La Salle's all-time blocks record in just two seasons. For the Mountaineers to improve in 2013, they'll need to get back to playing Huggins' defense and find a way to knock down some jumpers.

What's in store for 2013: Building a program back up with transfers has become a popular trend (see Iowa State), and Huggins is giving it a try. Along with Murray, the Mountaineers will likely start Dayton transfer point guard Juwan Staten, and Boston College two-time transfer guard Matt Humphrey. Staten was one of the best assist men in the country as a freshman, and Humphrey averaged double figures on a bad BC team. They should provide some much needed help offensively to Kilicli, the skilled Turkish big man. The Mountaineers also return Jabarie Hinds and Gary Browne, two sophomore guards who got a lot of experience as freshmen.

MEET THE MOUNTAINEERS

Deniz Kilicli (6-9, 260, Sr.): When his sweeping hook shot is falling, Kilicli is surprisingly tough to defend. He can finish with both hands and does a good job establishing position in the post.

Juwan Staten (6-1, 190, So.): Staten played on a solid Dayton team as a freshman and was one of the nation's top assist men with a 39.8 rate. He has a nice handle and an understanding of how to put his teammates in a good position to score. His passing should give West Virginia's offense a big lift.

Aaric Murray (6-10, 245, Jr.): Several top programs coveted Murray when he decided to transfer from La Salle, including Kansas. He led the Explorers in scoring as a sophomore and does a good job using his athleticism. Murray also can hit the face-up jumper and even knocked down 20 of 57 threes his sophomore season.

Matt Humphrey (6-5, 200, Sr.): When he was on the court, Humphrey took more shots at Boston College than any other player, but that wasn't necessarily a good thing. He made only 40 percent of his twos and 31 percent of his threes. He's certainly a willing shooter and the Mountaineers need to find someone to knock down threes.

Jabarie Hinds (5-11, 185, So.): A lefty, Hinds showed a nice ability to attack off the dribble as a freshman. He was also West Virginia's best perimeter defender. Hinds has quick hands and led the Mountaineers in steal percentage.

Gary Browne (6-1, 190, So.): The Puerto Rican guard was West Virginia's best player at getting to the free throw line. Like Hinds, he also attacked well off the dribble. He's a good rebounder for his size, and though he was out of control at times his aggressiveness and confidence were impressive for a freshman.

Aaron Brown (6-5, 220, So.): The lefty was the one Mountaineer who shot consistently from the three-point line, making 39 percent of his threes. If he shoots well this season, he could earn more playing time.

Terry Henderson (6-3, 190, Fr.): The three-star freshman guard is another player who could earn playing time if he shoots well. Henderson has a nice high release on his jumper and is a rangy athlete. He scored more than 3,300 points and won four state championships in high school in North Carolina.

Keaton Miles (6-7, 210, So.): Miles started 30 of 32 games last season but strangely played just 31 percent of available minutes. He's a good athlete who Huggins asked to simply play defense and rebound.

Volodymyr Gerun (6-10, 240, So.): The Ukrainian big man played on the U-18 national team and averaged 18 points and 11 rebounds during the European Championships. His post moves are methodical but effective. Gerun can score over either shoulder and like Kilicli, he should improve each season as he gets used to the American game.

Prospectus says: Like Iowa State a year ago, this is a tough team to figure out. The Mountaineers at least have better pieces than last year's squad, but Jones was one of the best players in the country and will be tough to replace. Kilicli was one of the Big East's most improved players last season and combined with Aaric the Mountaineers have one of the better frontlines in the conference. If they shoot the ball better from outside, they could finish near the top of the Big 12. It's tough to see anyone on this roster emerging as a sharpshooter, however, so a finish somewhere in the middle of the pack is more likely.

Big East

BY JOHN GASAWAY

It's common to say there are winners and losers in conference realignment, but among the major conferences it would be more accurate to say there are winners and the Big East. This fall Andy Katz tried to strike the proper tactful note with regard to the conference, and it came out like this: "I agree with new Big East commissioner Mike Aresco that the league's demise is not an issue." There's your Big East slogan for 2013 right there: "Our Demise is Not an Issue."

The slogan's correct. The league still has the venerable basketball likes of Louisville, Connecticut, Georgetown, Marquette, and Villanova, among others. The Big East isn't dying, but it is severely and uniquely diminished.

West Virginia has already left to join the Big 12, of course, but next year is when the chaos really descends. Syracuse and Pittsburgh will move to the ACC, while Memphis, Temple, UCF, SMU, and Houston will join the Big East. The net gain of three new programs in this 2013 swap was supposed to put the league at a numerically tidy 18 teams, but then Notre Dame spoiled that vision in September by announcing that they too will take their hoops to the ACC as soon as they can negotiate a non-punitive exit.

As usual we are discussing the basketball implications of decisions driven largely by football, and obviously Memphis and Temple are great basketball additions. But we're used to seeing "great additions" in the context of a conference that's already retaining its best teams. Syracuse and Pitt are "great additions" for the ACC because that conference gets to hang on to Duke and North Carolina. Memphis and Temple alone, on the other hand, can't make up for the departures of the Mountaineers, the Orange, and the Panthers, all of whom have made the Elite Eight within the past four seasons.

When the dust clears the Big East will have said goodbye to programs that have won 52 NCAA tournament games since 2000. In return the conference is welcoming new members who have won 19 tournament games over the same time period (and you can thank Memphis for 14 of those), thus incurring a net loss of 33 tournament wins. For comparison's sake, the Big 12 recorded a net loss of four tournament wins by losing Missouri, Texas A&M, Colorado, and Nebraska, and picking up West Virginia and TCU. No other major conference has lost any tournament wins.

Meaning in basketball terms realignment has singled out the Big East among the major conferences and hit it with a targeted fury. The league's loss in status is summed up in one word: Temple. Less than

JOHN'S 2013 STANDINGS

	2012 Record	Returning Poss (%)	Returning Min (%)	2013 Prediction
Louisville	10-8	66	60	13-5
Syracuse	17-1	42	48	13-5
Notre Dame	13-5	89	89	12-6
Pitt	5-13	63	66	12-6
Marquette	14-4	59	64	10-8
Cincinnati	12-6	66	70	10-8
Georgetown	12-6	46	55	9-9
Rutgers	6-12	83	85	9-9
Villanova	5-13	58	63	8-10
St. John's	6-12	69	72	8-10
Seton Hall	8-10	52	66	7-11
Connecticut	8-10	48	48	7-11
South Florida	12-6	54	52	7-11
DePaul	3-15	84	77	5-13
Providence	4-14	74	73	5-13

a decade ago the Owls were unceremoniously expelled from the Big East for not being good enough at football. Now the conference has come crawling back. The Big East is still a major conference, it still has great teams, and its demise is not an issue, but its overall quality is not what it used to be. In a relative heartbeat the league's hoops have gone from steak to hamburger.

The aforementioned new commissioner, Mike Aresco, is expected to save the day because he's a former CBS Sports executive, and, after all, TV drives the football dollars, which in turn drive this whole discussion. Aresco may indeed save the day for the Big East as a conference—that is after all his job—but that's something quite separate from returning the league to its former glory in basketball. The conference is currently negotiating a new TV deal while it pursues the likes of BYU, Air Force, and Army as football-only members. Navy is already scheduled to join the league as a football-only member in 2015. In other words the best-case scenario is a football conference with all three service academies and, possibly, BYU. That would ensure the survival of the Big East as a logo, but it won't bring back the good old days in hoops.

Of course what's done is done, and Mick Cronin is exactly right when he says the new watered-down Big East is "good for Cincinnati." Actually, if you want to look at this in purely Cronin-esque utilitarian terms, the new watered-down Big East is good for everyone that's still here, from Louisville right down to DePaul. It's easier, on balance, to win conference games against Memphis, Temple, UCF, Houston, and SMU than it is to win them against West Virginia, Syracuse, Pitt, and Notre Dame.

So much for the Big East's impending qualitative hit. In its more familiar yet suddenly elegiac present, Syracuse and Pitt are still around. The Orange will be less amazing than they were last season, when they won 17 of 18 conference games on their way to a No. 1 seed and a trip to the Elite Eight. Conversely the Panthers will be much less hapless than when you last saw them (5-13), thanks to programmatic regression to the mean and future lottery pick Steven Adams, in that order. On their way out the door, both programs should push Louisville for the conference title.

The Cardinals have the worst offense of any team so highly esteemed in recent years. Why in the world is everyone expecting a team that can't score to win the Big East? Probably because they got to the Final Four last April. I am gingerly placing one foot on this bandwagon myself, and my reasons are as follows. I anticipate another year of superb defense, fewer turnovers, a great leap forward from the already very good Chane Behanan, and, most crucially, a cease-and-desist order from the U.S. District Court for the Western District of Kentucky prohibiting Russ Smith from attempting two-point shots.

Before they join Syracuse and Pitt and head for the exits, Notre Dame and their All-Underrated star Jack Cooley will try to repeat their performance from last year, when just for novelty's sake the Irish played defense and very well too. Marquette has to replace Big East Player of the Year Jae Crowder and his co-conspirator in surprising excellence from a junior college transfer, Darius Johnson-Odom. That's no small task, but Buzz Williams' history suggests the offense in Milwaukee likely won't fall too far.

In 2012 there were three teams that finished 12-6 in the Big East, and don't be surprised if none of those three do as well this season. Cincinnati has the best shot at winning two out of every three again, and Cronin's been busy telling one and all that his backcourt (Sean Kilpatrick, Cashmere Wright, and Jaquon Parker) is the best one he's ever had. He's correct, but it's the rest of the roster that has me wondering if the Bearcats aren't due to drop a win or two compared to last season. As for Georgetown, I love Otto Porter, you love Otto Porter, and, most importantly for Otto Porter, the NBA loves Otto Porter. But the Hoyas will be hard pressed to repeat the level of D they played last year. Take the previous sentence, replace "Hoyas" with "Bulls," and you have South Florida in a nutshell, as well.

On the other hand Rutgers is very likely to be moving in the opposite direction, coming off a 6-12 year and blessed as they are with a flock of returning sophomores who were pretty fair as freshmen. Add Kansas State transfer Wally Judge, and you have a team that stands an excellent chance of beating last year's record with ease.

At nearby Villanova there may have been a few ruffled feathers last year when everyone acted so surprised that Pitt in particular was imploding, even though both of these proud programs (and veterans of a classic 2009 regional final) went 5-13 in 2012. This season's Wildcats will foul less, win more, and think twice about leaving early: Maalik Wayns and Dominic Cheek were both passed over on draft night, though Wayns has since signed as a free agent with the conveniently located Sixers.

Meantime congratulations and best wishes are in order for St. John's head coach Steve Lavin, who says he's beaten the prostate cancer that sidelined him last year. In his short time with the Red Storm, Lavin has already achieved considerable success on the recruiting front. That should start to pay dividends this season, though Moe Harkless did dampen expectations a bit by going one-and-done.

Seton Hall revolved around Herb Pope and Jordan Theodore on offense last season, and both players are gone. The good news is Seton Hall was not very good on offense last season. Thus Kevin Willard has a not entirely unwelcome opportunity to reboot, and in Fuquan Edwin he also has a player with one of the most imbalanced hype (zero) to performance (promising) ratios in the league.

The league's sole coaching change has taken place in the one spot outside Syracuse, New York, where coaching changes never take place, in Storrs, Connecticut. In September Jim Calhoun called it a career after 866 wins and three national championships. Nominal head coach Kevin Ollie has a contract that's shorter than most apartment leases, extending only through April 4, 2013. No pressure, Coach. You'll be auditioning for the full-time gig with a solid backcourt (Shabazz Napier, Ryan Boatright, and freshman Omar Calhoun), but a repeat of last year's 8-10 finish, or something close to it, seems likely.

Both Providence and DePaul have relatively new coaches who are still putting their stamps on their programs. Both coaches have chosen to mark their arrivals indelibly through that most traditional of stylistic media, the emphatic change in pace. (The Friars have slowed down dramatically; the Blue Demons have sped up appreciably). Most of all, both teams desperately need some defense, at any speed, before they can reasonably anticipate a modicum of success.

CINCINNATI

2012: 26-11 (12-6 Big East); Lost to Ohio State 81-66, Sweet 16
In-conference offense: 1.04 points per possession (4th)
In-conference defense: 0.99 points allowed per possession (8th)

What Cincinnati did well: *Repetition.*

You never would have known there was a brawl with Xavier. For a second consecutive season, Mick Cronin deployed the same basic nucleus of players (Sean Kilpatrick, Dion Dixon, Yancy Gates, and Cashmere Wright), outscored the Big East by 0.05 points per possession, and secured a No. 6 seed in the NCAA tournament. This time around his Bearcats even managed to make the Sweet 16, beating Texas and Florida State by six points apiece before falling to Ohio State.

This kind of year-to-year consistency seemed most unlikely last December. The Bearcats had just lost to Xavier by 23, and Gates was suspended for six games in the wake of the fracas that erupted in the game's closing seconds. Little did anyone guess that both teams would end up making the Sweet 16.

The repercussions of the brawl are still being felt. Starting this season the Crosstown Shootout will be rechristened as the less belligerently titled Crosstown Classic, and will move to neutral territory, specifically US Bank Arena in downtown Cincinnati.

What we learned in 2012: *Shooting is way overrated.*

This was, easily, the best offense we've ever seen from Cronin-era Cincinnati (indeed it's the only Cronin-era Bearcat offense that has outperformed the Big East average in conference play), and they owed it all to their ability to hang onto the rock.

In Big East play last year the Bearcats averaged just 1.22 points per turnover-less or "effective" possession, a pitiful mark that represented a big drop from the previous year and in fact ranked No. 15 in what was then a 16-team league. (Take that, Rutgers!) But the fact that Cincinnati gave the ball away on just 14 percent of their in-conference possessions meant that this was actually the Big East's fourth most effective offense. Cronin's men simply got more bites at the apple.

What's in store for 2013:

Gates and Dixon have departed, and little-used freshman Octavius Ellis was kicked off the team in May. Over the summer Cincinnati lost out on freshman-to-be Chris Obekpa, who spurned the Bearcats' advances and signed instead with St. John's.

MEET THE BEARCATS

Sean Kilpatrick (6-4, 215, Jr.): Kilpatrick is widely expected to have a "breakout" junior year, especially now that he'll be found at his more "natural" shooting guard position. But he's charted a rather curious sequence in his first two seasons, and if you're trying to project future performance a curious sequence is sufficient cause for caution. As a freshman Kilpatrick actually played a much larger role in his team's offense than he did as a sophomore, but his shooting percentages from both sides of the arc in both seasons stayed right where they were—very good but not mind-blowing. That's noteworthy, because ordinarily an added year of maturity plus a smaller workload would lead us to anticipate a bump in efficiency. Granted, Kilpatrick's minutes did go way up in his second season, so the net impact of his solid performance was greater. And, anyway, breakout junior seasons do happen. (It should be called the Kenny Boynton Effect.) Add it all up and here's a prediction: Kilpatrick earns first-team All-Big East honors as a junior (he was second-team as a sophomore), hitting half his twos and 38 percent of his threes.

Cashmere Wright (6-0, 175, Sr.): Wright has become a dependable point guard. True, he presents little scoring threat inside the arc, and it's not entirely clear to me why a Big East point guard who's listed at 6-0 and doesn't draw fouls is attempting nearly 200 twos a year (with predictably meager results). But Wright's improved both his three-point accuracy and his turnover rate in each season he's played. He also ended the year on a high note, hitting 4-of-6 threes and scoring 18 points in the Bearcats' 15-point loss to Ohio State in the Sweet 16.

Jaquon Parker (6-3, 210, Sr.): Cronin says the Kilpatrick-Wright-Parker trio comprises the best backcourt he's ever had. I'll buy that. Parker saw serious minutes for the first time as a junior. He proved to be a capable three-point threat, as well as a surprisingly effective defensive rebounder.

Justin Jackson (6-8, 210, Jr.): Jackson started 20 games as a sophomore and distinguished himself as a shot blocker. A very foul-prone shot blocker. When he's uninhibited by foul trouble, however, Jackson can be formidable. In the Bearcats' loss to Louisville in the Big East tournament title game, he blocked six shots in 28 minutes.

Ge'Lawn Guyn (6-1, 175, So.): You're probably thinking you've never heard of Guyn, but I know you've seen him countless times on replay. It was Guyn that Xavier's Tu Holloway pushed to the floor, thus triggering the brawl between the two teams last December.

Jeremiah Davis III (6-3, 205, So.): Between roughly mid-December and Valentine's Day, Davis was given a steady diet of about 12 minutes a game. He made 12-of-31 threes while showing a starter's willingness to shoot, but his playing time dropped off sharply late in the season.

Jermaine Sanders (6-5, 225, So.): Sanders failed to crack the rotation last year after arriving as a four-star wing from New York City. Cronin did give him a long look when the schedule offered up a series of post-Xavier December cupcakes, but the freshman logged just 18 total minutes in three NCAA tournament games.

Cheikh Mbodj (6-10, 245, Sr.): Like his more celebrated teammate Gates, Mbodj was also suspended for six games following the Xavier altercation. When he returned to action he never played more than 16 minutes in a game. For those willing to throw small-sample-size caution to the winds, the numbers suggest Mbodj might have potential as an offensive rebounder and as a shot blocker—and that he should never be allowed to glimpse the ball on offense.

David Nyarsuk (7-1, 230, Jr.): Cronin added Nyarsuk to the roster in August. The native of Sudan originally committed to West Virginia in 2009 but ended up playing two seasons for NAIA member Mountain State in Beckley, West Virginia. Cronin says Nyarsuk will be the "rim protector behind our pressure defense," and a quick check reveals the big guy's block rate (10.7 percent) last year against NAIA competition was a little better than what Jackson recorded (8.3) against Big East and other Division I types for the Bearcats. Nyarsuk also averaged nearly five fouls per 40 minutes.

Titus Rubles (6-7, 220, Jr.): At Blinn College in Brenham, Texas, Rubles averaged 15 points and 10 boards per game. He's about to don his fourth uniform in as many seasons: God's Academy (Grand Prairie, Texas), Independence CC (Independence, Kansas), Blinn, and now Cincy.

Prospectus says: Cincinnati will turn the ball over more often in 2013. Gravity says so. Past that the outlook is murkier. I have no problem with a team that gets almost all of its points from its guards—Missouri fared pretty well last year against teams other than Norfolk State—but I do at least pause when confronted with an entire roster that has, at best, 3.5 known quantities. We know in advance that two of the players on the court for Cincinnati at any given time are going to be very green on offense. Kilpatrick, Wright, and Parker are legit, but there are an awful lot of minutes that will go to teammates less proven than Kilpatrick, Wright, and Parker. And note as well that something as mundane as one injury or as common as threes not falling would hit Cincinnati with unusual force. Cronin's done a nice job bringing the program to this point. If he sustains the Bearcats' customary level of success (again, outscoring the league by about 0.05 points per trip and getting a No. 6 seed or thereabouts) for a third consecutive year, I for one will be impressed.

CONNECTICUT

2012: 20-14 (8-10 Big East); Lost to Iowa State 77-64, NCAA round of 64
In-conference offense: 1.02 points per possession (7th)
In-conference defense: 1.02 points allowed per possession (9th)

What Connecticut did well: *Blend in with the tumult in Storrs.*

Last year played out amidst what many called uncertainty at Connecticut. Actually what the Huskies faced was perhaps the most debilitating certainty of all, the knowledge that Jim Calhoun would, at some point in the not too distant future, step down.

And that was just off the court. In terms of such mundane qualities as actual basketball performance, UConn was no less puzzling last year. Andre Drummond's decision in August of 2011 to forego a final year of prep school and instead play at UConn was supposed to have what Sports Illustrated said would be a "massive" impact and to lift the Huskies into the top five nationally. It did not. Jeremy Lamb was supposed to follow up on his amazing 2011 NCAA tournament with what John Gasaway said would be a suitably dazzling sophomore season. He did not. (In fairness to Lamb, he had a season that would be exemplary for any run-of-the-mill major-conference shooting guard. But expectations for Lamb were even higher than "exemplary," and his three-point accuracy dipped from 37 percent to 34.)

Connecticut presented a perceptual dead-end in 2011-12. They were thoroughly mediocre all season long, but it was difficult to sustain an objection on that front because of course the previous year's team had been similarly unimpressive until flipping a switch in March of 2011 and gliding to a national championship. Maybe, it was thought last year, this team would do the same.

They did not. Aside from a Tuesday win over DePaul to tip off a second consecutive Big East tournament, nothing in last year's script stayed the same. It was an entirely new story in Storrs. Or was it?

What we learned in 2012: *If anything March and April of 2011 appear even more amazing in retrospect.*

If I'd grabbed you in the summer of 2009 and locked you in a room with no TV and no Internet where all you knew about any Big East team was their performance during the conference season, you would think that Connecticut is currently mired in a three-year slump. And, in a way, you'd be correct. The Huskies are 24-30 in Big East play over the past three seasons. Since Hasheem Thabeet, A.J. Price, and Jeff Adrien left campus on the heels of a run to the 2009 Final Four, UConn has outscored Big East opponents by a total of just 14 points over the course of 54 games.

Obviously the Huskies have been handed some bad bounces to find themselves six games under .500 while outscoring their opponents (albeit by a razor-thin margin). But the larger point pertains to the contrast between this three-year run and what came before. That 2009 team was beastly. UConn that year scored 1.10 points per trip in Big East play and allowed just 0.95. The following year the offense and the defense both took big steps back, and they've both been locked in at "mediocre" ever since. Except, of course, for the duration of the 2011 Big East and NCAA tournaments.

What's in store for 2013: Calhoun announced on September 13 that he was stepping down. UConn named assistant Kevin Ollie as the new head coach, but gave him a contract that runs only to April 4, 2013, in effect making 2012-13 a season-long audition for Ollie. Meanwhile the NCAA has prohibited Connecticut from postseason play in 2013 due to the men's basketball team's substandard Academic Progress Rate (APR) scores between 2007 and 2011. Lamb and Drummond were lottery picks in June. And Alex Oriakhi, Roscoe Smith, and Michael Bradley all transferred. So the combination of a postseason ban along with a high number of player departures made UConn a very interesting case study in recruiting this offseason. Prospects committing (or sticking to their commitments) to the Huskies in the summer of 2012 knew they would not be playing in the 2013 NCAA tournament—and that was pretty much the only certainty they had. They couldn't know if there would be more player departures before the season. They couldn't know if Calhoun would stay around to coach them in 2012-13. They couldn't even know what conference they'd be playing in if they were still in Storrs for their sophomore or junior years. Yet somehow UConn cobbled together a decent class. I guess available playing time and three national championships will do that.

MEET THE HUSKIES

Shabazz Napier (6-0, 170, Jr.): As a sophomore Napier made significant strides as a scoring point guard, but on Calhoun's way out the door the ex-coach declared an intention to have his junior star play "off the ball" in 2012-13. It appears new head coach Ollie shares that vision. Napier will have every opportunity to assume a larger role in the offense, assuming he's healthy. In early September he underwent surgery to repair a stress fracture in his right foot.

Ryan Boatright (6-0, 160, So.): Last year Boatright was, in effect, a co-point-guard alongside Napier, and this season UConn's apparent plan is to hand that task over to the sophomore more or less exclusively. Boatright clearly has the chops to be The Man at the point. Any freshman that can maintain a respectably low turnover rate while (co-) running a Big East offense and looking for his own shot is on an All-Conference trajectory.

Omar Calhoun (6-3, 185, Fr.): A top-50 shooting guard from Brooklyn, Calhoun committed to Connecticut in 2011 and then averaged 26 points and eight rebounds as a high school senior.

Tyler Olander (6-9, 225, Jr.): Olander scored the first basket in the 2011 national championship game. That likely supplies his Facebook page with a really cool GIF, but otherwise he's something of an enigma. Calhoun gave Olander nine starts and 600 minutes last season, and the young man responded by displaying a marked aversion to quantifiable basketball actions such as shots, rebounds, and blocks. His playing time waned as the season progressed.

DeAndre Daniels (6-8, 195, So.): Though he was given 12 starts, Daniels averaged just 12 minutes a game as a freshman. He was the only player in the UConn rotation to attempt more threes than twos. Daniels didn't make many of those threes (24 percent), but 20-of-25 shooting at the line suggests that could change.

Niels Giffey (6-7, 210, Jr.): Calhoun gave Giffey a serious look in January, when the Berlin native averaged 32 minutes per outing against Notre Dame, Cincinnati, and Tennessee. As it happens the Huskies went 0-3 over that stretch. Maybe Calhoun blamed his sophomore wing; Giffey averaged just eight minutes a game the rest of the season.

Enosch Wolf (7-1, 245, Jr.): The combined actions of the NCAA (that whole postseason ban thing) and the NBA (and their annual ritual of taking college players they like) have been such that Wolf may at last get a glimpse of the floor. "He understands the game," associate head coach Glen Miller has said. "But he has to get in better condition to be able to play effectively at this level."

R.J. Evans (6-3, 200, Sr.): Evans is a transfer from Holy Cross who has one season of eligibility remaining. "The coaches told me that what I bring to the table is what they need," Evans said. "Intangibles, toughness, leadership."

Phillip Nolan (6-10, 200, Fr.): Nolan stands out as a forthright hunter of minutes. He committed to UConn after the NCAA imposed its postseason ban, when Calhoun specifically pointed out to him that a depleted frontcourt could offer a lanky three-star prospect an unusually good shot at regular playing time.

Prospectus says: Connecticut won't be as talented this season under Kevin Ollie as they've been the past couple years, but then again each of the past two UConn teams underperformed during the regular season.

DEPAUL

2012: 12-19 (3-15 Big East); Lost to Connecticut 81-67, Big East first round
In-conference offense: 1.00 point per possession (11th)
In-conference defense: 1.12 points allowed per possession (15th)

What DePaul did well: *Improve.*

In year two of the Oliver Purnell era, DePaul performed better on both sides of the ball. In fact last year marked the first time since 2007 that the Blue Demons were not ranked No. 16 in the Big East in either offense or defense in conference play. By the slimmest of margins this defense was better than what Providence put on the floor in league play in 2012.

What we learned in 2012: *Improvement is relative.*

Even though their defense was better than it was in 2011, it's still very hard to be as bad as DePaul was on D last year. Keep in mind those 2011 Blue Demons from two seasons ago comprised arguably the single worst major-conference defensive team I've ever tracked. You can think of Purnell's defense this way: DePaul has improved over the past two years from the first percentile to the fourth. That's a step in the right direction, of course, but it's also true that roughly 96 percent of major-conference defenses have still been better than what you saw from the Blue Demons last season.

In the past six years there have been 16 major-conference defenses that, relative to their league averages, were as bad or worse than DePaul's last season. Two of those defenses occurred last year: DePaul, of course, and Providence. Of the 14 defenses that preceded last year's Blue Demons in chronology and matched or exceeded them in futility, every one of them improved the following year. That's the good news. The bad news is that, with the single exception of the miracle 2009 Auburn Tigers, not one of those defenses improved to the level of "average" within their conference the following season.

Purnell's biggest issue by far is his defense. History suggests in 2013 his D will improve but will still be significantly below average.

What's in store for 2013: In November DePaul will play in the Cancun Challenge, renowned to early-season viewers as the basketball tournament that, for reasons never explained to my entire satisfaction, takes place in a resort ballroom. Don't be too surprised if the Blue Demons waltz off (har!) with that title. Purnell returns six of his top seven scorers, and, more importantly, the Challenge's eight-team field isn't exactly going to make anyone forget the 2008 Final Four. DePaul won't rate out as the favorites, but in a bracket where that heavy burden falls on Iowa the Demons could shock the world.

MEET THE BLUE DEMONS

Cleveland Melvin (6-8, 210, Jr.): DePaul as a program likes to give its nominal star player a strikingly generous helping of shot attempts. It's a proclivity that predates Purnell's arrival on the North Side, and the current beneficiary of that tendency is Melvin. Last year the only Big East player that took a higher percentage of his team's shots than Melvin while on the floor was Louisville's Russ Smith. Melvin takes good care of the ball, but for a featured scorer listed at 6-8 to make just 48 percent of his twos is unusual. Also note that last year Purnell allowed his star to start jacking up an occasional three, to the tune of about one attempt per half. Melvin didn't make them (he shot 23 percent), and he's not likely to start making them anytime soon (he shot 64 percent at the line as a sophomore). On defense last year he improved his previously questionable rebounding to the point where it was average.

Brandon Young (6-3, 190, Jr.): Young's threes didn't fall last year, goodness knows, but that may have been a blip from a career 74 percent free throw shooter. He gets to the line, holds on to the rock, and while averaging 31 minutes a game for a 3-15 Big

East team he came shockingly close to making half his twos. In an overtime loss to Louisville at Allstate Arena last February, Young scored 27 points on 13 shots. For a scoring point guard who arrived in the Big East as a three-star recruit, it was an impressive sophomore year.

Jamee Crockett (6-4, 200, So.): Considering he doesn't record very many rebounds, steals, or blocks, Crockett is rather inexplicably foul-prone. If the sophomore can get that aspect of his game squared away, however, he can help this team. Among DePaul players that looked for their own shots last year (a group that also included Melvin, Young, and Moses Morgan), Crockett was the only one that was accurate from both sides of the arc.

Moses Morgan (6-6, 220, Jr.): As a sophomore Morgan averaged 20 minutes a game, mostly off the bench. He had a very nice season shooting threes (39 percent) and a disastrous season shooting twos (33 percent).

Worrel Clahar (5-11, 180, Sr.): Clahar may want to rethink his role. In theory he's a pass-first point guard, but in truth he coughed up the ball too frequently to carry off that persona convincingly (five times in 13 minutes against West Virginia; seven times in 27 minutes against St. John's). Conversely on the rare occasions when Clahar actually shot the ball, it went in.

Charles McKinney (6-3, 180, So.): Purnell gave McKinney 15 starts as a freshman. At first blush the young man has what would appear to be a high per-possession turnover rate, but that's mostly attributable to the fact that McKinney didn't get into the box score with any other quantifiable actions.

Donnavan Kirk (6-9, 220, Jr.): Kirk's minutes increased as the year progressed, no thanks to his playmaking ability. In 415 minutes he recorded five assists.

Durrell McDonald (6-2, 165, Fr.): A combo guard from Henderson, Nevada, McDonald's nickname is "Nugget," because his father once remarked that his son's head looks like a chicken McNugget. McDonald has this to say about his new team: "Their style of play is fast-paced." He's right!

Prospectus says: Purnell upped DePaul's tempo dramatically last year, but, even though the team did improve their performance on both sides of the ball, two troublesome issues remained stubbornly in place even at the new faster pace. First, conference opponents attempt many more free throws than do the Blue Demons. And, second, those same opponents absolutely love to attack Purnell's somewhat diminutive team in the paint. I can envision DePaul achieving something close to respectability on offense in 2013, but until those two issues are addressed the team will stay well under .500 in the Big East.

GEORGETOWN

2012: 24-9 (12-6 Big East); Lost to NC State 66-63, NCAA round of 32
In-conference offense: 1.02 points per possession (8th)
In-conference defense: 0.95 points allowed per possession (2nd)

What Georgetown did well: *Defend.*

Last year Louisville attracted a lot of attention for playing very good defense, and justifiably so. Then again Georgetown's D was just as good in Big East play, but somehow the word didn't get out. Maybe it was the visual contrast provided by an excellent Cardinal D and a sub-par Cardinal offense that did the perceptual trick.

In any event, John Thompson III's team made life very difficult for opposing offenses in 2012. In particular this was easily the Big East's best defensive rebounding team in conference play. The Hoyas pulled down 71 percent of their league opponents' missed shots, or about 11 percentage points better than what storied rival Syracuse was mustering at the same time.

Georgetown's overall performance on defense represented a sizeable improvement over 2011, and indeed comprised the Hoyas' best showing on that side of the ball in conference play since the days of Roy Hibbert. It was an underreported surprise.

What we learned in 2012: *Issues in need of improvement can be tough to spot, but very real.*

As seen above, this was merely the league's No. 8 offense in 2012, and what's odd there is that Georgetown looked very good in many categories that are ordinarily the precursors of superior offense. Most notably, this was the Big East's third-most accurate team in terms of shooting from the field. The Hoyas were also above average on the offensive glass, and no team in the league was better at getting to the line. So why was this a middle-of-the-pack offense?

One reason, of course, was turnovers. Georgetown gave the ball away on 21 percent of their possessions in conference play. And while the Hoyas excelled at getting to the line, they were largely ineffective once they got there, hitting less than 68 percent of their free throws in Big East action (good for No. 14 in the league). Just a few more shots from the field and a few more makes from the line could have made a noticeable difference for a team that already played D and shot the ball with a fair degree of accuracy.

What's in store for 2013: Georgetown featured three players on offense last year—Jason Clark, Hollis Thompson, and Henry Sims—and all three are gone. In the offseason the Hoyas narrowly missed out on Nerlens Noel (Kentucky) and Devonta Pollard (Alabama). The situation now confronting Thompson reminds me a little of what Jamie Dixon faced at Pitt the year after DeJuan Blair, Sam Young, and Levance Fields left.

MEET THE HOYAS

Otto Porter (6-8, 205, So.): If you were looking for a Roy Hobbs figure in D-I last year, Porter was your man. In high school he stayed away from the AAU circuit, opting instead to hide his light under a bushel in Sikeston, Missouri (pop. 16,000). A player of his size and obvious talent was duly christened top-100 anyway, but no one really knew what to expect. Well, you know the rest: Porter was a mainstay for an upper-tier Big East team, averaging 30 minutes a game and sinking 61 percent of his twos. Seeing a freshman do that was enough for the NBA scouts, and the young Hoya's now projected to be an early pick in the 2013 draft. Too much too soon for a wing who shot 23 percent on his infrequent threes? That's what sophomore years are for. Is Porter really another Doug McDermott (a 6-8-ish guy who's insanely accurate from everywhere), or merely another Ricardo Ratliffe (a 6-8-ish guy who's insanely accurate from the paint)? The answer to that question matters most to the NBA, somewhat less to Georgetown (either would be awesome, but a McDermott clone would be extra awesome thank you), and least of all to Porter, who'll very likely have the opportunity to go in the 2013 lottery regardless. For his part Thompson wants you to know this: "I can say with confidence that [Porter] will be not just one of the better players in our league, but in the country." When coaches talk like that about their underclassmen, my experience has been that, with the obvious exception of Fab Melo's freshman year, the player very often delivers.

Markel Starks (6-2, 175, Jr.): He'll customarily be the smallest guy on the floor, so Starks will usually be labeled the point guard by outside observers in a hurry. Certainly he'll do his share of ball-handling, but keep in mind the highest assist rate on last year's team (by far) belonged to the 6-10 Sims. For his part Starks functioned like a wing (albeit in a supporting role), one who was equally likely to shoot a two or a three. Like many a Hoya guard over the years, he rang up a two-point percentage (56) that others his height would kill to possess. Also note that for about 13 days in mid- to late-December Starks was hypnotized into thinking he was Damian Lillard, scoring 52 points on just 28 shots in games against American, Memphis, and Louisville.

Greg Whittington (6-8, 210, So.): Whittington's contributions were modest last year as a freshman, but he showed those proverbial flashes that people like to talk about, so he'll have every chance to show he can do more. Though he averaged just 20 minutes a game, those minutes increased as the year progressed. Whittington shot about as many twos as threes, and came close to doing as well on the latter (37 percent) as he did on the former (43).

Nate Lubick (6-8, 235, Jr.): Lubick's an excellent passer who's also a capable rebounder at both ends of the floor, though an unusual proportion of his statistical heft here was furnished by one 14-board effort in just 26 minutes against IUPUI in November. In 608 minutes he attempted just 88 shots.

Jabril Trawick (6-5, 210, So.): Can we draw inferences from a freshman season where Trawick averaged just 11 minutes a game? Why not. Drawing five fouls per 40 minutes and shooting 78 percent at the line suggests good things to come (though Trawick did commit about as many fouls as he drew).

Mikael Hopkins (6-9, 225, So.): Hopkins arrived in DC last year with about as much recruiting hype as Porter, but he couldn't earn consistent minutes and scored just 37 points in 20 games after New Year's. As is often the case with a freshman big man in limited minutes, Hopkins recorded both offensive rebounds and fouls in abundance.

D'Vauntes Smith-Rivera (6-3, 215, Fr.): A shooting guard from Indianapolis by way of Oak Hill Academy, Smith-Rivera turned down an impressive list of suitors (including Michigan State, Louisville, Florida, and Memphis) in order to say yes to the Hoyas. Maybe those coaches were thinking back to Eric Gordon, another 2-guard from North Central High School in Indy.

Stephen Domingo (6-6, 205, Fr.): After reclassifying from the class of 2013, Domingo has arrived in DC a year ahead of schedule. The wing from San Francisco is being talked up for his outside shooting. If the talk is correct, there are definitely minutes available now that Hollis Thompson and Jason Clark are gone.

Brandon Bolden (6-10, 205, Fr.): Bolden is pegged as a project big man, and the recent history of Hoya freshmen not named "Otto Porter" suggests he, and perhaps **Bradley Hayes (7-0, 250, Fr.)**, will get to observe a lot of basketball in addition to playing some.

Prospectus says: A lot is riding not only on Porter but indeed on the entire sophomore class. Last year these guys could afford to fade into the background as Sims, Thompson, and Clark carried the load. (Even Porter had a shot percentage below 19.) This year a large number of possessions and shots will fall to the sophomores by default. Assuming Porter walks the walk now that Coach Thompson has talked the talk, this projects to be a solid upper-tier Big East team yet again, one with a lot of size and even more youth.

LOUISVILLE

2012: 30-10 (10-8 Big East); Lost to Kentucky 69-61, Final Four
In-conference offense: 0.99 points per possession (12th)
In-conference defense: 0.95 points allowed per possession (4th)

What Louisville did well: *Peak at the right times for maximum perceptual impact.*

To the casual fan it must have seemed like Louisville was always embarked on winning streaks last year. The Cardinals overcame injuries to Mike Marra, Rakeem Buckles, and Wayne Blackshear (among others) and finished 30-10, but it was an oddly sequenced 30-10. Rick Pitino's team started the season 12-0 and rose to No. 4 in the nation in both major polls. They ended the year in the Final Four, of course, riding an 8-0 run that included a Big East tournament title.

By now you've done the math and figured out that in their other 20 games the Cards went 10-10. True, but put an asterisk by that record. Two of those 10 losses came to Kentucky, and if you're blaming a team for losing to that UK group you are one tough grader. Let's think of that stretch instead as the functional equivalent of 10-8—in other words, the games the Cards played during the Big East regular season.

Which was the "real" Louisville team? That 12-0 and later 8-0 bunch, or the 10-8 version? I'd say the former, with all the great defense and worrisome offense that that entails.

What we learned in 2012: *It's possible to win in March with defense.*

Louisville's 8-0 run came at the end (leading up to the loss to Kentucky in New Orleans), so it's reasonable to assume it's the best and specifically most current information we have on this team.

Playing 517 possessions on neutral floors against Seton Hall, Marquette, Notre Dame, Cincinnati, Davidson, New Mexico, Michigan State, and Florida, the Cardinals scored right at one point per possession. So even during their remarkable postseason run the offense struggled. Despite the fact that they brought what had previously been a high turnover rate down in March, the Cards were just 140-for-315 from inside the arc.

They won eight times anyway, because their defense was incredible, even better than it had been during the Big East regular season. Don't be surprised if this defensive improvement carries over to 2012-13. This D should be excellent.

What's in store for 2013: Pitino says he's not concerned about his team's perimeter shooting this season. Well, I am. Kyle Kuric and Chris Smith have wrapped up their eligibility, and together the two seniors hit 36 percent of their 399 attempted threes last season. The rest of the roster shot 27 percent on 334 attempts. Then in September senior guard Mike Marra re-tore the same ACL that sidelined him for all but two games last season. At the moment he is said to be done for the year.

MEET THE CARDINALS

Peyton Siva (6-0, 185, Sr.): Assuming Pitino's right not to be worried about perimeter shooting, here's one theory: I wouldn't be shocked if Siva, seemingly out of nowhere, became a somewhat dependable three-point threat as a senior, meaning one who picks his spots and shoots a normal percentage on a relatively low number of attempts. Now, at first glance that may seem like a really dumb theory. He's made just 26 percent of his threes over the past two seasons. Still, Siva's accuracy at the line has quietly shot up by 13 percentage points (to 74 percent) since he was a freshman. Otherwise I expect we'll see more of what we've come to expect from Siva. He'll spray assists all over the place, play outstanding Pitino-style defense, commit a few too many turnovers, and be incredibly fun to watch yet statistically just average when he tries to finish in the paint.

Gorgui Dieng (6-11, 245, Jr.): Dieng provides reliable excellence in shot blocking (Draymond Green still sees Dieng in his nightmares), and he's also a very good offensive rebounder. Anything else will be gravy. His two-point accuracy dropped off sharply last season, as he navigated the transition from being a seldom-glimpsed reserve his freshman year to very nearly leading an injury-blighted club in minutes in as a sophomore. (Kuric ended up wresting that title away by 57 minutes.) On paper Dieng's still drawing four fouls per 40 minutes, but, encouragingly for Cards fans, that dropped to three whistles per 40 in the NCAA tournament. Indeed, after the Davidson game fouls were never an issue for the big guy.

Russ Smith (6-0, 165, Jr.): In theory Smith's a reserve (he made seven starts) who averaged just 22 minutes a game as a sophomore. That's a remarkable number for minutes, when you consider last season Smith recorded five or more steals in a game no fewer than five times. Clearly Smith makes Louisville's outstanding defense even better, but, oh, how Pitino pays for that on offense. In this book in leagues like the SWAC or MEAC you'll occasionally run across a featured scorer who carries a huge load of possessions during his minutes and misses an astonishingly high proportion of his shots. But in major-conference basketball we're simply not used to seeing what Russ Smith does on offense. To make just 38 percent of your twos and still attempt 285 of the things (he led the team) in just 837 total minutes is surely carrying perseverance too far. Two silver linings: Smith drained 7-of-11 threes in the NCAA tournament, and he's a combo guard with a nice assist rate. Assuming his finishing skills in the paint stay where they are, however, he must call his teammates' numbers more often than he's been doing.

Chane Behanan (6-6, 250, So.): Behanan had the kind of freshman year that, rightly, has everyone keyed up to see what he can do as a sophomore. (How keyed up? His head coach has compared him to Charles Barkley.) His season totals range from good (eerily similar rebounding on both ends of the floor to Dieng) to great (significantly more efficient in the paint than Dieng despite giving away five inches in height). Then again forget season totals. Behanan looked fantastic in spots in the NCAA tournament. Tom Izzo specifically named Behanan to me as someone who had "killed" his team in the Sweet 16. The only question is whether he should just give up on threes, and, if so, how soon he can do so. A 59 percent shooter at the line, Behanan hit just 17 percent of his 36 attempts from beyond the arc.

Wayne Blackshear (6-5, 230, So.): Shoulder surgery kept Blackshear out of action until February, but Pitino was clearly interested in discovering what his freshman could bring to the table. The coach gave Blackshear 20 minutes in his first college game, a 77-74 win at West Virginia. And while I don't want to read too much into what was a microscopically small sample size (Blackshear logged just 105 minutes total), surely it's significant that Pitino was fine with the freshman attempting a whopping 28 percent of his team's shots during his brief minutes. Blackshear's a popular candidate for "breakout star" status, a nice way of saying he's talented, strong, and his fortunes this year could go either way.

Luke Hancock (6-6, 200, Jr.): This fall Pitino wrote on his blog that he hopes George Mason transfer Hancock can help the Cardinals improve their passing. Hancock is indeed an outstanding passer, even if he's trapped in the body of a wing. The last time we saw him he was a very good point guard (GMU obeyed height stereotypes and listed him as a forward) and an even better scorer for a Patriot team that spent 2010-11 being insanely underrated, only to show up on the wrong end of a 98-66 evisceration by Ohio State in the round of 32. Hancock could be an important addition in precisely the areas where Louisville needs the most help.

Prospectus says: I'm picking Louisville to win the Big East, but I harbor no illusions about this offense. Lots of observers believe this team has Final Four potential, for the eminently rational reason that the Cardinals—hobbled by injuries and questionable on offense—made the Final Four last season. So let's look at that. If you take the 16 teams that have made the last four Final Fours and rank all of those offenses and defenses from 1 to 32, you'll find that the 2012 Louisville offense ranks No. 32. By a large margin. Or if last season you pointed out that Indiana's defense, for example, wasn't all that good, you were of course correct. And that shabby and so very worrisome Hoosier D was significantly better than the Louisville offense. It's been a long time since so much was expected of a team that the last time we saw them was this bad at half the sport. So when I say I'm picking the Cardinals to win the Big East anyway, I'm doing so with my eyes open and for three reasons: I anticipate they'll cut down on turnovers; I expect the defense to be amazing again; and I will be surprised if any Big East team, including this one, can compare to last year's 17-1 Syracuse outfit.

MARQUETTE

2012: 27-8 (14-4 Big East); Lost to Florida 68-58, Sweet 16
In-conference offense: 1.07 points per possession (2nd)
In-conference defense: 0.98 points allowed per possession (6th)

What Marquette did well: *Improve dramatically on defense.*

There was a 17-1 predator called Syracuse roaming the Big East savannah last year and garnering all the available attention. That's too bad, because what Marquette was simultaneously doing to reach 14-4 was in its own way just as remarkable.

The Golden Eagles were outstanding on offense, but that wasn't the remarkable part. Buzz Williams' teams are usually outstanding on offense, and last year was no exception. Meanwhile on defense what in 2011 had been a somewhat permissive group that had allowed Big East opponents to score 1.06 points per trip was transforming itself into a much faster-paced Pitino-like menace that limited conference foes to a mere 0.98 points per possession.

There's simply no precedent for a team this small (often as not the tallest player on the floor was 6-7) and led by two junior college transfers playing defense this good in a major conference. The catalytic change on defense was a significant uptick in opponent turnovers, one achieved without (and this is the important part) any corresponding increase in opponents' trips to the line. Big East opponents coughed the ball up on 23 percent of their possessions against Marquette. Williams got to have his defensive cake and eat it too.

Helping that uptick along was a decided acceleration in tempo, all the way up to 69 possessions per 40 minutes in conference play. They weren't the fastest-paced team in the Big East, or even close to it, because last year DePaul was conducting their season-long "Why not?" experiment in extreme running. Call Marquette the fastest-paced normal team.

Every coach says they're going to play an exciting up-tempo brand of basketball and pressure opponents into turnovers. What an odd spectacle to find one coach actually doing it.

What we learned in 2012: *No one should ever disparage junior college transfers again.*

The challenge presented by Jae Crowder and Darius Johnson-Odom was never analytic—their numbers were self-evidently terrific—but said challenge was all the more real for being purely tonal. Basically Crowder and DJO presented us with a huge surprise, but the surprise arrived slowly and cumulatively, and there was never an appropriate moment to say, in effect, "No, seriously, this is incredible." By the time Crowder won 2012 Big East Player of the Year, deservedly, it seemed like he was just another star player, up there on the same bleachers with Dion Waiters and Kevin Jones.

So this is late, but I'll say it anyway: No, seriously, this was incredible. In this day and age it's simply not possible for Big East Player of the Year-level stars to come from the junior-college ranks, right? Today's remorseless talent-spotting industry is supposed to sort out tomorrow's stars in plenty of time to steer these precious vessels of potential toward the basketball "academies" whose very raison d'etre is to get their kids credentialed for the freshman year at the Division I level.

Ricardo Ratliffe was pretty fair for Missouri, surely, and big things are expected of Pierre Jackson at Baylor this season, but in Crowder and DJO, Williams may have had the two best junior college players of recent years on his team at the same time. It was quite a sight while it lasted.

What's in store for 2013: Not only did Crowder and DJO soak up an astonishing share of the possessions and shots on offense, they were the only players on the floor for Williams more than 80 percent of the time. If you want to think of the rest of the Marquette roster as one big collective George and Ringo to those guys' Lennon and McCartney, you're actually not far off.

MEET THE GOLDEN EAGLES

Vander Blue (6-4, 200, Jr.): Todd Mayo has said Blue improved by leaps and bounds over the summer. Blue had room to do so. Nominally a scoring guard, Blue is yet to present any threat from the perimeter, and last year he made a so-so 44 percent of his twos. If there's anything in his performance to date that would lend credence to Mayo's bullishness, it's that Blue did draw a fair number of fouls even while playing in the shadow of Crowder and DJO. You will remember that Blue arrived highly touted out of high school, a prized recruit who occasioned an intense recruiting war between Marquette and Wisconsin.

Junior Cadougan (6-1, 205, Sr.): Over the past two seasons Cadougan has logged a lot of possessions as Marquette's pass-always point guard, and he filled that role as the starter last year. On paper he's always carried a high turnover rate and, no, he won't be showing the grandkids the tape of that eight-turnover effort against Louisville on March 8 anytime soon. But keep in mind Cadougan's assists and his willingness to never shoot have demonstrably netted out as a positive for a team with a low collective turnover rate and a high level of offensive efficiency.

Davante Gardner (6-8, 290, Jr.): Last year Gardner missed eight games in January and February with a left knee sprain. Even when healthy, however, he was limited by foul trouble: Gardner had played nine conference games before the injury, and he recorded his fourth foul in five of those. If he and Williams can unite on a foul-avoidance and conditioning regimen that yields more minutes on the floor, the rewards could be substantial. Gardner draws even more fouls than he commits, he's a 76 percent shooter at the line, and he gives every appearance of being an offensive rebounding man among Big East children.

Trent Lockett (6-5, 210, Sr.): A Twin Cities product, Lockett played three seasons at Arizona State before returning closer to home to finish his career in Milwaukee. After his mother was diagnosed with cancer, Lockett was granted a hardship waiver by the NCAA and will be eligible immediately. In his last season as a Sun Devil he was his team's leading scorer and had a great year shooting the ball from both sides of the arc, but Lockett also committed a good many turnovers.

Jamil Wilson (6-7, 225, Jr.): As a sophomore Wilson recorded a big jump in minutes and indeed made 15 starts, even though, aside from a two-game 33-point outburst against DePaul and Cincinnati in February, he was relegated to the background on offense. On D he recorded a very nice block rate for someone listed at 6-7, and he had the foul rate to prove it.

Todd Mayo (6-3, 190, So.): Mayo had an encouraging freshman year. As a reserve averaging 21 minutes a game, he displayed a laudable assertiveness in looking for his shot, attempted roughly equal numbers of threes and twos, and made 33 percent of the former and 48 percent of the latter.

Steve Taylor (6-7, 230, Fr.): Williams says Taylor "might be the best player we've signed out of high school since I've been here." More: "He's a true face-up forward that will be great with what we do.

Chris Otule (6-11, 275, Sr.): Break glass in case of big opponent: Otule's deployed for use purely as a shot blocking specialist. By November 18 Crowder and DJO had each attempted more shots from the field than Otule would all year.

Prospectus says: Jae Crowder and Darius Johnson-Odom absorbed an incredible number of possessions for Marquette last season and recorded an incredibly low two-player turnover rate. So expect turnovers to be up this season in Milwaukee. The shots that the big two used to take will now fall to Blue, Gardner, and others (Taylor?). Yet even though all of the above will be new to their responsibilities, Williams has earned at least the presumption of good offense. Year after year this team scores points, and their defense has ranged from average to good. I expect both trends to continue in 2013.

NOTRE DAME

2012: 22-12 (13-5 Big East); Lost to Xavier 67-63, NCAA round of 64
In-conference offense: 1.04 points per possession (5th)
In-conference defense: 0.98 points allowed per possession (5th)

What Notre Dame did well: *Wander off script.*

For years Notre Dame has had a fantastic offense and a bad defense. So durable were these traits that explanatory theories were formulated that linked the two qualities. The Irish are good on offense, it was said, *because* they're bad at defense. Mike Brey recruits kids who can knock down jump shots, and jump shooters can't be bothered to play D—in high school or at any other time.

It was a good theory, but then it ran up against last year's team. For the first time since 2007, Notre Dame had a defense that was better than average in Big East play. Indeed for the first time in memory, the Irish had a D that was significantly better than average.

Part of that was luck. Big East opponents made just 26 percent of their threes, easily the lowest percentage recorded by any major-conference team's league opponents last year. Certainly the Irish helped those numbers along by closing out and chasing opponents off the line. Still, all teams endeavor to close out and chase opponents off the line, and none of them managed to get the other team to miss 74 percent of the time.

Then again those same opponents never went to the line, and at this underrated defensive activity ND ranked No. 1 in the Big East. The turnaround on defense was dramatic.

What we learned in 2012: *One pace does not fit all.*

If you're making your way through this Big East section sequentially, you've just read about how Marquette recorded a big defensive improvement last year while speeding up their tempo significantly. Not to be outdone, Notre Dame recorded a big defensive improvement last year while slowing down their tempo significantly. While everyone was busy yelling at South Florida for playing a "boring" brand of "slow-down" hoops, it was in fact the Irish who were the slowest-paced team in this league, averaging 59 possessions per 40 minutes.

I've wheeled out this idea before, but I do think it's helpful to remember that we see teams every year who fill all four cells on the good/bad defense vs. fast/slow matrix. North Carolina has traditionally played good defense at a fast pace, while last year DePaul played very bad defense at a very fast pace. By the same token last year Notre Dame played good defense at a slow pace, while for years now Northwestern has played bad defense at a slow pace. Choose the tempo that works for you, knowing that pace is not destiny.

What's in store for 2013: Just about everyone's back from the team that surprised many observers by successfully negotiating life after Ben Hansbrough and Tim Abromaitis and going 13-5. The only loss of note is Alex Dragicevich, a 6-6 wing who transferred to Boston College.

MEET THE FIGHTING IRISH

Jack Cooley (6-9, 245, Sr.): Cooley is a fantastic example of the player who serves an apprenticeship as a reserve and posts incredible per-possession numbers, then finally gets his chance as a starter and posts, you guessed it, incredible per-possession numbers. (See also Thomas Robinson.) Last year as a team the Irish displayed the kind of balance on offense that Kentucky was utilizing to such memorable effect. Such balance is a very long way from the Harangody days in South Bend, but Cooley and company proved it can work. Now Cooley enters his senior season as the presumptive best offensive rebounder in major-conference hoops. He's also a capable defensive rebounder, and as a junior new to the starting lineup he shot 63 percent on his twos. The previous two sentences go a long way toward illustrating why in the offseason I named Cooley one of the nation's five most underrated players.

Jerian Grant (6-5, 185, Jr.): I nominate Grant's year as the ultimate in "breakout sophomore" seasons. He didn't even play as a freshman, then last year he averaged 36 minutes a game and scored in double figures 26 times. True, Grant's struggles to finish in the paint (he made 41 percent of his twos) might fairly be characterized as Russ Smith-like, but he takes outstanding care of the rock, is north of 80 percent at the line, and shoots fairly well (35 percent) outside the arc. It was a great first year, and it's just too bad it ended with Grant committing the lane violation that sealed the Irish's fate with 2.8 seconds left in their round of 64 loss to Xavier.

Eric Atkins (6-1, 175, Jr.): Depending on how you look at it, Atkins was either a co-point guard or a co-combo guard alongside Grant last year. Both were on the floor more or less the whole season, and while Atkins shared his running mate's struggles in close he was even more effective from the perimeter, hitting 38 percent of his threes.

Scott Martin (6-8, 220, Sr.): In May the NCAA granted Martin a sixth year of eligibility, and as a result the 24-year-old gives the Irish that veteran and savvy look one usually sees only from BYU. Just to touch a few geriatric bases here, Martin is older than Michael Beasley, Eric Gordon, and Blake Griffin. A fair defensive rebounder, he can be counted upon to make 48 percent of his twos. At the same time Martin's attempted 300 threes in three seasons (the first at Purdue, back during the Bush administration) despite the fact that he's a career 30 percent shooter from out there.

Pat Connaughton (6-5, 205, So.): Connaughton got steady minutes as a wing all through the season and ended up making 18 starts, but he disappeared for long stretches of December and January before coming on strong at the end of the year. The 34 percent three-point shooting he displayed last season may turn out to be his floor, based on the fact that he was a freshman who shot 76 percent at the line.

Garrick Sherman (6-10, 240, Sr.): At Michigan State Sherman started 29 games for Tom Izzo, but it's unclear what Brey has here beyond mere size. (Not that Notre Dame can't use some of that.) With the possible exception of "starting games," Sherman did not specialize in any specific activity in East Lansing, be it scoring, rebounding, or blocking shots.

Cam Biedscheid (6-7, 175, Fr.): Biedscheid averaged 32 points a game as a high school senior in St. Louis, and is billed as a versatile wing with excellent range. "He can play anywhere on the perimeter," Brey has said.

Zach Auguste (6-10, 220, Fr.): A highly ranked power forward from Marlborough, Massachusetts, Auguste is expected to crack a rotation that under Brey has not always been particularly welcoming to freshmen.

Prospectus says: Think of Notre Dame this way. Their per-possession performance in conference play last year was better than Louisville's, they lost less from last year's team, and they have an equally good recruiting class coming in. If Jerian Grant had refrained from committing that lane violation with 2.8 seconds left against Xavier and simply allowed Eric Atkins to shoot his two free throws, who knows what kind of expectations we'd be seeing placed on this team right now.

PITT

2012: 22-17 (5-13 Big East); Beat Washington St. 71-65, CBI Championship Series Game 3
In-conference offense: 1.00 points per possession (10th)
In-conference defense: 1.06 points allowed per possession (12th)

What Pitt did well: *Surprise us and, probably, themselves.*

The last time you saw Pitt they were busy falling off a cliff, going 5-13 in the Big East despite the fact that they entered the season having won a whopping 71 percent of their games in the league's 18-game era. Yes, the Panthers lost a lot of points and minutes from the group that had a rather extraordinary encounter with Butler in the 2011 round of 32. Brad Wanamaker, Gilbert Brown, and Gary McGhee were all key contributors on a team that won the Big East regular season title outright.

But, with all due respect to Wanamaker, Brown, and McGhee, should losing those three really have been any tougher than losing the likes of DeJuan Blair, Sam Young, and Levance Fields was after the 2008-09 season? In fact, it was guys like Wanamaker and McGhee who stepped into major roles in the post-Blair era and led Pitt to a very surprising (in a good way) 13-5 Big East record in 2010.

We all thought Jamie Dixon had this "replacing starters" thing figured out, and we had very good reason to think so. History was in our corner on this one. But last year the Panthers wrote a new chapter.

Looking at the season as a whole, the offense and defense both collapsed completely, and almost precisely in equal measures. Tray Woodall missed 11 games in December and January due to an abdominal injury, and highly touted freshman Khem Birch left the program in mid-December and eventually transferred to UNLV.

What we learned in 2012: *Offensive rebounds don't matter. I kid, I kid. Still...*

In 2010, offensive rebounds were in. Teams that excelled at offensive rebounding—Duke, West Virginia, Michigan State—did things like win national championships or at least get to the Final Four. As a result, offensive rebound percentage enjoyed a brief vogue as the predictive stat du jour.

That is until Pitt had to go and ruin the fun last year. Amid the chaos and collapsing at the Petersen Events Center, the one thing the Panthers could cling to was their offensive rebounding. They were really, really good at it, hauling in 40 percent of their misses and ranking second only to perennially offensive-board-obsessed West Virginia in Big East play. And being really good at offensive rebounding was not enough to help a really bad offense, one that scored just 1,153 points in 1,147 conference possessions.

What's in store for 2013: If you watched last year unfold, you'll be forgiven for wondering if Pitt might not be doomed again this season. After all, losing Ashton Gibbs and Nasir Robinson (as Dixon has heading into this season) is at least in the same ballpark hit-wise as losing Wanamaker, Brown and McGhee (as Pitt had heading into last season). But maybe there's a small piece of good news to be found in last year's rubble. Once the Panthers got that December-to-January losing streak out of their system, they finished the regular season on a somewhat more respectable 5-6 run, one where they both scored and allowed 1.04 points per trip. We've seen hints of normalcy from this team. Besides, there's another big piece of good news called Steven Adams. Read on.

MEET THE PANTHERS

Tray Woodall (6-0, 190, Sr.): Woodall reportedly still experiences discomfort in his abdomen, despite or perhaps because of undergoing sports hernia surgery in the offseason. The conventional wisdom says that even when Woodall returned to action last season he wasn't 100 percent, but the funny thing is the rate stats from his junior year look fine. He made big improvements in his assist rate and in both his two- and three-point accuracy, albeit while remaining a bit too turnover-prone. Right now there's a good deal of talk to the effect that freshman point guard James Robinson (see below) may be needed sooner rather than later, but we should be under no illusions as to the alternatives here. If Robinson posts the rate stats as a freshman that the putatively hobbled Woodall recorded last season, people will run around screaming with their hands above their heads about this incredible new point guard. Meaning simply Woodall is a proven Big East point guard, abdominal pains and all.

Lamar Patterson (6-5, 220, Jr.): If you've been hoping to get out in front of The Next Big Thing in hoops, grab Patterson and show him off to your friends as the The Point Wing of the Future. On the one hand he has the Draymond Green thing where he's a 6-5-ish guy with soft hands who is both comfortable with and effective at distributing the rock. On the other hand he has said no to that whole "amazing defensive rebounding" thing that Green did so well, choosing instead to knock down threes. Or at least Patterson did that last year, hitting 41 of an even hundred attempts from out there. Given that he was just 8-of-36 as a freshman, that pretty much came out of nowhere. So was Patterson's three-point shooting last season a fluke? We'll find out. No one tastes success like that from beyond the arc without coming back for more.

Steven Adams (7-0, 250, Fr.): Among the good people who give us the mock draft boards that occasion so much dissection and critique, the only question presented by Adams is when he'll be a lottery pick. Some mocks have the big New Zealander shaking David Stern's hand in 2014, while others see it happening next summer. Meantime, he should be an immense help where Pitt needs it most. Last year Big East opponents ate the Panthers alive in the paint, making 51 percent of their twos. Assuming Adams is as good as advertised, those days should be over.

J.J. Moore (6-6, 215, Jr.): Moore had surgery in the offseason to repair a fractured metatarsal in his right foot, and is reportedly fully recovered. Lost amid last year's gloom was a solid year from Moore as a wing, one in which he made more than half his twos and a third of his threes as Dixon's sixth man. From Valentine's Day until pandemonium reigned supreme and Pitt cut down the nets on March 30 (do they do that at the CBI?), Moore scored 12 points per outing.

Trey Zeigler (6-5, 205, Jr.): Part of me says Zeigler is about to do the proverbial "breakout" thing now that he'll no longer have to carry the entirety of the offense for a very bad team, as he did at Central Michigan the past two seasons. A data point in my favor there is the fact that Zeigler's two-point accuracy shot up all the way to respectability as a sophomore. Then again the other part of me says Zeigler's a career 53 percent shooter at the line. Besides, we've seen this movie before, haven't we? It's called "Mike Rosario," and the plot revolves around a player who was rated one of the nation's top guards out of high school. Our protagonist transfers from a meh program where he gobbled up every doomed possession to a top program where he'll play a much smaller role. The good news for Zeigler is he won't be competing for playing time against the likes of Bradley Beal, Kenny Boynton, and Erving Walker, the way Rosario had to at Florida last year.

Talib Zanna (6-9, 230, Jr.): Zanna made 13 starts and only touched the ball if he got an offensive board, which he did quite often. In addition he was the team's best defensive rebounder by a wide margin.

Dante Taylor (6-9, 235, Sr.): One of the finest offensive rebounders in the country, Taylor made 20 starts and averaged 19 minutes a game. If you ever want to make the case that coaches can arrange the sun, moon, and the stars in this game however they see fit, you could do worse than to point at Taylor and Zanna. The former's from Westchester County, NY, while the latter lived in

Nigeria until 2006. Send both to Pitt to play for Dixon and they come out with rate stats that are very nearly indistinguishable.

James Robinson (6-3, 200, Fr.): If Woodall's really as hobbled as reports suggest, we'll be seeing a lot of Robinson, a DeMatha product billed as a "true" point guard. In the past I've lobbied for the abolishment of that term on the grounds that point guard effectiveness comes in all shapes and sizes. That being said, when observers say, "James Robinson is a true point guard," I know exactly what they're trying to convey. So maybe we can keep the term after all. It carries descriptive water.

Prospectus says: Pitt's one-year hiccup last season will prove to have been just that. The worst-case scenario for the Panthers' final year in the Big East is that Woodall's still hurt and Adams isn't entirely beastly right away. Grant both conditions and you're still looking at a team that's a rung or two above where the Panthers ended up last year.

PROVIDENCE

2012: 15-17 (4-14 Big East); Lost to Seton Hall 79-47, Big East first round
In-conference offense: 1.04 points per possession (6th)
In-conference defense: 1.12 points allowed per possession (16th)

What Providence did well: *Keep hope alive.*

You'd think that going 4-14 in the Big East for a third consecutive season and losing by 32 points to a not terribly formidable Seton Hall team in a win or go home setting would make it hard to be enthusiastic about the present. But oh how they like to talk about the future at PC.

Last season was head coach Ed Cooley's first at the helm with the Friars, and he marked the occasion by going out and signing a recruiting class that ranks alongside Pitt's for best-in-league honors. That doesn't mean the wins will start rolling in instantly, of course. (For one thing it's an open question when all these elite recruits will be on the floor together — see below.) But the most important recruiting class in any coach's entire career is the first class he signs after getting his first major-conference head-coaching gig. Cooley met that test and passed it with flying colors.

While we're on the subject, Cooley also landed two transfers who'll be eligible in 2013-14: Carson Desrosiers from Wake Forest, and Tyler Harris from NC State. Take that, ACC looters and pillagers!

What we learned in 2012: *Playing defense at PC is hard.*

For years observers yelled at former head coach Keno Davis for playing too fast a pace and not defending well enough. So out went Davis, in came Cooley, the tempo slowed down dramatically, and, wonder of wonders, the defense got even worse. (Cooley inherited Davis's players, granted.) Opponents rang up 1.12 points per trip against this D, which might fairly be termed remarkable in a year where Syracuse was setting a gold standard for efficiency on offense by scoring 1.10 points per possession in conference play. In effect Providence gave their opponents the gift of having, for one game, an offense even better than Syracuse's.

What's in store for 2013: Gerard Coleman, a 6-4 wing who made 21 starts last season, transferred to Gonzaga in June. Then in September freshman shooting guard Ricky Ledo was classified as a partial qualifier by the NCAA, meaning he can't play this season (but can practice with the team).

MEET THE FRIARS

Vincent Council (6-2, 180, Sr.): Your major-conference leaders in assist rate last year were Penn State's Tim Frazier, North Carolina's Kendall Marshall, and Council. That's impressive company, however, the crisp-passing Friar's offensive rating was nowhere near what those other guys posted. Nominally a scoring point guard, Council shot often and missed almost as often. There are few college players alive who have played more possessions than what Council has logged in 3,216 minutes, so at this point we should probably heed these career rates: 41 percent on his twos, 32 percent on threes. Speaking of excellence in the field of recording minutes, Cooley's already displayed a marked preference for sticking with his starters, and in Council the preference has become an iron law. From February 1 until the final horn in the Friars' lopsided loss to Seton Hall at the Big East tournament, Council sat for a grand total of one official box score minute.

LaDontae Henton (6-6, 215, So.): With my own eyes I saw Henton make 39 percent of his threes and 48 percent of his twos as a relatively high-volume shooter who never left the floor for a 4-14 Big East team in his freshman year. I say the kid bears further watching.

Bryce Cotton (6-1, 165, Jr.): Cotton led Division I in percentage of minutes played last season (96.0—Council and Henton were also in the top

15), and he was actually pretty efficient, hitting 38 percent of his frequent threes and 46 percent of his more rarely attempted twos. Those numbers were achieved as a role player on offense, to be sure. Still, there's always playing time available for a guy who takes very good care of the ball and shoots 89 percent at the line—in this case, a lot of available playing time.

Kris Dunn (6-3, 180, Fr.): In July Dunn underwent shoulder surgery, and he's expected to be unavailable until January. A McDonald's All-American point guard, Dunn averaged a double-double (31-10) as a high school senior in New London, Connecticut. McDonald's All-American point guards typically have a range of options in terms of where they can play ball, and many of those options will appear more attractive than a program that's gone 4-14 in the Big East three years in a row. If in 10 or 20 years Cooley is an Izzo figure with multiple Final Four appearances under his belt, he'll look back and single out Dunn's commitment, along with Ledo's, as the moment that turned things around.

Sidiki Johnson (6-10, 240, So.): Johnson transferred from Arizona (he scored one point in seven total minutes) and will become eligible on December 18 against Colgate. This past summer there was a flurry of rumors to the effect that Johnson would transfer out of PC before ever playing a minute (reportedly to Iona), but as of this writing the onetime top-100 big man from New York City is still a Friar.

Kadeem Batts (6-9, 245, Jr.): After an encouraging freshman season in 2010-11 where he posted an excellent offensive rebound rate, Batts saw his minutes dwindle last year. A lot of that was his own doing, as the big guy averaged an amazingly belligerent seven fouls per 40 minutes. On March 2 at Notre Dame, for example, Batts fouled out in eight minutes. He followed that up by fouling out of the Friars' season-ending loss to Seton Hall in Madison Square Garden in 20 minutes. Also note that when published reports label as "indispensable" a 6-9 player who made less than 40 percent of his twos as a sophomore, your program is rebuilding.

Josh Fortune (6-5, 195, Fr.): In ordinary circumstances Fortune might have to do a lot of sitting this year, but with Providence so strapped for bodies there's actually a good chance we'll see something of the shooting guard from Virginia.

Prospectus says: In November and December Providence will be very, very thin, as the Friars wait for Dunn to recover from surgery and for Johnson to become eligible. One report has Cooley giving a fearsome nickname ("White Lightning") to a walk-on (Ted Bancroft) and telling the young man to be ready for action. Mark that as the Cooley Era's humble beginnings. I expect PC will improve enough to get out of their 4-14 rut this season. I'm also frankly interested to see what a second year brings Henton's way. But the big change in the Friars' fortunes is still a year off. At about the same time that the league gets weaker by losing Syracuse and Pitt, Providence should be getting better.

RUTGERS

2012: 14-18 (6-12 Big East); Lost to Villanova 70-49, Big East first round
In-conference offense: 0.96 points per possession (16th)
In-conference defense: 1.03 points allowed per possession (10th)

What Rutgers did well: *Assemble quality wins.*

Imagine a parallel universe where Rutgers insinuated themselves into the 2012 bubble discussion during head coach Mike Rice's second season. In this alternative reality, the Scarlet Knights could have pointed to a number of real-world quality wins, the kind the selection committee puts such stock in. RU beat the likes of Florida, Connecticut, Cincinnati, and Notre Dame in Piscataway, and for good measure they put the finishing touches on Pitt's early-January fit of manic depression with a rather emphatic 62-39 win in Pittsburgh.

Unfortunately for fans of the Scarlet Knights, what I've just described is no mere representative sample but something closer to a complete census. Toss in wins against Seton Hall and St. John's, and you have the entire list of wins recorded by this team after December 28, 2011. All seven of them, against 13 losses.

What we learned in 2012: *Extraordinary failure can be the cumulative result of several more ordinary performances.*

Here's something you don't usually see: Rutgers had the worst offense in the Big East last season, but the Scarlet Knights were not the worst (or even second-worst!) team in the league within any one offensive statistical category. In terms of accuracy from the field, for example, Rice's team clocked in at a not-terrible No. 11 (West Virginia, to cite one eminently respectable rival, was much worse). Same thing for turnover rate (no. 14), offensive rebound percentage (10) and free throw rate (No. 13). But the sum of all those bottom-half performances was the single worst offense in the league.

In effect, this team was simply starved of shots. Giving the ball away on 22 percent of their possessions while at the same time never getting to the line proved to be too much for the Scarlet Knights to overcome on offense.

What's in store for 2013: Gilvydas Biruta, the only player to start all 32 games for Rutgers in 2011-12 (and the last recruit to commit to former head coach Fred Hill), transferred to Rhode Island after the season. Something was clearly amiss with Biruta in his sophomore season. After a freshman year where he played out of position as a center and succeeded brilliantly, he was widely expected to flourish in his more natural power-forward spot. Instead his rate stats tumbled. I fully expect that Biruta will be heard from, and I can't wait to see what he looks like when he's both happy and playing the correct position. But on paper, losing sophomore-version Biruta is no loss at all. An average Big East player getting those same minutes will be an improvement over what we saw from that spot last year.

MEET THE SCARLET KNIGHTS

Eli Carter (6-2, 195, So.): Though he was nowhere close to being the highest rated recruit in last year's highly ranked Rutgers freshman class, Carter emerged as The Guy. Nominally a point guard, he led the team in minutes, and was the only player on the roster to post a season scoring average in double-figures. Personally accounting for 28 percent of this team's shot attempts during his minutes, Carter's prominence within this offense was equivalent to that of Kevin Jones within the West Virginia offense. The shooting percentages that resulted weren't stellar (45 percent on twos, 35 percent on threes), but, seen within the context of a freshman who was carrying the load for a 6-12 Big East team, those numbers furnish ample grounds for optimism.

Myles Mack (5-9, 170, So.): Like Carter, Mack is a Paterson, NJ, product who functions as a combo guard, but, unlike Carter, Mack left the hometown touted as a top-100 prospect. He turned down offers from throughout the tristate area (Seton Hall, St. John's) and beyond (Miami, Boston College) to play for a new coach at a school that hasn't won an NCAA tournament game since Magic and Bird were still around. Give Rice credit: Mack was a nice recruiting win for a coach rebuilding a program. The young man in question made 14 starts and drained 45 percent of his twos. That second figure surely represents some kind of record for a 5-9 freshman playing in the Big East.

Wally Judge (6-9, 250, Jr.): This is where things get tricky for computer rating systems. Judge was a McDonald's All-American out of Washington D.C., and in the post-Beasley afterglow then palpable in the District he chose to play his ball at Kansas State. Whereupon Frank Martin had Judge foul, and foul, and foul some more. The rate stats that resulted are suitably terrible (a 6-9 McDonald's All-American should not shoot 44 percent on his twos), but, in Judge's defense, such numbers are the quantitative detritus of a few hundred instances where he was rarely more than a few seconds away from being pulled out of the game. We simply don't know how good Judge can be in a situation where he's asked to do something besides foul. If on the other hand it turns out that Judge really is this foul-prone in his own right, that raises some frightening possibilities of an entirely different sort, for he's joining a team that already had far and away the league's highest foul rate in conference play.

Dane Miller (6-6, 215, Sr.): Miller was a defensive specialist last season, which is a glass-half-full way of saying his role on offense became substantially smaller once the swarm of eagerly anticipated freshman teammates arrived. He started all but two games, cleaned the defensive glass, and recorded a very nice block rate for someone listed at 6-6. More importantly Miller did so for the most part without fouling.

Jerome Seagears (6-1, 175, So.): In a rotation without a "true" point guard, Seagears made 25 starts and posted the team's highest assist rate. Note that all three of last year's freshman guards—Carter, Mack, and Seagears—shot strikingly similar percentages (mid- to low-40s on twos, mid- to low-30s on threes), though Carter did so while carrying by far the heaviest usage load.

Mike Poole (6-5, 195, Jr.): If Rice had a sixth man last season, it was Poole, who averaged 22 minutes a contest despite making just three starts. On paper he has a really nice steal rate, a statistical artifact helped along by the fact that in consecutive games after Thanksgiving he dropped on UMBC and LSU like a jaguar out of a tree, recording 10 steals in 46 minutes.

Vincent Garrett (6-5, 210, Jr.): An athletic wing from Chicago by way of Lee Junior College in Texas, Garrett played on the same AAU team as Meyers Leonard, Tim Hardaway, Jr., and Wayne Blackshear.

Prospectus says: A young team that returns four starters is very likely to get better, the only question being how much. Dan Hanner's rating system really likes the Scarlet Knights' chances to make a big jump in performance this season, all the way up to a likely NCAA tournament bid. That's not as far-fetched as it may sound. (Good luck going back in time a year and persuading the people there that South Florida will come within two possessions of the 2012 Sweet 16.) In fact it's not far-fetched at all, and I too am a believer in sophomores improving upon what they did as freshmen. Still, I take a somewhat more cautious view of RU's potential this season. An inordinate share of this team's first-glance statistical respectability on defense (Rice's men were right at the league's statistical mean) was supplied by just one game, the 62-39 oddity at Pitt on January 11. Meanwhile seven of RU's last nine opponents during the Big East regular season rang up 1.09 points per trip or higher. Judge may help shore that up, but I can see all of the above netting out to a performance on D not terribly dissimilar to what we saw last season. That plus a significantly improved offense will lift Rutgers into the neighborhood of .500 in Big East play.

ST. JOHN'S

2012: 13-19 (6-12 Big East); Lost to Pitt 73-59, Big East first round
In-conference offense: 0.98 points per possession (14th)
In-conference defense: 1.09 points allowed per possession (14th)

What St. John's did well: *Tread water.*

Last season took place in something of a fog for St. John's, as a team filled with first-year stars waited for head coach Steve Lavin to recover from surgery for prostate cancer. Happily, all reports indicate that Coach Lavin is healthy and has made a full recovery: "All the blood work has been clean, and I'm cancer-free." Congratulations, Coach.

Now, back to the trivial stuff.

What we learned in 2012: *People should have just stopped yelling at Syracuse about their awful defensive rebounding—because St. John's was even worse.*

In Coach Lavin's absence, St. John's achieved the not inconsiderable feat of being even worse than Syracuse at defensive rebounding. The Red Storm hauled in just 59.2 percent of their Big East opponents' misses, while the Orange pulled down 59.8 percent of their foes' missed shots.

I was at some pains last year to suggest that, while of course all teams wish to be good at defensive rebounding, if you're as insanely efficient on offense as Syracuse was last season and you have a shot blocker the caliber of Fab Melo, you can at least hide this deficiency more effectively than a lot of other teams could. That being said, if you wanted to point to one game last year where terrible defensive rebounding really did "cost" a team, I for one nominate the Red Storm's OT loss at home to Villanova in January.

On an afternoon when SJU shot far better from the field than did the Wildcats, Jay Wright's team was able to eke out the win anyway thanks to 24 offensive boards. Coaches, if you're looking for the scare-tape that proves how important defensive rebounding really is, there you go. You're welcome.

What's in store for 2013: After a freshman year that screamed potential, Moe Harkless was drafted at No. 15 by Philadelphia. On the plus side of the ledger for St. John's, JaKarr Sampson is eligible after sitting out last season.

MEET THE RED STORM

D'Angelo Harrison (6-3, 200, So.): A little like an NFL coach heading off any hint of a quarterback controversy, Lavin has labeled Harrison as the St. John's point guard heading into this season. Harrison says he's grown taller since last season, and while his listed height has stayed the same he reconciles the discrepancy by claiming he is "6-3 for real now." When I put together my annual January list of top 25 freshmen last season, I included Harrison but left off co-featured scorer Harkless. I heard from a lot of St. John's fans on the error of my ways, of course ("How can you be so Harkless?"), and the NBA has subsequently added their thoughts to this mix as well. Had the Red Storm fans and the GMs at the next level hastened to tell me that subsequent to my honoring him Harrison would go on to miss his next 100 two-point shots, I would have conceded the point. I exaggerate, but only a little: Harrison ended the year having made just 38 percent of his twos. Fortunately for SJU fans he made about the same percentage of threes, while attempting roughly equal numbers of both. What really saved Harrison, though, was his ability to draw fouls and shoot 80 percent at the line.

Phil Greene (6-2, 180, So.): Greene is reportedly recovering from a hip injury, but is expected to be at full-strength when the season begins. The numbers he recorded as a freshman sometimes look like they're one column off: Greene's two-point percentage (39.2) would be an excellent three-point percentage, and his three-point percentage (26.0) would be a very nice defensive rebound rate. That being said, good passing and sheer durability offset at least some of Greene's struggles from the field.

God'sgift Achiuwa (6-8, 230, Sr.): Tip your cap to Achiuwa, who isn't all that large yet spent the balance of his junior season as clearly the largest St. John's player on the floor at any given time. Somehow the undersized Achiuwa held down the paint the whole year (he made 18 starts), drew more fouls than he committed, and did a commendable job converting loose balls and offensive boards into points.

Sir'Dominic Pointer (6-5, 190, So.): Lavin says Pointer will get some minutes at point guard in 2012-13. Last season the Detroit product started 25 games and posted a very nice steal rate while insisting on attempting roughly one three a game. He finished the year as a 19 percent three-point shooter who hit just 55 percent of his attempts from the line.

Amir Garrett (6-6, 190, So.): Garrett made 14 starts after becoming academically eligible on December 21. His season totals describe an afterthought on offense, but over St. John's last seven games Garrett averaged better than 10 points per contest. By the end of the year he was on the floor about as much as Harkless and Harrison. Garrett spent his summer pitching in the Cincinnati Reds' farm system.

JaKarr Sampson (6-8, 205, Fr.): After failing to qualify last year academically, Sampson will now have a chance to show what are said to be some formidable chops in the "very athletic wing" category. He certainly didn't lack for interest as a recruit: Sampson turned down offers from Kansas, Florida, Baylor, and Texas to say yes to Lavin.

Chris Obekpa (6-9, 220, Fr.): Obekpa is a top-100 prospect who committed to St. John's in June. He's billed as a formidable shot blocker who needs to polish his post game.

Jamal Branch (6-3, 170, So.): A transfer from Texas A&M, Branch will become eligible in December. In College Station Branch averaged 19 minutes per outing over 11 games as a reserve point guard. That's not a lot to go on, of course, but in that fleeting glimpse we saw many assists and almost as many turnovers.

Orlando Sanchez (6-9, 215, Jr.),
Marco Bourgault (6-6, 215, So.): In addition to all of the above, Lavin has brought in junior-college transfers Sanchez and Bourgault. Last year St. John's was undermanned. That shouldn't be an issue this season.

Prospectus says: By necessity rather than by choice, St. John's over the past few years has become a laboratory of chronological homogeneity. Dating back to the days of Dwight Hardy and Justin Brownlee and continuing right into the present, it seems like every time you scan a Red Storm roster you're looking at about 17 guys who are all the same year in school. That's not the normal way of doing things—heck, even Kentucky has an occasional old guy hanging around in any given year—and a lack of comparable examples makes prediction difficult. But here are three educated guesses. There will be a transfer or two at the end of the season by freshmen and sophomores who lost out in the scramble for playing time. St. John's will improve their defensive rebounding dramatically. And the Red Storm will save their really big push into the Big East's upper tier for 2013-14.

SETON HALL

2012: 21-13 (8-10 Big East); Lost to UMass 77-67, NIT second round
In-conference offense: 0.98 points per possession (13th)
In-conference defense: 0.99 points allowed per possession (7th)

What Seton Hall did well: *Start strong.*

Where the topic is the Big East, observers always yearn to see a program from the league's bottom tier finally break through the glass ceiling and get an NCAA bid. St. John's filled that bill in 2011, and last year for a good long while it looked like the next team in that particular line was going to be Seton Hall. (Actually it turned out to be South Florida. But I'm getting ahead of the story.)

It's easy to forget now, but this SHU team that we now know was ticketed for an NIT appearance was the subject of much "They've arrived!" talk in January. The Pirates were 15-2, and their only losses were a neutral-floor setback against Northwestern and a shellacking at Syracuse. They'd won at home against West Virginia and Connecticut, and Kevin Willard's team had earned a spot in the AP top 25.

The accolades were legit. Seton Hall really was playing well. Over their first five Big East games the Pirates outscored their opponents by 0.10 points per possession, and, again, that was with a 26-point loss at Syracuse tossed into the mix. This wasn't a case like Illinois last year, where people were looking past obvious warning signs. With Seton Hall there were no warning signs.

Then Willard's team went to South Florida and lost by a point. No shame there, surely, but it marked the first of what would be six consecutive losses. The defense fell off significantly and the offense charted an even steeper decline. Seton Hall couldn't sustain the success.

What we learned in 2012: *The three is powerful.*

The Pirates' offense was very weak in Big East play last season, but the truth is it very easily could have been even weaker. Last season was Willard's second at the Hall, and in year two turnovers went up and two-point accuracy dipped (SHU made less than 44 percent of their attempts inside the arc in-conference). That's a terrible combination, obviously, but overall Seton Hall's offense stayed more or less at the same (bad) level year to year.

The three-point shot was the only thing holding this offense up last year, and, give Willard credit, SHU shot more of them in Big East play than they had the previous season. Compared to what they did in conference play in 2011, the Pirates' perimeter accuracy improved by seven full percentage points to 37 percent. One thing that drives me reliably crazy is to see a team that can't make a particular kind of shot, be it twos or threes, record many attempts of that type of shot. Conversely Willard saw a team that struggled in the paint but thrived on the perimeter and changed the mix on offense accordingly. The end result was still the Big East's No. 13 offense, but it could have been even worse.

What's in store for 2013: The twin pillars of last year's offense, Herb Pope and Jordan Theodore, are gone. Statistically that creates an even larger absence than the one opened up at Marquette by the departures of Jae Crowder and Darius Johnson-Odom. Of course at Marquette replacing those stars is challenging because Buzz Williams is trying to sustain an offense that has played at a high level. On the other hand at the Hall, the available possessions and shots represent an opportunity to start over with an offense that performed well below the Big East average. Willard had hoped to have Texas transfer (and Seton Hall Prep graduate) Sterling Gibbs eligible this season, but in July the NCAA denied SHU's application for a hardship waiver.

MEET THE PIRATES

Fuquan Edwin (6-6, 205, Jr.): In an alternate universe where Jack Cooley was never born, Edwin would be able to mount a serious candidacy for the title of most underrated player in the Big East. For one thing he's inherited ex-Pirate Paul Gause's mantel as the SHU player who records a steal rate so good it looks like a typo. Indeed among major-conference players, only Louisville's Russ Smith can look Edwin in the eye when the topic turns to steals. Of course if Edwin then steers the conversation toward "accuracy from the field," it will be Smith's turn to fall silent. As a wing who attempted about twice as many twos as threes, Edwin drained 54 percent of the former and 37 percent of the latter. Those exemplary numbers were recorded as a supporting player behind Pope and Theodore, but Edwin will now have every opportunity to show he can stay efficient while carrying a much larger load on offense. He ended last season on an encouraging note, scoring 21 points on 8-of-14 shooting in the Pirates' NIT loss to UMass.

Aaron Cosby (6-3, 190, So.): The Pirates' shift toward a heavier perimeter orientation last season was good news for Cosby, who earned a spot in the starting lineup due solely to his 38 percent three-point shooting. That level of accuracy emerged from 175 attempts, so it would certainly seem to be a trustworthy number. But is it any more trustworthy than the 57 percent free throw shooting that emerged from the measly 42 attempts that a spot-up shooter could muster? We don't know. The kid was a freshman. We'll see what we see when Cosby returns from the knee injury he suffered in the preseason. He's expected to return to action in December.

Patrik Auda (6-9, 225, Jr.): Auda played very much in Pope's shadow in the Pirate frontcourt the past two seasons, but at least last year he demonstrated he could cut down on his fouls and stay on the floor (he made 26 starts). One question that will be important to Willard and indeed to the team as a whole is how much the Czech native can improve his rebounding numbers now that Pope's no longer around to gobble up every miss at both ends.

Brian Oliver (6-6, 225, Jr.): Oliver elected to transfer out of Georgia Tech when Paul Hewitt was let go after the 2011 season. What the New Jersey native can do for his new team as a high-usage wing comes down to whether we'll see freshman-version Oliver (38 percent three-point shooting) or sophomore-variety Oliver (29 percent).

Kyle Smyth (6-4, 185, Sr.): A transfer from Iona, Smyth is eligible immediately and gives Willard additional backcourt depth. He's a career 39 percent three-point shooter who functioned as a spot-up source of points for the Gaels in support of Scott Machado and Mike Glover.

Gene Teague (6-9, 290, Jr.): A transfer from Southern Illinois who sat out all of last year, Teague will clearly help the Pirates replace bulk that went out the door with Pope. In Carbondale Teague drew an exceptionally high number of fouls, and, no, that's not good news. He's a career 52 percent shooter at the line.

Brandon Mobley (6-9, 210, So.): Drawing inferences from 508 total minutes is hazardous, but Mobley appears to have the makings of a capable wing who can hit an occasional three and pitch in on the defensive glass.

Haralds Karlis (6-5, 185, So.): Seton Hall has a pipeline, of sorts, to the Canarias Basketball Academy in the Canary Islands. This pipeline has produced not only a Latvian like Karlis (still another wing in the making, apparently), but also Czech native Auda, and Great Britain's own **Aaron Geramipoor (6-11, 225, Jr.)**. Apparently the Canaries are quite the hoops talent entrepot.

Freddie Wilson (6-2, 175, So.): Wilson couldn't get on the floor as a freshman, but I wish to direct your attention toward the young man anyway. He's the only player listed here who has so much as shown an open mind toward recording the occasional assist.

Prospectus says: Seton Hall is not lacking in wings with decided spot-up tendencies. Improving upon last year's performance on offense should be no great challenge, but I'll be at least mildly surprised if there's not some slippage on D. The end result could be a record similar to last year's, but, coming from a roster with no seniors, a similar record in 2013 will furnish sufficient cause for optimism about the future.

SOUTH FLORIDA

2012: 22-14 (12-6 Big East); Lost to Ohio 62-56, NCAA round of 32
In-conference offense: 0.97 points per possession (15th)
In-conference defense: 0.95 points allowed per possession (3rd)

What South Florida did well: *Transform.*

Long an afterthought in the Big East and indeed a program that had been brought to the league for football reasons only, South Florida surprised everyone in 2012 by making their first appearance in the NCAA tournament since 1992.

Barely. The Bulls made the field of 68 by the thinnest of margins, earning a spot against Cal in the First Four. Stan Heath's team shut down the Bears and did the same to Temple in the round of 64 before coming up just short against Ohio.

USF did it with defense. What in 2011 had been the Big East's No. 14 defense improved all the way to No. 3 (behind Syracuse and Georgetown), and even that was a little misleading. By the end of the season there was a case to be made that this was easily the best defense in the conference.

Up through early February South Florida had been merely good on defense. But starting with their game on February 8 against Pitt, Heath's men reached a new level on D. Over their final eight games USF played 472 possessions and held opponents to just 399 points, or 0.85 points per possession. No opponent even came close to scoring a point per trip. The Bulls lost two of those eight contests by scoring just 48 (Syracuse) and 44 points (West Virginia). Still, it was the finest sustained performance on defense the league has seen in a long while.

What we learned in 2012: *Great defense plus good fortune is a really nice combination.*

Even with an amazing defense, South Florida managed to outscore their conference opponents by just 0.02 points per possession. Often as not that kind of performance will result in a 10-8 record over 18 games, but the 12-6 Bulls were virtually unstoppable in close games. They posted a 4-1 record in Big East games decided by five points or less. We can never know for sure, of course, but a team that ended up being seeded in the First Four likely needed every single one of those close wins.

What's in store for 2013: USF lost three members of what was effectively a seven-player rotation: Augustus Gilchrist, Ron Anderson, and Hugh Robertson. In addition, reserve point guard Blake Nash made a strong bid for this year's Ill-Advised Transfer Destination Award, choosing to take his game to Texas Tech on the very eve of the player revolt in Lubbock and Billy Gillispie's ensuing exit.

MEET THE BULLS

Anthony Collins (6-1, 175, So.): Collins made his name in March by making opposing guards miserable. His defense was relentless, and he scored 29 points in the Bulls' two NCAA tournament wins. Collins also made an impressive 53 percent of his twos as a pass-first point guard, but his turnover rate was about what you'd expect from a freshman playing the point for any coach besides John Calipari. One development to watch for this season is the appearance of a perimeter shot. Such a development would not be inconceivable coming from a player who shot 85 percent at the line.

Victor Rudd (6-9, 230, Jr.): Ordinarily Rudd's combination of high-volume and low-accuracy shooting would stand out, but on both metrics he was eclipsed last year by Gilchrist. Then again this is looking at Rudd—and South Florida—through the wrong end of the telescope. Last year the presence of Rudd, Gilchrist (6-10), and Anderson (6-8) on the floor at the same time, along with a perimeter defender like Collins, proved to be a very effective way of nullifying opposing offenses.

Toarlyn Fitzpatrick (6-8, 245, Sr.): Fitzpatrick made 11 starts last year, but mostly he got heavy minutes off the bench as still another big defender and, most especially, as the team's most effective defensive rebounder. Rather more surprising was the fact that Fitzpatrick launched 102 threes and made 42 of them.

Jawanza Poland (6-4, 205, Sr.): Over the past two seasons Poland has attempted 181 threes but made just 24 percent of those shots. His continuing struggles from the perimeter masked what was otherwise an effective season on offense, as Poland converted 53 percent of his twos as a high-volume shooter coming off the bench and averaging 22 minutes a contest.

Martino Brock (6-5, 205, Jr.): On paper Brock looks like a promising transfer, one who averaged 14 points a game as a sophomore at South Alabama. He did post a nice steal rate as an underclassman in Mobile, so he should fit right in with the Bulls defensively. But what an odd trajectory he charted in just two seasons on offense. Brock draws more than five fouls per 40 minutes, but as a sophomore his free throw accuracy tumbled by 11 percentage points, all the way down to 56 percent. That alone was sufficient to make him a net liability to the USA offense.

Shaun Noriega (6-4, 205, Sr.): Noriega was the starter on day one last year, and in the first game of the season he scored 15 points on 4-of-5 shooting from beyond the arc against Vermont. That turned out to be Noriega's season-high. After February 1 he logged a total of 40 minutes. Fun fact: Noriega's career three-point percentage (37) is nine points higher than his career two-point percentage.

Javontae Hawkins (6-5, 200, Fr.): It's been 11 years now since Heath was an assistant to Tom Izzo at Michigan State, but apparently he still has ties to his old recruiting haunts. Hawkins is a wing from Flint, Michigan, who's earned praise for his combination of size and athleticism.

Prospectus says: South Florida is due for a correction, possibly even two corrections. For eight games they played the most aberrantly sublime defense the Big East has seen in a very long while, and on top of that they were highly successful in close games. If the Bulls were bringing everyone back from last year I could believe that the great D could continue, but they lost three starters. And no matter who plays, USF isn't likely to duplicate their remarkable knack for winning tight games. This season South Florida may well be above average on D, and, who knows, they could still win more close games than they lose. That combination, which might be termed best-case, would still result in a dip in wins compared to last year.

SYRACUSE

2012: 34-3 (17-1 Big East); Lost to Ohio State 77-70, Elite Eight
In-conference offense: 1.10 points per possession (1st)
In-conference defense: 0.94 points allowed per possession (1st)

What Syracuse did well: *Peak.*

At the risk of stating the obvious with regard to a club that went 17-1, that was a great Syracuse team you saw last year. You can make a case that this was the best offense the league has seen in at least five years (the Orange beat the conference average by two standard deviations), and the same five guys on the court at any given time then turned around and functioned as the Big East's top defense as well. Syracuse improved from 12-6 in Big East play in 2011 to 17-1, and the biggest driver of that ascent was a much better defense.

Jim Boeheim's team did it entirely without rebounding, of course, so if you're a coach partial to crashing the boards you might want to change the subject the next time your players ask you about Syracuse 2011-12. The Orange were so-so on the offensive glass, and famously awful at defensive rebounding. Bear in mind the latter is not a foreordained outcome when you play a lot of zone. Boeheim also played a lot of zone in 2010-11, naturally, and that year his team was right at the league average for defensive rebounding. No, for whatever reason the defensive rebounding fell off a cliff last season, and it didn't seem to matter much.

It didn't matter because opponents who grabbed an offensive board were very likely to miss for the second time on the possession, often courtesy of a blocked shot by Fab Melo. It didn't matter because a lot of those possessions ended with the opponent giving the ball away: Syracuse forced turnovers on 23 percent of their league opponents' possessions, tops in the Big East. And, of course, it didn't matter because no one could keep up with that Orange offense anyway.

What we learned in 2012: *Minimizing turnovers is the most underrated factor in basketball.*

Last year Syracuse's shooting from the field in Big East play was worse than what we saw from the Orange in 2011, and in particular their perimeter shooting was much worse. (The 'Cuse made less than 32 percent of their threes in-conference.) Yet the result was what I've described as perhaps the best Big East offense we've seen in five years.

Boeheim was able to work this particular magic for two reasons. First, even though the shooting dipped slightly year to year and the perimeter was not kind, this was still the best two-point shooting team in the league. Second, the Orange unlocked the power of low-turnover basketball. Looking every bit as responsible with the rock as your most trustworthy Wisconsin team (only at a normal pace), Syracuse gave the ball away on fewer than 16 percent of their possessions in conference play.

Two-point shooting and a lack of turnovers accounted for why this offense was so good relative to the rest of the Big East, but it was the latter alone that explained why this offense improved from year to year. Literally every other stat went in the wrong direction, and it didn't matter. A big drop in turnovers was enough to cancel out everything else.

What's in store for 2013: Selected with the fourth pick by Cleveland, Dion Waiters joined the weirdest and most exclusive club of all, the I Was a Top-Five Draft Pick and I Never Started a Game For My College Team club. (Former North Carolina star Marvin Williams is another member. Still, it can't take long to take attendance at those meetings.) Fab Melo was taken at No. 22 by Boston, and the Celtics also took Kris Joseph late in the second round. Scoop Jardine was undrafted.

MEET THE ORANGEMEN

Brandon Triche (6-4, 210, Sr.): Commencing with a 75-43 win over Albany on November 9, 2009, and right up through the loss to Ohio State in the Elite

Eight, Triche has started every game since he arrived in Syracuse. (As Dion Waiters gently weeps.) His workload on offense has increased steadily over those three seasons, and a correspondingly gradual drop in his personal turnover rate over that same span has landed Triche where he is today, an effective and relatively high-usage performer on offense. A combo guard who posted the regular rotation's highest assist rate this side of Jardine, Triche favors twos over threes by about a 3-to-2 margin. Last year he shot 47 percent inside the arc, and 35 percent outside it.

Rakeem Christmas (6-9, 240, So.): Christmas was an honorary starter as a freshman, taking the floor for the opening tip yet averaging just 12 minutes a contest. He managed to be very foul-prone within a zone D, which isn't unheard of (Baye Keita was right there with him) but isn't all that common either. Christmas did at least get a fair number of shot blocks out of those fouls.

C.J. Fair (6-8, 215, Jr.): Fair is a dependable source of effective and low-foul coverage on the back line of the 2-3 zone. For 11 days in February he convinced himself his name was "Kris Joseph," and scored 61 points in four games before returning to a supporting role on offense. As a sophomore he did something "they" say can't be done, registering a big improvement at the line and hitting 74 percent of his freebies.

Michael Carter-Williams (6-6, 185, So.): If there's anyone here who's going to strike an "I could have been doing this all along" pose in response to regular playing time, it's Carter-Williams. His rate stats last year were fantastic, and he figures to be the heir apparent at the starting guard slot next to Triche now that Jardine's gone. Only thing: MCW may turn out to be a cause for concern (57 percent) if not an outright Onuaku-level abandon-all-hope menace at the line. Right now it's too soon (23 attempts) to tell.

DaJuan Coleman (6-9, 290, Fr.): What are they putting in the water up in Jamesville, New York? With a population of just 8,959, the town has managed to produce first Triche and now Coleman. Boeheim was smart to set up shop just down the road. Coleman is a McDonald's All-American who arrives on campus already earning praise for his back-to-the-basket game.

James Southerland (6-8, 215, Sr.): Southerland looked great when Syracuse needed him, scoring 30 points on 11-of-14 shooting in NCAA tournament games against UNC-Asheville and Kansas State. With the exception of the now departed Joseph, Southerland was the only player on the roster last year 6-7 or above who was assertive in looking for his own shot. Those shots were pretty evenly divided between threes (he made 34 percent) and twos (61).

Baye Keita (6-10, 215, Jr.): In the new post-Melo world order, Keita is Boeheim's best bet for blocking an opponent's shot. The big guy sports an ostentatiously high foul rate, but, even though he did foul out of the wild Sweet 16 game against Wisconsin, that was the exception to the rule. For the most part Keita's foul rate is the product of a lot of games where he plays 10 or 12 minutes and picks up two or three fouls.

Jerami Grant (6-8, 205, Fr.): A power forward out of DeMatha, Grant is the son of former Oklahoma and NBA force of nature Harvey Grant. The Sooners made an offer to Jerami, but apparently Dad couldn't close that deal for his alma mater.

Prospectus says: As always, Boeheim has plenty of guys between 6-8 and 6-10 to hold down the back line of the zone, while on the top he has Triche and the 6-6 Carter-Williams. One underrated portion of Waiters' game last season was his exceptionally high steal rate, and it's unlikely that the Orange can turn over opponents as often as they did during their 17-1 tear through the league. But with this much size and agility, the 2-3 will once again be a real pain for opponents. The offense will take a step back, but when the step in question is from "phenomenal" to "quite good," you can still feel content about this team if you're Boeheim. In their final year in the league Syracuse will contend for a second consecutive regular-season Big East title.

VILLANOVA

2012: 13-19 (5-13 Big East); Lost to South Florida 56-47, Big East second round
In-conference offense: 1.01 points per possession (9th)
In-conference defense: 1.08 points allowed per possession (13th)

What Villanova did well: *Carry a trend forward.*

On March 28, 2009, Scottie Reynolds scored on a driving layup in the closing seconds of Villanova's Elite Eight game against Pitt, giving the Wildcats a 78-76 victory and a trip to the Final Four.

Since that afternoon, Villanova has compiled a 59-40 record. With each succeeding year Jay Wright's team has won fewer games overall, while conference wins have declined from 13 (2010) to nine (2011) to last year's five. And each succeeding season has ended sooner, as the Cats have gone from the round of 32 (2010) to the round of 64 (2011) to a Wednesday night loss at the Big East tournament.

Going 5-13 marks the floor, surely, for a program of Villanova's caliber, and no one saw it coming. Wright's team was ranked just outside the top 25 in the preseason, and even the wary skeptics writing this chapter for last year's College Basketball Prospectus thought 'Nova would go a somewhat respectable 8-10. Instead the wheels came off in Philadelphia. What happened?

What we learned in 2012: *It's tough to foul often while rarely forcing turnovers, but if you can pull it off your defense is doomed.*

Villanova last season presented a case where the news and the problem weren't necessarily the same thing. The news was an offense that was suddenly much less effective than it had been the previous season. (An excellent year of offensive rebounding helped disguise a big increase in turnovers and a significant decrease in accuracy from the field.) Meanwhile the defense didn't change as much from year to year, but, rating out at No. 13 in the league, it was indeed the larger problem.

There are programs that don't set much store in going after steals (Connecticut certainly comes to mind), but typically such programs place an equal emphasis on avoiding fouls. Conversely Villanova experienced the worst of both worlds last season. Only Providence forced turnovers at a lower rate, yet, against the backdrop of a Big East where fewer fouls were being whistled, the Cats fouled at the third highest rate in the league.

In other words Wright's team paid the penalty for fouls—opponent free throws—but they received none of the good stuff that's supposed to arrive alongside a bunch of fouls. The Wildcats didn't block many shots and they didn't force many turnovers. It was too much for the defense to overcome.

What's in store for 2013: By signing as a free agent with the Sixers in July, Maalik Wayns achieved a rare trifecta, playing high school, college, and professional hoops all within the same city. Dominic Cheek also left early and went undrafted. Markus Kennedy transferred to play for Larry Brown at SMU.

MEET THE WILDCATS

Mouphtaou Yarou (6-10, 250, Sr.): Don't blame Yarou for Villanova's high foul rate. A capable rebounder at both ends of the floor, Yarou's shown an ability to draw many more fouls than he commits, a virtue that can pay even bigger returns if he improves his career 68 percent shooting at the line. There is one trend to fret about, however. Over the course of his career as Yarou's minutes have increased his two-point percentage has decreased, to the point where last year he hit just 47 percent of his attempts inside the arc.

JayVaughn Pinkston (6-7, 260, So.): A 2010 McDonald's All-American who sat out 2010-11 due to a code of conduct violation, Pinkston debuted last season and set a standard he should easily outperform as a sophomore. His best quality as a freshman was an ability to get the to line, though he shot just 67 percent once he got there. Beyond that there were many turnovers (seven in, incredibly, just 21 minutes against Rutgers in the Big East tournament) and a lot of missed twos (he shot 42 percent for the season).

James Bell (6-6, 225, Jr.): Bell missed three games in February due to a sprained ankle, and when he came back he was far less assertive on offense. Prior to that he had shown signs of developing into a solid wing, but if you're looking for a poster child for Villanova's foul problem you could do worse than Bell. He averaged 4.5 fouls per 40 minutes without recording any more steals or blocks than what happenstance would usually give a 6-6 player getting regular minutes.

Tony Chennault (6-2, 195, Jr.): A Wake Forest transfer who was the Demon Deacons' starter at point guard last season, Chennault was granted a hardship waiver by the NCAA and will be eligible immediately. He's a local product who nearly chose to play at Villanova originally. In two years in Winston-Salem his shooting from both sides of the arc was erratic, however he did bring his turnovers way down as a sophomore.

Maurice Sutton (6-11, 220, Sr.): Sutton cut down on his fouls drastically as a junior, but for a long while it didn't net him that much in the way of additional playing time. Then in mid-February Wright put Sutton in the starting lineup, and from that point on the big guy averaged 30 minutes a game. His best outing came in his first start, against Notre Dame, when he recorded a 12-10 double-double. If nothing else Sutton is capable of crashing the offensive glass.

Ty Johnson (6-3, 185, So.): Johnson was apparently thrown into more minutes as a freshman than he was prepared to handle. Nominally a pass-first point guard, he still recorded enough shots to uncover some very low percentages from both sides of the arc. Turnovers were also an issue.

Darrun Hilliard (6-6, 205, So.): From the start of last season up to early January, Hilliard averaged 26 minutes a game. From that point on, however, he averaged just eight minutes per contest. He shot just 21-of-72 on his threes, but decent (48 percent) if rare shooting inside the arc suggests maybe he should have tried more of those.

Achraf Yacoubou (6-4, 210, So.): Yacoubou was one of many Wildcats last season who shot more threes than twos in limited minutes without proving conclusively that such a shot distribution was a good idea.

Ryan Arcidiacono (6-3, 180, Fr.): A top-100 recruit as a point guard out of Langhorne, Pennsylvania, Arcidiacono has "the opportunity to become the next great Villanova guard." So says Wright.

Daniel Ochefu (6-11, 245, Fr.): Still another top-100 prospect, Ochefu is a Baltimore product touted for his shot blocking and rebounding.

Prospectus says: Villanova has painted themselves into a high-foul corner before only to prove they can change their hacktastic ways. In 2010-11 their foul rate was fairly normal, before ballooning again last season. I expect Wright to rein in the fouls this year, and that will be a big help for a defense that needs help. Last year the Wildcats bottomed out. This year the rebound will take them almost though not quite all the way back up to .500 in Big East play.

Big Ten

BY MIKE PORTSCHELLER AND JOSH REED

For the second consecutive season, the Big Ten was unquestionably college basketball's best conference. There are a myriad of reasons why the Midwest has become the epicenter for college hoops, but maybe the simplest explanation is that while everyone else got worse as we inch closer and closer to parity, the Big Ten managed to run in place. And while John Calipari has established Kentucky as the premier rest stop on the way to the NBA, and UCLA welcomes a class that can only be described as "unfair" this fall, as a conference no one is set up better than the Big Ten.

Sure, the addition of Nebraska probably brings the conference down a peg in terms of hoops. Lincoln has never been much of a basketball hotspot, and the state's entire population is two-thirds that of Chicago. Nonetheless, taking on the single acquisition of Nebraska dilutes things less than adding the likes of Colorado and Utah, or Miami, Virginia Tech, and Boston College.

Moreover, just as the legendary recruiting class of 2007 finally exits (almost—Trevor "Van Wilder" Mbakwe returns for his sixth season on a college campus), the Big Ten welcomes the fantastic class of 2012, which features 15 top-100 players. The influx of talent is largely driven by the reliably strong state of Indiana. The Hoosier state produced nine top-100 players in the class of 2012, seven of whom are headed to Big Ten schools.

Predictably, Indiana University did quite well for itself, securing commitments from three top-100 players, which it will add to a roster that returns the lion's share of minutes from last season's Sweet 16 team. This includes Cody Zeller, who appears to be the nation's frontrunner for the Naismith Player of the Year. And, frankly, why not? Zeller not only makes the most of his opportunities, but he also minimizes the miscues. There aren't a lot of players that shoot over 60 percent from the field, attempt two free throws for every three field goal attempts, all while being among the nation's best in terms of holding onto the basketball. Zeller was too good to be playing college basketball last year, and another year of physical maturation and better teammates is only going to make that even more obvious this season.

That isn't to say that Indiana figures to sleepwalk its way to Atlanta this coming April. What plagued Indiana last year—defense—figures to be a challenge for the Hoosiers this season as well. None of the incoming recruits are the kind of game-changing defenders along the lines of Anthony Davis, so the best shot that IU has for improving its defense figures to be the sort of marginal gains made by returning players over the offseason. Usually, that's not much, and I wouldn't expect any paradigm shifts on that end of the floor. The good news is that even just a little

MIKE AND JOSH'S 2013 STANDINGS

	2012 Record	Returning Poss (%)	Returning Min (%)	2013 Prediction
Indiana	11-7	83	78	14-4
Michigan State	13-5	59	59	12-6
Ohio State	13-5	55	63	12-6
Michigan	13-5	64	56	11-7
Wisconsin	12-6	71	76	11-7
Minnesota	6-12	84	85	11-7
Illinois	6-12	73	72	9-9
Iowa	8-10	67	65	8-10
Purdue	10-8	43	46	7-11
Northwestern	8-10	60	64	6-12
Penn State	4-14	70	63	4-14
Nebraska	4-14	23	26	2-16

improvement figures to go a long way. Keep in mind, the Hoosiers were every bit as good as Kentucky through the first 20 minutes of the two teams' Sweet 16 game. There's not a lot to fix.

Michigan State ignored all of the low preseason expectations that were written about the Spartans, and went on to win 29 games. Indeed, toward the end of the season, it was MSU that looked to be the Big Ten's best team. But then freshman phenom Branden Dawson tore his ACL in the Big Ten tournament, and it fundamentally changed how Michigan State played offense. The Spartans weren't nearly as effective on the glass, Draymond Green shouldered too much of the load, and the season ended with a 44-point effort against a stalwart Louisville defense. This season, the Spartans will start the Life After Green era, but there's still a ton of talent on the roster. Aside from Green, Austin Thornton, and Brandon Wood, the whole team comes back, and Tom Izzo might have the Big Ten's best freshman in Gary Harris.

Harris' biggest competition probably comes in the form of Wisconsin's Sam Dekker. Bo Ryan isn't known for landing blue chip recruits, but that's precisely what Dekker is. At 6-8, the athletic Dekker possesses a combo guard skillset. Think a tall Jeremy Lamb. Ryan will need Dekker to live up to his potential, because he's likely to take Jordan Taylor's spot in the starting lineup. Outside of Taylor, Wisconsin's offense was uncharacteristically terrible last season. Depending on one's outlook, that's either really bad or really good news. The glass-half-full outlook notes that there's only one direction this offense can go. The glass-half-empty view notes that Taylor was really good, and that there were still four Big Ten offenses that ranked worse than the Badgers last season. It can get worse.

The offensive end also was not kind to Michigan last year. While ranking sixth in a 12-team league isn't a badge of dishonor, remember that we're talking about a Beilein-coached team. When Beilein wins, it's supposed to be the offense that does the heavy lifting. But that hasn't been the case at Michigan. Indeed, Beilein has actually never finished higher than sixth in the Big Ten in terms of points per possession in conference play. Instead, the Wolverines have improved because the defense steadily gets better. That said, UM might be due for some regression to the mean. The 13-5 conference record the team sported last year is belied by its +0.06 efficiency margin. Even though Michigan loses only a couple of transfers from last season, and brings in arguably the best recruiting class in the Big Ten, there might not be much (if any) bottom-line improvement this season as karma evens itself out. But as long-term outlooks go, there might not be a team better positioned than the Wolverines over the next five years or so.

Last year's Big Ten consisted of a handful of elite teams (Ohio State, Michigan State, Wisconsin, and Indiana), a couple of pretty good teams (Michigan, Purdue), and then a pile of mediocre teams followed by the awful Penn State and Nebraska squads. This season's Big Ten figures to have a much murkier middle. Take Minnesota, for example. On paper the Gophers appear primed to make a jump into the contenders bracket this season. While the team loses Ralph Sampson III, it replaces him with the aforementioned Mbakwe. Other than that, all of the key pieces return.

But you could say the same things about Iowa. While the Hawkeyes lose a much bigger piece in Matt Gatens, they also have a great core of juniors to go along with the dynamic Aaron White. As good as his freshman season was, White's three-point activity suggests he's an excellent breakout candidate as a sophomore. Not only that, Iowa welcomes two top-100 players to campus this season, and one of them happens to be seven feet tall. That's a nice fit for a team that struggled with defending the paint last season.

Then there's Illinois, which begins a new era under John Groce. Groce led his Ohio Bobcats to a Sweet 16 appearance last season, and then parlayed that into a new gig in Champaign. Groce is a former Thad Matta assistant that appears to be cut from the same shooting cloth as his mentor. That's good news for an Illini team that finished dead last in the conference in three-point shooting last season. Plus, no team has more non-freshman top 100 players than the Illini, many of them sophomores. That's a good recipe for instant improvement.

But if all of these teams are getting better—in addition to the likes of Indiana and Michigan—then who is getting worse? Those extra wins have to come from somewhere, after all, and Nebraska isn't going to lose all 18. The first candidate, with plenty of wins to spare, is the team that went the deepest in the tournament last year, Ohio State. Once again Thad Matta has a roster that's among the most talented in the country. Even so, with the departures of Jared Sullinger and William Buford, one can't help but wonder if a window has been closed. And although they didn't play much, J.D. Weatherspoon and Jordan Sibert decided to take their talents elsewhere. Matta isn't one for deep benches anyway, but he only has eight players on the roster that have ever played a minute in a Buckeye uniform, and none of the new faces are of the five-star instant impact variety. Expect Ohio State to be good this season, but not much more than that.

Another candidate that figures to slide this season is Purdue. Between Robbie Hummel, Lewis Jackson, Ryne Smith, and Kelsey Barlow, the Boilermakers lose four starters from last season (Barlow was asked to leave in February). Purdue welcomes a solid batch of recruits this fall, but nothing short of a top-five class is going to prevent the Boilers from tumbling down the standings. It's a rebuild job in West Lafayette.

Northwestern is probably also rebuilding even though the only significant contributor they lose is John Shurna. But Shurna might have been the best player in school history, so he's not exactly easy to replace. While Drew Crawford figures to step into the limelight, he's going to need someone to fill the role of Robin to his Batman.

Bringing up the rear are Penn State and Nebraska. Both teams feature relatively fresh coaches that haven't spent a lot of time on a high major bench. Perhaps that inexperience is why they accepted the daunting tasks of building a program at these schools, where basketball gets the backseat treatment to the football spring game. The reality is that there probably isn't a player on either roster that will be part of the next NCAA tournament-caliber Penn State or Nebraska team. In a way, the apathy directed towards hoops on these campuses is a good thing. Collectively, the previous coaches at these schools won 32 percent of their conference games, and lasted a combined 14 seasons. Both coaches should have plenty of time to build a program while nobody is minding the store.

ILLINOIS

2012: 17-15 (6-12 Big Ten); Lost to Iowa 64-61, Big Ten first round
In-conference offense: 0.97 points per possession (10th)
In-conference defense: 1.05 points allowed per possession (6th)

What Illinois did well: *Construct a house of cards.*

It's hard to reconcile the 2012 Illinois that we know with the version of the team that existed as of January 10. On that date, the Illini improved to 15-3 after beating a top-ranked Ohio State team on the back of Brandon Paul, who poured in a historic 43 points. The only losses the team had suffered to that point happened outside of Champaign and were at the hands of formidable opponents (UNLV, Purdue, and Missouri). You would be forgiven for thinking that surely, Bruce Weber had found a way to keep his job for another season.

But even though Illinois had nine days to scout a hapless Penn State team, the Nittany Lions walked away with a two-point win thanks to Tim Frazier's floater with 8 seconds remaining. The visit to State College turned into something of a Waterloo for Weber, as the team went on a skid worse than anything the program had experienced in over a decade. The Illini lost 12 of their remaining 14 games, and by the time the team was bounced from the Big Ten tournament by an Iowa program trending in the other direction, torches and pitchforks had been brandished. In retrospect, we should have seen it coming. Since 2005, Weber is 6-7 against Penn State. Of course the Nittany Lions would be his undoing.

As is often the case, the breakup was not amicable. Even Michigan State coach Tom Izzo expressed his displeasure over Mike Thomas' handling of the situation. Still, the "it's not that I got fired, it's the way I got fired" complaint is all too similar to post-mortems one hears in junior high after a romance fizzles. As much as Weber might believe that Thomas dealt him an unfair hand, there aren't many coaches that can collect a buyout on top of landing a head coaching gig at another power conference program. This season, Weber will be paid nearly three million dollars to both coach and not coach basketball. He'll be fine.

As for Illinois, the coaching searched centered on candidates like Shaka Smart and Brad Stevens at first. There were reports that the school was willing to offer these men contracts guaranteeing in excess of $20 million. Soon after these reports surfaced, these respective coaches announced their respective intentions to remain at their respective mid-majors. Thereafter, Illinois hired John Groce.

What we learned in 2012: *If you think settling for jumpers is bad, you should see what happens when the team can't shoot.*

Illinois' incoming class of 2007 was somewhat of a mixed bag. While Demetri McCamey, Mike Tisdale, and Mike Davis were all quality players in their own right, they always seemed to fall a bit short of their collective potential. Some of that was tied up in the fact that those three individuals feasted on a diet of mid-range jump shots. Mid-range jump shots don't actually go in at a higher rate than three-pointers (in 2011, shots attempted within 6 to 19 feet were converted at a 34.8 percent clip; three-pointers were converted at a 34.6 percent rate), but they certainly count for fewer points. Otherwise, a mid-range offense offers the same pros and cons as a three-point offense: fewer turnovers, offensive rebounds, and free throws. All of which begs the question of why a team would adopt a mid-range offense instead of an offense built around three-pointers.

The good news for Illinois in 2012 is that all stopped. Once the class of 2007 left campus, the team was much more willing to take a couple steps back and attempt a three. The bad news was that this collection of players wasn't very good at making those shots. In conference play, the Illini converted under 30 percent of their long-range tries, dead last in the Big Ten. Fueled by his 8-for-10 performance against the Buckeyes, Brandon Paul led the way at 38 percent. No one else on the team reached 31 percent against conference foes.

What's more, the team didn't reap the benefits of reduced turnovers, either. Transfer Sam Maniscalco struggled with a chronic ankle injury all season, which left true freshman Tracy Abrams and shooting guard Brandon Paul carrying the load at the point guard position. Paul, for his part, performed admirably considering the circumstances. And though Abrams didn't look the part early in the season, he was a bona fide Big Ten point guard near the end of the year. Even so, the net result was far too many turnovers for the offense to stomach.

What's in store for 2013: In Weber's place comes John Groce, fresh off a Sweet 16 appearance with the Ohio Bobcats. Groce is a former Ohio State assistant who's credited with being the lead recruiter on the marquee parts of the Thad Five class of 2006. On the flipside, his Ohio teams went just 34-30 in the MAC. It's possible he'll fare no better in Champaign, but one would be wise to look beyond that MAC record. The team he built at Ohio should be even better this season. Illinois might have hired a star a year early at a significant discount. Groce inherits an Illinois roster that is largely the same as last season, with one big (literally and metaphorically) exception. Meyers Leonard moved on from being a college project to an NBA project.

MEET THE ILLINI

Brandon Paul (6-4, 200, Sr.): Even when he's at his best, Brandon Paul leaves you wanting more. When a player erupts for 43 points on 15 shots against the No. 1 team in the country, the number of turnovers that player has is rightfully relegated to the fine print. In ten years, when Illini fans reminisce on the last great moment of the Weber era, they likely will not remember that Paul's big night included seven turnovers. Groce's emphasis on shooting is likely to help Paul become a more consistent shooter, but if the combo guard is ever going to reach his potential, he's going to have to rein in the giveaways.

D.J. Richardson (6-3, 195, Sr.): It was a tale of two seasons for D.J. Richardson. That's a sentence you could have written about the shooting guard for each of his years in Champaign. Sure, Richardson won Freshman of the Year honors back in 2010, but his non-conference performance has always outshined his play against the Big Ten. Worse yet, his conference numbers are trending downward. Maybe a new coach will find what's plaguing the Peoria native every January through March. Maybe, but probably not.

Tracy Abrams (6-1, 185, So.): When it became clear that Bradley transfer Sam Maniscalco was not as healthy as the Illini hoped, Abrams was handed the starting point guard job. He wasn't ready, and it showed. The silver lining is that Abrams played much better right around the time his teammates nosedived. Perhaps that's why his peers selected him as the team's MVP, despite his alarming efficiency and usage numbers. If Illinois is going to be any good this season, Abrams has to show that last season's upward trajectory was a sign of things to come.

Joseph Bertrand (6-6, 195, Jr.): Prior to last year's matchup against Missouri, Bertrand had never played more than seven minutes against a major-conference opponent. So it was nothing short of lightning in a bottle when Bertrand made all nine of his shot attempts en route to a 19-point effort against the Tigers. Bertrand thus became a solid contributor throughout conference play, but Big Ten defenses soon figured out that the wing was reluctant to attempt shots outside of 20 feet. If Bertrand can expand his range, there's a lot of potential here.

Tyler Griffey (6-9, 220, Sr.): If you squint a little, you could make the case that last season was something of a turning point for Griffey. While he showed promise as a spot-up shooter as a freshman, he regressed severely as a sophomore. Last year, the St. Louis native shot well within the arc and even added a bit of offensive rebounding and defense to his game. Still, a power forward that only makes very occasional appearances at the free throw line is not something in high demand.

Nnanna Egwu (6-11, 235, So.): With the departure of Meyers Leonard to the NBA, Egwu is thrust into the starting lineup for a lack of alternatives. Although he wasn't very impressive in his limited minutes as a freshman, he did show some defensive ability. That said, he's only been playing basketball for a few years, and coaches all rave about his ability to pick things up quickly.

Sam McLaurin (6-8, 220, Sr.): What is it about Illinois that causes one to announce one's intention to matriculate through a profanity-laced statement of resignation? First it was Joel Goodson's "sometimes you gotta say 'what the f—-,' make your move: looks like University of Illinois!" announcement in "Risky Business." This past summer it was McLaurin's "f—- it I'm going to Illinois" tweet that announced his transfer from Coastal Carolina. Beyond providing a great slogan for a t-shirt, McLaurin is expected to rebound at both ends, dunk, and defend. From henceforth, such a player shall be referred to as an R2D2.

Prospectus says: Groce's offense appears to borrow heavily from the Matta School of Shooting. Ever since Thad showed up in Columbus, we've come to expect the Buckeyes to end up near the top of the conference in shooting accuracy. Groce's Ohio teams were similar. But there are legitimate concerns on the defensive side of the ball, notwithstanding the fact that the Bobcats were the very best defense in the MAC last season. It's the way they did it that is concerning. Ohio forced turnovers on over a quarter of opponents' possessions. This wasn't just a blip, either. This is a consistent theme with Groce's teams. That all sounds good, except for the fact that it definitely will not work in the Big Ten. Big Ten offenses do not turn the ball over. A defense predicated on denying this truth is not going to be successful, especially when all of this turnover-forcing comes at the expense of rebounding (a reliably weak area of Groce's teams). Thus, I think Groce is going to have to change his approach in the Big Ten. How well he does that will determine whether this roster plays to its potential.

INDIANA

2012: 27-9 (11-7 Big Ten); Lost to Kentucky 102-90, Sweet 16
In-conference offense: 1.11 points per possession (1st)
In-conference defense: 1.06 points allowed per possession (7th)

What Indiana did well: *Make it rain.*

It was both accurate and inaccurate to say that Indiana was a team that relied on three-pointers last season. Certainly, the public perception was that the Hoosiers' strength was outside shooting, and it's hard to quibble with that. On the year, Indiana shot just over 43 percent from three-point range, which amazingly was just second in the country (Northern Colorado's 45.1 percent mark was a record in the tempo-free era). But for all its shooting acumen, Indiana did not rely on those outside shots, devoting a paltry 27.5 percent of its attempts to threes. So in that respect, the Hoosiers did not rely on shots from outside of 20 feet.

But what happens to the Hoosier offense if we take away that three-point skill? The rest of the Big Ten shot a hair over 34 percent from long range—what if the Hoosiers shot at that accuracy instead?

That's still a very good offense, but not a great one (see table). Instead of sitting atop the Big Ten in offensive efficiency, the Hoosiers would rank just sixth.

And therein lies one half of the cold water to be found in previewing Indiana in 2013. Just about every preseason ranking you'll find is going to put IU as one of the top 3 teams in the nation this season. A Hoosier cynic might point to the otherworldly shooting put on by the 2012 squad, and confidently predict that the 2013 team won't match it. And they would be almost certainly correct.

Since 2004 there have been 16 major-conference teams that have shot better than 40 percent on their threes for the season, and all 16 of those teams saw their accuracy from beyond the arc drop the next year. For the most part, that drop was more than a couple of percentage points (the average decline is about five percentage points). So if you find yourself with the opportunity to place a prop bet on whether IU can repeat its three-point accuracy, you have found yourself some easy money.

But this doesn't mean the Indiana offense has to slow down. As mentioned above, the Hoosiers were extremely selective in the three-pointers they attempted last season. Even if that percentage drops significantly, there's a long way to go before the team hits average. Even if Indiana has to "settle" for making just 37 percent of its threes, that's still plenty good to power a great offense.

What we learned in 2012: *Defense is still a problem.*

There's no denying that the Hoosiers were a ton of fun to watch last season. Not only could the team shoot, but it was also not afraid to get itself into a track meet. Against Iowa, Indiana rung up 103 points in a 74-possession affair. Against the greatest defense in the country, and eventual national champion Kentucky, IU put up 90 points, easily the most that Calipari's team allowed all season.

Lost in those two anecdotes, however, is the fact that the Hoosiers also allowed 89 points to Iowa, and 102 to Kentucky. Then there were the 82 points rung up by Penn State, or the 79 points scored by plodding Wisconsin.

All of which is to say that the defense is still a work in progress. Much of the blame lies in the backcourt, where the likes of Verdell Jones, Jordan Hulls, and especially Matt Roth were all too easily beaten off the dribble. But there's plenty of blame to be found in

2012 INDIANA OFFENSE

	Three-Point Percentage	Offensive Efficiency
Actual 2012 Indiana	41.4	1.11
Hypothetical 2012 Indiana	34.3	1.07
Conference games only		

the frontcourt as well, where freshman Cody Zeller didn't have the bulk to be an elite rebounder, and he's not a natural shot blocker, either. Add to that the fact that the team fouled all too frequently (though not at the karate-inspired rates of years past), and you have a mediocre defense.

What's more, it's hard to see where the gains on defense will come from. One hopes Zeller's increased bulk will result in better rebounding, and maybe that's true. His best rebounding games came against Iowa, Michigan, Minnesota, and Northwestern—not exactly a murderer's row of imposing front lines. But even assuming Zeller becomes a solid rebounder, there are still plenty of other holes. Although Jones is gone, in his place steps 6-0 Yogi Ferrell. The freshman is a McDonald's All-American and figures to end up on a First Team or two before his time in Bloomington is up, but it's hard to expect any freshman, let alone one listed so suddenly and improbably as 6-0, to provide a significant defensive boost. Hulls will get his minutes, of course, though it appears Roth won't play for the Hoosiers this year (he still has a year remaining, but Indiana doesn't have a scholarship for him). Those are good steps, but they might not be enough. For Indiana to fulfill its promise in 2013, the defense needs to make some real strides.

What's in store for 2013: Gone are Jones, Roth, and Tom Pritchard. In comes the best recruiting class in recent memory, as well as the oft-injured Maurice Creek. You'd be forgiven for treating Creek as an afterthought, but back in the 2009-2010 season, there might not have been a better player (let alone freshman) in the Big Ten. But after 12 games, Creek missed the rest of the season with a knee injury. The next year, he was starting to round back into form when he suffered another season-ending knee injury. And last year, he missed the entire season with a ruptured achilles heel. When you read sentences that start out "if Creek can stay healthy," keep in mind just how massively huge that "if" really is.

MEET THE HOOSIERS

Cody Zeller (7-0, 240, So.): It's not often that a seven-foot freshman can start for a Big Ten team, shoot over 60 percent from the field, play defense, attempt over two hundred free throws, and turn it over on fewer than ten percent of his possessions. It's unheard of for a seven-foot freshman to do all that, and then come back to school for his sophomore season. The only real hole in Zeller's game, and I mean that in a relative sense, is his rebounding. In Big Ten play, the big man grabbed under 16 percent of the opponent's missed shots during his minutes. His improvement on the defensive glass is the lowest hanging fruit for improving the Hoosiers' defense.

Christian Watford (6-9, 230, Sr.): Maddening. That would be the word I'd use to describe Watford. Sure, he's a great player. And normally, NBA scouts would be salivating over a long, 6-9 forward that rebounds, gets to the line, makes his free throws, and can shoot over 40 percent from three-point range. But despite his size and touch, Watford converts two-pointers like he's under 6-0. After three years of watching him botch interior opportunities, it's probably time to concede that he probably is not going to suddenly dominate the paint. And that's fine. As it is, he's good enough to be All-Big Ten.

Victor Oladipo (6-5, 215, Jr.): Considering how terribly he shot last season, Oladipo had a spectacular season. His 14 percent three-point accuracy against conference opponents dragged his effective field goal percentage to just under 46, but everywhere else he was great. This includes defense, as he was not only easily the best defender on IU but also one of the best in the Big Ten. Oladipo's struggles from the field coincided with a massive improvement at the free throw line, so he's bound to put it all together sooner rather than later.

Jordan Hulls (6-0, 180, Sr.): Hulls presents a bit of a conundrum for Tom Crean this season. Offensively, he possesses deadly accuracy that's always in demand. But he's also one of the worst defenders in the conference on a team that needs to improve its defense in order to make any real strides. Moreover, if Hulls were to play alongside newcomer Yogi Ferrell, the Hoosiers would not have a lot of options for guarding bigger backcourts. Whether Crean trades offense for defense probably depends on how well Hulls' teammates shoot this season.

Yogi Ferrell (6-0, 180, Fr.): Ferrell headlines one of the best recruiting classes in the country, and should start immediately. He earns high marks for his quickness, distribution, and basketball acumen. That said, we're still talking about a freshman point guard. Outside of a precious few, most incoming floor generals will at least exhibit higher turnover numbers. The good news is that with so many weapons around him, Ferrell won't be asked to do too much. As long as he doesn't bite off more than he can chew, he should have a very good season.

Will Sheehey (6-7, 200, Jr.): It's hard to define Sheehey's role on the team largely because he's a jack of all trades, but a master of none. While he's an adequate two-point scorer, he doesn't frequent the line enough to be deadly on the interior. And while his perimeter shot was excellent last season, he's unlikely to repeat his 45 percent accuracy from three-point range in Big Ten play. He's not a skilled ball handler, and frankly a mediocre defender. On just about any other team he's a sure-fire starter. At Indiana, he's in danger of getting lost in the shuffle.

Hanner Perea (6-8, 225, Fr.): Perea was the centerpiece of an ESPN investigative piece surrounding his AAU team's relationship with the Indiana University coaching staff, and possible impermissible benefits. Like so many allegations of this nature, not much has happened to suggest anything will come of it. Assuming he's eligible, Perea is an athletic power forward whose defense is probably a bit ahead of his offense at this point.

Maurice Creek (6-5, 195, Jr.): As good as Indiana should be this season, there's a good chance that one of its best players won't have much of an impact. After suffering two severe knee injuries and then a torn Achilles last year, it's probably too much to expect Creek to stay on the floor for very long.

Prospectus says: Not only is there talent on the roster, but all of the pieces fit together. This team isn't missing anything at any position, except maybe defense. But the offense should be explosive enough to make IU one of the top teams in the Big Ten, one that will at least challenge for the conference title. The open question is whether the Hoosiers can defend well enough to move into the conversation for the national championship. But the fact that we're talking about whether or not Indiana can hang a sixth banner at Assembly Hall, a mere four years after the program imploded, is absolutely remarkable.

IOWA

2012: 18-17 (8-10 Big Ten); Lost to Oregon 108-97, NIT second round
In-conference offense: 1.03 points per possession (7th)
In-conference defense: 1.09 points allowed per possession (8th)

What Iowa did well: *Run, run, run…relatively speaking.*

Two seasons ago, Fran McCaffery came to Iowa City promising an energetic, up-tempo attack. He certainly had the track record at Siena to back it up, but fans could be forgiven for being skeptical. After all, "we're going to run" is about as cliché as it gets for college basketball coaches, and the Big Ten is not an easy conference in which to push the pace.

To this point, McCaffery has kept his promise. Iowa has become the Big Ten's fastest team. Granted, in this, the nation's second-slowest conference, that's a bit like being the best Jamaican bobsledder, but McCaffery's Hawkeyes have managed to drag the occasional Big Ten opponent into—gasp!—the neighborhood of 70 possessions. Not that a faster tempo guaranteed success for Iowa last season:

- 60-64 possessions: 7-4
- 65-69 possessions: 5-6
- 70+ possessions: 6-7

At first glance it looks like the Hawkeyes are actually better at a slower pace, though it should be noted that no one team can singlehandedly dictate a game's pace. It takes two to tango. Still, the Hawkeyes had great success against the conference's two slowest teams, going a combined 3-0 against Wisconsin and Michigan in games that weren't particularly fast. These are teams that otherwise lost only eight games total to non-Iowa conference foes. Perhaps McCaffery is onto something here as he goes against the grain.

What we learned in 2012: *You don't have to play slow to avoid turnovers.*

When Todd Lickliter was hired in 2007, the assumption was that his slow-paced, turnover-averse offensive attack that had worked so well at Butler would be a natural fit in the Big Ten. While the Hawkeyes did play at an exceedingly slow pace under Lickliter, they just couldn't stop turning the ball over, and the result was an offense that never quite got off the ground. In McCaffery's second season, conversely, turnovers were much less of a problem even at a faster pace. There's something to be said for getting off a quick shot instead of passing it around for an eventual turnover.

What's in store for 2013: Iowa is poised to be an improved team this season, but that may not show up in the Hawkeyes' conference record. The truth is that Iowa's efficiency margin didn't match up with their 8-10 Big Ten mark. The Hawkeyes' per-possession performance was actually worse than that of 6-12 Minnesota. With that in mind, projections of an NCAA tournament bid could be one season premature. This is still a young team, with lone scholarship senior Eric May likely playing a role off the bench.

The question for Iowa will remain its defense. Iowa was one of the shortest teams in the conference last season, and it showed in their poor two-point defense and rebounding. Opponents too often had their way inside. The addition of 7-1 freshman Adam Woodbury should help some, but it's more likely that the defense improves through forcing more turnovers. McCaffery's last three Siena squads, which all went to the NCAA tournament, were quite good at forcing turnovers without fouling. We saw some of that quality in McCaffery's first season at Iowa, but both areas regressed in year two. If the Hawkeyes are to compete for an NCAA tournament bid, they'll have to find a way to improve on the defensive end.

MEET THE HAWKEYES

Roy Devyn Marble (6-6, 195, Jr.): The son of Iowa's all-time leading scorer made big strides in his sophomore season, and his assist and turnover rates suggest that he could take over as the Hawkeyes' full-time point guard now that Bryce Cartwright has moved on. Marble still isn't a perimeter threat—he's a career 27 percent three-point shooter in Big Ten play—but he's adept at picking up points at the foul line and setting up others. His size and athleticism also allow him to be one of Iowa's better defenders. Further improvement can be expected.

Aaron White (6-8, 220, So.): It's safe to say White's freshman campaign was a huge surprise. The under-recruited Ohio native chose Iowa over programs like Duquesne, Boston College, Temple, and St. Bonaventure, so it's not like high-major coaches were beating down his door. Still, the active big man produced like a blue-chip recruit, leading the Big Ten in free throw rate and displaying a nice shooting touch in the process. While White's impressive freshman campaign creates the possibility of a sophomore slump, his three-point confidence suggests he's prepared to take a leap forward. Iowa appears to have a building block in place at the 4.

Zach McCabe (6-7, 235, Jr.): As a freshman, McCabe was basically a specialist, taking over half of his conference shots from beyond the arc. The result was a miserable level of production, as he shot only 18 percent on those threes. As a sophomore, McCabe made a concerted effort to get closer to the rim, and it paid big dividends in the form of better shooting, more free throws, and more offensive rebounds. Even with those improvements, McCabe still had foul and turnover problems, and those are the areas in which he'll need to improve to keep his spot in the lineup.

Melsahn Basabe (6-7, 220, Jr.): Let's face it, Basabe's sophomore campaign was a big disappointment. After a fantastic freshman season, the Glen Cove, New York native regressed in nearly every way. His two-point percentage dropped from 58 percent to 53, his free throw shooting went from a strength to a weakness, he grabbed fewer rebounds, and he turned it over more often. Still, even with all that regression, Basabe wasn't a bad player, and there's hope that he can regain the levels of production he achieved as a freshman. If not, he could find himself coming off the bench again.

Josh Oglesby (6-5, 200, So.): Oglesby showed his potential as a turnover-averse three-point specialist last season, but he did most of his damage during Iowa's soft non-conference schedule. He shot 45 percent from three against non-conference opponents, compared to just 29 percent in Big Ten games. It's safe to say that Oglesby will land somewhere in between as a sophomore, assuming his defense is adequate enough to keep him on the floor.

Eric May (6-5, 220, Sr.): As Iowa's lone scholarship senior, May is something of an enigma. His freshman season under Lickliter was promising enough, as he held his own while starting every Big Ten game. Each season since has been worse for May, with only his defense emerging as a real strength. Here's his last chance to figure it out.

Mike Gesell (6-1, 185, Fr.): If Marble doesn't seize the point guard role, Gesell could very well find himself starting as a freshman. Ranked No. 88 by RSCI, the Nebraska native has been described as a scoring point guard with a high motor.

Adam Woodbury (7-1, 235, Fr.): As Gesell's AAU teammate, this lanky lefty impressed enough to be rated No. 42 by RSCI. Woodbury isn't a plus athlete, but he's not afraid to mix it up inside. On a team with undersized post players, he'll see minutes, but they will likely come behind White, Basabe, and McCabe.

Prospectus says: At times last season, Iowa's offense was mighty impressive, and that was especially true in March. The loss of Gatens is a big one—he shot a ridiculous 48 percent on his threes in conference play—but the pieces are in place for a good offensive attack. With the team's reluctance to launch threes likely to get even more extreme without Gatens, it will be of the utmost importance to get to the foul line and keep the turnovers under control. This young team figures to alternately excite and frustrate Iowa fans, and a true NCAA tournament contender is probably a season away.

MICHIGAN

2012: 24-10 (13-5 Big Ten); Lost to Ohio 65-60, NCAA round of 64
In-conference offense: 1.06 points per possession (6th)
In-conference defense: 1.01 points allowed per possession (4th)

What Michigan did well: *Play Beilein Ball, with some wrinkles.*

There are a few things you can confidently predict about a team coached by John Beilein. They will play slow. They will shoot lots of threes. They will take good care of the ball. Offensive rebounds and free throws will not be weapons.

All of these things held true for Michigan last season, but it should be noted that this is no longer the same offense that Beilein brought with him from West Virginia. After a shift midway through 2010-11, Michigan now relies heavily on ball screens, a concept that would have seemed quite foreign to Beilein's first few Wolverine squads. The shift in philosophy worked wonders for Darius Morris, who then opted for the NBA, and we watched Trey Burke thrive as a freshman last season.

Unfortunately, the Wolverines ran into a buzz-saw in the NCAA tournament, succumbing to the hot shooting of John Groce's Ohio Bobcats. Still, the season as a whole was yet another validation of Beilein's coaching acumen, which should keep Michigan in the upper half of the Big Ten for quite some time.

What we learned in 2012: *Michigan recruits don't have to be highly touted to make an immediate impact.*

A season after Tim Hardaway Jr. exploded onto the scene, Trey Burke became the latest Michigan freshman to surprise with an all-conference type season. Burke wasn't exactly unknown as a recruit, but his offer list was littered with mid-majors and downtrodden high majors. There certainly was no inkling that Burke could be the leader of a Big Ten champion as a freshman.

Beilein has shown himself to be a keen evaluator of talent, but something must also be said for the structure that his offensive system gives to young players. In just the past two seasons, Michigan has hatched impressive debuts for Hardaway, Burke, and Jordan Morgan, with none of those players ranking in the RSCI top 100. Clearly, a combination of talent evaluation and fit-to-system allows freshmen to thrive early under Beilein.

What's in store for 2013: If Beilein can do so well with under-the-radar recruits, what happens when he lands the big dogs? That question will be answered this season, as Michigan welcomes a highly regarded freshman class. This season's freshmen are important, because the Wolverines lose a sizable chunk of last season's team, including Evan Smotrycz and stalwarts Zack Novak and Stu Douglass. It feels like those losses are being understated nationally, as many prognosticators have the Wolverines in their preseason top 10. This is a team that went just seven deep, and three of those seven are now gone. While the freshmen assuming these spots are clearly more talented, it may prove difficult for them to be more productive.

MEET THE WOLVERINES

Trey Burke (6-0, 190, So.): After seriously considering a jump to the NBA, Burke is back for his sophomore campaign. He has all the statistical excellence you look for in a point guard, but an underrated part of his game is his patience and control. When you watch Michigan play, keep an eye on how Burke uses ball screens. It's a bit of a lost art, but Burke is a master at positioning his body and being patient enough for the screener to arrive. It's a crucial part of the Michigan offense.

Tim Hardaway Jr. (6-6, 205, Jr.): Hardaway's sophomore campaign was seen as a disappointment after his impressive first season. While that's a fair assessment, it should be noted that Hardaway's numbers were nearly unchanged across the board save for three-point shooting. As a freshman, Hardaway hit a sizzling 44 percent from deep, which is probably a bit over his true ability. Some regression to the mean should have been expected, but that number crashed to 26 percent last season. Everything else was the same or slightly better, as Hardaway went from 49 percent to 52 percent on twos and increased his free throw rate. The smart bet here is that Hardaway settles in to a more normal three-point percentage and gets back to being an efficient scorer.

Jordan Morgan (6-8, 250, Jr.): This cerebral 22-year-old does the dirty work for Michigan, setting picks, grabbing rebounds, and generally only shooting within five feet of the tin. Morgan does all of these things quite well, and he's spent his entire career among the Big Ten's field goal percentage leaders.

Glenn Robinson III (6-6, 210, Fr.): The Big Dog's son is the highest rated of Michigan's incoming freshmen, clocking in at No. 23 according to RSCI. Robinson figures to start on the wing out of the gate, and he should provide a third scoring option after Burke and Hardaway.

Mitch McGary (6-10, 250, Fr.): McGary is ranked No. 26 by RSCI, and the big lefty should take over Smotrycz's minutes right away. McGary's already 20 years old, just a few months younger than a veteran like Hardaway, so he should be ready physically.

Matt Vogrich (6-4, 200, Sr.): His low usage rate tends to make him overlooked, but Vogrich is superb in his role. The Illinois native comes off the bench, plays solid defense, and knocks down open threes with aplomb. You're unlikely to see him shoot a free throw or commit a turnover. In 184 Big Ten minutes last season, Vogrich collected only two of each.

Nik Stauskas (6-6, 190, Fr.): This Canadian newcomer checks in at No. 78 on RSCI and brings a reputation as an outstanding shooter. With Novak and Douglass gone, there figure to be plenty of open looks available for Stauskas.

Prospectus says: If Michigan does fail to live up to this season's lofty expectations, the future will still be bright. Only one senior figures to play meaningful minutes this season, and another batch of top-100 recruits is set to arrive in Ann Arbor in 2013. The Wolverines should be a factor in the Big Ten race for the foreseeable future, even if they fall short of their sky-high expectations this season.

MICHIGAN STATE

2012: 29-8 (13-5 Big Ten); Lost to Louisville 57-44, Sweet 16
In-conference offense: 1.08 points per possession (4th)
In-conference defense: 0.92 points allowed per possession (1st)

What Michigan State did well: *Defense and Draymond.*

The Spartans entered last season unranked in both polls. Kalin Lucas, Durrell Summers, and Delvon Roe were gone from a squad that had stumbled to a round of 64 exit against UCLA the season before. It's safe to say that preseason expectations were lower in East Lansing than they'd been in awhile.

Draymond Green didn't get the memo. With the finest statistical season in all of college basketball, Green carried the Spartans to a Big Ten title, a No. 1 seed in the NCAA tournament, and a Sweet 16 berth. While Green's offensive contributions were obvious and well-lauded, his defensive excellence was often overlooked. Green was the Big Ten's leading rebounder and posted robust steal and block rates, spearheading one of the best defenses in the land. It could even be argued that this was Tom Izzo's best defense ever—heady praise in a program that has seen more than its fair share of great defenses.

What we learned in 2012: *Hot shooting can only last so long.*

When Branden Dawson tore his ACL in the final game of the regular season, there was immediate concern about what his absence would mean on the defensive end of the court. That was a reasonable concern: Dawson is indeed an excellent defender with a combination of size and athleticism that allows him to guard multiple positions. But an overlooked impact arose on the offensive glass. Dawson had been the Big Ten's best offensive rebounder, and Michigan State's offense has long relied heavily on second chances. Could the Spartans score enough without Dawson's ball retrieval skills?

At first, the answer was yes. The Spartan offense tore through the Big Ten tournament and the first weekend of the NCAA tournament, producing the team's best offensive stretch of the season. The second chances had indeed dried up, but that didn't matter with MSU shooting the ball so well. In that five-game stretch, the lowest effective field goal percentage posted by Michigan State was a sizzling 57. After making 35 percent of their threes in the regular season, the Spartans were connecting on 45 percent of them.

Then came the Sweet 16 matchup against Louisville. Izzo's team was ice cold from the field, and the Spartans couldn't get second chances despite facing a poor rebounding team. It was a painful end to Green's career, and you have to wonder if Dawson's presence on the offensive glass would have made a difference.

What's in store for 2013: Green is obviously a huge loss, and Michigan State also loses two solid role players in Brandon Wood and Austin Thornton. Consequently, there are only six returnees that played meaningful minutes last season, and one of them is the recovering Dawson. Izzo will be forced to rely on his incoming freshmen for depth early, which in the case of Gary Harris is not a bad thing at all. This will be a younger squad, with only one senior and two juniors in the rotation, but it is still supremely talented. Another Big Ten title is not out of the question.

MEET THE SPARTANS

Keith Appling (6-1, 190, Jr.): Appling became more of a point guard last season, though it could be argued that he shared that role with Green. The Detroit native became a real force going to the basket, and he consequently shot 51 percent on twos and scored a larger share of his points from the free throw line than any other Big Ten player. Appling still has plenty of room to grow: his three-point shot often looked broken, and his turnovers were still high. If he can get those areas shored up, Appling could be a dark horse contender for Big Ten player of the year.

Branden Dawson (6-6, 230, So.): Dawson's strengths as a freshman were offensive rebounding and active defense. His recovery from the ACL injury will be interesting to watch, as his game relied heavily on quickness and athleticism. Without an offseason to improve his skills, Dawson may not make the same leap we often expect from sophomores.

Gary Harris (6-4, 205, Fr.): This McDonald's All-American from Indianapolis should start from day one and is a clear contender for Big Ten freshman of the year. Harris has a reputation as a strong and athletic wing, and his playmaking will be needed to help cover for the loss of Green.

Adreian Payne (6-10, 240, Jr.): Payne is the more defensive-minded of the team's two centers, but he's no slouch when it comes to finishing inside. Fewer shots from outside the lane would serve Payne and his team well, though he did show an improved touch at the foul line last season.

Derrick Nix (6-9, 270, Sr.): Nix is a player that knows his strengths, and he's developed into one of the better post scorers in the conference. He shot 55 percent on a fairly heavy shot diet yet didn't go to the free throw line much. That's likely due to some laudable foul avoidance from the career 48 percent foul shooter.

Travis Trice (6-0, 170, So.): Despite his small size, Trice played more like a shooting specialist than a point guard in his freshman campaign. The Ohio native struggled with that role in conference play, shooting just 28 percent on threes, but his success from out there in all other games (47 percent) was encouraging. Expect more playmaking his second time around.

Denzel Valentine (6-5, 220, Fr.): Valentine is already garnering Draymond Green comparisons due to his playmaking ability and intangibles, and there are some that feel Valentine could make an early splash in the rotation as a big point guard. Those expectations could be a bit lofty for the Lansing native, but backcourt minutes are available.

Prospectus says: Tom Izzo himself has called his scheduling "insane," and this season's opening slate might top them all. The Spartans open against Connecticut on an air base in Germany, then they face Kansas in Atlanta just four days later. Given the unusual travel circumstances, it may be hard to draw any conclusions from these two games, but they sure make for a unique start. I expect the 2018 Spartans will open the season against the Lithuanian National Team in a game played on an oil tanker floating in the Arctic Sea.

MINNESOTA

2012: 23-15 (6-12 Big Ten); Lost to Stanford 75-51, NIT title game
In-conference offense: 1.00 points per possession (9th)
In-conference defense: 1.04 points allowed per possession (5th)

What Minnesota did well: *Break in the youngsters.*

When Trevor Mbakwe went down in late November with a torn ACL, the tone of the season changed for Minnesota. Many observers felt the Golden Gophers would be a pushover without their dominant big man, as what remained was mostly unproven young players. They took their lumps during conference play, losing a multitude of close games, but the Gophers finished the season strong with an impressive run to the NIT title game.

Along the way, potential stars emerged. Rodney Williams finally found his niche as an athletic power forward. Andre Hollins impressed as an aggressive freshman. Julian Welch and Austin Hollins emerged as solid backcourt options. In Mbakwe's absence, Minnesota found some building blocks, and the experience bestowed upon those young players sets the team up well for Mbakwe's return.

What we learned in 2012: *Turnovers can destroy an otherwise solid offense.*

With an inexperienced backcourt comes turnovers, and it was no different for Minnesota's young guards. The Gophers were quite good on the offensive glass and earned a steady stream of free throws, but they simply coughed the ball up too often. The hope is that another season of development will help in that regard, but Minnesota has never been all that careful with the ball under Tubby Smith. Anyway, with Mbakwe's put-backs and free throws rejoining the fray, a dip in turnover rate could be all that's needed to turn this into one of the Big Ten's better offenses.

What's in store for 2013: Minnesota returns the most minutes in the Big Ten, and the Gophers also welcome back the most freshman-to-sophomore minutes. These are both big positive indicators, and that's without factoring in the return of Mbakwe. Simply put, this could be the best Minnesota team of the Tubby Smith era, and the NCAA tournament should be the goal.

MEET THE GOLDEN GOPHERS

Trevor Mbakwe (6-8, 245, Sr.): Mbakwe will turn 24 this season, his fourth at Minnesota. Despite all that time on campus, he's played a grand total of 18 Big Ten games, in which he was a dominant defender and wreaked havoc on the interior. If Mbakwe can stay on the court, he's an all-conference player, but his college career could easily be over with one more legal slip-up. If Minnesota loses Mbakwe, the Gophers look a lot more like a bubble team than a top-25 contender.

Andre Hollins (6-1, 200, So.): Hollins put up an impressive season for a freshman ranked outside of the RSCI top 100. He displayed a soft shooting touch (92 percent on free throws, 38 percent on threes) and an ability to make plays going to the basket. Hollins struggled early in conference play, but by the end of the season he had become the focal point of the offense: Hollins averaged 17 points per game in the postseason. Expect big things in his second time around.

Rodney Williams (6-7, 200, Sr.): Williams was something of a disappointment in his first two seasons as a Gopher. As a highly rated freshman, he didn't get a lot of tick, then as a sophomore he displayed very little beyond some amazing dunks. Last season, Williams blossomed, and it came from focusing more of his efforts on the interior. Williams shot 58 percent on twos and posted career-best rebounding rates. He still struggled from the perimeter, making just 26 percent of his Big Ten three attempts, but at least he had the good sense to hoist fewer of those deep shots.

Julian Welch (6-3, 195, Sr.): This accurate shooter functioned as Minnesota's point guard until a February hip pointer took him out for a few games. It was in his brief absence that Andre Hollins took the reins of the offense, and Welch was relegated to more of a spot-up role when he returned. Still, this is a team that really needs Welch's outside shooting, so he'll remain a big part of the rotation.

Austin Hollins (6-4, 185, Jr.): While Austin is no relation to Andre Hollins, he also hails from the Memphis area and also became an indispensible part of the team as the season wore on. The elder Hollins made big strides with his perimeter shooting, though he remained a bit turnover-prone.

Joe Coleman (6-4, 200, So.): Early in conference play, it was Coleman that looked like Minnesota's most promising freshman, averaging 14 points over a six-game span. His role then diminished a bit, and he ended up with some woeful shooting numbers. Still, there's much to like about this athletic slasher, who can bring value with his defense and ability to get to the foul line.

Elliott Eliason (6-11, 260, So.): After a redshirt season, it was a successful debut for this true center from Nebraska. Eliason came off the bench in every Big Ten game, grabbing a large share of rebounds and showing great shot blocking potential in the process. He's not much of an offensive threat, but Eliason should continue to provide good backup minutes inside.

Maurice Walker (6-10, 290, So.): This large and talented Canadian has only been healthy enough to play in 12 games in his two years at Minnesota, all coming at the start of his true freshman campaign. He showed enough promise in that non-conference stint to include him in this preview. Walker is a versatile big man that can do a little bit of everything on the court. If his surgically repaired knee holds up, he could be a valuable member of this team.

Prospectus says: Minnesota's NIT run is more impressive when you consider that not a single game was played in Minneapolis. The Gophers won on the home floor of three solid teams—LaSalle, Miami, and Middle Tennessee—to reach Madison Square Garden. That experience should serve Minnesota well this season, as the team aims for the first single-digit NCAA tournament seed of the Tubby Smith era.

NEBRASKA

2012: 12-18 (4-14 Big Ten); Lost to Purdue 79-61, Big Ten first round
In-conference offense: 0.93 points per possession (12th)
In-conference defense: 1.09 points allowed per possession (10th)

What Nebraska did well: *When healthy, defend.*

There weren't many positives for Nebraska last season, but there were stretches where the Cornhuskers actually defended well. The obvious highlight was the mid-January stretch that produced an upset of Indiana, but this was also a solid defensive team early in the season. Those stretches of good defense correlated strongly with the availability of center Jorge Brian Diaz, which makes sense given his size, experience, and shot blocking ability.

When Diaz was out, the defense was no longer good enough to keep Nebraska in games, and the offense certainly wasn't going to carry the team. The resulting tailspin saw the Huskers lose nine of their final 10 games, and the writing was on the wall for coach Doc Sadler's dismissal.

What we learned in 2012: *Opponent three-point percentage can be a cruel lottery.*

Recent research has indicated that most defenses have very little control over an opponent's three-point percentage. That tidbit is especially important to defenses like the one deployed by Sadler at Nebraska, where his teams focused their defensive energies inside the arc. When things go well, you defend twos like mad, control the glass, and don't get hurt too badly by all the threes. That's how it went for the Huskers in 2010-11, when they held their own in the Big 12 on the strength of their defense.

Last season, the whole thing fell apart. There were problems all over the court, but one of the reasons for the poor defensive results was an uptick in opponents' three-point percentages. Nebraska could have done better in other areas to cover for this, but all the made threes were the straw that broke the camel's back.

What's in store for 2013: Sadler has been replaced by Tim Miles, who now has a complete rebuild on his hands. The encouraging news is that Miles started in a similar situation at Colorado State and was able to build an at-large tournament team by his fifth season. Similar patience will be required here, as the roster offers very little in the form of either immediate help or building blocks for the future. This isn't 2008-09 Indiana, but it's close, and without the prestige and recruiting base that Tom Crean had to work with. Miles has a tall task ahead of him.

MEET THE CORNHUSKERS

Dylan Talley (6-5, 215, Sr.): A season after providing scoring off the bench, Talley now becomes the team's main man. The New Jersey native has a solid outside stroke, but he's also got the size and athleticism to diversify his game. Given the roster surrounding him, Talley will have no shortage of opportunities.

Brandon Ubel (6-10, 235, Sr.): The team's lone returning starter, Ubel brings a mid-range jump shot and a willingness to hit the offensive glass. For a player with such a nice stroke (80 percent career on free throws), Ubel doesn't look for his own as much as he should.

Andre Almeida (6-11, 315, Sr.): The big Brazilian had a decent junior season off the bench, then redshirted last year while recovering from a knee injury. If he can stay healthy and in shape, his rebounding and shot blocking will come in handy.

Benny Parker (5-9, 165, Fr.): Kansas City product Parker originally committed to play for Doc Sadler, selecting Nebraska over offers from Creighton, Indiana State, and Murray State (among others). Parker is known for aggressive on-ball defense, and his point guard skills should get him plenty of playing time on a team that features few perimeter options.

Shavon Shields (6-6, 215, Fr.): Shields also hails from the Kansas City area, and his scoring ability will be called upon immediately. Like Parker, Shields stuck with his commitment after Miles came on, as he had originally chosen Nebraska over Long Beach State, Weber State, and Wyoming.

Sergej Vucetic (7-1, 235, Fr.): Vucetic will become the first seven-footer to play for Nebraska in over 20 years. The big lefty from Serbia garnered scholarship offers from programs like Minnesota, Vanderbilt, and Georgia Tech, so Miles wasn't the only high-major coach that took a liking to him.

Ray Gallegos (6-2, 180, Jr.): After getting semi-regular minutes as a freshman and sophomore, Gallegos took a redshirt last season to work on his game. That was likely a good decision, as he had struggled in nearly all phases. Gallegos has no real history of point guard play, but he may be forced into the role when Parker is off the floor.

Prospectus says: There are a few things we can glean from Miles' time at Colorado State. For one, whether by design or necessity, he recruited very little size, and last season's Rams featured no regular player taller than 6-6. This group was surprisingly competent on the defensive glass, but they won games with their offense. Accurate shooting and lots of free throws were the main drivers of Colorado State's success, and both of those things were sorely lacking in Lincoln last season. It will take time for Miles to mold the program into something of his liking, and this first season could be ugly.

NORTHWESTERN

2012: 19-14 (8-10 Big Ten); Lost to Washington 76-55, NIT second round
In-conference offense: 1.08 points per possession (5th)
In-conference defense: 1.12 points allowed per possession (12th)

What Northwestern did well: *Be Northwestern.*

There are a few things you can really count on in the Big Ten, and one of them is that Northwestern will play slow, score efficiently, and defend terribly. The numbers are incredibly consistent from season to season, and the result is a team that's regularly competitive but just not quite good enough to make the NCAA tournament. It's a real shame that John Shurna, one of the most productive scorers in the nation over the past four seasons, never got to play in the Big Dance, and now the Wildcats have to move on without him.

What we learned in 2012: *Bill Carmody is the greatest coach Northwestern has ever had.*

There's really not much argument about this point. Carmody has kept the Wildcats competitive in the Big Ten for four straight seasons, which in itself is an accomplishment given the program's history and academic standards. Still, fans have to wonder if this past season, in which Northwestern came somewhat close but still wasn't the first team left out of the NCAA tournament, is as good as it can get under Carmody. You certainly don't expect a team to lose a player of Shurna's caliber and get better, so there was some serious discussion after the season as to whether Carmody deserved to get another crack.

In late March, Northwestern AD Jim Phillips announced that Carmody would indeed return for this, his 13th season, but stressed that the on-court results are not satisfying. If things don't go well in 2012-13, Carmody's seat could start to get hot.

What's in store for 2013: Shurna is the big loss, but Northwestern also has to replace the interior minutes played by Davide Curletti and Luka Mirkovic. Given the limitations of those players, that might not sound like a big deal, but the Wildcats' other interior options have almost no Big Ten experience. Still, this will be one of the conference's older teams, with a rotation that includes four seniors and a redshirt junior. The suspension of JerShon Cobb hurts the team's depth, making it likely that a freshman or two will have to play regular minutes.

MEET THE WILDCATS

Drew Crawford (6-5, 210, Sr.): Now Northwestern's go-to scorer, Crawford will look to cap what has been a very good career. He's a career 38 percent shooter from three in Big Ten games, and he's more successful than most in the mid-range. Without Shurna to draw attention, Crawford figures to be the main focus of opposing defenses for the first time in his career, and the Wildcats will need him to knock down a high volume of shots.

Dave Sobolewski (6-1, 190, So.): Sobolewski is nominally the team's point guard, but his assist rate was not much different from that of Shurna, Marcotullio, or even Curletti. The truth is that Carmody's system doesn't need a true point guard to be successful, and Sobolewski did his part by knocking down his carefully selected shots and getting to the free throw line at a surprising rate. Expect more of the same from this hard-nosed shooter.

Alex Marcotullio (6-3, 195, Sr.): Marcotullio has spent most of his three seasons coming off the bench, and he's shown himself to be a reliable deep threat. More will be needed of him in his senior season, and Marcotullio has shown occasional flashes of playmaking ability and solid defense.

Jared Swopshire (6-8, 210, Sr.): This fifth-year transfer had a varied career at Louisville. The highlight came in 2009-10, when Swopshire played starter's minutes for an NCAA tournament team. He missed the following season due to injury, then saw more limited minutes for last year's Final Four entrant. Swopshire has never been much of a scorer, but his rebounding and defense should make him a valuable addition to a team in dire need of both.

Reggie Hearn (6-4, 210, Sr.): A former walk-on, Hearn worked his way into the starting lineup at the start of last season and never left it. Selective and accurate shooting enabled Hearn to lead the Big Ten in effective field goal percentage, and he's one of Northwestern's better defenders. Not bad for a player that didn't garner a single Division I scholarship offer out of high school.

Nikola Cerina (6-9, 245, Jr.): This TCU transfer becomes eligible this season, and his excellent rebounding ability should get him minutes immediately. Just don't expect much from Cerina on the offensive end. He struggled to score against the big men of the Mountain West, and things don't figure to come easier in the Big Ten.

Tre Demps (6-2, 200, Fr.): This son of an NBA GM actually started the 2011-12 season opener for Northwestern, but his season was shut down after four games due to a shoulder injury. Now a redshirt freshman, Demps figures to compete for backcourt minutes off the bench.

Mike Turner (6-8, 215, Fr.): A local product, Turner chose Northwestern over Penn, Harvard, and Valparaiso before redshirting as a true freshman. He has a reputation as a face-up four with a soft shooting touch.

Prospectus says: Normally the loss of a scorer like Shurna would spell problems for an offense, but Carmody has earned the benefit of the doubt on that end of the court. The Wildcats still feature enough shooters and passers to make Carmody's system work. As is the case before every season, Northwestern's success figures to hinge on how much improvement can be coaxed on the defensive end. The addition of a couple defensive-minded frontcourt transfers should help in this regard, but it seems unlikely that the Wildcats will break their NCAA tournament drought this season.

OHIO STATE

2012: 31-8 (13-5 Big Ten); Lost to Kansas 64-62, Final Four
In-conference offense: 1.10 points per possession (3rd)
In-conference defense: 0.93 points per possession (2nd)

What Ohio State did well: *Get over Jon Diebler.*

Ohio State has had to recover from the losses of many talented players in the Matta era. Greg Oden, Mike Conley, Evan Turner, Kosta Koufos, and now Jared Sullinger. But Jon Diebler's absence might have left the biggest hole of all. Dan Hanner's research suggests that replacing high-usage but only slightly above-average efficiency players is not as difficult as it might seem. Evan Turner's efficiency was even a bit higher than that, but the Buckeye offense actually improved after Turner picked up his hardware and headed off for the NBA. Sure, a big part of that was due to the contributions of incoming freshman Sullinger, but the real engine behind Ohio State's offense was Jon Diebler.

Yep. Jon Diebler.

Consider that the sharpshooter converted over 50 percent of his 227 three-point attempts in 2010-11. His effective field goal percentage in Big Ten play was a ludicrous 73.4. And because Diebler mostly hung out on the perimeter, and was not charged with initiating offense off the bounce or creating shot opportunities for others, he kept turnovers to a minimum (just 15 in 18 Big Ten games). The result was an eye-popping offensive rating that flirted with 150 in conference play. Only St. Mary's guard Todd Golden's 141.6 mark eclipsed Diebler's 140.6 for all games, and Golden's usage was lower.

When a player leaves the team, his possessions are gobbled up by his teammates. Sometimes that simply means the guy who replaces him in the lineup also takes ownership of those possessions. In someone like Turner's case, the substitute likely won't consume that many possessions. So other players will have to pitch in. But the calculus is the same—if those possessions are used more efficiently, the offense will be better. If not, the offense will be worse. That's an oversimplification, but it's not a bad way to think about offseason changes. In Evan Turner's case, the task was replacing a lot of possessions but at an achievable efficiency. In Jon Diebler's case, Ohio State had to replace many fewer possessions, but at an otherworldly efficiency.

It couldn't be done. The Buckeye offense was much worse in 2012 than in 2011. And yet, that still meant that Matta orchestrated the No. 7 offense in the country. This says more about how good the 2011 offense was, rather than any failings of the 2012 squad. With Diebler gone, OSU funneled the offense through the paint more often. More importantly, the Buckeyes got tough on defense. This was a sound strategy for the Big Ten's best two-point shooting team with long athletes, and Matta deserves another round of applause for suffering the loss of yet another hugely impactful player and guiding the Buckeyes to another outstanding season.

What we learned in 2012: *They're wrong about Sully.*

Every June, we hear the same Monday morning quarterbacking: who left school too early, and who left too late. In Jared Sullinger's case, the consensus was clearly with the latter. On the surface, it's hard to disagree. Sullinger put up the same 17 points a game while playing the same 30 minutes a game. He actually averaged one fewer rebound a game, and shot a lower overall percentage from the field. While steady production might have been all that was fair to ask for, given the stellar baseline set in his freshman season, what NBA general managers saw was a player who was basically the same as a guy who might have been a top-five pick last year—but a year older. That year makes a big difference to guys who are drafting 19 and 20 year olds on the basis of what they might become in their mid-to-late 20s.

But I think those that conclude that Sullinger merely ran in place were wrong. For one, he showed off a capable stroke from outside. Freshman Sullinger connected on just three of 12 shots from three-point range, while Sophomore Sully connected on 40 percent of his 40 attempts. But the real gains are found on defense. While grabbing six more steals is nice, Sullinger put forth a nice rebuttal to skeptics who claim that he's too short to defend the post by recording 39 blocks—which represents a 95 percent increase over his freshman campaign. While Sullinger's stock did take a tumble (in large part due to concerns over his back), I'm confident the Celtics got the steal of the draft.

Sullinger's improvement does not account for all of the gains on the defensive side of the ball for Ohio State. Coming into the season, you would be forgiven for believing that William Buford's defense consisted mostly of biding his time until he had another opportunity to shoot. But in his senior year, that all changed (see table).

Buford turned himself from a DeShaun-level defender into the team's best perimeter defender (yep, even better than that other guy). That he did so while fouling rarely is an even bigger accomplishment. Because defense is a difficult thing to track, it's natural that snubs are commonplace when All-Defensive teams are selected. So for a player to really get snubbed, it has to be egregious. This was egregious.

What's in store for 2013: Sullinger headed for the draft, Buford graduated, and the Buckeyes lost a pair of players to transfer. The Ohio State recruiting class is also not a typical Thad Matta class, so what you'll see is largely the players you would have seen last year if Sullinger and Buford were in foul trouble.

WILLIAM BUFORD STATS

Year	Blocks	Steals	Defensive Rebounds	Stops per 40 min.	Fouls comm. per 40 min.
Jr.	6	11	47	4.02	3.03
Sr.	4	17	86	6.84	2.14
Conference games only					

MEET THE BUCKEYES

Deshaun Thomas (6-7, 215, Jr.): Offensively, Thomas is as good as anyone in the Big Ten. Defensively, he's about as bad as one can be at 6-7. Teammate Lenzelle Smith is not known as an elite defender, but in 100 fewer minutes Smith grabbed more defensive rebounds, blocked more shots, and came away with nearly twice as many steals as Thomas. This isn't the first time that Thomas has heard this criticism. Before Thad Matta it was his high school coach that started calling him "Shaun." There doesn't seem to be any reason that Thomas can't improve. He's already an outstanding offensive rebounder, so he has the ability to at least rebound at a much higher level. It might just be a question of motivation. Frankly, defensive effort is the only thing standing in the way of a David Stern handshake.

Aaron Craft (6-2, 195, Jr.): Craft is something of the Derek Jeter of college basketball, in that he's the most overrated and underrated player in Division I. While he's a good perimeter defender, there's a limit to how much defense a player standing at 6-2 can really offer. The bulk of scoring is done inside the three-point line, and the best way to end an offensive possession is by rebounding missed shots. Altering two-pointers and rebounding are areas where it really helps to be tall. That said, his defense is about as good as it gets for a player of his size, and though he's never had to take on a large role in the offense, he's extremely efficient. That's a good player, albeit one you should leave off your All-America squad.

Lenzelle Smith, Jr. (6-4, 210, Jr.): Smith is another jack of all trades, but master of none. He's a capable outside shooter, has some ability to get to the free throw line, rebounds and defends well for his position, and he even shows some occasional point guard skills. In the absence of Sullinger and Buford, Smith and Craft are likely going to have to transition from their role player status. It will be a tall task for them to maintain their efficiency as their responsibility increases.

Amir Williams (6-11, 250, So.): Though it was in limited minutes, Williams' showed some jaw-dropping defensive promise in his freshman season. His rebounding and block numbers resembled those of a young Cole Aldrich. His offensive game is still very raw (though he's displayed some fantastic offensive rebounding), but his defense promises to be game-changing.

Shannon Scott (6-1, 185, So.): Big Ten fans are well aware of the fact that Matta typically employs a very short bench. So at first blush, it might be surprising to see that a guard that made only 36 percent of his two-point attempts and just six (yes, six) percent of his threes found his way into the rotation. And that's the nice way of putting it. The not-so-nice way is pointing out that Scott made one of his 18 three-point attempts. But Scott's defense is his ticket on the court. He accumulated steals at a Craft-like rate, and even rebounded more like a player who was a few inches taller. Even so, Scott's offense has a long way to go before he'll be able to play more than 10 or 15 minutes a game.

Sam Thompson (6-7, 200, So.): Division I is full of guys who all look great in a workout session, but never make much of an impact in the games. There's minutes up for grabs in Matta's rotation, so this season will go a long way in answering whether Thompson's someone that NBA general managers will keep tabs on.

LaQuinton Ross (6-8, 220, So.): At one point Ross was regarded as the top player in his class nationally. But his freshman season was a bit of a non-event, as he wasn't cleared to play until December. He's reportedly opened some eyes with his play over the summer.

Prospectus says: Buford and Sullinger are just too good to expect anything other than a decline. But there are still enough weapons to compete for the Big Ten championship. If Amir Williams lives up to his defensive promise, and Lenzelle Smith maintains his efficiency as his usage increases, then the Matta machine will keep on running.

PENN STATE

2012: 12-20 (4-14 Big Ten); Lost to Indiana 75-58, Big Ten first round
In-conference offense: 0.97 points per possession (11th)
In-conference defense: 1.10 points allowed per possession (11th)

What Penn State did well: *More than you think.*

You can make a lot of assumptions about a team based on how many three-pointers they shoot and allow defenses to shoot. Ken Pomeroy informed us all this year about just how much luck is involved at the three-point line, both offensively and defensively. Thus, a coach's propensity to allow three-pointers on either side of the ball is something akin to a coach's risk preference. Some coaches, like John Calipari, hate playing this sort of lottery. Last year the Cats allowed fewer than 30 percent of the opponents' shots to come from beyond 20 feet, a mark that was bested by Kentucky's own offense (under 27 percent).

There are other coaches that prefer the double standard. Coach K abhors three-pointers on defense, but his shooters always have the green light. We see similar strategies employed by the likes of Bo Ryan and Mike Brey.

From his time at Boston University and Penn State, we can surmise that Pat Chambers likes to play the lottery. His teams let it fly from beyond the arc, but they were also permissive in granting the opponent the same opportunity. As you would expect, sometimes this works out.

Last year, however, it didn't (see table).

Going forward, I expect the Nittany Lions to shoot even more threes. Chambers' BU teams were closer to 40 percent in terms of 3PA/FGA. And while I don't expect PSU to suddenly transform into Notre Dame East, they can't get any worse from the perimeter.

PENN STATE FOR 3

	Conference Ranks	
	3PA/FGA (%)	3FG%
Penn State	33.9 (7th)	29.8 (11th)
Opponents	42.0 (12th)	40.5 (12th)
Conference games only		

On defense, this is just bad luck. Combined, Big Ten teams (minus Penn State) shot about 35 percent on their threes. If that percentage is substituted for the 40.5 percent figure, it amounts to 57 less points scored against PSU during conference play. On a per possession basis, Penn State moves from the second-worst team in the Big Ten to sixth-best. Expect this unfortunate karma to even out in 2013.

What we learned in 2012: *Desperate times call for desperate measures.*

At first it seemed odd that Ed DeChellis quit his job right after he gave Penn State what was just its fourth NCAA tournament appearance for the school since 1985. The expectations aren't very high for the squad in Happy Valley, so you would think that making the tournament would make DeChellis the toast of the town.

But DeChellis knew what was in store for his squad. The Lions would be without the services of four starters, leaving only Tim Frazier (who was content to consume only 12 percent of the available shots while on the floor). So when DeChellis took a substantial paycut to coach a bad Patriot League team (Navy) that hasn't danced in nearly 15 years, it was kinda sorta understandable in a if-you-don't-think-about-it-for-long kind of way. It's not like DeChellis jumped at a plum offer. The Midshipmen were on the shortlist of one of the worst teams in Division I last season, going just 2-26 against other D-I opponents.

DeChellis likely concluded that bringing back only a single starter, who was a role player offensively, from a bubble team was not a recipe for success. And no, Penn State's 2012 season is not the stuff of movies. But it should have been a lot worse. And Tim Frazier's incredible transformation is what saved his team from a truly terrible season.

It's quite rare for a player to make this kind of me-

TIM FRAZIER'S TRANSFORMATION

	Shots	Points	Steals	Possessions Used (%)	Offensive Rating
Soph.	89	110	16	18.1	101.6
Jr.	300	353	43	33.1	103.8

Conference games only

teoric leap in usage, and rarer still for the player not to lose any efficiency in doing so. Even so, Frazier is not without his limitations. He's not going to finish around the rim, which limits his two-point accuracy (44 percent). And despite his solid free throw shooting, Frazier also isn't much of an outside shooter (31 percent). His value comes from his ability to gobble up possessions with an efficiency you can live with. What this team needs, though, are players who can make shots if they're afforded the opportunity to be picky about their attempts.

What's in store for 2013: Besides Frazier, there were only two willing shooters on the team. With the graduation of Cammeron Woodyard, that number drops to one (Jermaine Marshall). Trey Lewis and Matt Glover are transferring, and Billy Oliver is giving up basketball due to recurring concussions. In comes D.J. Newbill from Southern Mississippi. Patrick Chambers also welcomes his first real batch of recruits, two of them being post players.

MEET THE NITTANY LIONS

Tim Frazier (6-1, 170, Sr.): It's unlikely that Frazier will improve on last season's breakout performance. The fact of the matter is that Frazier is responsible for a heavy load of Penn State's offense, and it's extremely difficult for anyone to maintain a high level of efficiency with that kind of usage. While Frazier's inaccuracy might normally be considered low-hanging fruit (44 percent on twos and 31 percent on threes are not high bars) it isn't in this case. Frazier isn't inaccurate as much as he's being forced to take terrible shots. There aren't many players capable of posting enviable field goal percentages on 500 shots, at least among players that aren't already being paid to do so.

Jermaine Marshall (6-4, 205, Jr.): Like Frazier, Marshall is probably being asked to do a bit too much in this offense. Between the two of them, they handle over half of Penn State's possessions and shots while they're on the floor. Marshall is one of the Big Ten's better defenders, and he would probably be a good shooter if he didn't have to shoot so much. On a team like Iowa or Minnesota, he would be a key piece on a team that could make some noise. On Penn State, he's a chucker by default.

D.J. Newbill (6-4, 205, So.): Over the offseason, Pat Chambers dubbed his Frazier/Newbill combo as "the best backcourt in the nation." Newbill had a nice freshman season at Southern Mississippi, but averaging nine points a game in Conference USA is a ways from All-Big Ten. And Newbill was basically cut by Marquette, the school at which he originally signed his letter of intent. If he can simply reproduce his freshman line while moving up in competition, it will be a very successful season. The good news is that he's precisely the kind of player Penn State needs, someone who can make shots while defenses focus on Frazier.

Ross Travis (6-6, 225, So.): Travis has a high motor and isn't afraid to mix it up on the inside against bigger players, but he needs to play more to his strengths. He's a gifted offensive rebounder and converts on his attempts around the hoop, but he is a truly terrible shooter, as evidenced by his 48 percent accuracy from the free throw line. Travis nonetheless attempted 24 three-pointers last season, with little success. He'll be a better player this year if he attempts 24 fewer of those.

Sasa Borovnjak (6-9, 240, Jr.): Because he's from Serbia, some might mistake Borovnjak for a prototypical European big man. Don't. Borovnjak doesn't shoot jumpers, and he's certainly not someone you want to see dribble or try and create for others. He can score around the hoop, but he's not a particularly good rebounder or defender. This was his first season back from a torn ACL, so there's a chance he improves as he gains confidence in his rebuilt knee.

Jon Graham (6-8, 225, So.): Graham looks the part of a Big Ten power forward, but looks can be deceiving. Last year he was a turnover machine, despite the fact that he was rarely called upon to dribble. Once the game slows down for him, he could be an effective role player on the block. Unfortunately, he suffers from the same debilitating blindness while standing at the free throw line as the rest of PSU's front line.

Nick Colella (6-3, 195, Sr.): It's easy enough to dismiss Colella as a sharpshooter that can't shoot (Colella made only 24 percent of his three-pointers last season), but the guy is still a Division I player at a high major program. For someone who spent his first two seasons at Division III, and then a semester as a practice player for the women's team, that's quite an achievement. Colella probably won't make much of an impact this season, but it was also ridiculous to think he'd ever be in this position.

Prospectus says: Because he's only been a coach for three seasons, it's hard to separate Chambers' philosophies from the natural tendencies of the players that are on the roster. So we don't really know what kind of approach Chambers is going to bring over the long run to Bryce Jordan. At a minimum, however, we can expect Penn State and its opponents to shoot a lot of three-pointers. In order to win games, it therefore follows that you should try and stock the cupboard with players that can shoot. Right now, that's a scarce commodity in State College. Until that changes, this team is firmly in rebuilding mode.

PURDUE

2012: 22-13 (10-8 Big Ten); Lost to Kansas 63-60, NCAA round of 32
In-conference offense: 1.10 points per possession (2nd)
In-conference defense: 1.09 points allowed per possession (9th)

What Purdue did well: *Play to their strength.*

When Purdue's famed Baby Boiler class arrived in the fall of 2007, it set the basketball program off in a new direction. In the five years prior to the arrival of JaJuan Johnson, E'Twaun Moore, and Robbie Hummel, Purdue won 40 percent of their Big Ten conference games. In the five years with the Baby Boilers on campus, Purdue won over 70 percent of their conference games.

The fifth year of that era was Hummel's solo performance. Moore and Johnson were in the NBA while Hummel worked to prove that his knees could hold up over an entire season. Not only did his knees hold up, Hummel's low-turnover ways led Purdue to its best offense in the Baby Boiler era. This was the No. 8 offense on a per possession basis in Division I, and that came thanks mostly to a microscopic 13.6 turnover percentage.

Hummel, for his part, had the lowest turnover percentage in the country among players that saw at least 40 percent of their team's minutes. Mind you, this is not a ranking that filters out usage. So guys like Brady Heslip at Baylor, who stands in one spot behind the three-point line while future NBA players draw the defense and kick the ball out for an open jumper, are part of this group, yet Hummel put up lower turnover numbers than even those guys. He's been doing this his entire career, and you get some really strange stats. Like the fact that in Big Ten player over the past two seasons, Hummel has as many steals as turnovers. That's not a small feat for a power forward.

Although Purdue earned a blue-collar, defense-first reputation over the 2008-2012 seasons, it's probably more accurate to remember the Baby Boilers for their refusal to turn the ball over. Even when they were freshmen, Purdue had the lowest turnover percentage in conference play. In the subsequent seasons, it's ranked in the top 20 nationally.

Of course, all of this presents a question. Are low turnovers a function of the 2007 recruiting class, or are they a function of Matt Painter's style? The next few months will go a long way toward answering that question.

What we learned in 2012: *Even Purdue can play crummy defense.*

On offense, we can precisely measure how often a player makes a shot, and how often he misses. We don't have a good way of measuring the same on defense. While we can track steals, blocks, and defensive rebounds, that's a small portion of what players accomplish on the defensive end of the ball.

So we make assumptions, some better than others. But occasionally, we get a really nice piece of data that leads to an inescapable conclusion. Purdue's past two seasons comprise that data, and it tells us that JaJuan Johnson was a really good defensive player.

In 2011, the Boilers ranked as the Big Ten's best defense. In 2012, they were ninth. With that kind of drop-off, it's never just one thing, but it's worth noting just how small this team was last season. There were long stretches where Hummel functioned as the team's center. Indeed, there were even times when 6-5 D.J. Byrd filled that role. This is a stark contrast from 2011, when JaJuan Johnson was swatting away seven percent of the other team's two-point attempts. Johnson was also a strong rebounder, and best of all he rarely fouled. There was a reason this guy was the Big Ten Defensive Player of the Year.

What's in store for 2013: Finally, the Baby Boilers are gone. Also gone are point guard Lewis Jackson and sharpshooter Ryne Smith. Kelsey Barlow was also a starter for the Boilermakers until he was dismissed from the team in February. Throw in Hummel, and this team loses four starters. The good news is that Painter welcomes a strong recruiting class, headlined by center A.J. Hammons and point guard Ronnie Johnson.

MEET THE BOILERMAKERS

D.J. Byrd (6-5, 230, Sr.): Byrd is basically a taller version of the departed Ryne Smith. He doesn't do a lot out there other than shoot, but converting on 43 percent of your three-pointers isn't easy when you shoot as often as Byrd does. As a spot-up shooter, he's also unlikely to turn the ball over. Byrd excels in this role, the problem is he will likely be asked to do more this season.

Terone Johnson (6-2, 200, Jr.): Johnson is the yin to Byrd's yang. He can do a little bit of everything, except that he's a poor outside shooter. A source of frustration for Boilermaker fans is Johnson's abysmal free throw accuracy, coupled with his above-average ability to get to the line. If he could simply be an average shooter from fifteen feet, he'd have the makings of an All-Big Ten player. Nonetheless, the junior guard is perhaps the most important player for Painter's team. If his younger brother Ronnie Johnson isn't up to the task, Terone is probably Purdue's point guard this year.

Anthony Johnson (6-3, 190, So.): Believe it or not, Anthony Johnson was known as a shooter in high school. That reputation didn't bear out in his freshman season, as he made just 28 percent of his threes and only 49 percent of his free throws. Purdue desperately needs him to do better this year, because he's one of two ball handlers returning.

Jacob Lawson (6-8, 215, So.): There was a lot to like in Lawson's limited action in his freshman season. He finished his chances around the hoop, and he showed a lot of defensive promise as well. But as is the case with most freshmen, it wasn't all good. Lawson displayed mediocre rebounding, was careless with the ball, and his 35 percent free throw accuracy provided defenses with an easy strategy. Still, Lawson's a good bet to play starter's minutes this season.

Travis Carroll (6-9, 230, Jr.): Carroll was the only post player on Purdue that had any significant experience. By the end of the year, Painter was constantly looking for opportunities to simply play four guards plus Hummel. During the Big Ten tournament, there were stretches where 6-5 D.J. Byrd was the tallest Boiler on the court. With Lawson maturing and a new batch of frontcourt recruits headed to West Lafayette, Carroll's likely headed to the back of the rotation.

A.J. Hammons (7-0, 280, Fr.): Hammons is huge, but he also needs to work on his conditioning before he's able to play for long stretches. Not that it really matters. A seven-foot freshman basically enters the game with two fouls.

Ronnie Johnson (6-0, 170, Fr.): Ronnie is Terone's younger brother, but he's a couple inches shorter and probably a bit quicker. He's going to be given the first shot at the starting point guard job, but he's probably a year away from being ready for that.

Rapheal Davis (6-5, 210, Fr.): Davis is an aggressive slasher who led the team in scoring on its summer trip in Italy.

Prospectus says: Matt Painter has only been a head coach for eight seasons, but he's won his conference's Coach of the Year award four times. Only once has his team failed to win 22 games (his first season at Purdue). In 2013, he might face his most difficult challenge yet. Sure, there's still some talent on the roster, but Purdue lost a lot from a team that wasn't exactly dominant last season. Short of the class of 2012 rivaling the class of 2007, expect Painter to be in some unfamiliar rebuilding territory this season.

WISCONSIN

2012: 26-10 (12-6 Big Ten); Lost to Syracuse 64-63, Sweet 16
In-conference offense: 1.03 points per possession (8th)
In-conference defense: 0.97 points allowed per possession (3rd)

What Wisconsin did well: *Funnel traffic.*

Bo Ryan is typically thought of as a "system" coach. As best as I can tell, that's a coach that has a very unique approach, and recruits players specifically for that approach. Take a Badger and put him on UNC, and he's not nearly as effective. At the same time, if one took a talent such as Harrison Barnes and made him play for Bo, he might not be as useful as Jon Leuer would be in the same role. Or so goes the theory.

The thing about system coaches is, we like to think of them as consistent. Every year, they will run the same stuff, and the only question is whether the other team has adequately prepared for it. I'm not a huge fan of the system coach theory. Generally speaking, there are lots of coaches with very unique approaches to the game, but it's almost always the overachievers that get pinned with this label. Mike Brey is a system coach of the Big East, but when was the last time Syracuse played man-to-man defense? Ryan and John Beilein have the same reputation in the Big Ten, but Tom Izzo's set play weave-based offense is remarkably similar year-to-year.

But no matter how you feel about that label, the fact is that Ryan is evolving as a coach. In particular, the man is becoming obsessed with the three-pointer. Over the past four seasons, Wisconsin has steadily increased its three-point attempts while limiting those of the opponent. This synergy makes perfect sense, of course. If a coach believes shooting three-pointers is the key to a successful offense, then it follows that he would want to limit the opponents' opportunity to do the same.

This defensive strategy worked perfectly in 2012, when Wisconsin's closeouts forced teams to try their luck on the inside. That's where Jared Berggren resides, who proved to be one of the best interior defenders in the Big Ten. Conference opponents shot a mere 44 percent inside the arc against the Badgers, which was the primary reason why this was one of the Big Ten's best defenses.

What we learned in 2012: *If you're too careful, your whole offense can become a grind.*

Typically, when Wisconsin has a defense this good, it wins about 30 games or so. But last year's team fell short of that mark, largely because the offense was unusually inefficient, at least in conference play. The Badgers' eighth place finish in conference points per possession was easily the worst mark in the Ryan era. And one can't say that this simply wasn't Bo Ball because the team turned the ball over on just over 15 percent of its possessions.

No, the reason the team couldn't score was because it couldn't shoot. Only Penn State was worse from the field than the Badgers. Here's a scary stat for Wisconsin fans: Badgers not named Jordan Taylor managed a combined 45.7 effective field goal percentage. This stat is even worse than it sounds, considering how many possessions ended with Taylor attempting a near-impossible shot (to his credit, he made quite a few of these). Without Taylor as the safety valve, those shots will need to be taken by other, less accomplished players.

The good news is that Wisconsin doesn't need to shoot all that well to be successful. If the Badgers can simply return to being an average shooting team, this offense can be explosive. Well, at least as explosive as a team can be at 58 possessions a game. Still, average is a lofty goal, given the starting point and the fact that the supporting cast is going to have to take on more responsibility with Taylor gone.

What's in store for 2013: Besides Taylor, the team only lost fellow graduating senior Rob Wilson. In comes perhaps Ryan's best-ever recruit, swingman Sam Dekker. True, a few years ago Wisconsin welcomed McDonald's All-American Brian Butch (Dekker was not selected for the McDonald's game), but Butch sat out his first season with a redshirt. Dekker will almost certainly play, and probably start, right away.

It was all lining up nicely in Madison until late October, when presumptive starting point guard Josh Gasser was lost for the year to a torn ACL. Gasser's injury deprives the Badgers of their most capable returning ball handler, and places a lot of pressure on redshirt freshman George Marshall. Additionally, Gasser was probably this team's best perimeter shooter. At first glance, this roster now does not seem capable of the perimeter-oriented attack Ryan has become fond of in recent seasons. Either the likes of Frank Kaminsky and Ben Brust need to improve their accuracy, or Ryan will need to rethink his offense.

MEET THE BADGERS

Jared Berggren (6-10, 235, Sr.): Like everyone on the roster else not named Jordan Taylor, Berggren hit a rough patch once conference play began. Against Big Ten opponents, he converted just 41 percent of his two-pointers. Against everyone else, he made 59 percent of his twos. Whether he was exposed or just in a funk is anyone's guess. Regardless, the Badgers will need more out of him if they're to compete for the conference crown.

Ryan Evans (6-6, 210, Sr.): Berggren and Evans are a big part of why Wisconsin's defense was so formidable. Evans in particular rebounds like someone who stands a few inches taller. His offense has a nice upside too. Evans' solid free throw shooting suggests that there's room to improve from behind the arc.

Mike Bruesewitz (6-6, 225, Sr.): During a workout on October 9 Bruesewitz injured his lower leg and is expected to miss four to six weeks. Last season was something of a step back for Bruesewitz, and not just because he ditched the killer clown hairstyle (though the change couldn't have helped). It's not that he's a mediocre shooter, it's just that he has mediocre shot selection. He's a career 29 percent three-point shooter. So why is he hoisting as many of those as two-pointers?

Sam Dekker (6-7, 220, Fr.): This year's Big Ten freshman class is one of the best in recent memory, and Dekker just might be the best of them. Despite his size, he's really more of a two-guard with his ball handling and shooting ability. He's going to be a matchup nightmare.

George Marshall (5-11, 185, Fr.): The scuttlebutt out of Madison is that the coaching staff is excited about the long-term prospects for the redshirt freshman from Chicago. That said, it would be a bit of a surprise if he were ready for starter's minutes, but Gasser's injury rules out any mollycoddling.

Ben Brust (6-1, 195, Jr.): Brust hit 39 percent of his threes as a relatively high-volume shooter playing lower-volume minutes, memorably draining three treys apiece against Vanderbilt and Syracuse in the NCAA tournament. The loss of Gasser elevates his importance markedly.

Frank Kaminsky (6-11, 230, So.): Kaminsky earns high marks for his shooting, but didn't really showcase it last season. Still, the fact that he shot so many three-pointers (and continued to get minutes) suggests that he's showing something in practice.

Prospectus says: In the aftermath of the Gasser injury, Wisconsin looks a bit like it did last season. The defense should remain excellent, perhaps the best in the Big Ten. But offensively, this team has a lot of question marks. The outside shooting is entirely theoretical at this point, and given Ryan's recent infatuation with the three-point shot, that could spell trouble. Of course, it isn't hard to see the likes of Brust, Kaminsky, and Dekker putting down threes against high-major competition, but until that happens, it's probably best to play it safe with the Badgers. Figure a solid tournament team, but on the outside of the Big Ten title race.

Pac-12

BY KEVIN PELTON

A four-year downward trend for the conference formerly known as the Pac-10 reached its nadir during the league's first season with 12 teams. During 2011-12, the Pac-12 slipped across the divide that separates power conferences from their mid-major brethren.

For much of the year, it appeared the Pac-12 might be a one-bid conference. Ultimately, the league sent two teams, but not its regular-season champion, the Washington Huskies, whose poor non-conference performance and early exit from the conference tournament doomed them to the NIT. Newcomer Colorado won four games in as many nights at the Staples Center in Los Angeles to claim the Pac-12's automatic berth and was joined by Cal, which merited one of the last at-large bids and played in the First Four.

By the end of the first weekend of the NCAA tournament, the Pac-12 was eliminated. Just to get there, Colorado had to upset UNLV before losing to Baylor. However, the conference's fate was sealed long before March. During a disappointing non-league campaign, Pac-12 teams posted a combined 1-23 record against teams ranked in the top 50 by Ken Pomeroy.

Besides Cal, the other teams projected to contend for the Pac-12 title got off to slow starts. Arizona lost an exhibition game at home to D-II Seattle Pacific University and took a 9-4 record into conference play. Washington went 6-5 with only a single win over a top-100 foe. Worst of all was UCLA, which began the year 1-4. The Bruins' best non-conference win came by eight points over Richmond at home.

To the extent the conference salvaged anything from the months of November and December, it was unexpected teams carrying the flag. Those pair of top-50 wins came from Oregon State, which beat Texas and lost by two to Vanderbilt at the TicketCity Legends Classic in East Rutherford, New Jersey; and Stanford, which beat eventual Sweet 16 entrant NC State. The Beavers avoided their usual non-conference missteps and entered Pac-12 play 10-2, as did the Cardinal.

After the calendar turned, however, it was the usual suspects who controlled the league, joined by Oregon. Arizona, Cal and Washington battled for the conference lead with the Ducks making a late charge. None of them could separate themselves enough to overcome the nation's skepticism about Pac-12 teams.

The end of the season did not help matters. On the final weekend of conference play, the Huskies lost at UCLA, leaving the Bears a chance to share the league title—until they lost to Stanford the next night, giving Washington its second outright conference title since 1953. Neither team made it to the final of the Pac-12 tournament, and the Huskies' quarterfinal loss to Oregon State doomed their

KEVIN'S 2013 STANDINGS

	2012 Record	Returning Poss (%)	Returning Min (%)	2013 Prediction
UCLA	11-7	61	59	15-3
Arizona	12-6	48	48	14-4
Stanford	10-8	70	69	12-6
California	13-5	63	67	10-8
Colorado	11-7	56	55	10-8
USC	1-17	51	52	9-9
Washington	14-4	48	57	9-9
Oregon State	7-11	75	78	8-10
Oregon	13-5	43	42	7-11
Washington State	7-11	69	63	6-12
Arizona State	6-12	56	55	5-13
Utah	3-15	29	31	3-15

NCAA tournament hopes. Arizona and Colorado played for the automatic bid and the Buffaloes won to return to March Madness for the first time since 2003.

Fittingly, the Pac-12 capped a year where it was relegated to the second tier with a strong run in the other tournaments. Three of the conference's teams advanced to the quarterfinals of the NIT, and Stanford and Washington both reached Madison Square Garden, where the Cardinal knocked off Minnesota to win the title. Meanwhile Oregon State and Washington State faced each other in the semifinals of the CBI, though the Cougars lost the finals 2-1 to Pitt.

Despite the finish, the Pomeroy Rankings put the Pac-12 behind the A-10, though at least the league narrowly beat out the Mountain West for the title of best conference on the West Coast. The Pac-10 actually ranked worse (eighth) in 2003-04, but that was due to mid-majors playing exceptionally well. The Pac-12's aggregate performance in 2011-12 was the worst for any major conference during the decade for which KenPom.com has ratings. Sports-Reference.com, which dates back longer, showed the Pac-12 with the worst effort by the Simple Rating System (6.74) by a power conference since the SEC's 6.48 mark in 1988-89.

The Pac-12's performance was the result of a trend toward early entries and weak recruiting classes that had been building for years, leaving the league short on star talent. The conference's player of the year, Cal's Jorge Gutierrez, was a senior who went undrafted. Just three players from the Pac-12—Oregon State's Jared Cunningham, and Washington's Terrence Ross and Tony Wroten—were picked in June.

On top of that, depth was an issue for most of the Pac-12's best teams because of a combination of injuries and transfers. Cal, UCLA, and Washington all relied on seven-player rotations. At the bottom of the conference, injuries decimated USC and also hit Utah hard. Throughout the season, key players were lost to attrition. Three top recruits (Oregon's Jabari Brown and Bruce Barron, and Arizona's Sidiki Johnson) decided to transfer during their freshman seasons. Meanwhile, stars Reeves Nelson of UCLA and Josh Watkins of Utah were dismissed from their teams midseason. That continued an ugly trend of talent recruited to the Pac-12 contributing elsewhere. The Mountain West's top two teams were both led by transfers from Westwood in particular: Mike Moser and Chace Stanback (UNLV) and Drew Gordon (New Mexico).

The poor season on the court, however, had no apparent impact on the Pac-12's recruiting. In fact, UCLA and Arizona welcome two of the nation's top classes. ESPN.com ranks the Bruins No. 1 and the Wildcats No. 3, while Scout.com and Rivals.com have them second and third, respectively. UCLA landed the nation's top recruit in swingman Shabazz Muhammad, capping a group that also includes point forward Kyle Anderson and big man Tony Parker. Arizona landed a balanced class with four top-50 recruits, headlined by center Kaleb Tarczewski. Colorado, which has improved its recruiting under Tad Boyle, also signed a pair of top-100 players. Overall, using RSCIhoops.com's consensus rankings, this is the most talented group of Pac-12 freshmen in recent memory (see table).

Now, the question is whether the jewels of the class will take the court. The NCAA continues to investigate Muhammad and Anderson because of the possibility of impermissible benefits. Anderson is expected to be cleared, but Muhammad likely faces a suspension and may never be eligible to play at UCLA. Since Muhammad might be the conference's best player as a freshman, projecting the Bruins' performance without knowing his status

PAC-12 RECRUITING

Year	Top 10	Top 25	Top 50	Top 100
2006	2	5	6	13
2007	3	3	4	9
2008	2	3	9	13
2009	1	2	5	13
2010	0	0	4	10
2011	0	4	5	9
2012	3	6	8	15

is nearly impossible. Adding to the confusion, Oregon and USC were also awaiting word on waivers requested by Arsalan Kazemi and Omar Oraby, respectively, to see whether the Rice transfers might be immediately eligible.

Our predictions assume that Muhammad will be available for Pac-12 play but that Kazemi and Oraby will have to sit out a season as transfers. In that scenario, UCLA is the class of the conference. The Bruins and Arizona could both contend nationally, raising the perception of the Pac-12. Stanford, bringing back a quality young core from last year's NIT champs, slots third. Then comes a crowd, with five teams—Cal, Colorado, USC, Washington, Oregon State—and maybe a sixth, Oregon, that are difficult to distinguish. At the bottom of the conference, Arizona State, Utah and Washington State have all been hit hard by defections after struggling last year. The most important, and easiest prediction, is this: the Pac-12's regular-season champion will make the NCAA tournament during what figures to be a bounce-back year for the conference as a whole.

ARIZONA

2012: 23-12 (12-6 Pac-12); Lost to Bucknell 65-54, NIT first round
In-conference offense: 1.06 points per possession (5th)
In-conference defense: 0.96 points allowed per possession (2nd)

What Arizona did well: *Defend bigger opponents.*

Because their big men struggled so badly, Arizona threw out the conference's second-shortest lineups in terms of effective height. Weighted for playing time, Arizona's posts were 0.7 inches shorter than the NCAA average, which ranked ahead of only Utah. While ineffective 6-11 center Kyryl Natyazhko rode the bench, past Prospectus Foreword author Sean Miller started a frontcourt of 6-6 Solomon Hill and 6-7 Jesse Perry, spelled occasionally by 6-9 freshman Angelo Chol.

In theory, as predicted in this space a year ago, that should have spelled doom for the Wildcats' defense. Yet Arizona ranked second in Pac-12 play in points allowed per possession, a major improvement from their sixth-place finishes in Miller's first two seasons in Tucson. The smaller, quicker lineups proved ideal for Miller's version of the pack-line defense, as the Wildcats led the conference in defending both the two and the three. Meanwhile, Hill's rebounding allowed Arizona to hold its own on the defensive glass.

What we learned in 2012: *Point guard is the most difficult position for Sean Miller to fill.*

While the 'Cats overachieved on defense, the Arizona offense was unable to take full advantage of the opportunity thus afforded. One key reason was the disappointing campaign submitted by freshman point guard Josiah Turner, the conference's highest-rated recruit. Turner's inefficient play was reminiscent of predecessor Momo Jones, who transferred to Iona in the summer of 2011. Turner clashed with Miller and was suspended for the duration of both the Pac-12 tournament and the NIT (though the latter had a short duration for 'Zona). After the season, he announced plans to transfer to SMU, but after an extreme DUI charge he decided to turn pro and spent a couple of weeks playing in Hungary before asking for his release.

To replace Turner, Miller is going the transfer route. In the short term, he will be reunited with Mark Lyons, whom he recruited to Xavier before taking the Arizona job. As a graduate student, Lyons will be immediately eligible to start at point guard this season. He'll be followed by another transfer, Duquesne standout T.J. McConnell, who will have two years of eligibility after sitting out 2012-13.

What's in store for 2013: Besides Lyons, Miller adds four top-50 freshmen—collectively, one of the nation's top three recruiting classes—to five returning regulars. Suddenly, depth goes from a weakness to a strength for the Wildcats, who have the most talented roster of Miller's tenure.

MEET THE WILDCATS

Solomon Hill (6-7, 220, Sr.): During his junior season, Hill stepped up to fill the void left by Derrick Williams' departure for the NBA, emerging as the leader of a balanced offense. Hill made 55 percent of his twos and 39 percent of his threes while getting to the free throw line more than four times a night, the recipe for efficient scoring. The newcomers arriving this season will push Hill to small forward, where his size and rebounding will be strengths. However, Hill won't be able to beat slower defenders off the dribble as frequently as he did as a stretch 4.

Nick Johnson (6-3, 200, So.): While Turner was a disappointment, the Wildcats' other top recruit lived up to advance billing. Johnson played both guard spots and earned Pac-12 All-Freshman honors. The key task for Johnson in year two is stepping up his finishing after making just 41 percent of his twos last season. An improved three-point stroke could help Johnson boost his subpar true shooting percentage (49 percent).

Mark Lyons (6-1, 200, Sr.): Part of one of the nation's best backcourts alongside Tu Holloway at Xavier, Lyons now takes on a full-time point guard role. He's got the playmaking ability to handle the assignment, having handed out assists at a similar rate to Turner last season. Lyons will have to tighten his shot selection now that he has more weapons around him, which should help him improve 44 percent two-point shooting.

Kaleb Tarczewski (7-0, 255, Fr.): The most talented of Arizona's recruits, Tarczewski was the consensus No. 7 prospect in the country. That label may set expectations for his freshman season a little too high. Tarczewski will need some time to adjust to the Pac-12's level of athleticism. Eventually, his size and fundamental game should make him dangerous in the low post.

Brandon Ashley (6-8, 235, Fr.): Freshmen Ashley and Grant Jerrett (see below) will likely battle for a spot in the Wildcats' starting five. While Jerrett was the more touted recruit, Ashley's polished game could give him the upper hand. When Arizona played two games in the Bahamas this summer, Ashley was the team's leading rebounder. He also has the ability to step out on the perimeter at times.

Grant Jerrett (6-10, 235, Fr.): The skilled Jerrett is most comfortable in the high post, where he has range out to the three-point line and can also find teammates. Jerrett's 7-1 wingspan gives him defensive potential as he fills out his lanky frame.

Kevin Parrom (6-6, 220, Sr.): Just as he seemed to be fully recovered from an offseason gunshot wound to his right leg, Parrom broke a bone in his right foot, ending his season. His sophomore campaign, when he made 59 percent of his twos and 42 percent of his threes, is more indicative of his talent. He scored 37 points in the two games in the Bahamas and could be a major weapon off the bench as a senior.

Gabe York (6-2, 185, Fr.): The last of Arizona's fab four freshmen faces the most competition for playing time behind Johnson and Lyons. York's shooting ability will get him on the floor at times but he must improve defensively, especially against bigger opponents at shooting guard.

Jordin Mayes (6-3, 200, Jr.): Mayes gives the Wildcats an experienced option behind Lyons, though his inability to beat out Turner for minutes last season indicates that Arizona doesn't see Mayes as anything more than a reserve. After making 45 percent of his threes as a freshman, he slumped to 29 percent in 2011-12. Since he takes more threes than twos, bouncing back in that area is crucial to Mayes' success.

Angelo Chol (6-9, 225, So.): The skinny, athletic Chol was one of the conference's best shot blockers and made 56 percent of his two-point attempts by sticking to high-percentage finishes at the basket. Freshman mistakes limited his playing time, and now the newcomers will push Chol down to fourth on the depth chart up front.

Prospectus says: Arizona has star talent in Hill, Lyons and possibly the freshmen, and the Wildcats go two-deep at every position. This is Miller's best Arizona team, one that can legitimately aspire to contend nationally. A preseason ranking just outside the top 10 might be a little on the high side—though Dan Hanner's projections agree with the pollsters—but the Wildcats will indeed be that good if the freshmen live up to advance billing.

ARIZONA STATE

2012: 10-21 (6-12 Pac-12); Lost to Stanford 85-65, Pac-12 first round
In-conference offense: 0.93 points per possession (10th)
In-conference defense: 1.06 points allowed per possession (9th)

What Arizona State did well: *Dash their archrival's at-large hopes.*

It takes squinting hard to find positives from the Sun Devils' first 20-loss season since 2006-07. Arizona State did finish conference play with a two-game winning streak. While beating lowly USC was no cause for celebration, the Sun Devils did deliver their fans some schadenfreude by beating rival Arizona on the season's final weekend behind 20-point games from Carrick Felix, Jonathan Gilling, and Trent Lockett. The upset helped knock the Wildcats off the NCAA tournament bubble.

What we learned in 2012: *Turnover is high in Tempe.*

In recent seasons, embattled Arizona State coach Herb Sendek has had a tough time keeping players around. During the season, once-promising guard Keala King was dismissed from the team for a violation of team rules. Then after the season wrapped up, three players transferred. The departure of leading scorer Trent Lockett was personal; Lockett went to Marquette because he wanted to be closer to his family in Minnesota after his mother was diagnosed with cancer. However, the Sun Devils also lost a pair of key reserves in forward Chanse Creekmur (who decided to play football at Iowa State) and post Kyle Cain (headed to UNC Greensboro).

The defections weren't limited to players. Assistant coach Lamont Smith took the same position at Pac-12 rival Washington, and Scott Pera departed for Penn. Despite getting a two-year contract extension through 2015-16 in December, Sendek's future in the Valley of the Sun is precarious, which helps explain why coaches might look elsewhere. Sendek was still able to lure a pair of experienced pro coaches, former Golden State and Sacramento head coach Eric Musselman and long-time NBA advance scout Larry Greer, to fill out his rebuilt staff.

What's in store for 2013: After a year of waiting, prize class of 2011 recruit Jahii Carson becomes eligible to give Arizona State a dynamic presence at point guard. The Sun Devils also add mid-major transfers Bo Barnes and Evan Gordon to the backcourt to help ease the loss of Lockett.

MEET THE SUN DEVILS

Jahii Carson (5-10, 175, Fr.): Expectations are sky-high for Carson, who is the Sun Devils' best recruit since James Harden. Arizona State spent last season awaiting a decision on Carson's eligibility ... and waiting ... and waiting. Eventually, Carson was deemed a non-qualifier, though he was allowed to practice with the team. Now, Carson takes the reins as starting point guard and go-to guy from day one. His explosiveness with the basketball is a key reason behind Sendek talking at media day about his desire to play faster. Given Sendek's history of slow-paced hoops, you should take a wait-and-see approach there, but Carson may be impossible to slow down.

Jordan Bachynski (7-2, 250, Jr.): Over the course of his sophomore year, Bachynski developed quickly. He averaged 10 points an outing over the Devils' last 13 games, giving ASU a post presence. The lefty has a soft touch around the basket and is polishing his footwork with the basketball. That being said, the strength of Bachynski's game is still on the defensive end. Believed to be the tallest player in school history, Bachynski ranked second in the Pac-12 by swatting away nine percent of opponent two-point attempts. He's also solid on the glass for a shot blocking specialist.

Jonathan Gilling (6-7, 215, So.): The great Dane was one of the conference's top newcomers from beyond the arc, knocking down 53 triples at a 41 percent clip. Gilling topped 20 points twice, which is remarkable given how little time he spent inside. Nearly 80 percent of his shot attempts were threes. To round out his game, Gilling must get tougher on the glass. His rebound rate was anemic for a point guard, let alone someone listed at 6-7.

Carrick Felix (6-6, 195, Sr.): Felix led Arizona State in minutes, which says more about the chaos around him than his own performance. A generic athletic wing, Felix is a plus shot blocker but not otherwise a major factor at other end. Improving his three-point shooting from last year's 31 percent mark would make Felix more dangerous on offense.

Evan Gordon (6-1, 185, Jr.): Gordon is the younger brother of Eric Gordon, whose effort to join Evan in the greater Phoenix area was foiled when the New Orleans Hornets matched the Suns' offer sheet to him in restricted free agency. This Gordon began his career at Liberty and was the Flames' leading scorer as a sophomore before deciding to test his skill against better competition. Gordon wasn't especially efficient in a go-to role and made just 34 percent of his threes in 2010-11, so Arizona State is hoping he will be more effective relying on teammates to set up him on the perimeter.

Bo Barnes (6-4, 195, So.): By contrast, Scottsdale native Barnes will play more or less the same role he did at Hawaii as a freshman before transferring. Barnes made just nine two-pointers all season for the Warriors, but hit 57 threes at a 39 percent clip. If he can keep up defensively with Pac-12 athletes, Barnes will be a good fit for Sendek's perimeter-friendly system.

Chris Colvin (6-2, 185, Sr.): After starting 17 games in his first year in Tempe, Colvin likely moves back to a more appropriate role off the bench behind Carson. Colvin has enough size that he and Carson could team in the backcourt at times. Last season Colvin more than held his own as a playmaker, ranking second in the conference in assist rate. He struggled as a scorer and called his own number entirely too often given his 41 percent effective shooting. With more weapons around him, Colvin should be able to play more efficiently.

Ruslan Pateev (7-0, 255, Sr.): The Pac-12's preeminent Muscovite is the only four-year Sun Devil on the roster. Statistically, Pateev hasn't made much improvement over that span. Finishing at the rim remains the primary source of his offense; anything more is liable to lead to turnovers. Pateev is a fine shot blocker but only mediocre on the glass.

Kenny Martin (6-8, 220, Fr.): Arizona State's incoming recruiting class is unlikely to yield immediate returns. If Sendek's rotation goes nine deep, Martin could find some playing time as an active stretch 4. The Dave Mustaine look-alike is a good bet to become a fan favorite.

Prospectus says: After two seasons of being outmanned by conference foes, the addition of Carson gives the Sun Devils a chance to compete in 2012-13. Still, the team's limited depth and lack of athleticism will keep Arizona State solidly in the second division of the Pac-12.

CALIFORNIA

2012: 24-10 (13-5 Pac-12); Lost to South Florida 65-54, NCAA First Four
In-conference offense: 1.07 points per possession (2nd)
In-conference defense: 0.95 points allowed per possession (1st)

What Cal did well: *Turn things around defensively.*

In going from the NIT back to the four-letter tournament, Cal was only marginally improved at the offensive end. It was the Golden Bear defense that did a complete 180, going from last in the Pac-10 to first in the Pac-12. Mike Montgomery accomplished this with a similar rotation and despite losing his best rebounder and shot blocker (forward Richard Solomon) for much of the season.

Cal defended shots well and excelled both on the defensive glass and in terms of keeping opponents off the free throw line. Guard Justin Cobbs and forward Alan Crabbe were two of the best players in the country at avoiding fouls. Crabbe was a major factor in the team's rebounding by committee, which also got a boost from guard Jorge Gutierrez, the Pac-12 player of the year as well as the league's defensive POY. The last key piece was freshman post David Kravish, who more than held his own while replacing Solomon in the starting lineup. The group gave Montgomery an above-average defense for the first time in his four years in Berkeley.

What we learned in 2012: *Scheduling matters.*

More than any other team in the conference—more even than regular-season champion Washington—the Golden Bears suffered for the sins of their conference. Statistically, Cal belonged on the fringes of the top 25, finishing No. 28 in the Pomeroy rankings. Yet the Golden Bears got stuck in the First Four as one of the last at-larges in the field, largely due to a complete lack of any marquee victory. Per Pomeroy, the best team Cal beat all year was cross-Bay rival Stanford, which ranked No. 32.

The Cardinal was the best team the Bears had a chance to play in Pac-12 competition, since they couldn't face themselves. Cal's 10-3 non-conference performance was also missing notable wins. The best team the Golden Bears beat outside the conference was No. 80 Denver. Here the importance of scheduling becomes apparent. Cal never gave itself a chance to beat a mid-tier team at Haas Pavilion. All three of the team's marquee games were played either on the road (at San Diego State and UNLV) or at a not particularly neutral site (facing Missouri in Kansas City). A one-point loss to the Aztecs at Viejas Arena loomed particularly large in March, and the outcome might have been different had the game been played in the hills above the Bay.

The Runnin' Rebels are coming to Berkeley this time around, and Cal's tournament appearance (the Anaheim Classic) will be much more neutral. However, the Golden Bears' toughest game will be played away from home. On December 2, Cal visits Madison, Wisconsin, to face Bo Ryan's Badgers.

What's in store for 2013: Gutierrez, a fixture on all four of Montgomery's Cal squads, is now plying his trade in his native Mexico. The Bears also lose reliable big man Harper Kamp. Everyone else of note returns, which is good because Cal is unlikely to get much help this year from a somewhat thin recruiting class.

MEET THE GOLDEN BEARS

Alan Crabbe (6-6, 210, Jr.): Depending on how Pac-12 voters feel about giving the award to a freshman like Shabazz Muhammad, seasoned veteran Crabbe might just be the favorite to follow Gutierrez as conference player of the year. He was second behind Colorado's André Roberson in Pac-12 wins above replacement, putting up numbers similar to fellow sophomore Terrence Ross with a fraction of the hype. Crabbe wasn't especially accurate inside the arc last season, making 46 percent of his twos. Everything else about his game was star quality. His sure-handed play helped boost his efficiency, and Crabbe was excellent on the defensive glass. Expect him to take on more responsibility in Gutierrez's absence.

Justin Cobbs (6-2, 190, Jr.): The Minnesota transfer played an unexpectedly key role in his first year in Berkeley. Cobbs quickly unseated incumbent Brandon Smith as the starting point guard with his combination of solid playmaking and efficient scoring. He made 44 percent of his three-point attempts and got to the line four times a night. Cobbs' size was also an asset to the Bears against opposing point guards.

David Kravish (6-9, 220, So.): Expected to battle for minutes off the bench, Kravish took full advantage of the opportunity provided by Solomon's absence from the lineup due to injury and academics. He started 24 games and was an easy choice for the Pac-12 All-Freshman Team. The challenge for the lanky Kravish is to translate his high-percentage finishing into a larger role in the offense with the departure of Kamp, who was Cal's go-to guy in the paint. Kravish is also a fine shot blocker thanks to his long arms.

Richard Solomon (6-10, 235, Jr.): Solomon missed time due to a stress fracture in his left foot in December, then was ruled academically ineligible at the semester break and sat out the rest of the season. He returns for his junior year as the likely starter next to Kravish, supplying athleticism and activity in the paint. Solomon is a fine rebounder and shot blocker who can finish around the rim. A Kravish-Solomon frontcourt should be stout at the defensive end.

Ricky Kreklow (6-6, 210, So.): Cal suffered a blow when Kreklow, the projected starter next to Crabbe on the wing, underwent surgery to repair a stress reaction in his right foot in early October. He's expected to miss six to eight weeks. Kreklow transferred from Missouri, where he struggled as a freshman in a limited role. When healthy, he projects to help the Golden Bears with his combination of size and outside shooting.

Brandon Smith (6-0, 180, Sr.): One of the conference's most improved players as a sophomore, Smith gave back much of that development during his junior year, leaving his role in doubt entering his final season. Smith couldn't buy a three-pointer in 2011-12 and turned the ball over far too often, which forced Montgomery to cut his playing time nearly in half. Since Cobbs has enough size to play 2-guard, Smith has the opportunity to earn more minutes if he is more efficient this season.

Robert Thurman (6-10, 265, Sr.): Thurman walked on after transferring from D-III Norwich University. Thrust into the role of third big man last season, Thurman more than held his own, making 64 percent of his two-point attempts. However he was less effective at the defensive end, where he is slow footed and poor as a rebounder and shot blocker.

Jeff Powers (6-7, 225, Jr.): Having played fewer than 200 minutes in his two seasons with the Golden Bears, Powers could be the beneficiary of the team's unsettled wing rotation. He's got the most size of any of Montgomery's options and could improve his shooting with more regular action. If Powers falters or is unable to keep up defensively, tweener forward Christian Behrens (6-9, 225, So.) could be the alternative.

Bak Bak (6-9, 240, Sr.): Bak fell behind Kravish and Thurman in the rotation and likely enters his senior season as Cal's fourth post player. The Sudan native has yet to translate his potential into production beyond medium-high-percentage shooting in a limited role, and is not a major factor on defense.

Prospectus says: Cal's top three players are good enough to contend for a Pac-12 title. Too bad the rest of the roster is not to up to that standard. If Kreklow gets healthy and contributes and Smith bounces back, the Golden Bears could be back in the NCAA tournament. More likely, despite Crabbe's heroics, Cal will take a slight step back after losing two key seniors.

COLORADO

2012: 24-12 (11-7 Pac-12); Lost to Baylor 80-63, NCAA round of 32
In-conference offense: 1.01 points per possession (8th)
In-conference defense: 0.96 points allowed per possession (3rd)

What Colorado did well: *Get hot at the right time.*

During their first year in the conference, the Buffaloes tied for fifth during the Pac-12 regular season. That was actually superior to their performance over the full year; Colorado was ranked seventh in the conference by Ken Pomeroy's ratings. Nonetheless, it was Tad Boyle's crew that earned the first automatic bid in Pac-12 history. The Buffaloes became the first team to win four games in as many days since the Pac-10/12 tournament expanded, cruising by Utah, escaping against Oregon and dispatching Cal and Arizona to reach the NCAA tournament as a No. 11 seed.

The run continued in Albuquerque, where Colorado knocked off UNLV before getting blown out by Baylor. A few factors came together in the Buffaloes' favor besides good fortune. Boyle's tactics kept opposing coaches guessing throughout the run. Colorado got better as the season went on because of the development of the team's talented freshman guards. Lastly, the athletic department deserves credit for paying the way to Los Angeles (and later the NCAA tournament) for 50 members of the C-Unit, the school's student section. The rowdy fans provided the Buffaloes an unlikely home-court advantage at the otherwise sterile Staples Center during the league tournament's last year in L.A. (Starting this season, the tournament will be played in Las Vegas.)

What we learned in 2012: *Boulder is a big home-court advantage.*

The difficulty of playing at a high altitude isn't exactly a well-kept secret. Still, it appeared to help Colorado more than expected during year one in the Pac-12. The Buffaloes went 8-1 in conference home games as compared to 3-6 on the road. Colorado outscored Pac-12 foes by an average of 10.8 points per game at home and was outscored by an average of 4.0 points on the road for a home-court advantage of +7.4 points per game.

During the season, College Basketball Prospectus contributor Ken Pomeroy studied home-court advantage in conference games dating back to 1999-2000 for ESPN Insider. The Buffaloes' home-court advantage in 2011-12 was larger than any team enjoyed over that span. (Utah Valley, at +7.3, ranked No. 1). In part, that's a product of the smaller sample. However, Pomeroy's findings showed that the two biggest factors in home-court advantage are altitude and distance from other conference schools. Colorado obviously enjoys the former and is the most remote outpost in the Pac-12. So expect the Buffaloes to continue to be much more potent at the Coors Events Center.

What's in store for 2013: Colorado lost three senior starters, tied with Oregon for the most conference. Fortunately, star forward André Roberson returns to lead a talented young roster. The Buffaloes will start two sophomores in the backcourt and could replace the departed seniors with a pair of top-100 freshmen.

MEET THE BUFFALOES

André Roberson (6-7, 210, Jr.): Enjoy Roberson while he's still in Boulder. Despite concerns over his height, the NBA likely beckons for Roberson, considered a possible first-round pick after his breakout sophomore season. His freshman performance portended stardom, and Roberson obliged by improving his defensive rebounding (good for second in the nation) as a full-time starter. Because of his ability to get off the ground quickly, Roberson is an elite shot blocker and he also generates plenty of steals for a power forward. While Roberson's offensive game can't match his defense, he used plays at an above-average rate last season with decent efficiency. He can beat slower defenders off the dribble and even flashed occasional three-point range. The total package makes Roberson the best player in the Pac-12, even if he might not score enough to win conference player of the year honors.

Spencer Dinwiddie (6-5, 190, So.): A fixture from his first action in a Colorado uniform, Dinwiddie set the school record by starting all 36 games. Dinwiddie was at his best from downtown, and his 44 percent three-point shooting bettered another CU mark. The next step for the smooth Dinwiddie is to improve his finishing after making just 38 percent of his two-pointers. Dinwiddie's drives did often lead him to the free throw line, where he shot 82 percent. As a 2-guard, Diwniddie's size is an asset.

Askia Booker (6-1, 170, So.): As a sixth man, Booker was more inconsistent than Dinwiddie, but he flashed star potential during his freshman season. Booker led the Buffaloes with 31 points in two NCAA tournament games. Playing mostly off the ball, he used a team-high 25 percent of CU's plays while on the floor. After the graduation of point guard Nate Tomlinson, Booker will have to make strides as a playmaker. Because of his size, he's a poor finisher, so another key to his development is the ability to create contact and draw free throws.

Josh Scott (6-10, 215, Fr.): Scott is the keystone of the best Colorado recruiting class since anyone bothered to rank such things, and at No. 38 overall per RSCIhoops.com, the team's highest-rated incoming freshman since David Harrison in 2001. During the Buffaloes' five-game European exhibition tour, Scott lived up to the hype by leading the team with 17.4 points and seven rebounds per game. While Scott needs to add strength to battle Pac-12 centers, he's a certain starter and the team's best post scorer right away.

Xavier Johnson (6-6, 220, Fr.): Colorado's other top-100 recruit, Johnson stands a good chance of joining Scott in a youthful starting lineup. Johnson was effective in his own right during the exhibition tour, averaging 11.2 points and seven boards. His best asset is a wingspan CU lists at 6-11 3/4, which allows him to play bigger on the glass. Johnson will have to develop his outside shooting to stretch the floor.

Shane Harris-Tunks (6-11, 250, Jr.): With Booker heading to the starting five, Harris-Tunks is the Colorado reserve who saw the most action last season. A pick-and-pop big man, the Aussie relied on two-point jumpers as a higher percentage of his shots than any other Buffalo, per Hoop-Math.com. Alas, that's not a recipe for efficiency, and Harris-Tunks also struggled with turnovers. A year removed from the torn ACL that cost him 2010-11, he may prove more mobile at the defensive end.

Jeremy Adams (6-5, 220, Jr.): Adams has the size and experience to figure into the rotation on the wing. He struggled in his first season after transferring from the junior college ranks, however, making just three of his 21 attempts from long distance and shooting little more accurately closer to the hoop.

Sabatino Chen (6-4, 190, Sr.): The lone senior on the Colorado roster, Chen supplied energy off the bench in 2011-12 after transferring from the University of Denver. He was extremely judicious with his shot attempts and made 65 percent of his twos, but missed all 11 three-point tries.

Xavier Talton (6-1, 180, Fr.): Boyle gave 11 players regular minutes in Europe, so it's too early to tell which freshmen will fill out the rotation during the season. Talton could see action as a backup to Booker, while Wesley Gordon (6-8, 225, Fr.) also fills a need as a fourth big man. Chris Jenkins (6-7, 180, Fr.) averaged 7.4 points per game during the exhibition tour and offers size on the wing, and Eli Stalzer (6-3, 185, Fr.) could prove the team's best shooter off the bench.

Prospectus says: Expecting the Buffaloes to repeat last year's March magic is unrealistic. Still, with Roberson anchoring the talented young starting lineup, Colorado should be in the mix in the Pac-12's crowded middle tier.

OREGON

2012: 24-10 (13-5 Pac-12); Lost to Washington 90-86, NIT quarterfinals
In-conference offense: 1.12 points per possession (1st)
In-conference defense: 1.02 points allowed per possession (8th)

What Oregon did well: *Shoot the ball.*

After turning the Ducks around at the defensive end during his first year in Eugene, Dana Altman focused his attention on offense in 2011-12. With a more talented and experienced group—more on that in a second—Oregon shot the ball well from every area. The Ducks were second in conference play in two-point shooting (52 percent), three-point shooting (40 percent) and free throw shooting (73 percent). That drove the Pac-12's best offense, one that ranked No. 14 nationally. While the defense wasn't good enough to carry Oregon to the NCAA tournament, the team's 13-5 conference record was the best for the Ducks since they won the Pac-10 in 2001-02.

What we learned in 2012: *Who needs recruits when you have transfers?*

Oregon improved with virtually no help from incoming freshmen. Altman signed a solid class headlined by guard Jabari Brown, but Brown didn't even last a month on campus before deciding to transfer, ultimately to Missouri. He was followed out the door by guard Bruce Barron. Brett Kingma at least made it through the season, playing sparingly before transferring to Washington State. That leaves redshirt Austin Kuemper as the lone remaining player from the Ducks' 2011 recruiting class.

Altman still got plenty of help from newcomers, all of the transfer variety. Guard Devoe Joseph, formerly at Minnesota, became eligible at the semester break and immediately emerged as the Ducks' go-to guy. Joseph's valuable combination of volume and accuracy as a scorer with some playmaking added in was the biggest reason the Oregon offense was so potent in conference play. Like Joseph, post Olu Ashaolu spent only one season in Eugene but made major contributions.

The other two transfers, forward Carlos Emory and center Tony Woods, were also key players and both return for their senior seasons. They could be joined by yet another notable transfer, former Rice forward Arsalan Kazemi. The talented Iranian, who has averaged a double-double over three seasons in college, opted to change schools during the summer. He pursued a hardship waiver to become immediately eligible, and the matter was still pending as the book went to press.

What's in store for 2013: Besides Joseph and Ashaolu, the Ducks also graduated starter Garret Sim and reserve forwards Jeremy Jacob and Tyrone Nared. Add in Kingma and that's six of the team's 10 rotation players that departed, meaning another makeover for Altman. Senior forward E.J. Singler—perhaps in tandem with Kazemi—leads a frontcourt-heavy Oregon squad that will rely on their most prominent incoming freshman, point guard Dominic Artis.

MEET THE DUCKS

Arsalan Kazemi (6-7, 225, Sr.): Despite a leap in the level of competition, expect Kazemi to be a star from his first game in Eugene—whether that's now or next season. Adjusted for strength of schedule, only Colorado's André Roberson posted more wins above replacement than Kazemi among returning Pac-12 players. The undersized Kazemi ranked right behind Roberson as No. 3 in the nation in defensive rebound percentage. He was a high-percentage finisher against C-USA foes, making 60 percent of his twos, and he lived at the charity stripe, ranking eighth in the country in free throw rate.

E.J. Singler (6-6, 215, Sr.): The younger Singler has never been able to break free of the shadow of older brother Kyle, who starred at Duke and is now in the NBA. E.J. is a fine player in his own right. His 117 offensive rating was fourth in the Pac-12 among players who used at least 20 percent of their team's plays. Singler was efficient despite dropping from 40 to 37 percent from beyond the arc. He's solid closer to the hoop and automatic (91 percent) at the free throw line. In addition to drawing the defense, Singler is a solid contributor from the wing on the defensive glass. Only concern: Singler cut his flowing locks over the summer. Hopefully, his hair wasn't the source of his powers.

Dominic Artis (6-1, 185, Fr.): After originally committing to UCLA, Artis reopened his recruiting and became the centerpiece of Oregon's incoming class. The Ducks will put the ball in his hands right away and turn him loose. Artis should excel at getting to the basket off the dribble; setting up teammates when he drives, on the other hand, figures to take time. Defensively, Artis could struggle against more physical opponents. His listed height is two inches taller than recruiting sources indicated.

Tony Woods (6-11, 245, Sr.): In his first year in Eugene, Woods was part of a post rotation where no player saw more than 20 minutes per game. He served as the defensive anchor of the group, swatting away nine percent of opposing two-point tries—good for third in the conference. Since Woods isn't nearly as strong on the defensive glass, Kazemi would be a good partner for him in the frontcourt. Considered a legit NBA prospect when he started out at Wake Forest, Woods simply hasn't progressed enough on offense to justify the hype. He finishes decently but rarely creates his own shot.

Carlos Emory (6-5, 205, Sr.): Junior college transfer Emory came on down the stretch, scoring double figures in 10 of the season's last 14 games. In conference play, Emory made an incredible 69 percent of his two-point attempts, scoring against bigger defenders in the paint. Yet Emory's playing time still went down slightly during the Pac-12 season, suggesting that Altman was concerned about Emory's size on defense.

Johnathan Loyd (5-8, 165, Jr.): Because of Joseph's arrival, Loyd played less as a sophomore than he did as a freshman. He will likely play more this season, and could start if Altman can find a way to play him alongside Artis in a tiny backcourt. Loyd is the team's best playmaker, and last year's assist rate (29 percent) ranked sixth in the conference. He struggles to hit shots, however, making 37 percent of his threes and 29 percent of his twos. While obviously limited by his height on defense, Loyd does generate plenty of steals.

Waverly Austin (6-11, 270, Jr.): The Ducks picked up a late commitment from Austin, a junior college transfer, after he was unable to attain eligibility at South Florida before school started. (Austin had more time because Oregon is on a quarter system, not semesters.) Rated the No. 5 transfer in the country by Jucorecruiting.com, Austin will give the Ducks size when Woods is on the bench.

Ben Carter (6-8, 220, Fr.): Especially if Kazemi is not ruled eligible, the Ducks will need more help in the frontcourt. Carter, who was Shabazz Muhammad's running mate at Bishop Gorman HS in Las Vegas last season, will get the first crack. A stretch 4, Carter picked Oregon despite a heavy recruiting effort from UNLV, in part because it meant reuniting with still another high school teammate, Johnathan Loyd. Later in the season, Altman could add Arik Armstead (6-8, 280, Fr.) after the freshman wraps up a stellar debut campaign as a defensive end for Chip Kelly.

Fred Richardson III (6-4, 200, Fr.): The Ducks could also use another guard. In terms of contributing immediately, Richardson's shooting ability might give him the edge over the versatile, athletic Damyean Dotson (6-5, 200, Fr.). Expect both of these three-star recruits from Texas to get opportunities.

Prospectus says: It's impossible to project Oregon's performance without knowing Kazemi's status for the upcoming season. If he plays, the Ducks can compete with anyone outside of Arizona and UCLA. Without Kazemi, Oregon would be young and thin. In that scenario, even Altman's junk defenses would have a hard time pushing the Ducks above .500.

OREGON STATE

2012: 21-15 (7-11 Pac-12); Lost to Washington State 72-55, CBI semifinals
In-conference offense: 1.06 points per possession (4th)
In-conference defense: 1.08 points allowed per possession (10th)

What Oregon State did well: *Beat non-conference foes.*

The Beavers peaked early in 2011-12, starting the season 11-2 before entering Pac-12 play. This marked a major turnaround given that Oregon State had gone 16-16 in non-conference games during the regular season in Craig Robinson's first three years at the helm. Though the OSU schedule wasn't particularly daunting, the Beavers did pick up one of the Pac-12's marquee non-conference wins by beating Texas in overtime at the TicketCity Legends Classic in East Rutherford, New Jersey. Oregon State very nearly added a win over Vanderbilt in the tournament's championship, falling 61-59.

That's not to say the Beavers were entirely immune, however, to the inexplicable home losses that have marked their Novembers and Decembers under Robinson. Their other loss came by 14 at Gill Coliseum to Idaho. Still, Oregon State mostly took care of business and indeed was the rare Pac-12 team that took momentum into conference play. The Beavers added two more wins over non-conference opponents in the early rounds of the CBI before their season came to an end against Pac-12 foe Washington State in the semifinals.

What we learned in 2012: *The Beavers are due to improve their three-point defense.*

College Basketball Prospectus contributor Ken Pomeroy did terrific work on his blog during the 2011-12 season to research the variability of three-point shooting. Among his most provocative findings was that teams have essentially no control over the percentage their opponents shoot from beyond the arc. That's not to say that three-point defense doesn't exist, but the short NCAA season doesn't produce a large enough sample size for the stat to normalize.

Pomeroy's research should be hailed in Corvallis because Oregon State died by the three again and again last season. Opponents made 40 percent of their threes against the Beavers. Three-point defense is a known weakness of the 1-3-1 zone Robinson still uses on occasions. However, the issue is usually giving up three-point attempts, period, as opposed to allowing teams to make a high percentage of them. Oregon State did improve in that regard by playing far less 1-3-1, cutting the percentage of shots opponents took from downtown dramatically from 41 percent to 30 percent. So it's reasonable to expect better three-point defense this year.

What's in store for 2013: Of the eight Oregon State players who averaged at least 10 minutes per game, seven are back. Unfortunately, that group doesn't include Jared Cunningham, who entered the NBA draft after his junior season and was taken in the first round. The Beavers will count on juniors Devon Collier, Roberto Nelson and Ahmad Starks growing into larger roles to help fill the void.

MEET THE BEAVERS

Devon Collier (6-8, 215, Jr.): After relying on activity as a freshman, Collier flashed more skill in year two in Corvallis. He created more opportunities for himself, slashed his turnover rate, and improved his shooting both from the field and the free throw line. That last part was important, since Collier got to the line at the conference's top rate. Overall, the lefty's 122 offensive rating was second only to three-point specialist Brendan Lavender of Arizona among Pac-12 players. This year, Oregon State will put the ball in Collier's hands more frequently. He's best facing up and beating slower defenders with a quick move. Collier is also a fine shot blocker, though he could stand to put more focus on the defensive glass.

Ahmad Starks (5-9, 165, Jr.): A diminutive Chicago native, Starks made huge strides with his decision making during his sophomore campaign. Sure, he still likes to pull the trigger from deep, but more of those shots went in last season, as he went from 32 percent to 37 percent on threes. Starks also slightly improved his two-point accuracy and cut down on his turnovers. Since Cunningham often operated as the team's primary ball handler, Starks will have to do a better job of finding teammates this year. He will supplant Cunningham as OSU's top ball hawk on defense.

Joe Burton (6-7, 295, Sr.): The Beavers' best senior is Burton, whose size belies his impressive skills. Burton put things together during his third year in the program, becoming far more efficient as a scorer in a reserve role. Oregon State can throw the ball in to Burton in the post against smaller defenders, and he also excels in the high post, where his passing ability is a major strength. He doesn't get off the ground well, meaning few blocked shots, but his agility translates into a remarkable steal rate for a big man. Burton's also strong on the defensive glass.

Roberto Nelson (6-3, 195, Jr.): This is a crucial season for Nelson, a big-time recruit whose OSU career was delayed by academic ineligibility in 2009-10. By the time Nelson got on the floor, Cunningham was established as the Beavers' go-to guy. That meant an awkward fit with Nelson, a volume scorer who found better efficiency off the bench last year. If Nelson can avoid trying to do too much, he's the player most capable of stepping into Cunningham's role. One key will be getting to the basket more frequently, which would help Nelson's subpar two-point percentage.

Eric Moreland (6-10, 215, So.): Moreland moved into the starting lineup midway through his freshman campaign and ended up leading the Pac-12 in blocked shots. The lanky Moreland has long arms and excellent timing at the defensive end, and he's also an outstanding defensive rebounder (No. 2 in the conference in percentage), especially for a player who contests so many shots. On offense, Moreland mostly set screens and stayed out of the way. He could stand to improve his finishing, though teams generally preferred to make Moreland earn two points at the line since he made just half of his free throws.

Angus Brandt (6-10, 240, Sr.): Stop me if you've heard this before, but Brandt is an Oregon State player who dramatically improved his shooting percentages last season. The Aussie developed three-point range, making nearly half of his 59 attempts, and knocked down 55 percent of his twos. Floor spacing is Brandt's major statistical contribution. He is not a significant presence on the glass and racks up few assists, steals or blocks.

Victor Robbins (6-6, 195, Fr.): Robinson is high on Robbins, a three-star swingman from Compton who signed on after Cunningham's departure and could play a key role off the bench. A natural scorer, Robbins must improve his three-point range and stay focused on defense to help the Beavers as a freshman. Langston Morris-Walker (6-5, 215, Fr.) and Jarmal Reid (6-7, 225, Fr.) are also in the mix on the wing.

Challe Barton (6-3, 195, So.): The Pac-12's preeminent Swede saw limited action off the bench as a freshman and will continue to back up Starks at the point. That generally meant bringing the ball up and letting Cunningham or Nelson initiate the offense. Barton did not contribute much besides free throws last season, shooting just 6-of-29 from three-point range.

Daniel Gomis (6-10, 225, So.): The Beavers were excited about Gomis, rated a top-100 recruit in some circles. He ended up missing all of last season after breaking his leg while back home in his native Senegal over the summer. Now healthy, Gomis will battle for minutes up front and could step into a starting role after Brandt and Burton graduate. He'll have competition from newcomer Olaf Schaftenaar (6-9, 220, Fr.), the brother of former OSU standout Roeland Schaftenaar.

Prospectus says: Between Cunningham's departure and the improvement of the rest of the conference, Oregon State could make solid strides and still end up in exact the same spot. The optimistic but still reachable goal is going .500 for the first time since 1992-93.

STANFORD

2012: 26-11, (10-8 Pac-12); Beat Minnesota 75-51, NIT final
In-conference offense: 1.00 points per possession (9th)
In-conference defense: 0.97 points allowed per possession (6th)

What Stanford did well: *Win the NIT.*

While an invitation to the NIT means a snub from the NCAA tournament for many teams, the Cardinal was content to be there after two years without any postseason play at all. Stanford came from behind to defeat visiting Illinois State in overtime in the second round of the tournament, then romped the rest of the way to the title. Two of the Cardinal's five wins, including the final against Minnesota, came by 20-plus points. During the run, Stanford improved its Pomeroy ranking from No. 53 entering the NIT to No. 32 at season's end, which put the Cardinal behind only archrival Cal in the Pac-12.

What we learned in 2012: *Johnny Dawkins can coach an elite defense.*

During his first three seasons on the Farm, Anne and Tony Joseph Director of Men's Basketball Dawkins (more commonly called Coach) oversaw a series of middle-of-the-Pac defenses. Technically, last year's team fell into this category too, ranking just sixth in the conference in points allowed per possession. In fact this was misleading for a couple of reasons. First, the Pac-12 was very top-heavy defensively. The difference between sixth-place Stanford and first-place Cal (0.95 points allowed per possession) was less than half the difference between the Cardinal and USC, who ranked seventh at 1.01.

Beyond that, Stanford was far stouter defensively against non-conference foes, which explains both the NIT run and a 10-2 start to the season that featured three wins against teams ranked in the Pomeroy top 100. Factor all that in and the Cardinal ranked No. 19 in the nation in Pomeroy's adjusted defensive efficiency, their best such finish under Dawkins by some 55 spots.

With a deep group of competent big men, Stanford played aggressively in the paint. The Cardinal sent opponents to the free throw line more frequently than any other Pac-12 team. Dawkins lived with all those free throws because Stanford contested everything in the paint, forced turnovers, and controlled the defensive glass. While the Cardinal won't be able to use an identical formula this season, it's good to know that Dawkins' system can be so successful.

What's in store for 2013: Stanford said goodbye to longtime starter Josh Owens, as well as big men Jack Trotter and Andrew Zimmermann and wing Jarrett Mann. Besides Owens, the other three departed veterans played relatively small roles in the Cardinal attack, offering reason to believe their contributions can be replaced. Dawkins brings in a strong recruiting class featuring a pair of top-100 newcomers, forward Rosco Allen and center Grant Verhoeven.

MEET THE CARDINAL

Chasson Randle (6-1, 180, So.): During an impressive debut season, Randle set Stanford freshman records for starts, minutes and threes, finishing second in points. He averaged 14 points in the NIT, playing a key role in the Cardinal's run. Shooting was the strength of Randle's game as a freshman, as he made 44 percent of his attempts both inside and outside the arc. He was efficient because he took as many threes as twos. Billed as a combo guard, Randle essentially functioned as a 2 last year. He may have to run the point at times this season.

Aaron Bright (5-11, 180, Jr.): Randle could play off the ball last season because Stanford had a solid playmaker in Bright, who increased his assist rate from 21 percent to 26 percent as a full-time starter at point guard. Bright too is dangerous beyond the arc, having made 44 percent of his triples. As he becomes more aggressive and learns to negotiate shot blockers, Bright could emerge as one of the Pac-12's top lead guards. He competes defensively despite his small stature.

Dwight Powell (6-10, 235, Jr.): Consider Powell the Cardinal's enigma. A big-time recruit two years ago, Powell still had NBA prospect sheen entering his sophomore season before slumping badly and losing his starting job. Powell did improve his defensive rebounding and was a positive force on D, racking up both blocks and steals. However, he has to find a way to contribute on offense. The three-point line surely isn't it. Powell, who spent too much time on the perimeter given his athletic gifts, made just one of his 17 attempts from downtown.

Anthony Brown (6-6, 215, Jr.): Brown started 21 games last season and ranked fourth on the team in minutes played. His numbers don't justify such a large role, however, especially with Stanford bringing in talent on the wings. Brown's reputation as a three-point threat doesn't match his performance; he's made 35 percent of his triples over the last two seasons. Brown does have good size, and he emerged as a solid defensive rebounder for his position.

Josh Huestis (6-7, 230, Jr.): An incredible leaper with long arms, Huestis found his niche as a perimeter stopper late in the season. He earned Pac-12 All-Defensive honorable mention and should be considered a favorite for a spot this year. Huestis also blocks shots by the bushel (he ranked fifth in the Pac-12) and is a fine rebounder at both ends. Offensively, Huestis did no harm, though his free throw and three-point percentages indicate he is not a natural shooter.

Rosco Allen (6-9, 215, Fr.): Consider Allen, who was born in Hungary, a lock for Bill Simmons' Reggie Cleveland All-Stars. He has terrific size for a wing, and should challenge for heavy minutes right away after teaming with Shabazz Muhammad last year at Bishop Gorman HS in Las Vegas. Allen is considered an excellent shooter and could develop into a quality stretch 4 if he can improve defensively and on the glass.

Grant Verhoeven (6-9, 240, Fr.): The Cardinal is in a good spot with Verhoeven, who was ranked the nation's No. 19 center by ESPN. If Verhoeven plays well, there's nothing keeping him from the starting lineup. If he struggles like most young big men, Stanford has plenty of alternatives up front. So it's all on Verhoeven, who has good fundamentals and a strong motor. Our own Drew Cannon suggests Verhoeven may be a "secretly elite" shot blocker.

John Gage (6-10, 235, Jr.): When Gage checks in, watch for opposing coaches to yell "shooter" to their team. Gage took nearly three-quarters of his shot attempts from beyond the arc, making a solid 37 percent of his threes. He also knocked down 55 percent of his rare two-point tries, but Gage's shortcomings on the glass and defensively limit him to a part-time role.

Stefan Nastic (6-11, 245, So.): Nastic, henceforth to be known in this book as "Nasty Nas," is a Serbian by way of Canada who represented his birth country in the U-20 European Championships over the summer. As a redshirt freshman (his 2010-11 season, which ended after five games, got him a medical hardship), Nastic made just 33 percent of his two-point tries and struggled with turnovers, but he's got the size and skill to develop into a contributor.

Gabriel Harris (6-2, 190, Sr.): Dawkins has to go deep into his bench before finding a senior. Harris contributed a bit as a reserve early in 2011-12 before undergoing surgery on his right knee. Problematically, Harris is a career 29 percent shooter on twos, so he may lose his spot to sharpshooting Christian Sanders (6-4, 185, Fr.).

Andy Brown (6-7, 215, Sr.): In one of the season's best stories, Brown returned from tearing his left ACL three times in as many years to log his first action for Stanford. He saw some minutes down the stretch and could play a bigger role if he stays healthy.

Prospectus says: Nobody in the conference brings back more talent than Stanford, and this looks like the leader of the second tier after Arizona and UCLA. A return to the NCAA tournament for the first time since Trent Johnson coached the Lopez twins is the benchmark for success this season in Palo Alto.

UCLA

2012: 19-14 (11-7 Pac-12); Lost to Arizona 66-58, Pac-12 quarterfinals
In-conference offense: 1.06 points per possession (3rd)
In-conference defense: 0.97 points allowed per possession (5th)

What UCLA did well: *Generate copy.*

It was a busy year to be a Bruins beat writer. While UCLA fans probably won't want to relive the ups and downs—mostly downs—of 2011-12, let's recap. Playing the season at temporary venues (mostly the L.A. Sports Arena, with a few games at the Honda Center in Anaheim), the Bruins lost their opener at "home" to Loyola Marymount. Star Reeves Nelson did not participate in timeouts during the game, and after an argument with coach Ben Howland at practice the next day he was suspended for a subsequent home loss to Middle Tennessee State.

Nelson rejoined the team for the Maui Invitational, but, after beating Chaminade in the opener, UCLA lost to both Kansas and Michigan. After a home loss to Texas dropped the Bruins to 2-5, Nelson was dismissed from the team. The hope was that shedding the distraction of Nelson's off-court troubles would help UCLA. That never really panned out. The Bruins did go 11-7 in Pac-12 play, including a win over conference champion Washington in the last game of the regular season. However, after beating USC in the opening round of the Pac-12 tournament, UCLA lost to Arizona to end any hope of advancing to the NCAA tournament.

Late in the season, Pulitzer Prize winner George Dohrmann of Sports Illustrated published a story chronicling the Bruins' series of high-profile transfers and Nelson's ongoing discipline problems. While whispers to the effect that the story would reveal a serious drug problem in Westwood proved overblown—college players experimenting with recreational drugs dates back to at least the Wooden era, after all —Dohrmann's story did paint Howland as aloof, out of touch, and incapable of managing the difficult personalities he had recruited. Given that Howland had already lost favor with UCLA alumni based on the team's performance and style of play, the story seemed to spell doom.

What we learned in 2012: *UCLA is still UCLA.*

The down season, the SI article, and all the questions about his future should have made it impossible for Howland to recruit, right?

Wrong. Instead, the Bruins used their legacy to reel in a class that is rated either first or second in the country, depending on the source. Having first signed point forward Kyle Anderson, the consensus No. 3 prospect per RSCIhoops.com, UCLA won a heated battle for Las Vegas wing Shabazz Muhammad, the nation's top incoming freshman. After Muhammad signed up, the Bruins also landed top-25 recruit Tony Parker. Guard Jordan Adams, a fourth top-100 newcomer, rounds out the impressive class.

Already, Howland's class of 2013 is shaping up solidly. The Bruins landed one of the top point guards in the West, Zach LaVine, out of Washington's backyard. They also beat out the likes of Duke and Kansas for Allerik Freeman, a top-100 shooting guard from Charlotte.

What's in store for 2013: The most important moment of UCLA's season will be when the school finds out about the eligibility of Muhammad, who has been investigated by the NCAA because of his family's relationship to financial advisers. Muhammad did not join the Bruins on their offseason trip to China, which kept him from starting a 45-day clock on practicing with the team before his eligibility is determined. Howland told reporters Muhammad was also rehabbing a badly sprained ankle at the time. Anderson, who did play in China, also had yet to be cleared at the start of fall camp because of his family's dealings with agent Thad Foucher. However, all indications were that Anderson would be eligible for the season. Besides the talented freshmen, UCLA also adds former North Carolina guard Larry Drew II as a transfer. Drew will help replace departed seniors Jerime Anderson and Lazeric Jones in the backcourt.

MEET THE BRUINS

Shabazz Muhammad (6-6, 225, Fr.): Expectations for Muhammad might need to be tempered a bit. As elite wing prospects go, he's probably more Harrison Barnes than Kevin Durant. Muhammad is still the top offensive freshman in the country and one of the top players in the Pac-12 from the point when (and if) he's cleared. A compact lefty with a developed upper body, Muhammad excels from midrange but can shoot the NCAA three. He's also a threat off the dribble and a decent playmaker. Muhammad has the tools to be a quality defender if engaged in Howland's system.

Kyle Anderson (6-9, 235, Fr.): Few players do a better job of making the case that positions are obsolete than Anderson, who can defend either forward spot but operates primarily as a point guard on offense. Though the lanky Anderson could be vulnerable to pressure from smaller guards, his height allows him to see over the defense and find teammates. (Does that remind anyone of a former point guard plying his trade in L.A.? Name of Magic Johnson?) While not particularly quick (his nickname is "Slo Mo"), Anderson can get where he wants on the floor. He's a fine defensive rebounder and will also contribute blocked shots. The weakest part of Anderson's game is his perimeter shooting, which is why he's best with the ball in his hands.

David Wear (6-10, 230, Jr.),
Travis Wear (6-10, 230, Jr.): The Wears were reliable presences for an inconsistent Bruins team during their first year of eligibility. While David started more games (30) than Travis (24), the latter was the more effective of the two players. Travis used slightly more plays, made more of his two-point tries (54 percent vs. 49) and blocked five times as many shots (36 to seven). David's advantage is that he's a better shooter, which could allow him to play small forward at times. Whether the Wears start together or Howland brings one off the bench, they will continue to play key roles alongside the new talent.

Tyler Lamb (6-5, 200, Jr.): With Doron Lamb and Jeremy Lamb both heading to the NBA, Tyler Lamb can finally claim the title of best wing named Lamb in the NCAA. Lamb was effective at times during his sophomore season, including a 26-point outburst against Cal. Overall, however, his shooting percentages—45 percent on twos, 36 percent on threes—were too low for a player who used plays at a below-average rate. Defensively, Lamb contributed plenty of steals and has enough size to play either wing spot. He underwent arthroscopic knee surgery in early October, but should be back early in the schedule.

Joshua Smith (6-10, 305, Jr.): After coming into camp out of shape, Smith took an enormous step backward in his sophomore campaign. He was never in game condition, limiting him to brief stints and leading to constant foul trouble because he was unable to keep up with quicker opponents, especially when asked to play the pick-and-roll. When he was on the floor, Smith was as difficult to guard in the post as ever. He's got a soft touch and generates easy opportunities by overpowering defenders. At media day, Howland said Smith is in better shape than last year though not yet where he needs to be.

Tony Parker (6-9, 275, Fr.): The Bruins now have two behemoth post players with the addition of Parker, who will never, ever be confused with the diminutive NBA point guard of the same name. Parker is a bit more versatile than Smith and can step to the perimeter at times. Howland will want to limit those situations, though, because Parker figures to be most valuable on the offensive glass.

Larry Drew II (6-2, 180, Sr.): The son of the former NBA guard who is now coach of the Atlanta Hawks, Drew, like the Wears, is a SoCal product who left North Carolina to come back home. He will be one of the Pac-12's top playmakers, though in order to stay on the floor he must rein in the turnovers that aggravated Tar Heel fans. Hopefully Drew spent his transfer season working on his inconsistent three-point shot.

Norman Powell (6-4, 215, So.): As a freshman, Powell played a lot because Howland had so few options. Much of the year, Powell was the last member of a seven-player rotation, and he struggled to score. Powell made just 41 percent of his two-point tries, and decent three-point shooting (35 percent) wasn't enough to make him efficient offensively.

Jordan Adams (6-5, 220, Fr.): While Adams would be the jewel of most Pac-12 recruiting classes, he's an afterthought at UCLA. The Oak Hill product will battle Powell for backup minutes on the wing and stands an excellent chance of supplanting him. If Adams proves a knockdown shooter as advertised, Howland will get him on the court.

Prospectus says: Because of Muhammad's uncertain status, the Bruins might be more difficult to predict than any team in the country. One way or another, Howland brings his most talented team in years back to a renovated Pauley Pavilion. If Muhammad is cleared—even if he's suspended for some or all of non-conference play—UCLA will not only be the favorite to win the Pac-12 but one of the leading contenders nationally. Hopefully, the NCAA will not drag out the process so Howland and his team can move forward together.

USC

2012: 6-26 (1-17 Pac-12); Lost to UCLA 55-40, Pac-12 first round
In-conference offense: 0.82 points per possession (12th)
In-conference defense: 1.01 points allowed per possession (7th)

What USC did well: *Defend.*

The Trojans were battered by injuries in 2011-12. Starting with a torn ACL that ended Jio Fontan's season over the summer, USC was hit again and again. Starting forward Aaron Fuller missed 14 games after shoulder surgery. A variety of ailments cost starting center Dewayne Dedmon 12 games. And shoulder injuries limited Evan Smith to four games and kept Curtis Washington out the entire campaign.

By the end of the Pac-12 schedule, USC was down to six scholarship players and senior walk-on Eric Strangis, meaning literally every healthy body was given long minutes. Starting point guard Maurice Jones averaged more than 38 per game, which ranked him sixth in the country. Yet the undermanned Trojans continued to compete at the defensive end, ranking seventh in conference play in points allowed per possession and in the country's top 50 in adjusted defensive efficiency overall. Kevin O'Neill's ability to coach a solid defense is no surprise, but doing so with a makeshift cast was actually one of his most impressive accomplishments.

What we learned in 2012: *Depth matters.*

While no team would survive losing three of its top four players, USC's bad luck was exacerbated by O'Neill's tendency to feature small rotations, in part because of heavy turnover. With few alternatives on hand, the Trojans were surely the nation's least talented major-conference team by the time Dedmon and Fuller were sidelined midway through conference play. For all their solid defense, the Men of Troy simply could not score. Their adjusted offensive efficiency was the worst of any team from a major conference, and only Pac-12 rival Utah was anywhere close. As a result, USC finished 1-17 in conference play. After that lone win at home over the Utes, they lost their final 10 games of the season.

The Trojans again suffered multiple defections after the campaign ended. Washington, guard Alexis Moore and forward Garrett Jackson—the latter two having actually stayed healthy last season—all transferred. USC will have more depth this season because of a raft of newcomers and because of the players returning to the lineup. For that to last, however, O'Neill will have to keep players around.

What's in store for 2013: While the Trojans did not graduate a single scholarship player, besides the transfers they also lost Jones, who is academically ineligible for the coming season but will remain in school. At the same time, USC adds as much proven talent as any team in the conference. The Trojans have three Division I transfers (and possibly a fourth) becoming eligible along with junior college standout J.T. Terrell. USC's lineup will turn over almost entirely from the end of last season with massive talent upgrades.

MEET THE TROJANS

Jio Fontan (6-0, 175, Sr.): More than a year removed from his torn ACL, Fontan is back for his senior season. The Fordham transfer was second on the team in scoring and tops in assists in 2010-11. Assuming Fontan recovers his quickness, he's a proven playmaker. Before the injury, Fontan's biggest shortcoming was his height, which limited his ability to finish around the rim. He made just 43 percent of his twos as a junior.

Aaron Fuller (6-6, 235, Sr.): After playing as a stretch 4 before shoulder surgery ended his first season at USC, the former Iowa forward will probably spend time on the wing in 2012-13. The painful injury kept Fuller from shooting with his dominant left hand at times, yet he still made 52 percent of his two-point attempts. Fuller could improve that with a smaller role in the offense this season. He's a solid rebounder, especially on the offensive glass.

Dewayne Dedmon (7-0, 255, Jr.): As advertised, Dedmon showed raw potential as a starter in 2011-12. He did not pick up the game until his senior year of high school, and has made rapid improvement since then. During his first year with the Trojans, Dedmon couldn't shake injuries. A stress injury in his right foot limited him in December, and a torn MCL and bone bruise ended his season early. When Dedmon was on the floor, he was an active presence on the offensive boards, a high-percentage finisher, and a solid shot blocker. With plenty of size on the roster, USC is listing Dedmon as a forward. He can play the position defensively but won't be able to space the floor.

J.T. Terrell (6-3, 185, Jr.): A top-50 recruit entering Wake Forest, Terrell withdrew from school after a DWI arrest. He spent 2011-12 at Peninsula College in Port Angeles, Washington, and now returns to the D-I level. While Terrell's talent is undeniable, he still has to harness it. During his freshman campaign, he used more than a quarter of the Demon Deacons' plays with a poor true shooting percentage of 50. Decent from beyond the arc, Terrell made a disappointing 39 percent of his twos and will have to improve his shot selection to live up to the hype.

Eric Wise (6-6, 240, Sr.): Like Terrell, Wise was an indiscriminate shooter someplace else (UC Irvine) before transferring in to O'Neill's program, though he didn't have the same kind of talent around him. Wise's usage rate will surely come down from 30 percent. The concern is that Wise couldn't score efficiently in the Big West, and now the level of defense gets much better. On the plus side, he is a terrific rebounder from the wing, and according to Jeff Goodman of CBSSports.com, Wise dropped 50 pounds while sitting out last season.

Omar Oraby (7-2, 270, Jr.): At press time, the Trojans were still waiting to hear whether Oraby would be able to use a hardship waiver to become eligible immediately after transferring from Rice as part of a summer exodus from Ben Braun's squad. Whenever he takes the court at the Galen Center, Oraby will be one of the Pac-12's biggest players. The Egyptian put up remarkable numbers in limited minutes as a sophomore. His 15 percent block rate ranked third in the nation, and Oraby made 63 percent of his two-point shots and a solid 71 percent of his free throws. No wonder O'Neill is musing about the possibility of a giant Dedmon-Oraby frontcourt.

Byron Wesley (6-5, 210, So.): Believer it or not, the USC roster includes actual players recruited to the program out of high school! Wesley started all 32 games as a freshman, and considering the circumstances he acquitted himself decently. He won't have to use plays at an above-average rate this season, as he likely heads to the bench. Wesley has good size on defense and contributes on the glass. He must improve as a shooter after making just one three all season and hitting 52 percent at the free throw line.

Ari Stewart (6-7, 205, Jr.): Stewart played with Terrell at Wake Forest. After a decent freshman season in Winston-Salem, Stewart lost playing time as a sophomore because coach Jeff Bzdelik was displeased with his effort. Bzdelik's concerns might have included shot selection; Stewart tried 106 threes despite making them at a 27 percent clip. Stewart is a capable defensive rebounder.

James Blasczyk (7-1, 260, Sr.): Technically, Blasczyk wasn't part of the Trojans' injury list, as he was able to play through a mid-foot sprain and bone bruise that hampered him much of the year. Blasczyk started after Dedmon went out of the lineup and was the team's best defensive rebounder. Though he has good size, Blasczyk lacks the mobility to keep up with top Pac-12 big men, and he had a tough time finishing. His playing time as a senior will depend in large part on whether Oraby is cleared.

Renaldo Woolridge (6-9, 220, Sr.): The last transfer on the roster, Woolridge returns home after three seasons at Tennessee. The son of the late NBA player Orlando Woolridge, he is immediately eligible as a graduate student. As a Volunteer, Woolridge was unable to claim a key role. He does show some promise as a stretch 4, having made a career-high 37 percent of his threes in 2011-12, including five triples in a game against Kentucky where he scored 17 points.

Prospectus says: Assuming USC can build chemistry with an entirely rebuilt rotation, this team has more than enough size and talent to play the kind of defense O'Neill demands—especially since he'll actually be able to go to the bench this season. The question is how good the Trojans' offense will be. They've collected a number of volume scorers with middling efficiency. The optimistic viewpoint is that these players will no longer have to force shots. A pessimist would say they'll fight each other for shots all season. The outcome will determine where in the conference's middle tier USC lands.

UTAH

2012: 6-25 (3-15 Pac-12); Lost to Colorado 53-41, Pac-12 first round
In-conference offense: 0.86 points per possession (11th)
In-conference defense: 1.08 points allowed per possession (11th)

What Utah did well: *Not quit.*

It's safe to say that the Utes' debut in the Pac-12 did not go as they hoped. First-year coach Larry Krystkowiak inherited a team that had just gone 6-10 in the Mountain West, and while the move to a major conference turned out not to be as challenging as it appeared because the Pac-12 was so down, Utah's talent base was hit hard. Over the summer, starting guard Will Clyburn transferred to Iowa State. Then 7-3 starting center David Foster suffered a broken foot that ended his season before it started. Lastly, Krystkowiak had to deal with disciplinary issues for star guard Josh Watkins. Krystkowiak suspended Watkins for a game in December and later dismissed him from the team in January because of tardiness to practice and sleeping through classes.

The three departures left Utah facing life in the Pac-12 with a shell of the lineup that hadn't been good enough to compete in the Mountain West the season before. By December, we were musing on Basketball Prospectus about whether the Utes might be the worst major-conference team of all time. As it turned out, by the end of the season, Utah wasn't even the worst team in the Pac-12, a dubious honor held by USC. While the Utes did become the first team from a power conference ever ranked outside the Pomeroy rankings top 300, they avoided ignominy by playing hard despite the slow start. Give Utah's players credit for working hard in a situation where they had every excuse for quitting.

What we learned in 2012: *It's hard to go winless in conference play.*

Part of the discussion in December was whether the Utes might join the 2007-08 Oregon State Beavers by going 0-18 in conference play. College Basketball Prospectus contributor Ken Pomeroy was skeptical, pointing to the unpredictability of any given game. That looked prescient when Utah won not one, not two, but three conference games. The Utes eked out an overtime win over Washington State in the second week of conference play, crushed Arizona State by 21 in January (one of just two double-digit wins all season), and stunned a good Stanford team weeks before the Cardinal won the NIT.

The moral of the story: a team has to be both historically poor and remarkably unlucky not to win a conference game.

What's in store for 2013: Utah went through more turnover during the summer. Three starters transferred, with Chris Hines heading to Drake, Kareem Story going to the junior college ranks, and Dijon Farr landing at Division II Arkansas-Fort Smith. Lastly, Foster's college career came to an end when he re-injured his foot and was forced to undergo surgery. On the plus side the Utes added four D-I transfers, signed two junior college transfers, and added a top-100 recruit in wing Jordan Loveridge.

MEET THE UTES

Jason Washburn (6-10, 240, Sr.): After Watkins' departure, Washburn served as Utah's go-to scorer with impressive efficiency in that role. He made 56 percent of his twos. Washburn tends to be most effective from midrange and has good touch stepping away from the basket. On the downside, Washburn's style generates relatively few chances for him to show off his accurate free throw shooting. A fine shot blocker and defensive rebounder, Washburn ranked sixth in the Pac-12 in both categories.

Cedric Martin (6-4, 205, Sr.): As a junior college transfer, Martin was one of the Utes' most consistent performers in 2011-12 and is now one of two returning starters. Three-pointers were about the sum total of Martin's offensive contribution. He not only attempted more than twice as many threes as twos, but also shot a better percentage from beyond the arc (37 percent vs. 32 percent). Martin will be Utah's top perimeter defender.

Aaron Dotson (6-4, 202, Jr.): Dotson will miss time early with a stress fracture. A Seattle native, he spent two years at LSU before transferring back to the Pac-12. The hope is that Dotson, a top-100 recruit back in 2009, will be more efficient as a scorer at Utah. In Baton Rouge he made 41 percent of his two-point shots, undermining a solid free throw rate and effective three-point shooting. Dotson's athleticism has yet to translate on the glass or in terms of measurable defensive statistics.

Jordan Loveridge (6-6, 230, Fr.): Keeping Loveridge, who grew up in the suburbs of Salt Lake City, at home was important for Krystkowiak. That being said, the local favorite, who is capable of playing either forward position, might be a bit overexposed as a freshman. Drew Cannon's projections suggest that Loveridge will be an inefficient scorer this season, though he led the Utes in both scoring and rebounding during a summer trip to Brazil.

Glen Dean (5-10, 170, Jr.): Another Seattle product, Dean transferred from Eastern Washington looking for a step up in competition after leading the Eagles in scoring and assists in each of his first two seasons. Expect Dean, who has ranked in the nation's top 125 in assist rate twice, to focus more on playmaking. Because of his size, he's likely to struggle in the paint after making just 36 percent of his twos against Big Sky opponents in 2010-11. Dean will be more effective as a scorer from downtown, where he's a career 42 percent shooter.

Jarred DuBois (6-3, 170, Sr.): A full-time starter during his first two years at Loyola Marymount, DuBois saw his role decrease after missing nearly the entire 2010-11 campaign due to foot surgery. So he'll spend his fifth year of eligibility in Salt Lake City. As a graduate student, DuBois is immediately eligible. He will provide perimeter shooting, having made as many as 40 percent of his threes (as a sophomore). DuBois has been less effective inside the arc and saw his turnovers creep up last season, which could be problematic if he sees action at the point behind Dean.

Renan Lenz (6-9, 220, Jr.): A native of Brazil, Lenz averaged 13 points and nine rebounds at Arizona Western Junior College in 2011-12. One-time BYU center Rafael Araujo, another Brazilian, was also an Arizona Western product. Lenz scored a team-high 18 points in his home country during his first action in a Utah uniform. His size makes Lenz a fine defensive prospect if he can score enough to stay on the floor.

Justin Seymour (6-3, 205, Fr.): Utah could use another ball handler in the backcourt and Seymour may be able to fill the role. More a combo guard than a true point, Seymour did open eyes with his performance early in camp. Fellow newcomer Dakarai Tucker (6-5, 185, Fr.) is also in the mix for wing minutes.

Dallin Bachynski (7-0, 250, So.): The Pac-12 is now a two-Bachynski league after Dallin joined older brother Jordan, a 7-2 center at Arizona State. This Bachynski played sparingly at Southern Utah as a freshman before serving his LDS mission. He's one of two Utes returning from their missions, along with Jeremy Olsen (6-10, 230, Fr.). Jordan Bachynski developed dramatically after going on his mission, and Utah hopes Dallin will do the same.

Prospectus says: Things can't go as badly as last year, but Foster's re-injury and the transfers have left Utah little more capable of competing in the Pac-12. This looks like another rebuilding year for Krystkowiak, who may start feeling some pressure to win by 2013-14.

WASHINGTON

2012: 24-11 (14-4 Pac-12); Lost to Minnesota 68-67 (OT), NIT semifinals
In-conference offense: 1.03 points per possession (7th)
In-conference defense: 0.96 points allowed per possession (4th)

What Washington did well: *Win conference games.*

As we say here at Prospectus HQ, flags fly forever, and the Huskies can hang a Pac-12 conference championship banner from the 2011-12 season. It's the fourth consecutive year Washington has won either the regular-season title or the Pac-12 tournament, but only the second outright conference championship for the Huskies since 1953. Still, the season was bittersweet because Washington missed out on the NCAA tournament. The Huskies went just 7-5 in non-conference play and lost their opening game in the Pac-12 tournament, undermining their résumé. The conference championship understandably carried little weight with the selection committee during the Pac-12's dreadful year.

Washington was at its best during conference play, going 14-4—tied for the team's best performance in the Lorenzo Romar era. The Huskies went 8-1 at home and swept Arizona. The lone loss at Hec Edmundson Pavilion came against Cal, and Washington lucked out by avoiding a road trip to the Bay Area for a rematch. The Huskies also enjoyed good fortune in close games during Pac-12 play, going 5-1 in games decided by four points or fewer. Back-to-back two-point wins in Tucson and at home against UCLA helped Washington finish atop the conference.

What we learned in 2012: *NBA talent does not a great college team make.*

The Huskies were considered the Pac-12's most talented team because of stars Terrence Ross and Tony Wroten. Both players were taken in the first round of the NBA draft after declaring early. Ross went eighth overall to Toronto. Washington was certainly unique in having so much NBA talent and missing the NCAA tournament. Dating back to the 2005 draft, every other college with multiple first-round picks has reached March Madness. The closest comparison is probably Nevada in 2010. The Wolfpack had Luke Babbitt drafted 16th and Armon Johnson taken early in the second round (34th), both by the Portland Trail Blazers, yet never seriously contended for an at-large berth out of the WAC.

As talented as the Huskies were at the top of the roster, their depth was a major issue. Senior wing Scott Suggs opted to take a redshirt season after a broken bone in his right foot healed more slowly than expected. That left Washington playing a four-player perimeter rotation much of the year. When wing C.J. Wilcox missed three games—including the loss to Cal—with a stress fracture in his left hip, the Huskies were forced to use raw freshman Hikeem Stewart as their only perimeter reserve. Romar rotated through three different freshmen as backups in the frontcourt and never found a consistent contributor, meaning Washington struggled when its starters suffered foul trouble. Those shortcomings made the difference between a trip to the NCAA tournament and playing in the NIT.

What's in store for 2013: The loss of Ross and Wroten means the Huskies will have to replace their two leading scorers. A healthy Suggs returns as part of an experienced starting lineup. However, Washington may be even thinner than 2011-12. With one scholarship unused and two more going to transfers Perris Blackwell and Gilles Dierickx, the Huskies have just 10 active scholarship players, none of them incoming recruits.

MEET THE HUSKIES

C.J. Wilcox (6-5, 195, Jr.): Wilcox is about to make the unusual transition from sixth man to go-to guy. Last season, Wilcox was the odd wing out when Wroten forced his way into the starting five. The reserve role worked well because Romar had to limit Wilcox's minutes to avoid overtaxing his injured hip. He still finished as the team's third-leading scorer. A terrific perimeter scorer (he's a 40 percent career three-point shooter), Wilcox made strides in creating his own offense and will put those skills to use this season. Though unlikely to finish fourth in the conference in offensive rating (120) again, Wilcox could prove more valuable in a larger role.

Abdul Gaddy (6-3, 195, Sr.): Coming back from a torn ACL suffered in January 2011, Gaddy lost some quickness. And since he was no speedster to start with, that made it difficult for Gaddy to penetrate. Mostly he initiated the offense before spotting up. The court vision that made Gaddy the nation's No. 2 point guard recruit has never really panned out, though he could show more as the unquestioned lead ball handler during his senior year. Gaddy showed more promise as a scorer during the NIT, but overall his accuracy was poor on both two- and three-point shots. Playing at less than 100 percent also hampered Gaddy on defense.

Aziz N'Diaye (7-0, 260, Sr.): For all the talent on the UW roster, N'Diaye might have been the team's most irreplaceable player. The Huskies struggled defensively when he missed two non-conference games with a knee injury (including a blowout home loss to South Dakota State) or got in foul trouble. N'Diaye has harnessed his size to become a fine shot blocker and rebounder (fifth in the Pac-12 on the defensive glass). He grew into a larger role on offense, but tends to be prone to turnovers when he catches the ball in the post. Trips to the free throw line are an adventure for N'Diaye, who shot 40 percent in 2011-12.

Scott Suggs (6-6, 195, Sr.): As nice as Suggs would have been to have in reserve last season, his fifth year of eligibility will prove crucial to replacing Ross and Wroten. In 2010-11, Suggs was one of the conference's most efficient role players, knocking down 45 percent of his threes. While Suggs' other offensive contributions are limited primarily to transition, he's a fine, long-limbed defender who will take on the opposing team's top wing.

Desmond Simmons (6-7, 220, So.): As Washington began practice, four players were competing for the last starting spot at power forward. Simmons, who started much of his redshirt freshman campaign before giving way to senior Darnell Gant, should be considered the favorite. In time, Simmons may be able to stretch the floor with his shooting. He took 27 threes last year, though he made them at just a 22 percent clip. Simmons needs to stay energetic on the glass, where his intensity was up and down in 2011-12.

Andrew Andrews (6-2, 195, Fr.): Andrews, whose moniker has been voted the NCAA's easiest name to remember, spent last season developing as a redshirt and could immediately step into the role of sixth man. While redshirts often carry a negative connotation in basketball, Romar and his staff have used them effectively for player development. In addition to Simmons, Wilcox also redshirted before contributing immediately. A Portland native, Andrews is a true point guard with scoring chops, which will allow him to back up both guard spots.

Jernard Jarreau (6-10, 220, Fr.): Another redshirt, Jarreau could climb over last year's reserves and be the first big man off the bench. A late-blooming stringbean, Jarreau used last season to bulk up his frame to do battle with bigger opponents. He was a guard in high school before a growth spurt turned him into a post player. Now Jarreau is an active defender and fine shot blocker.

Shawn Kemp, Jr. (6-9, 255, So.): For the first time in more than a decade, Seattle fans got to enjoy a Kemp wearing No. 40. The son of the Sonics legend contributed at times as a freshman, though foul trouble and his limited offensive game kept him from establishing a regular role. Now in better shape, Kemp could prove an effective paint defender. He swatted a prodigious nine percent of opponents' two-point attempts. For another big body, the Huskies could again add star tight end Austin Seferian-Jenkins (6-6, 260, So.) at midseason.

Martin Breunig (6-8, 210, So.): Breunig began the season in the rotation and saw heavy minutes at times as a freshman before being phased out after the start of Pac-12 play. A fine athlete, the German must improve his defensive instincts to stay on the floor. Breunig did prove an accurate, high-flying finisher around the rim.

Hikeem Stewart (6-2, 185, So.): During his limited action as a freshman, Stewart was cautious to a fault. He went nearly all season without committing a turnover, but did not test the defense. To stay on the floor, Stewart must showcase long-range ability. He made one three-pointer in six attempts during 2011-12.

Prospectus says: Washington shook up its coaching staff over the summer, with Romar adding Lamont Smith from Arizona State and luring longtime Western Washington head coach Brad Jackson to Seattle as an assistant after the Vikings won the D-II national championship. The coaches have their work cut out for them to help the Huskies overcome the talent drain and short rotation. Consider this a rebuilding year for Washington, the most consistent team in the Pac-12 over the last decade.

WASHINGTON STATE

2012: 19-18 (7-11 Pac-12); Lost to Pitt 71-65, CBI Finals
In-conference offense: 1.04 points per possession (6th)
In-conference defense: 1.09 points allowed per possession (12th)

What Washington State did well: *Replace Klay Thompson.*

In 2010-11, the Cougars' attack was built around Thompson, a high-scoring 2-guard who used nearly a third of the team's plays while on the court, putting him 15th in the nation. Thompson parlayed the season into a spot in the lottery and proved his performance was legitimate by earning All-Rookie First Team honors with the Golden State Warriors.

Naturally, Washington State figured to miss Thompson, and indeed the team's offense dropped in conference play—all the way from sixth to seventh. Overall, the Cougars' adjusted offensive efficiency improved from 89th in the nation to 59th. WSU replaced Thompson with junior center Brock Motum, who ranked fourth in the Pac-12 in usage rate at 29 percent. Motum not only shot accurately but also proved effective at getting to the free throw line, helping the Cougars rank second in conference play in free throw attempts per shot from the field. With Motum drawing defensive attention, Washington State had a variety of efficient role players. Three Cougars (wing Marcus Capers, forward Abe Lodwick and center D.J. Shelton) had true shooting percentages north of 60.

What we learned in 2012: *DeAngelo Casto was harder to replace.*

Thompson wasn't the only WSU starter to leave early. Casto, the team's center and defensive anchor, left after his junior season to play overseas. The Cougars had a much more difficult time replacing Casto's size and athleticism down low. Lodwick and Motum got pushed around in the paint and WSU was undersized on the wing without Thompson, forcing Ken Bone to employ a heavy dose of zone defense. That opened things up for opponents' three-point shooters. Just three major-conference teams allowed a higher percentage of attempts from beyond the arc. During Pac-12 play, teams made 39 percent of their threes against Washington State.

Compounding matters, the Cougar zone was particularly passive in terms of forcing turnovers. Washington State ranked last in Pac-12 play in both steal rate and opponent turnover rate. Creating turnovers is not a necessary part of a quality defense—Cal, for example, was the lone team in the conference to come up with fewer steals per possession. However, the combination of few turnovers and hot shooting was impossible for the Cougars to overcome. Their defense ranked dead last in Pac-12 play, a huge decline from a fourth-place finish in 2010-11.

What's in store for 2013: Washington State graduated senior role players Capers, Lodwick and Charlie Enquist, as well as sixth man Faisal Aden. The bigger loss is starting guard Reggie Moore, who was dismissed from the team in September. Fortunately, the Cougars add Kansas transfer Royce Woolridge to their backcourt. WSU did take a hit when promising freshman Que Johnson was ruled a partial qualifier, making him ineligible to play this season. Johnson will join the team in 2013-14 along with guard Brett Kingma, who made a rare in-conference transfer from Oregon over the summer.

MEET THE COUGARS

Brock Motum (6-10, 245, Sr.): Few players in the country improved more than Motum, who increased his scoring average by more than 10 points per game to lead the Pac-12. Motum pushed his usage from average to elite without his true shooting percentage budging. An accurate shooter, the Australian can get off his lefty shot almost whenever he wants because of his size. Motum has three-point range and can be dangerous in the post, where he draws fouls on a regular basis. A solid defensive rebounder, Motum is nonetheless miscast in the middle because he can be overpowered down low and is a middling shot blocker.

DaVonté Lacy (6-3, 205, So.): The Cougars' other returning starter is Lacy, who will shoulder more responsibility during his second season because of Moore's departure. Already there were indications that Lacy was going to be the team's best guard. Though he and Moore took shots at similar frequency, Lacy was far more efficient because of his superior three-point shooting. Now, WSU will ask Lacy to do more playmaking. A combo guard, Lacy played largely off the ball as a freshman because of Moore's presence.

Mike Ladd (6-5, 195, Sr.): Early in his first season in Pullman after transferring from Fresno State, Ladd injured his thumb in practice. The injury caused him to miss 10 games and bothered him throughout the season. Ladd, who made 66 threes as a sophomore, attempted just 39 in 2011-12. His free throw shooting fell from 77 percent to 57 percent. Now healthy, Ladd is likely to start at one wing spot. He developed into a solid defensive rebounder last season and is a capable defender against players his own size.

Royce Woolridge (6-3, 175, So.): Woolridge committed to the Jayhawks as a sophomore in high school, but after finding playing time difficult to come by during his first season he transferred to WSU for more opportunity. Woolridge, the son of the late NBA forward Orlando Woolridge and half-brother of USC forward Renaldo, figures to start as part of a three-guard lineup. He can do a little bit of everything and will handle the ball some, though he's a shooting guard by trade. Expect Woolridge to match up against point guards, making his size an asset.

D.J. Shelton (6-10, 250, Jr.): During his first year on the Palouse, Shelton was the Cougars' best paint defender. He has enough size to handle opposing centers and moves well, allowing him to block shots as a help defender. Shelton stayed within himself offensively, shooting almost entirely around the basket and finishing a solid 62 percent of his attempts. To maintain his claim a starting spot in the frontcourt, Shelton would do well to improve his defensive rebounding. Cutting his foul rate will also keep him on the floor.

James Hunter (6-9, 250, So.): Washington State relied on assistant coach Ben Johnson, who played and coached in Australia, to land another Aussie. Hunter is a junior college transfer with size who will have three years to play for the Cougars. His coach at Gillette College, Shawn Neary, raved to CougFan.com about Hunter's ability to run the floor. Hunter's father, Todd, plays bass in Australian rock band Dragon, while his mother Johanna was the first woman to write a No. 1 hit Down Under.

Dexter Kernich-Drew (6-6, 180, So.): The team's third Aussie, Kernich-Drew played well during the Cougars' tour of Australia this summer. He averaged 8.4 points per game, third on the team behind Motum and Moore. Kernich-Drew flashed potential at times during his redshirt freshman campaign. Long arms give him major defensive potential, so if he can improve his three-point percentage from last year's 32 percent, Kernich-Drew could become a solid role player.

Junior Longrus (6-7, 230, Fr.): With Johnson ineligible, Richard Longrus, Jr.—aka Junior—is WSU's top incoming freshman. Longrus played extended minutes during the trip to Australia and was solid on the glass. By all accounts, Longrus is more advanced at the defensive end and will have to develop to become a threat as a scorer.

Dominic Ballard (6-4, 200, Fr.): The loss of Moore means Ballard, a walk-on who redshirted last season, is the team's backup point guard. Ballard isn't a natural ball handler either. Still, he's got good size and strength for the position and figures to be effective defensively.

Will DiIorio (6-5, 190, Jr.): Originally a walk-on, DiIorio earned a scholarship last season and even made one start during non-conference play. His energy and defense may help the Cougars off the bench.

Prospectus says: While none of the players Washington State lost is irreplaceable individually, taken together too much talent and experience left Pullman. Past their top six players, the Cougars have a lot of question marks, and the starting group will have to find a way to create shots without a true point guard. Those shortcomings will keep WSU in the second division of the Pac-12.

SEC

BY JOHN EZEKOWITZ

When Kentucky cut down the nets in New Orleans on April 4, they completed one of the most impressive seasons in the last decade of college basketball. The Wildcats ran through SEC play undefeated, and actually won 18 straight games against SEC foes before falling to Vanderbilt in the finals of the SEC tournament. Led by the fantastic freshmen duo of Anthony Davis and Michael Kidd-Gilchrist, Kentucky decimated the competition and won John Calipari the national title that will forever endear him to Big Blue Nation.

In SEC play, the Wildcats outscored their conference-mates by 0.26 points per possession. That is the largest efficiency margin recorded by any team in a major conference in the tempo-free era. Kentucky's offense put up 1.20 points per possession, the second-most efficient major conference offense behind Chris Paul's 2005 Wake Forest squad. What the Cats did last season was nothing sort of astonishing.

While that's bad news for the teams they beat, it's actually good news for the conference. Last season, I wrote that the perception of the SEC was greater than the reality because fans and media remember deep NCAA tournament runs rather than conference depth. There was an influx of talent into the SEC in 2011-12, but the conference actually finished the season in the same place as they did in 2010-11 in Ken Pomeroy's rankings: fourth.

While Kentucky, Florida and Vanderbilt have been consistently good to excellent over the last three seasons, no other team in the SEC has made the NCAA tournament in more than one of those years. Four teams, Arkansas, Auburn, LSU, and South Carolina, have failed to finish in the top 80 of the Pythagorean standings in each of the last three years. While the top of the SEC has been shining, the bottom has been shabby.

This poor performance has resulted in a lot of coaching turnover. The league's 14 current coaches have a combined 51 seasons at the helm of their current schools, and 29 of those seasons belong to Kevin Stallings at Vandy and Billy Donovan at Florida. The other 12 have recorded an average of 1.8 years of tenure at their SEC schools.

This turnover has produced an interesting trend in SEC play. In 2009, the conference was the fastest-paced league in the nations, averaging 69 possessions per 40 minutes. Last year, however, SEC teams averaged just 63 possessions per 40, an eight percent drop in four years.

JOHN'S 2013 STANDINGS

	2012 Record	Returning Poss (%)	Returning Min (%)	2013 Prediction
Kentucky	16-0	6	7	15-3
Missouri	14-4*	33	29	15-3
Florida	10-6	63	67	14-4
Tennessee	10-6	80	78	12-6
Arkansas	6-10	64	60	11-7
Ole Miss	8-8	66	71	10-8
Alabama	9-7	65	70	9-9
Vanderbilt	10-6	17	24	8-10
Georgia	5-11	64	67	8-10
Texas A&M	4-14*	48	51	7-11
Auburn	5-11	57	57	6-12
LSU	7-9	45	44	5-13
South Carolina	2-14	59	59	4-14
Mississippi State	8-8	16	22	2-16
*Big 12				

THE SLOWING SEC

Year	Average Tempo	Slowest Team
2009	69.0	Vandy (67.7)
2010	68.4	LSU (63.5)
2011	65.8	Florida (63.1)
2012	63.3	Georgia (60.7)

In fact, in 2012, the teams played so slowly that only Arkansas had a significantly higher tempo than the slowest team of any of the past three seasons (2011 Florida). The only other major conference to undergo such a dramatic slowing of the pace was the Pac-12, which went from an average of 72.5 possessions per 40 minutes in 2003 to 64.8 in 2006. Amazingly, of the six new coaches who have entered the SEC since 2009, none have played at a faster average tempo than their predecessor.

What could cause such a slowdown? It appears to be the interaction of coaches who do not mind playing slowly and a lack of talent at the bottom of the league. Take the case of Tony Barbee at Auburn. His UTEP teams played fast and had good offensive talent relative to Conference USA. He gets to Auburn, however, and the cupboard is bare. His teams struggle to get up good shots, and have to rely on digging in defensively to win. Barbee's two Tiger teams have played six possessions slower than his UTEP teams.

The slowdown may soon be ending, however. The five new coaches coming into the league all come from relatively up-tempo backgrounds. Frank Martin (South Carolina), Johnny Jones (LSU), and Rick Ray (Mississippi State) share another thing in common. Their teams will likely be in the cellar of the SEC this season. All three inherit rosters that are barren and are facing multi-year rebuilds.

The two new entrants, Billy Kennedy at Texas A&M and Frank Haith at Missouri, come from the Big 12 with dramatically different expectations. The Aggies are attempting to rebound after a disastrous 2012 campaign that saw them fall from the preseason pick to win the Big 12 to a 4-14 record in conference. Kennedy has a strong and experienced front line returning, but will be relying on freshmen in the backcourt. Haith, on the other hand, must work to fit his talented newcomers, transfers Alex Oriakhi, Keion Bell, Earnest Ross, and Jabari Brown, in with his returning backcourt stars Phil Pressey and Michael Dixon. Missouri has a chance to win the SEC in its first try.

Calipari, too, will be essentially coaching an entirely new team in 2013. He has reloaded on the recruiting trail with top-ranked center Nerlens Noel and other highly ranked recruits, but the most important player to the Cats' season is transfer point guard Ryan Harrow. The only way Kentucky can live up to their preseason ranking is if Harrow extends Calipari's recent run of stellar point guards.

The other league favorite is Florida. Donovan's squad is thin at the guards, where they will rely heavily on Kenny Boynton and the wild Mike Rosario, but strong up front behind Patric Young and Eric Murphy. The Gators will likely have a better start to the season than the Wildcats or Tigers because of their continuity, but their depth issues could pose a problem come SEC play.

A step below the top three is Tennessee. The Vols surprised last year, finishing 10-6 in league play. The frontcourt duo of Jarnell Stokes and Jeronne Maymon could be the best in the league, and point guard Trae Golden can play at an All-SEC level.

The two potential surprise teams are Arkansas and Ole Miss. The Razorbacks return a budding star in guard BJ Young and get Marshawn Powell back from injury. Ole Miss has an experienced and tough front line, a potential breakout performer in guard Jarvis Summers, and a potential impact transfer in Utah's Marshall Henderson. Andy Kennedy might finally get that NCAA tournament ticket he so desperately needs.

Finally, four teams sit in a building mode, likely not good enough to make a dent in the league this year. Vanderbilt and Alabama both lose substantial talent from NCAA tournament teams in 2012. Auburn and Georgia are attempting to build up to the middle of the pack in the league. Of these four teams,

Alabama likely has the best chance to make a push for a top-six league finish.

Despite the addition of Missouri, it is hard to see the SEC improving much as a whole this season. The bottom third of the league is still profoundly lacking in talent, and the middle third consists of teams with little depth or no standout players. At the top, every team has a question mark. There is no 2012 Kentucky to wow the nation, and, for the first time in three years, there may not be an SEC team in the Final Four. This might be the year that the national perception of the SEC catches up with the quantitative reality instead of the other way around.

ALABAMA

2012: 21-12 (9-7 SEC); Lost to Creighton 58-57, NCAA round of 64
In-conference offense: 0.99 points per possession (7th)
In-conference defense: 0.94 points allowed per possession allowed (1st)

What Alabama did well: *Play effective small-ball defense.*

Based on his previous record, we knew Anthony Grant was an exceptional defensive coach. SEC fans know their teams will struggle to score efficiently when playing the Crimson Tide. But the performance of Grant's team last season even exceeded those expectations.

Consider where the Crimson Tide stood at the beginning of February. The team's two best—and tallest—starters, JaMychal Green and Tony Mitchell, had been suspended indefinitely. Green would miss four conference games, and Mitchell would miss the remainder of the season. Grant was left with a roster with just one player taller than 6-6 (freshman Nick Jacobs), and whose only upperclassman, junior Andrew Steele, was coming back from what were initially thought to be career-ending concussions. In terms of effective height, Ken Pomeroy's measure that compares each player to the national average height for each position, the Crimson Tide were by far the shortest team in the SEC.

And yet despite these challenges, on a per-possession basis, Alabama put up the best defensive performance in SEC play and the No. 7 performance nation-wide. Compare their field goal defense and rebounding in SEC play to the four other shortest teams in the league.

SIZE MATTERS?

	Effective Height (in)	eFG% Allowed	Defensive Rebounding %
Alabama	+0.1	45.4	69.2
Florida	+0.3	51.1	68.4
Arkansas	+0.8	53.7	63.2
South Carolina	+1.1	53.4	59.9
Tennessee	+1.2	44.2	70.8

Only Tennessee, a team with an extra inch of effective height at each position, bested Alabama in field goal defense and rebounding. Credit Grant's coaching, and the strong play of the Crimson Tide's wings, for the remarkable defensive efforts that allowed Alabama to make the NCAA tournament for the first time since 2006.

What we learned in 2012: *Defense alone can only get you so far.*

Alabama's offense was as painful to watch as their defense was to play against. Alabama averaged 63.1 possessions per 40 minutes last season, putting them at No. 298 for tempo in Division I. Some of this languor can be attributed to the Tide's defense forcing opponents to use up the shot clock looking for an opportunity to score. More of it, however, can be explained by the Alabama offense's inability to produce quick and easy baskets.

Trevor Releford was putatively the point guard, but he was ill suited to the role, and was more successful attacking the basket than dishing effectively to teammates. In fact, Green's turns at point-forward were often the moments when the Bama offense ran at its best.

Additionally, there was the small matter of perimeter shooting. Two seasons ago the Crimson Tide shot 30 percent from three-point range. It wasn't easy but last season's team fell short of even that low standard, shooting 29 percent. Grant solved his team's lack of outside potency by designing an offense that ignored the perimeter shot altogether. Just 27 percent of Alabama's field goals came from beyond the arc, the 47th lowest total in all of college basketball. Of the starters, only Trevor Lacey and Mitchell managed to make even 30 percent of their attempts.

What you were left with, then, was an offense with limited spacing that struggled to score efficiently.

The Crimson Tide had the fourth-worst adjusted offensive efficiency of the at-large teams in last year's NCAA tournament. While they could look back with regret at several late-game lapses in their close round of 64 loss to Creighton, Alabama likely came very close to their performance ceiling given their offensive struggles.

What's in store for 2013: Green and Mitchell are gone, but the Crimson Tide will return battle-tested underclassmen. Alabama brings in only one recruit, but he's a big one: Devonta Pollard, a 6-7 swingman considered one of the top incoming freshmen in the nation.

What you will likely see is another Anthony Grant team that will have to rely on defense. Releford looks ready to take on a larger offensive role, but it's unclear where effective point guard play or three-point shooting will come from based on the existing roster. Pollard is an explosive playmaker but not yet a threat from the outside.

Bama will be undersized again inside, likely relying on Jacobs and perhaps the enigmatic 7-0 Moussa Gueye for rebounding. Pollard may even play some time at the 4.

MEET THE CRIMSON TIDE

Trevor Releford (6-0, 190, Jr.): Releford's development from his freshman to his sophomore year was impressive. He improved his free throw rate, free throw shooting, and shooting percentage. Releford excels at using his size and quickness to get to the free throw line, and is a pesky on-ball defender. To take the next step, however, he will have to improve his point guard play.

Devonta Pollard (6-8, 200, Fr.): Grant made Pollard his primary recruiting target, and Pollard chose the Tide over Georgetown. He is an explosive, athletic wing player who excels as a shot blocker on defense. Pollard needs to work on his outside game, but he should fit well in Grant's defensive scheme.

Levi Randolph (6-5, 205, So.): Randolph showed flashes of his potential in his freshman campaign. He is a good rebounder for his position, but needs to improve his jump shot (26 percent from beyond the arc) or stop taking so many threes.

Trevor Lacey (6-3, 215, So.): Like Randolph, Lacey was a moderately efficient offensive player as a freshman. He took the most threes on the team, connecting on 31 percent of his 101 attempts. Lacey has a penchant for turnovers (21 percent TO rate), but that's not always a bad trait to have as a freshman. He is a potential breakout candidate this season.

Nick Jacobs (6-8, 265, So.): Jacobs was a pleasant surprise for the Crimson Tide last season, and was the team's leading rebounder (by rate). He'll have to successfully assume a larger role in order for Alabama to be successful.

Moussa Gueye (7-0, 255, Sr.): Gueye tore his ACL before last season and played in just 12 games as a junior. He did have six blocks in a game against Tennessee, so perhaps he can help Alabama regain lofty ranking in team block rate, a category where they fell 37 spots nationally last season.

Prospectus says: The Crimson Tide will likely take a step back in 2013, but they will still be competitive. Unless Releford, Pollard, and one of Trevor Lacey or Levi Randolph play at an All-SEC level, it will be hard for Alabama to make a repeat trip to the NCAA tournament. Nevertheless, the future looks bright in Tuscaloosa as the Tide are a team dominated by underclassmen. No offense will get a night off against Grant's bunch this season.

ARKANSAS

2012: 18-14 (6-10 SEC); Lost to LSU 70-54, SEC first round
In-conference offense: 1.00 points per possession (5th)
In-conference defense: 1.09 points allowed per possession allowed (11th)

What Arkansas did well: *Find a star.*

Mike Anderson's first season at the helm of the Razorbacks was always going to be one of transition and upheaval. What was unclear before the start of last season was whether the transition process would lead to on-court success. That possibility was dealt a major blow in November when star forward Marshawn Powell tore knee ligaments and was lost for the season.

Despite some clear shortcomings (detailed below), Arkansas did succeed in one key area for the development of the program: they found a star player. If you have yet to see BJ Young play, make sure to watch an Arkansas game or two soon. As a freshman, the 6-3 playmaking guard shot 55 percent from two and 41 percent from three while using 29 percent of his team's possessions while he was on the floor.

Young's offensive rating of 110 was the fourth highest in the nation for major-conference players that used at least 28 percent of their team's possessions. The last four freshmen to post that level of efficiency while carrying that much of the scoring load for their major-conference teams were DeMarcus Cousins, Michael Beasley, James Harden, and Eric Gordon. Pretty good company.

Young's size, lankiness, explosive first step, and high socks are reminiscent of Rajon Rondo. Unfortunately, his passing ability, up to this point, is not: Young's assist-to-turnover ratio was only 1.0.

Clearly, Young is not a finished product and neither is Anderson's transformation of the Arkansas program. The Razorbacks struggled against SEC competition, but the return of Powell and Young means that the future is bright in Fayetteville.

What we learned in 2012: *40 Minutes of Hell needs offensive success.*

When most people think of Anderson's teams, they think of the frenetic pace and the non-stop full-court pressing defensive style. Anderson's tempo-free profile is a consistent one: his teams force more turnovers than almost anyone else in Division I, and his teams clearly prioritize blocked shots over defensive rebounds.

The 2012 Arkansas edition allowed 1.09 points per trip in conference play and 1.05 PPP overall, by far Anderson's worst defense in the tempo-free era. While some of that performance can be attributed to his new personnel's rookie mistakes, it can't explain all of it. Anderson's first-year teams at UAB and Missouri both produced substantially better defense, forcing more turnovers than the Razorbacks did last year.

I believe the reason 40 Minutes of Hell ended up being more like 40 Minutes of Transition Layups for SEC opponents last season had more to do with the Razorbacks' offensive struggles. Arkansas shot just 47 percent from inside the arc last season and registered the highest turnover rate in Anderson's career since his first Missouri team.

The full-court press can only be set up on made baskets. Anderson's teams thrive on turnovers, but can struggle in the half-court. With Arkansas not being able to set up its press as often last season because of an inability to put the ball in the basket, Anderson's defense faced more half-court possessions than it was designed to see. When offensive mediocrity breeds defensive mediocrity, you have a recipe for a 6-10 record in conference.

What's in store for 2013: It's hard not to see the Razorbacks taking a significant step forward in 2013. They return every significant player except Devonta Abron and Julysses Nobles, both of whom transferred, and get Powell back from injury. A frontcourt of Powell and sophomore center Hunter Mickelson will be much better suited to the rigors of the SEC, and guards Ky Madden and Mardracus Wade will have another year of practices in Anderson's system under their waistbands. If Young even slightly improves from his rookie campaign, he will be playing at an All-SEC level. Last year he was forced to take so many shots because the team around him lacked options. This year with the addition of Powell and growth around him, Young may take fewer shots but the Razorbacks will likely have more success.

MEET THE RAZORBACKS

BJ Young (6-3, 180, So.): I've spent a lot of time on Young already, so I will only add here that last year he ended up with the ball in his hands a lot without being a true point guard. Young's off-ball movement, however, is exceptional. He might benefit from a move to a more prototypical 2-guard role this season.

Hunter Mickelson (6-10, 245, So.): Mickelson quietly had a very intriguing freshman campaign. He was sometimes overmatched by opposing big men, but posted an impressive block rate (13.5 percent, fifth in the nation) and by the end of the season he was making jump shots. If he follows the typical freshman to sophomore improvement curve, he could be a breakout player for the Razorbacks.

Marshawn Powell (6-7, 240, Jr.): In his first two seasons, Powell carried a large possession load while getting to the free throw line efficiently (38 percent free throw rate). He is also a good defensive rebounder; Powell is likely going to have to step that up given Mickelson's predilection for gambling for blocks at the expense of rebounding position.

Rashad "Ky" Madden (6-5, 180, So.): Madden disappointed a bit offensively as a freshman, shooting just 24 percent on 71 attempts from three and turning the ball over 21 percent of his possessions. He was, however, a very good rebounder for his size with a 14.5 percent defensive rebound rate.

Mardracus Wade (6-2, 175, Jr.): Wade is a designated sharp shooter. Last season, 65 percent of his shots came from three, and he connected on 48 percent of his attempts. This performance is incredible in light of his 9-for-44 performance from deep as a freshman. Wade has gone from a non-entity to one of the best shooters in the SEC in the space of a single season.

Coty Clarke (6-7, 225, Jr.): Clarke is a junior college transfer who has a chance to make a significant impact as a rebounder and inside presence.

Prospectus says: For Arkansas to succeed this year, Young and Powell need to coexist successfully and one of the other young guards needs to play a large and efficient role in the offense. Additionally, with the loss of Abron, the Razorbacks will again be thin up front with only one player (Mickelson) taller than 6-7. The good news is Arkansas will play the upper-echelon likes of Kentucky, Florida, and Tennessee once apiece this year, and all three teams will visit Fayetteville. The schedule is set up for the Razorbacks to play a spoiler role in the SEC and perhaps make the NCAA tournament for the first time since 2008.

AUBURN

2012: 15-16 (5-11 SEC); Lost to Ole Miss 68-54, SEC first round
In-conference offense: 0.91 points per possession (12th)
In-conference defense: 0.99 points allowed per possession (4th)

What Auburn did well: *Play to its strengths.*

Anyone who watched Auburn's 2011 team from two seasons ago knew there simply was not SEC-caliber offensive talent on that roster. The Tigers lacked a true big man, and not a single player managed an effective field goal percentage of even 50.

Given that Auburn only brought in one new player in 2012, it was likely that any improvement would have to come on the defensive side of the ball. Admittedly, that new player was Varez Ward, a transfer from Texas. While Ward did play well in stretches last season, he was slowed by nagging injuries, and then suspended in February for potential involvement in a point-shaving scheme.

Nevertheless, the Tigers improved from a disastrous 2011 season to the level of mediocrity in 2012. Gone were the embarrassing losses to opponents who were paid to play in Auburn's new arena. The Tigers even beat an NCAA tournament at-large selection (South Florida) in their non-conference schedule.

This improvement can be directly traced to the defense. The Tigers held opponents to 44 percent shooting on twos and blocked 14 percent of their shots, a huge improvement from allowing 50 percent on twos in 2011. Big men Kenny Gabriel and Rob Chubb significantly improved their defensive rebounding and block rates, and 6-1 guard Frankie Sullivan managed to pull down 12 percent of the available defensive rebounds.

Make no mistake, the Tigers were not a good basketball team last season, and in fact they only won one more conference game than they did in 2011. Nevertheless, Auburn showed significant defensive improvement last. If Tony Barbee is completely honest, he probably could not have hoped for much more given the talent level of his team.

What we learned in 2012: *Improvement is incremental.*

Last season in this space, I wrote: "The Tigers will almost certainly improve as they return every player except for [one]." While that did turn out to be true, it probably was not nearly the improvement most Auburn fans would have liked.

Josh Wallace improved from shooting 35 percent from two to 47 percent. Chubb improved his rebounding, and Gabriel improved his rebounding and shooting. Chris Denson got to the free throw line twice as often, and improved his three-point shooting to 37 percent.

While all of Auburn's returning players had as good, if not slightly better seasons than they had in 2011, none of them broke out to become a star. As fans and observers of the game, we frequently get caught up in projecting vast improvements caused by players gaining more experience. While breakout improvements do happen, Auburn's 2012 team is evidence that most improvement is incremental.

What's in store for 2013: Auburn has a chance to accelerate its upward trajectory thanks to Barbee's recruiting. He landed the commitments of Jordan Price and Shaquille Johnson, both of whom are top 100-recruits. They will be expected to make an immediate impact and will likely be the two most talented offensive players on the roster in 2013.

Auburn's offense ranked No. 244 in the country in efficiency last season. The departure of Ward again leaves a gaping hole at the point guard position which will likely be filled by Wallace, who is not a good shooter but has shown the ability to run a team (29 percent assist rate in 2011). The Tigers badly need outside shooting, but it is unclear who will be able to provide it. Auburn's offense will likely remain an inefficient outfit.

MEET THE TIGERS

Jordan Price (6-5, 230, Fr.): Price is a large shooting guard who uses his size to get inside and score effectively. He has a smooth outside shot, and should provide an immediate shot in the arm to the Auburn offense.

Shaquille Johnson (6-5, 210, Fr.): Do yourself a favor and type Shaq Johnson into YouTube. Then watch his dunk compilation, which as I'm writing has almost 2.5 million views. I think it is safe to say you will see Johnson on Sportscenter at least once this season posterizing a poor defender.

Rob Chubb (6-10, 240, Sr.): Chubb is going to be thrust into a bigger role this season, whether he is ready for it or not. Despite improvement, he is still not a great defensive rebounder (16 percent rate in 2012). Given that Chubb is the only player taller than 6-6 with significant experience, that number needs to improve.

Chris Denson (6-2, 170, Jr.): Denson maintained his offensive efficiency while doubling his minutes and increasing his usage rate in 2012. He will be an important rotation player for the Tigers this year.

Josh Wallace (5-10, 170, Sr.): Wallace lost minutes to Ward last season, but will likely be asked to fill a starting point guard role in 2013. Auburn fans will hope he can finally cut down on his extremely high turnover rate (26 percent of his possessions last season).

Frankie Sullivan (6-1, 205, Sr.): Sullivan returned to the Tigers after missing a season with a torn ACL, and pick up where he left off as the team's designated three-point shooter. Unfortunately, Sullivan only connected on 32 percent of his 189 attempts last season.

Prospectus says: Barbee's turnaround job is still in its initial stages, but fans will be expecting a winning record and something closer to .500 play in conference this season. The Tigers should be able to hit those targets if the freshmen are as good as the recruiting analysts think. The question again will be on the offensive end: can Auburn score enough to beat mid-level SEC teams? That answer will ultimately decide the Tigers' fate.

FLORIDA

2012: 26-11 (10-6 SEC); Lost to Louisville 72-68, Elite Eight
In-conference offense: 1.10 points per possession (3rd)
In-conference defense: 1.04 points allowed per possession (8th)

What Florida did well: *Change identities.*

Two seasons ago Florida made the 2011 Elite Eight as one of the tallest teams in the nation, riding senior forwards Alex Tyus, Vernon Macklin, and Chandler Parsons. The Gators did not shoot many threes (31 percent of their attempts, good for No. 202 nationally). In many ways, the team succeeded in spite and not because of the erratic play of guards Kenny Boynton and Erving Walker.

Then came 2012. The Gators were below the national average in terms of size and effective height, they devoted more of their shots to threes than all but four teams in the country, and they relied heavily on the play of Boynton and Walker to get to yet another Elite Eight.

As you can see, despite becoming a much more guard-oriented team in 2012, the Gators were able to maintain the same level of rebounding performance. Much of the rebounding slack was picked up by fantastic freshman Brad Beal (19 percent defensive rebound rate) and Will Yeguete, who played a larger role in his sophomore campaign despite battling injuries.

While the teams shared tantalizingly close brushes with a trip to the Final Four, their journeys and identities were quite dissimilar. It is rare to see a team have that level of success in such different ways, and it is a testament to the program that Billy Donovan has built that he could manage such a transformation so successfully.

What we learned in 2012: *Florida lost the lottery in conference play, and was underrated as a result.*

Last year, Ken Pomeroy wrote a series of extremely interesting blog posts in which he showed why he believes that three-point percentage is essentially a lottery. Teams do not show consistent ability to maintain levels of three-point shooting or three-point defense. What they can do, however, is control whether or not they play the lottery by how many threes they take or allow to be taken.

Last season, Florida entered the month of February ranked in the top 10 in both polls, seemingly headed for a protected seed in the NCAA tournament. They then proceeded to lose five of their last eight conference games, and ended up receiving a No. 7 seed. What happened to the Gators?

Over that eight-game stretch, Florida scored three less points and gave up four more points on three pointers than they did on average over the rest of the season. It just so happened that their worst shooting stretch coincided with their worst defensive stretch. In those eight games, Florida lost the three-point lottery in a big way.

While I did pick arbitrary end points for this comparison, those end points are what the college basketball world was focused on as March Madness began. While Florida did benefit immensely from Norfolk State's stunning upset of Missouri, the Gators were definitely being underrated on the basis of their recent performance.

CH-CH-CH-CH-CHANGES

	2011 Gators	2012 Gators
Effective Height	+3.8 in	+0.3 in
FGA by Guards (%)	42	67
3PA/FGA (%)	31	45
Def. rebounding (%)	70	70

LOSING THE LOTTERY

	3FG%	3FG% allowed
Last eight SEC games	34	41
Rest of season	39	32

Recent games are not necessarily more predictive of future performance than games from earlier in the season, no matter how much better we remember the recent games. And if three-point shooting truly is a lottery, we should have expected some reversion to Florida's better mean performance over the course of the season. It's always harder to judge in the moment, but the perception of Florida last March was definitely more negative than it should have been given the nature of the three-point lottery.

What's in store in 2013: Florida will again be transformed with the departure of Walker and Beal. The Gators will likely be a more interior-focused team again in 2013. Patric Young and Erik Murphy return after very productive 2012 seasons. Both will likely be asked to shoot more often, and Murphy especially will have to work on staying out of foul trouble.

In the backcourt, Boynton returns for his senior season after a terrific junior campaign. The questions for Florida start at the point guard position. Senior guard Mike Rosario will be forced into a larger role. While Rosario is a dynamic playmaker, he is a score-first and score-second option at the point. The pesky Scottie Wilbekin is the only true point guard on the roster with significant experience.

Florida's biggest challenge will be depth. Besides the aforementioned five players and Yeguete, the Gators will be relying on low-minute players (Casey Prather) or freshmen like point guard Braxton Ogbueze and shooting guard DeVon Walker. There will likely be an adjustment period in the non-conference season. I would not expect the Gators to play their best basketball until conference play.

MEET THE GATORS

Kenny Boynton (6-2, 190, Sr.): For two years observers wondered why Donovan let Boynton attempt over 200 threes when he shot such a low percentage. The coach's faith was rewarded last season when Boynton connected on 41 percent of his 270 (!) attempts from deep. If he continues to connect at that rate during his senior season, he could finish second in three-pointers made in SEC history.

Patric Young (6-9, 250, Jr.): Young might be the biggest physical specimen in college basketball. He vastly improved last season, increasing his usage rate and his efficiency and shooting 62 percent from two. Young's rebounding still leaves something to be desired for someone with his physical gifts, but that is a minor blemish on his game.

Erik Murphy (6-10, 240, Sr.): It may be strange to think about Murphy as a breakout candidate as a senior, but I believe he is. He grew into his starting role last year, shooting 55 percent from two and 42 percent from three. Murphy could be All-SEC first team.

Mike Rosario (6-3, 185, Sr.): Rosario transferred from Rutgers with eyes on this year when he could star for the Gators. I am skeptical, however. Rosario benefited from the talented guards around him last season. Without that safety blanket, he might return to his low-efficiency ways from his time with the Scarlet Knights.

Will Yeguete (6-7, 240, Jr.): Yeguete impressed last season in his role as rebounding big man. A back line of Young and Yeguete may be undersized vertically, but both make up for it with bulk and hustle.

Braxton Ogbueze (6-0, 180, Fr.): Ogbueze has the opportunity to make a significant impact as a freshman with the clear hole at point guard on the roster. He is a heady guard with a great array of mid-range shots. The question will be whether he can compete physically as a freshman.

DeVon Walker (6-6, 190, Fr.): Walker is a freak athlete with a long wingspan. He needs to work on his outside shot, but could play an immediate role as a pesky perimeter defender.

Prospectus says: If Billy Donovan gets this team to the Elite Eight again, it may be his best coaching job yet. A more realistic expectation would be a top-four finish in the SEC and a trip to the Sweet 16. A lot rests on the performance of Rosario and the freshmen in the backcourt.

GEORGIA

2012: 15-17 (5-11 SEC); Lost to Vanderbilt 63-41, SEC quarterfinals
In-conference offense: 0.97 points per possession (9th)
In-conference defense: 1.05 points per possession allowed (9th)

What Georgia did well: *Take care of the ball.*

To be honest, the Bulldogs did not really do anything else well. UGA did not rank in the top 100 nationally of any of the other Four Factors on either offense or defense. Offensively, the Dawgs ranked No. 11 in what was then a 12-team SEC in effective field goal percentage and free throw rate, and No. 9 in offensive rebound rate.

But Mark Fox's team was able to avoid turnovers. The Bulldogs turned it over on just 17 percent of their possessions, good for No. 19 in the country. Freshman bright spot Kentavious Caldwell-Pope managed to take 28 percent of Georgia's shots when he was on the court while only turning the ball over 10 percent of the time. Point guard Gerald Robinson also sported a 1.8 assist-to-turnover ratio.

Interestingly, Georgia's ability to take care of the rock was essentially uncorrelated with the quality of the opponent. Perhaps this says more about the ability of Fox's players to get quality shots in his complicated triangle offense variants, and less about their ability to play good offensive basketball.

The Bulldogs took a lot of jump shots last season, both from two and from three. They struggled mightily getting to the free throw line and scoring in the paint. It's easy to avoid turnovers when your team only shoots jumpers.

What we learned in 2012: *In the SEC, Fox is moving at a more of a snail's pace.*

THE TORTOISE AND THE FOX

	Georgia Tempo	SEC Average
2010	65.7	68.4
2011	64.5	65.5
2012	60.7	63.3

When Fox coached in the WAC at Nevada, his teams played at a fairly average clip, settling around 67 possessions per game. After his move to the SEC and his aforementioned conversion to the triangle offense, however, his pace has slowed considerably.

Both Fox and the SEC as a whole have slowed down dramatically in the last three years. It is hard to tease out cause and effect, as the Bulldogs' slowdown brings down the SEC's tempo and other teams' decision to slow down brings down the Bulldogs' pace, but it seems clear that Fox has made a conscious decision to go slower and slower.

UGA's current offensive scheme and personnel essentially cede the free throw line as a facet of the offense. Georgia has finished at the bottom of the SEC in conference play free throw rate the last two years, putting more pressure on jump shots and stopping the clock less often.

This slows the game down and covers up some deficiencies in personnel, but Fox's slow tempo can't hide the fact that the majority of his players are currently not good enough to create their own shot against SEC level defenses. No amount of slowing down is likely to change that fact.

What's in store for 2013: The program-building at Georgia took a step back last year, and it is hard to see it regaining much forward momentum in 2013. Aside from Caldwell-Pope, the Bulldogs return forwards Nemanja Djurisic, Donte Williams, and Marcus Thornton. Djurisic was the most prominent of the three last season, but also the least efficient.

The depth problems will come in the backcourt. Georgia brings in three freshman guards, and at least one will have to contribute substantially: Caldwell-Pope is the only returning guard who played more than 12 minutes a game last season.

Fox will likely find it hard sledding offensively

again in 2013. This team struggles to shoot well from three (31 percent in 2012), and they lost their best deep threat in Dustin Ware. Defensively, the Bulldogs remain undersized and foul-prone. There is a chance the young bigs will improve, but that is not certain.

MEET THE BULLDOGS

Kentavious Caldwell-Pope (6-5, 205, So): Caldwell-Pope's freshman season was a statistical oddity. As a 6-4 guard, he shot better than 50 percent from two and pulled in 15 percent of the available defensive rebounds. He was not asked to handle the ball a lot last season, but with the departure of Robinson expect him to play more of a combo guard role. Caldwell-Pope has the ability to be a breakout star.

Nemanja Djurisic (6-8, 230, So.): Djurisic was a surprise last season. The Montenegrin national only played one season of high school basketball in America. Djurisic had some turnover issues last season, but shot 36 percent from three and showed flashes of real talent.

Donte' Williams (6-9, 225, Jr.): Williams improved by leaps and bounds last season, taking a starting role in the offense and becoming one of Georgia's most efficient players. He was the only player on the Bulldogs to shoot more than 100 free throws last season. He will need to improve his defensive rebounding this season.

Kenny Gaines (6-3, 195, Fr.): If there is a player who can solve Georgia's offensive explosiveness issues, it is Gaines. He is a big, athletic guard who specializes in thunderous dunks. Gaines can shoot from outside, but his shot involves a long motion that may be too slow against SEC defenders.

Charles Mann (6-4, 205, Fr.): Mann is a big point guard prospect from Georgia who will have the chance to play significant minutes as a freshman. He is not a good outside shooter, but is apparently a smart vocal leader.

Prospectus says: Fox's teams will always play hard and execute well, but there seems to be a lack of talent on the roster. There are certainly worse teams in the SEC this season, but it would be an accomplishment for the Bulldogs to finish in the top half of the league. If that does happen, it will likely be because of the emergence of Caldwell-Pope as a star, as well as the contributions of freshman guards.

KENTUCKY

2012: 38-2 (16-0 SEC); Beat Kansas 67-59, National Championship Game
In-conference offense: 1.20 points per possession (1st)
In-conference defense: 0.94 points allowed per possession (2nd)

What Kentucky did well: *Embody greatness.*

Sometime last fall, I stumbled across the complete broadcast of the 1991 national championship game. As someone whose college basketball consciousness essentially begins with Maryland's championship in 2002, this game was a revelation. UNLV played the game with a level of talent and abandon I did not recognize, but Duke executed so crisply and efficiently that they somehow surpassed UNLV on that one night. It was mesmerizing.

There have been a lot of great college teams in the last decade, but somehow all have felt a bit lacking. While teams like Connecticut in 2004, North Carolina in 2005, and Kansas in 2008 won titles and were loaded with NBA players, on an aesthetic level, they did not approach what I saw when I watched those great 1990s teams.

Which brings me to Kentucky in 2012. When the Wildcats played last season, it was an Event. The most indelible moments of the entire season nationally involved UK: the epic win over North Carolina, Indiana's Assembly Hall Miracle, and, ultimately, Michael Kidd-Gilchrist's block of Tyshawn Taylor to seal the championship.

John Calipari got the young Wildcats to cohere into a complete team. This was in no small part aided by the unselfish leadership of Anthony Davis, the most dynamic and dominating player college basketball has seen since Kevin Durant. Watching Kentucky on the fast break was breathtaking, and their interior defense was the best since the Connecticut teams of seven or eight years ago.

It is true that the 2012 Cats would likely be underdogs against the best teams of the 1990s (including the 1996 Wildcats), but the fact that they were able to play with the same aesthetic beauty and swagger helped make them a national sensation and earned Calipari the undying love of Big Blue Nation.

What we learned in 2012: *If you have enough talent, turnovers matter far less.*

It is widely acknowledged that the least efficient shots in college basketball are two-point jumpers. Such shots go in at rates similar to those of their cousins, three-point jumpers, but do not have the benefit of the extra point. Several very successful defensive systems (Tony Bennett's Pack Line defense at Virginia, Bo Ryan's defenses at Wisconsin) have been predicated on stopping drives to the basket and three-point shots, but allowing (contested) two-point jumpers.

All of Calipari's Kentucky teams have embraced these principles, but none has done it more effectively than the 2012 edition. The Wildcats allowed opponents to shoot only 29 percent of their attempts from beyond the arc, and blocked an incredible 19 percent of shots attempted at the rim. Even more impressively, Kentucky's opponents only shot 26 percent on two-point jumpers.

The combination of Davis and Terrence Jones patrolling the paint and MKG and Darius Miller harassing the wings effectively funneled UK opponents into areas where they could not score easily.

You will notice one defensive aspect has not been mentioned at all so far: forcing turnovers. That is because the Cats simply didn't do it. Their 18 percent opponent turnover rate was No. 301 in the nation. Calipari's team was so athletically gifted that they were able to prioritize forcing missed shots over forcing turnovers.

When Kentucky did force turnovers, however, they converted them into points. According to Synergy Sports, the Wildcats scored on 59 percent of their transition possessions, the tenth-best mark in the nation.

UK was able to succeed by forcing opponents to take shots they did not want to take. They made up for the lack of volume of their forced turnovers with ruthless efficiency in converting those that they did force into points. This combination was successful because of the unbelievable talent level Calipari was able to recruit to Lexington.

What's in store for 2013: That the Wildcats will start the season in the top five of most rankings despite returning one player (Kyle Wiltjer) who played even a small role in last season's NCAA championship run is both a testament to Calipari's ability to recruit and a potential cause for concern for Big Blue Nation. Expectations will be set sky high, and many of those expectations will rest on the shoulders of freshman center Nerlens Noel. While Noel, and the inevitable comparisons to Anthony Davis that he elicits, will draw the most attention, the most important player to Kentucky's success in 2013 will likely be transfer point guard Ryan Harrow. The onetime NC State player sat out last season, watching and learning during the Wildcats' run, but now will become the Calipari's sixth point guard in the last six years. If he plays as well as the previous five, Kentucky's lofty ranking will likely be justified.

MEET THE WILDCATS

Nerlens Noel (6-10, 230, Fr.): Probably the most well known freshman in the nation, Noel is an elite shot blocker and rebounder. This leads to inevitable comparisons to his predecessor at the center role for the Wildcats, but these are unfair to Noel: Anthony Davis was able to combine that defensive ability with fantastic offensive efficiency. If Noel produces simply average offense and his trademark defense, he will have lived up to his billing.

Ryan Harrow (6-2, 170, So.): As a freshman at NC State, Harrow improved throughout the year and put up an impressive assist rate (29 percent). Cats fans will hope he improved his outside shooting, which was an anemic 23 percent. I expect Harrow to have a breakout season.

Kyle Wiltjer (6-10, 240, So.): Wiltjer embraced his role as a designated shooter last season, taking half of his attempts from three and connecting on 43 percent of them. He is skilled enough to do more in Calipari's Dribble Drive Motion offense, and he should see more minutes this season.

Archie Goodwin (6-5, 200, Fr.): Goodwin is a strong wing who has the potential to lead Kentucky in scoring. He is a good shooter, but really excels off the dribble.

Alex Poythress (6-7, 240, Fr.): Calipari has built his success at Kentucky around strong defenders who can guard wings (and some bigs). Poythress will be the heir apparent to DeAndre Liggins, Darius Miller, and Terrence Jones. Defensively, he is ready for the SEC. It remains to be seen whether his offensive game will match up.

Julius Mays (6-2, 190, Sr.): Mays started his college career at NC State, played a year at Wright State, and will finish at Kentucky. He is a strong combo guard, but not a great athlete. Mays could fill a role as a shooter coming off the bench. He shot 43 percent from three last season.

Prospectus says: Kentucky's problem this season will not be talent, nor inexperience, but rather depth. The Wildcats' rotation will be at most seven deep, leaving them vulnerable to injury or poor play. Expect some growing pains in the non-conference as an entirely new team comes together, but if everything goes according to Calipari's plan, Kentucky is a legitimate threat to reach a third straight Final Four.

LSU

2012: 18-15 (7-9 SEC); Lost to Oregon 96-76, NIT first round
In-conference offense: 0.96 points per possession (10th)
In-conference defense: 1.01 points allowed per possession (5th)

What LSU did well: *Play well enough to lose the coach.*

Despite football being the official religion of the Tiger fanbase, the basketball team has had quite a bit of success in the last 20 years. From the Shaquille O'Neal years to the Glen Davis-led trip to the 2006 Final Four, LSU has been good enough to raise their fans' expectations for the months in between football and baseball seasons.

In 2010 and 2011, however, the Tigers played some of the worst basketball in that rich history. Trent Johnson's teams simply did not have enough talent to compete in the SEC. That changed in 2012. The arrival of highly touted freshman Johnny O'Bryant and transfer Justin Hamilton meant LSU was suddenly one of the biggest teams in the nation.

Johnson parlayed that size into a very good defense and a winning record despite poor shooting from the field. Another freshman, Anthony Hickey, provided point guard play that had been non-existent in the preceding two seasons. All of this added up to a good non-conference performance, which included a shocking win over Marquette, and a decent performance in SEC play.

After losing in the first round of the NIT, Johnson bolted for the newly minted major-conference job at TCU, and Hamilton left a season early to enter the NBA draft. It's not exactly a compliment to LSU's roster that Johnson was willing to leave for a school that will surely struggle in the Big 12 for the next few seasons.

New coach Johnny Jones had good success at North Texas, and has fantastic connections in the junior college circuit in the Southwest. He will recruit well, but it will take time to see that translate into wins. LSU fans will have to be patient, because last season's brief trip to the NIT may be the only postseason play they see for a year or two.

What we learned in 2012: *Johnny O'Bryant has nowhere to go but up... right?*

In this space a year ago, I discussed how the Tigers of 2011 had neither the size nor the talent to succeed offensively. This deficiency is part of the reason the arrival of O'Bryant was such a big deal. Here was a McDonald's All-American who contributed right away. Although he was sidelined by an injury for five games in SEC play, the putative star took on a featured performer's share of the offense right away.

The results, however, were less than stellar. In his minutes, O'Bryant carried an immense load for the Tigers, taking 26 percent of his team's shots. Unfortunately, he made just 40 percent of those shots. This was in no small part due to his fondness for mid-range jumpers. According to Hoop-Math's analysis of play-by-play data, 63 percent of O'Bryant's shots were two-point jumpers. He made just 28 percent of those attempts.

All of that inefficiency resulted in a shockingly low offensive rating of 84. It seems that O'Bryant, who clearly is talented, will only improve. While that may be true, of the 12 freshmen in the last five years who have carried a similar possession load with a similar level of inefficiency, only three have posted offensive ratings over 100 in their next season. I'm not saying that O'Bryant will not improve this season, but to assume that improvement to be a sure thing would be foolish.

What's in store for 2013: Regardless of O'Bryant's level of play, the Tigers will likely struggle in 2013. Gone are Hamilton and Storm Warren. Andre Stringer will return as a likely starter, but in his first two seasons in Baton Rouge he is yet to attain the caliber of an SEC starter. Stringer has not shot better than 40 percent from the field in those two seasons. Jones' roster is thus going to be lacking for talent. Hickey and O'Bryant will shoulder a lot of the load, and the Tigers will hope that at least one of Jones' class of junior college recruits can make an impact. From a style point of view, Jones will likely make the Tigers one of the fastest-paced teams in the SEC, as his previous teams have played at a tempo of around 68 possessions per game. Additionally, we can expect Jones to carry on Johnson's legacy of eschewing the three-point shot.

MEET THE TIGERS

Johnny O'Bryant (6-9, 260, So.): One area in which O'Bryant excelled last season was in drawing fouls. He drew five whistles per 40 minutes and had a free throw rate of 39 percent. If he can continue that rate in more minutes this season, he will be a major force in the paint.

Anthony Hickey (5-10, 180, So.): The diminutive point guard was a pleasant surprise as a pesky defender last season, averaging two steals per game. If Hickey is able to realize the freshman-to-sophomore improvement, he could be a breakout player for the Tigers.

Andre Stringer (5-9, 180, Jr.): Stringer was the putative point guard last season, but was superseded by Hickey. Stringer excels at getting to the free throw line, but has struggled to actually make shots (39 percent shooting from two) against bigger defenders.

Shane Hammink (6-7, 210, Fr.): Hammink's father Geert played at LSU when Jones was an assistant coach. The younger Hammink is a strong guard who plays good defense and can finish through contact. He is also likely the only player on a Division I roster from the Canary Islands.

Prospectus says: Jones is certainly a smart hire from a recruiting standpoint. Whether he can turn that recruiting network into on-court success will not be answered this season. The Tigers will struggle in 2013, but may find a playmaker in Hickey.

MISSISSIPPI

2012: 20-14 (8-8 SEC); Lost to Illinois State 96-93 (OT), NIT first round
In-conference offense: 1.00 points per possession (6th)
In-conference defense: 1.03 points allowed per possession (7th)

What Mississippi did well: *Play well through adversity.*

Last year, my Ole Miss preview was focused on the talent of Dundrecous Nelson and Jelan Kendrick. Both appeared to have the potential to give Ole Miss an outside shot at an NCAA tournament bid. By the end of the season, however, both had been dismissed from the team.

Nelson was jettisoned in January after being done in by the munchies. Campus police smelled marijuana in his room and followed the pizza deliveryman into the apartment. Kendrick's transgressions were more of an accumulation of small things, which included a practice fight with Reginald Buckner and alleged canoodling with his girlfriend during warm-ups before the Alabama game.

Without Kendrick or Nelson, the Rebels were left with no experience at point guard, and little scoring threat from the perimeter. Andy Kennedy combatted this problem by turning Ole Miss into an interior-oriented team. The Rebels led the SEC in offensive rebounding, corralling 37 percent of their misses in conference play, and shot 42 free throws for every 100 shots they attempted from the field. Murphy Holloway, Terrance Henry, and Buckner all took more than half of their shots at the rim, and drew fouls at extremely high rates.

As a result, the Rebels were able to manage to score a point per possession in conference play and finish with an 8-8 mark. It would have been easy for Kennedy's squad to slide to a 5-11 season, but Ole Miss actually won five of its last six games, including two at the SEC tournament, and made the NIT. That success is a credit to the remaining Rebels.

What we learned in 2012: *Ole Miss is stuck in Andy Kennedy Equilibrium.*

For a sixth consecutive year, Ole Miss finished between 7-9 and 9-7 in SEC play. And for the fourth time in the last five years, the Rebels went to the NIT. Ole Miss has managed a positive point differential in SEC play just once in those six seasons, and that was a measly 0.03 points per possession in 2009.

To be clear, Kennedy faces big disadvantages in recruiting and facilities when compared to many of his SEC peers. He has shown an ability to develop players, most notably Chris Warren, and has always put out strong teams on the offensive end of the floor. Nevertheless, after six years and two full recruiting cycles, fans have a right to expect at least one year of breakout success.

There is a sort of benign neglect that comes with being the basketball coach at football-crazy SEC schools. (Kentucky, of course, being the major exception.) Coaches get longer leashes and face less stringent expectations. There is no infinite patience, however, as Rick Stansbury found out down in Starkville last season. Ole Miss will soon have a new basketball arena, and a chance to jump-start the program. Kennedy needs to show improvement soon.

What's in store for 2013: The Rebels return a level of frontcourt depth and experience only matched by Florida in the SEC. In Buckner and Holloway, Ole Miss has a frontcourt duo that can rebound well, block shots at a high rate, and draw fouls. The question will be the backcourt. Nick Williams is a solid if unspectacular score-first 2-guard. Jarvis Summers provides more promise. He filled the point guard role as a freshman after the dismissal of Nelson, and did fairly well. His assist-turnover ratio was an unspectacular 1.1, but he showed the ability to stretch the defense and shot an amazing 6.5 free throws per 40 minutes.

The real hope for the Rebels comes in the form of two new players. Marshall Henderson averaged 11 points a game on 45 percent shooting from three as a freshman for Utah before transferring to be closer to home. He is joined by 6-9 freshman Anthony Perez, a small forward who can also shoot from deep. Last year, the Rebels took just 25 percent of their shots from three, one of the lowest rates in the nation. That is sure to change in 2013.

MEET THE REBELS

Reginald Buckner (6-9, 235, Sr.): Buckner returns as the leading shot blocker in Rebel history, and will be expected to continue his double-double form of last season. If he can somehow improve his free throw shooting, which has fallen from 49 percent his freshman year to 42 percent in 2011-12, he could be as effective an offensive force as he is a defensive one.

Murphy Holloway (6-7, 240, Sr.): Holloway's return to the Rebels after a sojourn at South Carolina was a major reason for their success last season. He is the leading returning rebounder in the SEC, which is not simply a product of longevity: his offensive rebound rate has been at or above 11 percent in all three of his previous seasons. Like Buckner, Holloway's offensive Achilles' heel is his free throw shooting, where he only managed to connect on 51 percent of his attempts as a junior.

Jarvis Summers (6-4, 185, So.): Summers had an under-the-radar freshman campaign that could signify a breakout performance in 2013. He is the rare player who combines perimeter shooting, good passing, and the ability to get to the free throw line consistently. If Summers cuts down on his turnovers and takes fewer shots, he could be a scarily efficient point guard.

Nick Williams (6-4, 210, Sr.): Williams is a glue guy on the perimeter, and not the first offensive option. Last year he took 112 threes, by far the most on the team, but only made 32 percent of them. I actually expect his usage rate to go down this year as new perimeter players enter the rotation.

Anthony Perez (6-9, 205, Fr.): Perez is from Venezuela, but he played his high school basketball at Montverde Academy in Florida. He is a tall wing who has good shooting ability. If he gets a bit stronger, he could make an immediate impact for the Rebels this season.

Marshall Henderson (6-2, 175, Jr.): Henderson's previous claim to fame at Utah was his ejection from a rivalry game against BYU in 2010 for pushing Jackson Emery to the floor. In his one season as a Ute, he shot the ball a often (accounting for 29 percent of the offense's shots during his minutes), but only made 44 percent of his twos. Nevertheless, his perimeter shooting and swagger should be welcome additions at Ole Miss.

Prospectus says: If the perimeter pieces fall into place, the Rebels are a darkhorse SEC contender. Ole Miss has a favorable schedule, playing Kentucky, Tennessee, and Florida just once apiece. Kennedy needs to make an NCAA tournament soon, and this has the potential to be the team that gets him to that promised land.

MISSISSIPPI STATE

2012: 21-12 (8-8 SEC); Lost to UMass 101-96 (2 OT), NIT first round
In-conference offense: 1.06 points per possession (4th)
In-conference defense: 1.08 points allowed per possession (10th)

What Mississippi State did well: *Hit the reset button.*

I'm pretty sure only the most addicted college basketball fans (read: me) watched Mississippi State's season-ending, double-overtime loss to UMass in the NIT. Those that did witnessed one of the sadder sights in the 2011-2012 season: a thoroughly defeated Rick Stansbury watching his players take ill-advised shots, play absolutely no defense, and seal his fate at the school he had led to five NCAA tournament appearances in 14 years as head coach.

Stansbury had taken a recruiting risk in those last few years, seeking talent even at the expense of minimal levels of acceptable player behavior. That strategy, which most notably yielded three bizarre and disappointing years of Renardo Sidney, ended up backfiring and costing him his job. The collection of offensive talent he put out on the court turned out to be a group that played selfish offense (the Bulldogs rated in the bottom half of assist-to-field goal ratio in Division I) while flatly refusing to defend.

It is not easy to win at a place like Starkville. Mississippi State's expenditure of $589,504 on its basketball program in 2010, the most recent year for which we have data, was the lowest of any SEC school. In fact that dollar amount was just 56 percent of the league's median budget that season. New coach Rick Ray, formerly an assistant at Clemson, will have to recruit against programs with larger budgets and better facilities. He will have to deal with the expectations of a fan base that, despite supporting the firing of Stansbury, has grown to expect the periodic runs in March that he produced.

The reset at Mississippi State is a complete one. Jalen Steele and Wendell Lewis are the only players of note who are back this season. The Bulldogs return just 22 percent of their minutes and 17 percent of their points. Ray kicked two more players off the team in August, and two of his recruits suffered significant injuries this summer.

Mississippi State will not play competitive basketball in 2013—and likely won't in 2014, either—but that does not mean that the decision to overhaul the program was not the right one. The Bulldogs are on the road towards receiving the right kind of attention for a change, but it may be a while before they get there.

What we learned in 2012: *This is what your stats look like when you give up on defense.*

Five years from now eager young college hoops statheads will look at the tempo-free numbers for Mississippi State's 2012 defense and likely be fooled. Here is a team that seemingly never fouled on defense, and pulled down the most defensive rebounds of any team in SEC play. Clearly they were able to both defend and box out effectively without sending opponents to the most efficient spot on the floor in basketball.

Those fans will then cue up game film courtesy of whatever brand of sorcery Google or Apple has cooked up by 2017, and then our future fans will see the true story: Mississippi State's lack of fouling didn't mean they were playing good defense. It meant they weren't playing any defense at all.

The Bulldogs rebounded at a very high rate, but that masks the fact that they allowed SEC opponents to shoot 48 percent from two and 40 percent from three. And Mississippi State forced by far the fewest turnovers (13.5 percent of opponents' possessions) of any team in the last decade of SEC play.

I am not sure we will ever again see a team this talented underachieve so greatly on one side of the ball while doing well on the other side of it. But if we do, we will know what the statistical signature will look like, thanks to 2012 Mississippi State.

What's in store for 2013: Futility. Steele and Lewis return, but neither played an integral role in the offense last season. Steele is primarily a three-point shooter, and Lewis is a big who only used 10 percent of his team's possessions while on the court last season. A decent recruiting class has filled out the remainder of the roster. The problem is a rotation of six freshmen and two upperclassmen does not cut it in the SEC unless you look in the mirror and see John Calipari. The highest rated recruit, Fred Thomas, underwent surgery for a stress fracture in August. The Bulldogs' November trip to Hawaii for the Maui Invitational, where they will play North Carolina in the first game, will be a baptism by fire for a young squad.

MEET THE BULLDOGS

Jalen Steele (6-3, 195, Jr.): Last year, Steele took 77 percent of his 231 shots from three, benefitting from his teammates' ability to create their own offense. This year, Steele won't have that luxury. Expect to see his usage rate explode, perhaps to the highest level of any player in the SEC, as he will have to be a main offensive cog this year.

Wendell Lewis (6-9, 250, Sr.): Like Steele, Lewis will likely see his role expand by necessity. He was efficient in his extremely limited duties on offense last season (63 percent shooting), but that efficiency will almost surely drop as he no longer limits himself to bunnies at the rim.

Fred Thomas (6-5, 180, Fr.): According to Ray, Thomas will be ready for the start of the season and will likely see time at the shooting guard slot. He is a wiry guard who can finish inside, but he might struggle with more physical defenders.

Craig Sword (6-3, 190, Fr.): Sword played shooting guard in high school, but with the season-ending injury to fellow freshman Jacoby Davis he will likely be moved over to the point guard slot.

Gavin Ware (6-9, 280, Fr.): Ware went to high school two miles from the Starkville campus. He will likely see playing time simply because of his size, though by all accounts he is still growing into his body and his game. For better or worse that process will be accelerated by the Bulldogs' thin roster.

Prospectus says: It's hard to tell just how much the Bulldogs will struggle, but they will almost assuredly be in the bottom tier of the SEC. If Ray can turn at least a few members of his recruiting class into viable SEC players, this season can be judged a success. Much like Tony Barbee's turnaround efforts at Auburn, the results of his tenure will not be clear until he is able to build a roster of his own players.

MISSOURI

2012: 30-5 (14-4 Big 12); Lost to Norfolk State 86-84, NCAA round of 64
In-conference offense: 1.15 points per possession (1st Big 12)
In-conference defense: 1.04 points allowed per possession (6th Big 12)

What Missouri did well: *Produce one of the most efficient offensive seasons in recent memory.*

In his first season at the helm in Columbia, Frank Haith was blessed with a senior class that played offense like a well-oiled machine. His charge was to first do no harm, but he did the job description one better. Missouri produced the fifth best adjusted offensive rating in the tempo-free era, and scored 1.15 points per possession in the second-toughest conference in the country.

At its best, the Tiger offense was a nightmare to defend. Frequently, it featured four sharpshooting guards (Kim English, Michael Dixon, Marcus Denmon, and Phil Pressey, playing around one uber-efficient big man (Ricardo Ratliffe). This set-up, reminiscent of Villanova's excellent mid-2000s teams, allowed the Tigers to create great spacing on the floor. Their crisp ball movement and penetration created open looks, which they converted at an unbelievable rate. Their effective field goal percentage of 58 trailed only the 2007 Florida group that repeated as national champions among major-conference teams since 2003.

The amazing thing was that the Tigers were able to move the ball so well and so quickly without giving it up. Their turnover rate was the third-best in the entire nation. Essentially, Missouri was able to take shots on a greater percentage of their possessions and make those shots more often than any other team in the country.

What we learned in 2012: *Beware negative covariance come March.*

Of course, Missouri's season will mostly be remembered for its ending, a stunning upset at the hands of No. 15 seed Norfolk State in the round of 64. While I cannot claim to have predicted such an upset, I did identify the Tigers as the team most at risk for an early round upset for the top seeds because of their negative covariance during the season.

Negative covariance refers to the tendency of a team's offensive and defensive efficiencies in single games to move in opposite directions. Teams who exhibit negative covariance win big and lose big, with correspondingly high offensive ratings and low defensive ratings (or vice versa).

Missouri's negative covariance last season was over two standard deviations below the norm for all teams since 2004. This puts them in the top 2.5 percent of over 2,800 team seasons in terms of negative covariance. Below are the Tigers' best four and worst four offensive performances against BCS teams last season.

While Missouri's ability to blow out teams served them well both on the court and in Ken Pomeroy's rankings, their tendency to have poor performances on both ends of the floor on the same night made them vulnerable in a single-elimination playoff format. It's true their loss to Norfolk State was a product solely of shocking defense (amazingly, Missouri scored more efficiently than anyone had all season against the Spartans), but the negative covariance throughout the season illustrated that Haith's team was at risk for an off night.

THE BEST OF TIMES...

Opponent	Offensive rating	Defensive rating
Oklahoma	144.0	81.4
Texas Tech	139.3	101.0
Oklahoma State	133.0	104.5
California	132.0	76.0

... THE WORST OF TIMES

Opponent	Offensive rating	Defensive rating
Kansas State	86.9	110.0
Kansas State	101.0	116.5
Texas	102.6	101.0
Oklahoma State	102.7	112.0

What's in store for 2013: Haith faces a tougher task this season, as his roster will experience quite a bit of turnover. At its heart, however, remain Pressey, the efficient passer, and Dixon, the dynamic scoring guard (assuming the dynamic scoring guard returns after being suspended "indefinitely" by Haith in the preseason). Haith gets Laurence Bowers back after he missed all of last season due to injury. Bowers will likely split time at the power forward spot with Auburn transfer Earnest Ross. Alex Oriakhi, eligible immediately because of Connecticut's postseason ban, will be in the paint. On the wing, Haith will likely rely on Keion Bell. Even though he was an inefficient volume scorer at Pepperdine, Bell may fit in much better when he is not asked to take over 30 percent of his team's shots. Haith will also get Oregon transfer and former top-25 recruit Jabari Brown in time for conference play. On paper this team looks as talented, if not more so, than the 2012 edition. But what made Missouri click last season was the fact that the players had played with each other for so long. While Bell, Ross, and Brown did practice last season, Bowers and Oriakhi did not. It will be a test of Haith's coaching ability to see how he molds this team.

MEET THE TIGERS

Phil Pressey (5-11, 175, Jr.): Pressey emerged as one of the best point guards in the country last season. He excelled at penetrating and either getting to the free throw line or passing to shooters. However, Pressey will have to be a different kind of point guard this season, as Mizzou's personnel is now more weighted towards slashing scorers and traditional big men.

Michael Dixon (6-1, 190, Sr.): Dixon was suspended indefinitely by Haith for unspecified reasons in October. Assuming he returns, his 58/37/88 shooting line from last season illustrates his immense value as a scorer, but he is also a good passer. He has averaged a 1.8 assist-turnover ratio over the last two seasons.

Laurence Bowers (6-8, 225, Sr.): Bowers is known for his efficient offense, but I think his defense deserves special mention. In his two seasons as a starter, he put up good block rates (over seven percent) and good steal rates (three percent), a rare combination for a big man. The question is whether he lost some of his explosiveness during his recovery from the ACL tear that sidelined him all of last season.

Alex Oriakhi (6-9, 255, Sr.): Oriakhi took a big step back last season at UConn, but then again, so did the rest of the Huskies. At his best, Oriakhi is an efficient post player who is great on the offensive glass. Even if he just gives the Tigers that same level of rebounding, he will have an impact.

Earnest Ross (6-5, 220, Jr.): In effect Ross is an undersized post player who can also play on the perimeter, and that versatility will earn him minutes this season. In his last season as a starter at Auburn, he showed an ability to rebound well (an 18 percent defensive rebound rate at 6-5 is impressive) as well as getting to—and converting from—the free throw line.

Keion Bell (6-4, 200, Sr.): Bell shouldered one of the heaviest loads in all of college basketball in 2010 when he played 78 percent of Pepperdine's minutes and took 33 percent of their shots. He won't be asked to do nearly that much this season, but will likely excel at drawing fouls (eight per 40 minutes in his abbreviated 20-game 2010-11).

Jabari Brown (6-5, 205, So.): Brown was a very highly regarded, athletically gifted guard coming out of high school, but his freshman year at Oregon did not go as planned. After struggling to clashing with coach Dana Altman, Brown transferred to Columbia. He will be eligible for SEC play in the second semester.

Prospectus says: The Tigers have the pieces to make a big splash in their first season in the SEC. Realizing that potential, however, is no sure bet. Expect some struggles in the non-conference as the players and Haith learn on the fly, but the Tigers should be firing on all cylinders come conference play. This team has the potential to put to rest the lingering questions about Haith's ability to win in March with a run to the second week of the NCAA tournament.

SOUTH CAROLINA

2012: 10-21 (2-14 SEC); Lost to Alabama 63-57, SEC first round
In-conference offense: 0.94 points per possession (11th)
In-conference defense: 1.10 points allowed per possession (12th)

What South Carolina did well: *Hire the right coach.*

Last season was a disastrous one for South Carolina basketball. It started in the offseason, when two key starters transferred out of the program and point guard Bruce Ellington decided to play football for the first semester. It only got worse once the actual basketball games began. Without Sam Muldrow in the middle, the interior defense of the Gamecocks disappeared.

After four years, it was clear that the Darrin Horn era in Columbia was coming to an end. Horn had been unable to bring in the quality of recruits needed to compete in the SEC, and he was not able to get his dribble drive offense to work effectively.

The inevitable parting of ways in March left South Carolina AD Eric Hyman with the challenge of how to get a high-level coach to accept a job at a school that spends at an amount that ranks in the bottom third of its conference, not to mention a school that has been to the NCAA tournament just three times in the last 20 years.

Hyman was handed a gift when Frank Martin got into yet another conflict with his AD at Kansas State. In his five years in the Little Apple, Martin built a perennial Big 12 contender that matched his hard-nosed, hustle-based approach. He can rant and rave with the best of them, but he clearly cares immensely about his players. The evidence for that can be seen in his press conference after Jamar Samuels was suspended by the NCAA last March.

Martin faces an uphill climb at South Carolina, as the Gamecocks' roster is bare this year. Nevertheless, it bears mention that Martin has climbed hills before.

What we learned in 2012: *South Carolina's defense was historically awful.*

In 2010 and 2011, South Carolina's saving grace was its defense. The Gamecocks put up defensive efficiencies in the top 100 nationally through a combination of not allowing opponents to shoot many threes and blocking a lot of shots on the interior. That formula collapsed in 2012.

In conference play, the Gamecocks allowed opponents a true shooting rate (which takes free throw shooting into account) of 57.5 percent, the third-worst mark in the last 13 SEC seasons. What made the defensive performance even more terrible was that in addition to allowing opponents to make a lot of shots, the Gamecocks fouled at the third-highest rate in the conference.

The final piece of the collapse was defensive rebounding: South Carolina's opponents were able to collect 40 percent of their own misses, the second-worst rebounding performance of any SEC team in the last decade.

Thus South Carolina allowed opponents to make more shots than almost any other SEC team in recent memory, and when they did force a missed shot, they were unable to gather in the rebound. Even with a bare cupboard, the defense under Frank Martin can only improve from last year's debacle.

What's in store for 2013: South Carolina will likely remain in the cellar of the SEC. The two most efficient players on last year's roster, Malik Cooke and Damontre Harris, were lost to graduation and transfer, respectively. Harris, an extremely athletic 6-9 junior, is an especially big loss, and to add insult to injury he'll be staying within the conference and putting his talents to work for Florida starting in 2013-14. Anthony Gill also transferred out of the program (Virginia) after a promising freshman season. Ellington is again playing for the football team, and will only return in December. The starting lineup will likely include guards Eric Smith and Damien Leonard, junior forward R.J. Slawson and undersized forward Lakeem Jackson. Past that, there are very few other options with any experience. Note that one of Martin's 2012 recruits, Thaddeus Hall of New York City, is not listed on the Gamecocks' official roster at this writing, presumably due to academic issues.

MEET THE GAMECOCKS

Bruce Ellington (5-9, 195, Jr.): I could comment on Ellington's relative inefficiency as a scoring guard, but instead let us praise the workload he is handling. Ellington is turning into an All-SEC-level wide receiver for Steve Spurrier, which requires full commitment during the summer and fall. He then immediately steps into the role of a fairly competent lead guard on a major college basketball team. My hat is off to him.

R.J. Slawson (6-8, 220, Jr.): Slawson was by far the Gamecocks' best rebounder last season, and will likely see his minutes and role increase under Martin. He might want to stop shooting threes, however. Slawson made just 26 percent of them last season.

Damien Leonard (6-4, 190, So.): Leonard managed to hoist up 171 three-point attempts last season while making just 32 percent of them. Even more incredibly, he took a mere five percent of his shots at the rim and made 29 percent of his twos.

Brenton Williams (5-11, 175, Jr.): In limited minutes, Williams showed an ability to connect from outside (40 percent on 66 attempts). Perhaps he will get a larger role this season.

Carlton Geathers (6-10, 255, So.): Geathers played sparingly as a freshman, but could see more time as he provides size inside that South Carolina lacks otherwise.

Prospectus says: Martin's team will certainly play hard, but neither the talent nor the depth is present for success on any large scale this season. Nevertheless, if the new coach is able to bring in similar quality recruits as he did at Kansas State, SEC teams will soon come to dread the trip to Columbia.

TENNESSEE

2012: 19-15 (10-6 SEC); Lost to Middle Tennessee 71-64, NIT second round
In-conference offense: 0.99 points per possession (8th)
In-conference defense: 0.95 points allowed per possession (3rd)

What Tennessee did well: *Exceed expectations.*

At the start of the 2011-12 college basketball season, expectations for Tennessee were low. The Volunteers had lost four starters from the 2011 squad, and had changed coaches, saying goodbye to Bruce Pearl and hello to Cuonzo Martin. The returning roster featured just one player, Cameron Tatum, who had averaged more than 12 minutes a game the previous season. Most fans and pundits were braced for a long season on Rocky Top.

In this space last season, however, I was a bit more bullish on the Vols' prospects, mainly because of the potential of rising sophomore guard Trae Golden. I predicted an 8-8 finish in the SEC, but the Vols exceeded even that, notching a 10-6 record on the strength of winning eight of their last nine games in conference.

Golden lived up to his breakout potential, playing the role of scoring point guard very well. The other two catalysts for Tennessee were less expected. Jeronne Maymon, the Marquette transfer who had disappointed in his first season in Knoxville, became a force in the post. He shot almost 200 free throws and had an offensive rebound rate of 13 percent.

Maymon was able to do this in part because of the arrival of Jarnell Stokes. Originally recruited for the class of 2012, Stokes graduated high school in December and joined the Volunteers near the start of SEC play. At 6-8 and 250 pounds, Stokes was physically ready immediately, and his entrance allowed the shorter Maymon to move to power forward and face somewhat smaller players.

Martin's young team was able to succeed behind a beefy front line that generated more free throws than all but two teams in the league. The good news for the future is that six of the eight rotation players return in 2013. The Volunteers are not sneaking up on anyone this year. Golden, Maymon, and Stokes announced their presence loud and clear at the end of last season.

What we learned in 2012: *Tennessee has a clear division of offensive roles.*

On most teams, there is a guy who takes more threes than seems prudent. He may be a big man who thinks he can shoot, like Lance Goulbourne, or a guard who thinks he has to, like Andre Stringer. The distribution of three-point attempts on a team is usually fairly diffuse rather than concentrated.

That was not the case last season for Tennessee. This is not to say the Vols shied away from three-pointers. On the contrary, Tennessee was smack in the middle of the SEC in terms of three-point attempted as a percentage of shots. The difference is essentially four players took all of the Volunteers' three-pointers.

On the evidence, Martin's rationing of three-point attempts was fairly rational. McBee and Golden, the two best shooters on the team, took almost 40 percent of the team's threes. Tatum, who improved on his percentage from his junior season, and Jordan McRae were at least average three-point shooters. As shown by the chart, the rest of the team barely passed that average mark on 90 attempts that were likely more wide open than most of the attempts by the four main shooters.

This distribution actually fits Martin's track record at Missouri State, where Adam Leonard and Kyle Weems took the vast majority of the team's three-point attempts. It will be interesting to see if Martin

LONG RANGE QUARTET

	Attempts	% Made
Skylar McBee	161	39.1
Cameron Tatum	137	34.3
Trae Golden	129	38.8
Jordan McRae	119	32.8
Rest of team	90	32.0

attempts to impose a similar distribution of attempts on his team this year.

What's In store for 2013: The Volunteers lose Tatum, but not much else from the 2012 squad. The team will likely be interior-focused again, with Maymon and Stokes forming one of the most underrated and formidable frontcourt duos in the country. Golden will be the team's general, and McBee and McRae will provide outside shooting. The real questions for Tennessee in terms of personnel will be at the wings. Josh Richardson struggled in limited minutes last season, but may be ready for more playing time as a sophomore. Martin has also indicated he expects 6-5 junior college transfer D'Montre Edwards to contribute right away. The Vols will lack depth and defensive ability on the perimeter. The final issue facing Tennessee is whether they can take care of the ball. They turned it over the most of any team in SEC play in 2012, and those turnovers really hurt them in close losses to Kentucky and Georgia. Finishing more possessions with shots will be a key in 2013.

MEET THE VOLUNTEERS

Trae Golden (6-1, 205, Jr.): If not for BJ Young, Golden would be the best kept secret in the SEC. He gets to the free throw line at an elite rate and had an assist rate of over 31 percent. If he cuts down on his turnovers (22 percent last season), he could be one of the most efficient lead guards in the nation.

Jarnell Stokes (6-8, 270, So.): Stokes spent the summer starring for the US team that won the U-18 World Championships. While his offensive numbers were a bit pedestrian last season, remember that he came in with no practice time and a year younger than everyone else. He is poised for a breakout season.

Jeronne Maymon (6-7, 260, Sr.): Maymon struggled with some knee issues this summer, and in October Martin announced that his senior had "suffered a minor setback, so we probably won't have him at the start of the season." Assuming he's healthy, Maymon bullies opponents in the post. Last season he drew six fouls for every 40 minutes he played.

Skylar McBee (6-3, 195, Sr.): Everyone's favorite goofy mustachioed shooting guard is back for his senior campaign. McBee still needs to be hidden a bit on defense, but his offensive production makes up for his liabilities on the other side of the ball.

Jordan McRae (6-5, 180, Jr): McRae is a physical perimeter player who struggled a bit to make shots last year. His block rate (4 percent) was fairly high for a guard or wing player.

D'Montre Edwards (6-6, 205, Jr.): Edwards played well on the Vols' trip to Italy in August, averaging eight rebounds a game. If he can bring an element of physicality to the small forward position, he will be a valuable addition to the Tennessee rotation.

Prospectus says: Martin's team has enough talent to finish in the upper echelon of the SEC and return to the NCAA tournament far more quickly than most would have predicted. Tennessee's ceiling will ultimately be determined by how dominating their front line can be and how their guard play holds up on defense. The Vols have the potential to not only make the NCAA tournament, but also win a game or two when they get there.

TEXAS A&M

2012: 14-19 (4-14 Big 12); Lost to Kansas 83-66, Big 12 quarterfinals
In-conference offense: 0.93 points per possession (9th Big 12)
In-conference defense: 1.03 points allowed per possession (7th Big 12)

What Texas A&M did well: *Rebound as a team.*

In truth, not a lot went well for Texas A&M last season. First-year head coach Billy Kennedy was diagnosed with early-onset Parkinson's before the season started, and star wing Khris Middleton was sidelined for much of the season with a partially torn meniscus. Middleton returned for Big 12 play, but lacked the explosiveness that made him a preseason All-Big 12 selection.

The season went downhill from there. Kourtney Roberson was lost for the year after breaking his ankle in December, and backup point guard Jamal Branch decided to transfer in January. The Aggies regressed in most statistical categories and slumped to a desultory 4-14 finish in the basement of the conference. That was a far worse finish than almost anyone had predicted in the preseason.

The one area in which the Aggies did not regress or disappoint was rebounding. Despite not having a single player grab more than 18 percent of the available defensive rebounds, Texas A&M finished No. 56 in the country and No. 3 in Big 12 play in defensive rebound rate. They did this through a team effort. Dash Harris, the 6-1 senior point guard, had the lowest rebound rate of any significant player at 10 percent. Guard Jamal Branch pulled in 12 percent of the available rebounds at 6-3, as did 6-5 wingman Elston Turner Jr.

The big men, David Loubeau, Ray Turner and Keith Davis, were effective rebounders, but it was really the guards and wings that did the job. This impressive effort sadly did not help the Aggies win many games last season, but at Prospectus we like to recognize effort when we see it.

What we learned in 2012: *When the free throws go away, efficiency follows.*

From 2009 through 2011, Texas A&M lived at the free throw line. Their free throw rates were in the top 15 nationwide, and their offensive efficiency was high. In 2012, however, the Aggies' free throw rate fell off a cliff.

While the Aggies did shoot worse from the field in 2012, their decline there does not account for scoring almost one tenth of a point less per possession. Their 2012 free throw rate was No. 321 in the country.

This was not brought about by a change in coaching styles. Kennedy's teams at Murray State were in the top 100 (and top 25 in 2011) in free throw rate. Nor was it a case of personnel change. With two exceptions, Texas A&M returned its entire rotation from 2011. And with no exceptions, each player who remained shot fewer free throws in 2012.

The Aggies only took 29 percent of their shots at the rim last season, well below the national average. Whatever caused the decline in their inability to penetrate and score inside was at the heart of the Aggies' offensive struggles in 2012.

What's In store for 2013: The Aggies lose quite a bit coming into this season with the departure of Middleton to the NBA and the graduation of Loubeau and Harris. Nevertheless, Kennedy has the bones of what could be a better team than last season's outfit. Elston Turner returns as a potent threat from deep, and rising sophomore Jordan Green might get more minutes at the 2-guard. Addition-

THE DISAPPEARING FREE THROW

	Free Throw Rate (%)	eFG(%)	Adj. Offensive Rating
2009	46.5	50.4	113.6
2010	48.4	49.6	111.9
2011	47.3	49.3	108.2
2012	29.4	47.6	99.9

ally, two freshman guards, J'Mychal Reese, who might get the call at starting point guard, and Alex Caruso will compete for minutes. In the frontcourt, Ray Turner and Keith Davis provide experience and rebounding prowess. Roberson also returns from injury. Davis is extremely limited offensively, but these three should provide the Aggies with solid frontcourt play.

MEET THE AGGIES

Elston Turner (6-5, 210, Sr.): Turner played well in his first season for the Aggies, hitting 39 percent of his 180 attempts from three. He needs to improve his performance from inside the arc, however, where he only shot 42 percent.

Ray Turner (6-9, 230, Sr.): The other Turner was extremely efficient inside last season, taking a whopping 61 percent of his shots at the rim and shooting 58 percent from two. Expect Turner to take more shots this season.

Keith Davis (6-10, 230, Jr.): Davis was essentially invisible on offense last season, somehow only taking five percent of his team's shots while he was on the court. He turned it over on an amazing 40 percent of his possessions. Offensively, there is nowhere for Davis to go but up.

Jordan Green (6-4, 185, So.): Green struggled offensively as a freshman, making 23 percent of his threes and turning the ball over on 29 percent of his possessions. He likely can only improve by cutting down his turnovers this season.

Kourtney Roberson (6-9, 230, So.): Roberson had a good start to his sophomore year before his injury. He was a rebounding machine as a freshman, and should bring great offensive rebounding to the Aggies this season.

Alex Caruso (6-5, 175, Fr.): Caruso is a highly regarded recruit from College Station. The floppy-haired Gordon Hayward lookalike is a talented shooting guard who can also pass well.

J'Mychal Reese (6-1, 175, Fr.): Reese, too, is a consensus top-100 recruit and will compete for the starting point guard role. He is a strong lefty with a great pull-up jumper.

Prospectus says: What Kennedy's team lacks is a playmaker. In order for Texas A&M to have a positive season, someone (perhaps one of the freshmen) will have to step into that role. The Aggies have enough talent and experience to avoid the cellar of the SEC, but probably cannot finish above .500 in league play.

VANDERBILT

2012: 25-11 (10-6 SEC); Lost to Wisconsin 60-57, NCAA round of 32
In-conference offense: 1.12 points per possession (2nd)
In-conference defense: 1.01 points allowed per possession (6th)

What Vanderbilt did well: *Improve over the 2011 season.*

Last season I wrote that because Vanderbilt was returning all of its major contributors from 2011, Commodore fans would be looking for "the same as 2011, except better." That is exactly what Kevin Stallings' team delivered in 2012.

Vanderbilt's Achilles' heel in 2011 was defense. They gave up over 1.05 points per possession in SEC play and barely finished in the top 100 overall. In 2012, the Dores improved dramatically in one key area: defending shots from the floor.

Stallings was blessed with one of the biggest teams in the NCAA last season, with an effective height as measured by Ken Pomeroy of +2.5 inches. They used that height on the perimeter to hold SEC opponents to the lowest percentage from three (30 percent) in conference play for the second year in a row. This season, however, Vandy extended that strong defense inside the arc, holding SEC opponents to only 46 percent from two. This contributed to Vandy's defensive efficiency increasing by 0.05 points per possession last season.

Offensively, the Dores delivered the same high level of efficiency we have come to expect from a Kevin Stallings offense. Jeffrey Taylor played exceptionally well, and John Jenkins made 134 three-pointers and posted a true shooting percentage of 65, which was in the top five for major-conference players. Festus Ezeli slipped a bit offensively, but Steve Tchiengang and Lance Goulbourne picked up the slack.

Vanderbilt came into the NCAA tournament rolling after convincingly beating Kentucky for the SEC tournament title. Unfortunately for Commodore fans, their team was bracketed in an NCAA tournament pod with Wisconsin, one of the most efficient No. 4 seeds in NCAA history. Vandy dropped a close game to the Badgers, and an exceptionally talented generation of Commodores graduated without so much as a trip to the Sweet 16. While Vanderbilt improved from 2011, they never quite played to their potential when it mattered most.

What we learned in 2012: *"Live and die by the three" isn't always a cliché.*

Stallings loves the three-point shot, and throughout his tenure at Vanderbilt, he has assembled rosters that allow him to shoot it often and with success. With the exception of two seasons, Vanderbilt has consistently been in the top third of Division I in terms of percentage of shots that come from three. And with the exception of one season, the Commodores have been in the top 75 in the nation in terms of three-point accuracy.

Last season Stallings had a trio of experienced guards who enjoyed shooting threes and made them at high rates: Taylor, Jenkins, and Brad Tinsley. It makes sense, then, that Vandy finished in the top 30 in the country in both threes attempted as percentage of shots and field goal percentage from three.

This success from outside bordered on overreliance, however. Over the course of their 36 games, Vanderbilt's three-point shooting percentage alone explained 30 percent of the variance in their offensive rating, significantly more than any other offensive factor.

Despite having one of the tallest teams in the country, the Dores were only average in terms of rebounding. Because their proclivity for three-point shooting pulled Vandy's players away from the hoop, they were not effective at creating second chances on offense. When the prolific backcourt misfired from three, Vanderbilt's offense became a lot of one-and-done empty trips. That inefficiency often led to losses.

What's in store for 2013: If you've noticed, there has not been a single returning player mentioned in the preceding two sections. That is because the Commodores graduated, or lost to early entry in the NBA draft, six players and 83 percent of their possessions from the 2012 team.

What remains for Vandy? The most experienced player will be Rod Odom, a 6-10 small forward who will likely be asked to play inside this year. In the backcourt, Kedren Johnson and Dai-Jon Parker both saw rotation minutes last year with limited success. Both are talented and will be asked to play much bigger roles this season. Neither showed particularly good form from three last season, so Stallings may have to adjust his style to fit his roster. The Commodores are extremely thin up front. Josh Henderson and Shelby Moats saw very limited action last season and will be thrust into larger roles in 2013.

MEET THE COMMODORES

Rod Odom (6-10, 215, Jr.): Odom was essentially the fifth option when he was on the court last season, but that will change now. If nothing else his rebounding numbers will likely improve if he moves inside. Odom has also shown the ability to shoot the three (38 percent on 40 attempts last season).

Kedren Johnson (6-4, 215, So.): Johnson played erratically in his minutes last season, turning the ball over on 28 percent of his possessions. He is very big for a point guard, and that size allows him to bully smaller guards on defense. Johnson has the talent to have a breakout season in 2013.

Dai-Jon Parker (6-3, 190, So.): Parker, too, was a bit wild last year, committing turnovers on 22 percent of his possessions. He is also a strong defender and a good rebounder for his size, but he enters the season suspended "indefinitely," and his status is uncertain.

Josh Henderson (6-11, 230, So.): Henderson played sparingly last season, but showed a good offensive game when he did play. The question for him will be whether he is big and physical enough to play inside successfully in the SEC.

Shelby Moats (6-8, 225, So.): It is tough to read much into Moats' limited play last year, but he made just five of his 25 attempts from the floor. Hopefully he will do better than that in 2013.

Prospectus says: In Odom, Johnson and Parker, the Commodores have enough talent to finish in the middle of the pack in the SEC. Anything higher than that will require a breakout performance from unlikely sources in the frontcourt and on the wing. Vandy's stretch of three NCAA tournament appearances in a row is likely to come to an end.

Previewing the "High-Mids"

Atlantic 10

BY MATT GILES

The new-look, while-supplies-last, 16-team Atlantic 10 should be fairly incredible in 2012-13, but it's downright unfair that the good times can't last.

For one season only, all of the following will be playing in the same league: Temple, Virginia Commonwealth, Xavier, Butler, and Saint Louis. And those are just the marquee names. Actually the Musketeers project to be substantially less mighty than what's come to be expected in Cincinnati, while programs like Saint Joseph's, UMass, and possibly Dayton could give all of the above a run for their money in 2013.

The A-10's top half will have remarkable depth, and it's not a stretch to imagine any one of, say, six A-10 teams reaching the second weekend of the NCAA tournament. And if you like continuity in personnel, the entire 2012 All-A-10 Second Team is back: Kevin Dillard (Dayton), Chris Gaston (Fordham), Ramon Galloway (La Salle), Langston Galloway (Saint Joseph's), and Khalif Wyatt (Temple). The league has even thrown in a token holdover from last season's First Team: Chaz Williams of UMass.

And that's speaking purely of the "old" A-10. The two teams new to the league this season are likely to introduce themselves by carving out spots near the top of the standings. VCU came within a possession of making the 2012 Sweet 16 hard on the heels of their appearance in the 2011 Final Four—alongside fellow A-10 newcomer Butler.

But it won't be a 16-team A-10 for long. Next season Temple will take its basketball team to the Big East (the Owls' football team is already there), while Charlotte will return to Conference USA, the same league the 49ers left in 2005.

Membership isn't the only change you'll notice in this season's A-10. Jim Crews will pilot the ship at Saint Louis in 2012-13 while Rick Majerus takes a leave of absence to tend to his health. (Get well soon, Coach.) Danny Hurley will start from scratch with a Rhode Island team that fell all the way to 7-24 last season. And after guiding Long Island to back-to-back appearances in the NCAA tournament, Jim Ferry was brought to Duquesne to see if he could work the same magic for a program that hasn't tasted March Madness since 1977.

Even the league's annual March get-together will be altogether new and different. After a six-year stay in Atlantic City, the A-10 tournament will be held in Brooklyn, at the Barclays Center. Interestingly the league chose to stay with its 12-team format for the 2013 tournament. In recent years this arrangement has visited a special brand of shame upon two of the league's 14 teams, an unfortunate duo mocked annually as "Fordham and someone else." That group of outcasts will swell to four teams this season.

Teams listed in Matt's predicted order of finish.

VCU

2012: 29-7 (15-3 CAA); Lost to Indiana 63-61, NCAA round of 32
In-conference offense: 1.03 points per possession (2nd CAA)
In-conference defense: 0.88 points allowed per possession (2nd CAA)

VCU is joining the A-10 without a clear leading scorer. Bradford Burgess led the Rams in percentage of shots taken and points per game, but he was the lone senior on last season's squad. Except for Burgess, the A-10 will see essentially the same team that came within a missed **Troy Daniels**' three of cracking the Sweet 16 for a second straight season. Sophomore wing **Treveon Graham** has been labeled a breakout candidate. As the first sub off the bench last season his role was to attack the basket, though Graham wasn't efficient from the field (converting 39 percent of his A-10 twos). VCU is blessed with an abundance of guards. Daniels, a victim of guard depth his first two seasons, is one of the top three-point shooters in the country, converting 38 percent of his 247 attempts. Many of VCU's offensive possessions included a three-point attempt, and **Darius Theus** handed out an assist on a good chunk of those possessions. The senior arrives in the A-10 as perhaps his new league's best pure point guard. The squad's offseason trip to Italy was key for the development of backups **Teddy Okereafor** and **Briante Weber**. Both will see time running point guard, and while Weber's nationally known for his absurd steal rate—seven percent, tops in Division I—Okereafor was one of the trip's standouts. Shaka Smart has mentioned playing Weber and Theus together, a pairing that will make it difficult for any offense to set up comfortably. (Theus' steal rate was four percent.) In addition, Smart will also have to find minutes for freshman **Melvin Johnson**, reportedly a prolific shooter. While Smart has praised the development of **Jarred Guest** and **D.J. Haley**, **Juvonte Reddic** is essentially the sole frontcourt option. The 6-9 forward has demonstrated the ability to gamble for a steal but then recover for the block and avoid a foul. However, several A-10 squads are deep on the interior, and Haley, Guest, and Smart's tall freshman class could see extra minutes. Perhaps VCU's most interesting challenge will be importing HAVOC, the squad's trapping and pressing defense, to their new conference. Just five CAA squads had turnover rates under 20 percent (and one of those was VCU). The A-10, however, is filled with sure-handed offenses. If HAVOC fails to create havoc, there could be concern in Richmond.

SAINT JOSEPH'S

2012: 20-14 (9-7 A-10); Lost to Northern Iowa 67-65, NIT first round
In-conference offense: 1.05 points per possession (6th)
In-conference defense: 1.03 points allowed per possession (8th)

Saint Joseph's partisans who've waited nearly a decade for a team capable of storming through the A-10 have pinned their hopes on Phil Martelli's latest squad. The entire roster, fresh off an NIT appearance, returns and the Hawks have been placed atop the A-10's preseason rankings. Saint Joe's does not often force turnovers, and would rather funnel opponents to the paint where 6-8 **Halil Kanacevic**, 6-8 **Ronald Roberts**, and 6-9 **C.J. Aiken** are all skilled at rejecting shots. The trio swatted nearly 15 percent of in-conference two-point attempts, and did it without committing many fouls. The ten-plus pounds Aiken added in the offseason should help him at both ends of the floor. Kanacevic was the only starter with a sub-100 offensive rating, but he was still the team's best passer from the post, sporting a 26 percent assist rate. Best known for his dunk on Creighton's Antoine Young, Roberts' game is more diverse. He grabbed 12 percent of SJU's misses and efficiently scored 1.24 points per offensive board. Roberts could lose his title as the A-10's reigning sixth man of the year by becoming a starter. **Daryus Quarles**, who Roberts usually replaced, has struggled with his efficiency and is not a rebounding force. In the backcourt last season **Carl Jones** struggled to replicate his impressive numbers from 2010-11, but he was still among the top tier of A-10 guards. Most troubling was Jones' increased turnover percentage, a combination of a lower usage rate and 14 extra giveaways (from 2011). **Chris Wilson** posted the backcourt's top assist rate and showed proficiency as a point guard. There aren't many D-I returnees with a usage rate under 20 percent and an offensive rating above 120, but **Langston Galloway** fits the description (19 percent, 124.9). An A-10 player of the year candidate, the guard is underrated nationally but is the prime concern on opponents' scouting reports. Ranked among the nation's top 50 in both effective field goal and true shooting percentages, Galloway's trusty handle means he's essentially instant offense.

SAINT LOUIS

2012: 26-8 (12-4 A-10); Lost to Michigan State 65-61, NCAA round of 32
In-conference offense: 1.06 points per possession (4th)
In-conference defense: 0.92 points allowed per possession (1st)

While Rick Majerus takes a season-long leave of absence for health reasons, former Army coach Jim Crews now leads SLU. The interim coach will do so, at least for part of the season, without **Kwamain Mitchell**, who underwent surgery for a broken foot in October and will be sidelined until at least calendar 2013. That's a big loss for the Billikens: Mitchell found his groove during A-10 play last season, converting 56 percent and 42 percent of his twos and threes, respectively. Crews will depend on a mix of youth and experience to offset Mitchell's absence. Majerus has raved about freshman **Keith Carter**, and though the guard would have likely spent his first season as a reserve, Carter could now see immediate playing time. Crews and Majerus must hope Carter develops the way **Mike McCall Jr.** has, for the junior is now a potential all-conference performer. McCall is effective in the half-court (SLU scored over a point per play with him as point guard), limits giveaways, and is poses an offensive threat in his own right, hitting at a 49 percent rate inside the arc. More possessions will also go to **Jordair Jett**, a guard who fuels the Billikens' defensive intensity. SLU is well versed in Majerus' defensive techniques, so again expect a team that holds opponents under a point per possession. The Billikens' vice-like interior, though, will be tested without Brian Conklin, who brought toughness to SLU's frontcourt. **Cody Ellis** doesn't often leave the perimeter, so **Rob Loe** could be the next Billiken to anchor the paint. Previously a stretch-5, the 6-11 Loe reportedly spent his offseason working on post moves. The match-up problem known as **Dwayne Evans** also returns, and his offensive role should increase with Conklin's departure. Evans is already a rebounding force, grabbing 25 percent of opponents' misses. The real surprise, though, could be **John Manning**. The 6-11 center is strong in the paint and while his offense is progressing, his game will improve with consistent minutes.

BUTLER

2012: 22-15 (11-7 Horizon); Lost to Pittsburgh 68-62 (OT), CBI semifinals
In-conference offense: 0.96 points per possession (7th Horizon)
In-conference defense: 0.94 points allowed per possession (1st Horizon)

Butler's offense fell to new depths last season, but Brad Stevens' team should score much more effectively in their first A-10 season. Arkansas transfer **Rotnei Clarke** is eligible for his final college season, and he should slide seamlessly into the point guard spot left vacated by coach-on-the-floor Ronald Nored. It may seem odd that a 47 percent three-point marksman would play the point, but Stevens believes the 6-0 Clarke can direct Butler's offense as well as score for himself. **Alex Barlow** will get minutes at backup point guard if for no other reason than his defense. Chrishawn Hopkins was dismissed from the squad in September, and his minutes will be split between two returnees and one newcomer. **Jackson Aldridge**'s high turnover rate explains why his playing time decreased during conference play, but the experience may have helped the guard's maturation. Fifth-year senior **Chase Stigall** underwent offseason surgery on his shooting wrist, and his long-rang woes should be fixed. And, despite a crowded backcourt, freshman **Kellen Dunham** will play. Known as a prodigious three-point shooter, Dunham doesn't solely rely on screens and can create his own shot. A Dunham-Clarke pairing could mean more pick and rolls;

ball handler pick and rolls accounted for roughly 10 percent of Butler's offensive possessions, but that rate should rise. **Roosevelt Jones** is this team's version of former Butler star Willie Veasley. Like Veasley, Jones can guard multiple positions. A propensity for turnovers hampered his effectiveness, and while Jones may never be an offensive star—he has virtually no mid- to long-range game—Butler needs his versatility and open-court skills. The frontcourt of **Khyle Marshall** and **Andrew Smith** posted high offensive ratings, and both are skilled at crashing the offensive glass. **Erik Fromm** will likely again contribute off the bench. **Kameron Woods** was a role player last season who happened to be Butler's best interior defender, grabbing 22 percent of the opponents' misses while also sporting an eight percent block rate.

DAYTON

2012: 20-13 (9-7 A-10); Lost to Iowa 84-75, NIT first round
In-conference offense: 1.11 points per possession (2nd)
In-conference defense: 1.06 points allowed per possession (11th)

Picked in the preseason to finish eighth, Dayton is this season's A-10 team flying under the radar. Perhaps the ranking is a testament to the A-10's depth, but it feels low for a squad containing a potential conference player of the year in **Kevin Dillard**. After Archie Miller installed a structured offense that still allowed play-calling freedom, Dillard was arguably the conference's top guard. He used 81 percent of Dayton's available minutes and assisted on 39 percent of the team's field goals (the conference's top mark). His shooting percentages weren't stellar, but since Dillard was the top option on each opponent's scouting report, he took advantage of the overplaying to create easy scoring opportunities for teammates. He's also one of Dayton's best on-ball defenders. Two transfers will be given extensive minutes to lighten Dillard's offensive load. **Vee Sanford** spent two seasons at Georgetown and he's added 13 pounds to his 6-3 frame. His presence will shift a portion of ball-handling duties from Dillard and allow the senior to work within Dayton's offensive flow. An injury to either, however, would spell trouble—freshman **Khari Price** is essentially the sole backup. The arrival of stretch-4 **Matt Derenbecker** could signify more pick and roll possessions. Nearly 12 percent of Dayton's possessions were pick and rolls—specifically high picks—to free Dillard and potentially allow a pass to a big camped beyond arc. The 6-7 Derenbecker made 34 percent of his threes in one season at LSU and his shooting should create spacing for teammates like **Dyshawn Pierre**. UD does not run often, but the notion of Dillard and Sanford lobbing passes to the uber-athletic Pierre is enticing. Last season it took the Flyers a while to understand Miller's pack-line defense, but during their final eight A-10 games something clicked and opponent shooting percentages dropped dramatically. Sophomore **Alex Gavrilovic** will bolster the pack-line's interior presence. **Josh Benson** tore his ACL in the midst of a statistically spectacular junior season, but his rehab is complete and he'll bring both quickness and heft—he added nearly 25 pounds—to the frontline. A double-double threat during A-10 play, **Devin Oliver** shined as a nationally ranked rebounding force in Benson's absence. A full season of Benson and Oliver together can only mean good things in the Flyers' second go-around with the pack-line D. Dayton's rotation did take a hit in October, however, with the announcement that 6-9 senior Matt Kavanaugh had been suspended for the season due to unspecified "violations of the University of Dayton Standards of Behavior and Code of Conduct."

TEMPLE

2012: 24-8 (13-3 A-10); Lost to South Florida 58-44, NCAA round of 64
In-conference offense: 1.13 points per possession (1st)
In-conference defense: 1.02 points allowed per possession (6th)

Ramone Moore and Juan Fernandez are no longer on campus, so Fran Dunphy must find a capable point guard. **Khalif Wyatt** is one option, a senior who is both his team's best defender and its most efficient performer on offense. Increased minutes didn't diminish Wyatt's percentages: he made over 55 percent of his twos and nearly 40 percent from deep. However, much of Wyatt's career has been spent off the ball so why would Dunphy hamstring his best scorer when the coach has to replace 38 percent of Temple's points? Either **T.J. DiLeo**—another phenomenal defender in his limited minutes—or **Will Cummings** will direct Temple's offense. Cummings reportedly shined during a Philadelphia-based pro-am league this summer. After a season watching Moore and Fernandez run Temple's offense, he could be the squad's next breakout player. **Dalton Pepper** will have a much larger role than he did at West Virginia, and **Scootie Randall**, who posted Temple's best offensive rating before his redshirt season, is a skilled long-range shooter who rarely commits turnovers. The Owls were heavily dependent on threes last season, but without Fernandez and Moore there is considerable pressure on the frontcourt to produce. **Rahlir Hollis-Jefferson** is Dunphy's best one-on-one scorer and the 6-6 forward used the offseason to refine his mid-range game. An injury to Michael Eric last season forced **Anthony Lee** into more minutes than he may have been ready for, but he did post his team's best defensive rebounding rate. If Lee can decrease his foul rate and stay on the floor, his block rate, already at seven percent, should rise. Boston University transfer **Jake O'Brien** hasn't played in more than a season, but he may prove capable of carrying the frontcourt scoring load. Already a versatile wing as a freshman, **Daniel Dingle** could become an early Dunphy favorite due to his defense. **Devontae Watson** possesses a 7-8 wingspan and his physical traits suggest he can impact the game even in limited minutes. If Cummings is pressed into extended minutes, expect the Owls to up the pace. Though the team used roughly 67 possessions per 40 minutes in 2012—the fastest Temple has played in five seasons—Cummings has said he enjoys "the fast-break element." The Owls could play even faster this season.

MASSACHUSETTS

2012: 25-12 (9-7 A-10); Lost to Stanford 74-64, NIT semifinals
In-conference offense: 0.99 points per possession (10th)
In-conference defense: 0.98 points allowed per possession (2nd)

Virtually the entire UMass roster returns, and the popular sentiment among college basketball analysts pegs the Minutemen as a threat to win the A-10 title. Despite much praise for their chaos-inducing defense, UMass was good but not great at forcing turnovers: A-10 opponents gave the ball away on 21 percent of their possessions. Still, the Minutemen did defend the perimeter well, mainly due to a preponderance of absurdly long wingspans. At 6-8, **Raphiael Putney**'s length negates his lack of body mass and allowed him to post a 20 percent defensive rebounding rate. **Terrell Vinson** and **Sampson Carter** are also long-armed forwards with strong defensive skills, but the key is **Cady Lalanne**. If healthy, the 6-9 Lalanne could be the favorite for A-10 defensive player of the year. Constantly plagued by injuries, Lalanne has created a body of work on D that's impressive even under the scope of a limited sample size: block rate of 10 percent while also grabbing 23 percent of the available defensive boards. **Maxie Esho**, a 6-8 sophomore, averaged just five points as a freshman but was a pleasant surprise toward the end of the A-10 schedule and has the speed to circumvent opposing forwards. Without **Javorn Farrell**, who will likely miss the season with an ankle injury, there is significant pressure on the backcourt of **Chaz Williams** and **Jesse Morgan** (with **Freddie Riley** in line for additional minutes). Williams and his 34 percent assist rate kept the UMass offense balanced. Since the Minutemen are perimeter-oriented, the squad excels when Williams' penetration puts pressure on opponents and creates open threes and interior cuts. That being said, Morgan needs to improve his shooting accuracy.

LA SALLE

2012: 21-13 (9-7 A-10); Lost to Minnesota 70-61, NIT first round
In-conference offense: 1.04 points per possession (8th)
In-conference defense: 1.00 points allowed possession (4th)

Following Aaric Murray's transfer after the 2011 season, La Salle coach Dr. John Giannini borrowed a roster alignment popularized by fellow City 6 head coach Jay Wright. The Explorers' four-guard lineup catapulted La Salle to a 21-win season and an NIT invite. With the exception of Earl Pettis, the entire backcourt returns. La Salle will continue to utilize an undersized lineup with Virginia Tech transfer **Tyrone Garland** filling Pettis' spot. Garland rarely played in Blacksburg, but he was known as one of the top scorers in Philadelphia high school history. He won't be eligible until December, though, so Giannini will move **D.J. Peterson** to the starting lineup. La Salle hit a whopping 41 percent of their threes last season, and Peterson was the most accurate Explorer. **Ramon Galloway**, **Tyreek Duren**, and **Sam Mills** complete the backcourt. During the A-10's first half, Galloway made 51 percent of his threes before sliding to 30 percent in the final eight games. Duren became less turnover-prone in 2012. Mills is a skilled defender but he isn't a one-dimensional player. He made over 40 percent from deep while also diversifying his shot selection by taking and consistently converting more twos. The big in Giannini's four-out offense is 6-8 sophomore **Jerrell Wright**, who should have a larger impact this season after cracking the conference's all-rookie team. Though he played a scant 49 percent of La Salle's minutes, Wright posted the team's highest usage rate, and his two-point efficiency (57 percent) kept opponents from pressuring La Salle's guards. Typical of most freshman bigs, Wright struggled with fouls, turnovers, and a tendency to rush his shot, but what separates him is his ability to move without the ball. Over 12 percent of La Salle's possessions involve pick and rolls, and Wright converted 1.25 PPP rolling to the basket. To top if all off he's a strong offensive rebounder: Wright is very effective in the paint. Last season the Explorers followed Syracuse's lead and showed that a team can be really bad at defensive rebounding (only Duquesne was worse in A-10 play) yet still play good D. And if 6-11 **Steve Zack** can spell Wright—or even join him in the frontcourt—La Salle's defense could actually be their strongest asset.

RICHMOND

2012: 16-16 (7-9 A-10); Lost to La Salle 80-72, A-10 first round
In-conference offense: 1.04 points per possession (7th)
In-conference defense: 1.05 points allowed per possession (9th)

Fran Dunphy was deserving, no doubt, but a case can be made that Chris Mooney was your true 2012 A-10 coach of the year. Mooney lost four players that accounted for 74 percent of the Spiders' A-10 point production in 2011. Yet somehow UR went 16-16 with just one returnee who'd logged more than 50 percent of the available minutes the previous year. Richmond's guard-heavy motion offense features dribble control and numerous threes. As a trio **Cedrick Lindsay**, **Kendall Anthony**, and **Darien Brothers** made nearly 40 percent of their shots from long range. The guards used roughly 593 A-10 possessions and only committed a turnover on 13 percent of those touches. The sub-6-0 Anthony was lights-out at the beginning of A-10 play, but dipped once opponents hard-hedged and went over screens. Just the second Spider under Mooney to be named the A-10 freshman of the year, Anthony's goal will be to apply more of his team-high usage rate toward getting to the bucket and drawing fouls. Both Lindsay and Brothers are standout shooters. Lindsay is the squad's catalyst, and it's impressive that while the trio plays so many minutes, they consistently limit mistakes. **Derrick Williams** benefitted most from the newly available minutes. At 6-6 and 270 he connected on 58 percent of his twos and posted UR's best offensive rating. Williams was an efficient half-court option, but when the ball went into the post it rarely left. And the fact that the Spiders' "big" is 6-6 flags another concern: Richmond lacks proven height now that Darrius Garrett has completed his career. Mooney redshirted three freshman forwards before last season tipped: **Alonzo Nelson-Ododa** (6-9), **Trey Davis** (6-5), and **Luke Piotrowski** (6-11) spent the year developing and watching. Between the three newbies, Williams, and senior "glue guy" **Greg Robbins** (Mooney's description), UR should be able to improve its standing on the defensive glass.

ST. BONAVENTURE

2012: 20-12 (10-6 A-10); Lost to Florida State 66-63, NCAA round of 64
In-conference offense: 1.08 points per possession (3rd)
In-conference defense: 0.99 points allowed possession (3rd)

How does a team recoup when a conference player of the year winner graduates? Without Andrew Nicholson (and without his fellow starter in the frontcourt, Da'Quan Cook), Mark Schmidt must replace nearly 36 percent of St. Bonaventure's total defensive boards. **Demitrius Conger** helps and he will need assistance from **Youssou Ndoye** and **Marquise Simmons**. Seven-footer Ndoye was effective in limited minutes, hoarding rebounds and showing a decent touch around the basket. Simmons missed all of last season with an Achilles injury. Newcomers **Dion Wright** and **Jean Yves Toupane** can also play on the interior but may have been redshirted if Schmidt had more depth in the paint. On the other hand a plethora of backcourt Bonnies could shift some of the offense toward the little guys (though Conger will likely receive the majority of the offensive touches). In fact Schmidt says he wants use his backcourt depth to push the pace. Well versed with the intricacies of Schmidt's offense, **Matthew Wright** is a converted point guard, and **Charlon Kloof**'s emergence should permanently move Wright to the 2-guard. The 6-3 Kloof grew more assertive as the season progressed and is capable of orchestrating an up-tempo offense. His A-10 assist rate (31 percent) was one of the conference's best and his perimeter game fits Schmidt's stated strategy. Kloof will likely be paired with Wright and **Jordan Gathers**, a 6-3 sophomore who averaged over 20 minutes in postseason play. **Chris Johnson** and **Eric Mosley** will again come off the bench. **Michael Davenport** finished rehabbing a shoulder injury, and his return guarantees another experienced ball handler. For a team without much size, SBU will need to reduce their turnovers. In the sure-handed A-10, giving the ball away 21 percent of the time, as the Bonnies did last season in conference play, is good for last place.

GEORGE WASHINGTON

2012: 10-21 (5-11 A-10); Lost to Dayton 67-50, A-10 first round
In-conference offense: 1.01 points per possession (9th)
In-conference defense: 1.08 points allowed per possession (12th)

Second-year coach Mike Lonergan must replace Tony Taylor and his team-leading 27 percent assist rate. A combination of returning guard **Brian Bynes** and freshmen **Kethan Savage** and **Joe McDonald** will subsume Taylor's minutes, but inexperience shouldn't be an issue. McDonald performed well during GW's offseason trip to Italy, and Lonergan believes the freshman could start when the season begins. Before the team's overseas sojourn, 6-9 Villanova transfer **Isaiah Armwood** was the only announced starter, but when **David Pellom** finishes rehabbing his wrist injury, the 6-8 forward will quickly regain a full share of minutes. The senior was the Colonials' sole inside presence, getting open through a variety of down and cross screens, and he secured nine percent of his team's misses. Armwood excels without the ball and is comfortable converting around the bucket. He also possesses a mid-range game that should create high-low opportunities with Pellom and establish cross-court looks for GW's shooters. In particular, teams will be forced to play **Nemanja Mikic** straight-up. If Armwood can direct the offense from the foul line, Mikic may find more open shots. Lastly, Armwood will help solidify GW's defense. His length affects shooters, and he has the speed and versatility to cover three positions. The staff may have also nabbed the steal of the A-10's 2012 recruiting class in the form of 6-10 Denmark native **Kevin Larsen**. Despite spending just two years playing in the U.S., Larsen is not a project. **Lasan Kromah** missed two seasons recovering from a foot injury, and could see his role transition to a supporting one. He's still the Colonials' best on-ball defender, forcing a turnover on four percent of his defensive possessions, but he doesn't have to carry GW offensively anymore. In fact freshman **Patricio Garino** could take some of Kromah's minutes. Lonergan has said he expects Garino to play "a major role" and his shooting touch made him a standout during the trip to Italy. It may seem strange to envision two freshmen, Garino and McDonald, in the backcourt after a season filled with much trial and error, but GW's 2012 recruiting class could be the foundation of future success.

CHARLOTTE

2012: 13-17 (5-11 A-10); Lost to Saint Joseph's 80-64, A-10 first round
In-conference offense: 0.96 points per possession (13th)
In-conference defense: 1.03 points allowed per possession (7th)

Charlotte will move to Conference USA after the season, and the team's final A-10 offseason did not begin well. Jamar Briscoe and K.J. Sherrill transferred, newcomer Shawn Lester was declared ineligible, and leading scorer **Chris Braswell** broke his foot. Good thing head coach Alan Major fed his first recruiting class extensive minutes last season. That four-player group—**E. Victor Nickerson**, **Pierria Henry**, **Terrence Williams**, and **DeMario Mayfield**—will form the 49ers' non-Braswell scoring nucleus in 2012-13. Braswell missed the squad's August trip to the Bahamas, but should be ready for the season opener. Charlotte's offense flowed through him last season, and the arrival of Virginia Tech transfer **JT Thompson** should help Braswell (assuming the oft-injured ex-Hokie can stay healthy). **Mike Thorne** will also boost interior depth after taking a redshirt last season. Charlotte improved defensively during Major's second season as Nickerson and Henry, two newcomers who prided themselves on stops, contributed to A-10 opponents' 20 percent turnover rate. In particular, Henry was one of two freshmen nationally with a steal rate over 4.5 percent. Offensively, though, the 49ers are still a work in progress. Henry's continued development as the team's point guard is crucial, and he and his fellow sophomores should lift the offense above a point per possession. Mayfield moves well without the ball and is dynamic once he gets into the lane, but he needs to improve his shot selection. Nickerson and Williams will become offensive focal points, and both were among the high scorers in the Bahamas. Position-wise, Major's second full recruiting class is diverse. Since Henry is really the team's only point guard, **Denzel Ingram**'s role could be as backup. **Willie Clayton** and **Darion Clark** add frontcourt depth and 10 extra fouls, but it's likely the 49ers won't need the two freshmen to do more than rebound and defend.

RHODE ISLAND

2012: 7-24 (4-12 A-10); Did not qualify for A-10 tournament
In-conference offense: 0.99 points per possession (12th)
In-conference defense: 1.08 points allowed per possession (13th)

Danny Hurley is accustomed to rebuilding projects after turning around Wagner, but even Hurley faces a cumbersome task at Rhode Island. Sharpshooter Billy Baron followed URI's former coach, his father Jim Baron, to Canisius, and A-10 all-rookie pick Jonathan Holton is no longer enrolled at the school. Fortunately for Hurley he does have some strong returnees. Point guard **Mike Powell** posted an assist rate of 23 percent, and though he struggled with turnovers a year spent under Hurley (and assistant coach Bobby Hurley) should help. **Nikola Malesevic**, the only remaining big, is a stretch-4, and Hurley has a penchant for players who spread the floor from the perimeter. The coach also convinced 6-10 freshman **Jordan Hare** to honor his commitment to the previous staff. **Mike Aaman** initially committed to Wagner, but followed Hurley to the A-10, and has been described as a very physical rebounder. URI will need the interior boost—no current Ram grabbed more than 10 percent of the defensive rebounds last season. Although 6-8 forward Ifeanyi Onyekaba has enrolled, it's unknown if he will be eligible, making the arrival of 6-5 Northeastern transfer

Alwayne Bigby all the more timely. Bigby will round out Rhody's newcomer frontcourt and add a needed dose of experience. **Andre Malone**, a wing under Baron who will serve as an undersized forward, should also see playing time simply because he's accustomed to the speed and physicality of A-10 ball. **Xavier Munford**, a junior college transfer who played for Hurley in high school, is at least familiar with the coach's style and was known as a scorer at Iowa Western College. Depth concerns, however, could also alter Hurley's preferred pace and defensive intensity. On paper Wagner under Hurley had one of the worst defensive free throw rates in the nation, but thanks to a deep bench the Seahawks had the luxury of multiple fouls to give. That freedom vanishes at Rhode Island this season, and Hurley may be forced to play a less aggressive style of defense.

XAVIER

2012: 23-13 (10-6 A-10); Lost to Baylor 75-70, Sweet 16
In-conference offense: 1.05 points per possession (5th)
In-conference defense: 1.01 points allowed per possession (5th)

Outside of Lexington, Kentucky, there are few Division I rosters that have seen as much turnover as Xavier's since last spring. Mark Lyons transferred to Arizona, Dez Wells was expelled for "a serious violation of the Code of Student Conduct" (he has landed at Maryland), and the Musketeers five-man recruiting class was hit hard when the NCAA declared Myles Davis and Jalen Reynolds ineligible. Add the Cincinnati brawl last December, and Chris Mack hasn't had the easiest 12 months. Experience is not an issue. There are several returnees from a squad that made the Sweet 16 last season. But it's difficult to sugar coat the fact that Xavier must replace 78 percent of its scoring. **Dee Davis** was an understudy to Tu Holloway and Lyons but now he'll be thrust into a starting role. Freshman **Semaj Christon** should absorb a large amount of the newly available possessions. A natural point guard, the 6-3 Christon will likely be forced off the ball because Davis is 6-0. **Travis Taylor** was Xavier's best overall rebounder, hauling in 11 percent of his team's misses during his limited minutes. This season he'll be joined on the glass by 6-9 newcomer **James Farr**. Towson transfer **Isaiah Philmore** is still a question mark—he spent the majority of his offseason rehabbing and his conditioning isn't superb—so Mack plans to rely heavily on **Jeff Robinson**. Inconsistency has plagued the 6-10 Robinson, but there was a five-game stretch last January when he converted 77 percent of his twos and averaged 11 points. Like Robinson, 6-6 sophomore **Justin Martin** could benefit from a less crowded interior. Perhaps the silver lining to Xavier's tumultuous offseason is that Mack is now free to play at a faster pace, his stated desire when he took the job four years ago. There are no plodding Musketeers, and the Christon-Davis duo is perfectly suited to push the pace. Of course the first requirement for a fast break is a defensive rebound. If XU's frontcourt can do its part, the Musketeers may speed up the tempo in 2013.

FORDHAM

2012: 10-19 (3-13 A-10); Did not qualify for A-10 tournament
In-conference offense: 0.93 points per possession (14th)
In-conference defense: 1.15 points allowed per possession (14th)

For the first time in several seasons, Fordham is not predicted to finish in the Atlantic 10's cellar. Home victories against Georgia Tech and Harvard last season set the stage for a program that can now set a realistic (if still doubtful) goal of finishing in the league's top 12. If Tom Pecora can pull it off he'll give the Rams their first trip to an A-10 tournament since 2008. Pecora signed a contract extension that will keep him in the Bronx through 2017, and rather than aim for a quick rebuild, Fordham will have one of the nation's youngest teams this season. Only three upperclassmen dot the roster, and one of them is **Chris Gaston**, the first Ram named to an all A-10 preseason team since 2006. The 6-7 Gaston has averaged a double-double in each of his three seasons (we'll wink at last year's 9.9 rebounds per game). Another crucial presence on the glass will be 6-9 sophomore **Ryan Canty**, especially if the NCAA doesn't clear 6-8 freshman **Ryan Rhoomes**. Those are some young running mates for Gaston in the frontcourt, so Fordham will depend on their guards to take the pressure off their star. **Branden Frazier** was a noted scorer in high school, but defenses gladly sagged off him last season since he converted just 27 percent of his three-point attempts. **Devon McMillan** and **Bryan Smith** were placed in the unenviable position of running Fordham's offense as freshmen last season, and shot a combined 36 percent on their twos. This season McMillan, Fordham's true point guard in their three-guard lineup, needs to tighten his handle. **Mandell Thomas**, **Jermaine Myers**, and **Jeffrey Short** will all see varying degrees of playing time, with Myers potentially starting at some point. Pecora has sought to strengthen his team's defensive focus, and though allowing 1.14 points per possession in-conference seems awful, much of that came courtesy of opponents' 39 percent three-point shooting. The percentages say Fordham's defense is likely to "improve" in that respect this season, though clearly the Rams could do a better job limiting the number of threes attempted by opponents. Better D and one more season of Gaston may be enough to get this team to the Barclays Center in March.

DUQUESNE

2012: 16-15 (7-9 A-10); Lost to UMass 92-83, A-10 first round
In-conference offense: 0.99 points per possession (11th)
In-conference defense: 1.05 points allowed per possession (10th)

Ron Everhart was officially fired on March 23, but his tenure's true end occurred during a February road trip. The Dukes pestered opponents into giving away 23 percent of their possessions through the first half of the Atlantic 10 slate, a strategy that jump-started their transition-heavy offense. In the first St. Bonaventure game, the Dukes forced 18 turnovers and scored 0.96 points per possession. During the rematch, though, the Bonnies cut their giveaways by a quarter, held Everhart's squad to 0.73 PPP, and won by over 20 points. Duquesne lost five of their next seven games, Mike Talley and T.J. McConnell transferred, and after the season Jim Ferry, the impresario behind the fast-paced Long Island teams of recent years, replaced Everhart. Duquesne's recruiting class imploded following Everhart's firing, so Ferry had to move quickly. Two potential standouts are **Quevyn Winters** and **Derrick Colter**. Winters is the prototypical Ferry player, a versatile 6-5 wing who excels scoring off the dribble. Colter was a standout in Pittsburgh's pro-am league. The arrival of Colter and **Marvin Binney**, a noted on-ball defender, allows **Sean Johnson** to focus on his offense. The 6-2 returnee led Duquesne in percentage of shots taken and should resume his role as offensive leader, but Ferry must challenge the guard to focus on his offense within the arc. **Jerry Jones** and **Kadeem Pantophlet** both attempted more threes than twos, and both will benefit from a half-court offense predicated on ball movement. In particular, the 6-5 Jones could be an A-10 breakout star. If he can avoid unnecessary fouls, 6-6 **Andre Marhold** will receive consistent paint touches, but he needs to finish stronger. Also, more minutes for a much stronger **Mamadou Datt** and 7-1 **Martins Abele** will enable the Dukes to handcuff some (but not all) opponents on the defensive glass. If UAB transfer Ovie Soko could play, the Dukes' interior depth would be much improved, but the forward won't be eligible until 2013-14.

CAA

BY CRAIG POWERS

The Colonial Athletic Association could very well have been two separate leagues in 2011-12, with a clear line between the upper half of the conference and the bottom. The top teams dominated the league, and built up big win totals on the backs of the last five.

The discrepancy between the haves and the have-nots is spelled out in the data. Drexel, VCU, George Mason, and Old Dominion all finished in the top five in points per possession and points per possession allowed. Those four teams went a combined 58-14 in league play.

Georgia State, Delaware, and Northeastern didn't have quite the same success as the top four, but all were clearly better than the last five teams. Georgia State had the third-best defense, while Delaware finished with the third-best offense. Northeastern wasn't great on either end, but managed not to fall into the muck of the last five teams on either offense or defense.

With a number of programs rising to the status of at-large potential come tournament time, the CAA looked well on its way to becoming a perennial multi-bid conference. The league has been in the national spotlight multiple times recently, with George Mason and VCU making Final Four runs. Those successes served to bring better talent, and the conference had been moving towards four or five teams each year having the chance to play into the tournament, with two or three surviving for bids.

Which is where the bottom five teams come into play. While the best teams in the league had a dominant combined record, the worst were an inversely poor amalgam. James Madison, UNC Wilmington, William & Mary, Hofstra, and Towson were a combined 18-72 in conference games. James Madison and UNC Wilmington tied for the high mark of the low at five wins, well behind Northeastern's nine.

Schools that have come to expect NCAA bids, like VCU and Old Dominion, don't want those bottom-dwellers bringing down their RPI come selection time. A win over a 1-31 Towson team does nothing to improve one's chances for an at-large bid, and having the Tigers on the schedule is more likely to hinder the possibility. Thus, the CAA is going through major changes. VCU has already left for the Atlantic 10. Old Dominion and Georgia State are both gone in 2013, with ODU headed to Conference USA and Georgia State to the Sun Belt.

With all the shuffling, this will indeed be an awkward season for the league. Old Dominion and Georgia State will be like teenagers stuck at a parents' party, forced to hang out with the host's kids. The rest of the CAA wasn't going to take these moves lying down. They've effectively "grounded" ODU and the Panthers for their final season in the conference. Instead of curfews and loss of cell phone privileges, the Monarchs and GSU won't be allowed to compete for the league's automatic bid to the NCAA tournament. The league has made it clear that they don't want programs that are bolting for supposed greener pastures to represent the CAA on college basketball's biggest stage. If Old Dominion and Georgia State want to go dancing, they'll need an at-large bid.

ODU and GSU won't be the only teams barred from the conference tournament this season. Towson and UNC Wilmington received NCAA sanctions, including postseason bans, for not adhering to Academic Progress Rate (APR) standards. So, in one of the more bizarre scenarios in all of college basketball this season, there are now just seven teams eligible for the CAA tournament in March. The format had been four rounds with the top four seeds earning byes to the quarterfinals. Now, the rounds will be trimmed to three with the top overall seed earning a bye into the semifinals. The other six teams will have to play an extra game to win the tournament. This will put extra incentive for a school to take home that regular-season title—unless of course the regular-season champion is ineligible for the conference tournament.

That's not beyond the realm of possibility, but the one possibly great team in the league this year figures to be a program that's actually sticking around: Drexel. Past the Dragons, there are several good teams that will make the conference race interesting in this, the CAA's strangest year to date.

Teams listed in Craig's predicted order of finish.

DREXEL

2012: 29-7 (16-2 CAA); Lost to UMass 72-70, NIT quarterfinals
In-conference offense: 1.08 points per possession (1st)
In-conference defense: 0.92 points allowed per possession (4th)

Drexel was a victim of their conference last season, as they were certainly a tournament-level team but weren't afforded enough opportunities to play against other talented teams. The Dragons recorded a school record for wins (29) and took the regular season CAA title by winning their last 16 conference games. Combined with a Bracketbuster win over Cleveland State and two victories in the CAA tournament, Drexel was on a 19-game winning streak heading into the conference championship game against Virginia Commonwealth. It turned out that was a must-win for the Dragons, as VCU would be the only CAA team to make the tournament after winning the title game in their hometown 59-56. This season Bruiser Flint's team will shoot for those all-important resume wins at the Anaheim Classic. The Dragons will open against Saint Mary's, and could get Xavier in the second round with a win. Cal and Georgia Tech are on the other half of the bracket. With all but one rotation player returning, Drexel is set up for another big year. Junior point guard **Frantz Massenat** will lead the Dragons' slow-paced offense. Massenat is a coach's dream, with the ability to drive the lane without turning the ball over, a high assist rate, and an almost automatic jumper. Alongside Massenat is **Damion Lee**, who notched an impeccable effective field goal percentage of 55. **Derrick Thomas** and **Chris Fouch** will also see plenty of backcourt minutes, with Fouch being the more aggressive offensive player. The one place where attrition might pinch is in the frontcourt: Samme Givens is gone after an excellent senior season. **Dartaye Ruffin** and **Daryl McCoy** aren't nearly as offensive-minded as Givens was, but both are good rebounders at both ends of the floor. Drexel featured the most efficient offense in CAA play, as they knocked down 40 percent of their threes while also driving the lane and getting to the line. They were solid on the defensive end too, leading the league in both field goal defense and (by a mile) defensive rebounding. With all the returning talent, the CAA is the Dragons' to lose.

DELAWARE

2012: 18-14 (12-6 CAA); Lost to Butler 75-58, CBI first round
In-conference offense: 1.02 points per possession (4th)
In-conference defense: 0.98 points allowed per possession (6th)

Last season Delaware put together a nine-game winning streak in February and March that ensured they'd finish with a winning record, something the school hadn't yet accomplished under Monte Ross. The streak netted the Blue Hens an invite to the CBI, their first postseason exposure since an NIT appearance in 2000. Every significant player from that team returns. Junior guard **Devon Saddler** carried the load on offense, playing 87 percent of the minutes and using 30 percent of the possessions while he was on the floor. He struggled with his shot, but made up for it at least partially by hitting 80 percent from the free throw line. Still, Saddler would do well to pass more of the tough shots off to his teammates this season. Some of those shots could go to sophomore point guard **Jarvis Threatt**, who was very good at getting to the free throw line and converted at an 82 percent rate when he got there. Threatt's efficiency at the line and his low turnover rate (unusual for an attacking guard, much less an attacking guard who's a freshman) were the main drivers behind a stellar 110 offensive rating. **Kyle Anderson** will see minutes as his team's three-point specialist after knocking down 34 percent of his 200 attempts as a freshman. In the paint senior **Jamelle Hagins** will look to continue his overachieving ways on both sides of the ball. A reliable source of points inside, Hagins grabbed 27 percent of the available defensive boards during his minutes and blocked nearly nine percent of opponents' twos. There weren't many rebounds left to grab after Hagins was done, so **Josh Brinkley** isn't impressive in that area, but he does convert his touches while also getting to the line. The Blue Hens didn't draw a lot of attention last season, but that's about to change. Delaware will jump some teams and finish near the top of the CAA.

OLD DOMINION

2012: 22-14 (13-5 CAA); Lost to Mercer 79-73, CIT quarterfinals
In-conference offense: 1.00 points per possession (5th)
In-conference defense: 0.87 point allowed per possession (1st)

Old Dominion was expecting some drop-off in 2011-12 after two consecutive NCAA tournaments and the departure of four graduating seniors. The drop-off certainly came, but only on one end of the court. The Monarch defense was every bit as good, and often times better, than what we saw from the group that won the 2011 CAA tournament. The defense masked some of ODU's offensive shortcomings and indeed deserved most of the credit for the 13 conference wins, just one less than the year before. But three important pieces from the D are gone. Kent Bazemore and Trian Iliadis helped lock down the outside and create turnovers. Chris Cooper was Blaine Taylor's best defensive rebounder. Perhaps ODU can make up for those losses by improving on the offensive end this season. **Donte Hill** and **Dimitri Batten** are in line for more minutes. Hill was capable enough in enough categories to post a 102 offensive rating. Batten's an excellent shooter, hitting 40 percent from three while also contributing on defense. The Monarchs should get a boost from NC State transfer **DeShawn Painter**, who was granted immediate eligibility. Painter wasn't a great rebounder in the ACC, but at 6-9 and 225, he should see those numbers improve in the CAA. Senior shot blocker **Nick Wright** is the only returning frontcourt player that saw regular minutes last season, and he made just 39 percent of his twos. Incoming freshman **Ekene Anachebe** may provide some inside punch. He's big (6-9, 265), and seems to have solid rebounding and shot blocking instincts. Old Dominion should have a good defense again, just like they have every year under Taylor. However, repeating last season's level of dominance on D will be a tall task. The offense may see some improvement, as the departing seniors were all lacking in that area, but another drop-off, however slight, is likely in the offing in terms of conference wins. The timing there is unfortunate. ODU's regular season will have special importance, with the program banned from the conference tournament due to their impending jump to Conference USA.

GEORGE MASON

2012: 24-9 (14-4 CAA); Lost to VCU 74-64, CAA semifinals
In-conference offense: 1.02 points per possession (3rd)
In-conference defense: 0.94 points allowed per possession (5th)

In 2011-12 the Patriots were masters of the interior under new head coach Paul Hewitt. Mason led the CAA in two-point field goal percentage, while placing in the top three in both free throw rate and defensive 2FG percentage. This came as GMU was adjusting to Hewitt's faster pace. Ryan Pearson and Mike Morrison were the key cogs on the inside. Those two are now gone, and Hewitt will try to piece together a new frontline with players who haven't seen the floor much: **Jonathan Arledge**, **Johnny Williams**, and **Erik Copes**. Arledge is arguably the most proven performer of the lot, as he provides decent rebounding on both ends as well as an ample supply of made free throws. Williams was injured last season; Copes averaged 15 minutes a game but was a liability on the offensive end. Conversely the backcourt doesn't hold as much mystery, though whether that's a good thing remains to be seen. **Bryon Allen** returns as the starting point guard, one who's certainly capable of recording assists—and turnovers. Allen also attempted 48 threes as a sophomore, which was about 48 too many given his 17 percent success rate. **Sherrod Wright** and **Vertrail Vaughns** are both efficient in their own ways. Wright shot the lights out (heavy on the twos, though with an occasional three) as a supporting player. Vaughns worked mainly as a catch-and-shoot guy and turned the ball over just 11 percent of the time. Both will need to pick up some scoring slack with the departures of Pearson and Morrison. George Mason is losing what made them a top team in the CAA last season, and the Patriots will see a dip this year.

GEORGIA STATE

2012: 22-12 (11-7 CAA); Lost to Mercer 64-59, CIT second round
In-conference offense: 0.96 points per possession (9th)
In-conference defense: 0.89 points allowed per possession (3rd)

After opening conference play 3-0 with wins over the likes of Drexel and VCU, it appeared GSU would challenge for the league title. However luck was not on the Panthers' side. From that point forward Georgia State went 3-8 in games decided by five points or less, including an 0-3 record in games that went to overtime. This season the Panthers are saying their goodbyes to the CAA, as the program prepares to takes its hoops to the Sun Belt. That leaves GSU, like Old Dominion, banned from this year's Colonial tournament, and this team's chances of earning an at-large NCAA bid don't look promising. Second-year coach Ron Hunter loses four starters, which is kind of a big deal when you rank No. 312 nationally in bench minutes. The lone returning starter is guard **Devonta White**, a jump shooter who hit 43 percent of his twos and 34 percent of his threes as a sophomore. Virginia Tech transfer **Manny Atkins** will certainly be in the mix. As a Hokie the wing was an efficient afterthought; as a Panther he'll be one of the primary options. **Rashaad Richardson** is a three-point specialist who launched 65 percent of his shots from behind the arc, where he hit at a 35 percent rate. At 6-10 and 260, **James Vincent** will provide a shot blocking presence and make an impact on the offensive glass. Newcomers include freshmen **R.J. Hunter** and **Markus Crider,** as well as junior college transfer **Denny Burguillos**. Hunter's a 6-5 guard that reportedly impressed the coaches in summer workouts, though it surely helps when you can greet your new head coach with "Hi, Dad." Crider was the team's most highly touted recruit and may back up Atkins on the wing. Burguillos brings some much-needed size to a thin frontcourt. Coach Hunter hasn't had a losing team since 2001, but he has his work cut out for him this season. Still, with a large gap between the top half of the CAA and the bottom, the Panthers have a shot at a winning season in conference play, and possibly overall.

NORTHEASTERN

2012: 14-17 (9-9 CAA); Lost to VCU 75-65, CAA quarterfinals
In-conference offense: 0.98 points per possession (6th)
In-conference defense: 1.01 points allowed per possession (7th)

The Huskies achieved respectability in 2011-12, adding three wins to their CAA total from the previous season to finish at .500 in conference play. This season head coach Bill Coen returns his top four players. Seniors **Jonathan Lee** and **Joel Smith** form one of the league's best backcourts. Both are dangerous from beyond the arc; Lee is the playmaker of the two, posting a nice assist rate and getting to the line with regularity, though he'll miss time early with a broken foot. In the frontcourt, **Quincy Ford** and **Reggie Spencer** return after making an impact in their freshman seasons. Ford's a long wing who can guard multiple positions. He was solid inside the arc but may be better served shooting fewer threes. Spencer is turnover-prone for an interior player, but he blocks shots, draws fouls, and last season he grabbed 10 percent of the available offensive boards during his minutes. Junior center **Dinko Marshavelski** will also see minutes. At 6-11, he'll provide some interior scoring but his most important contribution could be defensive rebounds, an area where Northeastern was seriously lacking in 2011-12. The gap between the top of the league and Coen's team is still real, but these Huskies may close that gap in a hurry.

HOFSTRA

2012: 10-22 (3-15 CAA); Lost to Georgia State 85-50, CAA first round
In-conference offense: 0.96 points per possession (10th)
In-conference defense: 1.02 points allowed per possession (8th)

The highlight of Hofstra's 2011-12 was a home-court upset over eventual NCAA at-large Iona right before New Year's. From that point on, though, the Pride went just 4-15 on their way to a CAA record that only Towson could envy. Now head coach Mo Cassara has lost his two best players from that team (Mike Moore and Nathaniel Lester). It doesn't sound promising so far, but Cassara's prescription for what ails his team is transfers. In a league where no team even made the 2012 NCAA tournament (VCU now being in the A-10), it's pretty amazing to have a player who's won a national championship. That's what Cassara has in **Jamal Coombs-McDaniel**, a veteran of the 2011 Connecticut team that won it all. At 6-7 Coombs-McDaniel was efficient at UConn in a reserve role, but he'll be called on for more at Hofstra. He even has major-conference company: **Taran Buie** grabbed a cup of coffee as a reserve 2-guard in 2010-11 on a Penn State roster that featured his half-brother, Talor Battle. Both transfers are suspended for the first two games for a "violation of team rules." Still another transfer, 6-10 junior **Daquan Brown**, has arrived from the junior college ranks (Barstow College). Brown will share time in the frontcourt with some combination of **David Imes**, **Stephen Nwaukoni**, and **Moussa Kone**. Imes and Kone are shot blockers; Nwaukoni is a solid rebounder, especially on the offensive glass. The transfers may provide a boost, but whether they can exceed what the Pride got from their graduating seniors is an open question. Still, improving on 3-15 seems reasonable enough, and the good news is none of Hofstra's key players will be seniors.

JAMES MADISON

2012: 12-20 (5-13 CAA); Lost to UNC Wilmington 70-59, CAA first round
In-conference offense: 0.98 points per possession (7th)
In-conference defense: 1.06 points per possession allowed (9th)

It's not often that a team has poor rebounding percentages on both ends of the floor, as the difference between the two can sometimes boil down to a choice of style. Anyway, that's the theory, but James Madison was an exception to that rule last season. Head coach Matt Brady's squad finished No. 11 in the CAA in offensive rebounding percentage (take that, William and Mary!) and dead last in the league on the defensive glass. This team wasn't good on the inside, and on offense they avoided it at every turn as four Dukes shot more threes than twos. Actually **Andrey Semenov** may want to consider taking even more shots from beyond the arc, since he hit on 44 percent of his attempts from out there. Be that as it may 6-6 **A.J. Davis** returns as the featured scorer. The onetime Wyoming Cowboy draws five fouls per 40 minutes and connects on 51 percent of his twos. Rather remarkably, he arrived at JMU a 10 percent career three-point shooter. Davis brought that all the way up to 33 percent last season, but he'd still be better served by taking the ball inside more often. To rectify some of the team's interior issues, Brady will hope for more from last year's reserves, guys like **Enoch Hood** and **Gene Swindle**. Hood put on some badly needed weight in the offseason. Swindle doesn't rebound at nearly the rate one would expect from a 6-11, 265-pound major-conference (Virginia Tech) transfer turned loose in the CAA. While returning most of your rotation is a good thing, JMU's veterans will have to improve to pull this team up to the CAA's midsection.

TOWSON

2012: 1-31 (1-17 CAA); Lost to Delaware 72-65, CAA first round
In-conference offense: 0.80 points per possession (12th)
In-conference defense: 1.06 points allowed per possession (10th)

Towson was certainly generous on defense, but their performance on that side of the ball wasn't anything out of the ordinary, as the Tigers finished tenth in a 12-team league for points allowed per possession. The offense however, was absolutely atrocious. In a league where the average possession yielded 0.98 points, Towson scored just 0.80, or 18 percent worse than the mean. The next lowest team was UNC Wilmington, and the Tigers were 16 percent worse than No. 11. Head coach Pat Skerry will be looking for much better results as he brings in three Big East transfers. **Bilal Dixon** was an effective 6-9 role player at Providence, making 56 percent of his twos and hitting the defensive glass last season as a junior. He's eligible as a senior this season under the NCAA's graduate transfer rule. Also parachuting in from the Big East are **Mike Burwell** (South Florida) and **Jerrelle Benimon** (Georgetown), both of whom struggled mightily (read: offensive ratings around 80) as sophomores in 2010-11. That being said, Benimon is a large specimen (6-8, 240) for the CAA, and maybe Burwell can hit some threes. The best-case scenario is that the Big East refugees take some of the possession load off **Marcus Damas**, who fared about as well as you'd expect in attempting 371 shots from the field for one of Division I's worst offenses. Towson won't jump to the top of the league, but they should win more than a handful of conference games. It's a shame the Tigers won't have a chance to roll the dice in the league tournament, having been ruled ineligible for postseason play due to the NCAA's APR standards.

UNC WILMINGTON

2012: 10-21 (5-13 CAA); Lost to Drexel 59-47, CAA quarterfinals
In-conference offense: 0.96 points per play (11th)
In-conference defense: 1.08 points per play allowed (12th)

Buzz Peterson has some rebuilding to do after four players transferred out of the program. The most important departure was that of Adam Smith, the team's most voluminous shooter. On the other side of the ledger Peterson has welcomed a small army of new arrivals, as well as players coming off redshirt seasons. **Marcus Graham**, a junior college transfer, and **Tyree Graham**, a graduate transfer from Rutgers, should see minutes in an all- or mostly-Graham backcourt. **Craig Ponder** and **Dylan Sherwood** both suffered season-ending injuries early last year and will see minutes. But the most important Seahawk will be senior forward **Keith Rendleman**. He's very good on the boards at both ends, and the offense will go through him. If UNC Wilmington can get some points from the new guys, they can take a step forward this season. Unfortunately, UNCW will sit out the CAA tournament because of NCAA sanctions related to academic progress. The best the Seahawks can do is make life difficult for the other teams in the conference, and a player like Rendleman will always give them a chance to do so.

WILLIAM AND MARY

2012: 6-26 (4-14 CAA); Lost to Northeastern 57-49, CAA first round
In-conference offense: 0.97 points per possession (8th)
In-conference defense: 1.07 points per possession allowed (11th)

Under Tony Shaver the Tribe has shot threes on more than 40 percent of their attempts in CAA play in each of the last six seasons. William and Mary made threes at a 33.5 percent clip in-conference last season, making the long ball the most efficient part of this offense. The problem was they didn't excel anywhere else. The Tribe was decent on the defensive glass, but when you allow the other teams in your league to make half their twos that particular skill isn't all that vital. Basically the guys that shot threes weren't around to play much D on the other end. We can make an exception, though, for returning junior **Tim Rusthoven**. He was an excellent rebounder on both ends while also furnishing the team's only shot blocking. Rusthoven and guard **Matt Rum** are the only returning players who posted above average offensive ratings, a distinction the latter veteran can credit to 37 percent shooting on his threes. On the other hand **Marcus Thornton** and **Brandon Britt** combined to miss 142 threes. That played a big role in William and Mary putting up just 0.97 points per possession in CAA play. The Tribe will be a more experienced group this season, and an improvement in three-point shooting is certainly possible (and probably necessary). The defense is unlikely to improve by leaps and bounds, and the only way to make up for it will be to score more efficiently.

Conference USA

BY JOEY BERLIN

Ah, the old "no respect" card. If you're a coach, whether you're talking about your team or your league, it never gets old to you.

For one prominent example, take Larry Eustachy and Tom Herrion after Herrion's Marshall team beat Eustachy's Southern Miss squad 73-62 in the Conference USA semifinals last March.

"That was the sixth place team in our conference," Eustachy told Marshall's student newspaper, the Parthenon. "We are in the NCAA tournament, and they have beaten us back-to-back. This league does not get the recognition it deserves."

The winning coach's thoughts were akin to an echo. "We just don't get the national respect," Herrion said. "This league has great players, great coaches and we've got really good teams. Teams that can not only get into tournaments but win games in postseason basketball."

While Eustachy has since moved on to Colorado State, Herrion's still in the league. If he and the rest of C-USA's remaining coaches think their conference gets no respect now, they might do well to enjoy the modest recognition the league still receives in 2012-13.

Next year, Memphis heads to the Big East. Since the departures of Cincinnati, Louisville and Marquette to the same league in 2005, the Tigers have been C-USA's unchallenged standard-bearer, with three straight Elite Eight appearances from 2006 to 2008. In fact, John Calipari's 2008 squad was 2.1 seconds away from a national championship. Setting aside that the Tigers' wins from that season were later vacated, it would have been the first national title for a school from outside one of the current major conferences since UNLV's 1990 title. Though Josh Pastner hasn't been able to duplicate Calipari's overall success thus far, the Tigers are still the class of the league, the first (and often only) school that comes to mind in a spontaneous word association game involving C-USA hoops.

The other three programs C-USA is losing to the Big East for the 2013-14 season have either already shown promise or are at least could show signs sometime soon. UCF will serve a one-year postseason ban this season, but the Knights made the NIT for the first time last year. Houston, with a highly rated local freshman coming in, may have more raw talent on its roster than any team in the league other than Memphis. SMU is relying on the considerable coaching credentials of Larry Brown and Tim Jankovich to return the Mustangs to relevance, which isn't the worst bet in the world. Above all, though, losing Memphis hurts the perception—as well as the reality—of a league that ranked No. 10 in Ken Pomeroy's conference rankings last season.

The six schools C-USA will be adding after this year—Charlotte, FIU, Louisiana Tech, North Texas, Old Dominion and Texas San Antonio—do boast a few recent NCAA tournament appearances among them. Still, as a group, they're more quantity than quality, and in the present, they won't move the league's perception needle in a positive direction. Cumulatively, those six were barely .500 teams both overall (97-96) and in their respective conferences (48-48) last season. Only Old Dominion, with two wins in the CIT, made a trip to the postseason, its eighth straight. So, more respect will be hard to come by for Herrion and other conference coaches hoping to elevate C-USA to something more than a two-bid league.

For one last year, Memphis is the conference's most loaded team, and by extension the clear favorite to win another league title. The Tigers lose conference player of the year Will Barton, but Tarik Black,

Joe Jackson, Chris Crawford and Adonis Thomas are all back. After the Tigers, a league that's been crowded in the standings the last couple years could easily be crowded again. Herrion's Marshall squad had the highest RPI of any team that didn't make the field of 68, and with Dennis Tinnon and DeAndre Kane both returning, the Thundering Herd have one of the league's best inside-outside tandems. Tim Floyd's UTEP squad was green in 2011-12 and had trouble winning on the road, but back-to-back victories over Memphis and Southern Miss showed that the Miners had the talent to do damage in the league. This year, Floyd's team is more experienced, and they've added a high-level recruit in Chris Washburn. Houston, with TaShawn Thomas and Joseph Young returning and Danuel House entering, is a potential sleeper pick for a high league finish.

Four teams—Southern Miss, UAB, SMU and Tulsa—welcome new coaches. At USM Donnie Tyndall inherits easily the best situation of the four, at least at the start. The former Morehead State coach takes over an NCAA tournament team that has two all-conference performers back: second-team guard Neil Watson and third-team forward Jonathan Mills. Brown will try to revive an SMU team that hit devastating offensive lows in Matt Doherty's final season, while Brown's star player from Kansas' 1988 national championship team, Danny Manning, will be starting essentially from scratch in his first head coaching job at Tulsa. Jerod Haase, who played for Roy Williams at Kansas and coached under him at both KU and North Carolina, will take his initial shot as a head coach at UAB.

Rice will have to make do without the ultra-efficient inside play of Prospectus favorite Arsalan Kazemi. UCF is something of a wild card. There's no postseason to shoot for, but with Keith Clanton and Isaiah Sykes back and Oklahoma transfer Calvin Newell eligible in December, the Knights still have appreciable talent after last year's NIT berth. Tulane will ride Kendall Timmons and reigning conference freshman of the year Ricky Tarrant, while East Carolina will count on another big season from point guard Miguel Paul.

Teams listed in Joey's predicted order of finish.

MEMPHIS

2012: 26-9 (13-3 C-USA); Lost to Saint Louis 61-54, NCAA round of 64
In-conference offense: 1.12 points per possession (1st)
In-conference defense: 0.90 points allowed per possession (1st)

Most teams are happy to single out one turning point in a season. For Memphis, there were two. First, after a 70-59 loss to Georgetown dropped the Tigers to 6-5, Josh Pastner held an Oliver Stone director's cut of a team meeting—one hour and 45 minutes—immediately after the game. Whether it was the meeting, the fact that Memphis' somewhat nasty early schedule got easier immediately, or a combination of the two, the Tigers went on a tear worthy of their talent, winning 13 of their next 15 games. Then came February's two-point home loss to UTEP, in which the Tigers blew a nine-point halftime lead and gave the Miners their only road win of the season. For that monstrosity, Pastner took the names off the back of the jerseys, took away practice attire with "Memphis" emblazoned on it, denied the team access to the locker room and withdrew hot meals. The extreme anti-selfishness measures appeared to send the intended message. The Tigers rolled unchallenged through their last four regular-season games, then crushed UTEP, UCF and Marshall in the C-USA tourney by an average of 25 points. That got the Tigers and conference player of the year Will Barton a date in the round of 64 against Saint Louis and one of the nation's best defenses. You know the rest. Still, Memphis' play down the stretch represented a talented group finally blooming. Barton is gone, but once again, Pastner has enough talent on hand to field two C-USA teams—and this time, his team has a little experience, too. **Tarik Black** needs to, and will, get more opportunities to put the ball in the hoop this year. The junior forward posted the nation's second-highest effective field goal percentage last year, as well as the country's sixth-best true shooting percentage, earning second team all-league honors. Juniors **Joe Jackson** and **Chris Crawford** return to give Memphis scoring and passing in the backcourt. Jackson averaged 11 points and hit 84 percent at the free throw line, and Crawford was the team's assist leader and a third-team all-league selection. An ankle injury limited former McDonald's All-American **Adonis Thomas** to just 19 games and also likely kept him from jumping to the NBA. In his limited time on the floor as a freshman, the 6-7 forward posted an eFG of 54 percent. With more new talent headed in, including another McDonald's honoree in 6-8 power forward **Shaq Goodwin**, don't forget about junior guard **Antonio Barton** or senior forward **Ferrakohn Hall**. Barton couldn't miss from either side of the arc, and the 6-8 Hall, a Seton Hall transfer, started 24 of the Tigers' last 27 games.

MARSHALL

2012: 21-14 (9-7 C-USA); Lost to Middle Tennessee 86-78, NIT first round
In-conference offense: 1.04 points per possession (5th)
In-conference defense: 1.03 points allowed per possession (9th)

Tom Herrion's team started the year strong, with nine wins in 11 games (with losses at home to Ohio and in a close game at Syracuse) and made a nice run to the C-USA tournament final, highlighted by an 11-point win over Southern Miss in the semis. Though Memphis hammered them by 26 in the title game, and they finished tied for fifth in the league, the Thundering Herd were the highest-RPI team left out of the NCAA tournament. Offensively, the Herd were the nation's sixth-best team at getting a second chance to score, grabbing more than 40 percent of the available offensive rebounds, and they relied on the scoring of shooting guard **DeAndre Kane**, who put up nearly 30 percent of the Herd's shots while he was on the floor. Now a junior, Kane followed up his C-USA freshman of the year campaign with a season that earned him a second team all-conference selection. Herrion is elated to have 6-8 forward **Dennis Tinnon** back after the NCAA granted him one more year of eligibility over the summer. A newcomer to Marshall last year, Tinnon arrived from Kansas City Kansas Community College after a winding journey plagued with legal problems and a protracted, but ultimately successful, effort to earn his high school diploma. In his first season at Marshall, Tinnon made 55 percent of his twos and established himself as one of C-USA's best rebounders at both ends of the floor. Senior **Robert Goff** gives the Herd a third returning starter after averaging six points and five rebounds last season. Freshman point guard **Kareem Canty** may get the chance to step in after the departure of Damier Pitts.

UTEP

2012: 15-17 (7-9 C-USA); Lost to Memphis 65-47, C-USA quarterfinals
In-conference offense: 0.96 points per possession (9th)
In-conference defense: 0.98 points allowed per possession (3rd)

Last season UTEP lost six seniors from Tim Floyd's first Miner team, which had won 25 games, and started the year with eight freshmen and one senior. They got the results most mid-majors can expect when they start all over. UTEP lost five of its first seven games, then rebounded to win four of its next five, starting with a win over eventual NCAA tournament entrant New Mexico State. The Miners were similarly streaky in conference play, following a four-game losing streak with a four-game winning streak. The last two wins in that run showed promise for the future: a 60-58 upset of Memphis (UTEP's only road win all season), and a double-OT victory over Southern Miss. As he usually does, Floyd got his young team to play tough defense. Offensively, the Miners relied on hitting from two; they made just 144 threes and no C-USA team got a lower percentage of their points from outside. Not surprisingly, it was an interior player, **John Bohannon**, who emerged as the team's top performer. The 6-10 Bohannon grabbed nearly 29 percent of opponents' misses in conference play to lead C-USA in defensive rebound percentage, and his 65 percent eFG in C-USA play ranked second in the league. Swingman **Julian Washburn** made the C-USA all-freshman team. Washburn averaged 11 points per game, led the Miners with 45 dunks and quickly gained a strong defensive reputation. **Jacques Streeter** ably stepped into the point guard role as a newcomer, averaging seven points and four assists. Headlining this year's recruiting class is Julian Washburn's 6-9 younger brother, **Chris Washburn**, though 6-6 small forward **Twymond Howard** could also contribute immediately.

SOUTHERN MISS

2012: 25-9 (11-5 C-USA); Lost to Kansas State 70-64, NCAA round of 64
In-conference offense: 1.06 points per possession (2nd)
In-conference defense: 1.03 points allowed per possession (8th)

Though the Golden Eagles lost six of their last 11 games, it was a notably successful season, as Southern Miss set a school record for wins. For every deficiency Larry Eustachy's squad had, there was something to counteract it. Southern Miss was C-USA's smallest team, but scrappiness and experience made up for that. In fact the Eagles were among the conference's best teams at both grabbing and preventing offensive rebounds. They did not shoot well from the field (and their conference opponents did against this defense), but USM took outstanding care of the ball and was the league's best free throw shooting team. An amazing 11 Eagles wins came by five points or less, and they went to OT five times. A 75-72 win over Memphis on the first day of February marked the season's high point. Not only did that win in Hattiesburg give Southern Miss a 20-3 record and sole possession of first place in C-USA, it also ended an 18-game losing streak against the Tigers. With Eustachy headed to Colorado State, new coach Donnie Tyndall will be hard pressed to duplicate last year's success right away. Four of last year's five leading scorers are gone, but the guy at the top of that list is back, in the form of senior point guard **Neil Watson**. Though he started just four games, Watson played more than 73 percent of the available minutes, averaging 12 points and ranking third in the league in assist percentage. At 6-5, **Jonathan Mills** led the Eagles in rebounding and made the league's all-defensive team. **Daveon Boardingham**, a 6-7 Newark product by way of Seward County (Kansas) Community College, made noise in last season's NJCAA national tournament.

UCF

2012: 22-11 (10-6 C-USA); Lost to Drexel 81-56, NIT first round
In-conference offense: 1.04 points per possession (3rd)
In-conference defense: 1.01 points allowed per possession (7th)

UCF jumped from six conference wins to 10 and improved dramatically at the offensive end, going from 10th in C-USA play to third. The result was the program's first NIT appearance in 28 seasons of action. Though they bowed out quickly with a loss to Drexel, the Knights looked like a decent bet to take the next step. But they won't get that chance: UCF is under a one-year postseason ban for recruiting violations and impermissible benefits. Personnel-wise, losing 5-9 distributor/pest A.J. Rompza hurts, and for the first time in a while the Knights are fresh out of Michael Jordan offspring. On the plus side, first-team all-conference selection **Keith Clanton** decided to return for his senior year, despite having the option to transfer elsewhere and play immediately due to the postseason ban. (Clanton turned down overtures from Kentucky, Ohio State, and others.) The 6-9 forward is an all-around star, scoring, grabbing rebounds at both ends and blocking shots. Coach Donnie Moore is also likely to rely heavily on athletic 6-5 junior **Isaiah Sykes**, the team's most improved player in 2012 and a force on the offensive glass (though listed officially as a guard). Sykes likes to get to the basket but needs to improve his long-range and free throw shooting (29 and 55 percent, respectively). Another junior, 6-8 forward **Tristan Spurlock**, is likely to play an expanded role. Oklahoma transfer **Calvin Newell** will give Moore another backcourt option when the he becomes eligible mid-season. Newell was OU's second-leading scorer in their first five games last year before deciding to transfer.

HOUSTON

2012: 15-15 (7-9 C-USA); Lost to UTEP 67-62 (OT), C-USA first round
In-conference offense: 0.99 points per possession (8th)
In-conference defense: 1.09 points allowed per possession (12th)

The Cougars are on a clear upward trend as coach James Dickey enters his third season. Despite being the league's most turnover-prone team in conference play and once again fielding C-USA's most porous defense, Houston finished just short of .500 in league play by ending the regular season on a three-game winning streak, including a one-point win at Rice. To continue the upward trend Dickey will have to offset personnel losses. Leading scorer Jonathon Simmons declared for the NBA draft (but did not end up hearing his name called), No. 2 scorer Alandise Harris transferred to Arkansas, and role player Kirk Van Slyke left for Arkansas State. Those departures make this year's new arrivals all the more important. Dickey brought in a pair of local blue-chippers: 6-7 wing **Danuel House**, a consensus top-30 recruit, and 6-10 forward Danrad "Chicken" Knowles, ranked in the top 60 on both the ESPNU and Rivals lists. In September, however, UH announced cryptically that they "look forward to [Knowles] joining our program for the 2013-14 season." A third in-state freshman, 6-10 center **Valentine Izundu**, is considered raw but gives the Cougars more size and shot blocking. Add that group to the best of last year's freshman class—**TaShawn Thomas** and **Joseph Young**—and Dickey suddenly has a core of talent that many coaches would envy. The 6-9 Thomas posted a 113 offensive rating, grabbed 14 percent of the available offensive boards and blocked a fair number of shots. Former Providence signee Young averaged 11 points per game and shot the ball well from long range (38 percent). Both players were C-USA All-Freshman selections. Point guard **J.J. Thompson** also returns for his sophomore season after making 19 starts.

UAB

2012: 15-16 (9-7 C-USA); Lost to UCF 64-54, C-USA quarterfinals
In-conference offense: 0.99 points per possession (7th)
In-conference defense: 0.99 points allowed per possession (5th)

Mike Davis was let go after last season, and a critic of that decision may note that UAB had won its first C-USA regular season title and made the NCAA tournament just a year earlier. On the other hand, a critic of our critic might say 2012 was on the whole an unredeemable season. The Blazers started the year 5-11, including a November home loss to Tennessee Martin, one of the Skyhawks' four wins on the year. UAB went 1-8 against teams that made the NCAA tournament, and those five wins down the stretch came courtesy of SMU, East Carolina, Tulsa and Tulane (twice). Athletic director Brian Mackin cited fan apathy as a reason for Davis' ouster, and the attendance figures back him up on that. At any rate, Jerod Haase gets his first shot as a head coach after 13 years on Roy Williams' staffs at both Kansas and North Carolina. Haase won't have do-it-all forward Cameron Moore, who averaged a double-double as a senior and was the conference's defensive player of the year. He will have two good long-range shooters in juniors **Jordan Swing** and **Preston Purifoy**, who were the reasons UAB ranked second in three-point shooting in conference play. Junior point guard **Quincy Taylor** was recovering this summer from a torn ACL suffered in the regular season finale. As of this writing, Haase's first roster was without freshmen—the Blazers' newcomers are all transfers. **Terence Jones**, a 6-2 senior, is eligible immediately after averaging 14 points a game at Texas A&M Corpus Christi last season. **Fahro Alihodzic**, a transfer from Southeastern Iowa CC, will give UAB a 6-10, 240-pound presence.

TULANE

2012: 15-16 (3-13 C-USA); Lost to UAB 72-64, C-USA first round
In-conference offense: 0.94 points per possession (11th)
In-conference defense: 1.05 points allowed per possession (10th)

Undoubtedly, Tulane's season would've turned out at least a little differently if not for the season-ending Achilles injury that then-junior guard **Kendall Timmons** suffered during a double-overtime loss to Southern Miss in early January. Entering that game, the Green Wave had ridden a friendly nonconference schedule (with the exception of a loss at Syracuse) to a 12-3 record. Without the multitalented Timmons, however, Tulane struggled in nearly every facet of the game and again finished at the bottom of the league. And that was with point guard **Ricky Tarrant** (109 offensive rating) emerging as C-USA's top freshman, scoring in double figures in all but one of the Wave's conference games and earning a selection to the all-league first team. If Tarrant, Timmons, senior guard **Jordan Callahan** and junior forward **Josh Davis** all stay on the floor, Tulane should finally show real improvement in coach Ed Conroy's third season. The 6-8 Davis averaged 11 points and nine rebounds, and finished in the conference's top 10 in both offensive and defensive rebounding percentages. Size was an issue for the Wave last year: among conference foes, only Southern Miss ranked lower in average and effective height, and just three teams in the nation had a higher percentage of their shots blocked. The incoming freshman class won't help in that department. Three of the signees are guards, and the fourth, Orlando forward **Marc Eddy Norelia**, is 6-7.

TULSA

2012: 17-14 (10-6 C-USA); Lost to Marshall 105-100 (3 OT), C-USA quarterfinals
In-conference offense: 1.04 points per possession (4th)
In-conference defense: 0.97 points allowed per possession (2nd)

Fewer and fewer fans were going to see the Golden Hurricane, which had as much to do with the firing of Doug Wojcik as the mediocre results in his seventh season. Tulsa did tie for third in the league and was among C-USA's most efficient teams at both ends of the floor, but a nonconference stretch of seven losses in nine games—including losses to Missouri State, Oklahoma State and Arizona State—set a bad early tone. Even the 10-6 conference mark, which included a seven-game win streak, had some nasty warts, namely, back-to-back losses to Houston and SMU. And Tulsa trailed Memphis by 25 points in the second half of the regular-season finale before cutting the final deficit to 12. So Danny Manning takes over the Tulsa program after developing a reputation as a stellar big-man tutor on Bill Self's staff at Kansas. The transfers of two likely starters in the backcourt—all-conference first teamer Jordan Clarkson to Missouri, and Eric McClellan to Vanderbilt—don't leave Manning much in the way of returning firepower. Senior **Scottie Haralson** is back with the remnants of last year's most accurate long-range shooting team in C-USA. The 6-4 Haralson put up 221 threes last year (out of 293 total shots) and knocked down 41 percent of them. **Tim Peete**, another 6-4 guard, averaged five points mostly as a reserve. All three of Wojcik's 2012 recruits elected to stick with Tulsa. Shooting guard **James Woodard** and power forwards **Zeldric King** and **D'Andre Wright** are listed as three-star recruits by Rivals. And if 6-2 Southern Idaho transfer **Pat Swilling Jr.** returns from wrist surgery, he'll give the Hurricane a nice boost in the backcourt.

EAST CAROLINA

2012: 15-16 (5-11 C-USA), Lost to Southern Miss 81-78 (OT), C-USA quarterfinals
In-conference offense: 1.00 point per possession (6th)
In-conference defense: 1.05 points allowed per possession (11th)

In 2010-11, when East Carolina recorded their first winning season in 14 years, the Pirates got to the free throw line at a better rate than all but five teams in the nation. Last season, only one C-USA team was worse at getting to the line. Other than that, though, ECU's year on the offensive end was similar to its performance the previous season. The Pirates were once again a high-assist squad that relied heavily on threes. At the other end, Jeff Lebo's team finished next-to-last in the league in defensive efficiency. This year, Lebo has a senior-laden core led by point guard **Miguel Paul**. The Missouri transfer proved to be a tremendous playmaker in his first year at ECU, posting an assist rate good for ninth in the nation, along with leading the Pirates with 15 points per game. Senior **Maurice Kemp** and junior **Robert Sampson**, both solid rebounders at 6-8, are back and will try to pick up the production lost with the departure of forward Darius Morrow. Guard **Shamarr Bowden**, another senior, hit a team-high 59 threes a year ago with 40 percent accuracy. Rhode Island transfer **Akeem Richmond** will give the Pirates another backcourt option and another avid shooter. He played two years with the Rams and led all A-10 players with 231 three-point attempts in 2011, making 75.

RICE

2012: 19-16 (8-8 C-USA); Lost to Oakland 77-70, CIT quarterfinals
In-conference offense: 0.96 points per possession (10th)
In-conference defense: 0.98 points allowed per possession (4th)

Strong defense, particularly inside the arc, and the continued all-around excellence of Arsalan Kazemi propelled Rice to its first postseason appearance in seven years, and in the CIT the Owls notched their first two postseason victories since 1993. Coach Ben Braun's team gave up less than half of its points from two-point range, and in conference play only Memphis blocked a higher rate of shots. The Owls didn't have any marquee wins, but a comeback victory over UCF in February gave Braun career win No. 600. However, this season the coach's career total won't grow as fast as it would have had Kazemi not chosen to transfer to Oregon. Braun will also be without promising point guard Dylan Ennis and 7-2 shot blocker Omar Oraby, who transferred to Villanova and USC, respectively. Who's left? Senior guard **Tamir Jackson** averaged 10.5 points but didn't have a good season shooting the ball. Philadelphia-area freshman **Keith Washington** might get the chance to replace Ennis at point guard, and **Austin Ramljak**, a transfer from Ventura (Calif.) College, will be expected to bring long-range shooting. Ramljak averaged 19.2 points and hit 41 percent on threes last season.

SMU

2012: 13-19 (4-12 C-USA); Lost to Marshall 74-56, C-USA first round
In-conference offense: 0.93 points per possession (12th)
In-conference defense: 1.00 point allowed per possession (6th)

All the gains Matt Doherty's squad made in 2010-11—the year when SMU had the nation's second-best effective field goal percentage, won 20 games, and made the CIT semifinals—quickly became a distant memory last season. The Mustangs had C-USA's worst offense, and just when SMU fans thought they'd hit bottom with a 43-39 loss at Rice in February, they found a new low four days later with a 47-28 home loss to UAB, setting a C-USA record for fewest points scored in a game. By bringing Larry Brown back to the college game and making Tim Jankovich the head coach in waiting (and the nation's highest-paid assistant), the Mustangs hope they're set to build a program for the long haul. Brown quickly proved he wasn't coming to SMU just to draw a leisurely golden-years paycheck, cutting four players within a week of taking the job, including starting point guard Jeremiah Samarrippas. No players remain on the roster from Doherty's only good season just two years ago. The Mustangs were one of C-USA's smallest teams in 2012, which contributed to their troubles. They were the worst team in conference play both at grabbing offensive rebounds and preventing them, and they allowed a league-worst 54 percent shooting inside the arc. Brown's first freshman class will at least address that by adding size in 6-11 Doherty recruit **Blaise Mbargorba** and 7-0 **Jordan Dickerson**, a late signee. The best of the returners include junior guard **London Giles** (38 percent from three-point range), sophomore center **Cannen Cunningham**, and sophomore guard **Jalen Jones**. But any major step forward will likely have to wait until 2013-14, when key transfers Crandall Head (Illinois), Markus Kennedy (Villanova) and Nic Moore (Illinois State) become eligible.

Horizon League

BY JEFF HALEY

When you think of the Horizon League you probably think first of Butler, and with good reason. The Bulldogs have won or shared in nine of the last 13 conference regular season titles, and made two trips to the NCAA championship game. The Bulldogs have been the signature team of the Horizon League for the last decade. Starting this season, however, Brad Stevens' team will be plying its trade in the Atlantic 10. When you think of the Horizon league, you're going to have to start thinking of someone else.

The Horizon has been through this before. Back when it was still called the Midwestern Collegiate Conference, it was dominated by Xavier. When the Musketeers left in 1995 to join the A-10, the MCC was left without its signature program. In stepped Butler. Now the cycle of life repeats.

With the departure of the Bulldogs, the Horizon's potential as a multi-bid league takes a hit. In the 1990s, the MCC sent more than one team to the NCAA tournament fairly frequently. Between 1989 and 1998, the MCC sent two or more teams to the tournament in six separate seasons. Of course, in four of these six years, Xavier was the school that received the at-large bid. Since the start of the millennium, the Horizon has earned three at-large tournament invitations. In all three cases these bids went to Butler.

This brings up an important point encountered when considering mid-major hoops in general, and one that's of particular importance in the Horizon. What is required to have a multiple-bid league? At a minimum, getting two teams in the NCAA tournament requires having a team good enough to earn an at-large bid, and another team good enough to beat that team in the conference tournament. For almost the entire history of the Horizon League, either Xavier or Butler has been the conference's best candidate to earn an at-large bid. The only exceptions came in 1996, when UW-Green Bay earned an at-large bid, and in 1998, when both Detroit and UIC went dancing without winning the conference tournament.

There are still good teams in the Horizon. Over the course of the regular season last year Valparaiso and Cleveland State finished first and second in the conference. Detroit won the conference tournament and earned the league's automatic bid. Roster turnover hits Cleveland State hard this season, while Detroit returns several key players, including Ray McCallum Jr., one of the most exciting players in the conference.

Are any of these teams likely to justify an at-large bid in the near future? It won't be easy. Since head coach Gary Waters took over at Cleveland State in 2006, Ken Pomeroy has ranked the Vikings in the top 100 in three separate seasons, peaking at No. 60 in 2009. Detroit hasn't cracked the top 100 in the Pomeroy ratings since 2004, while the last time Valparaiso made the top 100 was 2003. On the other hand, in the three seasons where Butler earned at-large bids its Pomeroy rankings were Nos. 45, 25, and 32. Over the last 10 seasons of Horizon League play, the highest season-ending Pomeroy ranking by a school other than Butler was Milwaukee's ranking at No. 53 in 2005.

Valparaiso is likely to be the best Horizon team this season. The Crusaders are relative newcomers to the league, having joined in 2007. Valpo also has some NCAA tournament magic in their recent history. Current head coach Bryce Drew's game-winning shot in the first round of the 1998 tournament propelled the Crusaders on an NCAA tournament run that ended in the Sweet 16. Valparaiso has the best shot of being the fun underdog from Indiana next March, keeping the Horizon League in the eye of the wider basketball viewing public. The Crusaders return several of the top players in the conference, including 2012 Horizon player of the year Ryan Broekhoff. In addition, Drew has brought in several transfers from major-conference programs.

But while there are good teams left in the Horizon League, the loss of Butler, in terms of national prestige, is a huge blow. The Horizon's status as a "high mid-major" is in danger.

Teams listed in Jeff's predicted order of finish.

VALPARAISO

2012: 22-12 (14-4 Horizon); Lost to Miami 66-50, NIT first round
In-conference offense: 1.05 points per possession (3rd)
In-conference defense: 0.99 points allowed per possession (5th)

Last season was Bryce Drew's first as head coach of Valparaiso after he took over for his father, Homer. In fact this season marks the 25th consecutive year where a member of the Drew family is calling the shots for Valpo—Scott Drew was also head coach of the Crusaders for one year before moving on to Baylor. The Crusaders had one of the best offenses in the Horizon League last season, leading the conference in effective field goal percentage (55). A large part of Valpo's success on offense was due to shot selection. Coach Drew's squad took 40 percent of their field goal attempts from three-point range, and when they weren't taking shots from beyond the arc, they were working to get the ball inside. Coming into his second year, Drew returns a strong front line that includes conference player of the year **Ryan Broekhoff**. The 6-7 senior from Australia is a handful for opponents. Broekhoff is a career 40 percent three-point shooter, outstanding rebounder, and a threat to score around the rim. Senior forward **Kevin Van Wijk** also had a strong season as an effective scorer inside. **Bobby Capobianco**, a 6-9 transfer from Indiana, will be eligible to play this season, adding more depth at forward. While the front line appears to be in good hands, there are some questions as to who will get the minutes in the backcourt for the Crusaders. Three-point specialist **Will Bogan** and starting point guard **Erik Buggs** return, while Jay Harris has transferred out of the program. Look for South Florida transfer **LaVonte Dority** to push for minutes at point guard once he becomes eligible mid-season. Senior guard **Matt Kenney**, who has a knack for getting to both the rim and the foul line, and 6-4 Hawaii transfer **Jordan Coleman** will also be in the mix. The Crusaders look deeper and more talented than any other team in the Horizon League.

DETROIT

2012: 22-14 (11-7 Horizon); Lost to Kansas 65-50, NCAA round of 64
In-conference offense: 1.06 points per possession (2nd)
In-conference defense: 1.02 points allowed per possession (7th)

Detroit is one of the few Horizon League teams that looks to score in transition. They should. The Titans' offense last season was fantastic in transition, but ordinary in the half-court. With junior point guard **Ray McCallum Jr.**, it makes sense to run. There are very few holes in McCallum's game, and his careful stewardship of the offense was a major reason why Detroit was so good at limiting turnovers. If there's a weak spot in McCallum's game, it's that he struggles with his jump shot. But when he can get out on the break with 6-5 senior **Doug Anderson**, the combination is terrifying for opponents. Anderson is an explosive finisher who has a knack for getting to the free throw line. At 6-7 **Evan Bruinsma** is another inviting target for McCallum's dishes on the break. And maybe McCallum will find a new running mate this season in 6-6 sophomore wing **Juwan Howard Jr.**, a transfer from Western Michigan. The other returning starter is 6-2 junior **Jason Calliste**, a career 37 percent three-point shooter from the wing who's reliably drawn four fouls per 40 minutes for two seasons. This is a good team on the fast break, but the other side of the ball is another story, as Detroit struggled on defense last season. Despite leading the Horizon league in block percentage, the Titans were ninth in opponents' effective field goal percentage—a strange combination. Horizon opponents hit 41 percent of their three-point attempts against coach Ray McCallum Sr.'s squad, which feels a lot like a fluke that is unlikely to repeat this year. On the other hand, most of those blocked shots were swatted by Eli Holman and LaMarcus Lowe, who were both seniors last year. Detroit will look to no fewer than three junior college transfers (6-11 **Olumide Solanke**, 6-10 **Ugochukwu Njoku**, and 6-8 **Jermaine Lippert**), along with Bruinsma, to fill the void inside. With Holman gone, Coach McCallum also hopes 6-9 senior **Nick Minnerath** can reprise his highly efficient ways on offense after missing all but five games last season with a knee injury. Detroit will be a fun team to watch, but to be really good the Titans will need one or more of the big men to step up their game at both ends of the floor.

CLEVELAND STATE

2012: 22-11 (12-6 Horizon); Lost to Stanford 76-65, NIT first round
In-conference offense: 1.08 points per possession (1st)
In-conference defense: 0.95 points allowed per possession (2nd)

Even with a late-season swoon that saw Cleveland State drop five of their last seven regular-season games, the Vikings led the Horizon League in point differential per possession last season. Having the best offense and second-best defense in the conference will do that. Duplicating that feat this season will be difficult, as coach Gary Waters' team is young. A large portion of the Vikings success on offense in conference play came from making 41 percent of their threes and crashing the glass to generate second chance points. The problem for Waters is that three of his most important perimeter players last season were seniors. Jeremy Montgomery and the aptly named Trey Harmon accounted for many of those made threes, while ball hawk D'Aundray Brown is no longer around to mess with opposing ball handlers. Now it's up to 5-9 sophomore **Charlie Lee** to do most of the ball handling. As a freshman he struggled with turnovers and his shot, so Viking fans will have to hope for a sophomore breakout this season. Lee will likely be joined in the backcourt by 6-6 **Marlin Mason** and 6-4 **Sebastian Douglas**, two sophomores who saw very limited minutes last season. In the frontcourt 6-7 senior **Tim Kamczyc** has been highly effective in a limited role in the offense, but he'll need to carry more of the load this year. There's no question Kamczyc can shoot the three and is effective at finishing at the rim, Waters just needs him to do it more often. On defense, the Vikings will rely on 6-8 sophomore **Anton Grady** to be their anchor. Grady's an outstanding rebounder and shot blocker who's also no slouch on offense. Cleveland State led the conference in opponents' effective field goal percentage, and was the second best team in the league when it came to forcing turnovers. These two areas have generally been strengths for CSU under Waters, and there is no reason to believe this will change. Then again Waters' teams also generally have trouble on the defensive glass and with fouls, so if there is some drop off in forced turnovers with the loss of Brown, the Viking defense will take a step back.

GREEN BAY

2012: 15-15 (10-8 Horizon); Lost to Youngstown State 77-60, Horizon first round
In-conference offense: 1.03 points per possession (5th)
In-conference defense: 1.02 points allowed per possession (8th)

Last year Green Bay was a young team with a lot of size. This year the Phoenix will be a somewhat more experienced team with a lot of size. **Alec Brown** was the focal point of coach Brian Wardle's offense, but Brown's 47 percent two-point shooting was inefficient coming from a 7-1 featured scorer in the Horizon. A high proportion of Brown's attempts were away from the rim, which accounts for his relatively low field goal percentage. On the defensive end, Brown's an effective shot blocker and a solid rebounder. Wardle's frontcourt also includes 6-9 senior **Brennan Cougill**, a skilled big man who can score near the basket, as well as step out and hit the three. Running the point will be 5-10 sophomore **Keifer Sykes**. As a freshman Sykes took care of the ball and got to the rim, but his 67 percent free throw shooting left something to be desired. Green Bay can take a significant step forward if their point guard improves as a shooter. Sykes will be joined in the backcourt by three-point phenomenon **Kam Cerroni**, a 6-2 junior who drained 47 percent of his 129 three-point attempts last season. Also capable of knocking down long range shots are 6-1 junior college transfer **Sultan Muhammad** and 6-4 sophomore **Cole Stefan**, a La Salle transfer who'll be eligible after the first semester. Despite all the size on the interior, the Phoenix were not good on defense last season. Even with a height advantage over the rest of the Horizon, Green Bay struggled to control their defensive glass. Wardle's team was also hurt on the perimeter, as conference opponents shot 40 percent from three-point range. The Phoenix were good at defending the two-point shot, however, thanks to Brown and Cougill. If things break right for Green Bay, they seem like a good bet to surprise this year in the Horizon. At the very least, they should be in the middle of the pack on both offense and defense, assuming opponents stop killing them from three.

YOUNGSTOWN STATE

2012: 16-15 (10-8 Horizon); Lost to Detroit 93-76, Horizon quarterfinals
In-conference offense: 1.04 points per possession (4th)
In-conference defense: 1.01 points allowed per possession (6th)

Youngstown State excelled at avoiding turnovers and making threes last season. Coach Jerry Slocum's team hoisted threes early and often (four starters attempted more than 100), shooting them in transition situations, as well as out of half-court sets. The Penguins are led by 6-0 junior point guard **Kendrick Perry**, who upped his minutes, usage, and efficiency markedly during an exemplary if underpublicized sophomore season. His low turnover rate is critical to the team's success. Both Perry and 6-1 senior **Blake Allen** will let the shots fly, and both will be on the floor more or less all the time. Playing time at a third guard position (filled last season by senior Ashen Ward) will be up for grabs. Candidates include 6-4 sophomore **Shawn Amiker** and 6-4 freshman **Ronnye Beamon**. Minutes are also available in the frontcourt now that DuShawn Brooks has departed after his senior season. That playing time could go to a veteran (6-9 junior **Josh Chojnacki** or 6-8 sophomore **Fletcher Larson**), or it may fall to one or more of Slocum's freshmen: **Bobby Hain** (6-10), **Ryan Weber** (6-6), **Kamren Belin** (6-7), or walk-on **Larry Johnson, Jr.** (6-4), son of the former UNLV and NBA great. The recipient of those minutes will slide in alongside 6-7 senior **Damian Eargle**, who's made his presence known on both sides of the ball the past two seasons. Eargle's efficiency has been hampered by his struggles from the free throw line—he's a 55 percent career shooter at the stripe—and he made just 45 percent of his twos last season. As a junior, he attempted large proportion of his shots away from the rim, which is rarely a recipe for success as a big man. Eargle's shot distribution highlights a larger issue with the Penguins last season: YSU was a jump shooting team. That's fine when a high proportion of those jumpers are three-point attempts and those threes go in, but in general teams that take a large number of two-point jump shots tend to struggle with their shooting efficiency. On defense Slocum's men finished in the middle of the conference in terms of points allowed per possession, even though Eargle led the Horizon (and placed No. 11 nationally) in block percentage. The Penguins did a nice job of not putting their opponents at the free throw line, but struggled on the defensive glass.

MILWAUKEE

2012: 20-14 (11-7 Horizon); Lost to TCU 83-73, CBI first round
In-conference offense: 0.99 points per possession (6th)
In-conference defense: 0.97 points allowed per possession (4th)

Coach Rob Jeter believes in the power of the three-point shot. The Panthers shoot a lot of them, and they work hard to limit opponents' attempts from three. It's a strategy employed by many top coaches, including Bo Ryan. And it is no accident that Jeter takes this approach, as he spent 10 seasons as an assistant to Ryan. You can see why this approach is appealing to coaches—the number of threes a team attempts and allows is at least partially within a coach's control. Once the ball's in the air, though, it's a different matter. Who will be launching it from three this season for the Panthers? Kaylon Williams, Ryan Allen, and Tony Meier were seniors last season, and Shaquille Boga and Ja'Rob McCallum have transferred out of the program. The only remaining perimeter player who saw significant minutes last season is 6-2 senior **Paris Gulley**, and he'll miss time early in the season with a broken hand. Junior college transfers **Jordan Aaron** and

Thierno Niang will be needed to contribute right away, with Aaron likely ending up as the primary ball handler. The Panthers look to have more continuity on the front line. Senior **James Haarsma** returns, and could wind up being an all-conference player. At 6-7, the one time transfer from Evansville is an inside-outside player who can shoot the three, score inside, and is tough on the offensive glass. Haarsma will be joined in the frontcourt by some combination of 6-9 junior **Kyle Kelm**, 6-7 senior **Demetrius Harris**, and/or 6-10 freshman **J.J. Panoske**. All three are big, and all three will be expected to rebound. Like his old boss, Jeter demands that his teams control the defensive glass.

WRIGHT STATE

2012: 13-19 (7-11 Horizon); Lost to Butler 70-52, Horizon first round
In-conference offense: 0.93 points per possession (9th)
In-conference defense: 0.96 points allowed per possession (3rd)

Last season Wright State had the third best defense in the Horizon League, but the way that the Raiders did it was strange. Billy Donlon's defense reduced the number of shots their opponents took by forcing turnovers on 26 percent of their possessions in conference play, tops in the Horizon. In fact in all of Division I, just three teams forced a higher rate of turnovers than did Wright State. Donlon's team was also strong on the defensive glass, further reducing opponent shot attempts. In possessions where Wright State wasn't forcing turnovers, however, things were often ugly. In conference play, WSU's opponents made a scorching 54 percent of their twos. In effect the Raiders provided no protection for the rim, aside from fouling. And Wright State fouled a lot, putting opponents on the line more frequently than any Horizon defense except perennially foul-happy Cleveland State. Opponents also launched 40 percent of their field goal attempts from three-point range. Generally, it's bad to give up so many threes, but with so little interior D Donlon's squad was actually better off letting opponents shoot from out there. While the Raiders liked to apply pressure on defense and play for steals, they made little effort to score in transition on non-steal possessions. They didn't attempt many threes, but they also struggled to get to the rim. Throw in a bunch of turnovers and little in the way of second chances, and the result is a bad offense. To make matters worse, Wright State's best offensive player, Julius Mays, transferred to Kentucky, so this season Donlon will look to 6-10 junior **AJ Pacher** to carry the load on offense. Pacher saw limited action last season (averaging nine fouls per 40 minutes will do that), but when he played he was the focal point of the offense. **Reggie Arceneaux** can hit the occasional shot from outside, though the 5-9 sophomore had problems with turnovers in his first college season. **Matt Vest** could also see a fair number of touches on offense, assuming the 6-5 junior has recovered from the foot and ankle injuries that plagued him in 2011-12. With so many young players on the roster, expect 6-8 junior **Cole Darling** and 6-1 junior college transfer **Miles Dixon** to also play important roles.

UIC

2012: 8-22 (3-15 Horizon); Lost to Milwaukee 68-55, Horizon first round
In-conference offense: 0.96 points per possession (8th)
In-conference defense: 1.09 points allowed per possession (9th)

Head coach Howard Moore has a roster full of new faces for 2012-13, and several of the best players from last season's 8-22 team return, giving the Flames a realistic chance to improve. **Hayden Humes** should look for his shot more, as the 6-8 junior is by far UIC's most effective jump shooter. **Gary Talton**, a 6-1 senior, and 6-3 sophomore **Joey Miller** (an Eastern Illinois transfer eligible this season due to an NCAA hardship waiver) will compete for minutes at point guard, while 6-4 sophomore **Marc Brown** has already shown an ability to get to the line. In addition to Miller, there are many new players on UIC, and some of them are going to have to contribute. Junior college transfer **Jay Parker** could push for minutes in the backcourt, but the real need is along the front line, where only Humes and little used 6-10 sophomore **Will Simonton** return. Two freshmen, 7-0 **Matt Gorski**, and 6-8 **Jake Wiegand**, could see rotation minutes. Though Humes' return and the infusion of new talent gives UIC a chance to climb out of second-to-last in the Horizon this season, the gap between the Flames and Wright State last season was rather large in terms of both won-loss record and point differential per possession. To put someone besides crosstown rival Loyola beneath them in the standings, Moore's team will have to be substantially better this season.

LOYOLA

2012: 7-23 (1-17 Horizon); Lost to Detroit 80-71, Horizon first round
In-conference offense: 0.92 points per possession (10th)
In-conference defense: 1.09 points allowed per possession (10th)

Loyola had both the worst offense and the worst defense in the Horizon last season, and the Ramblers' only conference win came at home against a UIC team that was on its way to a 3-15 finish in league play. A BracketBusters win (on the road, no less) against Bradley may have lifted spirits a little on the lakeshore, but basically there's nowhere to go but up. **Ben Averkamp** was second-team all-conference last season, and pretty much the only bright spot for Loyola. The 6-8 senior has a nice stroke from three-point range, makes plays for others, rebounds, and even blocks the occasional shot. **Cully Payne**, a 6-1 Iowa transfer, is now eligible, and the former member of the Sporting News All-Big Ten freshman team will likely do most of the ball handling for coach Porter Moser. **Jordan Hicks** has been granted an extra year of eligibility by the NCAA, which is only fair because the 6-6 senior has never really been healthy during his career. During the Ramblers' August trip to Italy, Hicks was a starter and this season he'll be expected to contribute. Sophomores **Joe Crisman** and **Christian Thomas** will likely fill out the starting five for Moser. For depth Loyola will call on freshmen: **Matt O'Leary** scored 22 points in one of the team's games in Italy, and **Jeff White** and **Devon Turk** are also likely to play. The Ramblers took their lumps in Moser's first season, and while improvement's the safe forecast for a team that just went 1-17, that improvement is likely to be modest in 2012-13. Averkamp, Payne, and Hicks notwithstanding, this is a very young roster.

Missouri Valley

BY MATT GILES

There are few certainties in Division I basketball, but in the second oldest league in Division I, the Missouri Valley Conference, some things never change. Each team will have several upperclassmen on the roster. Defense is held in almost reverential regard. And, perhaps most crucially of all, realignment does not exist in the Valley.

The last team to join the MVC was Evansville in the mid-1990s, and since then there have been virtually no membership changes. Unlike the formation of mega-conferences across the nation, the Valley has been a paragon of stability. Sure, there have been coaching changes, and players do transfer, but the members who annually contend for the Arch Madness crown have remained the same for the past 16 seasons.

There were two coaching changes this past offseason. Barry Hinson replaced Chris Lowery at Southern Illinois, and the hiring was a pseudo-homecoming for Hinson, who spent five seasons coaching Missouri State. His Bear squads were known for efficient offenses that continuously pushed the pace. There is promise in Carbondale, but SIU will likely camp within the conference's bottom tier, jostling for position with Bradley and Missouri State.

Tim Jankovich trekked to SMU to serve as Larry Brown's coach-in-waiting, but Dan Muller inherited a plum situation at Illinois State. Nic Moore followed Jankovich to Dallas, but study rebounder Jackie Carmichael returns with the potential to average a double-double, a feat not accomplished by a Redbird in decades.

The consensus top squad is Creighton, one of the two MVC teams to make the 2012 NCAA tournament, and a likely bet to again make the field of 68. The Bluejays have vowed to amplify their defensive intensity, but if the efforts occasionally short-circuit, the offensive core of Greg McDermott, Grant Gibbs, and Gregory Echenique should still carry the squad to the Dance. Rather than parlay his sophomore campaign into NBA highlight reels, McDermott returned to Omaha to build off his USBWA first-team All-America selection—the first Valley player so honored in over 20 years.

Wichita State was the other MVC squad to make a tournament appearance, and coach Gregg Marshall will depend on a mix of junior college players, returnees, and a Pac-12 transfer for a repeat occurrence. The Shockers, though, could fall to third place because Northern Iowa is back. UNI's defense faltered in recent years, but the Panthers have arguably the conference's best frontcourt. Seth Tuttle, like many players in the Valley, spent 2011-12 in McDermott's long shadow, but the forward will not be undervalued after his sophomore season.

For perhaps the first time in his career, Evansville's Colt Ryan is surrounded by enough Purple Aces to help relieve him of some of the team's scoring load. The question, though, centers on whether defensive miscues, which hampered Evansville a season ago, will continue.

Drake and Indiana State have legions of newcomers, so it is difficult to judge how quickly they will pick up their respective game plans. The Sycamores' trip to the Bahamas certainly helped the squad mesh, but injuries, which plagued Jake Odum, have already begun to hinder the team: Michael Samuels is potentially done for the season due to a broken foot.

Bradley enters the second year of a rebuild under Geno Ford and should show progress this season. Missouri State may be entering year one of a rebuild they didn't see coming, as the Bears adjust to life without Kyle Weems and Michael Bizoukas and do so without Jarmar Gulley, out for the year with a torn ACL.

Teams listed in Matt's predicted order of finish.

CREIGHTON

2012: 29-6 (14-4 MVC); Lost to North Carolina 87-73, NCAA round of 32
In-conference offense: 1.15 points per possession (2nd)
In-conference defense: 1.05 points allowed per possession (7th)

Creighton's 29 wins in 2011-12 were the most for the Bluejays in nearly a decade, and **Doug McDermott** became a poster boy for possession-based statistics. A season that ended with a loss to a No. 1 seed (North Carolina) and the return of virtually the entire team has fueled an almost unsustainable amount of hype surrounding Creighton. The Bluejays, however, have violated the code of the Missouri Valley: defense is essential to success. Creighton applied scant ball pressure, ranking last in conference turnover and steal rates. Coach Greg McDermott's top priority is improving the squad's defensive focus. The Bluejays' practice uniforms bear the number "222," a reminder of the team's defensive field goal percentage ranking. **Josh Jones** might prove useful in a defensive rebuild. He didn't play often, but his steal rate was one of the squad's best. And **Gregory Echenique**, the returning MVC defensive player of the year, was the only Bluejay with a block rate over four percent. A woeful foul rate kept 6-11 **Will Artino** tethered to the bench, though during his brief appearances he did haul in 25 percent of opponents' misses. (This season 7-0 redshirt freshman **Geoffrey Groselle** could challenge Artino for those frontcourt minutes.) If Creighton still can't contain opponents' scoring, though, the nucleus of McDermott, Echenique, and **Grant Gibbs** will again boost the squad. McDermott made 63 percent of his twos and 49 percent of his threes; no other D-I player used as many possessions and scored as many points. His accuracy from the field was unrivaled—he ranked in the nation's top ten for effective field goal and true shooting percentage. The definition of a mismatch, Gibbs stretches the defense with perimeter shooting and uses his 6-4 frame to make perfectly placed interior passes. Echenique grabbed 15 percent of Creighton's misses during his minutes, and should expand his game to include more post-ups and cuts around the basket. A potential breakout Bluejay is 6-1 junior **Jahenns Manigat**, a 47 percent three-point shooter. If the elder McDermott plays Manigat and noted freshman shooter **Isaiah Zierden** together, the Bluejays could create better spacing for McDermott and Echenique. Though his assist rate led Creighton, Gibbs is not a point guard, and without Antoine Young, the squad must find a player to direct the offense. **Austin Chatman** backed up Young and is the likely replacement.

NORTHERN IOWA

2012: 20-14 (9-9 MVC); Lost to Drexel 65-63, NIT second round
In-conference offense: 1.03 points per possession (5th)
In-conference defense: 1.01 points allowed per possession (4th)

Northern Iowa may best known for their defense, but there's a new quality that could define them: depth. Johnny Moran is the only 2011-12 Panther no longer on the roster, and this is the deepest UNI squad Ben Jacobson has had. Consequently, Northern Iowa is the only team in the Missouri Valley without any incoming recruits. Featured scorer **Anthony James**, a 6-0 senior, is suspended for the first three games, and 6-1 sophomore **Deon Mitchell** will likely replace him. Mitchell struggled mightily with turnovers, though he did post a high assist rate. **Marc Sonnen** will reprise his off-the-ball role. The Panthers were the slowest-paced team in MVC play, and a three-point shot is typically their first offensive option. The best perimeter shooter on a good perimeter shooting team may turn out to be 6-4 redshirt freshman **Matt Bohannon**. And, as remarkable as it may sound in a league that has Doug McDermott, UNI may have the Valley's most skilled frontcourt. **Nate Buss** added 20 pounds to his 6-9 frame, and the sophomore's outside shot and speed will cause match-up problems. **Seth Tuttle** made two All-MVC teams (All-Newcomer and All-Freshman—they make fine distinctions in the Valley) and became the first freshman to ever lead the Valley in field goal percentage, yet somehow avoided the hype. He's reportedly bulked up, which should help the 6-8 sophomore on the offensive glass and in the post. Tuttle excels at drawing fouls; he made 66 percent of his twos and nearly two-thirds of his attempts are the result of cuts, put backs, or paint touches. Of all D-I freshmen, only Tuttle and Cody Zeller had usage rates of 20 percent or more while also notching offensive ratings over 120. **Jack Koch** often deferred to his teammates as a 6-9 pseudo point-forward. If Mitchell's ball handling is no longer a concern, Koch's shots could increase since the big is still capable of converting inside the arc. When UNI advanced to consecutive NCAA tournaments in 2009 and 2010, the team's defensive focus was manifest. Then something slipped on that side of the ball. It took some time to rebuild a frontcourt without Jordan Eglseder and Lucas O'Rear. But now a combination of the bigs' weight room efforts, maturation, and the better defensive shooting percentages seen last season could signal a return to March Madness for the Panthers.

WICHITA STATE

2012: 27-6 (16-2 MVC); Lost to VCU 62-59, NCAA round of 64
In-conference offense: 1.15 points per possession (1st)
In-conference defense: 0.94 points allowed per possession (1st)

To some, Wichita State could be characterized as a typical rebuilding team. The squad has lost essentially four starters from last season, and Gregg Marshall must find a way to replace 73 percent of his team's scoring. However, depth has never been a concern for the Shockers. Marshall distributes minutes generously to his bench, so the returnees are experienced. Add in a recruiting class chock full of junior college players, and WSU is primed to defend their Valley regular-season title. Oregon transfer **Malcolm Armstead** has one season of eligibility, and the 6-0 senior is skilled at finding the open teammate. Additionally Marshall could bring highly-regarded 5-11 freshman **Fred Van Vleet** off the bench. Landing Van Vleet was regarded as a recruiting coup, and playing Armstead and the freshman together alongside WSU's bevy of wings could pay dividends in a conference where size doesn't necessarily equate to success. Marshall can also pair Armstead with either 6-2 sophomore **Tekele Cotton** or 6-2 senior **Demetric Williams**. Primarily a role player as a freshman, Cotton was arguably the team's best on-ball defender. Williams can play either guard position and, most importantly, he significantly decreased his turnover rate as a junior. And Marshall has named 6-3 redshirt freshman **Ron Baker** as the team's best shooter. At 6-8, **Carl Hall** is the only Shocker big who's not a project on offense. He struggled during the latter half of MVC play last season, but conventional wisdom stipulates junior college transfers bloom in their second go-round so there are high expectations for the senior. Hall will team with rebounders off the bench like 7-0 senior **Ehimen Orukpe** and 6-9 junior college transfer **Chadrack Lufile**. Perhaps the Shockers' most interesting position is the small forward. Both of Marshall's junior college transfers on the wing, 6-6 **Nick Wiggins** and 6-8 **Cleanthony Early**, are known for their ability to slash to the basket. Both are skilled in the open court, and their presence could speed up the tempo for the Shockers, especially if WSU goes small with both Wiggins and Early on the wings.

ILLINOIS STATE

2012: 21-14 (9-9 MVC); Lost to Stanford 92-88 (OT), NIT second round
In-conference offense: 1.04 points per possession (4th)
In-conference defense: 1.05 points allowed per possession (8th)

Illinois State took eventual champion Stanford into overtime before losing in the second round of the NIT, only to lose both their point guard and their coach to SMU in the offseason. Nic Moore transferred after a promising freshman season to stay with the coach who recruited him, Tim Jankovich. The departures were sudden, but new coach Dan Muller, formerly an assistant to Kevin Stallings at Vanderbilt, inherits a deep and experienced team. Well-known among Valley coaches, 6-9 senior **Jackie Carmichael** is strangely underappreciated nationally. Last season he converted 53 percent of his twos and drew six fouls per 40 minutes. Carmichael is tenacious on the glass, and grabbed nearly 30 percent of opponents' misses during his minutes, good for fifth nationally. Muller says his senior might be the "best rebounder I've been around." Carmichael should receive help on the interior from 6-9 senior **John Wilkins** and 6-10 sophomore **Jordan Threloff**. Wilkins was a starter last season as a stretch 4; he had a miserable season beyond the arc but made up for it by making better than half his twos. Threloff missed the Redbirds' postseason with an injured hand, but he's outstanding on the glass at both ends. In the backcourt Muller could hand the reins to 5-11 senior **Anthony Cousin** to start the season, though 6-3 sophomore **Johnny Hill** may also see minutes and the future could belong to 6-1 freshman **Kaza Keane**, who was on schedule to join the college ranks in 2013-14 until he reclassified. Point production should not be an issue: ISU has two of the conference's most efficient wings in 6-4 senior **Tyler Brown** and 6-7 junior **Jon Ekey**. They combined to shoot 43 percent from the perimeter on 319 attempts last season. Ekey posted the Redbirds' best offensive rating, and Brown carried the team in the NIT with his (not a typo) 93 percent three-point shooting over two games. **Bryant Allen**, a 6-0 junior who started his collegiate athletic career on the University of Minnesota football team, was a scoring spark off the bench in his first Redbird season and should continue in that role. Interestingly, ISU's defense was excellent (0.93 points allowed per possession) during three games of Arch Madness, after a nothing-special regular season. If that's carried forward into this season, Mullen will look very good very early in his head coaching career.

EVANSVILLE

2012: 16-16 (9-9 MVC); Lost to Princeton 95-86, CBI first round
In-conference offense: 1.08 points per possession (3rd)
In-conference defense: 1.04 points allowed per possession (6th)

Colt Ryan is one of the nation's top scoring talents, but, unfortunately for coach Marty Simmons and his staff, he was essentially the only Purple Ace opponents were concerned about in their scouting reports last season. However, there are some who believe that Evansville's capable of an NCAA appearance in 2013 thanks to the collective improvement in the players around the 6-5 senior. The Valley's sixth man of the year in 2012, 6-1 senior **Ned Cox** directs the offense when he's on the floor. Last season his assist rate jumped to 26 percent, and his already low turnover rate dropped even lower. **Troy Taylor** doubled his minutes from 2010-11 and still converted 51 percent of his twos. The 6-0 senior should continue to see minutes this season, even with the arrival of two highly regarded freshmen: **D.J. Balentine** and **Adam Wing**, 6-2 and 6-4, respectively. The development of Cox and Taylor has lessened Ryan's scoring burden, though he's still the alpha dog on offense. Without Doug McDermott or Jackie Carmichael, Ryan might be a consensus conference player of the year winner. He made just 45 percent of his shots inside the arc, but when he's fouled he shoots 84 percent at the line—and he draws six fouls per 40 minutes. Almost half of his possessions are on the perimeter, either spotting up or using a screen, and he converted 44 percent of his threes. The Aces needed the extra points because having one of the nation's shortest frontcourts hindered the defense. Evansville compensated by forcing turnovers on 25 percent of their defensive possessions. That was important, because Valley opponents made an amazing 55 percent of their twos against the Aces. Simmons went out and got two freshman bigs, 6-8 **David Howard** and 6-10 **Egidijus Mockevicius**, to remedy the size disadvantage. Their presence should allow 6-8 sophomore **Ryan Sawvell** to play at his more natural power forward position.

DRAKE

2012: 18-16 (9-9 MVC); Lost to Rice 74-68, CIT second round
In-conference offense: 0.99 points per possession (8th)
In-conference defense: 1.00 points allowed per possession (3rd)

After posting 18 wins in 2011-12 with the second-youngest team in the Valley, Drake's roster will be vastly different in 2012-13. Of the seven departing Bulldogs, none was more crucial that Rayvonte Rice, who transferred to Illinois after his sophomore year. Rice had a usage rate of 29 percent, and he was the sole Bulldog to get to the free throw stripe. Without Rice, though, Mark Phelps' team might be better at moving without the ball. The Bulldogs' assist rate ranked last in the MVC, and just one player had an assist rate above 20 percent. Beating Drake meant stopping Rice, Kurt Alexander, and **Ben Simons**, the three Bulldogs with shots-attempted rates over 25 percent. Since Alexander and Rice are no longer on the squad, Drake's offense may become less of an oligopoly and more socialistic. There are seven newcomers now on the roster, but the returnees' development will largely determine the team's success. A 6-8 senior, Simons posted Drake's best offensive rating last season, and hit his shots from both sides of the arc. He needs support, though, and two options could be 6-8 senior **Jordan Clarke** and 6-6 sophomore **Jeremy Jeffers**. Clarke grabbed 12 percent of Drake's misses during his minutes, while Jeffers made 43 percent of his threes. **Karl Madison** will likely serve as point again, but the 5-9 sophomore will compete with 6-1 junior **Gary Ricks Jr.** and 6-2 freshman **Micah Mason** for minutes. **Chris Hines**, a transfer from Utah, is immediately eligible and the 6-1 senior should provide an offensive spark. Accuracy has never been Hines' forte, but he's an additional ball handler who rarely commits turnovers. And Phelps has described 6-4 freshman **Kori Babineaux** as a wing possessing Rice-like qualities. Babineaux should bolster Drake's rebounding efforts, especially on the offensive glass. Also helping out on the boards will be 6-11 junior **Seth VanDeest**, who missed all of last season after shoulder surgery. VanDeest has also added about 40 pounds since arriving at Drake, so he can better compete with the conference's more physical frontcourts.

INDIANA STATE

2012: 18-15 (8-10 MVC), Lost to Robert Morris 67-60, CIT first round
In-conference offense: 1.00 points per possession (7th)
In-conference defense: 1.04 points allowed per possession (5th)

There are plenty of new names on Indiana State's roster. The squad underwent heavy turnover during the offseason, a mix of transfers and expiring eligibilities, and coach Greg Lansing must unearth a few Sycamores ready to contribute and mesh with 6-4 junior playmaker **Jake Odum**. In 2010-11 Odum encapsulated ISU's underdog narrative as a redshirt whose 30 percent assist rate helped the program make its first NCAA tournament in ten years. But last season he struggled with the increased attention opposing defenses paid him. He also suffered from plantar fasciitis most of the season, and in February he was diagnosed with a stress fracture in his shin. Not surprisingly, Odum's effectiveness dipped compared to his first season. His teammates weren't consistent either—even though Odum's 35 percent assist rate led the Valley, the squad scored just a point per possession. Odum is now reportedly healthy, however, few of his teammates saw many minutes last season, so there could be some non-conference scoring pains. Gonzaga transfer **Manny Arop**, a 6-6 junior, could develop into a featured target for Odum. Another option is 6-6 freshman **Khristian Smith**, a wing known for his athleticism and slashing abilities. Redshirt freshmen **Devonte Brown** and **Brandon Burnett** are familiar with Lansing's offensive pace and game plan, and could contribute early. But the newcomer who might provide the most significant impact is 6-4 junior **Dawson Cummings**. The junior college transfer is reputed to be a long-range threat who can play either guard position, and his presence will allow Odum to shift off the ball and showcase his new-found perimeter accuracy. Lansing's frontcourt does not share this same depth, however. **Michael Samuels**, who was supposed to replicate Myles Walker's interior production, is potentially lost for the season with a broken foot, leaving **Jake Kitchell** and 6-8 sophomore **Justin Gant** as the last remaining interior options. Lansing has already praised Kitchell as the team's most improved player. We'll see how accurate that is, because the 6-10 sophomore will garner extensive minutes immediately.

SOUTHERN ILLINOIS

2012: 8-23 (5-13 MVC); Lost to Indiana State 66-51, MVC first round
In-conference offense: 0.97 points per possession (9th)
In-conference defense: 1.09 points allowed per possession (9th)

Hired at Southern Illinois after Chris Lowery was dismissed, Barry Hinson faces a massive rebuilding project, but the Salukis do have some talent that could net out to a somewhat efficient offense. **Dantiel Daniels** was selected to the Missouri Valley's all-freshman team, and though he asked for his release after Hinson's hiring, the forward eventually decided to return to the school. His offense consists almost entirely of interior possessions, and Daniels is good at those: he made 57 percent of his twos, and is a strong offensive rebounder. He played just 54 percent of the Salukis' minutes, but if he can stay healthy the 6-5 sophomore should lead the squad in two-point attempts. Last season Lowery gave a total of 36 starts to two junior college imports from Monroe College in New York. Now 6-3 senior **T.J. Lindsay** and his 6-1 classmate **Jeff Early** have to show they can find an offensive groove. Early has shown some defensive promise, and Lindsay, along with 5-9 senior **Kendal Brown-Surles**, occupied the role of perimeter threat, but actually there weren't many perimeter threats on a Saluki team that ranked last in three-point accuracy (30 percent) during Valley play. This season's offensive leader will likely be Wyoming transfer **Desmar Jackson**. The 6-5 junior is a career 26 percent three-point shooter, and should probably just throw in the towel there. But in two seasons in Laramie he made 53 percent of his twos and drew between five and six fouls per 40 minutes while functioning as the Cowboys' featured scorer. He even posts very high steal rates. If nothing else Jackson should provide a shot of energy for Hinson, who on November 12 will take the court as a head coach for the first time since his Missouri State Bears lost to Illinois State in the quarterfinals of the 2008 Missouri Valley tournament.

BRADLEY

2012: 7-25 (2-16 MVC); Lost to Drake 65-49, MVC first round
In-conference offense: 0.90 points per possession (10th)
In-conference defense: 1.10 points allowed per possession (10th)

While it will be another challenging season for Bradley and second-year coach Geno Ford, there are several indications that the squad will likely avoid the Missouri Valley's cellar. Five of Ford's top six scorers return. **Walt Lemon Jr.** registered the biggest improvement of any BU player, and though turnovers still plagued him, the 6-3 junior enters this season as Ford's most efficient player. As a sophomore Lemon connected on 52 percent of his twos, and he's one of the few Braves capable of creating offense off the bounce. Player development will be a key theme this season, and expect more minutes for 6-2 sophomore **Jalen Crawford**, an offensively creative guard who scarcely played his first year. He'll compete for minutes with 6-1 freshman **Ka'Darryl Bell**, who has the reputation as a combo guard who needs to improve his decision-making. **Dyricus Simms-Edwards** transitioned to a scoring role last season with mixed results. His perimeter shooting was adequate (34 percent), but his degree of success inside the arc can be inferred from an offensive rating of 88. And it was an influential 88, as Simms-Edwards led Bradley in minutes. This season Ford will need better results from his 6-3 senior. Similarly, 6-8 sophomore **Shayok Shayok** is a work in progress. Last season his offensive rating was 20 points lower than what Simms-Edwards posted. This team's best performer on the glass is **Jordan Prosser**, a 6-9 junior who rebounds 10 percent of the Braves' misses during his minutes, but he needs to get more points out of those offensive boards. A redshirt center, **Nate Wells** could provide rebounding support and he might be the squad's best interior defender at 7-1. **Jake Eastman** has progressed each season, but the 6-5 senior is more of a face-up big—over 40 percent of his possessions are spot-up attempts—and may lag behind 6-9 senior **Will Egolf** and 6-6 junior **Tyshon Pickett**. Egolf missed last season with a torn ACL; when healthy two-thirds of his offensive possessions are used in the paint. Ford believes junior college transfer Pickett could be a season-altering addition. Pickett matches up well with most MVC frontcourts and has no illusions of perimeter scoring. Using his physicality, he concentrates on converting from the block and the free throw line.

MISSOURI STATE

2012: 16-16 (9-9 MVC); Lost to Evansville 72-64, MVC quarterfinals
In-conference offense: 1.01 points per possession (6th)
In-conference defense: 0.99 points allowed per possession (2nd)

Even though Missouri State finished at .500 a year ago, the season was still regarded as somewhat of a disappointment. Before departing for Tennessee, Cuonzo Martin left Paul Lusk the pieces to challenge for a Missouri Valley title, but even though preseason conference player of the year selection Kyle Weems converted 40 percent of his threes, the offense sputtered to just over one point per possession. Now Lusk and his staff have to rebuild, and the Bears will struggle. Nearly 50 percent of the team's scoring is no longer at MSU, and the squad has yet to find a replacement for Michael Bizoukas, who posted the team's top assist rate of 32 percent. Tevin Bracey, a junior college transfer, was supposed to slide into the vacated point guard spot, but he left the school in mid-September. Jarmar Gulley, a senior wing, tore his ACL during the offseason, depriving the Bears of their most efficient player. Gulley made 53 percent of his twos and was primed to assume the mantle of leading scorer. Lusk will rely on 6-4 junior **Keith Pickens** and 6-1 senior **Anthony Downing** to shoulder the offensive burden. Pickens has been consistently plagued with injuries, and though he played the full 2011-12 season he wasn't completely healthy. Downing had an impressive inaugural year after arriving in Springfield as a junior college transfer. He was already taking 23 percent of the Bears' shots during his minutes, and this season that number should jump even higher. Though they each averaged less than 17 minutes a game last season, 6-5 junior **Nathan Scheer** and 6-7 sophomore **Christian Kirk** will see much more playing time. The squad adds six newcomers, who must quickly learn that though minutes are plentiful, defense is Missouri State's priority. There will be a Mount Everest-like learning curve this season but the additional minutes should prep the squad to improve significantly in 2013-14.

Mountain West

BY JEFF NUSSER

Like many conferences previewed in this book, the Mountain West is in a state of flux. BYU, a founding member of the conference, bolted for independence in football and the West Coast Conference in all other sports a year ago, and it was fair to wonder just what the departure of one of the premier basketball programs in the conference would do to the MWC's stature.

The league held up just fine, thank you very much. For the second time in three years, the MWC sent four teams to the NCAA tournament: New Mexico, San Diego State, UNLV, and Colorado State. The Rams were the surprise entry of the group, however, they were also the biggest testament to just how deep the league has become as the Pac-12 has faltered. Heck, if the Cougars had stuck around for another year, this would have been a five-bid league with just nine teams.

But change is afoot again. TCU has left the conference for the Big 12, and Nevada and Fresno State have arrived. Given the Wolf Pack's hoops history, that's probably a net gain. However, San Diego State and Boise State will be departing at the end of this year, and while nobody will shed any basketball tears over the loss of the Broncos (we hardly knew ye!), losing the Aztecs to the Big West is a big deal. When that day comes, SDSU will be replaced by Stew Morrill's Utah State Aggies, and by San Jose State.

That's a concern for another day, though. In the meantime, conference fans ought to set their sights on what certainly could be another four-bid year for the league. Let's start with the usual suspects: UNLV, San Diego State and New Mexico.

Dave Rice promised to put the "run" back in the Runnin' Rebels, and he wasn't kidding. UNLV's adjusted tempo jumped up to 70 possessions per 40 minutes, good for No. 29 nationally. The end-to-end style definitely made the Rebels more entertaining, certainly not something to be dismissed out of hand in Las Vegas. The fascinating thing about the Rebels' acceleration, though, is that it didn't translate into a higher two-point percentage, or even in more free throws—both rates were down from 2011. Instead, UNLV shot just about every transition three it could muster and made a good share of them (37 percent).

Despite the style change, the results for the Rebels ended up looking remarkably similar to the previous year, something that won't sit well with Rice for another season. UNLV is loaded with talent, thanks to the return of all-conference selections Mike Moser and Anthony Marshall, and the addition of freshman Anthony Bennett, ranked the No. 6 recruit in the nation by RSCI. At 6-8 and 240 pounds, Bennett exemplifies the term "power" forward.

As for San Diego State, we're guessing there weren't many out there who doubted Steve Fisher's coaching ability before last season, but in case there were a handful of holdouts, all questions should have been answered by last March. The Aztecs lost their top four scorers from their historic 2011 team—including an NBA first-round pick in Kawhi Leonard—and all they did was win at least 20 games for the seventh consecutive year, earn a share of the MWC regular-season championship, and advance to their third consecutive NCAA tournament as a No. 6 seed. And SDSU did it all while being rated for most of the season between Nos. 50 and 60 by Ken Pomeroy's skeptical laptop.

Such is the power of beating the teams you're supposed to beat, winning a couple of games against the Pac-12, prevailing against a couple of the better teams on your schedule, and generally only losing to the very good teams. Some might chalk that up to coaching; some might ascribe that to the players. Whichever way you lean, here's the good news:

Fisher and virtually the entire roster return, led by 2012 conference player of the year Jamaal Franklin. The Aztecs will dream big in their MWC swan song.

New Mexico tied with San Diego State for the league title, but statistically speaking the Lobos were the class of the Mountain West last season. In conference play, Steve Alford's squad finished first in no fewer than nine different statistical categories, including both offensive and defensive efficiency. A large part of that statistical preeminence was due to New Mexico's large presence in the middle, Drew Gordon, who led the charge on both ends of the floor.

But now Gordon's gone, and the Lobos will rely on what might be the best collection of guards in the league. Kendall Williams in particular could make a push for conference player of the year. Still, there are some big question marks up front in Albuquerque, as Alford's relying on the return of Alex Kirk after the 7-0 sophomore missed all of last season with a back injury.

Can any team mount a serious challenge to the Mountain West's big three? Colorado State and Nevada seem to be the most likely candidates, and both will scoff at the notion that this can only be a four-bid league. They'll want five.

Tim Miles is now at Nebraska, but his fingerprints are still all over a CSU program that improved from seven wins in his first year to 20 wins and an NCAA tournament berth in his fifth and final season. That's great news for new coach Larry Eustachy, who, for the first time in a long time, isn't tasked with a rebuild. The Rams return 78 percent of their minutes and 83 percent of their offensive production.

The Wolf Pack are new to the MWC, but they're unlikely to be intimidated after reclaiming their ownership of the WAC last season. Every year, there's a deserving regular-season conference champion that gets left out of the NCAA tournament because it loses in the conference tournament. Nevada was the poster child last year after winning its conference by three games before losing to Louisiana Tech (of all teams) in the WAC semis. While the road to a conference championship will be littered with more road blocks than ever before, the Wolf Pack do have a tremendous weapon in WAC player of the year Deonte Burton, perhaps still the best kept secret in the country.

Further down the Mountain West pecking order are Wyoming, Air Force, Boise State, and Fresno State. The Cowboys (Leonard Washington) and Falcons (Michael Lyons) have established all-conference second team performers leading the way, while the Broncos have an emerging young star (Derrick Marks). Fresno State will be looking to its most touted recruit in years (Robert Upshaw).

Teams listed in Jeff's predicted order of finish.

UNLV

2012: 26-9 (9-5 MWC); Lost to Colorado 68-64, NCAA round of 64
In-conference offense: 1.05 points per possession (3rd)
In-conference defense: 0.97 points allowed per possession (3rd)

The Runnin' Rebels are a three-point shooting team in a three-point shooting league. Top returning shooters **Mike Moser**, **Anthony Marshall**, and **Justin Hawkins** combined to attempt 335 threes but connected just 31 percent of the time. And unfortunately for Dave Rice the guy who hit 36 percent of his threes, Oscar Bellfield, has graduated. Marshall, a 6-3 senior who was primarily a shooting guard last season, takes over for Bellfield. While Marshall's assist rate (27 percent) suggests he can handle the duty, he's still somewhat turnover-prone. Moser will also change positions, moving into the wing spot occupied last year by Chace Stanback. Whether he plays from the 3 or the 4, though, the 6-8 Moser is still fairly unrefined offensively, and he struggled in the second half of the season as teams learned his tendencies and took them away. That being said, Moser can change a game with his defense alone. He was second in the league in defensive rebounding (28 percent), sixth in blocks, and fourth in steals. A lot of transition opportunities start with Moser. In the paint, 6-9 sophomore **Khem Birch**, a Pitt transfer and 2011 McDonald's All-American, will be eligible after the fall semester. And both 6-11 junior **Carlos Lopez-Sosa** and 6-8 senior **Quintrell Thomas** are excellent offensive rebounders who also are efficient with their limited offensive touches. If either player can get his tendency to foul under control and play more than 15 minutes a game, it would be a huge boost to the Rebels. The ultimate success of the season, however, will likely hinge on how quickly Rice can get production out of one of the top recruiting classes in the nation. At 6-8, **Anthony Bennett** is a specimen with both an inside and an outside game. He is the highest rated recruit to hit the Mountain West in at least eight years. Three other freshmen will also play: 6-6 wing **Savon Goodman** impressed during the team's summer international tour; 6-5 guard **Katin Reinhardt** displayed nice touch from deep; and 6-1 **Daquan Cook** supported the notion that he's the point guard of the future. The newcomer who was set to potentially make the biggest splash of all was sophomore **Bryce Dejean-Jones**, a USC transfer who sat out last season. He's all scorer, but he'll have to wait. A broken bone in his non-shooting hand had Dejean-Jones sidelined as practice began.

SAN DIEGO STATE

2012: 26-8 (10-4 MWC); Lost to NC State 79-65, NCAA round of 64
In-conference offense: 1.02 points per possession (5th)
In-conference defense: 0.97 points allowed per possession (2nd)

Jamaal Franklin proved to be one of the more remarkable players in Division I last season, pulling down 23 percent of opponents' misses during his minutes at a listed height and weight of 6-5 and 185. This prowess, along with a relative lack of formidable frontcourts in the Mountain West, allowed Steve Fisher to play Franklin as a 4 toward the end of the year. A high-volume shooter who used 31 percent of SDSU's possessions when he was on the floor, Franklin was also the Aztecs' top offensive threat, drawing enough fouls (6.4 per 40 minutes) to offset so-so outside shooting. **Chase Tapley** transitioned seamlessly from role player to impact player, posting a 112 offensive rating on excellent outside shooting (43 percent on 178 attempts). Joining the 6-3 senior in the backcourt is 6-3 junior **Xavier Thames**, termed "steady, if unspectacular" in last year's book. As he fought through a nagging knee injury, Thames lived up to that description last season. Senior **James Rahon** and junior **LaBradford Franklin** round out the guard rotation. Rahon battled an injured foot all year and is supposedly healthy now. If so, he'll be looking to get back to his sophomore shooting form, when he hit 43 percent of his threes. However, Fisher's frontcourt is questionable. LSU transfer Garrett Green provided a one-year stopgap—an unexpectedly good one, actually—but now the responsibility will fall to 6-8 senior **DeShawn Stephens**, 6-9 sophomore **James Johnson** (a Virginia transfer), 6-7 sophomore **Dwayne Polee** (a St. John's transfer), and some freshmen. Stephens doesn't shoot much, using just 16 percent of possessions, but he's efficient in the opportunities he does take and is an excellent offensive rebounder (grabbing 13 percent of his teammates' misses). The problem is Stephens draws a lot of fouls, possibly because he makes just 40 percent of his free throws. Johnson was a highly touted recruit (RSCI No. 58 in 2010), but couldn't break into the rotation for Tony Bennett. He's the wild card in this bunch and could provide a major boost when he becomes eligible in December. **Winston Shepard**, a 6-8 power forward, is rated by RSCI as the No. 33 player in the 2012 class, but an arrest for marijuana possession over the summer has dampened some of the enthusiasm.

NEW MEXICO

2012: 28-7 (10-4 MWC); Lost to Louisville 59-56, NCAA round of 32
In-conference offense: 1.08 points per possession (1st)
In-conference defense: 0.91 points allowed per possession (1st)

Offensively the Lobos should be fine without Drew Gordon's production. Junior **Kendall Williams** is a true triple-threat who creates opportunities off the dribble to dish (28 percent assist rate), finish (50 percent on twos) and/or get to the line for a stellar offensive rating of 113. Although Williams did it while using a relatively modest 23 percent of possessions, it won't be surprising if the 6-4 junior is able carry a larger workload. Junior **Tony Snell** didn't take a ton of shots, but when he did the 6-7 swingman was deadly: 39 percent on 186 threes. He was efficient on his twos on the rare occasion he took them, but with that kind of length and shooting touch, simply shooting more often from beyond the arc could contribute mightily. Sophomore **Hugh Greenwood** was one of the last cuts from the Australian national team after a solid debut season, 5-9 senior **Jamal Fenton** is a shorter version of

Williams (without the free throws), and 6-2 junior **Demetrius Walker** flashed the ability that made him one of the most coveted recruits in the nation. Yes, the Lobos are just fine at guard and should be able to score with the best of them. The interior is where Alford could be searching for answers. Replacing Gordon and A.J. Hardeman are **Alex Kirk** and **Cameron Bairstow**. Kirk missed all of last season with a back injury; Bairstow played limited minutes last season, is foul-prone, and misses a remarkable number of shots around the basket (connecting on just 45 percent on his twos) for someone listed at 6-9 and 250. They are huge question marks. For his part, Alford insists the 7-0 Kirk is healthy and poised to become one of the premier big men on the west coast. It might seem hyperbolic at first, but Kirk did rebound 21 percent of opponents' misses and block 4.5 percent of their twos in his freshman campaign. Alford appears set to go with a roughly seven-man rotation, so health will be a key.

COLORADO STATE

2012: 20-12 (8-6 MWC); Lost to Murray State 58-41, NCAA round of 64
In-conference offense: 1.03 points per possession (4th)
In-conference defense: 1.03 points allowed per possession (5th)

New coach Larry Eustachy inherits players that have already made 191 starts for CSU, plus an incoming class headlined by two major-conference transfers. **Wes Eikmeier** and **Dorian Green** were the Rams' two leading scorers a year ago, and both return as seniors. The 6-3 Eikmeier transformed himself from a supporting player to the go-to guy, using 27 percent of CSU's possessions during his minutes, but he didn't sacrifice anything in the way of efficiency. Still, his 102 offensive rating isn't quite what you'd like to see from a high-usage player; more trips to the free throw line (where he's an 88 percent shooter) instead of settling for 263 two-point attempts (where he made just 42 percent) would be a good start. Green, on the other hand, was ultra-efficient, posting a 117 offensive rating while hitting 43 percent of his threes and 53 percent of his twos. Here's a guess that Eustachy will get the 6-2 Green to shoot more. Speaking of woefully underused assets, how about 6-5 senior **Pierce Hornung**? Using just 18 percent of possessions, his otherworldly 126 offensive rating was fueled by hitting 70 percent of his twos. Hornung was also one of the premier rebounders in the country, grabbing 18 percent of his team's misses (second in the nation) and 23 percent of opponents' misses. To cement his value on the defensive end, Hornung was also No. 22 nationally in steal percentage. He's raised his offensive rating each year while simultaneously increasing his offensive load. Why not see what he's capable of doing while using 20 percent of the possessions? Hornung will be paired with 6-10 Minnesota transfer **Colton Iverson**, who's limited offensively but a solid rebounder (13 percent offensive rebounding, 18 percent defensive) and a shot-altering presence around the rim. Filling out the frontcourt will be 6-6 senior **Greg Smith**, who actually trailed only Green in usage despite posting just a 96 offensive rating, and 6-9 junior college transfer **Gerson Santo**. In the backcourt, 6-4 Arizona transfer **Daniel Bejarano** is yet another interesting piece for which Eustachy can thank ex-coach Tim Miles. Reputed to have a sweet shooting stroke, Bejarano was a top-100 recruit in the 2010 class but couldn't rise above the glut of guards in Tucson. Glue guy **Jesse Carr**, a 6-2 senior, had the team's highest assist rate and specializes in rare but very accurate (43 percent) three-point shooting.

NEVADA

2012: 28-7 (13-1 WAC); Lost to Stanford 84-56, NIT quarterfinals
In-conference offense: 1.11 points per possession (1st WAC)
In-conference defense: 1.00 points allowed per possession (2nd WAC)

At some point, the entire country will be forced to sit up and take notice of **Deonte Burton**, the guy who posted a 115 offensive rating while using 24 percent of his team's possessions during his minutes. He shoots (37 percent on 156 threes), slashes, and dishes (28 percent assist rate). A nitpicker might say the 6-1 junior's two-point percentage is low (42 percent), and they'd be correct. If he improved that while also using 26 to 28 percent of possessions, the NBA would probably come calling. Pairing with Burton in the backcourt is 6-5 senior **Malik Story**, an efficient high-volume shooter who hit 42 percent of his 226 threes a year ago. The help behind them, however, is spotty. **Jerry Evans**, a 6-8 junior, is a nice piece who uses his length to great effect from beyond the arc, where he shot 39 percent on 77 threes. **Jordan Finn**, **Patrick Nyeko** and **Jordan Burris**—who posted offensive ratings of 89, 84 and 97 respectively—were used sparingly as David Carter was able to get by with a short rotation (three players averaged at least 31 minutes, and five averaged 25 minutes or more). Up front, 6-10 junior **Devonte Elliott** and 6-9 junior **Kevin Panzer** appear to be in line to replace stalwarts Olek Czyz and Dario Hunt, but both have struggled mightily offensively in their two seasons. Panzer has made some strides, but Elliott's offensive ratings each of the last two years have been in the low 80s. They'll get some needed help from junior college transfer **Ali Fall**, a big body at 6-9 and 250. If you want to brand the Wolf Pack "a year away," you'd have reason. Just two seniors, Story and Nyeko, figure to play rotation minutes this season.

WYOMING

2012: 21-12 (6-8 MWC); Lost to Washington State 61-41, CBI quarterfinals
In-conference offense: 0.98 points per possession (6th)
In-conference defense: 0.98 points allowed per possession (4th)

Using a formula that's worked so well for others—play defense, secure missed shots, walk the ball up, work the clock, forsake offensive rebounding to defend in transition, repeat cycle—Wyoming overcame the transfers of its top two scorers from 2011 and advanced to its first postseason since 2005. Under Larry Shyatt, the Cowboys went from a below average defensive club to membership in Division I's top 10 percent in adjusted defensive efficiency. **Leonard Washington** had a lot to do with that. The 6-7 senior is a force in the paint on both ends of the floor, but especially defensively, where he grabbed more than 27 percent of opponents' misses (No. 11 nationally) and led the MWC in block percentage. It's nothing less than a travesty that Washington was left off the MWC all-defense team. In his year off after transferring from USC, Washington developed an offensive game that, while still a bit raw, was good enough for him to post a 106 offensive rating while using 27 percent of possessions as Wyoming's go-to guy. He's superb around the basket (62 percent on twos) and draws lots of fouls. (Washington ran afoul of Shyatt's rules after the season and was suspended, but he was reinstated in September.) Not that Wyoming was a one-man show. **Larry Nance Jr.** was fourth in the conference in block percentage while proving that he had his father's nose for the basketball by rebounding 20 percent of opponents' misses as a lithe 6-8 freshman. The other returning starter is 6-4 senior **Luke Martinez**, a three-point devotee who shot twice as many times from beyond the arc (242) as anyone else on the team but connected on just 34 percent of his attempts. **Derrious Gilmore** is a 5-10 senior who figures to step in to the starting point guard spot, but turnovers were a serious problem for him, as they were for presumed backup **Riley Grabau**. Wyoming lost three starters and six players overall to graduation, so Shyatt filled the roster with a mix of freshmen and junior college transfers. Australian **Nathan Sobey**, a 6-4 junior, figures to provide immediate help in the backcourt, while fellow transfers **Derek Cooke Jr.** and **Matt Sellers**, at 6-9 and 6-10 respectively, will fill in behind Washington and Nance. Of the freshmen, 6-2 point guard **Josh Adams** will likely play significant minutes immediately.

AIR FORCE

2012: 13-16 (3-11 MWC); Lost to New Mexico 79-64, MWC quarterfinals
In-conference offense: 0.90 points per possession (8th)
In-conference defense: 1.05 points allowed per possession (7th)

The vagaries of relying heavily on one player were on display when **Michael Lyons**' injuries hampered his effectiveness. After producing at the level fans had come to expect in the Falcons' first nine games, Lyons hurt his ankle and missed the next six. Upon his return, he wasn't the same player, as his free throw rate, one of the driving factors in his efficiency, fell off a cliff. His two-point percentage also suffered as he battled a shoulder issue all year. As Lyons' offensive rating fell all the way to 96, the Falcons' overall efficiency suffered as well, to the point where this was the league's worst offense during Mountain West play. Even if the 6-5 senior is healthy this year, Lyons needs help. One of AFA's biggest problems on offense was poor three-point shooting, and that certainly wasn't Lyons' fault.

Point guard **Todd Fletcher**, wing **Mike Fitzgerald** and big man **Taylor Broekhuis** are the most likely candidates to supply non-Lyons efficient scoring. The AFA offense was the worst in the MWC at giving the ball away, something a team simply can't do if it chooses to do without offensive boards, as Dave Pilipovich apparently does. That starts with Fletcher. Fitzgerald is a superb shooter, hitting 39 percent of his 110 threes, while the 6-10 Broekhuis is most comfortable around the basket, but will also step outside. The problem with these three guys? Last season, they allowed less efficient players such as **Kamryn Williams**, **Max Yon** and **Kyle Green** to take (and miss) a lot of shots. If Lyons is healthy and Pilipovich can get the ball into the hands of the right guys, Air Force could be poised for a nice season—just a year later than we thought.

BOISE STATE

2012: 13-17 (3-11 MWC); Lost to San Diego State 65-62, MWC quarterfinals
In-conference offense: 0.93 points per possession (7th)
In-conference defense: 1.05 points allowed per possession (6th)

Head coach Leon Rice started 12 different players last year, but a lot of them came back, so Rice now has a deep and experienced squad. **Derrick Marks** burst onto the scene as a freshman and became the Broncos' highest usage player, putting up an admirable 100 offensive rating thanks to a tremendous ability to get to the free throw line. The 6-3 Marks also proved to be a capable passer, and even pitched in on the defensive glass, although his turnovers could stand to come down. Australian wing **Anthony Drmic** led the team in minutes played as a freshman and posted an excellent 109 offensive rating on 21 percent of possessions used, a remarkable feat considering he shot just 32 percent on 180 threes. Shooting was an issue for the whole team, and it doesn't help that the team's best three-point shooter, Drew Wiley, has transferred out. **Jeff Elorriaga** could fill that void, but he'll need to shoot more to do it (39 percent from three, but just 11 percent possessions used). **Igor Hadziomerovic** missed a number of games with a foot injury, but he did show a knack for getting to the free throw line. **Ryan Watkins** and 6-5 junior **Thomas Bropleh** both took a step back under their increased workloads. The 6-9 Watkins is foul-prone, but his rebounding rates (especially offensively, where he also pulls in 14 percent of his team's misses) were fantastic. Bropleh simply suffered a shooting slump as his effective field goal percentage sagged from 54 to 47, and his rebounding, assists and steals tailed off, too. Lining up next to Watkins in the frontcourt, **Kenny Buckner** makes 60 percent of his twos and grabs a stellar 14 percent of his teammates' misses. Newcomers include guard **Mikey Thompson**, **Jake Ness** and **Darrious Hamilton**, each of whom redshirted last season, and 2012 signees **Edmunds Dukulis**, **Joey Nebeker** and **Vukasin Vujovic**.

FRESNO STATE

2012: 13-20 (3-11 WAC); Lost to New Mexico State 65-49, WAC quarterfinals
In-conference offense: 1.00 points per possession (8th WAC)
In-conference defense: 1.05 points allowed per possession (5th WAC)

It sure didn't take long for former Texas assistant Rodney Terry to deliver on his reputation as a stellar recruiter, convincing RSCI No. 55 prospect and Fresno native **Robert Upshaw** to stay home for college. The seven-footer originally committed to Kansas State, but when Frank Martin bolted for South Carolina, Terry swooped in for what might have been the coup of the entire recruiting cycle. The Bulldogs face a stiff challenge moving into the MWC, but Upshaw augments what is already a pretty solid core. Terry leaned heavily on **Kevin Olekaibe** last year. The 6-2 shooting guard played nearly 90 percent of the Bulldogs' minutes and seemingly had the green light to shoot whenever he felt like it. That wasn't always a good thing, as he hit just 41 percent of his 236 twos and 34 percent of his 272 threes. The second busiest shooter was 6-8 **Kevin Foster**, who used 26 percent of the Bulldogs' possessions but posted just an 89 offensive rating. Foster should share more of the load with **Tyler Johnson** and **Jerry Brown**, two juniors who posted 106 offensive ratings. The 6-2 Johnson presumably will take over the point guard role, while the 6-7 Brown—one of the best in the nation at getting to the free throw line—likely starts next to either Foster or Upshaw. The trio should form one of the more formidable defensive lines in the MWC, as it's not every day you drop a seven-footer in between a pair of guys who already have posted excellent block percentages. Also available is 6-4 senior **Garrett Johnson**, who's been serviceable off the bench. The wild card is point guard. **Cezar Guerrero**, an Oklahoma State transfer, has applied for immediate eligibility, and if it's granted the 6-0 sophomore could be the starter. If not, Terry's other options include **Allen Huddleston**, a 6-2 transfer from Pacific, and 6-3 freshman **Aaron Anderson**.

WAC

BY ASHER FUSCO

Conference realignment is an oft-vilified character in the narrative of modern college athletics. It's about money, football, and, well, more money, and it seems to help university presidents at the expense of all other involved parties. But if the ultimate optimist wanted to try to embrace the new and constantly shifting world order of college sports, he or she could start by paying attention to the Western Athletic Conference this coming season.

The WAC is dealing with the nightmarish symptoms of conference realignment in a more up close and personal manner than perhaps any other league. This year's basketball WAC features 10 teams. Five are new additions to last season's eight-school WAC, which lost three of its old teams, including 2012 regular season champion Nevada.

It doesn't stop there. Because of the disintegration of the league's football-playing core, the 2013-14 WAC will look completely different than the 2012-13 edition. This year's WAC is a single-season petri dish, a chance to see what happens when 10 programs come together for one random season, tossing tradition aside for the sake of football, money, and the chance to enjoy Texas State at Idaho.

The new-look WAC drops perennial contender Nevada out of the picture, along with Hawaii and Fresno State, two teams that haven't threatened the top of the standings in the past five years. The five newcomers come from the Sun Belt (Denver), the Southland (UT Arlington, UTSA, and Texas State), and the independent ranks (Seattle). The factor that rescues the WAC from being an immediate casualty of conference realignment is its relative strength in 2012-13. The conference loses one of its best programs, but it also replaces two of its weakest basketball members with two of the Southland's better teams (along with an also-ran in Texas State) and an unusually strong independent in Seattle. The five teams the WAC added had a combined Pomeroy ranking of 171. The three departing programs' average position was 167. The five holdovers held an average position of 161. Sure, adding Texas State (No. 263) isn't great, but getting rid of Hawaii (213) doesn't hurt.

That isn't to say the WAC is ready to revisit the halcyon two-bid days of 2010 thanks to its recent reshuffling, but each of the league's top three teams is good enough to be dangerous as a No. 13 seed in the round of 64. There isn't an odds-on favorite in the WAC this season, as plodding-but-efficient Denver will compete against the conference's remaining legacy programs—Utah and New Mexico State—and a transitional UT Arlington team coming off a dominant season in the Southland.

In their inaugural season in the new conference, Denver and its ultra-efficient Princeton-style offense could conquer the WAC. The Pioneers lose Brian Stafford, the Sun Belt's best pure shooter in 2011-12, but they return Chris Udofia, a dynamic 6-6 wing who could stack up as the WAC's best two-way threat as a junior. With Udofia, the inside-out scoring and rebounding acumen of sophomore Royce O'Neale, the defense of Chase Hallam on the wing, and the 46 percent three-point shooting of sophomore Brett Olson, Denver has all the pieces in place to excel this season.

New Mexico State's attempt to make its second straight NCAA tournament appearance will be made more difficult by the loss of well-rounded star Wendell McKines. Post players Bandja Sy, Sim Bhullar and Tshilidzi Nephawe have big shoes to fill, but the team does return two solid starters on the wing. Utah State, looking to recover from an uncharacteristically pedestrian 8-6 conference record, will look to scoring guard Preston Medlin and efficient forward Kyisean Reed to fill in for departed seniors Brockeith Pane and Morgan Grim.

Outside of the league's presumptive top three, the league has a deep middle filled with teams that could finish near .500 or step up a rung into 10-victory territory. UT Arlington, which dominated the Southland to the tune of a +0.16 efficiency margin last season, will face substantial personnel losses during the move to a tougher conference. Kevin Butler and Jordan Reves will be one of the league's top frontcourt combinations, and the Mavericks will have the benefit of a Big 12 transfer in guard Reger Dowell. Idaho looks primed to improve this season, even if its in-conference win-loss record doesn't budge. The Vandals, who managed a 9-5 WAC record despite carrying a negative efficiency margin, lose their top two shooters but return a pair of hot shooters in Stephen Madison and Connor Hill alongside a strong class of junior college transfers.

Louisiana Tech has the makings of a program on the rise, thanks to a cast of veteran contributors and the defense-first approach of second-year coach Michael White. UTSA, a consistently successful program of late in the Southland, could field one of the league's top defenses but doesn't have the talent to hang with the WAC's frontrunners.

The bottom third of the conference should include Seattle, an independent with some noted success against big-name opponents over the past couple of seasons, along with San Jose State and Texas State. San Jose State has a lot of ground to make up after a dismal 1-13 season, and Texas State goes from being a struggling program in the Southland to a struggling program in the WAC, a more difficult conference.

All this shuffling isn't good for college athletics, and mid-major basketball isn't on the good end of many of these football-inspired transactions. The WAC's future as a league is unsettled, and many of these teams will be members of the Mountain West and conferences farther afield within the next year. At this point, all a WAC fan can do is sit back, take things season-by-season, and watch what happens.

Teams listed in Asher's predicted order of finish.

DENVER

2012: 22-9 (11-5 Sun Belt); Lost to Western Kentucky 67-63, Sun Belt semifinals
In-conference offense: 1.11 points per possession (1st Sun Belt)
In-conference defense: 0.97 points allowed per possession (5th Sun Belt)

The always good, never great Princeton-style offense coach Joe Scott brought to Denver from, you guessed it, Princeton, became a well-oiled machine in 2012. The Pioneers posted the Sun Belt's best points-per-possession mark, in the process generating the nation's best assist-per-field goal made ratio and the country's third-best effective FG percentage. Scott's 2012 team had just the right combination of sure-handed passers and lights-out shooters, as five of the Pioneers' most frequent long-distance shooters made 39 percent or more of their threes. Denver's pace figures to be less of an outlier in the WAC, where Utah State and Idaho aren't afraid to play low-possession contests. The Pioneers do lose three important pieces from the 2012 team, however. Never-miss shooter Brian Stafford is the biggest loss, followed by Rob Lewis, a solid defensive rebounder. Left over is a cast of contributors, highlighted by do-it-all 6-6 swingman **Chris Udofia**. The lanky 6-6 junior earned the Sun Belt's defensive player of the year award for his shot blocking and rebounding prowess while taking the largest share of the Pioneers' shots and making 61 percent of his twos. The WAC player of the year candidate will be joined by no fewer than three 6-5 mainstays: **Brett Olson**, a sophomore who buried 46 percent of his threes; **Chase Hallam**, a three-year starter who had his best season as a freshman; and **Royce O'Neale**, a sophomore who emerged as the team's best rebounder off the bench last season. One of the keys on offense could be 6-3 freshman **Nate Engesser**, who certainly fits the mold of a star under Scott, ranking fourth in Colorado state high school history in career threes made. The team will also look to 6-7 junior **Blake Foeman** for minutes. If Udofia continues to blossom into one of the nation's most well-rounded mid-major stars, and Engesser slides into the offense seamlessly, Denver could easily end up at or near the top of the WAC standings. But the Pioneers have a lot of productivity to replace given the loss of Stafford.

UTAH STATE

2012: 21-16 (8-6 WAC); Lost to Mercer 70-67, CIT championship game
In-conference offense: 1.08 points per possession (3rd)
In-conference defense: 1.04 points allowed per possession (4th)

Can Utah State revert to form and earn their fourth NCAA bid in five seasons? Or will Stew Morrill's program finish its stay in the WAC with a repeat of their "down" 2012. It's no surprise the Aggies didn't post a fourth straight 27-plus-win season in 2012 given the loss of do-it-all big man Tai Wesley and three other senior contributors (not to mention Brady Jardine's career-ending foot injury during the season). Still, it was a bit shocking to see Utah State fall out of the national spotlight, and there's no guarantee the Aggies will be back at the top of the WAC this season. Morrill has lost two starters, so the anchor of this Utah State squad will be 6-4 junior **Preston Medlin**, who posted the WAC's top offensive rating among players using 20 percent or more of their team's possessions. If Medlin can take on even more of the offensive load while maintaining anything near his current shooting accuracy (43 percent on threes, 58 percent on twos), he could be the conference's most valuable player.

TeNale Roland, a 6-1 junior college All-American, arrives with a reputation as a scoring point guard and may start. **Danny Berger**, a 6-6 junior, gives USU another three-point threat on the wing, where 6-4 junior college transfer **Marvin Jean** will provide depth. The most likely Aggie to step into Jardine's large shoes is 6-6 senior **Kyisean Reed**, one of the league's most efficient offensive performers in 2012. Morrill's options for minutes alongside Reed in the post include 6-10 sophomore **Jordan Stone**, who showed flashes of potential in nine minutes per game last season, 6-11 sophomore **Matt Lopez**, who could make an impact in his first full season after transferring from La Salle, and 6-10 Oklahoma State transfer **Jarred Shaw**, a junior who has the size and reputation if not track record to be a solid performer in the WAC. The Aggies need to find two solid starters from a cast of unknowns, but the potential of Medlin and Reed make Utah State a serious WAC contender.

NEW MEXICO STATE

2012: 26-10 (10-4 WAC); Lost to Indiana 79-66, NCAA round of 64
In-conference offense: 1.09 points per possession (2nd)
In-conference defense: 0.97 points allowed per possession (1st)

If not for a pesky 13-1 Nevada squad, New Mexico State would have run away with the 2012 WAC regular season title. Instead, Marvin Menzies' team had to settle for the league's best efficiency margin and its second-best record. The Aggies made their second NCAA tourney trip of the Menzies era anyway, thanks to a dominant run through the WAC conference tournament. NMSU might have a tough time matching that performance in 2013, even with Nevada now playing in the Mountain West. Wendell McKines, Hernst Laroche, and Hamidu Rahman are gone. Remaining are four proven players; arriving is a collection of newcomers from the high school and junior college ranks. **Tyrone Watson** and **Daniel Mullings**, the team's two starting wings, return for their senior and sophomore seasons, respectively. Watson's a 6-5 role player who took a step back statistically as a junior. Mullings is a promising 6-2 guard who hit 51 percent of his twos and showed some solid defensive chops, but turned the ball over too often. Menzies will need to either move Mullings to the point or turn to 6-1 sophomore **K.C. Ross-Miller**, a New Orleans transfer. Newcomers **Kevin Aronis** (a 6-3 junior college transfer) and **Matej Buovac** (a 6-7 freshman) should be able to step in and provide some immediate help on the wing. **Bandja Sy**, a 6-8 senior, could blossom into an all-conference performer this season. Returning 6-10 center **Tshilidzi Nephawe** will have a crack at the starting job as a junior. He excelled off the bench as a sophomore by drawing plenty of fouls and converting at a 74 percent clip from the free-throw line. Nephawe will compete with the team's most intriguing player for minutes. **Sim Bhullar**, top-100 recruit who nearly became a Xavier Musketeer, happens to be a 7-5 360-pound center who received some press from the New York Times for his Indian heritage and size before redshirting the 2011-12 season. It could be an uphill climb to a fourth NCAA tournament trip in seven seasons, but it's not out of the question for Utah State program making one last tour of the WAC before heading to the Mountain West in 2013-14.

UT ARLINGTON

2012: 24-9 (15-1 Southland); Lost to Washington 82-72, NIT first round
In-conference offense: 1.06 points per possession (2nd Southland)
In-conference defense: 0.90 points allowed per possession (2nd Southland)

When play wrapped on December 20, 2011, UT Arlington stood at 4-5 with a bad home loss to Samford and no victories of note. Then the Mavericks beat Kent State on a neutral court. Next came wins against two low-quality non-conference opponents. Then 13 more victories. Just like that, the Mavericks were 20-5 heading into a BracketBusters matchup at Weber State. UT Arlington dropped that game, despite leading at halftime, but won three of its final four regular season games to finish at 15-1 in the Southland. But their stellar run through a one-bid league wasn't enough after they lost to McNeese State in a fairly momentous Southland tournament upset. Even after building one of the college basketball season's most impressive streaks, the Mavericks were NIT-bound. The NIT is a destination Scott Cross's team will be lucky to reach in 2013, thanks to their move to the WAC and the exhausted eligibility of All-Southland performers LaMarcus Reed and Bo Ingram. Reed, the league's leading scorer, will be the toughest to replace. Physical 6-5 senior **Kevin Butler**, who earned All-Southland third team honors, will start alongside 6-10 senior **Jordan Reves**, who ranked fourth in the league in both offensive and defensive rebounding rates. Incumbent point guard **Shaquille White-Miller**, a 5-9 junior, will need to limit turnovers to fend off 6-1 junior **Reger Dowell**, an Oklahoma State transfer who started 11 games for the Cowboys over two seasons and change in Stillwater. Cross will lean on a number of newcomers during his first season in the WAC. Texas Tech transfer **Jamel Outler**, a 6-2 sophomore, could earn minutes in the backcourt, while 6-5 junior college transfers **Vincent Dillard** and **Greg Gainey** will add depth behind Butler and Reves up front. The substantial personnel losses will set the team back in their first and only WAC season (the Mavericks are just passing through on their way to the Sun Belt), but UT Arlington won't be a walkover by any means.

IDAHO

2012: 19-14 (9-5 WAC); Lost to Utah State 76-56, CIT second round
In-conference offense: 1.05 points per possession (4th)
In-conference defense: 1.06 points allowed per possession (6th)

A 19-14 record and a trip to the CIT constituted Idaho's most successful season since the late 1990s. The cornerstone of that success was perimeter shooting. Seniors Deremy Geiger and Landon Tatum hit 44 and 41 percent of their threes, respectively. Starting wing **Stephen Madison** made 37 percent of his threes, and reserve gunner **Connor Hill** drained 38 percent of his attempts from out there. This season the Vandals will look to two junior college transfers, 6-1 junior **Antwan Scott** and 5-10 junior **Robert Harris**, for outside shooting help. Scott made 37 percent of his threes last season at Ranger College, while Harris hit 42 percent of his tries at Eastern Arizona. The team's new starting point guard will also most likely come from the junior college ranks, as 5-10 Casper College product **Denzel Douglas** will fight for time with Harris. On top of replacing one of the steadiest backcourt combinations in the league, Don Verlin will need to replace forward Djim Bandoumel, the team's top post defender last season. Incumbent center **Kyle Barone**, who begins the season on an indefinite suspension, will pick up some of the slack in Bandoumel's absence, but the 6-10 senior will need to improve his 63 percent shooting at the line. The 6-5 Madison is a sure source of rebounds and efficient scoring on the wing, and 6-2 sophomore Hill, along with 6-2 senior **Mike McChristian** and 6-5 sophomore **Matt Borton**, provides scoring off the bench. Someone will need to step into a prominent role in the front court alongside Barone, and the most likely man for the job is yet again a junior college transfer, the 6-8 **Marcus Bell**. The top-50 junior college recruit will compete with 6-8 freshman **Ty Egbert** and seldom glimpsed returnees like 6-8 senior **Wendell Faines** and 6-9 junior **Joe Kammerer** for playing time up front. Idaho has a good mix of solid veterans (Madison and Barone) and high-upside newcomers (Bell, Scott and Harris), and it's easy to imagine the Vandals at or near .500 for a fifth straight season.

LOUISIANA TECH

2012: 18-16 (6-8 WAC); Lost to New Mexico State 82-57, WAC championship game
In-conference offense: 1.02 points per possession (5th)
In-conference defense: 1.03 points allowed per possession (3rd)

Two seasons ago Louisiana Tech finished 2-14 in the WAC and lost to Utah State in the last game of the season 72-30. At home. Thus endeth the Kerry Rupp era. In came Ole Miss assistant Michael White, who was handed an inexperienced roster short on star players. It looked like another long season was in store, but the Bulldogs were respectable thanks to an aggressive defense predicated on forcing turnovers. Now the team's top three perimeter defenders are back in the form of 6-3 sophomore **Raheem Appleby**, 6-1 junior **Kenyon McNeail**, and 6-3 sophomore **Kenneth Smith**. The go-to scorer in last season, Appleby should grow into an even more prominent role as he picks up the slack left by the graduation of wing Trevor Gaskins. Smith and McNeail give White options at the point guard position. Both committed too many turnovers last season, but have the potential to turn into solid distributors. Louisiana Tech has plenty of players to fill minutes on the wing, as offense-minded 6-5 junior **Cordarious Johnson** returns alongside 6-4 freshman **Alex Hamilton** and a pair of 6-6 junior college transfers, **Jaron Johnson** and **Chris Anderson**. For post scoring White will turn to some combination of 6-10 freshman **Gilbert Talbot**, 6-8 sophomore **Isaiah Massey** (who followed in White's footsteps from Ole Miss to Ruston), and solid if unspectacular veterans like 6-8 senior **J.L. Lewis** and 6-9 sophomore **Michale Kyser**. Louisiana Tech has the look of an average WAC squad with plenty of room to grow, thanks to the youth of some of its most important contributors. Things are trending up for White and the Bulldogs just in time for their move to Conference USA in 2013-14.

UTSA

2012: 18-14 (10-6 Southland); Lost to McNeese State 78-74 (OT), Southland quarterfinals
In-conference offense: 1.00 points per possession (4th Southland)
In-conference defense: 0.94 points allowed per possession (3rd Southland)

Comfortably competitive in the Southland for the balance of the last decade, Brooks Thompson's Roadrunners are getting a cup of WAC coffee this season before stepping up another rung to Conference USA for 2013-14 and beyond. To improve on the program's solid performance—28-20 in-conference the past three seasons, with one NCAA appearance—UTSA will need to compete against not just the UT Arlingtons and Texas States of the world, but also the UTEPs and UABs. Regardless of what the future holds, UTSA will be competitive in the 2012-13 WAC. **Larry Wilkins** received a sixth year of eligibility after an injury forced him to miss all of last season. The 6-4 senior's 250-pound frame should help the Roadrunners on the glass, where they struggled last season. Junior **Jeromie Hill**, a second-team All-Southland selection, joins Wilkins up front, providing a 40 percent touch from three and some rebounding at 6-8. **Lucas O'Brien** arrives with more acclaim than your average WAC newcomer, and the 6-10 freshman could make an instant impact. In the backcourt, 5-9 senior **Michael Hale** displayed an uncanny knack for getting to the basket, drawing fouls, and taking care of the ball last season. UTSA's ability to keep up in the more offensive-minded WAC could depend on the progression of the oh-so appropriately named **Kannon Burrage**. The 6-3 senior operated as Brooks Thompson's shoot-first sixth man last season, nailing 38 percent of his threes and earning regular trips to the stripe. Burrage has the touch and shot-creating ability to end up as one of the league's top scorers, and whether he does or not could be the difference between a solid season and a disappointing one for the Roadrunners. Burrage will get help in the backcourt from **Hyjii Thomas**, a 6-1 junior college transfer, and **A.J. Price**, a solid 6-2 recruit from the 2011 class who redshirted.

SEATTLE

2012: 12-15 (Independent)
Offense: 0.97 points per possession
Defense: 1.03 points allowed per possession

After three relatively successful seasons as a Division I independent (40-49 overall), Seattle University has a conference to call home. Coached by former UCLA star and Washington assistant Cameron Dollar, the Redhawks will take on the WAC with a much different group than last season's senior-led squad. Holdovers like 6-6 junior **Clarence Trent**, 6-0 junior **Sterling Carter** and 6-2 senior **Prince Obasi** will have to shoulder the load. Trent is a rugged post player who racked up solid rebounding and defensive numbers to go along with 55 percent shooting on twos. He'll presumably start alongside three-point gunner **Chad Rasmussen** and some combination of 6-9 senior **Louis Green** and 6-11 freshman **Jack Crook**. The backcourt will feature a pair of experienced players in Carter and Obasi. Carter shot 36 percent on 190 three-point attempts, and will likely split the scoring duties with Trent. At the point, Obasi is a serviceable shooter who could stand to cut down his turnover rate. Seattle's depth is unproven at best—a mixture of freshmen, junior college transfers, and seldom-used veterans should see plenty of playing time. The Redhawks fared well for an independent last season, but the step up to the WAC from the 289th-toughest schedule in the nation, coupled with Aaron Broussard's departure, doesn't bode well. At least they'll be fun to watch: SU played at the nation's fastest clip last season, and were not far off that mark in the two previous years.

SAN JOSE STATE

2012: 9-22 (1-13 WAC); Lost to Nevada 54-44, WAC quarterfinals
In-conference offense: 1.01 points per possession (7th)
In-conference defense: 1.16 points allowed per possession (8th)

A 1-15 record never looks good, and when the "1" comes at home in double overtime against Fresno State things may be even worse than they appear. Add in the fact that George Nessman has to replace three departing Spartans who posted above-average offensive ratings last season, and the outlook could be downright dire. There is, however, good news. San Jose State welcomes what looks to be a fairly solid class of six newcomers, and there are a couple of promising veterans, starting with **James Kinney**. The 6-2 senior took more than 30 percent of the team's shots during his time on the court, converting at a decent rate while dishing a healthy number of assists. Kinney will be joined in the backcourt by 6-2 sophomore **D.J. Brown**, who joined the starting lineup midway through last season and showed potential. If Brown and Kinney don't split time at the point, 6-4 junior college transfer **Xavier Jones** might see some minutes there. **Stephon Smith**, a 6-8 sophomore who took over as a starter late last season, is the team's most proven post player. His freshman season was solid at best and unspectacular at worst, meaning Nessman might need to look to newcomers to contribute big minutes down low. **Chris Cunningham** should be first in line. The Santa Clara transfer provides ideal size at 6-9 and shot 62 percent in limited minutes for the Broncos as a sophomore in 2010-11. Junior college transfer **Alex Brown** (6-11) and freshman **Mike VanKirk** (7-1) will give the Spartans one of the conference's largest front lines. This is San Jose State's last chance to make some WAC noise before joining the Mountain West in 2013-14, but a relatively quiet departure looks more likely.

TEXAS STATE

2012: 13-17 (5-11 Southland); Did not qualify for Southland tournament
In-conference offense: 0.97 points per possession (8th Southland)
In-conference defense: 1.00 points allowed per possession (9th Southland)

Despite the Bobcats' struggles to score and rebound (and defend) last season, several players emerged as go-to contributors, one of whom is still in San Marcos. The departed star is Brooks Ybarra, a wiry wing who led the conference in true shooting percentage and offensive rating. The one who remains is senior **Matt Staff**, a 6-10 New Mexico transfer who transformed from a so-so reserve as a sophomore to a dominating post player as a junior. TSU's lone standout on the glass and in the paint defensively, Staff showed a diverse offensive game that included an impressive 54/42/78 percent line on twos, threes and free throws. Staff will play alongside a cast of newcomers (mostly junior college transfers) and several proven contributors. **Vonn Jones** is the incumbent at point guard, where the 5-11 senior will be joined by junior college transfers **Phil Hawkins** (6-0) and **Deonte' Jones** (6-2). Promising 6-3 sophomore **Wesley Davis** should see quite a bit of playing time at the wing, along with 6-4 sophomore **Darius Richardson**, a UT Arlington transfer who served as a long-distance gunner during his freshman season. Coach Doug Davalos has a few options at forward, including junior **Reid Koenen**, whose size (6-7) belies a willingness to shoot threes and an inability to rebound, and sturdy 6-7 junior college transfer **Joel Wright**. The one-season stint in the WAC shapes up as an important year in San Marcos. If the Bobcats' win total craters during their first season in a tougher conference, Texas State may need to reassess the program as they join the Sun Belt in 2013-2014.

West Coast

BY NIC REINER

No league has escaped the effects of the conference realignment over the past two years. Invariably, the shifts happen because of money, TV contracts, exposure, greater recruiting access or, most simply, football. The fact that football is the driving force is not a bad thing and it's delusional to begrudge schools that do what's in their best interest, even if it costs others.

However, it's within this ruthless framework that a league like the West Coast Conference must operate. On the one hand, they have so little control over what happens because they have so little power. On the other, because they are completely disconnected from the source of that power, their cohesion can remain largely intact. That combined with a shrewd move to bring BYU on board in non-football sports has served to keep the WCC ahead of other conferences whose futures are far more flimsy.

During this process, the WCC has remained unified and has actually improved in basketball. With BYU, an already strong basketball conference became even stronger. Next year, the WCC will add Pacific to bring the league to an even ten teams. UOP is a historically strong basketball program and a small private school. The latter is important because the West Coast Conference has achieved reasonably strong synergy in its commitment to private, primarily religious member schools.

The WCC is firmly entrenched in Division I basketball's upper third (some years, in its upper quarter), a fact reflected by the changes the league will make to its conference tournament when UOP joins in 2013. As it stands now, the WCC's conference tournament operates on a double-bye format that protects higher seeds. However, this summer, WCC commissioner Jamie Zaninovich told ESPN that, come 2013, the league would reformat its conference tournament into a traditional 10-team structure. According to the report, the conference will eliminate the double-bye system because it feels it can secure multiple NCAA tournament bids without shielding the favorites.

Further testament to the WCC's clout is the long-term contract it signed with ESPN in the summer of 2011. Because of that relationship, this year, the ESPN family of networks will air a minimum of 43 games nationally involving WCC schools, including 20 conference games. The deal was the most comprehensive ESPN had ever signed with a non-football conference. The exposure schools like Santa Clara, San Francisco, and San Diego get from this arrangement is invaluable and speaks to how Gonzaga's domination of the WCC actually enabled the league to blossom.

The Bulldogs' annual steamrolling of the conference kept the WCC in the public eye because Gonzaga's name (and by extension, the WCC's name) was everywhere. It's fair to say, though, that dominance was not enough. When other schools were able to challenge the Zags the resulting TV was even better. The Saint Mary's–Gonzaga rivalry, while obviously more important on the left coast, means something far away from the Western seaboard now, too.

Last year Saint Mary's, Gonzaga, and BYU each finished with at least 26 wins and an NCAA tournament trip. This season those three will likely be the strongest teams in the conference once again. The Bulldogs have reloaded in their usual fashion and are the favorites to take back the league crown from SMC. The Gaels return WCC player of the year Matthew Dellavedova and will go toe-to-toe with the Zags. BYU may fall back slightly but the Cougars do get a number of players back from injury and from obligations related to LDS missions.

Outside the top tier, Loyola Marymount broke new ground last year, finishing a surprising 11-5. However, it would be just as surprising if the Lions reached that point again in 2013, and it's more likely that LMU will return to the peloton. The team poised to rise up to challenge the top three is Santa Clara, as the Broncos will have a strong and seasoned trio in Marc Trasolini, Kevin Foster, and Evan Roquemore. San Diego returns one of the conference's best young players, Johnny Dee, and could crack the top half of the conference if things fall into place. Portland returns nearly every important piece and the Pilots expect to win more than three conference games this season. On paper just Pepperdine and San Francisco have no real shot at competing for a regular season title, as both, for different reasons, are in rebuilding mode.

Teams listed in Nic's predicted order of finish.

GONZAGA

2012: 26-7 (13-3 WCC); Lost to Ohio State 73-66, NCAA round of 32
In-conference offense: 1.09 points per possession (2nd)
In-conference defense: 0.93 points allowed per possession (1st)

Gonzaga finally relinquished their stranglehold on the WCC after losing both the regular season and conference tournament titles to Saint Mary's. The Bulldogs had won at least a share of the previous 11 regular-season championships (nine of them outright), finished conference play 14-0 three times, and 13-1 three times. That amazing streak is over, but a new one could start in 2013. The Zags are the favorites again to win the WCC. Though their centerpiece and leader Robert Sacre is gone, Mark Few's team returns four key contributors and adds another seven-footer to the lineup. Sophomore point guard **Kevin Pangos** had a stellar first season, finishing with an offensive rating of 119, an effective FG percentage of 56, and assist rate of 22 percent. The "other" sophomore guard **Gary Bell** also parked his offensive rating north of 115, while sinking 51 percent of his twos and a fantastic 48 percent of his threes. Not to be outdone by the new guys, 6-7 senior **Elias Harris** shot just as well as Pangos from the field (recording an eFG percentage of 55), while posting an offensive rating of 111 and corralling 25 percent of the available defensive rebounds during his minutes. Harris has been to three NCAA tournaments and is poised to have an excellent senior year. Reserve guard **David Stockton** plays well in support of Pangos but must lower his high turnover rate. Coach Few hopes the void left by Sacre is filled by the tandem of 6-9 junior **Sam Dower** (an efficient and active presence on offense in limited minutes last season) and freshman **Przemek Karnowski**. The seven-footer from Poland was coveted late by several big-name programs, has a wealth of international experience, and is expected to contribute immediately because of his skills down low and his physical presence inside. Fellow seven-footer **Kelly Olynyk** returns after a medical redshirt and, while it's been two years since he's logged real minutes, he has the potential to contribute, especially on the defensive end. Gonzaga didn't win the WCC in 2012, but it's still worth noting that 11 of their 13 conference wins came by double-digits. Moreover, the team they barely lost to in the round of 32, Ohio State, made it to the Final Four. Comfortably nestled in several pre-season top 25s, the Zags are the class of the WCC.

SAINT MARY'S

2012: 26-9 (14-2 WCC); Lost to Purdue 72-69, NCAA round of 64
In-conference offense: 1.17 points per possession (1st)
In-conference defense: 1.00 points allowed per possession (4th)

Saint Mary's finally broke through the Gonzaga wall in 2012. Led by West Coast Conference player of the year **Matthew Dellavedova** and fellow All-WCC honoree Rob Jones, the Gaels ended Gonzaga's regular-season WCC title streak at 11. Then for good measure Randy Bennett's team won the conference tournament as well, prevailing against the Zags in overtime in a thrilling 78-74 title game. Even though it was a momentous event to finally wrest both titles away, in truth the gap between the Gaels and the Zags had closed significantly in recent years. Now that the mission has been accomplished, Bennett loses Jones, a high-efficiency performer who used more possessions than even Dellavedova. On the other hand the 6-4 Dellavedova was on the floor an absurd 93 percent of the time as a junior. That coupled with 24 percent of the Gaels' possessions makes his already excellent 118 offensive rating even more impressive. Three other starters return, and they all took supporting roles on offense in SMC's "Rob and Matthew Show" last season. **Stephen Holt** posted the team's highest steal rate. The 6-4 junior picks his spots on offense, but when he does shoot from either side of the arc there's a high probability of points being scored. Though less efficient than Holt, 6-1 junior **Jorden Page** will similarly be asked to do more on offense. And **Brad Waldow** will be especially important, as the 6-9 sophomore will function as the Gaels' main force inside. Waldow was the conference's best offensive rebounder as a freshman, and, considering graduations, is now its best returning shot blocker. **Mitchell Young** had an injury-blighted season, but in 2010-11 he was one of the team's best rebounders and an efficient high-usage contributor as well. If the 6-9 senior returns to form, this front line improves even more. Last season the Gaels' recipe was to shoot well and grab the miss on the rare occasions one happens. SMC finished first in both categories in conference play, and thus put a startling 0.08 points of daylight per possession between themselves and the second-place Gonzaga offense. But that was then. Saint Mary's faces an uphill battle defending its hard-won titles.

BYU

2012: 26-9 (12-4 WCC); Lost to Marquette 88-68, NCAA round of 64
In-conference offense: 1.07 points per possession (3rd)
In-conference defense: 0.94 points allowed per possession (2nd)

Replacing Noah Hartsock and Charles Abouo isn't like replacing a certain Jimmer, but even with their relatively normal first names Hartsock and Abouo were seasoned starters who also happened to be the team's two most efficient contributors on offense. Dave Rose will try to replace those possessions as seamlessly as possible, and he'll have help in the form of three returning starters: 6-9 senior **Brandon Davies**, 6-2 sophomore **Matt Carlino,** and 6-6 senior **Brock Zylstra**. Davies inherited the most post-Jimmer responsibility on offense, using 28 percent of BYU's possessions when he was on the floor. In addition to being clearly the first option on offense, Davies is also his team's best rebounder and best defender. Carlino now has a year of experience running the offense and his 31 percent assist rate is a sign of good things to come. Zylstra's highly effective on offense in an exceedingly small role. He could likely carry a heavier load quite capably, but it's a good sign for his team that he probably won't have to: **Tyler Haws** is back from a two-year LDS mission, and there's little doubt the 6-5 "sophomore" can provide valuable support to Davies on offense. As a freshman in 2009-10 Haws hit 37 percent of his threes, and that was actually the worst number available from a wing who also made 54 percent of his twos and shot 92 percent at the line. (Pity Fredette, who drained 89 percent of his free throws that season and still wasn't the best choice to shoot technicals.) Haws is back, but 6-8 senior Stephen Rogers is gone. A torn meniscus forced him to miss 15 games last season, and in October Rose announced that lingering issues from that injury had effectively ended his senior's career. For additional size alongside Davies, BYU will turn instead to 6-8 junior **Agustin Ambrosino**, a junior college transfer. Also arriving from the juco ranks is 6-2 junior **Raul Delgado**, who once made 12 threes in a game for Western Nebraska CC. The Cougars have ranked in the top 30 nationally in defense each of the past five years, so good D is the default assumption in Provo. And if BYU draws some old-school buzzer-beater inspiration from the family connections claimed by 6-0 freshman **Cooper Ainge**, all the better. In their second season in the West Coast, Rose's team will have the personnel to again challenge the league's big two.

SANTA CLARA

2012: 8-22 (0-16 WCC); Lost to Portland 74-70, WCC first round
In-conference offense: 0.99 points per possession (7th)
In-conference defense: 1.17 points allowed per possession (9th)

When 6-9 senior leader **Marc Trasolini** tore his ACL shortly before the 2011-12 season, expectations at Santa Clara were tempered. Trasolini had posted a 117 offensive rating in 2010-11, and appeared ready to replicate, if not improve upon, an exceptional year. But when ultra-high-usage 6-2 combo guard **Kevin Foster** was suspended after the first five games of the conference season, the wheels really came off the bus. With 6-3 guard **Evan Roquemore** as the only efficient major contributor, the Broncos recorded the first winless WCC campaign since Saint Mary's did it in 2001. Kerry Keating's team couldn't stop anybody. Literally: SCU didn't allow less than a point per possession in a single conference game. Safe to say the Broncos will be putting last year far behind them. Foster and Trasolini are now seniors while Roquemore is a junior; all three are capable of offensive ratings upwards of 110. Foster has an incredibly high usage rate, Trasolini does most everything well, and Roquemore developed into an excellent distributor and driver during his time as the offense's focal point. The returning Broncos who now know what its like to have a ton of possessions fall on you out of nowhere—namely, 6-8 senior **Niyi Harrison** and 6-4 senior **Raymond Cowels**—will take more of a back seat this year, but maybe the experience did them good. Anyway, with Trasolini, Foster, and Roquemore together again, all will be well or at least much better in Santa Clara. Barring more injuries or off-court trouble, the Broncos will be competitive, and a top-four finish is within reach.

LOYOLA MARYMOUNT

2012: 21-13 (11-5 WCC); Lost to Utah State 77-69, CIT quarterfinals
In-conference offense: 1.04 points per possession (5th)
In-conference defense: 0.99 points allowed per possession (3rd)

Loyola Marymount enjoyed their best season in a decade in 2011-12. **Anthony Ireland** and Drew Viney made All-WCC, and Max Good was named WCC coach of the year. Using the SRS rating favored by the archives at Sports-Reference.com, the Lions posted their best performance since the 1990 Elite Eight team led by you-know-who. True, Good caught some good breaks last season, and his team's actual per-possession improvement wasn't quite as drastic as 11-5 made it seem. But so what? LMU unquestionably turned a corner defensively. Ireland played 90 percent of the minutes, used 25 percent of the Lions' possessions, and posted a respectable 107 offensive rating. Also an excellent distributor, the 5-10 junior will assume even more responsibility for carrying his team this season. **Ashley Hamilton** is back after missing part of last season with an injury. The 6-7 senior's not particularly efficient, but he is relied upon on both ends of the floor. And 6-5 sophomore **C.J. Blackwell** was a high-volume shooter off the bench last season, one who took 28 percent of his team's shots during his limited minutes. His respectable offensive rating implies good things may come if his role is expanded. Overall, it will be interesting to see whether "The House That Hank Built" is home to another winning team in 2012-13. Viney was the most efficient Lion and his absence will hurt. Also Jarred DuBois, a 6-3 guard whose numbers were not dissimilar to Hamilton's, transferred to Utah. It's unlikely the Lions will go 11-5 again, but they may be able to stay above .500.

SAN DIEGO

2012: 13-18 (7-9 WCC); Lost to BYU 73-68, WCC second round
In-conference offense: 1.01 points per possession (6th)
In-conference defense: 1.07 points allowed per possession (6th)

After a combined five conference wins in the previous two seasons, last year's 7-9 campaign represented progress for the Toreros. For their seven wins, Bill Grier's team swept the league's three worst teams and scored a road victory over a much-improved LMU team. Being swept by the four most efficient teams in the WCC, though, was also part of that equation so more progress is needed. Needed and possible: San Diego brings back all five starters. (Which actually is a bit misleading. Last season as a senior Darian Norris made 15 starts and, more importantly, was third on the team in minutes.) **Johnny Dee** was honorable mention All-WCC as a freshman and functioned as the featured scorer in Grier's offense, taking 28 percent of his team's shots while on the floor. With a year under his belt, the 6-0 sophomore will only be asked to carry even more possessions. **Christopher Anderson** finished in the top 30 nationally in both assist rate and steal rate last season as a 5-7 freshman. He and Dee provide a reliable and sound backcourt and if the oft-fouled Anderson can improve his 61 percent free throw shooting USD will be in even better shape. **Chris Manresa**, a 6-9 senior, will continue to provide both defensive boards and a high-usage spark off the bench, and 6-11 junior **Dennis Kramer** is coming off a season where he improved in essentially every important category. Another returning starter, 6-5 senior **Ken Rancifer**, saw his role reduced significantly on offense last season but, as would be expected, his efficiency improved, as his two-point percentage climbed north of 50 for the first time in his career. The final returning starter is 6-10 sophomore **Simi Fajemisin**, who averaged an astonishing 9.2 fouls per 40 minutes but did get offensive boards during the occasional moments when he was in the game. Key reserve **John Sinis** is carried on the USD roster as a "G-F," but the shooting percentages recorded by the 6-9 sophomore to date suggest the Greek native may want to forget about the "G." With the teams at the top showing few signs of regression, it seems realistic to assume that a successful conference season for San Diego would be another win or two above what the Toreros achieved in 2012.

PORTLAND

2012: 7-24 (3-13 WCC); Lost to San Francisco 87-66, WCC second round
In-conference offense: 0.94 points per possession (8th)
In-conference defense: 1.09 points allowed per possession (8th)

Outside of Santa Clara's extenuating circumstances, Portland had by far the WCC's most disappointing 2011-12. Picked to finish fifth in the conference by Ken Pomeroy in the preseason, the Pilots won just six games all year against Division I opponents. Three of those wins came against Santa Clara, so, with all due respect to the Broncos, Portland's performance may have actually been worse than it appeared. The good news is improvement's a safe guess after a 3-13 season, and most of the team is back. (Nemanja Mitrovic graduated, and starting point guard Tim Douglas transferred across the Willamette and up I-5 a couple exits to Portland State.) In particular, Eric Reveno's three most efficient performers on offense return: 6-7 junior **Ryan Nicholas**, 6-5 sophomore **Kevin Bailey**, and 6-11 sophomore **Thomas van der Mars**.

Nicholas had usage and shot percentage rates over 20, led the team in rebounding, and finished with an effective FG percentage of 52. Bailey posted a high usage rate and frequently reached the foul line, where he shot a healthy 76 percent. But it's van der Mars who has the greatest ability to impact the game, and he will see his role increase in his second year. Senior guard **Derrick Rodgers** likely will assume the point guard role, although his assist rate was significantly lower than his turnover rate. For what it's worth, Eric Reveno's team was one of the most inexperienced teams in Division I last year. But there are too many good teams in the WCC to see even a slightly more experienced Portland move up the ranks. Finishing at .500 overall and in conference is probably the team's ceiling.

SAN FRANCISCO

2012: 20-14 (8-8 WCC); Lost to Washington State 89-75, CBI first round
In-conference offense: 1.07 points per possession (4th)
In-conference defense: 1.04 points allowed per possession (5th)

San Francisco suffered a mass exodus in the offseason. Six players transferred out of the program. Two of those, Perris Blackwell and Michael Williams, had the highest usage rates among possible returners. Each of the four less-involved players who departed had been on the team for two years and thus took a goodly amount of experience with them. With two of the Dons' biggest pieces graduated, the complete decimation of the USF roster forced Rex Walters to unexpectedly rebuild on the fly. To be fair, the roster isn't completely new. One starter returns, 6-2 junior **Cody Doolin**. And while the career of 5-10 junior **Dominique O'Connor** has been ravaged by injuries, he should start at the other guard position. He'll need to improve his shooting and limit his turnovers to have a positive impact. **Cole Dickerson**, a 6-7 junior, was on the floor less than 50 percent of the time last season, but he made shots from both sides of the arc and was probably the best overall rebounder on the team. Incoming freshmen **Frank Rogers** and **Matt Christiansen**, both at 6-9, will have opportunities to contribute immediately on the interior. And 6-6 junior **De'End Parker** originally chose UCLA coming out of junior college but ended up at San Francisco for family reasons. He has the talent to make an impact from the outset. The story going into this season is whether or not Walters' team can rebound from the offseason departures. Expectations on the Hilltop are now lower, even after two straight winning seasons and postseason appearances (CIT 2011, CBI 2012). A finish in the lower half of the conference is likely for the Dons this year.

PEPPERDINE

2012: 10-19 (4-12 WCC); Lost to San Diego 76-54, WCC second round
In-conference offense: 0.92 points per possession (9th)
In-conference defense: 1.08 points allowed per possession (7th)

Pepperdine's 2012 offense reminded me of a Jim Mora postgame rant when he was coaching the New Orleans Saints. No, it wasn't his infamous "Playoffs!" outburst, but it was equally outrageous and incisive. When asked about his team's performance, Mora muttered in a resigned tone, "We couldn't run the ball. We didn't try to run the ball. We couldn't complete a pass. We couldn't make a first down." Mora goes on but you get the gist. Extend the logic to Pepperdine and we can hear Mora rattling off how awful the Waves were offensively. They couldn't shoot the ball (effective field goal percentage of 44). They made only 26 percent of their three-point shots. When they got to the line, they sank only 63 percent of attempts. They turned the ball over 20 percent of the time. And the list can go on. It's imperative coach Marty Wilson improve his team's offense in his second season. One hopeful sign on that front is the return of 6-2 senior **Lorne Jackson** from a medical redshirt. In 2011 as an All-WCC honorable mention, he posted strong numbers. He'll almost certainly lead this offense. Pepperdine also retains 6-4 sophomore **Jordan Baker**, who had high assist and steal rates but must improve his shooting. Wilson can also call on 6-2 senior **Caleb Willis**, who assists on 28 percent of baskets when he's on the floor. And 6-4 junior **Nikolas Skouen** might be able to contribute if he can get his two-point accuracy to a place where it looks down on his 31 percent shooting from beyond the arc. The 75th season of Pepperdine basketball doesn't look like it'll be a gem.

Previewing the Mid-Majors

America East

BY MATT GILES

Some of the America East's most recognizable names are no longer members of the America East. A few, like Boston Univeristy's Darryl Partin and Stony Brook's Bryan Dougher, no longer have eligibility, while several others—including the Albany duo of Gerardo Suero and Logan Aronhalt, as well as Vermont's Four McGlynn—have either decided to transfer or join the professional ranks.

Yet while there's been significant roster upheaval, much remains the same in the conference. Despite losing key parts of their lineups, Vermont and Stony Brook will contend for the league title. Losing McGlynn will hurt the Catamounts' bench production, but point-forward exemplar Brian Voelkel and a cast of multiple returnees will again put the squad in contention for the America East title. Vermont also has a newcomer who could surprise the league in Marist transfer Candon Rusin, a 6-4 guard known for his penchant for long-range attempts.

Meanwhile, Tommy Brenton returns for his final season at Stony Brook under Steve Pikiell, and though Dave Coley will help Brenton shoulder the scoring burden, the Seawolves will have to depend on their large and acclaimed recruiting class.

Many experts expect Boston University to round out the conference's top tier. This will be the final season for the Terriers in the America East before leaving for the Patriot League, and the combination of D.J. Irving and freshman Maurice Watson should rank as one of the AE's top backcourts. But don't forget Maine. Despite the Black Bears' sub-.500 record in-conference last season, Justin Edwards is primed for a breakout sophomore campaign, and the frontcourt tandem of Alasdair Fraser and Mike Allison will again make it difficult for opponents to score within the arc.

Albany claimed the America East's most efficient offense last season, and the departures of Suero and Aronhalt will allocate more possessions not only for Mike Black, but also for Jayson Guerrier and Blake Metcalf. However, the Great Danes will sorely miss Suero's ability to draw fouls and connect from the free throw stripe.

New Hampshire was too dependent on perimeter scoring, and the addition of Iona transfer Chris Pelcher should balance the point distribution. At Hartford the development of sophomores, specifically Mark Nwakamma, will be crucial. The Hawks' offensive rebounding percentage ranked last among America East teams, and without the scoring of Andres Torres it will be necessary for the squad to grab as many additional possessions as possible.

UMBC and Binghamton will round out the America East cellar, and both squads have new head coaches. Randy Monroe waited until two days before the start of official practices to resign as the Retrievers' head coach, and interim coach Aki Thomas, who was credited by some for keeping the team together during the offseason, will lead a roster that has enough pieces to win more than three conference games. And at Binghamton, Tommy Dempsey enters his first season as head coach. Dempsey turned Rider around in the MAAC, and there's an expectation that he'll do the same for the Bearcats in the America East.

Teams listed in Matt's predicted order of finish.

VERMONT

2012: 24-12 (13-3 AE); Lost to North Carolina 77-58, NCAA round of 64
In-conference offense: 1.10 points per possession (2nd)
In-conference defense: 0.93 points allowed per possession (3rd)

First-year coach John Becker clearly stressed the advantages of an unguarded 15-foot shot and urged the Catamounts to get to the line in 2011-12. The additional free throws fueled Vermont's offense, and the squad posted their highest efficiency since 2009. Two Catamounts have since left Burlington. Matt Glass' eligibility expired, and Four McGlynn transferred to Towson. Some have speculated that McGlynn's absence will hurt the offense in Burlington, however, on paper if McGlynn had not played last season the Catamounts' in-conference number for points per possession would have still been 1.10. A volume shooter who struggled with accuracy inside the arc, McGlynn was also a defensive liability. Last season Vermont's point production was essentially allocated to four players, but because 6-7 junior **Luke Apfeld** is the only returnee of that group, **Sandro Carissimo**'s offensive share will grow. The 6-2 guard cut his turnovers by 20 percent and upped his two-point accuracy as a sophomore. Carissimo is the sole Catamount capable of creating off the dribble, and Becker will often rely on him during pick and roll possessions. Another option for backcourt points is Marist transfer **Candon Rusin**, who attempted 61 percent of his shots from beyond the arc in two seasons as a Red Fox. Apfeld played roughly 50 percent of Vermont's minutes, but the forward's minutes will grow as he comprises most if not all the squad's interior offense. Nearly 65 percent of his possessions resulted in a paint touch, and Apfeld converted 55 percent of his twos. However, if he continues to be flummoxed by fouls, former walk-on **Clancy Rugg** could prove integral. The 6-8 junior grabs 18 percent of opponents' misses during his minutes, which thus far have been limited. Vermont does not have a de facto point guard so 6-6 junior **Brian Voelkel** operates the offense as a point-forward. Voelkel's 31 percent assist rate led the America East, and no other player in D-I Voelkel's size or taller handed out a higher percentage of assists. His defensive rebounding rate is ranked nationally, and the combination of Voelkel, Apfeld and Rugg ensured Becker's team hauled in 35 percent of its own misses.

STONY BROOK

2012: 22-10 (14-2 AE); Lost to Seton Hall 63-61, NIT first round
In-conference offense: 1.09 points per possession (3rd)
In-conference defense: 0.91 points allowed per possession (1st)

Winning 14 of 16 conference games proved bittersweet when Stony Brook ran up against rival Vermont in the AE title game and managed just 43 points in an eight-point loss. While 2012-12 won't be a rebuilding season, there will be some growing pains as the Seawolves must replace 40 percent of their minutes. **Tommy Brenton** is more of a scoring threat than Vermont's Brian Voelkel, but overall he plays a similar role for SBU. The 6-5 senior essentially directs the offense, and his assist rate leads the squad. On D he claims both the team's best defensive rebound percentage and a high steal rate. **Carson Puriefoy** will lean on Brenton to help orchestrate SBU's offense. The 6-0 freshman is known for his ability to create his own offense, and head coach Steve Pikiell could pair Puriefoy with 6-2 junior **Dave Coley**. Last season Coley attempted nearly 100 more two-point field goals than he had as a freshman, yet his accuracy improved. Coley will likely attempt the highest percentage of Stony Brook's shots, so the improvement there is encouraging. **Anthony Jackson** and 6-5 senior **Ron Bracey** will also garner extra possessions. Just a quarter of SBU's shots in conference play were from long-range, but Jackson, a 6-0 junior, has bucked that trend and attempted more threes than twos over his two seasons. And Pikiell has high expectations for 6-8 freshman **Jameel Warney**, saying the Plainfield, New Jersey, product could be "the best big man that will ever play [at Stony Brook]." Warney is reportedly a skilled shot blocker and rebounder, but the Seawolves will be watching closely to see how quickly the 255-pound freshman becomes acclimated to the speed and physicality of D-I frontcourts.

MAINE

2012: 12-17 (6-10 AE); Lost to Vermont 50-40, AE quarterfinals
In-conference offense: 0.97 points per possession (5th)
In-conference defense: 1.00 points allowed per possession (5th)

Maine was an anomaly last season. The Black Bears allowed conference opponents to convert nearly 40 percent of their threes, grab 32 of their misses, and take excellent care of the ball. Yet Ted Woodward's defense held AE squads to a point per possession, and if Maine's offense had shown some life the team might have finished in the conference's top tier. Eight of the Bears' conference losses, including an exit in the AE quarterfinals, were decided by 10 points or less. Maine's defense is fueled on the interior, specifically by the duo of 6-7 junior **Alasdair Fraser** and 6-9 senior **Mike Allison**. Fraser posted a defensive rebounding rate of 17 percent during his minutes, and while his block rate dipped slightly this was likely caused by Allison swatting away nearly nine percent of opponents' two-point attempts while he was on the floor. Fraser and Allison were a significant factor in the Bears' league-leading block rate and two-point defense. Allison, though, has yet to develop an offensive game, whereas Fraser has established himself on the block. He took over 150 additional twos during his sophomore season, and still managed to increase his conversion rate to 55 percent. **Till Gloger**, a 6-8 freshman, will bolster Woodward's frontcourt depth. Two products of Maine's mini-NYC pipeline, 6-5 freshman **Shaun Lawton** and 6-3 sophomore **Xavier Pollard**, will headline the backcourt. Lawton appears to be the rare freshman that enjoys playing defense, and Pollard was efficient insider the arc during limited minutes last season. **Justin Edwards**, a 6-3 sophomore, was the team's second-leading scorer last season, and his usage rate led the team. But during the conference season opponents learned he predominantly drove right, and his two-point percentage plummeted. Still, Edwards was the only Black Bear to draw more than four fouls per 40 minutes—he has the ability to register an All-AE caliber season.

BOSTON UNIVERSITY

2012: 16-16 (12-4 AE); Lost to Hartford 53-49, AE quarterfinals
In-conference offense: 1.05 points per possession (4th)
In-conference defense: 0.92 points allowed per possession (2nd)

If 6-0 junior **D.J. Irving** is selected as the America East player of the year this season, he'll be the third consecutive winner from Boston University, following a path mapped out by John Holland (2011) and Darryl Partin (last season). Irving will also be the final BU winner. With the Terriers joining the Patriot League for 2013-14, Joe Jones' squad will not be eligible for the 2013 AE tournament. That's too bad, because BU returns a highly efficient offense, even without Partin. Still, a scoring void exists, and Irving's offensive role should increase. **Maurice Watson**'s arrival may help that along. Watson's decision to become a Terrier was regarded as a recruiting coup, and while Jones has yet to declare the 5-10 freshman a starter, it's likely he'll be handed the offensive reins. His presence will move Irving off the ball. The junior guard's game is heavy on pick and rolls and he may now be run through a good many screens in the half-court. The key, though, will be the development of BU's wings and their frontcourt: 6-7 junior **Dom Morris**, 6-5 junior **Travis Robinson**, and 6-7 sophomore **Malik Thomas**. Morris showed mettle keeping opponents off the glass, and he'll be crucial around the bucket on offense. Robinson is a role player but he can stretch a defense, converting 40 percent from deep (which could create gaps for Irving and Watson to attack the basket). Thomas was once nicknamed "Skittles" after his favorite candy. He was a bit player for the Terriers a year ago, but he posted a defensive rebounding rate of 22 percent in limited minutes. If he's afforded additional playing time, Thomas could be one of the conference's top rebounders.

ALBANY

2012: 19-15 (9-7 AE); Lost to Manhattan 89-79, CIT first round
In-conference offense: 1.10 points per possession (1st)
In-conference defense: 1.05 points allowed per possession (7th)

Albany had the best offense in the America East last season, and other than Vermont and Stony Brook no conference team came close to matching the Great Danes' mark of 1.10 points per possession. Now Will Brown's team has lost Gerardo Suero (to the professional ranks overseas) and Logan Aronhalt (to Maryland where he is eligible immediately as a graduate student), guards who attempted nearly half of the squad's twos. But all is not lost. Albany sought to use pick and rolls to spread opposing defenses, and since 6-0 senior **Mike Black** returns, the Danes should again resume their pick and roll onslaught. Black used a pick on a third of his offensive possessions, scoring just under a point per play, and he converted 51 and 36 percent of his twos and threes, respectively. He also posted an assist rate of 27 percent, an effective stat line for a player who played 82 percent of Albany's minutes. Black is clearly an AE player of the year candidate, and the departures of Suero and Aronhalt will free more minutes for 6-4 senior **Jayson Guerrier** and 6-9 senior **Blake Metcalf**. Guerrier's 124 offensive rating led the team, and he scored in double digits in six of his final nine games. While his usage rate was only 15 percent, he was the team's best long-range shooter (42 percent). Albany rebounded an AE-best 40 percent of their misses last season, and the combination of Metcalf and 6-8 junior **Luke Devlin** will keep producing second chances. The Danes' offense should continue to hum, but defensively, the squad has some clear problems. Brown's team limited opponents on the defensive glass, but rarely gambled for steals and allowed offenses to make a high percentage of their twos, in part, because their transition defense was poor. Suero struggled with turnovers, and since his usage rate ranked second in the nation (38 percent), Albany was often racing back on defense. Black's turnover rate wasn't pretty either, so Brown could heavily rely on 5-9 junior college transfer **D.J. Evans**.

NEW HAMPSHIRE

2012: 13-16 (7-9 AE); Lost to Albany 63-45, AE quarterfinals
In-conference offense: 0.94 points per possession (6th)
In-conference defense: 0.99 points allowed per possession (4th)

Patrick Konan, a 6-6 sophomore whose 38 percent shooting on threes led New Hampshire, returns. So do 6-0 sophomore **Jordan Bonner**, the Wildcats' starting point guard, and 6-4 junior **Chandler Roads**, UNH's No. 2 scorer. However, AE opponents had a fairly easy time defending New Hampshire, a squad that fell in love with their perimeter game. UNH took 340 threes, the second-most of any AE team, and opponents were able to successfully monitor the perimeter and hold the Wildcats to well under a point per possession. If Bill Herrion's team can continue to play solid defense, the Wildcats should improve—but this offense needs some significant boosts. **Ferg Myrick** was injured midway through his sophomore season, and it was clear the 6-6 wing was tentative at times. When healthy, Myrick put pressure on defenses by drawing fouls, and he proved to be a threat both on the perimeter and in the paint. **Scott Morris** is reportedly a skilled shooter, and the 6-2 sophomore should shine with additional minutes. Iona transfer **Chris Pelcher**, a 6-10 junior, is now eligible, and could balance UNH's offense. There's an expectation that Pelcher will receive frequent paint touches, and his heft necessitates double-teams which should create openings for the Wildcats' numerous shooters.

HARTFORD

2012: 9-22 (7-9 AE); Lost to Vermont 77-73 (2OT), AE semifinals
In-conference offense: 0.93 points per possession (7th)
In-conference defense: 1.02 points allowed per possession (6th)

Under John Gallagher, Hartford has been good at forcing turnovers. The Hawks have led the American East in opponent turnover percentage each of the past two seasons, as the squad has pressured their foes into giving the ball away on at least one in four possessions. The Hawk with the highest steal rate, Andres Torres, is no longer eligible, but Gallagher will depend on a mix of seasoned sophomores who have played extensive minutes. **Mark Nwakamma** is the squad's most efficient scorer, converting 57 percent of his twos while using 24 percent of the team's possessions during his minutes. Hartford made 52 percent of their shots within the arc, tops in the AE, and the 6-6 Nwakamma's return will help maintain that interior accuracy. He'll again be paired with 6-6 classmate **Nate Sikma**, who connected on half his twos. While Sikma primarily operates on the perimeter, he's shown proficiency in pick and rolls (1.3 points per play) and Gallagher might develop his offensive role further. Hartford will still pressure ball handlers, but one glaring weakness they need to address is their lack of rebounding. Getting to a few more of their own misses would have helped last season, as 6-0 reserve **Wes Cole** (still another sophomore on this season's roster) accounted for a whopping 35 percent of UH's shots during his appearances—and missed 67 percent of the time. Nwakamma will again help, but more minutes could be allocated to 6-8 sophomore **Jamie Schneck** if he can avoid foul trouble. Gallagher and his staff also landed a frontcourt-heavy recruiting class, headlined by 6-6 junior college transfer **Glenn Akerland** and a pair of freshmen, 6-7 **Antoine Burrell** and 6-5 **Parker U'u**.

UMBC

2012: 4-26 (3-13 AE); Lost to Binghamton 73-67 (OT), AE first round
In-conference offense: 0.92 points per possession (8th)
In-conference defense: 1.12 points allowed per possession (9th)

Three of UMBC's four wins last season came against Towson and Binghamton, opponents who combined to post a 3-60 record overall. Randy Monroe's six-year contract extension, signed after a 24-win 2007-08 season, ran through 2013-14, but rather than wait for the inevitable he resigned on October 10. Assistant coach Aki Thomas has been tapped as acting head coach, and he'll look to 6-6 junior **Chase Plummer** to again carry the scoring load. Just three other Division I players posted usage rates over 34 percent, and, as would be expected for a high-volume shooter on a 4-26 team, Plummer wasn't overly efficient. Then again it's not clear that any of the other Retrievers would have fared better. Maybe 6-2 senior **Ryan Cook** and 6-4 senior **Brian Neller**, who last season combined to shoot 355 threes but made just 30 percent of them, will benefit from the arrival of 5-11 freshman **Aaron Morgan**. A combo guard, Morgan will see extensive minutes as the team's point guard, and his ability to break down opposing defenses could free Cook, Neller, and 6-0 sophomore **Joey Goetz** for perimeter attempts. However the most important newcomer could be 6-10 junior **Brett Roseboro**, who landed in Baltimore by way of both Marquette and St. Bonaventure. Roseboro could be effective simply because there aren't many players his size in the America East. UMBC ranked last in both defensive rebounding and two-point defense during AE play, and Roseboro, described fondly by a former coach as having a "mean streak," should boost the Retrievers' interior defense.

BINGHAMTON

2012: 2-29 (1-15 AE), Lost to Stony Brook 78-69, AE quarterfinals
In-conference offense: 0.88 points per possession (9th)
In-conference defense: 1.07 points allowed per possession (8th)

After seven seasons and nearly 120 wins at Rider, Tommy Dempsey decided he was ready for a new challenge. Many considered his move to Binghamton unusual, and it's likely Dempsey's first season will indeed be rough. Four of the Bearcats' top five scorers from last season will not be available. Chris Longoria, Ben Dickinson, and Omar Richards transferred, and Robert Mansell, owner of the team's highest offensive rating in 2011-12, tore his ACL in the offseason. That leaves possessions and shots available for 6-0 senior **Jimmy Gray**, whose 33 percent shooting from the perimeter led the team. Gray was Binghamton's nominal point guard, but the arrival of 6-1 junior **Rayner Moquete**, a Fordham transfer, may shift Gray off the ball. After 6-4 freshman **Jordan Reed** serves a three-game suspension to start the season, he should contribute some offensive pop from the bench. BU has to replace 65 percent of its scoring, though, and the available possessions could establish 6-4 freshman **Karon Waller** as a prolific scorer in the conference. Initially set to join Manhattan, the guard will likely be a focal point of Binghamton's offense. Dempsey does have some interior size on the roster, and 6-8 juniors **Roland Brown** and **Brian Freeman** could provide him with frontcourt athleticism. Brown is a wide-bodied forward who should boost BU's offensive rebounding, and Freeman should be the perfect complement to what is about to become an up-tempo system. Dempsey's Rider squads rarely dipped below 68 possessions per 40 minutes.

Atlantic Sun

BY CRAIG POWERS

The Atlantic Sun bids adieu to its most successful member of the last few seasons this year, as Belmont heads to the Ohio Valley Conference. The gut reaction of many will be to declare this the end of national relevancy for the A-Sun, as the Bruins reached levels of dominance and efficiency that no one had ever touched in the league before.

However, the Bruins weren't the only A-Sun team improving the last few years. The league jumped from No. 21 in Ken Pomeroy's conference rankings in 2011 to 14 in 2012. Naturally there's no statistical way for the A-Sun to achieve a ranking that lofty absent Belmont's remarkable success. The year-to-year improvement, however, plainly had little to do with the Bruins, since Rick Byrd's team was more or less equally outstanding in both seasons.

Last season the A-Sun still would have ranked as the No. 19 conference nationally without the Bruins, higher than the league ranked the year before with them. That's a vast improvement over the conference's average finish of No. 26 between 2003 and 2010. The A-Sun isn't better just because of one team, it's been a top-to-bottom effort. Belmont leaves behind a mid-major conference that's a rising star, one that may be well on its way to challenging for some at-large bids in the near future.

East Tennessee State may be down this year, but the Buccaneers are an established power. ETSU has finished in the top half of the A-Sun every year since their arrival in 2006, and have ranked in the top 150 nationally each of the past four years. ETSU could very well rebuild and maintain their success. By the same token Mercer's steadily improved over the past five years and jumped into the top 100 nationally last season. The Bears return a lot of talent and should be even better in 2012-13.

Then there are programs that are relatively new to Division I: North Florida, South Carolina Upstate, and Florida Gulf Coast. All are young and improving, and all are bringing in solid talent through recruiting year after year. Each is on the way up, and sure to be tougher in 2012-13. The newest provisional member is Northern Kentucky, who won't be eligible for the postseason yet.

Stetson finished ninth a season ago, but their best players were young and the Hatters are likely to provide stiffer competition going forward. Even Kennesaw State, which went winless in league play, has hope. Lewis Preston brings in a solid recruiting class this season.

But conference wins are a zero-sum proposition, and not everyone can be on the upswing. Lipscomb and Jacksonville are each suffering from the defections and dismissals that accompany programmatic turmoil.

And, obviously, the league's overall quality of play will take a hit this season. In effect, the A-Sun has traded Belmont for Northern Kentucky. Still, five of the conference's top teams return the bulk of their rosters from a year ago, so there should be improvement across that board, at least. The race for the conference title will feel more wide open than it has the past two seasons, when Belmont was dominating the league.

College basketball fans would do well to pay attention to the A-Sun, which makes many of its games available online. Much like a music fan constantly looking for the next great under-the-radar band, you can acquaint yourself now with the programs and faces in the league. Then, when the conference blows up and the national media talk about the suddenly great A-Sun, you, the college hoops hipster, can proudly exclaim, "I liked them before they were cool."

Teams listed in Craig's predicted order of finish.

MERCER

2012: 27-11 (13-5 A-Sun); Beat Utah State 70-67, CIT championship game
In-conference offense: 1.07 points per possession (2nd)
In-conference defense: 0.96 points allowed per possession (1st)

Even though it came in the little known and even more little watched tournament known as the CIT, Mercer was one of few teams in Division I that, like Kentucky, ended their season with a win. The Bears look to continue that success this season as they return all but one of their rotation players from a team that rated out No. 1 on defense in A-Sun play. **Daniel Coursey** was a major factor in that defense, as he blocked almost 14 percent of the two-point attempts launched while he was on the floor, fourth-best in the nation. Thanks in large part to the 6-10 junior, Mercer should play strong defense on the interior again this season. Out top 6-4 junior point guard **Langston Hall** towers over most A-Sun opponents. Add 6-3 senior **Travis Smith** at the off-guard, and Bob Hoffman has a backcourt that's able to limit open looks on the perimeter. Hall is also one of Mercer's playmakers on offense; the other is 6-6 junior **Jakob Gollon**. Both players have fine assist rates, and each is above average in terms of free throw rate. But the Achilles heel for the Bears may be an inability to hang on to the ball. Mercer was ninth in the A-Sun in turnover rate, giving away the rock on 22 percent of their possessions. The only starter that had any success taking care of the basketball last season was senior Justin Cecil. With him gone the rest of the team is going to have to improve. That being said, the Bears are the most talented team in the A-Sun. With Belmont out of the way, they look to be the favorites to take the league title.

USC UPSTATE

2012: 21-13 (13-5 A-Sun); Lost to Old Dominion 65-56, CIT second round
In-conference offense: 1.05 points per possession (3rd)
In-conference defense: 0.98 points allowed per possession (3rd)

There are turnarounds, and then there's what the USC Upstate Spartans did in 2011-12. Going into last season Eddie Payne's team had posted a 22-52 mark in four tours through the A-Sun. When the season was finished the Spartans could look back on a 13-5 conference record, 21 wins overall, and the program's first D-I postseason victory (in the CIT first round, against Kent State). Now Upstate returns every rotation player from that record-setting season. A big factor in Upstate's breakout was the improvement of **Torrey Craig**, who emerged as a bona fide star. Craig was named A-Sun player of the year, as well as AP All-America honorable mention. The 6-6 junior rebounds at an astounding rate for a player his size, grabbing almost 23 percent of opponents' misses during his minutes. Craig also blocks shots and records steals before heading down to the other end of the court and hitting 35 percent of his threes and 53 percent of his twos. If in addition to all of that he could draw fouls, it would be time to stop giving him the POY and start naming it after him. Alongside Craig is 6-8 junior **Ricardo Glenn**, one of the top offensive rebounders in the country and the main reason the Spartans led the A-Sun in that category. **Ty Greene** had an excellent freshman season in 2011-12, draining 40 percent of his threes, though the 6-3 guard wasn't nearly as good inside the arc. In fact that was a problem that plagued much of the team, as the Spartans were last in the conference in two-point percentage. Nevertheless Eddie Payne's team was able to work around that weakness (thanks mainly to excellent offensive rebounding), and will likely do so again. The Spartans should battle it out with Mercer for the 2013 A-Sun title.

NORTH FLORIDA

2012: 16-16 (10-8 A-Sun); Lost to East Tennessee State 68-66, A-Sun quarterfinals
In-conference offense: 1.03 points per possession (6th)
In-conference defense: 1.05 points allowed per possession (6th)

In Matthew Driscoll's third season at the helm in 2011-12, North Florida was able to post its first .500 year overall and its first winning record in the A-Sun. That accomplishment looked out of reach in January when the Ospreys were 9-12 overall and 3-5 in-conference, but UNF won seven of their last 11. Driscoll returns the bulk of his roster's offensive production this season, starting with 6-3 senior **Parker Smith**. The shooting guard was lights-out from outside last season, knocking down 41 percent of his threes on his way to a stellar 114 offensive rating. Flanking Smith in the backcourt are 5-11 senior **Will Wilson** and 6-5 senior **Jerron Granberry**. In line to take over at point guard, Wilson rarely shoots and that's a good thing. If he is to be his team's primary facilitator, however, he has to bring down his alarmingly high turnover rate. Granberry will roam the outside and provide another lethal three-point threat, as he hit on 39 percent of his long-range attempts last season. **Travis Wallace**, 6-8 senior **Andy Diaz**, and 6-7 junior **David Jeune** return in the frontcourt. Wallace is the best of the trio, a 6-6 junior who hits 51 percent of his twos and rarely turns the ball over while also serving as the team's best rebounder on both ends. Diaz and Jeune are solid offensive rebounders but both are turnover-prone. Diaz gets to the line a fair amount, but a 38 percent free throw shooter's better off avoiding that spot altogether. Assuming Diaz can be safely stashed someplace far away from the charity stripe, and with so many key players returning, North Florida should improve their win total for a fourth straight season. The Ospreys may very well be headed to a top three-finish in the A-Sun.

FLORIDA GULF COAST

2012: 15-17 (8-10 A-Sun); Lost to Belmont 83-69, A-Sun championship game
In-conference offense: 1.05 points per possession (4th)
In-conference defense: 1.10 points allowed per possession (8th)

For a team that prior to last year had never even made the A-Sun tournament, much the NCAA tournament, Florida Gulf Coast came amazingly close to hearing their name called on Selection Sunday. The Eagles knocked off No. 3 seed USC Upstate and No. 2 seed Mercer to reach the final against top seed Belmont. In that game Andy Enfield's team came out hot and built a nine-point lead in the first half, but the Bruins stormed back to claim the title and the league's automatic bid. Still, it was an impressive run for a team with two freshmen in the backcourt. This season those ex-freshmen are back in the form of 6-3 sophomores **Brett Comer** and **Bernard Thompson**. As freshmen the pair proved predictably turnover-prone, however Comer did show his playmaking ability by getting to the free throw line, dishing assists, and doing both with regularity. Meanwhile Thompson generated points from both sides of the arc and at the line. Also capable of burning defenses from outside are 6-4 senior **Sherwood Brown**, 6-2 junior **Christophe Varidel**, and 6-9 sophomore **Filip Cvjeticanin**. Last season the trio combined to make 41 percent of their 395 three-point attempts. FGCU's primarily a perimeter team, but Enfield does have some effective options inside, namely 6-8 junior **Chase Fieler** and 6-8 senior **Eddie Murray**. Both players make their twos while serving as valuable second fiddles on offense, though this season they'll compete for minutes with Iowa State transfer **Eric McKnight**, a 6-9 sophomore. The Eagles should be fine on offense, but they do have some defensive concerns. Their best rebounder last season was 6-4 (Brown), and not surprisingly FGCU was unable to control their defensive glass. A little improvement on that side of the ball could yield big rewards in a season where every important player returns. The Eagles will likely be above the .500 mark in league play, building toward 2013-14 when two more major-conference transfers will become eligible: Nate Hicks (Georgia Tech) and Jamail Jones (Marquette).

EAST TENNESSEE STATE

2012: 17-14 (10-8 A-Sun); Lost to Belmont 69-61, A-Sun semifinals
In-conference offense: 1.02 points per possession (7th)
In-conference defense: 0.99 points allowed per possession (4th)

East Tennessee State has posted seven consecutive winning seasons under Murry Bartow, but extending that streak to eight is going to be a tall task. The Buccaneers lost their top three players in minutes from last season, so keeping the streak alive will be up to four returning seniors, all of whom saw significant playing time in Bartow's tight seven-man rotation. **Marcus Dubose** returns as the team's most voluminous shot-taker. The 6-2 off-guard hit almost half his shots inside the arc, but if Dubose is to be more effective he needs to pose more of a threat from outside. A little more aggression going to the hoop might also serve him well, since he's a solid free throw shooter. Dubose, 6-3 **Sheldon Cooley**, and 6-2 **Jarvis Jones** will likely share ball-handling duties. Jones (who becomes eligible after the fall semester) and Cooley will keep ETSU's tradition of an attacking, turnover-oriented defense alive, as both are adept at getting steals. That's a lot of experience in the backcourt, but the interior will be a question mark. **Lukas Poderis**, the Bucs' 6-8 senior and a strong offensive rebounder, suffered an Achilles injury and his status is uncer-

STETSON

2012: 9-20 (6-12 A-Sun); Did not qualify for A-Sun tournament
In-conference offense: 1.04 points per possession (5th)
In-conference defense: 1.10 points allowed per possession (9th)

Stetson missed its third consecutive A-Sun tournament in 2012, but the good news for the Hatters is that they return every important piece of their rotation from a season ago. Senior **Adam Pegg** will be the primary offensive threat. At 6-9 and 260 pounds he has a surprisingly good shooting touch, hitting not only 55 percent of his twos but also 35 percent on threes and 73 percent on free throws. Pegg is a poor rebounder for his size, though, pulling down just 13 percent of the available defensive rebounds during his minutes. Casey Alexander's rotation has size in Pegg and in 6-8 senior **Liam McInerney**, but for whatever reason that size hasn't translated into successful defense. Out top the Hatters don't have a playmaking guard that draws defenders and distributes to open teammates. **Chris Perez** returns as a shoot-first guard that does most of his damage inside the arc, where the 6-3 junior makes 51 percent of his twos. Unlike Perez, 6-4 senior **Joel Naburgs** and 6-3 junior **Aaron Graham** are more likely to dish the ball off; the vast majority of shots for both players will come from beyond the three-point line. With this much experience returning, Stetson has an opportunity to move up in the standings. To do so, however, they have to improve on defense, specifically on the interior. The Hatters allowed A-Sun opponents to shoot 54 percent on their twos. Bringing that number down could return Alexander's team to their first A-Sun tournament since 2009.

LIPSCOMB

2012: 13-18 (8-10 A-Sun); Lost to Mercer 61-53, A-Sun quarterfinals
In-conference offense: 0.99 points per possession (8th)
In-conference defense: 1.03 points allowed per possession (5th)

Head coach Scott Sanderson went through a tumultuous season in 2011-12. Four players left the team due to various transgressions, be they academic or unspecified. The most important departure was the February loss of Jordan Burgason, the nation's leader in three-point percentage. Coming into this season Sanderson will have to deal with still more turnover. Two seniors are gone, as well as four transfers, and Jacob Arnett, who left to attend pharmacy school. The roster now has nine new faces, including seven freshman and two junior college transfers. For veteran leadership Sanderson will have to turn to sophomore brothers **Malcolm** and **Martin Smith**, as well as 6-1 senior **Deonte Alexander**. Malcolm (at 6-5, an inch taller than his brother) led the nation in fouls drawn per 40 minutes. Martin is a much different player, preferring to do most of his damage on the perimeter. He knocked down 41 percent of his threes and half his twos. Alexander's a spot-up shooter who struggled with his accuracy in his first season after arriving in Nashville as a junior college transfer. The Bison are hoping 6-8 junior **Oscar Garcia** and 6-5 junior **Khion Sankey** make an immediate impact after following Alexander's path from the junior college ranks. Garcia has size, and Sankey looks like a candidate to take over at point guard. Even if both newcomers flourish, however, there will still be available playing time. The most likely candidate to get major minutes may be 6-4 freshman **John Ross Glover**, who despite his height plays an interior-oriented game. The newcomers provide hope for the future, but in the near term Lipscomb will have a tough time matching their eight conference wins from last year.

JACKSONVILLE

2012: 8-22 (6-12 A-Sun); Lost to Belmont 76-62, A-Sun quarterfinals
In-conference offense: 0.99 points per possession (9th)
In-conference defense: 1.06 points allowed per possession (7th)

Four players transferred out of the Jacksonville program in the offseason. The biggest loss was guard Aloys Cabell, who carried the team offensively at times. Now the Dolphins are down to just three experienced players in 6-6 senior **Glenn Powell**, 5-9 senior **Russell Powell** (no relation), and 6-1 junior **Keith McDougald**. Glenn Powell is an effective scorer on the interior and a capable rebounder, but shoots just 43 percent at the line. Russell Powell is a solid pass-first point guard. McDougald is a high-volume shooter who sticks to the outside and rarely gets to the free throw line. With so few returning players, head coach Cliff Warren needs immediate production from newcomers. Of the incoming freshmen, 6-4 guard **Jarvis Haywood** is the most likely to make an immediate impact. Likewise, transfers like 6-6 junior **Javon Dawson** (Utah) and **Dylan Fritsch** (Otero Junior College, also a 6-6 junior) will have opportunities right from the start. Dawson wasn't effective in the Pac-12 last season, but he's eligible immediately and should have an easier time in the A-Sun. Fritsch will provide long-distance shooting. With so many new arrivals it's going to be another tough year for Jacksonville. The Dolphins likely won't improve on the 6-12 conference record they posted last season, and may even have a difficult time matching it.

KENNESAW STATE

2012: 3-28 (0-18 A-Sun); Did not qualify for A-Sun tournament
In-conference offense: 0.94 points per possession (10th)
In-conference defense: 1.16 points allowed per possession (10th)

Head coach Lewis Preston has only one way to go this season, and he'll head that direction without his offensive leader from a year ago, Spencer Dixon. **Markeith Cummings**, 6-0 sophomore **Delbert Love**, and 6-7 senior **Aaron Anderson** return after logging major minutes last season, with Anderson and 6-6 senior Cummings pairing up in the front court. Anderson was much more productive all around, as he hit on 55 percent of his twos, and rebounded 12 percent of offensive chances and 24 percent of defensive chances while turning the ball over just 12 percent of the time. Cummings didn't produce much in the way of rebounding for his size and position, but he does draw fouls. Also available will be 6-7 junior **Brandon Dawson** and 6-7 freshman **Nigel Pruitt**. Like Cummings, Dawson was effective at getting to the free throw line. Pruitt is likely to be more of a slasher, spending time outside until he bulks up his 185-pound frame. Love will be joined in the backcourt by some combination of freshmen, as **Jordan Montgomery** (6-5), **Myles Hamilton** (6-1), **Cole Hobbs** (6-7), and **Yonel Brown** (5-9) all vie for minutes. Montgomery and Hobbs project as scoring guards, while Hobbs and Brown are more likely to be distributors. Preston does appear to be raising the talent level through recruiting, but a ninth-place finish is very likely for the Owls.

NORTHERN KENTUCKY

2012: 23-7 (Division II)

Northern Kentucky is the newest member of the A-Sun, moving up from the ranks of Division II. As provisional members of Division I, the Norse won't be eligible for the A-Sun tournament until 2017, but they will be counted in the RPI this season. Head coach Dave Bezold led his team to a Division I upset last season, when Northern Kentucky took down West Virginia in an exhibition game. Nebraska transfer **Eshaunte Jones** hit the game-winner against the Mountaineers, and the 6-4 senior returns for NKU. He was deadly from long range last season, knocking down 44 percent of his threes. Also back is 6-4 junior **Chad Jackson**, a James Madison transfer who started all 30 games for the Norse a season ago. Completing what is likely to be a three-guard starting lineup is 6-1 senior **Ethan Faulkner**, who led the team last season in minutes played. In the frontcourt Bezold will turn to 6-7 senior **Ernest Watson** and 6-6 sophomore **Jalen Billups**. Watson was solid on the boards, grabbing 14 percent of offensive and 19 percent of defensive rebounds. Billups was a good finisher, hitting on 65 percent of his two-pointers. Of course many of these stats won't hold up once the Norse are playing a full D-I schedule, but it does help to have a few guys that can knock down open looks if they find them. Still, we've seen how this works. NKU is hardly the first program to transition to D-I as a member of the A-Sun. USC Upstate, North Florida, and Florida Gulf Coast blazed this particular trail, and those programs went a combined 12-37 in their first conference seasons. Northern Kentucky will start life in the A-Sun at the bottom.

Big Sky

BY KEN POMEROY

You can rank conferences by various means, but if I were Big Sky commissioner Doug Fullerton, I'd use a new system I recently developed which rates conferences by the highest draft pick in the subsequent NBA draft. Here's how my power ratings would look for last season:

1. SEC
2. Big East
3. Big 12
4. Big Sky
5. ACC
6. Pac-12
7. Big Ten

The Big Sky was represented by Weber State point guard Damian Lillard, who went sixth overall. It was an accomplishment worth celebrating for the conference, and for Lillard himself, who could have had a number of power-conference suitors should he have decided to leave the mid-major level after his sophomore season. However, my new rating system masks a sad truth for the Big Sky: Overall the quality of the league fell to its lowest level in many years. Weber State and conference champion Montana were steady as usual, but the rest of the league took a nosedive. Counting tournament games, the Wildcats and Griz went a combined 29-1 against the other seven schools in the conference. (And it was very close to 30-0. The lone loss was by Weber State to Idaho State when a Wildcats' victory was denied by a Kenny McGowen buzzer-beater.)

Better days should be ahead for the Big Sky in 2013. Lillard aside, a majority of the conference's other teams return their key players. The two programs making their Big Sky debuts this season, North Dakota and Southern Utah, should also improve on their 2012 performances. The conference had its share of coaching drama last season with two of its programs (Northern Arizona and Idaho State) losing coaches mid-season. Both situations eventually involved allegations of NCAA violations. Elsewhere, however, stability reigns. The only other coaching change occurred at Southern Utah where Roger Reid retired in a non-controversial move.

In administrative news, expansion has caused some changes in the way the Big Sky will do business this season. The conference will maintain the double round-robin approach which means each team has a 20-game league schedule, with games starting as soon as December 17 to fit it all in. The tournament format will also change with the field expanded by one to include the top seven teams in the standings. In addition, all six games will be played at the regular-season champion. The most likely destination for that event is Missoula, Montana, but here's guessing the rest of the league hands the Griz more than one loss this season.

Teams listed in Ken's predicted order of finish.

MONTANA

2012: 25-7 (15-1 Big Sky); Lost to Wisconsin 73-49, NCAA round of 64
In-conference offense: 1.08 points per possession (3rd)
In-conference defense: 0.88 points allowed per possession (1st)

Relative to its conference, the Grizzlies had the most dominant defense of any team in the land. The difference between Montana's defensive efficiency in conference play (0.88 points per possession) and that of the second-best defense, Weber State (1.01), was greater than the difference between Weber State and the conference's worst defense. The 0.88 points allowed per possession came in a conference where the average possession league-wide resulted in 1.05 points. The Griz also led the conference in two-point percentage defense, three-point percentage defense, and turnover percentage, the former two by wide margins. This was the biggest reason Montana lost just one game between December 17 and March 7. The Griz are the favorites once again because they return their starting backcourt of 6-1 senior **Will Cherry** and 6-5 junior **Kareem Jamar**. (Well, sort of. Cherry broke his foot in a September pickup game and is expected to miss the first five to 10 games of the season.) Both guards are extremely disruptive defensively and steady on offense. Cherry was highly touted when he arrived in Missoula three seasons ago, and he's made improvements in his game each offseason since. On the offensive side of the ball, he's a consistent scorer whether it's off the dribble or the pass, inside the three-point line or outside of it. He also draws a bunch of fouls and has made himself into a very good free-throw shooter after hitting just 55 percent of his freebies as a freshman. Assuming a full recovery, he'll be the best player in the conference. A shred of good news for the rest of the conference is that Montana may play a bit smaller. Seven-footer Derek Selvig is gone after a solid four years for Montana. The only big option in the middle for coach Wayne Tinkle is 7-0 freshman **Andy Martin**. However, Martin doesn't have the polish that Selvig, nor Brian Qvale before him, did, and is not expected to see the court much as a freshman.

WEBER STATE

2012: 25-7 (14-2 Big Sky); Lost to Loyola Marymount 84-78 (OT), CIT second round
In-conference offense: 1.16 points per possession (1st)
In-conference defense: 1.01 points allowed per possession (2nd)

The Wildcats aren't exactly decimated in terms of how many minutes they lose from last season—just three rotation players are gone—but replacing Damian Lillard means the offense will get a makeover. Weber finished with the fourth-lowest turnover rate nationally mainly because Lillard could monopolize possession of the ball without risk of losing it. So realistically, the offense figures to take a step back. But don't expect a collapse: Lillard missed the entire 2011 conference season, and Weber still led the conference in offensive efficiency. In rare moments when Lillard sat last season, **Gelaun Wheelwright** or **Jordan Richardson** picked up point guard duties. However, neither posted an assist rate over 20. While high assist rates have never been the hallmark of a Randy Rahe offense, he'll need his point guard to do a better job of setting up his teammates. The Wildcats retain the services of 6-2 senior **Scott Bamforth** as a shooting guard for one more season. Bamforth is a high-volume three-point shooter who drained more than 40 percent of his threes for a second straight season. That's notable because the first of those two seasons was played largely without Lillard on the floor. Also back is 6-10 junior **Kyle Tresnak**, an efficient scorer who prefers to work facing the basket. He'll get some help up front from 6-9 freshman **Joel Bolomboy**, mainly in the rebounding and shot-blocking departments. Weber's the perennial leader in Big Sky attendance, and they bring a 17-game home winning streak into this season, the sixth-longest in the country.

NORTHERN COLORADO

2012: 9-19 (5-11 Big Sky); Did not qualify for Big Sky tournament
In-conference offense: 1.05 points per possession (4th)
In-conference defense: 1.11 points allowed per possession (8th)

Last season figured to be a rebuilding year in Greeley and in this case, it wasn't a cliche. The signs were apparent early with a loss to NAIA Westminster in UNC's sixth game. The Bears did manage to collect five conference wins, but it wasn't enough to qualify for the conference tournament. The defense struggled tremendously, primarily on account of B.J. Hill's team "leading" the country in three-point accuracy allowed at 45.1 percent against Division I opponents. This was the highest figure allowed by any D-I team in a decade. While the D struggled, the offense performed nicely considering the possessions that needed replacing from the 2011 conference-champion team. However, turnovers got in the way too often—a whopping 24.9 percent of their Big Sky possessions ended in a TO—and put pressure on an already weak defense with additional transition chances for opponents. UNC should improve on their effort last season if only because they got a lot of contributions from freshmen and sophomores. Redshirt freshman **Tevin Svihovec** led the team in minutes and the 6-2 combo guard was acceptably efficient, if a bit limited by a few too many turnovers. Indeed, one could repeat this analysis for nearly every returning Bear. Simply put, better care of the basketball will allow Northern Colorado to challenge for Big Sky offensive supremacy.

SACRAMENTO STATE

2012: 10-18 (5-11 Big Sky); Did not qualify for Big Sky tournament
In-conference offense: 1.01 points per possession (7th)
In-conference defense: 1.06 points per possession (5th)

On the surface, the Hornets were still pretty much the Hornets we all know and love last season. Meaning, they were not good at many basketball-related skills. For a tenth consecutive season, they failed to crack the top 200 in two- or three-point percentage defense. But on the bright side, they did show general improvement in season four of the Brian Katz era. After four consecutive finishes in the Big Sky basement, Sac State posted a 5-11 conference record, finishing four games clear of last-place Northern Arizona. The improvement could be traced to an offense that scored five more points per 100 conference possessions than it did in 2011. Amazingly, had the Hornets protected a 22-point lead with a little over ten minutes to go against Idaho State on January 14, they would have qualified for the six-team Big Sky tournament for the first time since 2006. Sac State was one of the few teams in the nation to end its season with a win, and the good vibes of a 5-3 finish will continue into this season as the cornerstones of last season's modest success are back in the form of 6-6 senior wing **John Dickson** and 6-2 sophomore point guard **Dylan Garrity**. In addition, 6-8 senior **Konner Veteto** has the potential to be the most dynamic player to suit up for the Hornets since their jump to D-I. That potential rests on his desire to curb an enthusiastic foul rate that forced him to sit much more often than Katz would have liked last season. For the first offseason in a while, an optimistic view of the team means more than just avoiding last place. Given the league's talent void below Montana and Weber State, a winning record is likely if the Hornets play some defense.

NORTH DAKOTA

2012: 17-15 (6-4 Great West); Lost to Drake 70-64, CIT first round
In-conference offense: 0.98 points per possession (4th Great West)
In-conference defense: 0.95 points per allowed possession (2nd Great West)

Perhaps the best thing that North Dakota has going for it in its inaugural season in the Big Sky is its lack of proximity to the rest of the conference's members. Montana State is the closest and it's nearly 800 miles away, making the trip to Grand Forks a chore for league members. A decent home-court advantage should ease the transition of UND ramping up its talent to compete with the top of the Big Sky. That's not to say that the only nicknameless team in Division I (note the alternating references between "North Dakota" and "UND") will be a pushover away from the Betty Englestad Sioux Center. UND only loses one senior from last season's rotation that technically made it to the postseason, (getting a bid to the CIT on the basis of winning the five-team Great West conference tournament). In a few respects North Dakota felt like a Big Sky team last season: Brian Jones' men loved to shoot the three and were not terribly interested in grabbing offensive rebounds. But in other ways, they aren't so similar. For instance, UND make a legitimate effort to prevent opponents' scores. Their adjusted defensive efficiency ranked No. 209 nationally, which was behind only Montana among Big Sky teams. Oh yeah, keep an eye for a big improvement from frequent shooter **Troy Huff**, who became the first D-I player in seven seasons to hoist 100 three-pointers and make fewer than 20 percent of them. Here's guessing the 6-5 junior does better this season. You don't shoot that much and keep your scholarship unless you have some ability. (And he made a third of his three-pointers as a freshman.)

SOUTHERN UTAH

2012: 14-17 (8-10 Summit); Lost to South Dakota State 63-47, Summit semifinals
In-conference offense: 0.99 points per possession (10th Summit)
In-conference defense: 1.02 points allowed per possession (2nd Summit)

The Big Sky's other rookie member has led the country in fewest three-pointers taken two years in a row (threes represented 17.6 percent of SUU's field goal attempts last season). However, that was under Roger Reid, who retired in March after five seasons in Cedar City. The Thunderbirds' new head coach is former Stanford player Nick Robinson, but don't expect to see more long-range shots flying. Robinson has spent all but one of the past eight seasons playing or coaching under Trent Johnson, who also makes perimeter shooting a low priority. One indication that Robinson will employ a philosophy similar to his mentor was the signing of 6-11 **Jayson Cheesman** from Salt Lake Community College. Cheesman will give SUU quality size in the middle. Better news for Southern Utah's prospects: Despite the coaching change, everyone that could have stayed with the program is back. The offense, which struggled tremendously last season, will once again revolve around 6-4 senior **Jackson Stevenett**, whose game has grown dramatically since being an offensive wallflower as a freshman. Like North Dakota, Southern Utah gets some enjoyment out of playing good defense, and this fact alone will make them immediately competitive.

MONTANA STATE

2012: 12-17 (7-9 Big Sky); Lost to Portland State 75-53, Big Sky first round
In-conference offense: 1.01 points per possession (6th)
In-conference defense: 1.04 points allowed per possession (4th)

The Bobcats struggled to find an identity last season, with Brad Huse throwing nine different players into the starting lineup at some point. MSU finished the first half of conference play at 6-2, but won only one game (against a shattered Northern Arizona team) over the last half before getting routed in the first round of the Big Sky tournament. The offseason wasn't filled with good news, either, and in fact left a few unexpected holes in the roster. Among the losses was junior forward Tre Johnson, who started 20 games last season and was dismissed from the team after an arrest over the summer. Johnson's departure leaves the Bobcats without a returning big man on the roster, and thus the team figures to go small. Their efforts will be led by 6-0 junior point guard **Antonio Biglow**, who will make his debut in Bozeman after two years at Mt. San Antonio College. He's expected to bring the kind of athleticism that is at a premium in the Big Sky. The returning player likely to make the biggest contribution is combo guard **Xavier Blount**. The 6-4 senior is a solid three-point shooter and gets to the line plenty, but his 40 percent mark on twos kept his overall efficiency down last season.

PORTLAND STATE

2012: 17-15 (10-6 Big Sky); Lost to Weber State 69-63, Big Sky semifinals
In-conference offense: 1.14 points per possession (2nd)
In-conference defense: 1.09 points allowed per possession (7th)

In a conference that doesn't seem to spring many major surprises in the league standings from year to year, Portland State qualified as one last season. Led by the versatile scoring duo of Charles Odum and Chehales Tapscott, the Vikings were able to put an offense on the floor that rivaled the Big Sky's big boys in terms of effectiveness. Like nearly every other coach in the conference, however, Tyler Geving is apparently waiting for Wayne Tinkle to publish "Basketball Defense for Dummies," because PSU's inability to prevent points kept them from greater achievements, like upsetting Weber State in the Big Sky tournament, for example. The Vikings held a lead for all but a few seconds of the first 35 minutes, only to see the game slip away as they allowed 69 points in a 60-possession game. Both Odum and Tapscott were seniors and will be difficult to replace (Tapscott in particular since he was the only capable defender in the starting lineup, not to mention an incredible rebounder given he was listed at 6-5). The result will be an expanded role for 6-5 senior **Renado Parker**, who, like Tapscott, plays bigger than his height. Portland State will also have one of the more experienced point guards in the Big Sky in 5-11 senior **Lateef McMullan**, who's a capable perimeter shooter. But outside of Weber State, the Vikings lose more production than any team in the league.

EASTERN WASHINGTON

2012: 15-17 (8-8 Big Sky); Lost to Montana 74-66, Big Sky semifinals
In-conference offense: 1.05 points per possession (5th)
In-conference defense: 1.02 points allowed per possession (3rd)

Jim Hayford trotted out the most experienced lineup in the conference last season, as eight of his nine rotation players were either juniors or seniors. More notably, that roster was incredibly foul-happy, with opponents taking 59 free throws for every 100 field goal attempts, far and away the highest figure in the land. Center Laron Griffin fouled out of 13 games on his own and his teammates combined for another 24 disqualifications. At least the team got something for its fouls. They were second in the conference in both steal rate and block rate, and in conference play they had the most efficient defense outside of the Montana-Weber State cabal. For his part, Griffin also led the conference in offensive rebounding rate at 13.6 percent. But studies have shown that it's possible to play effective defense and grab offensive boards without constantly getting in foul trouble.

The challenge for Hayford this season is to make that concept a reality. All in all, it was a successful season in Cheney, where the Eagles went 8-8 and gave Montana a stern test in the Big Sky semifinals. While Eastern Washington has some parts to replace this season, they aren't going to worry too much about where the shots will come from. That's because **Collin Chiverton** is back for his senior season. Chiverton took 38 percent of the Eagles' shots while he was on the floor, second-most in the country. There's a tendency to think a player like that needs to be reigned in, and since the 6-6 Chiverton made just 32 percent of his twos and had a grand total of 17 assists some criticism is justified. But despite doing a lot of his work off the dribble, he posted a microscopic turnover rate and was reasonably efficient in a mediocre Big Sky offense.

NORTHERN ARIZONA

2012: 5-24 (1-15 Big Sky); Did not qualify for Big Sky tournament
In-conference offense: 0.91 points per possession (9th)
In-conference defense: 1.12 points allowed per possession (9th)

The 2011-12 season was simply a disaster for the Lumberjacks. Head coach Mike Adras resigned in early December after being the subject of an internal investigation the previous summer. According to the Arizona Daily Sun, that report concluded that Adras violated NCAA and university regulations, and that there was an environment of "extreme fear" in the program under his watch. NAU would lose its final 16 games and finish 5-24. Making matters worse was that home games took place in the cramped Rolle Activity Center while the spacious Walkup Skydome was being renovated. The new head coach in Flagstaff is former Memphis assistant Jack Murphy. The early vibe on Murphy is positive, as is usually the case when a fresh face comes to town after a five-win season. He couldn't keep all possible returnees in the program, but he inherits the services of two quality seniors in the backcourt, **Stallon Saldivar** and **Gabe Rogers**. Last season Rogers struggled while recovering from a torn labrum, but he's just one year removed from making 47 percent of his threes. The Jacks will still be one of the shortest teams in the nation, however. NAU fans cleverly invite opponents to "kiss my axe." It will be at least another season until that will be realized, but with Murphy's reputation as a recruiter and his connections to the Las Vegas area, NAU should be relevant again soon.

IDAHO STATE

2012: 9-21 (7-9 Big Sky); Lost to Eastern Washington 81-75, Big Sky first round
In-conference offense: 1.00 points per possession (8th)
In-conference defense: 1.08 points allowed per possession (6th)

The Bengals are in a tough spot. Head coach Joe O'Brien resigned in mid-December after a double-digit loss to Utah and handed the reigns over to assistant Deane Martin. Martin guided the Bengals to a 7-9 record and a berth in the conference tournament, but was let go at the end of the season. Only after his dismissal did Martin inform his athletic director, and later the NCAA, that a booster once offered him financial help to obtain players. The NCAA investigation is ongoing, but in the meantime, former Montana assistant Bill Evans gets to pick up the pieces. Those pieces do not include Idaho State's two best offensive players from last season, Kenny McGowen and Chase Grabau. McGowen was personally responsible for three game-winning shots in conference play. It seems likely that 5-11 senior **Melvin Morgan** will lead the team in scoring. Just how efficiently he does so will tell us how effective the Bengals' offense becomes. The defensive side of the ball should get most of Evans' attention. Opponents have made baskets with alarming frequency, and in fact Idaho State is one of the few teams that consistently allowed opponents to make a high percentage of their threes over the past three seasons. ISU ranked Nos. 330, 329, and 337 nationally in opponents' three-point accuracy. That should improve with the protective zone employed by the previous coaching staff a thing of the past.

Big South

BY MIKE PORTSCHELLER

With conference realignment and its trickle-down effects crippling smaller conferences around the nation, the Big South has calmly added to its ranks. A season after welcoming back a solid Campbell program, the conference now adds a 12th member in former Division I independent Longwood. With this expansion comes the advent of two divisions, named North and South, and a 16-game schedule that will see each team play home-and-away against their division rivals and one game against each crossover opponent. The all-important Big South tournament will now be seeded by division standing, and the top two teams from each division will receive first-round byes.

This change in format is not the only way in which the Big South will look different this season. The expansion coincides with a large chunk of roster attrition, as just four teams return more than 51 percent of their conference minutes. All six all-conference first-teamers are gone, and just three second-teamers return. This is a conference ripe for the taking, as last season's best teams are among the hardest hit. It's unlikely that a team as good as 2011-12's UNC Asheville carries the Big South banner into the NCAA tournament, which means the door is cracked open wider than normal for those programs thirsty for a chance.

This doesn't mean that Asheville is out of the discussion, far from it. The Bulldogs should again be a contender, but they'll have some unfamiliar company at the top. Charleston Southern broke through last season with a surprising cast of newcomers, and it is those young players that have made the Buccaneers a reasonable pick as preseason favorites. Coastal Carolina is seemingly always in the discussion, and that shouldn't change this season. Campbell and Liberty both add several talented transfers that could have them in the mix. A dark horse contender could be Gardner Webb, which enters season three of the Chris Holtmann era with a solid defensive backbone and a healthy dose of upside. It is from this half of the conference that the Big South champion is likely to emerge.

At the other end of the spectrum, Presbyterian and Longwood finally enter a season that will end with them in a conference tournament. Winthrop ushers in a new era, and Radford enters season two of theirs. High Point looks to replace a prolific backcourt, and VMI will keep running and hoisting threes. These programs are in various states of rebuild, but it's not impossible that one of them rises up to surprise. The Big South is as wide open as it's been in a long time, and some one is going to win it.

Teams listed in Mike's predicted order of finish.

CHARLESTON SOUTHERN

2012: 19-12 (11-7 Big South); Lost to UNC-Asheville 91-64, Big South semifinals
In-conference offense: 1.10 points per possession (2nd)
In-conference defense: 1.03 points allowed per possession (5th)

In a conference littered with roster attrition, Charleston Southern bucks the trend. Head coach Barclay Radebaugh welcomes back nearly 80 percent of the minutes from last season's surprise team, though it should be noted that the lone loss is a quite big one: Kelvin Martin. A two-time Big South defensive POY, Martin was also an efficient part of the offense—his absence will surely be felt. Still, given the personnel losses suffered by other contenders, the Buccaneers have to be considered the preseason favorites in the Big South. A big reason for that lofty expectation is the sophomore class, which burst onto the scene last winter. **Saah Nimley** was an efficient 5-8 floor general in spite of some shooting woes, and should be even better this time around as a sophomore. Shooting guard **Arlon Harper** nailed 40 percent from deep and scored in a variety of ways, while **Paul Gombwer**, at 6-6, was one of the Big South's better rebounders. Joining these sophomores will be senior wings **Mathiang Muo** and **Jeremy Sexton**, both capable outside shooters in their own right. This group can shoot and pass with anybody in the conference, but the glaring lack of size raises questions about the defense. Without Martin, can the Buccaneers remain a solid rebounding team? Can they continue to force turnovers at a high rate? Will opponents with competent big men be able to score at will? After all, this was Division I's shortest team (by average height) a season ago, and that won't change much. If Charleston Southern can answer these questions and defend at a solid level, the Bucs could bring home their first Big South title in 26 years.

CAMPBELL

2012: 17-15 (11-7 Big South); Lost to Winthrop 71-55, Big South quarterfinals
In-conference offense: 1.06 points per possession (5th)
In-conference defense: 1.06 points allowed per possession (6th)

When head coach Robbie Laing was hired in 2003, Campbell had posted just seven winning records in 24 D-I seasons. With that backdrop of futility, it's quite impressive that the Fighting Camels have now finished above .500 two of the past three seasons. Despite the loss of all-conference forward Eric Griffin, Laing's squad is well positioned to notch another winning campaign, and a run at the Big South title is not out of the question. Like much of the conference, Campbell loses about half of its minutes from last season, but the players that remain are talented. Most notable are senior wing **Darren White** and sophomore point **Trey Freeman**, as both should contend for all-conference honors. Joining the fray are several promising transfers—from junior colleges and elsewhere—headlined by 6-0 sharpshooter **Darian Hooker** (Mineral Area CC), 6-6 scorer **Antwon Oliver** (SW Tennessee CC), and 6-9 **Darius Leonard** (Kent State). It seems a safe bet that Campbell will have one of the Big South's better offenses. The big question mark is defense. The Fighting Camels were quite permissive on the defensive end last season, and even that mediocre performance was boosted by some good fortune. Big South opponents shot a ton of threes against Campbell but converted just 31 percent of them. This type of thing is normally not repeatable (in fact, Laing's coaching resume shows a litany of teams that allowed high three-point percentages), and after the loss of a plus defender like Griffin, a big defensive improvement seems unlikely. The Fighting Camels may have to win shootouts in their quest for Big South glory.

UNC ASHEVILLE

2012: 24-10 (16-2 Big South); Lost to Syracuse 72-65, NCAA round of 64
In-conference offense: 1.14 points per possession (1st)
In-conference defense: 1.01 points allowed per possession (3rd)

We hear it every March. A 16 seed has never defeated a 1 seed in the NCAA tournament. UNC Asheville nearly rendered that statement obsolete in a controversial loss to Syracuse. Setting officiating critiques aside, the main reason Eddie Biedenbach's team was able to hang with an eventual Elite Eight team was its excellent offense, which was led all season by senior guards Matt Dickey, J.P. Primm, and Chris Stephenson. That prolific trio has moved on, leaving Biedenbach to replace an awful lot at both ends. The loss of four starters figures to pull the Bulldogs back to the pack, but Asheville looks very solid on the wings, where returnees **Jeremy Atkinson**, **Jaron Lane**, and **Keith Hornsby** were highly efficient in smaller roles. The interior should get a boost from the return of 6-10 junior **D.J. Cunningham**, who sat out last season with a knee injury. When healthy, Cunningham is one of the Big South's top rebounders and shot blockers, and his potential impact shouldn't be overlooked in a conference so lacking in size. Beyond this point, however, Asheville's rotation gets a bit shaky. Junior **Trent Meyer** figures to get first crack at the point guard spot, as Biedenbach will have to find some ball handlers and distributors if his team is to successfully defend its Big South title.

COASTAL CAROLINA

2012: 19-12 (12-6 Big South); Lost to Old Dominion 68-66, CIT first round
In-conference offense: 1.06 points per possession (4th)
In-conference defense: 1.00 points allowed per possession (2nd)

In the Cliff Ellis era, Coastal Carolina has found success with interior defense. The Chanticleers were the Big South's tallest team last season, a trait that helped them hold conference opponents to frigid 43 percent shooting on twos. That interior defense will be put to the test this season, as the squad has only one returnee taller than 6-4 (that would be 6-7 senior **Bisi Addey**, who played a grand total of 55 Big South minutes last season). Basically, Ellis has two unappealing frontcourt options: go extremely small or go extremely young. Fortunately, there's enough perimeter ability on hand to keep Coastal Carolina afloat. This team now belongs to the slightly-built duo of **Anthony Raffa** and **Kierre Greenwood**, two seniors who just might comprise the Big South's best backcourt. Raffa is a gunner who has no problem hoisting shots, while Greenwood is an unselfish distributor that can find teammates time and again. Of course, they'll need some major help if CCU is to maintain its customary spot near the top of the conference. A small boost could come in the form of new digs. This season the Chants will begin play in a new $35 million facility, which will more than triple the capacity of former home Kimbel Arena. Most importantly, this new facility will be the home of the Big South tournament for the next three seasons, lending Coastal Carolina an edge in its quest to return to the NCAA tournament for the first time in 20 years.

GARDNER WEBB

2012: 12-20 (6-12 Big South); Lost to High Point 68-58, Big South first round
In-conference offense: 0.98 points per possession (9th)
In-conference defense: 1.02 points allowed per possession (4th)

The striking thing about Chris Holtmann's second season at Gardner Webb was how similar it was to his first season, despite a very different cast of characters. Only three rotation members returned from 2010-11, yet the Runnin' Bulldogs posted the same conference record, the same defensive efficiency, and only a marginally improved offensive efficiency. In a way, this was an impressive accomplishment, as we had forecast a more permissive defense and a real battle to avoid the Big South basement. With a full four games separating Gardner Webb from the cellar, you'd have to call 2011-12 a mild success. Now, in Holtmann's third season, GWU seems poised to move up in the standings. A full 65 percent of last season's minutes return (second in the conference), and a significant chunk of those minutes are of the high upside freshman-to-sophomore variety. The leader of this team, however, will be senior **Tashan Newsome**. The 6-3 transfer from Mississippi Valley State is one of the Big South's best rebounders, despite his height, and he also brings a low turnover rate and a penchant for drawing fouls. Improved accuracy from the field could have Newsome contending for an all-conference spot. Of the sophomores, the most promising are 6-2 shooter **Max Landis** and athletic wing **Donta Harper**. Joining the fray is UCF transfer **Jarvis Davis**, a 6-0 sophomore who could take over some of the point guard duties left behind by Jason Dawson and Laron Buggs. If this collection of players can shoot the ball better while maintaining the solid defense Holtmann has installed, the Runnin' Bulldogs will be looking at an upper half finish.

LIBERTY

2012: 14-18 (9-9 Big South); Lost to Charleston Southern 88-74, Big South quarterfinal
In-conference offense: 1.03 points per possession (8th)
In-conference defense: 1.06 points allowed per possession (7th)

The Jesse Sanders era is over. Liberty's four-year starter at point guard finished his career by leading the Flames in nearly every statistical category and earning all-conference honors. On top of that, Sanders was one of only 13 D-I players to record a triple-double last season. Normally, losing a player of Sanders' caliber would doom a team to a down year, but that might not be the case here. Even with Sanders, the Flames started Big South play 2-8. A strong finish pulled Liberty back to .500 in-conference, but this was clearly not a good team. Now, five of Dale Layer's top seven are back, including two prime candidates for a sophomore leap in big men **Joel Vander Pol** and **Tomasz Gielo**. **John Caleb Sanders**, arguably a better pure scorer than his big brother, figures to take over as the team's leading consumer of possessions, and 6-6 senior **Antwan Burrus** supplies proven interior scoring. A serious bugaboo for the Flames has been perimeter shooting, as only six teams in all of D-I made fewer threes last season. That deficiency could be addressed quickly by Layer's latest recruiting class, which includes junior college sharpshooters **Davon Marshall** and **Chad Donley**. Both of these transfers shot better than 38 percent on threes and 82 percent on free throws last season, so we shouldn't be surprised if they garner immediate playing time on a team starved for accuracy. It's never easy to replace a four-year starter, much less at point guard, but Liberty could very well do that and end up with a stronger team.

HIGH POINT

2012: 13-18 (8-10 Big South); Lost to UNC Asheville 86-61, Big South quarterfinal
In-conference offense: 1.07 points per possession (3rd)
In-conference defense: 1.06 points allowed per possession (8th)

No longer does this team belong to Nick Barbour and Shay Shine. Last season, that dynamic duo consumed over half of the team's possessions, and they did so with fantastic efficiency. The result was one of the Big South's best offenses, which was usually good enough to keep the Panthers in games. Unfortunately, a porous defense spoiled the party, and High Point ended up with back-to-back losing seasons. Now that outstanding backcourt is gone, making a stay among the Big South's better offenses seem unlikely. That prospect has to be a bit scary, as Scott Cherry has yet to prove his ability to coach defense in his three seasons at High Point. The Panthers have finished seventh, ninth, and eighth in defensive efficiency under Cherry, and there's no real defensive strengths to build upon. Some help could arrive in the form of **Allan Chaney**, a 6-9 transfer who began his career as a highly-touted freshman at Florida and spent the past three seasons sitting out at Virginia Tech with a heart condition. Chaney has been cleared to play in 2012-13 and could make an instant impact on both ends of the floor. He'll join a returning group that's highlighted by 6-6 senior **Corey Law**, an active rebounder and defender. Without Barbour and Shine, this will be a very different High Point team, and that's probably not a good thing.

PRESBYTERIAN

2012: 14-15 (8-10 Big South); Ineligible for Big South tournament
In-conference offense: 1.05 points per possession (6th)
In-conference defense: 1.07 points allowed per possession (10th)

The time has finally come for the Blue Hose. After five transitional seasons, Presbyterian now gains full-fledged membership in Division I, and with it a spot in the Big South tournament. Regardless of what the regular season brings, dreams of a magical run to the Big Dance can now be entertained well into March. Head coach Gregg Nibert has overseen steady improvement during the transition, to the point where last season's Blue Hose scored a stunning win at Cincinnati (an eventual Sweet 16 team) and made a valiant run at .500 by winning six of their last seven conference games. Had the team been eligible for the Big South tournament, it might well have been considered one of the dark horse contenders to claim the automatic bid. Leading the attempt to do exactly that will be senior **Khalid Mutakabbir**, a solid 6-4 guard whose most distinguishing feature might be his durability. He has led the Big South in minutes for three straight seasons and has yet to miss a collegiate game. Point guard **Eric Washington** showed promise as a freshman last season, and he can be expected to cut down on the turnovers and post better shooting numbers in his second campaign. **Jordan Downing**, a 6-5 transfer from Davidson, will look to provide scoring from the wing. A winning season doesn't seem likely quite yet, but with a roster that includes just three upperclassmen, Blue Hose fans can be forgiven for feeling optimistic about the future.

VMI

2012: 17-16 (8-10 Big South), Lost to UNC Asheville 80-64, Big South championship game
In-conference offense: 1.04 points per possession (7th)
In-conference defense: 1.09 points allowed per possession (11th)

VMI has shot better than 33 percent on their threes twice in Duggar Baucom's seven seasons, and both of those campaigns resulted in winning Big South records. In each of the other five seasons (including 2011-12), the Keydets shot poorly from deep and finished below .500 in conference play. More than any other team, VMI's fate rests in their ability to knock down threes. With less than half the squad's Big South minutes returning, it will be a very different cast of characters launching those shots this season. The biggest presence will be 6-6 senior **Stan Okoye**, an excellent rebounder who's had quite a career in spite of an inconsistent perimeter shot. Diminutive junior **Rodney Glasgow** will look to bounce back from a disappointing season from the field (his career 77 percent shooting from the line suggests that he will). Regardless of what happens on the offensive end, there's a limit on how high VMI can climb. The Keydets have had the conference's most permissive defense for three years running, and only the Big South's addition of Longwood—owners of the worst defense in all of Division I last season—gives reason to think this streak will end. As always, Baucom's team will give up and score a lot of points, but it likely won't be enough to pull VMI out of the bottom half of the conference.

RADFORD

2012: 6-26 (2-16 Big South), Lost to VMI 55-53, Big South first round
In-conference offense: 0.96 points per possession (11th)
In-conference defense: 1.07 points allowed per possession (9th)

Mike Jones has been busy. After a first season in which his Highlanders won just four games against D-I opponents (two more than the season prior), Jones' overhaul of the program continues. This season eight freshmen are on the roster, and the key returnees are sophomores. Radford will be among the nation's youngest teams, but there is some promising talent on hand. Foremost on that list is 6-4 sophomore **Javonte Green**, a tenacious rebounder and defender who's displayed quite a knack for scoring despite a less-than-accurate stroke. Green could make a run at the all-conference team this winter. His main running mate is 6-0 point guard **R.J. Price**, an excellent distributor who shot 41 percent on Big South threes but only 33 percent on twos. One of the best reasons for optimism at Radford is the progress that's been shown on the defensive end. Even while the Highlanders struggled to win games, there were clear signs of the VCU approach that Jones brings. Radford's defense was second only to Winthrop in forced turnover percentage, and opponents took a conference-low 26 percent of their shots from beyond the arc—both hallmarks of Shaka Smart's VCU defenses. A review of the season shows a clear trend: after a choppy November and December, RU's defense got better and better as 2012 wore on, culminating in an excellent effort that almost won the Highlanders a Big South tournament game. This is still not a good team, but fans can expect more progress and an influx of young talent. Given the state of the program Jones inherited, that's a good start.

WINTHROP

2012: 12-20 (8-10 Big South), Lost to VMI 75-55, Big South semifinals
In-conference offense: 0.96 points per possession (10th)
In-conference defense: 0.97 points allowed per possession (1st)

The young and energetic Pat Kelsey now takes the reins at Winthrop. Kelsey made his name as a well-regarded assistant under Skip Prosser and Chris Mack, and he inherits a major rebuild. Winthrop's four best players are gone. The top returning scorer and rebounder is 6-5 junior **Joab Jerome**, at just five points and four boards per game. None of the other returnees provided much of value last season, with dismal shooting percentages the norm. While it's not hard to envision the offense getting better simply because it can't really get much worse, the defense will almost certainly be more permissive. Frankly, Kelsey has some serious recruiting to do. The only silver lining for the current roster is the presence of several sophomore leap candidates, including guys that received solid minutes as freshman last season, namely 6-8 **James Bourne** and 5-10 **Andre Smith**. Short of major progression from these young players, it will be a rough debut season for Kelsey, and only the Big South's addition of Longwood figures to keep the Eagles out of the conference cellar.

LONGWOOD

2012: 10-21 (Independent)
Offense: 0.94 points per possession (No. 282 D-I)
Overall defense: 1.23 points allowed per possession (No. 345 D-I)

Buckle up, Big South fans. If you thought playing VMI was a boon to your team's offensive statistics, wait till you get a load of Longwood. Mike Gillian's program, which has admirably made the long journey from Division III to the Big South, plays nearly as fast as VMI but with even worse defense. Last season, Longwood had the worst defense in all of Division I, and it wasn't close. Now, the Lancers return only 30 percent of their minutes and have to replace the school's all-time leading scorer in Antwan Carter. Longwood seems like a lock for the Big South cellar, but there's still reason for a glimmer of excitement in Farmville. For the first time ever, the Lancers will have a chance to make the Big Dance. Sure, it's extremely unlikely that Longwood runs the table at the Big South tournament, but a long shot is better than no shot at all. This small school in rural Virginia has a proud basketball past, including longtime NBA forward Jerome Kersey and a D-III Final Four. With the tantalizing statistic accumulation offered by matchups with Longwood, Big South fans should find it in their hearts to forgive the school for once instructing Jason Mraz.

Big West

BY EDDIE ROACH

Long Beach State left little doubt as to who the best team in the Big West was last season, rolling through the conference with ease. UC Santa Barbara was expected to be a stiff test for the 49ers, but failed to apply as much pressure on the eventual conference champ as anticipated. The 49ers and the Gauchos met in the title game for a third straight year, but UCSB proved an unworthy opponent. Big West coach of the year Dan Monson (a repeat winner) and his team seized the opportunity and capped a fantastic 2012 campaign with the school's first NCAA tournament berth since 2007.

In a league that had two clear favorites last season, a clear path was set for a couple teams to shine and for the rest to languish in their shadow. This season things figure to be a little more ambiguous. Parity abounds with several teams in the mix and looking to incorporate their influxes of young talent. In fact many Big West teams will rely heavily on underclassmen to play significant roles.

With the only returning All-Big West first-teamer in D.J. Seeley on their roster, Cal State Fullerton appears to be a slight favorite for the title this season, though hardly a lock. Pacific will look to go out firing in what will be their final season in Big West play before departing to the West Coast Conference next year. Long Beach enters the season with far less clout than last year, but looks to prove it still has the pieces to remain in the top tier of the conference.

With the Big West realignment under way, the league welcomes Hawaii into the conference this season, but the changes don't end there. San Diego State and Boise State will join the fray in 2013-14 in a move that will give the conference's national exposure a continued boost and round the league out at 10 teams.

Teams listed in Eddie's predicted order of finish.

CAL STATE FULLERTON

2012: 21-10 (12-4 Big West); Lost to Loyola Marymount 88-79, CIT first round
In-conference offense: 1.13 points per possession (1st)
In-conference defense: 1.08 points allowed per possession (7th)

After a Cal State Fullerton team carrying a No. 2 seed into the Big West tournament lost in the quarterfinals to No. 7 seed UC Irvine, several Titans on the roster threatened to quit the team rather than continue playing for head coach Bob Burton. In June the school announced that Burton would not return, and in August associate head coach Andy Newman was named interim head coach. Not the backstory you usually see from a conference favorite, perhaps, but Newman has **D.J. Seeley**. The 6-4 senior had an impressive opening season in the Big West after transferring in from California. Seeley was the focal point of the Titan offense and was named first team All-Big West. Although not nearly as highly touted, 6-3 senior **Kwame Vaughn** has proven to be just as good if not better than Seeley, producing comparable offensive numbers across the board at a more efficient rate. Vaughn posted an offensive rating better than 115, good for third in the conference among players who used at least 20 percent of possessions while on the floor. Cal State Fullerton was fantastic offensively last year, finishing No. 1 in the Big West at 1.13 points per possession. The Titans relied heavily on the long ball, and that proved to be a good idea as they drained 43 percent of their threes in conference play. This season Newman will look to **Givon Crump**, a 6-7 transfer from Pasadena City College, to make an immediate impact by serving as another athletic perimeter threat. However defense was once again a sore spot for the Titans, as they surrendered a robust 1.08 points per trip to Big West opponents. If CSUF is serious about contending for the Big West title, improvement on the defensive end is a must. It remains to be seen whether Newman will continue to employ the high-tempo offense that his predecessor ran. But considering last year's success, the interim head coach may want to leave that side of the ball more or less alone. If he does the Titans may just feature two all-conference first team selections.

PACIFIC

2012: 11-19 (6-10 Big West); Lost to UC Santa Barbara 72-52, Big West quarterfinals
In-conference offense: 1.01 points per possession (6th)
In-conference defense: 1.04 points allowed per possession (5th)

Never mind what you saw last season. Pacific actually has the pieces in place to make some noise in head coach Bob Thomason's 25th and final year. Thomason will retire at season's end, and the Tigers will move to the West Coast Conference for 2013-14. Meantime keep your eye on 6-7 junior **Ross Rivera**. In 2011-12 he posted an offensive rating of 118 while using 23 percent of his team's possessions during his minutes. Rivera also drew more than six fouls per 40 minutes (tops in the Big West) and made opponents pay dearly for those whistles by shooting 85 percent at the stripe. Senior **Lorenzo McCloud** wasn't too far behind in terms of production at the line, and he also assisted on 29 percent of UOP's baskets while on the court. The duo will look to continue attacking the paint and making opponents pay from the line—and that's important because Thomason's team wasn't overly efficient offensively otherwise. What the Tigers did have going in their favor, however, was a very nice turnover margin, ranking first in the Big West in both lowest turnover percentage and highest opponent TO rate. This season Thomason will look to 6-8 junior **Khalil Kelley** to provide a physical presence inside and create extra opportunities for the offense as he did last season, grabbing 12 percent of his team's misses during his minutes. An improvement in Kelley's 37 percent free throw shooting would also be a nice bonus for a team that looks to be in the Big West mix one last time.

LONG BEACH STATE

2012: 25-9 (15-1 Big West); Lost to New Mexico 75-68, NCAA round of 64
In-conference offense: 1.11 points per possession (2nd)
In-conference defense: 0.91 points allowed per possession (1st)

Coming off a strong and perhaps even dominant 2011-12, Long Beach State will have plenty of holes to fill. The 49ers have lost their three best playmakers: Casper Ware, T.J. Robinson, and Larry Anderson, all of whom earned All-Big West first team honors. Dan Monson's only returning starter is 6-7 senior **James Ennis**, who, not surprisingly, will be tasked with assuming a bigger role offensively. As a junior the swing forward posted an offensive rating of 112 on 18 percent of possessions used, numbers encouraging enough to make him this season's focal point on offense. You may even hear Ennis' name being mentioned among the candidates for Big West player of the year. Sophomore **Mike Caffey** will also see an expanded role since he's the only other returning player that logged significant minutes. While Ennis and Caffey at least give Monson two efficient sources of points, things are more uncertain on the other end of the floor. The 49ers will be without their defensive anchor, Robinson, for the first time since 2008. Strong defensive play has been a program staple, as Long Beach State has finished in the top three in conference-only defensive efficiency in each of the last four years. The 49ers will need to continue that strong play defensively if they're to have any chance of defending their title. Monson's team isn't the clear-cut favorite like last year, but Long Beach State should compete for another Big West crown.

CAL STATE NORTHRIDGE

2012: 7-21 (3-13 Big West); Did not qualify for Big West tournament
In-conference offense: 1.02 points per possession (5th)
In-conference defense: 1.13 points allowed per possession (9th)

The Matadors had a rough 2011-12, but that was to be expected after losing four starters and handing over a large chunk of possessions and minutes to the talented but inexperienced **Stephan Hicks**. The Big West freshman of the year looks to be a star in the making and posted a very respectable offensive 108 offensive rating while using 25 percent of Northridge's possessions during his minutes. Hicks struggled a bit from the field, but made up for it by getting to the line frequently and shooting 81 percent from there. For Bobby Braswell's team to take another step in the right direction, though, Hicks will need help. As the Matadors' second option offensively, 6-0 junior **Josh Greene** must improve his efficiency, particularly inside the arc, if he plans to again take 25 percent of the team's shots while he's on the floor. Another option will be foul-prone 6-7 sophomore **Stephen Maxwell**, his team's best rebounder at both ends of the floor. The Matadors should be much improved and simply getting a year older should help this offense a good deal, but a defense that finished dead last in the league last season does need to be addressed. Braswell may want to find a few more minutes for 6-10 junior **Frankie Eteuati** to provide some shot blocking inside. Watch for Northridge to be tested early, with three true road games against Pac-12 opponents (UCLA, Arizona State, and Utah) coming in quick succession between Thanksgiving and Christmas.

CAL POLY

2012: 18-15 (8-8 Big West); Lost to UC Santa Barbara 64-52, Big West semifinals
In-conference offense: 1.07 points per possession (4th)
In-conference defense: 1.03 points allowed per possession (4th)

Cal Poly repeated as the slowest-paced team in the Big West for a second consecutive year and figures to utilize the same strategy again this season. Not spectacular at any one thing but steady on both sides of the ball, Joe Callero's team finished fourth in both offensive and defensive efficiency in-conference. One sore spot offensively was the Mustangs' inability to get to the free throw line; another was the frequency with which their shot attempts were swatted away by opposing defenses. And at the other end of the floor Cal Poly was the league's most foul-prone defense. On a roster that just lost three starters to graduation, 6-7 junior **Chris Eversley** looks to be the guy primed to take over on offense, though he'll do so alongside senior guards **Dylan Royer** and **Drake U'u**. Eversley posted a solid offensive rating of 111 on just over 24 percent of possessions used, and he'll likely see increased minutes this season. The Mustangs didn't attempt a whole lot of threes last season, but Royer was easily the team's biggest threat from long distance, shooting a blistering 47 percent from downtown on a team-high 155 attempts. While the amount of possessions used during his time on the floor was nothing to write home about, Royer posted an off-the-charts offensive rating of 136, a figure good for second in the nation. Just the fact that he's standing outside the line should help spread opposing defenses. Callero will look to U'u to again make an impact on the defensive end.

UC IRVINE

2012: 12-20 (6-10 Big West); Lost to Long Beach State 68-57, Big West semifinals
In-conference offense: 1.00 points per possession (7th)
In-conference defense: 1.07 points allowed per possession (6th)

Russell Turner's team remained remarkably consistent in a middle-of-the-pack way, ranking seventh and sixth in offensive and defensive efficiency in-conference, respectively, for a second straight season. But the Anteaters have hopes of breaking out of that rut this season, as they return their top five players in minutes from 2011-12. UCI's backcourt is led by 6-3 senior **Daman Starring** and 6-0 senior **Derick Flowers**, both of whom (particularly Flowers) struggled with turnovers as juniors. But give the seniors credit (or perhaps give the official scorer at the Bren credit). A remarkable 67 percent of the Anteaters' baskets in Big West play came off of assists. Sending a few more of those dishes **Michael Wilder**'s way might not be a bad idea. The 6-2 senior posted easily the best offensive rating on the team last season, and could stand to add a few more possessions to his workload. Defensively UCI was great at blocking shots, but were unable or unwilling to create turnovers, as Big West opponents ended their possessions with some kind of shot 83 percent of the time. With opponents getting that many chances to score, Turner will look to 6-8 sophomore **Will Davis** to cement his emergence as one of the top shot blocking threats in the conference. It will also be helpful if conference opponents no longer make 39 percent of their threes against this defense, the way they did last season.

UC SANTA BARBARA

2012: 20-11 (12-4 Big West), Lost to Idaho 86-83, CIT first round
In-conference offense: 1.11 points per possession (3rd)
In-conference defense: 0.99 points allowed per possession (3rd)

After losing several key contributors, most notably three-time All-Big West first team selection Orlando Johnson, UCSB enters the season in a bit of a rebuilding mode as Bob Williams will take a very inexperienced roster into battle in 2012-13. The exceptions to the inexperienced rule are 6-2 junior **Kyle Boswell** and 6-7 sophomore **Alan Williams**, and each should see a spike in minutes. Boswell's offensive rating of 129 was good for fourth in all of D-I, although he wasn't exactly a high-usage machine. He won't be the focus of the offense, but he should be a steadying presence for a team featuring five freshmen. Williams returns as the team's starting center and should see the bulk of the minutes inside as long as he can stay out of foul trouble. He posted the highest offensive rebounding rate in the nation last season (23 percent) and was the primary reason the Gauchos finished first in that category in conference play. Williams was no slouch on the defensive end either, proving to be nearly as effective on the defensive glass and a capable shot blocker. Doing all of the above as a freshman has UCSB fans (not to mention the team) excited about what's to come for Williams once he's given a heavier workload. Coach Williams will have plenty of talent at his disposal, and by next season, these young guns will be making a serious run at the top of the Big West.

HAWAII

2012: 16-16 (6-8 WAC); Lost to New Mexico State 92-81, WAC semifinals
In-conference offense: 1.02 points per possession (6th WAC)
In-conference defense: 1.08 points allowed per possession (7th WAC)

After 33 years in the WAC, Hawaii is set to make its debut in the Big West this season and will get its first taste of league competition against Cal State Northridge in late December (a familiar opponent, actually, and one they handled with ease in their 2011-12 season opener). As chance would have it, however, the change in leagues is catching the Warriors at a time of high turnover, as Gib Arnold has just two returning starters to blend with eight newcomers. All-WAC first team selection **Vander Joaquim** returns as UH's clear leader—or will eventually. The 6-10 senior suffered a torn MCL in a preseason workout and is expected to miss the early part of the season, but should be ready to go by the time league play comes around. If he's healthy, Joaquim seems poised to have another strong season in his senior campaign. If he's not, abandon all hope for a defense that even with Joaquim gave up a dismal 1.08 points per trip in WAC play. Though maybe 6-8 Nebraska transfer **Christian Standhardinger** can offer some support on the glass. **Senior Hauns Brereton**, the only other familiar face from last year's starting lineup, should see a boost in usage to go along with an increase in minutes. One encouraging sign for Arnold's up-tempo offense is that many of last season's highest turnover rates have been made to disappear through the magic of graduation. Hawaii is young and unlikely to set the Big West on fire in their debut, but the Warriors will ultimately go as far as their decorated if gimpy big man can take them.

UC RIVERSIDE

2012: 14-17 (7-9 Big West); Lost to Cal Poly 66-54, Big West quarterfinals
In-conference offense: 0.91 points per possession (9th)
In-conference defense: 0.96 points allowed per possession (2nd)

UC Riverside enters the season knowing they won't play in the Big West tournament or anywhere else in the postseason due to failure to meet NCAA academic requirements. The Highlanders' presence on the NCAA's very small postseason blacklist fits in with the UCR's status as a team of extremes. Just one season ago Jim Wooldridge could claim the sixth most experienced roster in Division I. Now four of those starters are gone, which actually may not be a bad thing offensively. Last season's group clearly had difficulties scoring points, but, to be fair to the recent graduates, Wooldridge will have a tough time getting his young team to duplicate the level of defense seen from UCR last season. Senior guard **Robert Smith** and 6-4 junior **Chris Harriel**, a Portland State transfer, will have to provide leadership for a team that enters the season looking plenty different from last year's. With so many newcomers, playing time is up for grabs.

UC DAVIS

2012: 5-26 (3-13 Big West), Lost to Long Beach State 80-46, Big West quarterfinals
In-conference offense: 0.96 points per possession (8th)
In-conference defense: 1.12 points allowed per possession (8th)

Coach Jim Les had a tough time in his debut for UC Davis. The Aggies finished 3-13 in the conference and had a lot of trouble on both ends of the floor. While UCD fared well on the perimeter, their 39 percent three-point shooting was within reach of their appalling 42 percent success rate from inside the arc. On the other side of the ball the Aggies' strength was their outstanding free throw defense, as conference opponents made just 67 percent of their attempts from the charity stripe. Assuming that performance isn't duplicated, Les will want to find improvements elsewhere on D. Individually, coach's son **Tyler Les** was the main ingredient in UCD's long-range recipe on offense, hitting 41 percent of his 200 three-point attempts. Another efficient scorer is 6-9 junior **Josh Ritchart**, but these guys are going to need some help. Maybe 6-4 junior **Ryan Sypkens** can provide it. Sypkens looked great in the first four games of the season before a knee injury sidelined him for the remainder of 2011-12.

Great West

BY JOHN GASAWAY

The Great West has been playing Division I basketball for just three seasons, but the league's already old enough for its founding assumptions to look a little dated. If you were starting a basketball conference in the fall of 2009 as an adjunct to what was, comparatively speaking, a storied old football conference (est. 2004), you could have been forgiven for thinking you'd enroll some ambitious programs in your new venture, stick together, pay some dues, and come out in a few seasons with an automatic NCAA tournament bid.

Then again no one came up to you that fall and said, "Oh, by the way, all heck's going to break loose in a year and a half, and programs will start hopping around, or threatening to, like kernels in a popcorn popper." Conference realignment has already claimed the Great West as a football victim, as the league stopped participating in that sport after the 2011 season. In basketball it's not clear the picture is much brighter.

When a program like Northern Kentucky can jump directly from Division II to provisional D-I status and membership in an established conference (the Atlantic Sun) that already has an automatic bid, the Great West's operating model can be called into question. True, the Norse won't be eligible for their spiffy new conference's tournament until 2017. But that's a definite date on the calendar, one NKU can market to recruits. Similarly, CSU Bakersfield and even long-suffering independent Longwood have also found the D-I promised land without having to do time in the Great West.

In the past two offseasons the Great West has seen South Dakota and North Dakota leave for the Summit and Big Sky, respectively. After this season Houston Baptist is headed to the Southland, and Utah Valley is slated to join the WAC. An exhaustive quantitative evaluation by highly trained technicians in white lab coats has revealed that the Great West will then be down to three members, meaning someone's getting a bye all the way to the 2014 conference title game.

Teams listed in John's predicted order of finish.

UTAH VALLEY

2012: 20-13 (9-1 Great West); Lost to Weber State 72-69, CIT first round
In-conference offense: 1.05 points per possession (1st)
In-conference defense: 0.93 points allowed per possession (1st)

The Wolverines are the Gonzaga/Kansas of this here conference, having posted a 20-2 record in league play over the past two seasons. So don't be overly concerned about Dick Hunsaker losing 2011 Great West POY Isiah Williams. (Last season's winner was NJIT's Isaiah Wilkerson. In the entire history of the Great West POY award, a whopping 67 percent of its recipients have been named some variant of "Isaiah.") In Orem they don't rebuild, they reload. **Holton Hunsaker** returns and will shoot many threes. Thus far the 6-0 junior has connected on just 32 percent of those attempts over his career, but he does shoot 85 percent at the line so there's a good chance he'll start connecting at a higher rate at some point. Conversely if he had a different last name his coach would likely draw him aside to discuss his 31 percent shooting inside the arc. Far more successful in close is 6-9 junior **Ben Aird**, who's poised to see a big jump in his defensive rebound percentage now that Geddes Robinson has graduated. That being said and with all due respect to the respective listed heights, this roster's best option for a made two-point shot is actually 6-4 senior **Alfonzo Hubbard**. Before heading out the door to join the WAC, UVU will wrap up its Great West career with a third consecutive regular season title.

NJIT

2012: 15-17 (5-5 Great West); Lost to North Dakota 75-60, Great West championship game
In-conference offense: 1.03 points per possession (2nd)
In-conference defense: 1.03 points allowed per possession (6th)

Last season the Highlanders played like they'd read only the even-numbered pages in Frank Martin's book of hoops. Jim Engles' team fouled like crazy—so far, so good. But you know the part of Martin's magnum opus where he points out it's also important to draw fouls? That's the part the young men in Newark somehow missed. Redressing this imbalance in whistles could pay big rewards, because Engles has three seniors who give his team a chance at a first place finish. **Chris Flores** carried a load on offense that was nearly as heavy as that hauled by Great West POY and teammate Isaiah Wilkerson, and did so pretty well. At 6-2 Flores dishes assists and is capable of scoring from either side of the arc. **Ryan Woods** hit 42 percent of his 130 attempted threes last season. And while he's turnover-prone, **PJ Miller** gives Engles still another experienced option on offense.

TEXAS-PAN AMERICAN

2012: 11-21 (5-5 Great West); Lost to North Dakota 63-59, Great West semifinals
In-conference offense: 1.00 points per possession (3rd)
In-conference defense: 1.02 points allowed per possession (4th)

The Broncs have said goodbye to last season's featured scorer, Jared Maree, and that's a big loss because the 6-3 senior translated possessions into points in a highly effective manner. Then again coach Ryan Marks does return a flock of seniors, including co-featured scorer **Aaron Urbanus**. At 5-10, Urbanus is a good perimeter shooter who would be well advised to stay on the perimeter. An even better option from beyond the arc is **Brandon Provost**, a career 46 percent three-point shooter. Other experienced veterans include **Jesus Delgado** and **Ruben Cabrera**. And just to make things interesting, there are even a couple non-seniors to note. Meet 6-7 sophomore **Lauri Toivonen** (nickname: "Latte"), a Finn that Marks says will be heard from. And if 6-6 junior **Josh Cleveland** can stay out of foul trouble, the young man has proven beyond question that he can get you offensive boards.

HOUSTON BAPTIST

2012: 10-20 (3-7 Great West); Lost to NJIT 65-64, Great West first round
In-conference offense: 0.96 points per possession (5th)
In-conference defense: 1.02 points allowed per possession (5th)

Ron Cottrell gave a large share of possessions and shots to a freshman last season, and, with the exception of that whole 18 percent three-point shooting thing, the experiment didn't go too badly. Now **Tyler Russell** is a 6-0 sophomore. His accuracy from beyond the arc is certain to improve (he shoots 80 percent at the line), and the rest of his game isn't too bad as is. Also back is 6-5 senior **Marcus Davis**, a wing who pushed his offensive rating north of 100 by drawing fouls and shooting 86 percent on his free throws. And at 6-9, **Art Bernardi** is an effective scorer in the paint when he can stay out of foul trouble. The real question, however, is on defense, as the Huskies posted their best showing in program history last season at No. 312 nationally.

CHICAGO STATE

2012: 4-26 (2-8 Great West); Did not qualify for Great West tournament
In-conference offense: 0.94 points per possession (6th)
In-conference defense: 1.01 points allowed per possession (3rd)

Yes, you're reading those figures correctly. On paper the Cougars played defense better than three other Great West teams, but Tracy Dildy's group won just twice in 10 tries. You might therefore conclude the offense wasn't very good, and you would be correct. If you're looking for seeds of hope within a program where the words "Did not qualify for Great West tournament" are applicable, here you go: **Jeremy Robinson**, 2012 Great West newcomer of the year. He's back, a 6-9 senior who should give up on threes, but does make half his twos and cleans the defensive glass. The Great West tournament is played annually on the Cougars' home floor, at the Emil and Patricia Jones Convocation Center, and in the new slimmed-down five-team bracket, CSU is guaranteed to participate. Did someone just say "magical run to the CIT"?

Independents

BY JOHN TEMPLON

Independence in college basketball is going out of style faster than tamagotchis. Right now, not being affiliated with a conference means difficulty scheduling and practically no chance of reaching the NCAA tournament. Those trends are why just two teams will play as independents during the 2012-13 season—and both will leave those ranks soon. Already putting the "ex-" in "ex-independent" as of this season are Seattle University (WAC), Longwood (Big South), and Omaha (Summit). It's becoming an awfully lonely place.

CSU BAKERSFIELD

2012: 16-15
Offense: 0.99 points per possession (No. 211 D-I)
Defense: 1.08 points allowed per possession (No. 279 D-I)

The Roadrunners took a huge step forward for independents by playing in the postseason. Yes, it was the CBI, but for a team that battled through one of the oddest schedules in the nation it was a justly deserved reward. CSUB also acquitted itself well, with a 75-69 loss at Utah State. The highlight of the season, though, was undoubtedly sweeping two Big West programs: Cal Poly and Cal State Fullerton. In other words the Roadrunners were sweeping members of the league that had rejected CSUB's bid for membership on at least one occasion, so they took the logical next step and joined a conference that's better than the Big West. As of 2013-14, CSU Bakersfield will be a member of the WAC.

NEW ORLEANS

2012: 17-15 (1-7 vs. NCAA Division I)

The rambling UNO program has returned to Division I after a two-year hiatus. The Privateers return to the highest level of college basketball after considering moves to either Division II or Division III. The last time UNO played D-I basketball the Privateers went 8-22 as members of the Sun Belt in 2009-10. The temporary drop down to Division II did lead to talent depletion, but UNO managed to defeat Alcorn State and hang with San Diego last season. This team will be back on its feet in no time, as independence is a one-season deal with UNO accepting an invitation to join the Southland Conference in 2013-14.

Ivy

BY JOHN EZEKOWITZ

Last year felt like an inflection point for basketball in the Ivy League. The league had easily its best performance, as measured by Ken Pomeroy, in the tempo-free era. In their non-conference schedules, Harvard and Princeton managed four wins against major-conference schools, including two against NCAA tournament at-large selection Florida State. Harvard earned a spot in the national polls for several weeks, and held their own in a nationally televised showdown with Connecticut. The Ivies sent four teams to the postseason for the first time in league history.

Administratively, the conference capitalized on their increasingly high profile in the college basketball landscape to land a TV deal for basketball. NBC Sports Network will broadcast between six and 10 games this season. For a league that was not able to secure more than Internet streaming for its marquee one-game playoff for an NCAA tournament berth in 2011, this is a major step forward.

These signs point to a positive inflection: a league on the rise will continue to rise, and possibly even at a faster pace in terms of national recognition. But this is the Ancient Eight, and nothing is that simple. Off the court, there is still unease about the newfound prominence of Ivy sports on the national stage. And there are still Ivy-specific rules that hurt basketball programs.

This summer, the NCAA changed its bylaws to allow players to practice formally with coaches during the summer as long as they were enrolled in summer school. Coaches nationwide hailed this rule change as an unalloyed positive. Nationwide, that is, except for in the Ivy League. That is because Harvard and Princeton do not offer summer school to any students. Because not all of the schools have it, no one can have it. And Harvard and Princeton are not about to start offering summer school because of a basketball rule change.

Additionally, teams are still feeling out the impact of the increase in the Academic Index (AI) standards passed by the Ivy League presidents last summer. The AI is composed of a recruit's GPA and standardized test scores, and represents a minimum standard for admission that is far above any other conference's standards. The increased AI limits the pool of players Ivy coaches can attempt to recruit.

Finally, there was the news in September that Harvard senior stars Kyle Casey and Brandyn Curry were implicated in a cheating scandal in a government class that had ensnared over 100 students and made the front page of the New York Times. Casey and Curry will miss this season as punishment. While the scandal was a Harvard student problem, not a Harvard athletic or basketball problem, and although Penn, Princeton, and Yale have all suspended players for similar offenses in recent years, reactionaries in Ivy administrations must have been vindicated in their condemnation of pursuing athletic success.

On the court, too, the Ivy will likely take a step back this season. The league will lose eight of the 11 players selected to either the first or second teams All-Ivy. Player of the year Zack Rosen, who almost won the Ivy crown for Penn by himself, is gone, as is defensive player of the year Reggie Willhite from Yale. While the drop in talent will not be as steep as it would have been in the past, it's unlikely that the 2013 Ivy season will end with four teams in the postseason, let alone a team in the top 50 in Pomeroy's rankings.

Princeton is the preseason favorite to win the so-called "14-game tournament" because the Tigers return the most talented front line and my pick for Ivy POY, Ian Hummer. Despite the suspensions, Harvard will contend, too, behind the play of dynamic guards Laurent Rivard and Wes Saunders.

The most intriguing team in the league is Columbia. The Lions have not finished above 7-7 in league play since the 20th century, but they should be able to better that mark this season. They return All-Ivy point guard Brian Barbour, uber-efficient post player Mark Cisco, and three-point gunner Meiko Lyles. If the Lions can tighten their defense, they have a chance to make their first NCAA tournament appearance in 45 years.

The league's middle is a muddle. Yale, Cornell and Penn must deal with a lot of roster turnover having graduated star players in 2012. The Big Red has the most continuity in returning players and will benefit from the return of athletic wing Errick Peck, who missed all of last season with a knee injury. Any of these teams could finish as high as third or as low as sixth.

At the bottom, Dartmouth continues its slow but steady ascent from the cellar of the league. Despite winning only one league game last year, the Big Green showed improvement and return talented sophomores Gabas Maldunas and Jvonte Brooks. They could challenge Brown for seventh place. Under their new 30-year-old coach, Mike Martin, the Bears must find a way to play better defense. Brown has offensive talent in Sean McGonagill and Tucker Halpern, but the defense gave up over 1.11 points per possession in Ivy play last season.

While the Ivy League might take a step back in 2013, the future is bright. There is still pushback on the increased commitment to basketball from some corners of the league, but the TV deal is a huge advance. If alumni get used to seeing their teams playing well on TV on Friday and Saturday nights in February and March, there may be no amount of harrumphing that will pull back the improvements that have been made in recent years. This fan of Ivy basketball can only hope that we did not witness the peak of the league in 2012.

Teams listed in John's predicted order of finish.

PRINCETON

2012: 20-12 (10-4 Ivy); Lost to Pittsburgh 82-61, CBI quarterfinals
In-conference offense: 1.09 points per possession (1st)
In-conference defense: 0.96 points allowed per possession (3rd)

In his first year as head coach, Mitch Henderson proved himself to be an excellent in-game manager and X's and O's teacher. In their first 10 games, the Tigers averaged 0.93 points per possession offensively against opponents with an average Pomeroy ranking of No. 139. In their last 10 games, the Tigers averaged 1.14 points per trip against opponents with an average rank of 156, an unbelievable improvement registered against similar competition. Henderson's version of the Princeton Offense is not especially slow (Princeton was fourth in the conference in tempo), but is brutally efficient. The Tigers posted an effective field goal percentage of 56 in conference play while leading the Ivy League in turnover rate. A lot of that efficiency can be attributed to 6-7 senior **Ian Hummer**, who led the Tigers in points, rebound rate, and assist rate, an unbelievable feat. The sweet-passing big man is the perfect player for Henderson's system. The Tigers are extremely tall for an Ivy League team, boasting an effective height of +3.6 inches, good for No. 16 nationally. **Mack Darrow**, a 6-9 senior who shot 53 percent from two and 36 percent from three last season, will again pair with 6-11 senior **Brendan Connolly**. Sophomore **Denton Koon** will back them up. In the backcourt a lot will rest on 6-5 junior guard **T.J. Bray**, who's been very efficient and is a good defender but sometimes has trouble creating his own shot. The Tigers will definitely feel an impact from the graduation of Doug Davis, the do-everything guard who frequently bailed them out last season. Jimmy Sherburne is also out for the year with an injury, leaving Princeton thin in the backcourt. But the Tigers return experience and skill up front, and they benefit from the disconcerting shooting backdrops at Jadwin Gymnasium, a venue where they've lost one game in the last two seasons. If Bray gets injured or does not live up to expectations, Princeton will be in trouble, but the Tigers must be made the favorite to make their second NCAA tournament appearance in the last three seasons.

HARVARD

2012: 26-5 (12-2 Ivy); Lost to Vanderbilt 79-70, NCAA round of 64
In-conference offense: 1.07 points per possession (2nd)
In-conference defense: 0.90 points allowed per possession (1st)

Last season, Harvard finally made it to the promised land. They won the Ivy League outright for the first time in program history, and made the NCAA tournament for the first time in over 60 years. Surprisingly, the Crimson improved over the 2011 edition primarily because of their defense. The Crimson limited Ivy opponents to just 0.90 points per possession, and posted effective field goal percentage defense and defensive rebound rate marks that were inside the top 35 in the nation. Harvard exhibited tremendous offensive balance with no fewer than seven players leading the Crimson in scoring in at least one game. Senior point guard Oliver McNally finished his career with three straight seasons of true shooting percentages of over 60 percent, an incredible mark. This summer, the Crimson were certainly the favorite to retain their Ivy League title. In September, however, it was revealed that senior co-captains Kyle Casey and Brandyn Curry would miss the season as punishment for their role in a large-scale cheating scandal in a government class. Both Casey and Curry are All-Ivy quality players. The loss of Curry stings especially because he was the only point guard on the roster with any experience. Freshman **Siyani Chambers** will get the call to start right away. The Crimson do return a lot of talent, however. Junior shooting guard **Laurent Rivard** shot 57 percent from two and 44 percent from three last season. Sophomore guard **Wes Saunders** was impressive in limited minutes last season and was the leading scorer on the Crimson's trip to Italy in August. Inside, **Steve Moundou-Missi** and **Jonah Travis**, two sophomores who were efficient scorers and good rebounders as freshmen, will likely start. Highly regarded freshman wing **Agunwa Okolie** might also get some minutes. Harvard has the talent to win the 14-game tournament, but lacks depth. There will be a lot of pressure on Chambers right away. The Crimson might get beat up in non-conference play, where they play an extremely challenging slate. Given the question marks about depth and point guard play, Harvard cannot be regarded as the favorite to win the league.

COLUMBIA

2012: 15-15 (4-10 Ivy)
In-conference offense: 1.03 points per possession (3rd)
In-conference defense: 1.06 points allowed per possession (7th)

Yes, Columbia finished 4-10 last season in league play, but that record reflects a lot of bad luck. In league games decided by five or fewer points (or in overtime), the Lions went 2-7. They lost overtime games to Penn and Harvard, by one to Yale, and by two in another game against the Quakers. The Lions dramatically improved their shooting in conference play last year, going from 44 percent from two and 30 percent from three in 2011 to 48 and 37 percent, respectively, in 2012. They also remained an elite defensive rebounding team, pulling in 73 percent of opponents' misses last season, the 18th-best rate in the nation. Columbia returns every major rotation player from last season, and they are the only team in the league that can make that claim. They are led by All-Ivy point guard **Brian Barbour**, who had a Zack Rosen-esque season last year. Barbour shot 90 percent from the free throw line on 162 attempts and boasted an almost 2:1 assist-turnover ratio. Barbour's backcourt mate is junior **Meiko Lyles** who shot 44 percent from three last season. The main man in the frontcourt is power forward **Mark Cisco**. The 6-9 bruiser had a breakout season in

2012, shooting 59 percent from the floor and pulling in 23 percent of the available defensive rebounds. Senior **John Daniels**, an excellent rebounder, will likely pair with Cisco in the starting lineup. They will be backed up two sophomore big men, **Alex Rosenberg** and **Cory Osetkowski**, who both played well in more limited roles last season. Columbia has the offensive firepower and experience to potentially win the Ivy League. The major question will be their defense. Opponents shot 40 percent from three against the Lions and made a living at the free throw line last year. Ultimately, their defensive shortcomings will likely keep them from making their first NCAA tournament appearance since 1968.

CORNELL

2012: 12-16 (7-7 Ivy)
In-conference offense: 0.96 points per possession (6th)
In-conference defense: 1.00 points allowed per possession (5th)

Cornell's 2012 season was one of transition. The team was led by senior Chris Wrobleski, the last remaining meaningful player from Steve Donahue's dominating 2010 Cornell team. With the start of this season, Cornell will be using only players developed and recruited by coach Bill Courtney. Last season, Courtney's charges beat who they were supposed to beat. They were 5-1 against the teams below them in the league, but only 2-6 against the upper division of the Ivy. The Big Red struggled to score; they averaged an effective field goal percentage of only 37 against the four teams that finished above them in the league. This season, Cornell could improve their league standing because of their returning talent. Wing **Errick Peck,** who missed last season due to injury, returns, as does promising sophomore big man **Shonn Miller**. In the backcourt, **Galal Cancer**, an exciting (27 percent assist rate) but wild (28 percent turnover rate) and poor-shooting (39 percent from two) guard will likely start at point guard. The frontcourt will also benefit from the return of **Eitan Chemerinski** and **Josh Figini**, both rotation-quality bigs. In addition Cornell welcomes freshman **Braxton Bunce**, a 6-11 commit who has been rated the best center recruit from Canada. Cornell's offensive talent is not overwhelming. They struggle to shoot from three in a league where connecting from deep is usually a big part of the offense. What they do have, however, is continuity and size inside. With the Ivy League experiencing a lot of turnover this season, that could be worth a good deal.

YALE

2012: 19-10 (9-5 Ivy); Lost to Fairfield 68-56, CIT first round
In-conference offense: 0.98 points per possession (5th)
In-conference defense: 0.97 points allowed per possession (4th)

Despite Yale compiling their best league record since 2007, their 2012 campaign has to be considered a disappointment. The Bulldogs returned All-Ivy starters Greg Mangano and Reggie Willhite, and lost only one rotation player. Unfortunately, it turned out that losing that player, Porter Braswell, turned out to be a much bigger problem than first anticipated. Braswell provided steady point guard play and leadership; the Bulldogs struggled to find both in conference play last season. After starting 2-0, Yale took on Harvard in front of a sold-out crowd at the John J. Lee Amphitheater in a game of huge import. The Bulldogs proceeded to get blown out, 65-35. After an overtime loss at Cornell and another lopsided loss to Harvard, Yale's chances for an Ivy League title were essentially over. This season, coach James Jones returns **Austin Morgan**, the scoring guard who had a strong season last year (posting a 112 offensive rating), but was not the point guard the Bulldogs hoped he would be. Center **Jeremiah Kreisberg** has the potential to be an All-Ivy player with his deft offensive touch and defensive rebounding ability. Beyond that, however, the roster is short on experience. Senior guard **Michael Grace** did not have a good season, turning the ball over on 27 percent of his possessions. **Brandon Sherrod** will fill in inside. The Bulldogs need to solve the same two problems that plagued them last season. Senior leader Reggie Willhite has graduated, and Yale does not have a proven answer at point guard. Kreisberg and Morgan are the nucleus of a good team, but it is unclear where their support will come from. Yale likely does not have the depth to contend for the Ivy title.

PENNSYLVANIA

2012: 20-13 (11-3 Ivy); Lost to Butler 63-53, CBI quarterfinals
In-conference offense: 1.03 points per possession (4th)
In-conference defense: 0.94 points allowed per possession (2nd)

If you are reading this preview, you are likely an Ivy League fan and know all about Zack Rosen. But if by some chance you are not, you should know that last season Rosen almost single-handedly dragged his team to the Ivy League title. Rosen played 94 percent of the possible minutes, and used 27 percent of his team's possessions, shooting 49 percent from two, 40 percent from three, and had an assist rate of 34 percent. He made three game-winning-shots, including a 28-footer against Dartmouth. Rosen scored his team's final 16 points in another game against the Big Green, and the last nine in a dramatic 55-54 win at Harvard. This year, however, Rosen has graduated, along with three other contributors, and the Quakers' roster is far more uncertain. Explosive junior guard **Miles Cartwright**, who has shown flashes of brilliance, will be tabbed by Jerome Allen to run the team. Cartwright has not had to run a team in his first two seasons, but he has the talent to do it well. He will likely be joined in the starting lineup by junior **Steve Rennard**, a three-point threat. Up front, the Quakers will be very thin. **Henry Brooks** played well as a freshman, but needs to cut down on his turnovers. Junior **Fran Dougherty** is the best rebounder on the team. Unfortunately for Allen, while these two could be quality Ivy big men, they are the only interior players on the roster with any experience. The middle of the Ivy this season is very tightly bunched, and Penn could finish as high as third or as low as sixth. I have them on the lower end of that scale because of their depth issues, but the Quakers have overachieved for two seasons in a row.

BROWN

2012: 8-23 (2-12 Ivy)
In-conference offense: 0.93 points per possession (7th)
In-conference defense: 1.11 points allowed per possession (8th)

Everything that could go wrong for Brown last season did, and it cost coach Jesse Agel his job. Potent wing Tucker Halpern was lost for the season to mononucleosis. Starting big Andrew McCarthy missed quite a bit of the season with injuries, and star recruit **Rafael Maia** was ruled ineligible for the year. That left the Bears very thin up front, which showed on the defensive end. Brown allowed Ivy opponents to shoot 51 percent from two and 40 percent from three last season. After a disastrous 2012, the Bears attempt to restart their program by hiring Penn assistant and former Brown player Mike Martin. At age 30, Martin is one of the youngest head coaches in Division I. His first team will have experienced guards, as **Sean McGonagill**, the prolific if inefficient scoring point guard, and **Stephen Albrecht**, the sharp-shooting off-guard, return. Senior **Matt Sullivan**, also a 39 percent three-point shooter, will play on the wings with Halpern. Brown's troubles will come up front. Both McCarthy and backup big Dockery Walker are out for the year. Senior **Tyler Ponticelli**, who has not rebounded well for his size, will likely start. Martin must hope that the much-hyped 6-9 center Maia lives up to his billing and stays healthy. **Cedric Kuakumensah**, a 6-8 freshman, might get some minutes, too. The Bears' defensive and rebounding issues do not have clear answers. The players found themselves overmatched size-wise last season; this season they will have bigger players, but less depth. Martin's first season in Providence could be a struggle if he cannot find a way to play better defense.

DARTMOUTH

2012: 5-25 (1-13 Ivy)
In-conference offense: 0.88 points per possession (8th)
In-conference defense: 1.02 points allowed per possession (6th)

Dartmouth finished with the exact same record in the basement of the Ivy League in 2012 as they did in 2011, but the strides that Paul Cormier has made are becoming evident. The Big Green improved their defense substantially and, despite being one of the shortest teams in the country by effective height, finished in the top 30 nationally in defensive rebound rate. The Big Green came ever so close to two wins over Penn last season, but were denied by Zack Rosen's heroics in both instances. The prospects for this season look brighter. Promising sophomore bigs **Gabas Maldunas** and **Jvonte Brooks**, who had the highest free throw rate (90 percent) of any starter in the entire country, return, as does sophomore wing **John Golden**, who was potent from three. The question will be at point guard: sophomore **Mack McKearney** was wild (25 percent turnover rate) in his limited minutes last season. Freshman **Alex Mitola** might challenge for some time. Cormier is slowly turning Dartmouth from one of the worst programs in Division I into a respectable team. That process takes time, however, and while the Big Green have better talent returning, they lack depth and proven guard play. Dartmouth will likely struggle to avoid finishing eighth in the league for a fourth straight season, but I expect them to win three or four games and possibly get their first road conference win since 2009. The gap between Dartmouth and the rest of the league is closing steadily.

MAAC

BY JOHN TEMPLON

The Metro Atlantic Athletic Conference was front and center on Selection Sunday last season, as Iona, which had fallen to eventual conference tournament champion Loyola MD in the semifinals, received one of the final at-large bids. It marked the first time since the 1996 that the conference received two invitations to the NCAA tournament.

Iona had planned for that moment. The Gaels got there by playing a challenging schedule that basically put them on the road for the first two months of the season. When the calendar turned to 2012, Tim Cluess' team had played at home just twice. But obviously the gamble paid off. Wins over Saint Joseph's, Maryland, Denver, Richmond and Vermont were enough to put Iona in the Big Dance.

Unfortunately for the MAAC, the Gaels weren't able to secure the conference's first NCAA win since Siena defeated Ohio State in 2009. Iona came oh so close. The Gaels led by as many as 25 points at one point and by 15 at halftime before BYU made the largest comeback in NCAA tournament history.

That 78-72 loss meant the end of an era for the Gaels. Star seniors Scott Machado and Mike Glover finished their careers, and junior Kyle Smyth transferred to Seton Hall. Now Cluess is picking up the pieces and rebuilding the team using junior college players, transfers and a solid recruiting class. But he's got a number of rivals that want to take the title away.

The MAAC promises to be one of the most entertaining leagues in the country this season. Most of the conference's teams should at least be competitive, and five have a good shot at taking home the title. That includes Loyola, which will be moving on to the Patriot League next season, but is still eligible to win the title.

While Iona will be trying to break in some new players, most of the league's teams have familiar stars to lean on. Twelve of the 16 players named to the league's three postseason all-conference teams return this season. The favorites to replace Machado as the conference player of the year are George Beamon of Manhattan, O.D. Anosike of Siena and Erik Etherly of Loyola.

Beamon leads a Manhattan team that in its second season under former Louisville assistant Steve Masiello thinks it can compete at a very high level. The Jaspers finished second in the conference in both offensive and defensive efficiency last season and return 80 percent of their possession-minutes. The return of hard-nosed point guard Mike Alvarado along with versatile forward Emmy Andujar and defensive presence Rhamel Brown will provide extra support. Playing in the back of Manhattan's pressing defensive scheme, Brown's block rate of 14.9 percent trailed only Kansas' Jeff Withey nationally.

Taking a cue from the Gaels, the Jaspers have scheduled aggressively this season in hopes of raising their national profile. Manhattan plays just one true home game until a January 1 tilt against America East favorite Stony Brook. Along the way the Jaspers will face Louisville, Harvard, South Carolina, and a few Atlantic 10 teams.

Of course the team that dethroned Iona last season, Loyola, also could be the one that this season takes home the league title. Last season Loyola broke through and won a school record 24 games. While this will be the Greyhounds' final season in the MAAC, they obviously have something to prove. Jimmy Patsos has a number of key players back, including Etherly and point guard Dylon Cormier. Loyola doesn't play the pretty style of basketball that Iona employed to reach national prominence last season, but the slow-down style was certainly effective during conference play.

Both Niagara and Marist return even more minutes than Loyola. The Purple Eagles are especially intriguing due to the projected growth of their Three Musketeers: Juan'ya Green, Antoine Mason and Ameen Tanksley all played significant minutes as freshmen. If the three of them continue to improve, Niagara could be a sleeper.

Then there's the biggest mystery of all, Canisius. After a 5-25 season, Jim Baron replaces Tom Parrotta, but the roster isn't devoid of talent. Harold Washington was an all-conference performer last season and transfers Freddy Asprilla (Kansas State) and Baron's son Billy (Rhode Island) should help out as well. It seems like climbing out of the basement might be one of the easier goals to accomplish this season.

This season Manhattan, Loyola, Siena and Niagara all believe they have a chance to compete for a league title. Iona is an odd class by itself as Cluess tries to rebuild without taking any time off to do it. Fairfield, Marist and Canisius also have the potential to be dangerous. Unless St. John's transfer Nurideen Lindsey makes a bigger difference than expected at Rider, the Broncs wil be rebuilding under new head coach Kevin Baggett, and St. Peter's is waiting for next season.

Teams listed in John's predicted order of finish.

MANHATTAN

2012: 21-13 (12-6 MAAC); Lost to Fairfield, 69-57, CIT second round
In-conference offense: 1.05 points per possession (2nd)
In-conference defense: 0.94 points allowed per possession (2nd)

In Steve Masiello's first season at the helm, the Jaspers played a style very reminiscent of Louisville under Rick Pitino. That's no surprise considering Masiello was a walk-on at Kentucky and then an assistant under Pitino. By shutting down the three-point line, Manhattan managed to be the second-best defensive team in the MAAC last season. What people don't realize is that it was also the second-best offensive team. While there were way too many turnovers, the rest of the offense flowed nicely through **George Beamon** and point guard **Michael Alvarado**. The problem was Alvarado was injured near the end of the season, which led to Manhattan dropping five of their final eight conference games, including an 84-82 overtime loss to Siena in the MAAC quarterfinals. But a healthy Alvarado and the development of point forward **Emmy Andujar** should give Masiello a variety of options to kick-start the offense into an even higher gear. Last season Manhattan struggled a bit early during non-conference play while adjusting to Masiello's system. The adjustment period is over, but the Jaspers have a daunting schedule in front of them with road games against Louisville, Harvard, Long Island, and Dayton. If navigated correctly, it's a schedule designed to leave Manhattan in much the same place Iona was going into the conference tournament last season—in good shape for an at-large bid.

LOYOLA MD

2012: 24-9 (13-5 MAAC); Lost to Ohio State 78-59, NCAA round of 64
In-conference offense: 1.03 points per possession (4th)
In-conference defense: 0.97 points allowed per possession (3rd)

The twin towers of **Erik Etherly** (6-7) and Shane Walker (6-10) forced shorter opponents to head out to the perimeter, especially during MAAC play last season. The presence of those two players helped Loyola defeat Iona pretty convincingly at home and run up a 13-5 league record overall. Thanks to Siena knocking off Manhattan and Fairfield defeating Iona, the Greyhounds got a nice gift of playing the Nos. 7, 6, and 4 seeds in the MAAC tournament on the way to an NCAA tournament berth. Fairfield had defeated Jimmy Patsos' club a month earlier, but this time both teams turned it into a slow (58 possessions), defensive slog, which Loyola won 48-44. The Greyhounds were comfortable playing at that pace all season. In part due to their height, Loyola tried to slow things down whenever possible and finished at 65 possessions per 40 minutes, well behind the run-and-gun show of Iona. Star sixth man Justin Drummond transferred to Toledo at the end of the season and Walker graduated, but the presence of former Xavier forward **Jordan Latham** and the return of Etherly should allow the Greyhounds to dominate the paint once again.

IONA

2012: 25-8 (15-3 MAAC); Lost to BYU 78-72, NCAA First Four
In-conference offense: 1.18 points per possession (1st)
In-conference defense: 0.97 points allowed per possession (4th)

From Robbie Hummel's season-opening buzzer beater to BYU's stunning comeback, Iona had a roller coaster of a year, especially for a team that was consistently the favorite in the MAAC. The Gaels put on entertaining offensive displays, scoring triple-digits four times and featuring the 20th fastest pace in the nation. However this same team was also prone to stunning defeats. Looking back it's hard to figure out how Hofstra or Siena managed to defeat the Gaels, except for the fact that sometimes Iona just took games too lightly. Tim Cluess' team appeared content to play only one half at Hofstra, for instance, and it almost worked, but a 15-point deficit at the break was too much to overcome. Scott Machado was the engine that drove Iona's attack and his battle with North Carolina's Kendall Marshall for the NCAA's official assist crown was entertaining, though Machado actually finished with just the fourth best tempo-free assist rate in the country. All that is in the past. Former Arizona point guard **Momo Jones**, forward **Taaj Ridley**, and three-point gunner **Sean Armand** are the Gaels' three returning rotation players. (It was Armand who dropped 10 threes on Siena in just 22 minutes at Madison Square Garden.) Those three will be complemented by an influx of transfers and talented youngsters. Two key ones will be former Iowa State point guard **Tavon Sledge** and former Toledo forward **Curtis Dennis**, a 6-5 senior. Dennis is a swingman who should bring some much-needed toughness.

NIAGARA

2012: 14-19 (8-10 MAAC); Lost to Loyola MD 86-73, MAAC quarterfinals
In-conference offense: 1.00 points per possession (6th)
In-conference defense: 1.04 points allowed per possession (7th)

According to Ken Pomeroy's experience metric, the Purple Eagles were the fourth youngest team in the nation in 2011-12. Of course, the sixth youngest was Kentucky, and we know how that turned out. Things take a little longer to develop at the mid-major level where super recruits aren't the norm, however, and Niagara certainly went through some growing pains. Joe Mihalich's team went .500 in conference play until late January, when a five-game slide left them in a position from which they couldn't recover. Niagara did manage to do some good things during the month of February, winning four of its final five conference games and then defeating Canisius in a first-round MAAC tournament match up, but this team has enough talent to go further in 2012-13. **Juan'ya Green** was an outstanding surprise last season. The 6-3 freshman played a ton of minutes and used a lot of possessions while showing a passing acumen and scoring knack that was beyond his years. With a season under their belts the Purple Eagles should be one step closer to making a big impact and possibly finishing better than .500 in-conference for the first time since the 2009.

SIENA

2012: 14-17 (8-10 MAAC); Lost to Loyola (MD) 70-60, MAAC Semifinals
In-conference offense: 0.96 points per possession (8th)
In-conference defense: 1.00 points allowed per possession (5th)

Siena had the worst luck of any MAAC team last season, and it consistently impacted the product on the court. From the NCAA forcing **Lionel Gomis** and **Imoh Silas** to spend a year in residence to **Rakeem Brookins**' season-ending injury, Mitch Buonaguro was never playing with a complete deck. Because of this the rotation shortened down to just seven players. This also had an impact on the court, as the Saints played a lot of zone to protect star **O.D. Anosike** down low. Sometimes it didn't work too well, such as when Iona scored 95 points in an early January match up as the Gaels lit up the scoreboard from three. Then again the Saints also upset Iona and Manhattan (twice). The second of those victories over the Jaspers was an overtime affair in the conference tournament and helped ease some of the sting from an 8-10 conference record. Anosike is back and one of the favorites for MAAC POY, but he'll need some help from his teammates, many of whom are now both eligible and healthy, in order for the Saints to move back up the conference standings.

FAIRFIELD

2012: 22-15 (12-6 MAAC); Lost to Mercer 64-59, CIT semifinals
In-conference offense: 1.01 points per possession (5th)
In-conference defense: 0.92 points allowed per possession (1st)

Things probably didn't go quite how Sydney Johnson wanted them to during his first season in charge of Fairfield. Yes, the Stags managed to reach the finals of the MAAC tournament and the semifinals of the CIT, but expectations were higher thanks to a number of high-profile transfers. It took a while, but Fairfield seemed to find its stride during a 10-game conference stretch in which it won nine games, only falling to Iona at home. Even though Johnson brought tenets of the Princeton offense to Farifield, the team still leaned heavily on Boston College transfer Rakim Sanders. The All-MAAC first team selection used 29 percent of the team's possessions when he was on the court. This season the offensive load will have to be more spread out, and the health and skill of senior point guard **Derek Needham** is of the utmost importance. Needham broke a bone in his left foot near the end of the season, and his full recovery is essential. Fairfield will be looking to find offensive life after Sanders for a team that had the MAAC's top rated defense last season by a pretty solid margin. The Stags managed to force teams to both turn the ball over and miss shots, which might be harder to do this season without seven-footer Ryan Olander patrolling the paint.

MARIST

2012: 14-18 (7-11 MAAC); Lost to Iona 87-63, MAAC quarterfinals
In-conference offense: 0.97 points per possession (7th)
In-conference defense: 1.04 points allowed per possession (8th)

Things seemed to be headed south fast in February when Marist was 2-9 in-conference and in the midst of an eight-game losing streak. But give the Red Foxes credit, they turned it around and closed on a 6-2 run with their only losses coming against Iona and Fairfield. A victory over St. Peter's in the first round of the MAAC tournament continued the momentum. Like Niagara, Marist was running out a very inexperienced team and needs to build on that success. **Chavaughn Lewis** was the freshman star for Chuck Martin. Learning on the job had its ups and downs, though Lewis scored in double-figures in every conference game, including a 25-point outburst in the season finale against Iona. One problem an additional year of experience can't fix, however, is a lack of height. Opponents did a lot of their damage in the paint against the Red Foxes last season because the roster had but two players over 6-6. A third 6-10 player has been added this season, but the development of forwards **Adam Kemp** and **Pieter Prinsloo** could make or break the season.

CANISIUS

2012: 5-25 (1-17 MAAC); Lost to Niagara 80-70, MAAC first round
In-conference offense: 0.93 points per possession (9th)
In-conference defense: 1.10 points allowed per possession (10th)

Wins were hard to come by last season for Canisius and that ultimately cost Tom Parrotta his job. The Golden Griffins' lone MAAC win came at home in mid-January against Marist. There were some close calls, like an overtime loss at Niagara, but no good results. Now former St. Francis (PA), St. Bonaventure, and Rhode Island head coach Jim Baron will take over. Baron, who has gone through mid-major reclamation projects before, has a knack for finishing around .500 at every coaching stop, and is actually 368-368 overall in his career. He'll be charged with fixing a defense that was by far the worst in the conference. Canisius held opponents to under a point per possession just four times during MAAC play last season, including in its one victory. The addition of transfers **Freddy Asprilla** and **Billy Baron**—the coach's son—should help on the talent side.

RIDER

2012: 13-19 (10-8 MAAC); Lost to Fairfield 65-63, MAAC quarterfinals
In-conference offense: 1.04 points per possession (3rd)
In-conference defense: 1.03 points allowed per possession (6th)

Expected to be a contender in the MAAC, Rider stumbled out of the gate during non-conference play last season and struggled to a 1-10 record by mid-December. Losses to Manhattan and Marist during the opening weekend of MAAC play put Rider immediately behind the eight ball. After that point, Tommy Dempsey was able to get things turned around, and the Broncs went 12-9 the remainder of the season. The mid-season turnaround was impressive, but Dempsey still bolted for Binghamton after Rider lost a close game to Fairfield in the quarterfinals of the MAAC tournament. As it turns out, all but two of those opening 10 losses were to top-150 teams. Long-time assistant Kevin Baggett replaces Dempsey. Unfortunately for Baggett, he won't have any of the top three players from last season's team. Novar Gadson, Brandon Penn and Jeff Jones all graduated and took a large chunk of Rider's possession-minutes with them. On the other hand a key piece of the rebuilding effort, former St. John's guard **Nurideen Lindsey**, received a waiver and will be eligible immediately for the Broncs, instead of having to sit until after the fall semester.

ST. PETER'S

2012: 5-26 (4-14 MAAC); Lost to Marist 64-57, MAAC first round
In-conference offense: 0.87 points per possession (10th)
In-conference defense: 1.05 points allowed per possession (9th)

The fact that the St. Peter's offense struggled a season after making the NCAA tournament wasn't much of a surprise. What was a surprise was that a defense that had ranked in the top half of the league each of the past three seasons plummeted down to ninth. A lack of height was difficult for the Peacocks to overcome on the defensive end, as MAAC opponents feasted in the paint and on the boards. John Dunne's team did manage to sweep two conference opponents, Canisius and Siena. In fact victory over the Saints during the opening weekend of conference play gave St. Peter's a short-lived perfect record in-conference. The second win over Siena on February 3, however, was the last win the Peacocks managed to wrangle all season. The addition of Delaware State transfer **Desi Washington** should help the offense, as he brings a scoring dimension to the backcourt that was definitely missing in St. Peter's attack last year. What this season really hinges on is if Dunne can get this team back to its defensive roots.

MAC

BY JEFF HALEY

Ohio's appearance in the 2012 Sweet 16 marked the deepest run for the Bobcats in the NCAA tournament since 1964, when Ohio won games against Louisville and Kentucky to reach the regional finals. In the 48 years between 1964 and 2012, Ohio had won a total of two NCAA tournament games. It isn't an exaggeration to call the 2012 NCAA tournament a once-in-a-generation event for the school and its fans.

The example of Ohio illustrates how catching a few good breaks and capitalizing on them can propel a team on a great postseason run. During the regular season John Groce's squad had been a perimeter-oriented team, despite the fact that they didn't shoot very well from the perimeter (31 percent in conference play). In the Mid-American Conference tournament, the style stayed the same but the results suddenly changed for the better. In three games against Toledo, Buffalo, and Akron, the Bobcats shot 39 percent on their threes. This was break number one for Ohio—having an extra handful of three-point shots go down each game. Outside shooting had been a weakness for the Bobcats during conference play, but in the postseason it became a strength.

In the first round of the NCAA tournament, Ohio faced off against Michigan in a slow, low-possession game. Like the Bobcats, the Wolverines also liked to shoot threes. In a game that Groce's team won 65-60, Ohio shot 6-of-16 from three point range, while Michigan shot 7-of-23. UM's cold shooting from outside was lucky break number two for the Bobcats.

The third lucky break for Ohio came in the form of another round of 64 upset. After South Florida's upset of Temple, the Bobcats and USF met in the round of 32. Rather than having to beat two high seeds in a row, Groce's squad was granted a fairly even match up with the Big East's No. 8 team in per-possession terms. The Bulls' strong defense had frustrated Cal (in the First Four) and Temple, but sometimes the best way to attack a tough D is to shoot over it. That's exactly what Ohio did. The Bobcats went 9-of-18 from three-point range, and won 62-56 to advance to the Sweet 16.

And now these guys were stars. Groce and D.J. Cooper were doing interviews on national television. Everyone in America learned that Clark Kellogg's son Nick played for Ohio. It was 15 minutes of, if not fame, then at least attention that the basketball program in Athens had never known before. Groce would soon parlay this into a significant pay increase, when he accepted the head coaching job at Illinois. It is hard to imagine him in Champaign today without the postseason run the Bobcats made. Groce owes a lot to a handful of shots that went down during 10 days in March of 2012.

None of which is meant to diminish Ohio's accomplishments. Most tournament runs involve catching a few breaks. The Bobcats created an opportunity to catch breaks, by shooting all those threes. Then they took advantage of their luck, by playing well generally.

In fact, the breaks almost carried the Bobcats even further. Against North Carolina in the Sweet 16, Ohio went 12-of-28 from three-point range during regulation. But Groce's men missed all four of their threes in overtime, and lost 73-65. Ohio's luck had finally run out.

Teams listed in Jeff's predicted order of finish.

AKRON

2012: 22-12 (13-3 MAC); Lost to Northwestern 76-74, NIT first round
In-conference offense: 1.07 points per possession (1st)
In-conference defense: 0.97 points allowed per possession (4th)

Akron had the best record in the MAC during the 2012 regular season, but lost to Ohio in the conference tournament championship game. This season Keith Dambrot returns most of his key players. This includes 7-0 senior **Zeke Marshall**, the 2012 MAC defensive player of the year. Marshall is one of the top shot blockers in Division I, and can also score. He's an active offensive rebounder who gets to the line frequently. Marshall's offensive game has steadily improved over the course of his career and took a major leap when he made 71 percent of his free throws as a junior. Part-timer **Demetrius "Tree" Treadwell** is very active on the glass at both ends of the floor. He should soak up some additional minutes with the departure of Nikola Cvetinovic, but this Tree's skills haven't yet branched out to include free throw shooting. Junior point guard **Alex Abreu** is very fast, with a knack for getting to the line, where he's highly effective. He also went 43-of-100 from long range last year. Overall, Abreu's a good playmaker who does enough well to make up for his turnover problems. **Chauncey Gilliam** and **Brian Walsh** are dangerous outside shooters. With so many good shooters, it's surprising Akron didn't attempt more threes, but it's hard to be critical on this point since the Zips made 52 percent of their twos in MAC play. The ability of Marshall and Abreu to get to the line was an important part of the team's success: almost one quarter of Akron's points came on free throws. On defense, Dambrot's team excelled at not fouling and did a good job limiting opponent damage from three-point range. The roster did take a hit in October, however, when reigning MAC sixth man of the year Quincy Diggs was suspended for the season due to unspecified violations of Akron's code of conduct.

OHIO

2012: 29-8 (11-5 MAC); Lost to North Carolina 73-65 (OT), Sweet 16
In-conference offense: 1.02 points per possession (7th)
In-conference defense: 0.93 points allowed per possession (1st)

After last season's Sweet 16 run, Ohio coach John Groce took the head job at Illinois. His replacement is Jim Christian, who spent the last four seasons as head coach at TCU, and before that coached in the MAC at Kent State. Watch how Christian addresses his new team's shot distribution. Last season the Bobcats shot a lot of threes yet finished last in the conference in three-point accuracy. This combination resulted in a few head-scratching losses, such as a 68-55 defeat at the hands of Eastern Michigan. At least Christian knows this season the shots will be taken by veterans. Virtually the entire roster returns, with the exception of part-time player TyQuane Goard, who transferred to Marshall. Senior point guard **D.J. Cooper** led the perimeter-oriented attack last season, taking 244 three-point attempts and making 31 percent of them. A very good playmaker who rarely turns the ball over, Cooper is joined in the backcourt by **Walter Offutt**, a slasher who gets to the rim and free throw line, and can also knock down threes. The best outside shooter for the Bobcats is junior guard **Nick Kellogg**. Inside scoring and rebounding will mostly come from **Ivo Baltic** and **Reggie Keely**. Ohio had the top defense in the MAC last season, and their strength was forcing turnovers. During conference play, opponents gave the ball away on 26 percent of their possessions. Look for Christian to continue pressuring the ball. Christian's TCU teams didn't always force a lot of turnovers, but his Kent State teams did.

EASTERN MICHIGAN

2012: 14-18 (9-7 MAC); Lost to Northern Illinois 55-52, MAC first round
In-conference offense: 0.91 points per possession (11th)
In-conference defense: 0.95 points allowed per possession (2nd)

Under first-year head coach Rob Murphy, Eastern Michigan took a major step forward last season, finishing with a winning conference record, and placing first in the MAC's west division. The Eagles did it by crushing their opponents defensively while playing offense at a shockingly slow pace. Murphy's front line is one of the most imposing in the conference if not all of mid-majordom, with 6-9 senior **Jamell Harris**, 6-10 senior **Matt Balkema**, and 7-0 onetime Syracuse transfer **Da'Shonte Riley** patrolling the paint. With the rim protected, guards like **J.R. Sims**, **Austin Harper**, and **Anthony Strickland** can play in the passing lanes. Like many teams that play zone defense, the Eagles give up their share of offensive rebounds, but by holding down opponent field goal percentages and taking the ball away EMU compensates for the second-chance points they give up. On offense, however, things are different. The Eagles struggled with shooting, struggled with turnovers, and didn't generate much in the way of second-chance shots. Harper's turnover problems become more of a concern this season, as he's likely to be the primary ball handler. **Derek Thompson** is the only member of this team that could hit a shot last year. The best chance for offensive improvement comes from the big guys; it's strange that a team with so much size finished the season ranked ninth in the MAC in offensive rebounding percentage. Murphy's team will likely rely on its D again.

BOWLING GREEN

2012: 16-16 (9-7 MAC); Lost to Oakland 86-69, CIT first round
In-conference offense: 1.04 points per possession (5th)
In-conference defense: 0.96 points allowed per possession (3rd)

Bowling Green coach Louis Orr is not a believer in the three. In MAC play last season the Falcons launched just one quarter of their field goal attempts from three-point range, the lowest rate of any team in the conference. This is not unusual for Orr's teams, which almost always record 70 percent or more of their attempts inside the arc. Ignoring the three-point line is fine, provided a team's effective from two-point range and gets to the line. The problem is Orr's teams generally don't draw that many fouls either. So the BGSU offense sinks or swims largely on the strength of its two-pointers, turnover rate, and ability to create second-chance points. Turnovers have been a struggle for the Falcons in recent years, in part because 5-6 point guard **Jordon Crawford** has problems hanging on to the ball. The pluses for Crawford are that he is both a good playmaker and a defensive pest. **A'uston Calhoun**, the Falcons' primary scorer inside, is tough around the rim and a good offensive rebounder. Unfortunately, Calhoun also has a tendency to take too many mid-range shots. Simiarly, while the strength for Bowling Green the last several years has been forcing turnovers, Scott Thomas, who lived in the passing lanes, was a senior last year, so it is possible that the defense will take a step back. Or maybe this loss will be offset by more minutes for 6-10 junior shot blocker **Cameron Black**, who can help improve what was a fairly weak interior D last season.

BUFFALO

2012: 20-11 (12-4 MAC); Lost to Oakland 84-76, CIT second round
In-conference offense: 1.05 points per possession (3rd)
In-conference defense: 0.98 points allowed per possession (5th)

Buffalo ranked among the best teams in the MAC last season. The Bulls were second in the conference in effective field goal percentage, and first in opponents' effective FG percentage. The biggest question for coach Reggie Witherspoon is how he'll make up for the loss of center Mitchell Watt, who was the key player for UB at both ends of the floor. Watt's scoring inside was the biggest reason Buffalo led the conference in two-point percentage. He was also the best shot blocker on a team that played excellent interior defense. The burden of making up for Watt will fall on 6-7 **Javon McCrea**. Though he was a key part of the Bulls' defense in the paint, McCrea is undermined by his struggles at the free throw line. McCrea will have help, though, in the form of 6-8 sophomore **Will Regan**, a Virginia transfer who has come home to Buffalo after playing very little in Charlottesville as a freshman. Witherspoon's backcourt was shaky last season, as point guard **Jarod Oldham** struggled with both turnovers and his shooting for a second consecutive season. And while 6-2 senior **Tony Watson** is a good shooter who excels (92 percent) at the line, his game isn't the sort that generates frequent trips there. In addition to losing Watt, the Bulls also lost Zach Filzen, their best outside shooter.

WESTERN MICHIGAN

2012: 14-20 (6-10 MAC); Lost to Kent State 76-72, MAC quarterfinals
In-conference offense: 1.04 points per possession (4th)
In-conference defense: 1.02 points allowed per possession (7th)

Western Michigan was the MAC's hard luck team last year, posting a 6-10 record despite outscoring their opponents over those 16 games. Steve Hawkins' team was 1-5 in conference games decided by five points or less. Conversely all but one of the Broncos' MAC wins were by at least eight points. Flenard Whitfield, Mike Douglas, and Demetrius Ward were all seniors, while physical center Matt Stainbrook transferred to Xavier. This season Hawkins has a roster that includes eight freshmen and three sophomores, but he does still have 6-7 senior **Nate Hutcheson**, who logged more playing time last season than any other returning Bronco. Hutcheson's a good inside-outside player who's comfortable stepping out and taking a three but can also rebound and get himself to the line. At 6-10, **Shayne Whittington** was effective in limited minutes last season, and will have to play more as a junior. Sophomore **Austin Richie** also earned some minutes, but otherwise WMU has no guards who saw more than token possessions last season. With an untested backcourt, the Broncos could be in for a rough ride this year. One thing that we know is Hawkins' teams will rebound and find a way to get to the free throw line, even when they're below average at everything else.

KENT STATE

2012: 21-12 (10-6 MAC); Lost to USC Upstate 73-58, CIT first round
In-conference offense: 1.07 points per possession (2nd)
In-conference defense: 1.02 points allowed per possession (6th)

Playing time at Kent State last season was reserved primarily for upperclassmen. But this year the roster has four freshmen, five sophomores, and three transfers. Rob Senderoff returns just two players who saw significant minutes last season. Senior **Chris Evans** is a good inside scorer and provides some defensive presence in the middle at 6-8. And 6-1 senior **Randal Holt** is an effective three-point shooter. But that's it in terms of experience for Senderoff, so where will the minutes go? Look for 5-11 freshman **Kellon Thomas** to handle the ball, while 6-6 Tulsa transfer **Bryson Pope** and 6-9 junior **Mark Henniger** should also soak up some of the available minutes. Another option might be 6-9 junior college transfer **Melvin Tabb**, a onetime ESPNU top-100 recruit who formerly played at Wake Forest and now gets a second chance with Kent State. Still another junior college transfer, 6-5 **Darren Goodson**, will also be in the mix. Last year the Flashes were weak on the glass at both ends despite having decent size. Additionally, while Kent was second in the MAC in shot blocking percentage, opponents still made 48 percent of their twos. You don't often see a defense more likely than most to block a shot and to give up a layup as well.

TOLEDO

2012: 19-17 (7-9 MAC); Lost to Robert Morris 69-51, CIT second round
In-conference offense: 1.03 points per possession (6th)
In-conference defense: 1.02 points allowed per possession (8th)

Toledo spent a lot of time playing with a small lineup last year, which, predictably, hurt their rebounding and interior defense. Opponents rebounded 38 percent of their own misses, and the Rockets' two best rebounders were both 6-4 (**Rian Pearson** and **Reese Holliday**). Without much size inside, Tod Kowalczyk's team allowed conference opponents to make nearly half their twos. **Matt Smith**, at 6-7, was the only Rocket who was a credible threat to block a shot (in addition to being an effective scorer inside). Then again this roster does have 6-9 junior **Delino Dear**, 6-9 junior **Richard Wonnell**, and 6-9 freshman **Nathan Boothe**, so maybe it's time for Kowalczyk to find some minutes for the big guys. Shooting threes was Toledo's strength on offense last season, but they didn't do it particularly often, preferring to work from in close. Pearson dominated the shooting, recording 82 more attempts than the next closest player, point guard **Julius Brown**, who was the team's leading playmaker and frequently pulled up for jump shots. Onetime Iowa State transfer **Dominique Buckley** is Kowalczyk's best three-point shooter, though both Smith and Holliday can also hit shots from out there. Guard Curtis Dennis transferred to Iona, but the rest of the team is back so some improvement is possible. But if Toledo continues to run out extremely small lineups, opponents will continue to score easily.

MIAMI OH

2012: 9-21 (5-11 MAC); Lost to Toledo 60-53, MAC first round
In-conference offense: 1.02 points per possession (8th)
In-conference defense: 1.06 points allowed per possession (10th)

Miami's new coach is John Cooper, formerly of Tennessee State. During a three-season stint in Nashville, Cooper's teams improved each year. Conversely, Miami was terrible last season, and their best player (Julian Mavunga) was a senior. But the situation for Cooper isn't as awful as it sounds. Part of the reason the RedHawks were so bad last year is that, other than Mavunga, everyone who played was a freshman or a sophomore. Another issue was the passive perimeter defense played by all those freshmen and sophomores. Add to that an inability to rebound opponent misses, and the Miami defense was bad. Cooper's Tiger teams forced turnovers, so look for the RedHawks to apply more pressure this season. Junior point guard **Quinten Rollins** is a likely candidate to provide some of that defensive pressure. Despite the loss of Mavunga, Miami does return a few decent offensive players. Junior **Jon Harris** is a good outside shooter, and 6-11 junior **Drew McGhee** is a capable scorer inside, though his minutes and touches have to date been limited with so much of the offense revolving around Mavunga.

BALL STATE

2012: 15-15 (6-10 MAC); Lost to Western Michigan 69-63, MAC first round
In-conference offense: 0.99 points per possession (9th)
In-conference defense: 1.03 points allowed per possession (9th)

Ball State suffered through a tough season last year, giving many minutes to underclassmen. Unfortunately, despite playing so many younger players, their two best players were seniors. Additionally, the Cardinals do not return a point guard, as Randy Davis was a senior, and Tyrae Robinson left the program. Billy Taylor's team broke tendency a bit last year, hoisting up many more three-point shots than their historical norm. Ball State made just 33 percent of those threes in conference play, but when you consider they shot 47 percent on their twos, 33 percent shooting from beyond the arc doesn't sound so bad. At the same time, conference opponents murdered Ball State from three, hitting 42 percent. The core of this team is now its large junior class. Guard **Jesse Berry** is a solid outside shooter, and **Chris Bond**, at 6-4, is an active defender and good on the boards. **Tyler Koch** can hit outside shots, and 6-8 **Matt Kamieniecki** is the only returning inside player with any experience. These four juniors, along with senior guard **Jauwan Scaife**, will be asked to carry the team (though Koch may miss time early as he recovers from hip surgery). Coach Taylor does have a large incoming class of freshmen, however, including 6-11 **Mading Thok**, who will probably have to play.

CENTRAL MICHIGAN

2012: 11-21 (5-11 MAC); Lost to Toledo 75-72, MAC second round
In-conference offense: 0.96 points per possession (10th)
In-conference defense: 1.06 points allowed per possession (11th)

Keno Davis, who last coached at Providence, takes over at Central Michigan for the fired Ernie Zeigler. Davis knows how to set up an offense. His teams at Providence and Drake never had trouble scoring, and this is definitely one area where the Chippewas need help. (The other area where Central Michigan needs help is defense.) When a coach is fired, it often results in a flurry of transfers. Sure enough, CMU's best player last season was the coach's son, Trey Zeigler, and he transferred to Pitt when his father was fired. Austin McBroom and Derek Jackson also departed, leaving Davis with very little experience in the backcourt. **Finis Craddock** and **Austin Keel** are the two remaining guards who played significant minutes last season. Junior college transfer **DeAndray Buckley** will help out right away, while 6-7 senior **Olivier Mbaigoto** is a good rebounder who struggles on offense. **Zach Saylor**, a 6-8 senior, is the only other returning inside player with any experience. Rather than opening the doors to junior college transfers to make it through the season, Davis brought in a large freshman class. Perhaps his offensive wizardry can turn things around right away, but it's more likely the Chippewas will take their lumps this season as they start rebuilding.

NORTHERN ILLINOIS

2012: 5-26 (3-13 MAC); Lost to Western Michigan 71-54, MAC second round
In-conference offense: 0.90 points per possession (12th)
In-conference defense: 1.10 points allowed per possession (12th)

Northern Illinois coach Mark Montgomery had a rough first year. The Huskies were by far the worst team in the MAC, one that claimed both the league's worst per-possession offense and its worst such defense. But the news in DeKalb wasn't all bad. Despite a poor showing in almost every other statistical category, NIU ranked first in the conference in offensive rebounding percentage, and second on the defensive glass. **Abdel Nader** was the focal point for the offense last season. A high percentage of the 6-7 sophomore's shot attempts come on jumpers, and thus far he hasn't converted many of these. The Huskies would probably benefit from getting more shots for 6-7 junior **Aksel Bolin**, who was an effective scorer from everywhere on the floor. Turnovers frequently derail Montgomery's offense before a shot can be hoisted. Better ball handling by sophomore point guard **Marquavese Ford** would be a big help here, though it's true many Huskies got in on the turnover action last season.

BY CRAIG POWERS

Much like fans of stock car racing who watch to see exciting crashes, there are many college basketball fans that want to see a fast-paced, athletic brand of basketball, one that puts an attacking style at the forefront. Those fans would love the Mid-Eastern Athletic Conference.

With an average tempo of 68 possessions per 40 minutes, the MEAC is one of the fastest-paced leagues in Division I. And the league is all about attacking. Most teams have high offensive rebounding rates, high turnover rates, high free throw rates, and high block rates. In fact, the league ranked in the top five nationally in all of those categories last season.

That style doesn't necessarily translate to efficiency, as the MEAC was among the worst leagues in the country in terms of points scored per possession. Combined with the high turnover rate mentioned above, MEAC teams ranked 29th in shooting in D-I, with a collective effective field goal percentage of 48.

The benefit of this style on a national stage is that even poor shooting teams have big days from the field occasionally. With the athleticism on display in the MEAC, a good shooting day for one of their teams can spell trouble for a non-conference opponent.

Norfolk State was a prime example of this, as they put the MEAC on the map with the most shocking upset of the 2012 NCAA tournament. The Spartans defeated No. 2 seed Missouri, a team that started out with an initial win expectancy rate of over 96 percent. For one game the MEAC brand of attacking ball aligned with shooting accuracy. NSU was on fire, posting a 62.7 effective FG percentage against the Tigers. And on the rare occasions when Norfolk State did miss a shot, the experience from MEAC play kicked in and they were able to grab almost 44 percent of those rebounds. It all added up to one of the most unpredictable outcomes of the entire season, courtesy of the MEAC tournament champs.

The bulk of that team is now gone, and the conference lacks an obvious star player with NBA talent like Kyle O'Quinn. The successful MEAC teams in 2012-13 will be the ones who can exploit those conference-wide deficiencies the best.

All four of the slowest-tempo teams in MEAC play in 2011-12 were in the top five of the league standings, while the fastest-paced team went winless in conference play. It's entirely likely that the coaches at Savannah State, Delaware State, Bethune Cookman, and North Carolina Central may be on to something when they make the choice to walk, not run. It should not come as a surprise that three of those teams, SSU, DSU, and BCU, all were among the top four teams in offensive efficiency in league play.

The slower teams in the league had lower turnover percentages, and higher shooting percentages in general, with the exception of Coppin State, who had a number of excellent shooters. It appears that taking their time is allowing these teams to find better shots, take better care of the ball, and be more successful.

Some of the coaches who finished near the bottom of the league standings may take a look at the top half and start trying to play copycat. It is quite often beneficial for teams with less talent to slow the game down, limit possessions, and keep the score closer. This provides the opportunity to spring an upset, and schools like Maryland-Eastern Shore and South Carolina State may see the need to quit pushing the ball and value possessions more.

Even history suggests that the slower teams in the MEAC are more successful. Only twice since 2003 has the regular-season league champ finished in the top half of tempo during MEAC play.

Norfolk State, for example, slowed their tempo down for 2011-12. With largely the same cast that finished in fifth place as the fastest team in the league the year before, head coach Anthony Evans brought the pace down and success followed.

Coaches are stubborn creatures, and they like to stick with what they know, but they also hate losing as a rule. If some of these head coaches that are stuck with less talent than the year before want to improve in the win/loss column, taking a look at something as simple as how many times a team passes the ball before they shoot could make a world of difference in efficiency.

Of course, that would mean those car-crash-loving, slam dunk-YouTubing, edge-of-your seat thrill ride fans may be left disappointed. On the flipside, the stat-loving, calculator-wielding, efficiency nerds that write, read, edit, and publish books like this would be happier. The MEAC will just have to decide who it wants in its corner.

Teams listed in Craig's predicted order of finish.

SAVANNAH STATE

2012: 21-12 (14-2 MEAC); Lost to Tennessee 65-51, NIT first round
In-conference offense: 1.04 points per possession (4th)
In-conference defense: 0.85 points allowed per possession (1st)

After years as a Division I independent, Savannah State and head coach Horace Brodnax got called up to the "big leagues" last season, joining the MEAC and at last getting a shot at an automatic bid to the NCAA tournament. The Tigers made a splash instantly, using a stifling defense to go 14-2 in league play and take the conference crown. Alas, in the MEAC quarterfinals SSU fell to Hampton, an opponent they'd beaten twice in the regular season. The first-round NIT game against Tennessee, however, marked the first national postseason game in the school's history. The Tigers will look to build on that result as they return all of their significant contributors from 2011-12. **Rashad Hassan** and **Arnold Louis** are a formidable frontcourt duo that made offensive rebounding difficult for MEAC opponents. Hassan was also the team's usage leader and their go-to-guy on the inside, hitting on 58 percent of his two-pointers. Louis is stellar on the offensive glass, ranking No. 16 nationally. Backing those two up will be **Jyles Smith**, who provides an intimidating interior presence with his 11 percent block rate. The backcourt will be led by point guard **Preston Blackman**, whose 41 percent assist rate was bested by only seven players in the nation last season. Flanking him will be **Deric Rudolph** and **Cedric Smith**. Rudolph will primarily stick to the outside and shoot spot up-threes, while Smith prefers to attack the basket and draw fouls. **Joshua Montgomery** will come off the bench with the confidence that comes from having been the most efficient Tiger a season ago. With a senior-laden lineup and all the important pieces returning for 2012-13, it is likely that Savannah State will be contending for the league title once again. This group of seniors has grown the program from a middling independent to a potential NCAA tournament team, and they have a good shot to make amends for last season's untimely detour to the NIT.

BETHUNE-COOKMAN

2012: 18-17 (11-5 MEAC); Lost to Norfolk State 73-70, MEAC championship game
In-conference offense: 1.08 points per possession (3rd)
In-conference defense: 1.03 points allowed per possession (10th)

With a first-year head coach (Gravelle Craig) at the helm and their top player (C.J. Reed) having transferred out of the program (to UCF), the Wildcats were expected to take step back last season. They did, in that they couldn't capture the regular-season MEAC title for a second straight year. However, for the first time in school history, B-CU was one win away from the NCAA tournament, only to fall in the MEAC title game to Norfolk State. Bethune-Cookman loses three seniors off that historic team, and will be especially hard hit in the rebounding department. Craig tried to address that issue in recruiting, bringing in two junior college transfers who are 6-6 and 6-8, respectively: **Malik Jackson** at shooting guard, and **Myron Respress** at center. **Adrien Coleman** returns as the team's usage leader. Coleman's primarily an inside player (just 11 percent of his shots come from behind the arc), an orientation that can be challenging when you're a 56 percent foul shooter. From the outside, the primary threat will be senior point guard **Kevin Dukes**. He knocked down 38 percent of his threes last season and was tops on the team in offensive rating among those who played significant minutes. The Wildcats should have production from the backcourt and wing positions, but the frontcourt is a mystery, as junior college transfers are quite often unpredictable. If the newcomers can maintain or improve upon the rebounding and replace some of the interior scoring, there's no reason why Bethune-Cookman can't contend for the MEAC title again.

DELAWARE STATE

2012: 15-14 (12-4 MEAC); Lost to Florida A&M 65-55 (OT), MEAC quarterfinals
In-conference offense: 1.09 points per possession (1st)
In-conference defense: 0.98 points allowed per possession (5th)

Tahj Tate carried the load on offense for Delaware State last season. The 6-4 guard took 28 percent of the Hornets' shots while he was on the floor, and maintained a 102 offensive rating. That's impressive for a freshman carrying such a heavy burden in the MEAC. The Hornets will return three other starters. Forward **Marques Oliver** was Greg Jackson's primary inside threat, grabbing offensive rebounds and drawing fouls. Alongside him in the frontcourt will be **Tyshawn Bell**, who was the team's most efficient scorer last year, hitting 39 percent of his threes. **Casey Walker** pairs with Bell to form a solid catch-and-shoot duo. The biggest question will be the man distributing the ball to these shooters. Point guard Jay Threatt graduated, and took his ability to drive and create for others with him. DSU plays at a slow tempo in one of the fastest conferences in the nation, but they don't show some of the statistical attributes that are generally associated with "slow" teams. The Hornets have been one of the worst defensive rebounding teams in the country the past few seasons, and they take chances on steals quite often. Usually those two things are indicative of team trying to run out in transition. Even with these deficiencies, the Hornets are still likely to contend for the league title again. Returning four starters will give them enough talent to make some noise in the MEAC.

NORTH CAROLINA A&T

2012: 12-20 (7-9 MEAC), Lost to Howard 51-50, MEAC first round
In-conference offense: 0.98 points per possession (8th)
In-conference defense: 1.00 points allowed per possession (7th)

There were three weeks in January when it looked like North Carolina A&T could contend for the MEAC title. The Aggies rattled off five straight wins and moved to 5-2 in conference play. After that stretch, however, A&T would lose eight of its last 10 games, with the only victories coming against a South Carolina State team that went winless in conference. The late-season skid eventually cost head coach Jerry Eaves his job. The Aggies brought in former South Carolina State and Tennessee State head coach Cy Alexander to replace Eaves. A&T will likely be an up-tempo team under Alexander, as his past squads have often finished near the top of D-I in pace. He runs an aggressive man-to-man defense that results in a high number of steals, but an even higher number of easy looks for the opposition. Five seniors and a junior return, so the Aggies will be nothing if not experienced. Two guys likely to see an increase in shots are **Adrian Powell** and **DaMetrius Upchurch**. Powell's a solid shooter from anywhere on the court, and may be taking a lot of the catch-and-shoot looks that went departing senior Nic Simpson's way. Upchurch, one of only two Aggies to top 100 with his offensive rating, is a low-post player with solid offensive rebounding abilities. The biggest question mark is at point guard. **Jeremy Underwood** served as a backup last year, but posted a horrendous turnover rate. Still, with all the upperclassmen, the Aggies could be set for an improvement in 2012-13. A top-half league finish is likely.

MORGAN STATE

2012: 9-20 (6-10 MEAC), Lost to Hampton 69-65, MEAC first round
In-conference offense: 1.00 points per possession (6th)
In-conference defense: 1.01 points allowed per possession (8th)

Don't let the record fool you. Morgan State finished 1-8 in games decided by three points or less, including a 1-4 record in one-point games. The good news for the Bears is that performance in close games isn't something that is generally repeated from year to year. More good news is that one of their biggest issues on offense, turning the ball over, may have graduated along with several benevolent seniors. Morgan State's biggest defensive strength, interior defense, should remain with 7-2 **Ian Chiles** returning for his junior year. The Bears were second in the MEAC, allowing just 45 percent on twos, and Chiles blocked nine percent of the two-pointers taken while he was on the floor. Of course, with good shot blocking often comes bad rebounding, and that's an area where there is massive room for improvement. Chiles is well below what anyone would consider to be a good rebounding big man, and the problem for Todd Bozeman is that Chiles is his best returning rebounder. Then again as far as frontcourts go on the offensive end, the Bears have one of the best in the MEAC. With Chiles, 6-8 **DeWayne Jackson**, and 6-9 **Shaquille Duncan** all returning, Morgan State should feed the ball inside often. With some of their more inefficient offense players leaving, Morgan State should improve on that end.

NORTH CAROLINA CENTRAL

2012: 17-15 (10-6 MEAC); Lost to Bethune-Cookman 60-59, MEAC quarterfinals
In-conference offesnse: 0.99 points per possession (7th)
In-conference defense: 0.91 points allowed per possession (2nd)

Solid man-to-man defense can mask a lot of deficiencies, and North Carolina Central rode the second-best D in the MEAC to a 10-6 conference record. The defense was good enough that it nearly won the Eagles a game over an ACC opponent, as LeVelle Moton's team nearly erased a 13-point deficit to NC State in Raleigh with 10 minutes to play. That game was followed by a cross-country trip to Oregon, where NCCU held the Ducks, one of the best offenses in the country, to their second-worst performance of the year on that side of the ball. Of course, North Carolina Central was unable to come away with either victory because of some poor offense, and that doesn't look to be getting better this season as they lost their two most efficient scorers to graduation. The bulk of the usage will fall to senior **Ray Willis**, who led the team in possession percentage a year ago. Willis is turnover-prone but excellent at getting to the basket. Moton recruited a number of junior college transfers to try to fill the void left by his graduating seniors. The newcomers are unlikely to match the output on both ends from the departed likes of Dominique Sutton and Nick Chasten. It's likely the Eagles will take a step back in 2012-13.

NORFOLK STATE

2012: 26-10 (13-3 MEAC); Lost to Florida 84-50, NCAA round of 32
In-conference offense: 1.03 points per possession (5th)
In-conference defense: 0.97 points allowed per possession (3rd)

Norfolk State provided the most shocking upset of the 2012 NCAA tournament when they took down No. 2 seed Missouri 86-84 on the strength of an extraordinary shooting performance. MEAC player of the year Kyle O'Quinn was a leader and media darling by the end of the season, and parlayed that attention into his selection with the No. 49 pick in the 2012 NBA draft. With O'Quinn gone, the Spartans have some big shoes to fill, and in fact their star's departure is just part of a large outmigration of minutes and possessions. NSU will be looking to replace four starters, as well as one of their top reserves. **Pendarvis Williams** returns after a solid sophomore season and will likely see a big jump in possessions. How he handles the increased workload will be the key to the Spartans' season. **Quasim Pugh** will step in as the only other experienced backcourt option when he becomes eligible after the fall semester. Norfolk State faces a transition year with a young team. Williams could provide some star power, but he won't carry the team on both ends of the floor like O'Quinn did.

COPPIN STATE

2012: 14-16 (9-7 MEAC); Lost to Florida A&M 74-72, MEAC first round
In-conference offense: 1.09 points per possession (2nd)
In-conference defense: 1.06 points allowed per possession (12th)

Five of the Eagles' seven regular rotation guys from last season graduated, and Coppin State looks to field a young team in 2012-13. **Taariq Cephas** and **Michael Murray** are the only returning players who were part of the regular rotation last season. Cephas is a point guard who struggles with taking care of the ball, and isn't likely to replace much of the scoring the Eagles have lost. Murray is an inefficient wing. With all the new faces on the floor this season, Coppin State will find it hard to duplicate the winning conference record it had in 2011-12. It's likely they will return to a slower-paced, more defense-oriented style with all the firepower they lost. It has all the makings of a rebuilding year for Ron "Fang" Mitchell's team, and a spot in the bottom half of the MEAC is in the forecast.

FLORIDA A&M

2012: 10-23 (6-10 MEAC); Lost to Norfolk State 58-46, MEAC semifinals
In-conference offense: 0.97 points per possession (9th)
In-conference defense: 1.04 points allowed per possession (11th)

Featured scorer and top rebounder Amin Stevens is gone, but most of his supporting cast is returning, and the Rattlers should have an experienced crew of juniors and seniors this season. FAMU lacks a true point guard, as **Reggie Lewis** is a shoot-first scorer. As a result Clemon Johnson's team will play a lot of one-on-one offensively just like last season, when they were last in the MEAC in assists per field goal. Having upperclassmen and a star is important in the MEAC, where freshmen are not often ready to make immediate impact and one talented player can carry a team. FAMU will have both of those in 2012-13, so an improvement on their six conference wins is entirely possible.

HAMPTON

2012: 12-21 (6-10 MEAC); Lost to Bethune-Cookman 81-72, MEAC semifinals
In-conference offense: 0.94 points per possession (10th)
In-conference defense: 0.97 points allowed per possession (4th)

The Pirates have added some height in recruiting, with 6-7 **Dionte Adams** and 6-11 **Oumar Sall**, but offensively Edward Joyner Jr.'s team could well struggle this season. Hampton lacks someone who can be classified as a major contributor or go-to-guy to take the many shots available after the graduation of Darrion Pellum. Junior big man **David Bruce** will be a key part of the offense. He is a good offensive rebounder, but struggles to make shots, as he made just 49 percent of his two-pointers, a low number for a 6-10 guy who plays primarily in the paint. Seniors **Jasper Williams** and **Wesley Dunning** will need to expand their roles from three-point specialist and low-usage wing, respectively. It's hard to see the Eagles being better in 2012-13 with so much to replace and players stepping into new responsibilities.

HOWARD

2012: 10-21 (6-10); Lost to Norfolk State 71-61, MEAC quarterfinals
In-conference offense: 0.91 points per possession (12th)
In-conference defense: 1.00 points allowed per possession (6th)

Howard is a team full of bad shooters. Glenn Andrews is gone, and his shots will likely be absorbed by a combination of **Calvin Thompson**, **Prince Okoroh**, **Mike Phillips**, and **Simuel Frazier**. Thompson is excellent at getting to the free throw line, and hits 70 percent when he's there, however he's turnover-prone and struggles to make shots from the field. Actually high turnover rate is a theme throughout the Bison roster. Frazier, the point guard, gave the ball away almost 32 percent of the time. Pair that with the Bison's shooting struggles, and they end up as the No. 12 offense in the conference. The one thing Kevin Nickelberry's team will do well is get to the free throw line. On the flip side, Howard is prone to fouling on defense and games involving the Bison will likely be some of the longest in the MEAC. Turnover rate is something that can be improved on as players age, so there is a possibility that Howard will be more efficient on offense. However, it is not likely that this group will suddenly become great, or even average, shooters. The Bison will be making a late-season push for 10 wins again.

MARYLAND EASTERN SHORE

2012: 7-23 (4-12 MEAC); Lost to North Carolina Central 60-43, MEAC first round
In-conference offense: 0.90 points per possession (13th)
In-conference defense: 1.01 points allowed per possession (9th)

Every team needs to have something to hang their hat on. Even the teams that don't win much can possess that one quality they can be proud of and build on for the future. For 7-23 Maryland-Eastern Shore, that one thing was rebounding. The Hawks were the best offensive rebounding team in MEAC play, grabbing 40 percent of their own misses. They were also the fourth-best team in defensive rebounding. Offensive rebounding is something that the Hawks have consistently done well under head coach Frankie Allen, and one of their best rebounders returns for 2012-13 in **Ron Spencer**. The 6-9 junior is an imposing inside presence, as he was also ninth in the conference in block percentage. Spencer missed significant time last year, and if healthy all year, could help improve the UMES defense. **Louis Bell** is the team's best three-point shooter and will lead the attack from the perimeter, while sophomore point guard **Ishaq Pitt** shows promise but must cut down on turnovers. As a team, UMES was the worst in the MEAC at turning the ball over, and all primary culprits are returning. The offensive rebounding should remain solid, but the offense can't take advantage of that if it can't get shots in the first place.

SOUTH CAROLINA STATE

2012: 5-25 (0-16 MEAC), Lost to Bethune-Cookman 62-53, MEAC first round
In-conference offense: 0.93 points per possession (11th)
In-conference defense: 1.12 points allowed per possession (13th)

Going through a winless conference season is among the worst feelings in sports. It was no fluke that the Bulldogs struggled to win a game, even if doing so is unlikely. SCSU was the worst shooting team in the conference, as well as the worst defensive team in the conference. The shooting isn't likely to get better, as four of the top five players in terms of effective field goal percentage for SCSU were departing seniors. The two players still around with any offensive pop are senior point guard **Khalif Toombs** and sophomore forward **Luka Radovic**. Toombs was the facilitator last season, putting up a solid 26 percent assist rate. Radovic played in a limited role, but did show some offensive skill in hitting almost 49 percent of his twos and 72 percent of his free throws as a freshman. A look at the entire roster, however, doesn't inspire confidence that the Bulldogs will improve much this season. Then again they can't get any worse in terms of wins.

Northeast

BY JOHN TEMPLON

Last season was a strange one in the Northeast Conference. Three conference programs qualified for the postseason, but the best team by Ken Pomeroy's lights, Wagner, was left without a seat when the music stopped and chairs stopped shuffling. St. Francis NY was picked 11th in the preseason, beat that prediction by seven spots to place fourth, but went just 15-15 overall. One thing was the same, though. LIU Brooklyn finished as conference champions.

The growth and depth of the NEC is obvious. The conference is one on the rise, as evidenced by the four teams with solid postseason credentials. LIU went to the NCAA tournament after winning its second straight NEC regular season and conference titles. Robert Morris went to the CIT and made it to the quarterfinals before falling to Fairfield. Quinnipiac was invited to the CBI and fell to Penn in a first-round matchup. But, despite 25 wins and defeating then-No. 15 Pittsburgh on national television, Wagner wasn't invited to the NIT. The disappointed Seahawks were left sitting at home.

St. Francis NY actually finished fourth in the standings, which was even more impressive considering Glenn Braica's club was picked 11th in the preseason after losing two key contributors. The Terriers surprised a lot of people, but also showed the depth of the conference behind the top teams. SFC finished fourth even while playing the third hardest schedule inside of the NEC.

The conference is also showing its strength by attracting and promoting solid young coaches. Both Jim Ferry (LIU to Duquesne) and Dan Hurley (Wagner to Rhode Island) used success at the NEC level to move to the Atlantic 10 this offseason. Some hot young coaches in the conference include Andy Toole (RMU), Bashir Mason (Wagner), Jamion Christian (Mount St. Mary's) and King Rice (Monmouth). Rice is the oldest of those four at 33, and both Mason and Christian are still in their 20s as they embark on their first seasons.

The younger coaches seem to be bringing a more wide-open style of basketball to the league. Last season NEC teams averaged 68 possession per 40 minutes, the third-fastest tempo for a conference in the NCAA trailing only the Great West and the MEAC. LIU is driving this stylistic move, as the Blackbirds finished second in the nation in tempo. But there were three other teams—Robert Morris, Wagner and Monmouth—in the top 60 nationally in adjusted tempo.

Last season LIU, RMU and Wagner proved that the elite teams in the conference could hang with anyone in the country. Those three teams bagged wins over Pittsburgh, La Salle, Ohio and Princeton, to name a few. This season the top three teams are once again expected to be the class of the NEC. Robert Morris has the advantage of young stars on the way up (as well as not having had any coach turnover), but LIU has consistently outplayed its Pomeroy rank, and Wagner is a program on a dramatic rise. The Blackbirds are looking for a historic three-peat, something that hasn't been accomplished in the regular season since Rider completed the feat in the mid-1990s. No team has ever represented the NEC in three straight NCAA tournaments, something that's also within the Blackbirds' grasp.

The moment that would really announce the conference's arrival to a national audience, however, is pulling an NCAA upset. Given the right situation, all three of the top contenders should have the opportunity to do it. The closest any NEC team has come was in 2010 when Mike Rice's RMU team fell to No. 2 seed Villanova 73-70.

The remainder of the conference also has enough promise to keep things interesting for the top three. In 2011-12 St. Francis NY unexpectedly rose to fourth place in the standings. This season the Terriers should take on Quinnipiac, Sacred Heart and Monmouth for the final home game in the quarterfinals of the NEC tournament. Each of those four teams has some question marks, but all four have the personnel to compete with the top teams in the conference on a nightly basis. Bobcats forward Ike Azotam and Pioneers guard Shane Gibson are two of the seven all-conference performers that return from a season ago. On the other hand, the Hawks and Terriers are still looking for the dominant all-league type player that can take them over the top.

Below those teams Central Connecticut, Mount St. Mary's and Bryant are on another tier, fighting for the final spots in the conference tournament. For the Blue Devils it will be a bit of an unfamiliar spot. If CCSU fails to qualify for the NEC tournament, it would be the first time since 1998-99 – the program's first season in the conference. On the other side of that coin, this is the first time Bryant is even eligible to win the NEC crown after transitioning up from Division II.

Finally, Fairleigh Dickinson and St. Francis PA will have to surprise a lot of people in order to play some sort of postseason ball. The return of Umar Shannon, an all-conference player in 2010-11, from injury should help the Red Flash's chances, but the past three seasons have been a downward slide from mediocrity into irrelevance. Then again, as SFC proved last season, some wacky things can happen in the NEC.

Teams listed in John's predicted order of finish.

LIU BROOKLYN

2012: 25-9 (16-2 NEC); Lost to Michigan St., 89-67, NCAA round of 64
In-conference offense: 1.12 points per possession (1st)
In-conference defense: 1.02 points allowed per possession (8th)

For the second season in a row LIU was the class of the NEC, winning both the regular season and conference tournament titles. One the highest tempo teams in the nation, the Blackbirds ran past opponents with their wide-open style of play. Head coach Jim Ferry has moved on to Duquesne, but former assistant Jack Perri takes over the reigns and returns a team with six seniors in the rotation, including 2012 NEC player of the year **Julian Boyd**. The presence of Boyd and versatile frontcourt teammate **Jamal Olasewere** made LIU the second best team in the nation in free throw rate. Of course a strange aversion to fouling on the other end might have contributed to the below-average performance there. The Blackbirds might get off to a slow start in NEC play, however, because Boyd, Olasewere and two other players will miss the first two games due to an on-campus incident in the offseason. But when they're at full strength, LIU certainly has the most talent in the NEC. The Blackbirds look primed to make a run at a three-peat.

ROBERT MORRIS

2012: 26-11 (13-5 NEC); Lost to Fairfield, 67-61, CIT quarterfinals
In-conference offense: 1.07 points per possession (2nd)
In-conference defense: 0.98 points allowed per possession (4th)

Lately Robert Morris just can't finish. For the second straight season the Colonials were right there in the finals of the NEC tournament, but fell to LIU once again on the road. RMU struggled with bouts of inconsistency during the NEC season, problems that were driven by defensive performance. A particular two-game stretch when Robert Morris allowed St. Francis NY and Wagner to score 1.13 points per possession in back-to-back games was of concern. But Andy Toole is a good young coach, and by the NEC semis his team held that same Wagner squad to just 0.98 points per trip. Senior point guard **Velton Jones** is the player that drives both the Colonials' attack and their defense. He was among the national leaders in usage, assist rate and steal percentage in 2011-12. Most of RMU's rotation returns and, as the only top team without a coaching change, the continuity might help the Colonials finally get over that final game hump.

WAGNER

2012: 25-6 (15-3 NEC); Lost to Robert Morris, 71-64, NEC semifinals
In-conference offense: 1.07 points per possession (3rd)
In-conference defense: 0.91 points allowed per possession (1st)

A tough, gritty win at then-No. 15 Pittsburgh epitomized the dramatic transformation that Dan Hurley finished in his third season on Grymes Hill. That 59-54 win solidified Wagner as one of the NEC's elite teams and was part of a 10-2 record against non-conference opponents last season. Hurley did the work of pulling the Seahawks from just five wins in 2009-10 to 25 in 2011-12. Unfortunately, it still didn't lead to the postseason, as Wagner didn't hear back from the NIT. Hurley then took off for Rhode Island, where he inherits another difficult rebuilding process. In his place is former Drexel point guard and the youngest coach in Division I, Bashir Mason.

It'll be Mason's job to continue developing a defense that far surpassed the rest of the NEC last season. The interior is protected by junior center **Naofall Folahan**, who doesn't do much on offense, but is a commanding paint presence at 6-11. Athletic 6-7 sophomore **Mario Moody** showed a proficiency for blocking shots. Their inside presence allow NEC defensive player of the year **Kenneth Ortiz** to harass opponents on the perimeter. Wagner also gets one last gift from Hurley, as he recruited Michigan State transfer and former Michigan Mr. Basketball **Dwaun Anderson** to Staten Island before departing. He's a rare blue-chip recruit in the NEC.

QUINNIPIAC

2012: 18-14 (10-8 NEC); Lost to Pennsylvania, 74-63, CBI first round
In-conference offense: 1.07 points per possession (4th)
In-conference defense: 0.98 points allowed per possession (5th)

Tom Moore's team improved markedly after a 2-5 start in NEC play last season. The Bobcats did it by tightening up on the defensive end and holding eight straight opponents under a point per possession over a 6-2 run. What's odd is that the Bobcats were one of the best defensive teams in the paint with all-conference forward **Ike Azotam** and teammate **Ousmane Drame**, but this team couldn't turn around and score near the basket either.

Opponents shot just 44 percent on two-point attempts, best in the NEC, and the Bobcats also held their opponents to 29 percent on the offensive boards. On the offensive end, Quinnipiac shot 46 percent on twos, the worst in the NEC. Azotam and forward **Jamee Jackson** were the only players who shot above 50 percent on twos last season. If the Bobcats can improve their shooting, Moore's men could challenge the NEC's elite.

MONMOUTH

2012: 12-20 (10-8 NEC); Lost to Robert Morris, 87-68, NEC quarterfinals
In-conference offense: 1.00 points per possession (8th)
In-conference defense: 1.02 points allowed per possession (7th)

King Rice's debut at Monmouth certainly didn't get off to a sparkling start. The Hawks lost their first six games of the season, including some ugly ones to Brown, Albany and St. Francis PA. Wins over Navy and Fordham didn't stop the slide, and on January 14, Monmouth was 3-16 overall. What people didn't notice during the losing streak is that Rice had his team on the right track. By the time the meat of the conference schedule came around, the defense had picked up and Monmouth managed to win nine of its final 12 regular season games, including a resounding 106-78 victory over LIU Brooklyn on the final day. The Hawks are going to have to rely on that defense again in 2012-13, because Mike Myers Keitt, the only Monmouth player with an offensive rating above 100, graduated. Point guard **Jesse Steele** returns, but the offense continues to be devoid of a true go-to guy. Until Rice can find one, Monmouth won't be able to ascend much higher in the NEC standings.

ST. FRANCIS NY

2012: 15-15 (12-6 NEC); Lost to Quinnipiac, 80-72, NEC quarterfinals
In-conference offense: 1.01 points per possession (6th)
In-conference defense: 0.96 points allowed per possession (2nd)

St. Francis NY was picked 11th in the preseason NEC poll after losing Akeem Bennett and Ricky Cadell. The Terriers ended up finishing fourth. While SFC struggled out of conference as Glenn Braica tried to figure out how to put together a bunch of new pieces, the team raced out to a 10-2 record in the NEC before anyone knew what had happened. The highlight of the early streak was an 81-68 win at Robert Morris. Then the threes stopped falling quite as often and St. Francis finished 2-5 in its final seven games. Still, considering the circumstances the season was quite the success. The Terriers were the fourth best team in the league at shooting the three, and the second best at defending it. This season the undersized frontcourt of **Akeem Johnson** and **Jalen Cannon** are going to have to do more if SFC wants to be successful. Both players were efficient when called upon last season, but showed limited offensive games. If point guards **Brent Jones** and **Dre Calloway** can limit turnovers, the Terriers might be able to surprise people again.

SACRED HEART

2012: 14-18 (8-10 NEC); Lost to LIU, 80-68, NEC quarterfinals
In-conference offense: 1.02 points per possession (5th)
In-conference defense: 1.02 points allowed per possession (6th)

Sacred Heart's success begins and ends with shooting guard **Shane Gibson**, one of the most underrated players in the entire nation. Gibson put up a 113 offensive rating last season thanks to 56 percent shooting on twos and 43 percent shooting on threes. He used 29 percent of SHU's possessions while on the court, which was often. And while Gibson provided a steady presence, it was the Pioneers' frontcourt—especially 6-9 forward **Justin Swidowski**—that often decided games. Sacred Heart got to .500 twice during conference season, but both times followed it up with a three-game losing streak. The final one near the end of the regular season was evidence that SHU wasn't quite prepared to hang with the top teams in the NEC. After losing 103-91 in overtime to LIU Brooklyn, the Pioneers bowed out in much less competitive style during the NEC tournament. Dave Bike will have to find players to complement Gibson in the star's final season.

MOUNT ST. MARY'S

2012: 8-21 (6-12 NEC); Did not qualify for NEC tournament
In-conference offense: 0.97 points per possession (9th)
In-conference defense: 1.02 points allowed per possession (9th)

It has been a steady slide down to bottom of the NEC for Mount St. Mary's. Robert Burke is out after MSM missed the NEC tournament last season. In his place is Jamion Christian, who has promised to put some step in the Mount's lackadaisical offensive game plan. The former VCU assistant wants to attack early and often. One thing Christian will have to watch out for is if a rise in the tempo leads to more turnovers. Mount St. Mary's turned the ball over on 24 percent of its possessions last season, second worst in the NEC. Those empty possessions prevented talented players like **Kelvin Parker** from getting more touches on the offensive end. This season Parker and **Julian Norfleet** should flourish, and it's possible the Mount might compete for a return spot in the NEC tournament this season. But if MSM's going to do it they'll have to beat an NEC tournament team, something the Mount only did once last season. The lone victory was an 81-80 double-overtime victory over Sacred Heart.

CENTRAL CONNECTICUT

2012: 13-16 (10-8 NEC); Lost to Wagner 87-77, NEC quarterfinals
In-conference offense: 1.00 points per possession (7th)
In-conference defense: 0.96 points allowed per possession (3rd)

Central Connecticut took a step forward last season, and now Howie Dickenman has to build on that. The transition started last season as the offense began to revolve more and more around freshman **Kyle Vinales**. The 6-1 guard never stopped shooting and ending up leading all of the nation's freshman in scoring at 17.9 points per game. He had an offensive rating of 100.2 while using 29 percent of CCSU's possessions thanks to shooting 38 percent from three and 84 from the free throw line. As a sophomore Vinales will have to improve on his game inside the arc, where he shot just 40 percent. He might even get more opportunities, as the graduation of Ken Horton and Robby Ptacek leaves a big hole in CCSU's attack. Dickenman has a tall task in front of him, as he'll have to find a way to not disturb a defense that ranked third in the NEC last season while jumpstarting an offense suffering from those personnel losses.

BRYANT

2012: 2-28 (1-17 NEC); Did not qualify for NEC tournament
In-conference offense: 0.92 points per possession (11th)
In-conference defense: 1.12 points allowed per possession (12th)

The long transition to Division I hoops is finally complete, and Bryant is eligible to win NEC titles. That has to be a great feeling for Tim O'Shea, but he surely knows that the Bulldogs still have a long way to go. Last season Bryant won just two games, over UC Davis and St. Francis PA. To be fair, Bryant lost in overtime or by fewer than five points five times during conference play, with the closest loss coming on the road to Sacred Heart during "Rivalry Week." Unfortunately the Bulldogs couldn't translate that into a home victory in the return game, as O'Shea's men were blown out by 26. O'Shea needs to find a complement to forward **Alex Francis**. The junior has all-NEC potential if he's not the focal point of every opposing defense.

ST. FRANCIS PA

2012: 6-23 (5-13 NEC); Did not qualify for NEC tournament
In-conference offense: 0.95 points per possession (10th)
In-conference defense: 1.05 points allowed per possession (10th)

St. Francis PA was young last season and it showed, as the Red Flash turned the ball over more often than any NEC team. On the other hand it didn't help matters that SFU lost point guard **Umar Shannon** for the year before the season even began. He was one of the lone bright spots in the offense in 2010-11 and his return should help SFU improve this season. What won't help is the transfer of Scott Eatherton, the NEC's most improved player in 2011-12. While he would've given the Flash a nice inside-outside combination with Shannon, Eatherton transferred to Northeastern instead.

Even so, there's something to build on for SFU. The Red Flash sat at 4-4 in conference play on January 21, but then suffered through a seven-game losing streak. Yes, five of those losses were to teams that finished in the top four in the conference, but it showed how far this team has to go in order to be competitive, as just two of the losses were by fewer than five points. After the rough season, Don Friday resigned and was replaced by longtime assistant coach Bob Krimmel, who just happens to be the athletic director's son. The younger Krimmel has a tough road in front of him.

FAIRLEIGH DICKINSON

2012: 3-26 (2-16 NEC); Did not qualify for NEC tournament
In-conference offense: 0.89 points per possession (12th)
In-conference defense: 1.05 points allowed per possession (11th)

In 2011-12 the roster of Fairleigh Dickinson resembled a box of puzzle pieces that didn't quite seem to fit. Individually some of the players certainly had talent, but the collection of them resulted in a 3-26 season. Give credit to FDU for not giving up, the Knights got their final win of the season in their last game, defeating St. Francis NY 45-44. This season it might be smart for Greg Vetrone to take some possessions away from **Melquan Bolding** and funnel them to **Kinu Rochford**. The latter showed strong rebounding skills and athleticism that can help him succeed in the NEC during his senior season if given the opportunity. Otherwise it might be a long season, especially since George Goode, one of the team's only consistent offensive threats, graduated. Even with Goode, FDU was one of the worst offensive teams in the country. The Knights shot a dreadful 27 percent from beyond the arc in conference play.

Ohio Valley

BY COREY SCHMIDT

The Ohio Valley Conference has won at least one NCAA tournament game in each of the last four seasons, but all of those wins belong to either Murray State or Morehead State. And that's the problem for the OVC. It's historically been a top-heavy league dominated by Murray State, Austin Peay, and more recently Morehead State. The relative weakness of the league's remaining programs is a major reason why Murray State was a bubble team last year after losing just one game all season. Fortunately, the Racers secured the league's automatic bid, but there was a real possibility they could have been left out of the field of 68 because they didn't beat any programs of substance in OVC play.

Last year's addition of SIU Edwardsville to the conference didn't help that perception, as the Cougars were one of the worst programs in Division I in their time as an independent. It also didn't help that Austin Peay had a bad season by the Governors' standards, and even Morehead State took a step back after losing all-time rebounding leader Kenneth Faried to the NBA.

At the same time, however, Tennessee State had one of its best seasons and finished as runner-up to the Racers in the OVC tournament. Tennessee Tech fared well under a new coach, and Southeast Missouri State continued to improve under Dickey Nutt. The OVC needs these programs to continue their ascents, but in the immediate term the conference powers-that-be can pat their backs for bringing Belmont into the fold.

Belmont's move from the Atlantic Sun to the Ohio Valley didn't get much recognition nationally, but this is a major coup for the OVC. The Bruins should contend immediately in their new conference, which could lead to the blossoming of a rivalry with Murray State. The two programs will likely battle for championship as early as this season. If they can continue on their current trajectories of success, this could very well be the tandem that increases the quality of the OVC as Gonzaga and Saint Mary's have done in the WCC.

In the meantime, the league suffered a dual-blow when schools in higher-ranked conferences lured Donnie Tyndall and John Cooper away from Morehead State and Tennessee State, respectively. The new coaches at those posts have big shoes to fill. Tennessee State could challenge for a crown this year if the coaching succession plan works out, while Morehead State may be in for a middling year. Of the teams that finished in the middle of the pack last season, Southeast Missouri State is the most likely to improve, while Austin Peay seems positioned for a rebuilding year.

The bottom of the league will be just as poor as it was in 2011-12. While it's unlikely that Tennessee Martin will go winless in conference play again, the team won't win much. The same can be said for Eastern Illinois, which hit the reboot button this summer and hired a new coach to lead the Panthers out of the depths of the league standings.

Most of the programs in the OVC appear to be on the right track, but the conference as a whole is not yet poised to cash in on the success of Murray State. As such, it's probably a one-bid league again, though the addition of Belmont could certainly make things interesting come March.

Teams listed in Corey's predicted order of finish.

MURRAY STATE

2012: 31-2 (15-1 OVC); Lost to Marquette 62-53, NCAA round of 32
In-conference offense: 1.12 points per possession (1st)
In-conference defense: 0.93 points allowed per possession (1st)

Murray State's quest for an undefeated season was well documented last year, but what perhaps went overlooked at times was just how great this team was on defense. The Racers were a top-25 team in defensive efficiency, and their 0.93 points allowed per possession mark was a full 0.10 points less than the OVC in-conference average. On that front Steve Prohm will miss Donte Poole and Ivan Aska, who respectively led the team in steal rate and defensive rebounding percentage last season. While Murray may not be a top-25 defensive team this year, the program has a history of getting players to commit on defense—and thus far Prohm has done a fine job of carrying on that legacy. Of course, it helps that **Isaiah Canaan** will be returning for his senior season a year after winning OVC player of the year. Canaan is a threat to score from anywhere on the court, and he poses that threat with alarming efficiency (122 offensive rating) for a player who takes 28 percent of his team's shots during his minutes. Senior **Ed Daniel** will also be back and is sure to be a reliable option to score in the paint or swat shots. The pipeline behind the senior class continues to flow with talent as it always seems to in Murray, Kentucky. Prohm will have the Racers contending for the OVC crown yet again in season two of his tenure.

TENNESSEE STATE

2012: 20-13 (11-5 OVC); Lost to Mercer 60-68, CIT first round
In-conference offense: 1.04 points per possession (5th)
In-conference defense: 0.99 points allowed per possession (4th)

Tennessee State was the only team to beat Murray State during the regular season last year, but the Tigers fell to the Racers when it mattered most—in the OVC tournament championship. Neither team led by more than seven points in that game, but Murray State won 54-52 to end TSU's chances of going to the NCAA tournament and the OVC's chance for multiple bids. Tennessee State turned enough heads in its battles with the Racers for other schools to take notice of coach John Cooper. With Cooper now at Miami OH, former assistant Travis Williams takes over head coaching duties for the Tigers. Williams inherits a team with plenty of proven commodities, one that will again challenge Murray for the OVC's crown. Just about everyone's back, including one of the OVC's best in senior **Robert Covington**. At 6-8, Covington's big by Ohio Valley standards. He uses that advantage to clean up boards at rates of 20 percent (defensive) and 11 percent (offensive) and to connect on an amazing percentage of his two-pointers (57 percent). Oddly enough, he's also one of the league's best three-point shooters. He made 46 percent of his threes as a sophomore and 45 percent as a junior. For TSU to leap Murray State, Covington's teammates will need to follow his lead when it comes to offensive efficiency. Only one other returning contributor (**Kellen Thornton**) made more than half of his two-point attempts last year.

BELMONT

2012: 27-8 (16-2 A-Sun); Lost to Georgetown 74-59, NCAA round of 64
In-conference offense: 1.23 points per possession (1st A-Sun)
In-conference defense: 0.97 points allowed per possession (2nd A-Sun)

After a decade spent dominating the Atlantic Sun, Belmont will attempt to establish itself as a top-tier program in the Ohio Valley. Fresh off yet another NCAA tournament appearance, Rick Byrd's program should contend immediately against the likes of Murray State and Tennessee State. While the Bruins will certainly miss efficiency stud Drew Hanlen in the backcourt, they may still have one of the best guard tandems in the league in seniors **Kerron Johnson** and **Ian Clark**. It's a feat that Johnson made 60 percent of his frequent two-point attempts at a listed height of 6-1, and he was getting banged up too, as his 72 percent free throw rate indicates. Clark complements Johnson well as an efficient, low-usage guy on offense and a lockdown defender on defense. While Belmont should be fierce on the perimeter, the question mark with this team lies on the interior. Scott Saunders and Mick Hedgepeth, who last year provided much of the team's rebounding and low-post scoring, have graduated. Though Byrd will be relying on young and/or inexperienced players to fill those gaps this season, he's proven over the years that personnel losses rarely slow his program. Belmont should navigate the OVC waters just fine.

SOUTHEAST MISSOURI STATE

2012: 15-16 (9-7 OVC); Lost to Tennessee Tech 73-77, OVC quarterfinals
In-conference offense: 1.10 points per possession (2nd)
In-conference defense: 1.03 points allowed per possession (5th)

Southeast Missouri State bottomed out by going 0-18 in conference play in 2008-09. Dickey Nutt was brought in subsequent to that abysmal season, and he's slowly but surely shifted the tide in the three years since. In conference play, his teams went from three wins in 2009-10 to six in 2010-11 to nine last year. While it's unlikely SEMO will continue with the multiples of three progression to get to 12 wins this year, the team should be competitive for a second straight campaign. Last year's squad featured one of the top offenses in the OVC, largely due to its accuracy inside the arc and tenacious offensive rebounding. On those fronts, Nutt will miss Leon Powell, who made 59 percent of his twos and finished sixth nationally in offensive rebounding percentage. If they can replace Powell's production by committee, then the return of junior **Tyler Stone** and senior **Marland Smith** should ensure that the Redhawks will again wield a highly efficient offense. On defense, the team can improve its efficiency by forcing more turnovers (league-low last year), but SEMO will need to be careful not to over-foul as happened a year ago.

TENNESSEE TECH

2012: 19-14 (9-7 OVC); Lost to Georgia State 74-43, CIT first round
In-conference offense: 1.07 points per possession (3rd)
In-conference defense: 1.03 points allowed per possession (7th)

It's not often that guys are drafted out of the OVC, but that was the realty for a second straight year as former Tennessee Tech wing Kevin Murphy heard his name called at the 2012 NBA draft. In addition to losing a player of Murphy's talent, TTU will also be without its starting backcourt from a year ago. The team's two biggest players—who provided rebounding and high-percentage scoring off the bench—have also graduated. A squad that was the seventh-most experienced in D-I last year will likely be somewhere in the lower half this season. If Steve Payne's guys have a chance at being competitive, it will be on the backs of seniors **Terrell Barnes** and **Jud Dillard**, who have been playing together since high school. Barnes' role on offense is limited to grabbing offensive rebounds and hoping to get fouled. Dillard, though, is an offensive star. While Kevin Murphy was firmly a go-to guy in terms of possession usage, Dillard wasn't too far behind and he was far more efficient. Despite his relatively skinny frame at 6-4 and 190 pounds, Dillard excels at attacking the basket both for points and rebounds. He'll likely have to do a lot of that this season as he works to lead a team without much experience.

JACKSONVILLE STATE

2012: 15-18 (8-8 OVC); Lost to Morehead State 68-54, OVC quarterfinals
In-conference offense: 1.03 points per possession (7th)
In-conference defense: 0.99 points per possession (3rd)

While Jacksonville State could claim one of the Ohio Valley's best defenses a year ago, that effort was often mitigated by an offense that struggled to put the ball in the basket. Most of those offensive struggles can be traced to the perimeter, where the Gamecocks made only 26 percent of their three-point attempts. That was the worst rate in all of Division I last season. The worst offenders on the squad were **Tarvin Gaines** and **Darion Rackley**, who not only missed 75 percent of their threes but also attempted a lot of them. With a slight improvement in effective field goal percentage, JSU could be on its way to fielding an offense that's at least slightly better than the league average. On defense, the returning personnel would do well to stop fouling so much. Not only did they have a league-worst defensive free throw rate, opposing teams also burned James Green's team at the free throw line by making 76 percent of their freebies.

SIU EDWARDSVILLE

2012: 10-17 (6-10 OVC); Ineligible for OVC tournament
In-conference offense: 0.99 points per possession (9th)
In-conference defense: 1.07 points allowed per possession (8th)

That SIU Edwardsville won six league games in its first year in the OVC is an impressive feat considering this had been one of the worst programs in Division I since moving up in 2009-10. While the Cougars need to improve in a lot of areas—namely limiting turnovers and connecting on more free throws—they at the very least return a core of players who have had an offseason to get better. One of the greatest challenges for recent reclassifiers is just keeping a roster together year after year, and coach Lennox Forrester has managed to do that. The team will be led by a senior trio consisting of **Mark Yelovich**, **Jerome Jones**, and **Derian Shaffer**. The key for these guys will be to use their size—they're all between 6-5 and 6-7—to produce points in the lane, as opposed to taking shots from the perimeter where they struggle. They should leave the three-point duties to sophomore **Kris Davis**, who went a rather amazing 58-of-97 from beyond the arc last season. While Forrester has several nice pieces coming back, it remains to be seen if those pieces are talented enough to contend with the OVC's upper half.

AUSTIN PEAY

2012: 12-20 (8-8 OVC); Lost to Jacksonville State 70-75, OVC first round
In-conference offense: 1.05 points per possession (4th)
In-conference defense: 1.03 points allowed per possession (6th)

Last year's book predicted that Austin Peay would win the Ohio Valley Conference crown. Under Dave Loos, APSU has been a sure bet to finish at or near the top of the OVC, and given a senior-laden roster, it seemed likely that would occur again last season. Instead, the Governors had a rare letdown season that saw them lose at least four games in a row on three separate occasions. The Austin Peay faithful will need to be patient as Loos attempts to get the ship back on course with just two returners who played at least 50 percent of available minutes in 2011-12. Among the rest of the pack, sophomore **Chris Freeman** could be poised for a breakout season. In a limited role as a freshman, the 6-6 forward posted admirable rebounding rates, made 56 percent of his twos, and went 19-of-23 at the charity stripe.

MOREHEAD STATE

2012: 18-15 (10-6 OVC); Lost to Tennessee State 59-52, OVC semifinals
In-conference offense: 1.01 points per possession (8th)
In-conference defense: 0.98 points allowed per possession (2nd)

Donnie Tyndall did yeoman's work in turning around the Morehead State program during his six-year tenure, and now that he's moved on to Southern Mississippi, it'll be up to former Mississippi Valley State coach Sean Woods to ensure that MSU continues to rise. Woods' two best teams at MVSU played at warp speed, which is a philosophy that current Eagles won't recognize. Tyndall's squads were deliberately slow-paced. If a change of pace is afoot in Morehead, Kentucky, the results could be ugly early on. The Eagle offense was one of the worst in OVC play last season, largely due to the fact the team turned the ball over on a quarter of its possessions. Woods had just one adequate defensive team in his four years at MVSU, and that was conveniently last season. The Eagles may play much differently than they have in the past, and the results could be mixed in a year where the roster as presently constructed may not mesh with the new coach's historical approach. That roster figures to be led this season by 6-6 senior **Milton Chavis**, an offensive rebounding machine.

EASTERN KENTUCKY

2012: 16-16 (7-9 OVC); Lost to Southeast Missouri State 75-65, OVC first round
In-conference offense: 1.04 points per possession (6th)
In-conference defense: 1.08 points allowed per possession (10th)

So long as Jeff Neubauer is the coach at Eastern Kentucky, we can be sure that the Colonels will be a slow-tempo, low-turnover, three-point loving team. While that's worked well for them offensively, they've also had their struggles on defense, particularly when it comes to defending inside the arc. Neubauer has yet to field a squad that could hold OVC opponents to under 50 percent on two-pointers. That type of track record will always limit EKU's regular-season success, no matter how many threes they make. If there is hope for the Colonels' interior defense, it comes in the form of 6-8 sophomore **Eric Stutz**. The Indiana native has the potential to develop into a leading big man in the Ohio Valley, particularly in a year such as this one where standout bigs are few and far between.

EASTERN ILLINOIS

2012: 12-17 (5-11 OVC); Did not qualify for OVC tournament
In-conference offense: 0.96 points per possession (10th)
In-conference defense: 1.07 points allowed per possession (9th)

When the Eastern Illinois brass let go Mike Miller after seven seasons, they had to figure that his son Joey would end up transferring. Joey did indeed head to a new school (UIC), but so too did rising sophomore Alfonzo McKinnie (Green Bay). When combined with the loss of three other starters to graduation, the EIU roster was gutted. New coach Jay Spoonhour will have a clean slate this season in Charleston, though 6-8 sophomore **Josh Piper** should figure prominently in the rebuilding plan. As a freshman role player, Piper posted an offensive rating of 115, and he had a solid shooting touch as evidenced by his 93 percent free throw mark (24-of-26). Spoonhour may turn this program around, but it won't happen this season.

TENNESSEE MARTIN

2012: 4-27 (0-16 OVC); Did not qualify for OVC tournament
In-conference offense: 0.95 points per possession (11th)
In-conference defense: 1.16 points allowed per possession (11th)

To a national observer it doesn't seem like it's been four years since Lester Martin was stuffing the stat line every night for Tennessee Martin, but surely it seems like much longer than that for the UTM faithful. Since Hudson graduated to the professional ranks, the Skyhawks have had two seasons in which they won just four games total. The 2011-12 season represented a new low for the program as it went 0-16 in conference play. Jason James' squad had both the league's worst offense and its worst defense, with UTM ranking near or at the bottom of the conference in each of the four factors. Pick something and the Seahawks could surely shore it up.

Patriot

BY ASHER FUSCO

As head-to-head player-of-the-year competitions go, this is about as good as it gets. C.J. McCollum, the reigning conference MVP, is Lehigh's impossible-to-stop wing, whose dynamism spans both ends of the court and includes rebounding and passing. Mike Muscala is Bucknell's steady center, quietly the league's most efficient scorer and a spectacular rebounder and post defender. Toss in the fact that Lehigh and Bucknell appear to be the class of the Patriot League by a fairly wide margin, and you've got a sexy season-long storyline.

Choosing a favorite in the McCollum-vs.-Muscala competition might come down to personal preference—it's that hard to parse the stats and come out with a clear favorite. Do you prefer the rangy assassin who can score from anywhere on the court in almost any fashion, or the big man who quietly controls the game on both ends with rebounding, size and offensive acumen? Either way, the star-against-star race will be undeniably entertaining.

Lehigh, led by McCollum, will look to reprise its role as the Patriot League's representative in the NCAA tournament (and its role as round-of-64 giant slayer) with a solid core of McCollum, forward Gabe Knutson and point guard Mackey McKnight. Lehigh didn't lose much talent from its stellar 2012 squad, making the Mountain Hawks a good bet to finish in one of the league's top two spots this coming spring.

The other clear-cut competitor for the conference crown is Muscala's Bucknell squad, which finished the 2012 regular season with the Patriot's best record and top efficiency margin before faltering against Lehigh in the conference title game. Bucknell's strength sits in the post, where Muscala teams with the underappreciated Joe Willman. If Bucknell sees some improvement from young guards Ryan Hill and Steven Kaspar and continued consistency from wing Cameron Ayers, there's no reason the Bison can't finish atop the standings again. Just as they were in 2012, Lehigh and Bucknell are far and away the most talented teams in the conference, setting up a pair of high-stakes matchups in January and February, and potentially a third come March.

After Bucknell and Lehigh, American looks like the third-best team almost without question. The return of forward Stephen Lumpkins from professional baseball to a team with a solid point guard (Daniel Munoz) and steady post player (Tony Wroblicky) places Jeff Jones' Eagles above most of the conference but just shy of the talent level at Bucknell or Lehigh. The loss of Charles Hinkle and Troy Brewer shouldn't be understated, but it's tough to doubt a Jones-coached team.

Holy Cross looks like its steady self, fielding a strong defensive team centered on the solid all-around play of forward Dave Dudzinski and promising point guard Justin Burrell. If forwards Eric Obeysekere and Phil Beans can make positive contributions, the Crusaders could threaten the 10-victory plateau and make a run at American for third place. Lafayette's senior-centric 2012 lineup managed a positive efficiency margin, thanks to the stellar shooting of Jim Mower and the efficient post scoring of Ryan Willen. With both of those players—and two other veteran contributors—out the door, long-time Lafayette coach Fran O'Hanlon will have a challenge on his hands in 2013. Senior point guard Tony Johnson will be the Leopards' top contributor on both ends, and the only thing keeping the team from falling into the league's bottom third.

If one program is falling out of the league's middle ground, another has to be moving up. The ascendant team that could replace Lafayette near .500 this season is Army. The Black Knights have taken small steps forward during the tenure of coach Zach Spiker, stepping out of the basement last year thanks in part to the versatility and efficiency of forward Ella Ellis. The 6-7 Ellis, returns to the fold at West Point, making Army a real threat to push .500 in conference play for the first time in a long time. Ellis combines with solid post Jordan Springer and sharp-shooting wing Josh Herbeck to create a trio that could officially lift Army out of the doldrums.

Colgate and Navy each flirted with efficiency margins nearing -0.20 in conference play last season, and 2013 isn't looking much better for the Patriot's basement-dwellers. Colgate is in the early stages of a rebuilding project that won't really get rolling until it adds transfers in the 2013-14 season, while the Ed DeChellis plan at Navy has taken big hits lately with the transfer of star forward J.J. Avila and early departure of guard Jordan Brickman. The former Penn State coach wasn't at the top of the heap in State College, by any means, but he's buried even deeper in Annapolis.

You could look at the Patriot League and see its relative predictability as a negative. But when the dueling favorites boast stacked veteran rosters and individual stars as extraordinary as C.J. McCollum and Mike Muscala, sometimes a little predictability isn't a bad thing. Even outside of Bucknell and Lehigh, the Patriot League has some intriguing storylines and stars. The return of Lumpkins to American, the emergence of Ellis at Army, and the spectacular point guard play of Johnson at Lafayette provide plenty to watch in the Patriot League this coming season.

Teams listed in Asher's predicted order of finish.

LEHIGH

2012: 27-8 (11-3 Patriot); Lost to Xavier 70-58, NCAA round of 32
In-conference offense: 1.10 points per possession (1st)
In-conference defense: 0.95 points allowed per possession (2nd)

Lehigh authored one of the most shocking narratives of last season's NCAA tournament by knocking off Duke in a 15-over-2 upset. Upon closer inspection, however, the Mountain Hawks' 75-70 unseating of the vaunted Blue Devils wasn't all that shocking. Lehigh relied on the same strengths it had during the course of its 11-3 Patriot League regular season and three-game sweep of the conference tournament: the high-volume, ultra-efficient offense of guard **C.J. McCollum** and post **Gabe Knutson**, and a smart defensive scheme that forced turnovers while avoiding fouls. McCollum has been Lehigh's key player for the duration of his career. He carried the Mountain Hawks to an NCAA tourney appearance as a freshman before regressing in a sophomore season that saw Lehigh finish 6-8 in league play. In 2012, McCollum expanded the reach of his game to become one of the conference's best rebounders, perimeter defenders and distributors, on top of his status as one of the nation's top pure scorers. There isn't much more for McCollum to prove as a senior. He's the league's best perimeter player, a high-usage, high-efficiency terror who hits the glass and uses his long arms to excel on the defensive end. The second half of Lehigh's inside-outside tandem of senior stars is Knutson, a solid rebounder and defender who has grown more efficient on the offensive end as he has grown into the team's number two scoring option. The Mountain Hawks return another starter in **Mackey McKnight**, a well-rounded point guard who became one of the league's best as a sophomore. **Holden Grenier** will reprise his role as the team's stretch forward, using his 35 percent three-point shooting to lure defenses away from Knutson down low. Coach Brett Reed has some interesting options on hand to fill the void left by starting wing Jordan Hamilton, a capable, if infrequent, scorer who provided bulk alongside McCollum and McKnight. If Reed feels like going big, he could add promising sophomore post **Conroy Baltimore** or one of two 6-8 freshmen (**Justin Goldsborough** and **Jesse Chuku**) to the lineup. He could also elect to stretch defenses by utilizing the shooting of 6-3 freshman **Devon Carter** or junior **B.J. Bailey**. The Mountain Hawks have more than enough talent to fill the hole left by the departure of Hamilton, and the core of McCollum, McKnight and Knutson is only getting better.

BUCKNELL

2012: 25-10 (12-2 Patriot); Lost to Nevada 75-67, NIT second round
In-conference offense: 1.09 points per possession (2nd)
In-conference defense: 0.92 points allowed per possession (1st)

Bucknell came within five points of its second straight NCAA tournament appearance in 2012, as coach Dave Paulsen wrapped up the fourth campaign in a remarkable tenure. It only took Paulsen one down year to reposition Bucknell as one of the Patriot's most prominent programs. A big part of the turnaround has been one unbelievably steady frontcourt pair. Center **Mike Muscala** and forward **Joe Willman** enter their senior seasons with a firm grasp on the title of the top frontcourt combo in the conference. As a junior, the 6-11 Muscala was the league's most efficient scorer, second-best rebounder, second-best shot-blocker. The less celebrated Willman was the team's most important cog, putting up solid rebounding numbers while shooting 53 percent from the field and 85 percent from the free-throw line. In addition to anchoring the conference's toughest defense, Willman and Muscala shored up an offense that struggled to replace the productivity of sturdy point guard Darryl Shazier, who graduated after the 2011 season. In his stead, Paulsen turned to a combination of **Ryan Hill** and **Steven Kaspar**, who both hovered around the 40 effective FG percentage mark and handed out too many turnovers. The good news is the team's backcourt situation should improve this season as Hill and Kaspar age, and freshman **Ryan Frazier** is tossed into the mix. At the wing, 6-5 junior **Cameron Ayers** is one of the conference's strongest all-around performers, one who buried 46 percent of his threes in a stellar sophomore season. He'll play alongside 2-guard **Bryson Johnson**, a 40 percent three-point marksman who's ultra-efficient until he steps inside the arc. This season's Bucknell squad shouldn't look appreciably different from last season's, as Muscala will battle Lehigh's C.J. McCollum for player of the year honors and the Bison will battle the Mountain Hawks for Patriot supremacy.

AMERICAN

2012: 20-12 (10-4 Patriot); Lost to Buffalo 78-61, CIT first round
In-conference offense: 1.08 points per possession (3rd)
In-conference defense: 0.96 points allowed per possession (3rd)

The 2011-12 season didn't result in the best record of the Jeff Jones era, but it was one of his most impressive accomplishments at American. The Eagles lost the services of two stellar post players after the 2011 season—versatile scorer Vlad Moldoveanu to graduation and rebounder extraordinaire **Stephen Lumpkins** to pro baseball—but managed to finish third in the conference and earn a trip to the CIT. And now Lumpkins is back after spending parts of two seasons as a pitcher in the Kansas City Royals organization. If he can pick up where he left off, he'll be one of the conference's best big men. Lumpkins is an efficient and active post scorer and a strong rebounder, as well as a decent shot blocker. He'll team up with 6-10 junior **Tony Wroblicky** down low to create a frontcourt pair that will compete with Bucknell's for post supremacy in the Patriot. In addition to Wroblicky and Lumpkins, American returns starting point guard **Daniel Munoz** and starting shooting guard **John Schoof**. Munoz, a solid passer and a 43 percent three-point shooter, is one of the better lead guards in the conference. Schoof had a rough freshman season, shooting 28 percent from three and 34 percent from two. Those guards will miss the presence of **Blake Jolivette**, a 5-11 sparkplug who may miss the entire season due to a knee injury.. Jones will look to replace his top two reserves with promising freshman wing **Jesse Reed** and Serbian newcomer **Marko Vasic**.

HOLY CROSS

2012: 15-14 (9-5 Patriot); Lost to Lafayette 84-76, Patriot quarterfinals
In-conference offense: 0.99 points per possession (6th)
In-conference defense: 0.98 points allowed per possession (4th)

Holy Cross can compete consistently in the Patriot League—the Crusaders' strong resume says as much. The program has only finished below .500 in conference play once in the past decade, earning two NCAA tournament trips during that period. But on the heels of a so-so 21-21 stretch over the past three seasons, it's worth wondering whether Bucknell and Lehigh have gained some serious ground on Holy Cross in the bigger picture. This coming season, Milan Brown's third coaching the Crusaders, could tell us a lot about the program's place in the conference moving forward. With the loss of three of its top five guards, Holy Cross' strength has shifted from the backcourt to the frontcourt over the course of one offseason. The Crusaders' most crucial returner is **Dave Dudzinski**, a 6-9 junior who shined on both ends of the court last season. He's a 54 percent shooter on twos, a frequently fouled 83 percent free-throw shooter, and he doesn't have any substantial flaws in his game. **Phil Beans** and **Eric Obeysekere** are the other main cogs down low for Brown. With more playing time than the 18 minutes per game he saw in 2012, Obeysekere, a 6-8 senior, could emerge as one of the conference's top post defenders if he recovers from a preseason stress fracture. They'll be joined by promising freshman **Isaiah Baker** and sophomores **Taylor Abt** and **Malcolm Miller**. The Crusaders' backcourt isn't nearly as close to being a finished product. **Justin Burrell** showed solid passing skills and could turn into one of the league's top distributors this season. Senior wing **Jordan Stevens** upped his three-point accuracy to 44 percent last season to become one of the conference's best bench players. Aside from Burrell and Stevens, the Crusaders will turn to some combination of unproven wing **Malcolm Miller** or freshman **Cullen Hamilton**. Holy Cross appears to be a rung below Bucknell and Lehigh on the talent ladder once more, but the inside-out duo of Dudzinski and Burrell, as well as the development of the freshman Hamilton, should lend their games some intrigue.

ARMY

2012: 12-18 (5-9 Patriot); Lost to American 57-40, Patriot quarterfinals
In-conference offense: 0.97 points per possession (7th)
In-conference defense: 1.06 points allowed per possession (5th)

Army took a small step forward from eighth to sixth in the conference standings in Zach Spiker's third season as head coach, thanks in large part to versatile forward **Ella Ellis**. Spiker's 6-7 star, who returns for his senior season, took nearly one-third of the Black Knights' shot attempts during his minutes and used his athletic frame to excel on the boards and at both ends of the floor. Ellis is joined in the frontcourt by **Jordan Springer**, a stereotypical low-usage post player who scooped up more than his fair share of rebounds and shot 56 percent from the field. Wing **Josh Herbeck** returns as the team's primary floor-spacer and second-best offensive threat, coming off a season in which he made 40 percent of his threes. The Black Knights have plenty of depth at the point guard spot, as **Milton Washington** and **Maxwell Lenox** both return for their sophomore seasons. The pair split time at the lead guard position, helping spearhead an aggressive defense that forced more turnovers per possession than any other team in the league. Army has a few returning bench players who made positive contributions in 2012, including forward **Andrew Stire** and **Jason Pancoe**. Sixth man **Mo Williams** also returns, but he'll need to shoot better than the 41 effective FG percentage he posted in 2012 to make an impact. It's hard to make a case for Army as a contender in the Patriot League, despite Ellis' status as one of the conference's best and Herbeck's emergence as a quality sharpshooter. But if the Black Knights' offense catches up with its aggressive defense, this team can reach .500 in conference play.

LAFAYETTE

2012: 13-18 (7-7 Patriot); Lost to Bucknell 79-52, Patriot semifinals
In-conference offense: 1.07 points per possession (4th)
In-conference defense: 1.07 points allowed per possession (6th)

There are a lot of positives that come with having four seniors in your rotation, but "next year" is never one of them. Next year is here for Lafayette. Fran O'Hanlon's two best scorers, along with his starting combo guard and top reserve all graduated. This season the Leopards will depend heavily on point guard **Tony Johnson** on both ends of the floor. Johnson, who played well enough in just 12 games last season to earn second team All-Patriot honors, is everything a pass-first point guard should be. To whom Johnson should pass is another issue entirely. Sophomore sharpshooter **Joey Ptasinski** should have a chance to earn a starting spot, based on his 45 percent long-range shooting as a freshman. Returning starter **Seth Hinrichs** could be the team's leading scorer. That's where the sure bets stop for O'Hanlon. Returning starter **Dan Trist** will pair up with 6-9 senior **Levi Giese** down low, where neither has proven himself a competent scorer or rebounder. A pair of 6-10 freshmen, **Nathaniel Musters** and **Ben Freeland**, will have a chance to play early and often, and decorated freshman **Zach Rufer** will contribute minutes at the wing. No other team in the Patriot League lost as much talent as did Lafayette this offseason. If Johnson stays healthy, Hinrich continues his hot shooting and one of the post players develops into an above-average contributor, the Leopards could be a sleeper, but this team has more ifs than it does safe bets.

COLGATE

2012: 8-22 (2-12 Patriot); Lost to Lehigh 70-57, Patriot quarterfinals
In-conference offense: 1.00 points per possession (5th)
In-conference defense: 1.18 points allowed per possession (8th)

Matt Langel began his uphill climb at Colgate in 2011-12. The former Penn and Temple assistant didn't engineer a stunning turnaround in his first season at the helm, as the Raiders managed just eight overall victories and slid into seventh place in the Patriot for a second straight season. For better or worse the 2013 Raiders will look quite a bit different, as the team loses its starting center, shooting guard, and two of its most frequently-used wings. On the other hand two of the team's best offensive players return in senior point guard **Mitch Rolls** and junior wing **Pat Moore**. Rolls is a one-time offensive liability who added 43-percent three-point accuracy to his arsenal. Moore is a rangy 6-5 guard who blossomed into one of the league's best pure outside shooters as a sophomore, finishing with a conference-best 58 effective FG percentage. Langel will look for immediate contributions in the backcourt from junior college transfer **Damon Sherman-Newsome** and 6-1 freshman **Alex Ramon**. Returners **Brandon James**, **Matt McMullen** and **Luke Roh** will be in the rotation on the wing, where James showed a diverse set of skills last season. In the post 6-11 senior **John Brandenburg**, a onetime Virginia transfer, will start after coming off the bench for the past two years. Rolls and Moore can push Colgate to double-digit wins overall, but Langel's rebuilding plan won't really take shape until two transfers, **Austin Tillotson** (Monmouth) and **Ethan Jacobs** (Ohio), debut in the 2013-14 season.

NAVY

2012: 3-26 (0-14 Patriot); Lost to Bucknell 87-63, Patriot quarterfinals
In-conference offense: 0.91 points per possession (8th)
In-conference defense: 1.09 points allowed per possession (7th)

It's a bit of an understatement to say Ed DeChellis' first season at Navy didn't go all that well. Theoretically, the Midshipmen should be in somewhat better shape this year as their top contributors mature. Don't bet on it. The team's best player, forward J.J. Avila, was booted from the program in February and elected to transfer to Richmond. The team's second-best player, wing Jordan Sugars, graduated. Navy's starting point guard, Jordan Brickman, elected not to return for his senior season. That leaves DeChellis with two starters, a few rotation players, and no seniors on his 2013 squad. Navy's top returner is **Worth Smith**, a 6-6 forward who showed solid scoring ability from inside the arc in addition to solid defense and rebounding as a freshman. **Isaiah Roberts** played at both guard spots during the season, but the returning junior could be the team's best choice at point guard. DeChellis has an interesting prospect in 6-10 center **Jared Smoot**, who didn't show much in eight minutes per game as a freshman, but won't have much competition for playing time on the guard-heavy Navy roster. **Thurgood Wynn** and **Donya Jackson** will compete for minutes in Sugars' stead, while a litany of sub-6-0 returners and freshmen fight for minutes in the backcourt. Navy may not go winless in-conference again—after all, they weren't any worse than 2-12 Colgate in 2012—but the premature losses of Avila and Brickman won't help matters.

Southern

BY JOEY BERLIN

It doesn't take a basketball savant or a lot of fancy numbers to predict that Davidson is going to dominate the Southern Conference again in 2012-13. Because the Wildcats return the top eight scorers from a team that went 16-2, running the table in SoCon play wouldn't be a crazy prediction to make. Again, Bob McKillop's team is likely to be well represented in postseason honors. The Wildcats return Jake Cohen, the media's player of the year, and De'Mon Brooks, the coaches' pick, along with All-SoCon third-teamer Nik Cochran.

And once again, the league's balance of power appears to be tipped sharply toward the South division, which housed all three of the league's winning overall records last year (Davidson, Wofford and College of Charleston). The SoCon teams that struggled the most in 2012 will likely struggle the most in 2013.

But if there's a huge difference between "now" and "then," it may come from the emergence of UNC Greensboro as a North division team that actually pulls its weight. Seven games after 29-year-old Wes Miller became Division I's then-youngest head coach, the 2-14 Spartans started winning and then just kept on doing it, putting together a streak of 10 wins in 11 games and winning the North crown with a 10-8 mark. Miller was regarded as a revelation, taking the media's coach of the year hardware. In a league that looks weak after its top four teams or so, and a division that looks weak all the way down, Greensboro returns four starters and has at least a chance to separate itself from every school not named Davidson. All-SoCon first team selection Trevis Simpson, who's hunting for his next shot as you read this, and third-teamer Derrell Armstrong give Miller two backcourt talents who probably won't be pinnacles of efficiency, but will put plenty of points on the board.

After Greensboro, any noticeable shift in power toward the North will probably have to come from Elon, Western Carolina, or Samford. Elon managed a .500 league record and returns all-league second-teamer Jack Isenbarger and all-freshman point guard Austin Hamilton. WCU won seven games in a row in the regular season and league tournament before they darn near took out Davidson in the double-OT title game. This year they'll look for big things from Trey Sumler outside and Tawaski King inside. Samford begins a new era with the hiring of Indiana assistant Bennie Seltzer, and conference all-freshman picks Tyler Hood and Raijon Kelly give him a starting point.

Back in the South division, Georgia Southern and Wofford should be above-average SoCon teams again. The addition of former MEAC player of the year C.J. Reed could give a Georgia Southern another big scorer to take defensive attention away from Eric Ferguson, who might win the league's player of the year award if Cohen or Brooks don't do it again. Wofford will look for bigger things from the SoCon's freshman of the year, Karl Cochran. College of Charleston has point guard Andrew Lawrence, forward Trent Wiedeman and center Adheji Baru, who should all be impact players for new coach Doug Wojcik.

The SoCon cellar dwellers from 2012 aren't likely to move up. In the South, senior center Mike Groselle again projects to be a heck of a player for a struggling Citadel team, and Jeff Jackson's Furman squad will try to compensate for the loss of its best player, Brandon Sebirumbi. In the North, Jason Capel loses three key guys off last year's 13-18 Appalachian State team, but will welcome a former high-level recruit to his lineup in Xavier transfer Jay Canty. Chattanooga coach John Shulman will try his hand with a new nucleus after graduating four players.

Teams listed Joey's predicted order of finish.

DAVIDSON

2012: 25-8 (16-2 SoCon); Lost to Louisville 69-62, NCAA round of 64
In-conference offense: 1.17 points per possession (1st)
In-conference defense: 0.94 points allowed per possession (1st)

It wasn't 2008 all over again, but maybe this year will be? In about every way imaginable, Davidson was the class of the SoCon. Bob McKillop's squad had the league's best offense, its best defense and its best player (although the media and coaches disagreed on which Wildcat it was). They proved themselves against some good nonconference competition, too. The Wildcats hung tough with Duke at Cameron Indoor Stadium until early in the second half, and they got the better of eventual national runner-up Kansas for an 80-74 semi-road win in Kansas City. This year McKillop has everyone of significance back, so another conference title would be the minimum expectation. **De'Mon Brooks**, the coaches' pick for SoCon POY, takes a ton of the Wildcats' shots while he's on the floor, but McKillop won't complain as long as the 6-7 junior puts the ball in the hole, rebounds, and grabs steals the way he's been doing. **Jake Cohen** (the media's POY) is back for his senior year. The 6-10 inside-outside threat put up a 61.2 true shooting percentage and again posted a block percentage in the nation's top 100. **Nik Cochran** put up 21 points in the win over Kansas, and the 6-3 senior guard is also the Wildcats' top long-range shooter and top assist man. **Chris Czerapowicz**, a 6-7 junior, and 6-4 senior **JP Kuhlman** give McKillop two more backcourt mainstays and a total of five returners in double figures. In fact, the top eight scorers are all back. Davidson could be even more dangerous if sophomore **Tyler Kalinoski** finds his shooting touch. As a freshman, Kalinoski came off the bench and put up 123 threes, but made just 29 percent of them.

GEORGIA SOUTHERN

2012: 15-15 (12-6 SoCon); Lost to Elon 65-58, SoCon quarterfinals
In-conference offense: 0.99 points per possession (9th)
In-conference defense: 0.99 points allowed per possession (3rd)

Give major credit to coach Charlton Young and the Eagles for what was easily the league's biggest improvement. After a horrid 1-17 conference campaign in 2011, Georgia Southern saw its SoCon record jump by 11 wins. It helped that Young's team put together a six-game win streak, with five of the six victories coming by seven points or less. A big jump in defensive efficiency was the catalyst, as Georgia Southern forced turnovers at a higher rate than any team in the league. A Pythagorean winning percentage of .306 doesn't inspire a lot of confidence going forward, but Young does have his top player back and some other useful pieces. **Eric Ferguson** was first team All-SoCon as a sophomore. A top-100 defensive rebounder, the 6-7 forward put up nearly 30 percent of the Eagles' shots while he was on the floor, posting a 58 eFG percentage. Junior guard **Jelani Hewitt** is the only other returning double-figure scorer, a feat he accomplished by hitting nearly 40 percent of his threes. The graduations of guards Willie Powers and Ben Drayton leave holes in the backcourt, but Young looks to have solid options to fill those spots. **C.J. Reed**, a 6-3 point guard who transferred from UCF, was the 2011 MEAC POY while at Bethune-Cookman, where he averaged 19 points and five assists. His father, Cliff, was Bethune-Cookman's coach and is now a Georgia Southern assistant. Once again, Young landed a three-star recruit in 6-5 shooting guard **Cleon Roberts**. The one he landed last year, 6-8 forward **Kameron Dunnican**, played minor minutes off the bench as a freshman.

COLLEGE OF CHARLESTON

2012: 19-12 (10-8 SoCon); Lost to Appalachian State 93-81, SoCon first round
In-conference offense: 0.98 points per possession (10th)
In-conference defense: 0.95 points allowed per possession (2nd)

Former Tulsa coach Doug Wojcik takes over for the retired Bobby Cremins, and despite the loss of Antwaine Wiggins, the new coach has a few returning weapons on his roster. Senior **Andrew Lawrence** had a strong first season as Charleston's starting point guard, leading the league in steals per game and owning an assist rate in the national top 75. Lawrence competed for Great Britain in the Olympics over the summer. Inside, 6-8 junior **Trent Wiedeman** ranked in the top 75 nationally in defensive board rate and made the media's all-league third team. Sophomore center **Adheji Baru**, an all-freshman team pick, grabbed more than 10 percent of available offensive boards. **Anthony Stitt** is in line to start at off-guard after averaging nine points per outing. Notable newcomers include junior college transfer **Anthony Thomas**, a 6-7 forward, and **Canyon Barry**, a 6-6 freshman and the son of Rick Barry. Had Cremins stayed another year, Canyon would've become the third Barry to play for him, following half-brothers Jon and Drew.

UNC GREENSBORO

2012: 13-19 (10-8 SoCon); Lost to Western Carolina 82-77, SoCon semifinals
In-conference offense: 1.00 points per possession (8th)
In-conference defense: 1.03 points allowed per possession (7th)

When Mike Dement was fired as Greensboro's coach last December, former North Carolina guard Wes Miller became, at age 29, Division I's youngest head coach. His hire didn't make an immediate impact, as the Spartans lost the first six games of the Miller era to fall to 2-14. Greensboro broke the losing streak with a road win at Charleston, then won at The Citadel on a last-second inbound alley-oop dunk by **Trevis Simpson**, a moment which Miller later cited as a turning point. It was the second of what would become 10 wins in 11 games. By the end of the season, UNCG was the North division champion, and Miller was the media's pick for SoCon coach of the year. Four starters are back this year, putting Greensboro in great position to repeat as North champions. As a sophomore, Simpson put up the nation's highest percentage of his team's shots (38) while on the floor, shooting just 43 percent on his twos and 31 percent on his threes. Senior **Derrell Armstrong** is more likely to dish it off, but he used 31 percent of UNCG's possessions while in the game and posted similar shooting numbers to Simpson's. His steal rate ranked in the top 100. Senior **Korey Van Dussen** and junior **Drew Parker**, the Spartans' assist leader, are also back. Parker connected on 48 percent of his threes. **David Williams**, a 6-6 junior forward, should get more touches inside now that Aaron Brackett has graduated. Williams posted a 56 eFG percentage but hit just 46 percent of his free throws.

WOFFORD

2012: 19-14 (12-6 SoCon); Lost to Pitt 81-63, CBI first round
In-conference offense: 1.09 points per possession (2nd)
In-conference defense: 1.00 points allowed per possession (4th)

For a group that lost so much from back-to-back NCAA tournament teams, Wofford and coach Mike Young had to be pleased with last year's results. The Terriers' 12-6 league record would've won the North by two games, and they earned another trip to the postseason, albeit to the CBI. Only three coaches in the nation used their bench less than Young, who leaned heavily on guards Brad Loesing and Kevin Giltner. Now, both are gone. Wofford was both the SoCon's slowest team last year and its best-shooting one, posting a 53 eFG percentage. Guard **Karl Cochran** earned the conference's freshman of the year award and should become the Terriers' top scoring threat this year. The 6-1 Cochran finished third on the team in scoring and certainly wasn't a shy freshman, putting up 27 percent of Wofford's shots when he was on the floor. **Lee Skinner** also showed promise as a freshman, grabbing more than 13 percent of available offensive rebounds at 6-6. **Aerris Smith**, a 6-7 junior, hit 62 percent of his shots in 16 minutes per game. Australian native **Indiana Faithfull**, a former Maine Mr. Basketball, will join the backcourt after sitting out last season.

ELON

2012: 15-16 (9-9 SoCon); Lost to Davidson 83-67, SoCon semifinals
In-conference offense: 1.02 points per possession (4th)
In-conference defense: 1.04 points allowed per possession (8th)

Last season marked the first time Elon won at least 15 games since 2005-06, and the .500 SoCon record was good enough for second in the North and a bye in the conference tournament. Playing at the conference's second-fastest tempo (behind Greensboro), Elon was the SoCon's most accurate three-point shooting team. This year holds plenty of reasons to hope for more improvement, as Matt Matheny's team loses just one senior. Junior shooting guard **Jack Isenbarger** emerged as Elon's star last season. The 6-2 Isenbarger finished with a 115.6 offensive rating and a 57 eFG, hitting almost 40 percent from three and 87 percent from the line. **Austin Hamilton** showed promise, starting at the point and making the league's all-freshman team. Junior **Sebastian Koch**, a 6-8 perimeter player, put up more than twice as many threes as twos last season, hitting 35 percent from long range. Inside, 6-10 junior **Lucas Troutman** hasn't been a rebounding force, but he averaged 12.8 points and finished tied for second in the league with 44 blocks. **Ryley Beaumont**, a 6-7 junior, led Elon in rebounding (5.8 per game) and scored 20 points in the second win over Greensboro.

WESTERN CAROLINA

2012: 17-18 (8-10 SoCon); Lost to Davidson 93-91 (2OT), SoCon championship game
In-conference offense: 1.02 points per possession (5th)
In-conference defense: 1.07 points allowed per possession (11th)

With a staggering comeback in an epic SoCon title game, the Catamounts almost made their second-ever NCAA tournament appearance. Down 13 to Davidson with 2:47 to play, WCU stormed back with three-pointers and tied the score on three Keaton Cole free throws with 11 seconds left. The game stretched all the way to double-OT, where a baseline drive and dunk by Davidson's Clint Mann with a minute to go proved to be the clincher. Larry Hunter's Catamounts were playing by far their best ball at the end of the season, having entered the conference title game on a seven-game winning streak. Still, it was somewhat appropriate that Davidson's winning points came on an easy dunk, because defense was WCU's main problem all season. Hunter's effort to build on last year's strong finish will rest largely on junior guards **Trey Sumler** and **Brandon Boggs**. Sumler averaged nearly 14 points while distributing effectively, but he also turned the ball over a lot. **Rhett Harrelson**, a 5-10 freshman point guard, may allow Sumler to play off the ball more. In the frontcourt, 6-8 junior **Tawaski King** is a solid offensive rebounder and had 20 points and 10 boards in the title game loss. Freshman **Justin Browning**, a 6-4 small forward, could also see minutes.

SAMFORD

2012: 11-19 (8-10 SoCon); Lost to Furman 75-66, SoCon first round
In-conference offense: 1.05 points per possession (3rd)
In-conference defense: 1.08 points allowed per possession (12th)

Jimmy Tillette's 15-year run as Samford coach came to an end after his Bulldogs showed some improvement, but not enough to impress new athletic director Martin Newton. New coach Bennie Seltzer spent the last six years working under Tom Crean, at Marquette and Indiana. He'll have a pair of returning all-SoCon freshman team picks in 6-6 forward **Tyler Hood** and 6-4 guard **Raijon Kelly**. Hood posted an eFG percentage of 55 and averaged 11.1 points, second on the Bulldogs behind Drew Windler, who transferred to Belmont. Kelly had a 53 percent eFG and shot 77 percent from the line. Junior **Gregg Wooten** was expected to be last year's starting point guard, but a preseason knee injury forced him to take a redshirt. **Will Cook** grabs an unusual number of boards for a 6-4 guard. Seltzer signed five players in the offseason, including a pair of Florida high school players of the year, 6-6 forward **Clide Geffrard** and point guard **Russell Wilson**.

APPALACHIAN STATE

2012: 13-18 (7-11 SoCon); Lost to UNC Greensboro 65-55, SoCon quarterfinals
In-conference offense: 1.01 points per possession (7th)
In-conference defense: 1.03 points allowed per possession (6th)

Jason Capel's team was great at getting to the foul line, but not good at making foul shots. They were adequate defensively in SoCon play except for an inability to force any turnovers. Capel loses his best overall player from last season, guard Omar Carter, and his best inside guys. His best returners are 6-6 senior **Jamaal Trice** and 6-2 sophomore **Mike Neal**. Trice, who started his career at UConn, connected on 37 percent of his threes in his first year at ASU. As a freshman, Neal handed out assists at a high rate and showed an ability to grab steals, but also had an elevated turnover rate (30 percent). Capel might like to get more touches this year for 6-7 senior **Nathan Healy**, who averaged just 18 minutes per game but had a 117 offensive rating and added value defensively as well. **Tab Hamilton**, a 6-3 guard, will likely get more minutes as a sophomore, and 6-6 Xavier transfer **Jay Canty**, a four-star recruit in the class of 2010, is eligible after sitting out last season. Two-star power forward **Michael Obacha** will give the Mountaineers a third Oak Ridge graduate, joining Neal and Canty.

FURMAN

2012: 15-16 (8-10 SoCon); Lost to Davidson 73-54, SoCon quarterfinals
In-conference offense: 0.97 points per possession (11th)
In-conference defense: 1.00 points allowed per possession (5th)

The most notable thing about Furman last year was the way coach Jeff Jackson used his roster. Eleven players started games and averaged at least 10 minutes per game—and none cracked 28 minutes per outing. As a result, 40 percent of the minutes went to bench players. The Paladins played solid defense, and their best wins were home victories over Georgia Southern and North division champion UNC Greensboro. This year, Jackson's roster is chock full of sophomores and freshmen, but 6-5 junior **Charlie Reddick** is his best returner. Reddick lived outside the arc last year (38 percent), taking 52 more shots from out there than from inside. At the other end, he posted a very good steal rate as well. Two seniors, 6-7 **Bryant Irwin** and Charlie's twin brother, 6-9 **Colin Reddick**, are the Paladins' best frontcourt options. Irwin took nearly a quarter of Furman's shots while in the game, but shot just 36 percent from the floor. **Larry Wideman**, a 6-4 two-star recruit and South Carolina native, is one of four incoming freshmen.

CHATTANOOGA

2012: 11-21 (5-13 SoCon); Lost to Georgia Southern 76-70, SoCon first round
In-conference offense: 1.01 points per possession (6th)
In-conference defense 1.05 points allowed per possession (9th)

It was a tough year for the Mocs, who lost decisively in the nonconference both to very good teams (Kentucky, Indiana) and very bad ones (Kennesaw State, Gardner Webb). About the only things they did extremely well were getting to the line and keeping the opposition off the line. As John Shulman returns for his ninth season, he loses three regular starters off the SoCon's most experienced team and a fourth senior who started 17 games. The top returner is 6-9 senior forward **Drazen Zlovaric**, who performed solidly in his first year after transferring from Georgia. The Serbian shot just under 55 percent and had 15 points and nine boards against Kentucky. Senior guard **Dontay Hampton**, who posted a 111 offensive rating in mostly bench duty, had surgery in July to repair a torn ACL. Shulman hopes to have him back by Christmas. Forward **Z. Mason**, a former blue-chip football recruit who originally went to Ole Miss to play tight end, averaged six points a game in his first year of college basketball. The best of Chattanooga's freshman class might be **Casey Jones**, an athletic wing from Louisiana.

THE CITADEL

2011-12: 6-24 (3-15 SoCon); Lost to Western Carolina 68-56, SoCon first round
In-conference offense: 0.92 points per possession (12th)
In-conference defense: 1.05 points allowed per possession (10th)

Despite the school's name, the only impenetrable fortress at Citadel games was the opposing team's basket. Chuck Driesell's team was the worst in the SoCon with a bullet, struggling mightily at both ends, although they did win two games in a row late in the season. For one more year, center **Mike Groselle** will give Bulldog fans good reason to watch. The 6-8 Groselle led the league in rebounding and grabbed more than 13 percent of the Bulldogs' many misses while he was on the floor, placing in the top 60 nationally. He also finished second in the league in scoring and posted a 59 percent eFG, which ranked in the national top 70. If nothing else, Driesell's complementary pieces are still young. **Ashton Moore**, a sophomore guard, is the leading returning scorer after Groselle. Fellow sophomore **Marshall Harris III** posted a high assist rate as a freshman, and another one, **Lawrence Miller**, knocked down 42 percent of his threes in mostly bench duty. Freshman **Matt Van Scyoc**, a 6-6 swingman from Wisconsin, shot exactly 50 percent on his threes as a high school senior.

Southland

BY NIC REINER

In each of the past eight years, the Southland Conference has sent a different team to the NCAA tournament. This mind-boggling fact supports the assertion that the conference is one of the most dynamic, unpredictable basketball leagues in Division I.

And, of course, conference landscapes have shifted rapidly and boundlessly in the past two years. Texas-Arlington (a Southland charter member 50 years ago), Texas-San Antonio, and Texas State all have found different homes. Oral Roberts, a sterling basketball program, arrives this season and quite possibly could take the crown in its inaugural year. And the dust will finally settle in 2013-14 when four new teams join the Southland: Abilene Christian University (an original charter member!), University of the Incarnate Word, Houston Baptist University, and the University of New Orleans. Three of these teams will be making some sort of D-I transition.

The Southland includes teams from Texas, Arkansas, and Louisiana, where football is unquestionably supreme. And it's clear even the realignment that affects the Southland is greatly influenced by the sport. Houston Baptist and New Orleans will begin playing football a few years from now in conjunction with their migration to the Southland. However, since the men's basketball landscape has proven to be so egalitarian, it's definitely an attractive destination for schools looking to find a place in D-I. Low-major schools have trouble gaining recognition, even when they're successful. But the Southland is a good spot to try one's hand at success.

To make matters more interesting, consider that the Southland hasn't had fewer than 11 teams since the 1997-98 season. The league balloons next year, but in this season's 10-team formation, everybody has greater hope. Teams that finished at the bottom of the barrel last year have fewer rungs to climb. Those in the middle of the pack will get better seeds in the conference tournament.

Unfortunately, no amount of hope will be enough to extract Nicholls State, Texas A&M Corpus Christi, and Central Arkansas out of the cellar. The other seven are harder to predict. Schools like Northwestern State and McNeese State could rise to the top, though they could also conceivably be mediocre or worse. Sam Houston State is realistically at least a year away.

Southeastern Louisiana is the team that seems most poised to scale the ranks quickly, with the return of playmaker Brandon Fortenberry. Lamar likely will fall to the middle after graduating their whole rotation. And Stephen F. Austin looks ready to return to the top of the Southland, a space it occupied for several years during the past decade.

Irrespective of what happens during the season, Katy, Texas is the place to be the second week of March. The Southland Conference tournament has proven to be one of the most exciting and surprising ones for the better part of a decade. This year, with a strong Oral Roberts now on board, could that unreal streak of rotating NCAA bid recipients become nine?

Teams listed in Nic's predicted order of finish.

STEPHEN F. AUSTIN

2012: 20-12 (12-4 Southland); Lost to Lamar 55-44, Southland semifinals
In-conference offense: 1.00 points per possession (5th)
In-conference defense: 0.88 points allowed per possession (1st)

Danny Kaspar has built the Lumberjacks into a leader in Southland basketball. Stephen F. Austin has had nine winning seasons in the past 10 years and captured three regular season titles from 2009 to 2011. Kaspar's team is fantastic at forcing bad shots, disallowing offensive boards, and forcing turnovers. Kaspar has proven that SFA will bring that to the table, though this year the Jacks will be small once again (no player is over 6-8). **Antonio Bostic**, who tallied the largest share of his team's minutes last year, brings offensive capabilities to the table, although the 6-2 senior could improve as a shooter. He was the only non-senior last year to make first team All-Southland. **Taylor Smith** is poised to step into a leadership role, as he has posted a 108 offensive rating with the highest returning usage and shot percentage. The 6-6 Smith was also the tenth best defensive rebounder in the country, grabbing a whopping 27 percent of available boards while on the floor (in addition to corralling 14 percent of offensive boards). If he can even marginally improve his 35 percent free throw shooting, then opponents will no longer be able to send him to the line so smugly. In addition, Kaspar says 6-8 junior college transfer **Ice Asortse** will compete for minutes at forward. **Hal Bateman** will step in at the point, and if the 5-11 senior can turn the ball over less the Jacks can become even more potent. Junior **Desmond Haymon** is a returning starter who shoots from both sides of the arc but did so without great success. Last season, SFA ended the regular season strong with five straight wins, including a road victory over Lamar. If they have even a serviceable offense, they could be at the top of the Southland.

ORAL ROBERTS

2012: 27-7 (17-1 Summit); Lost to Nevada 68-59, NIT first round
In-conference offense: 1.19 points per possession (2nd Summit)
In-conference defense: 1.07 points allowed per possession (4thSummit)

In what amounts to a downward move basketball-wise, Oral Roberts has joined the Southland. The Golden Eagles moved primarily for geographical reasons, and the school argues that the conference is a better fit for recruiting both athletically and academically. From last season's team ORU loses Dominique Morrison, one of the best players in the country. Scott Sutton also loses Michael Craion who contributed significantly on offense, posted an 110 offensive rating with high usage and was the team's best defender. **Steven Roundtree** had a similar statistical profile to Craion in 2012 and the 6-8 junior should continue to thrive with an increased role. He'll become the team's most efficient high-usage offensive player. **Warren Niles** should also be in line for more possessions. An uptick in usage should ding the 6-5 senior's offensive rating a bit, but that's a trade Sutton will take. Lastly, 6-9 senior **Damen Bell-Holter** will be asked to do more, as well. Six of the 14 players on the roster are freshmen, which won't have as great effect this year as it will in years to come. It's impressive that ORU has gone 57-15 over the past four years but troubling that it's failed to make an NCAA tournament during that time. Still, the Golden Eagles are coming from a conference that churned out the occasional 14 seed and entering one more likely to send a 15 or 16. Based on their sustained basketball success over the past decade (they've finished comfortably in the top half of Division I throughout the KenPom era), Sutton's squad should finish yearly near the top of the Southland.

NORTHWESTERN STATE

2012: 16-16 (8-8 Southland); Lost to Lamar 76-69, Southland quarterfinals
In-conference offense: 0.97 points per possession (7th)
In-conference defense: 0.96 points allowed per possession (5th)

Northwestern State loses a first team All-Southland performer in William Mosley, but in great news for coach Mike McConathy and the people of Natchitoches, senior **Shamir Davis** returns. The 6-0 guard had the highest offensive rating of all high-usage Demons last year. Davis gets to the line a bunch and sinks over 70 percent of his free throws. He has a solid effective FG percentage (49) and was Northwestern State's best distributor. **James Hulbin**'s role will increase this year. The 6-8 junior has specialized in high-usage low-minute appearances to this point, but those minutes may now increase. **Marvin Frazier** will have an expanded role, as well, though the 6-9 sophomore will have to improve his poor shooting (30 percent from the floor) to make any real impact. Senior guards **Gary Roberson** and **Gary Stewart** posted offensive ratings hovering around 93 and will be asked to step up as scorers. Last season McConathy's team defended shots exceptionally well, forced an impressive amount of turnovers (23 percent of possessions), but allowed an atrocious 40 percent of opponent misses to be rebounded. Nevertheless, the approach hasn't made for a horrible recipe as the Demons again finished in the top half of the conference in defensive efficiency. To gear up for league play, Northwestern State has a strong non-conference slate this year, facing LSU, Texas A&M, Oklahoma, and Arkansas.

LAMAR

2012: 23-12 (11-5 Southland); Lost to Vermont 71-59, NCAA First Four
In-conference offense: 1.11 points per possession (1st)
In-conference defense: 0.96 points allowed per possession (4th)

What people remember about Lamar's season is Pat Knight's press conference after the Cardinals lost at home to Stephen F. Austin. Knight lambasted his seniors and called them out for, among other things, not knowing what it takes to win. At the time of the rant, Lamar was the Southland's second-best team by a comfortable margin. It's not surprising, then, that the Cardinals promptly started winning. And those seniors Knight doubted were responsible pre- and post-rant for what was unquestionably the Southland's most efficient offense. Now, the experience-laden six-man senior core is gone and Knight will rebuild, mostly with guys he's recruited. On record as saying he'd like to build the "Gonzaga of the Southwest," Knight has drawn talent from Chicago, Los Angeles, Australia, Utah, and Indianapolis. **Stan Brown** is the only returnee who logged relatively significant minutes, and the 6-8 senior may be called upon to do more than rebound. Knight does have an effective shot blocker in 6-11 junior **Osas Ebomwonyi**. As for the freshmen, **Donnell Minton** has the potential to get to the hole consistently at 6-0, and 6-5 **Rhon Mitchell** (a redshirt) figures to be a strong asset in the frontcourt. Lamar is the only school in the nation to have scheduled three Final Four teams, and the Cardinals play Ohio State and Kentucky in consecutive games in December.

SOUTHEASTERN LOUISIANA

2012: 12-17 (5-11 Southland); Did not qualify for Southland tournament
In-conference offense: 0.86 points per possession (12th)
In-conference defense: 0.97 points allowed per possession (7th)

Southeastern Louisiana played most of 2011-12 without their most efficient high-usage player, **Brandon Fortenberry**, after he suffered a season-ending foot injury in the team's seventh game. A healthy Fortenberry in the Lions' backcourt would have made it a much more interesting season. He'll be back this year and SELU will be in a position to at least ascend to the middle of the Southland pack. **Roosevelt Johnson** also returns and the 6-6 senior was the Lions' highest usage player last year. He wasn't phenomenal offensively but rebounded very well and will be a good complement to Fortenberry. The third-worst D-I offense last year must improve by shoring up their shooting and taking better care of the ball. (The Southland's worst offense by a full 0.05 points per possession, SELU posted a 44 percent effective FG percentage and turned the ball over nearly 25 percent of the time.) The third starter returning, 6-4 **Jeremy Campbell** will be asked to greatly improve his lackluster 44 true shooting percentage. Another returning shooter is 6-3 **Todd Nelson**, though he also shot an unimpressive 33 percent from beyond the arc. The most encouraging thing about last year's campaign was the best defense in Jim Yarbrough's seven-season tenure. With Fortenberry back, Yarbrough's team could crack the better half of the conference.

MCNEESE STATE

2012: 17-16 (10-6 Southland); Lost to Toledo 76-63, CIT first round
In-conference offense: 1.03 points per possession (3rd)
In-conference defense: 0.99 points allowed per possession (8th)

This year Dave Simmons' team will be without Southland Player of the Year, Patrick Richard, who, in addition to being one of the most efficient players in the conference, handled virtually all of the offensive responsibilities on the team. Fortunately, Simmons returns two players who tallied major minutes: 6-1 **Dontae Cannon** and 6-3 **Jeremie Mitchell**. Both will take on bigger roles. Cannon needs to work on complementing his exceptional free throw shooting with better percentages from the field. Mitchell was the team's three-point specialist, sinking 36 percent of his treys on 208 attempts. Sophomore forward **Desharick Guidry** was already the team's second best rebounder as a freshman. **Craig McFerrin** returns from an injury suffered in conference play, and it looks like the 6-7 sophomore is capable of forming a solid tandem with Guidry. He excelled on the glass and as a scorer inside before he went down. Still, with Richard gone, it's likely the Cowboys will see a dip in performance.

SAM HOUSTON STATE

2012: 13-19 (7-9 Southland); Lost to Stephen F. Austin 68-46, Southland quarterfinals
In-conference offense: 0.92 points per possession (9th)
In-conference defense: 0.96 points allowed per possession (6th)

Sam Houston State had a losing season for the first time since the 2003-04 campaign solely because they fielded a terribly inefficient offense. The reason Jason Hooten's team was not rotting in the Southland dungeon was because it finished in the top half of the conference in defensive efficiency. However, last year's two most efficient Bearkats, Konner Tucker and Steven Werner, are gone. Though neither was particularly efficient offensively, junior guard **DeMarcus Gatlin** and 5-11 senior **Darius Gatson** return, having been on the floor roughly 80 percent of the time last year. Gatson assists on 30 percent of Bearkat baskets and made 38 percent of his threes but only 26 percent of his twos. Gatlin will likely shoot the ball the most, though he needs to improve his accuracy. **Terrance Motley** is touted by the coaching staff for his versatility and the 6-7 junior college transfer is expected to contribute immediately. Another junior college transfer, 6-5 **James Thomas**, is an intriguing prospect for Sam Houston and has the body to work on the inside. If the defense stays above average and an offense with new pieces clicks better, Sam Houston State can finish closer to the middle of the Southland. The team only suits up one senior, so if Hooten has played his recruiting cards right he should have a team prepared to compete in the new-look Southland's future.

NICHOLLS STATE

2012: 10-20 (6-10 Southland); Lost to UT-Arlington 96-48, Southland quarterfinals
In-conference offense: 1.00 points per possession (6th)
In-conference defense: 1.11 points allowed per possession (12th)

J.P Piper's team sustained seven losses by 30 or more points (including a resounding 96-48 loss to UT-Arlington to end the season), and considering how inefficient the Colonels were over the course of the season, it's actually impressive Nicholls won six conference games. Guard **Fred Hunter** was supposed to be last year's leader but missed the whole season after a knee injury in November sidelined him. His return is good news for a team that needs some. Junior guard **Dantrell Thomas** will occupy a similar role (high-usage, lots of shots) but in a more limited fashion with Hunter returning. Sophomore forward **Sam McBeath** and junior guard **Jeremy Smith** both played significant roles last year and can serve as complements to Hunter. The team didn't have a single senior contribute last year, finishing No. 341 nationally in experience. This year, with everyone a year older and Hunter back on board, there's little doubt the Colonels will improve. It's conceivable they could finish in the middle of the Southland.

TEXAS A&M CORPUS CHRISTI

2012: 6-24 (4-12 Southland), Did not qualify for Southland tournament
In-conference offense: 0.92 points per possession (11th)
In-conference defense: 1.05 points allowed per possession (10th)

Last season Texas A&M Corpus Christi did everything poorly, and the Islanders were just slightly more efficient than conference mates Central Arkansas and Nicholls State. This year Willis Wilson doesn't have a single senior on the roster, and just two starters return: sophomores **Hameed Ali** (6-2) and 5-10 **Johnathan Jordan** (5-10). Jordan has the highest returning offensive rating, mainly because he assisted on 32 percent of Islander baskets during his time on the floor. **Nate Maxey** has potential to be a strong presence on the defensive end at 6-11. Willis will expect immediate contributions from junior college transfers: 6-9 **Zane Knowles**, 6-6 **William Nelson**, and 6-4 swingman **Joy Williamson**. Though few in number, the Islanders victories in 2011-12 were frequently of the thrilling variety: four of the team's six wins came by just two points and a fifth came by three in overtime. Wilson has hopes the wins will come in greater abundance and with fewer thrills this year but it's unlikely the team will move up very far.

CENTRAL ARKANSAS

2012: 8-21 (3-13 Southland), Did not qualify for Southland tournament
In-conference offense: 0.92 points per possession (10th)
In-conference defense: 1.05 points allowed per possession (11th)

Central Arkansas won three conference games in 2012, up from one the year before. The Bears were the second worst team in the nation at the free throw line, sinking only 56 percent of their freebies on the season. Coincidentally, the Bears' opponents also shot poorly from the line (63 percent), meaning UCA games collectively featured some of the worst charity-stripe shooting in the land. Corliss Williamson used a fluid rotation all year and allocated close to 50 percent of available minutes to his bench. **LaQuentin Miles** used a ridiculous 31 percent of the team's possessions, took 30 percent of shots, led the team in assist rate, steal percentage, and offensive rebounding. The 6-5 do-it-all junior's offensive rating (98) was not higher only because he drew seven fouls a game and shot an abominable 55 percent from the line. Three other players out of Williamson's seven-man rotation are back. **Jarvis Garner** will again be the second option, and the 6-7 senior has shown he can do so capably. Fellow senior **Robert Crawford** is poised to step up as a 6-5 complement to Garner and Miles. Finally, 6-8 junior **Jordan Harks** is the team's most complete rebounder and provides UCA with a presence on the interior. Williamson enters his third year with the Bears and, though excellence is unlikely, the expectation is improvement will be shown.

Summit

BY COREY SCHMIDT

For the second straight season the Summit League led all conferences in offensive efficiency in 2011-12. While there wasn't much defense to be seen, it was an exciting year for fans who like scoring. The league had five players among the top 20 scorers nationally, and those guys accomplished that counting stat with an average offensive rating of 114 and usage rate of 31 percent. Only South Dakota State's Nate Wolters and Fort Wayne's Frank Gaines are back from that bunch, and both are poised to score at will against Summit defenses yet again.

In addition to containing some of the most efficient, high-usage guys in the nation, the Summit League was full of great three-point shooters last year. The conference's teams made 38 percent of their collective three-point attempts, tops in Division I. The most accurate team was South Dakota State, which used a bevy of superb shooters and the aforementioned Wolters to power an offense that took the team to the NCAA tournament. With Oral Roberts now in the Southland, there's not a team in the league with as much returning firepower as the Jackrabbits. SDSU should again contend for the Summit's automatic bid.

For the first time since the Summit expanded into the Dakotas, Prospectus is projecting South Dakota State and North Dakota State to finish No. 1 and 2. The power axis of the conference is now firmly in the Dakotas, as evidenced by NCAA tournament appearances, television deals, and the location of the league tournament. Both programs have done a stand-up job of scouring Minnesota and the Dakotas for the best players who were previously overlooked due to the lack of any D-I programs in much of that area. Both SDSU and NDSU are stacked with talented guys from that region who stayed close to home and will make their teams tough to beat in 2012-13.

With the addition of South Dakota last year and Omaha this season, the Summit continues to build a footprint in the Badlands area. While neither team projects to do much damage this season, they are programs to keep an eye on in light of how quickly SDSU and NDSU got up to speed in D-I. This season, it will be the likes of Oakland and Western Illinois looking for a spot in the upper echelon alongside the Jacks and Bison. Oakland will again play at a frantic tempo with a focus on offense, while Western Illinois will break from the Summit mold to play at a snail's pace with a staunch commitment to defense.

IUPUI, Fort Wayne, and Kansas City will likely fall in the middle of the pack this season. Any one of these teams could be the surprise of the league depending on the contributions of transfers, in the same way that Western Illinois surprised by finishing as runner-up in the 2012 conference tournament. Whatever happens among the rest of the bunch, they'll all be fighting for a spot behind South Dakota State. The Jackrabbits played at an elite level a season ago and will be very much the class of the Summit League again in 2012-13.

Teams listed in Corey's predicted order of finish.

SOUTH DAKOTA STATE

2012: 27-8 (15-3 Summit); Lost to Baylor 60-68, NCAA round of 64
In-conference offense: 1.19 points per possession (1st)
In-conference defense: 1.01 points allowed per possession (1st)

Though Oral Roberts had a better record than South Dakota State in last year's Summit League race, those paying attention to the tempo-free stats knew better than to anoint ORU as the league's best. For much of the conference season, it was SDSU that trumped all others in efficiency margin. By the end of the year, the Jackrabbits possessed both the best offense and the best defense in the Summit on a per-possession basis. While offensive supremacy was expected with efficiency all-star **Nate Wolters** running the team, it was the defensive transformation that catapulted the Jacks into the NCAA tournament. Coach Scott Nagy focused his drills in the 2011 offseason on defense, and it paid off. With largely the same group of guys, Nagy's team took a big step forward on D. That commitment to defending should remain intact this season as SDSU loses only one contributor from a team that took Baylor to the brink in the round of 64. The centerpiece of this year's club is again Wolters, a 6-4 point guard and legitimate NBA prospect as he enters his senior campaign.

At this point, we know what we're getting from the Minnesota native: an uber-efficient, high-usage guy who draws a ton of fouls, rarely turns it over, and draws so much attention when driving that he's always dishing to wide-open teammates on the perimeter. Indeed, 68 percent of his assists in conference play were on made three-pointers. His favorite target, Griffan Callahan, has graduated, but **Jordan Dykstra**, **Chad White**, and **Brayden Carlson** all return, and, incredibly, all of those guys shot better than 45 percent on their threes last season. Another offensive weapon could emerge in the form of sophomore **Taevaunn Prince**. The 6-3 guard is a bulldog of a player who was second on the team in both defensive and offensive rebounding rate, and who connected on 58 percent of his two-point attempts. There's not another team in the Summit League that returns as strong a core as South Dakota State, let alone one with a player as talented as Wolters. The target will be squarely on the Jacks, but they're so seasoned at this point that it shouldn't rattle them.

NORTH DAKOTA STATE

2012: 17-14 (9-9 Summit); Lost to Wyoming 75-78, CBI first round
In-conference offense: 1.09 points per possession (5th)
In-conference defense: 1.08 points allowed per possession (5th)

Considering that North Dakota State's regular rotation in 2011-12 consisted of six sophomores and two freshmen, the season as a whole was something of a success to most observers. The Bison should be much improved over last year's squad because most of their struggles were a function of youth. For example, the team had the largest gap in the Summit League between its actual points per possession output and its points per effective (turnover-less) possession number. That means a ton of their possessions were wasted by committing turnovers. The biggest turnover offender has since transferred, but sophomore point guard **Lawrence Alexander** will also need to improve his control for his squad to take the next step. The Bison were also one of the worst rebounding teams in the league last year. Again, that stat is a function of the team's youth. As far as skill goes, NDSU has perhaps the most talented frontcourt in the league, but those guys have needed time to get stronger and more aggressive on the boards. If the team as a whole improves in those areas, Saul Phillips' guys will be tough to top this season. On the individual front, 6-7 junior **Taylor Braun** is bound for a breakout campaign. He's an athletic forward with a guard's handle who does a little bit of everything in efficient form for North Dakota State. Braun and his young Bison teammates also like to dunk, as they had 10 more dunks in conference play than the next most slam-happy squad.

OAKLAND

2012: 20-16 (11-7 Summit); Lost to Utah State 81-105, CIT semifinal
In-conference offense: 1.16 points per possession (3rd)
In-conference defense: 1.12 points allowed per possession (10th)

Though Oakland eventually finished third in the regular season standings, it took a late February push for the team to get to that threshold. There was a period in 2011-12 when the Golden Grizzlies looked as though they'd finish with a losing record for the first time in six years. They lost six straight at the mid-point of the year, including a 27-point setback to North Dakota State. Their offense was just too good (No. 25 nationally) for them to not contend in the end, but it was their poor defense (No. 320) that ultimately prevented them from doing more come conference tournament time. In the area where the defense has the most control—inside the arc—OU allowed its league counterparts to shoot 54 percent. The team was also scorched from the perimeter to the tune of 40 percent three-point shooting. Combined with very little turnover creation and below average defensive rebounding, the Grizzlies defense was just awful. The Oakland defense will get some help from Providence transfer **Duke Mondy**, who posted the Big East's highest steal rate in 2010-11. The 6-4 guard will also be tasked with taking over point guard duties from Reggie Hamilton, who was the nation's leading scorer a year ago. Chief among Mondy's duties will be to drive and dish to junior shooting guard **Travis Bader**, who's a career 42 percent three-point shooter. Greg Kampe's offense should be productive as always, but it remains to be seen if his team can generate enough stops for it to matter.

WESTERN ILLINOIS

2011: 18-15 (9-9 Summit); Lost to Oregon State 59-80, CBI first round
In-conference offense: 1.01 points per possession (6th)
In-conference defense: 1.02 points allowed per possession (3rd)

Just as it seemed that Western Illinois had finally turned the corner under Jim Molinari, the Leathernecks were dealt a major blow when freshman stud and leading scorer Obi Emegano announced he was transferring—and to Oral Roberts of all destinations. Molinari has had a tough time getting players to come to and stay in Macomb since taking over the program five years ago. Fortunately, his best player in that time, **Ceola Clark**, decided to stay for a sixth year. Clark was granted a sixth year of eligibility, and his steadying presence at the point guard position will be vital to WIU. Clark will combine with senior forward **Terell Parks** to form one of the best inside-outside duos in the league. About 40 percent of Clark's 91 assists in conference play were on baskets made by Parks, primarily as a result of pick-and-rolls. There's not a big man in the conference as versatile as Parks. Together, Parks and Clark are also the best defensive duo in the Summit. Parks is an intimidating force around the basket, and Clark has long been considered a defensive stalwart on the perimeter. With the loss of Emegano, however, WIU will need an unknown quantity to step up to provide much-needed scoring. Emegano was the one Leatherneck who could create offense on his own, and that type of player came in handy when Molinari's deliberate offensive schemes broke down. If someone emerges to fill that role, Western Illinois may again play spoiler in the Summit.

IUPUI

2012: 14-18 (7-11 Summit); Lost to South Dakota State 56-77, Summit quarterfinal
In-conference offense: 1.09 points per possession (4th)
In-conference defense: 1.10 points allowed per possession (7th)

For the first time in several years, IUPUI will enter a season without an established go-to guy. The days of George Hill, Robert Glenn, and Alex Young are long gone, and a new torch-bearer has yet to emerge. How the Jaguars fare will largely be determined by the strides made by their sizeable junior class. Up to this point, none of the six juniors eligible this season have had a breakout campaign. The closest to achieving a consistent level of high performance is **Ian Chiles**. The 6-1 guard thrived as a role player last year and possesses a tempo-free profile that suggests he could continue to produce in a larger role. It's also a make-or-break kind of year for junior big men **Donovan Gibbs** and **Mitchell Patton**. IUPUI was beat up badly in the paint last year by opposing bigs who scored at will and grabbed a high percentage of available defensive rebounds. There aren't any players in the team's pipeline who have size comparable to Gibbs and Patton, so if this duo is unable to make an impact in year three, expect the Jags to continue to be helpless in the interior. Coach Todd Howard will receive some perimeter help in the form of Purdue transfer **John Hart**.

FORT WAYNE

2012: 11-19 (5-13 Summit); Lost to Oral Roberts 67-71, Summit quarterfinal
In-conference offense: 1.01 points per possession (7th)
In-conference defense: 1.11 points allowed per possession (8th)

Second-year coach Tony Jasick will welcome seven newcomers to the fold this season: three from the high school ranks and four from junior colleges. Interestingly, all four junior college transfers hail from Florida. Perhaps Jasick and his staff are stacking the deck in hopes of catching lightning twice because the team's best player, **Frank Gaines**, also hails from the Sunshine State. In total there are six players from Florida on the roster this year, which is rather curious considering Fort Wayne's about as different from Florida as it gets. Gaines, of course, is the brightest ray among the Floridians. He wasn't always at his most efficient last season, primarily because he was asked to carry a huge load on offense, and that is worrisome given the amount of newcomers this season. Gaines is at his best when he has teammates who demand attention near the perimeter, which opens up the lane for him to drive and potentially get fouled. If one or more of his new teammates are unable to keep defenses honest, opponents will deny Gaines the lanes he needs to be most effective. If that happens, it'll be a long season for the Mastodons.

SOUTH DAKOTA

2012: 10-18 (5-13 Summit); Ineligible for Summit tournament
In-conference offense: 1.01 points per possession (8th)
In-conference defense: 1.11 points allowed per possession (9th)

South Dakota will have to reinvent its backcourt now that the double-threat of Charlie Westbrook and Louie Krogman has graduated. If the team's foreign trip is to serve as an indication, then expect to see Kansas State transfer **Juevol Myles** leading the charge from the perimeter. Junior center **Trevor Gruis** has the potential to be a game-changer for the Coyotes in the paint, but he has yet to assert himself night-in and night-out. With a bit of consistency, Gruis can give USD a reliable option inside. The rest of the roster is rounded out with newcomers or players who had limited roles last season. It's a good thing South Dakota took that foreign trip because they need improvement in just about every area.

KANSAS CITY

2012: 10-21 (4-14 Summit); Did not qualify for Summit tournament
In-conference offense: 1.00 points per possession (9th)
In-conference defense: 1.10 points allowed per possession (6th)

Kansas City has achieved roster stability over the past two seasons after enduring a rash of transfers in the early years of Matt Brown's tenure. While that's good for continuity's sake, the fact is that the group returning this season wasn't very good in 2011-12. The team had just two players with an offensive rating over 100, and the better of the two has since graduated. Brown's banking on the fact that his returners have improved in the offseason, chief among them junior **Trinity Hall** and sophomore **Estan Tyler**. Both players have performed at a high level at times, but over the course of the season they've been susceptible to committing lots of turnovers and poor shot selection. If the team as a whole is to improve, they'll have to start on the boards. The Kangaroos finished dead last in the league in both offensive and defensive rebounding percentage. If oft-injured center **Fred Chatmon** stays healthy, it'd be a step in the right direction for improving upon the Roos' rebounding woes.

OMAHA

2012: 11-18 as an Independent
Offense: 0.94 points per possession (No. 279 D-I)
Defense: 1.18 points allowed per possession (No. 343 D-I)

Omaha played a partial Division I schedule last year as it began its reclassification efforts, including seven games against Summit League teams. The Mavericks went 0-7, though they were at least competitive in games against the league's worst teams like Kansas City, Fort Wayne, and South Dakota. Expect Omaha to again be competitive against the bottom half of the league, while picking up one or two wins along the way. Transition is never easy, particularly for a squad losing its best player to graduation.

Sun Belt

BY NIC REINER

True to form, the Sun Belt will be doing something unconventional this year. In the year before morphing back into a 12-team conference, the 11 current Sun Belt teams will play a 20-game conference schedule. Each team will play a home-and-home with every other conference team. In addition to being the most egalitarian way to decide a champion, it will also make for a fun transitional year. Because the preseason will be shorter, conference play will start earlier and teams will shift into gear more quickly. Each team will see every other team's fans and travel to every arena in the conference. The new schedule has been the talk of the conference among coaches and media thus far. (To be fair, the Sun Belt is not the only conference to have adopted a 20-game schedule. The Atlantic Sun and Southern Conference have done this in recent years and the Big Sky will also do it this year.)

The 20-game schedule, obviously, is a harbinger of things to come because after the blitz the teams will endure this conference season, the dust will settle. North Texas and Florida Atlantic will leave for Conference USA in 2013. In will come Georgia State, UT-Arlington, and Texas State and the conference again will split seamlessly into East and West, with a line down the middle of Mississippi. When realignment ends, the calm the schools feel will be different from the unsteadiness they've felt over the past couple years.

Last year, the Sun Belt was the strongest it had been collectively since 2008 (when it sent both Western Kentucky and South Alabama to the tournament), largely because of how well Middle Tennessee and Denver performed. Knowing that, it's partly disappointing that a conference capable of sending a 12 or 13 seed to the NCAA tournament ended up represented by Western Kentucky, who went 7-9 in-conference, earned a spot on the 16 line, and was shipped to the First Four. It's no knock against the Hilltoppers—they won a play-in game in dramatic fashion and further solidified their brand as a worthy basketball school. Still, we were left wondering what would have happened if a 3, 4 or 5 seed had drawn Middle Tennessee or Denver.

Expect a two-horse race in this year's Sun Belt. Both North Texas and Middle Tennessee have the firepower to take control of the conference. The Mean Green have a gem of a player in Tony Mitchell and the Blue Raiders are coming off a year in which they set all kinds of records. The games in both Denton and Murfreesboro should be some of the year's best and will pit two programs in different places against each other. North Texas has tasted postseason success, having been to two NCAA tournaments in the past six years. They also went to the last two Sun Belt conference championship games, losing both. Middle Tennessee has had a strong program over the past decade but has been unable to fully get over the hump. The team hasn't been to the NCAA tournament since the late 1980s.

Outside of those two, it's genuinely difficult to predict what will happen. If South Alabama's defense improves, the Jaguars could ascend, because Sun Belt player of the year candidate Augustine Rubit has the ability to change a game by himself. Western Kentucky will be improved and could make noise in the conference outside of getting hot at the right time. The Arkansas schools and Florida Atlantic lost pieces but have shown they can compete the past couple years. Louisiana-Lafayette likely won't surprise anybody this year, while Lousiana-Monroe, Troy, and FIU are basically either rebuilding or in shambles.

Hot Springs, Arkansas is always the place to be during the second week of March. The Sun Belt's conference tournament usually makes for great theater and the conference's rich history comes alive in that space. Let's hope the slugfest that is the 20-game conference season sets up an excellent stage for Hot Springs. Whoever wins there will have played upwards of 23 conference games and, with the singular focus required to plow through a long slate, that team should be ready to win a game at the Big Dance.

Teams listed in Nic's predicted order of finish.

NORTH TEXAS

2012: 18-14 (9-7 Sun Belt); Lost to Western Kentucky 74-70, Sun Belt championship game
In-conference offense: 0.99 points per possession (6th)
In-conference defense: 0.92 points allowed per possession (2nd)

North Texas reached its second straight Sun Belt championship game, falling to Western Kentucky after losing a big lead late in the second half. The reason the Mean Green will reestablish themselves in the conference's upper echelon this year is the continued emergence of 6-8 sophomore **Tony Mitchell**. North Texas has a star on its hands. Mitchell was named Sun Belt freshman of the year, and was the only freshman named first team All-Sun Belt. Playing in UNT's last 23 games, Mitchell was the most efficient high-usage player in the Sun Belt last year; his 112 offensive rating was a function of shooting 61 percent from the field, sinking 74 percent of his 115 free throw attempts and rebounding nearly 30 percent of opponent misses. On defense he finished in the top 15 nationally in block percentage. At the time Mitchell stepped on the floor, the Mean Green was ranked No. 266 nationally on offense; by season's end, they were 159. Mitchell's ascendance is being entrusted to new head coach Tony Benford after long-time head man Johnny Jones left for LSU. Benford has last year's full starting rotation returning. Sophomore guard **Chris Jones** assisted on over 30 percent of Mean Green buckets, and is a threat to record a steal at any time. Junior guard **Alzee Williams** and senior guard **Brandan Walton** both posted above-100 offensive ratings and were among national leaders in taking care of the ball. Senior forward **Justin Patton** led Grambling two seasons ago in scoring but essentially did so because of how much he used the ball. The Mean Green will win at least 20 games, and Mitchell and company should take on Middle Tennessee for the conference crown.

MIDDLE TENNESSEE

2012: 27-7 (14-2 Sun Belt), Lost to Minnesota 78-72, NIT quarterfinals
In-conference offense: 1.04 points per possession (2nd)
In-conference defense: 0.89 points allowed per possession (1st)

Middle Tennessee's historic year significantly raised expectations in Murfreesboro. The 27 wins were the most in a single season for the program. In the Kermit Davis era, Middle Tennessee has now finished with a winning conference record in eight of ten seasons but has not been able to translate that into a single NCAA tournament appearance. (The Blue Raiders haven't been to the Big Dance since 1989.) Now four senior starters return, and they all posted offensive ratings higher than 100 last season. Davis may ask 6-8 **JT Sulton** to step into a larger role in the paint. If so the coach can point to guard **Marcos Knight**, who used 25 percent of the Raiders' possessions, shot well, assisted on one out of every five Blue Raider buckets, and kept the turnover rate low. Guard **Raymond Cintron** finished with a blisteringly high true shooting percentage (67) and must remain efficient in the expanded role he'll likely see this year. Guard **Bruce Massey** is a great defender and notched one of the highest steal rates in the country while distributing the ball at a healthy 26 percent clip. Junior **Shawn Jones**, the least experienced member of the rotation, will supplement Sulton at the other big man spot. Middle Tennessee's defense overall was the best in the Sun Belt for the second straight year, near the top in every defensive category, and shows no signs of dropping off. If the success of last year's squad catapulted Middle Tennessee to the cusp of national relevance, then this Blue Raiders squad must finish the job and make the NCAA tournament for the first time in 24 years.

SOUTH ALABAMA

2012: 17-12 (8-8 Sun Belt); Lost to Denver 61-50, Sun Belt quarterfinals
In-conference offense: 0.99 points per possession (7th)
In-conference defense: 1.04 points allowed per possession (9th)

Once again, 6-6 junior **Augustine Rubit** will be the go-to guy for coach Ronnie Arrow. The first team All-Sun Belt selection was the conference's third best offensive rebounder and was best in the conference at combining a high free throw rate (54) with a high free throw percentage (71). His usage and shot percentage rates increased noticeably from his freshman year yet his offensive prowess remained constant. The four other starters on last year's South Alabama team come back, too. **Freddie Goldstein** was on the floor as much as Rubit last year, and the 5-10 senior is a solid three-point shooting threat. Sophomore **Mychal Ammons** had a solid college debut, started for most of the year, and finished with a 96 offensive rating as the third-most used player on the squad.

Before junior **Xavier Roberson** went down in early January (and earned a medical redshirt), he had won a starting spot on the strength of all-around excellent shooting and recorded an offensive rating of 112. **Javier Carter** is the Sun Belt's best shot blocker and was just outside the top ten nationally last year at a listed height of just 6-6. Senior guard **Trey Anderson** is the team's main distributor but he also turns the ball over nearly 40 percent of the time. The defense was not particularly stalwart last year but if it can ascend to the middle of the pack in conference defensive efficiency, South Alabama will be in good shape. Expectations are growing in Mobile because of the returning talent and the hope that Rubit will build on an already impressive college career.

WESTERN KENTUCKY

2012: 16-19 (7-9 Sun Belt); Lost to Kentucky 81-66, NCAA round of 64
In-conference offense: 0.99 points per possession (8th)
In-conference defense: 1.01 points allowed per possession (7th)

Western beat Mississippi Valley State 59-58 in front of President Obama at the First Four, a game in which the Hilltoppers trailed 53-37 with five minutes to go. New coach Ray Harper is nothing if not adept at picking his moment. This will be Harper's first full year at the helm, as Ken McDonald was let go mid-season after a disappointing 5-11 start. WKU returns four starters, though highly touted guard Derrick Gordon is gone after one year. His absence will force other Hilltoppers to step up. Sophomore forward **George Fant** will become a bigger leader offensively. Posting an even 100 offensive rating in 2011-12, he showed even greater potential when his late-season excellence led to him being named the Sun Belt tournament most outstanding player. Senior guard **Jamal Crook** has a high career assist rate but hasn't proven to be very efficient in other areas. The other key guard, 6-3 sophomore **T.J. Price**, will be asked to increase his total usage and shot percentage this year. And while his season totals don't reflect it, 6-11 big man **Teeng Akol** played a larger role later in the season and will be given more opportunities to do work inside. Lastly, 6-0 sophomore **Kevin Kaspar** is WKU's best all around shooter outside of Fant. Those on The Hill probably shouldn't expect another tournament team but, with a driven Fant at the helm, WKU can finish in the top third of the conference.

ARKANSAS LITTLE ROCK

2012: 15-16 (12-4 Sun Belt); Lost to Western Kentucky 68-63, Sun Belt quarterfinals
In-conference offense: 1.00 points per possession (5th)
In-conference defense: 0.94 points allowed per possession (3rd)

The nice thing about efficiency measurements is that we can chart improvement in a more comprehensive way than through pure wins and losses. Arkansas Little Rock moved forward all of last year, beginning the season ranked as No. 260 nationally in efficiency and finishing No. 177. Nevertheless, even UALR's 12-4 sparkling in-conference record is a little deceiving. Steve Shields' team was at best the third or fourth most efficient team in the Sun Belt last season. In 2012-13, three starters come back. Two 6-10 forwards, junior **Will Neighbour** and sophomore **Michael Javes,** command higher expectations. Javes blocked an obscene 10 percent of opponent's two-point attempts. Neighbour shoots better from three-point land than he does from two but playing with a torn labrum late in the season lowered what probably would have been an above-100 offensive rating. Sophomore **Ben Dillard** is a shooter with opportunity for growth within the offense. Steve Shields is excited about 6-5 swingman **Leroy Isler**'s ability to defend the perimeter. On offense, the Trojans were a team of four-factor extremes. UALR was nearly the worst in conference effective FG percentage and offensive rebounding, but gave away the ball the least and got to the line over 40 percent of the time. It's hard to imagine Shields' team stays at the top of the conference again and it's likely they slip closer to the middle of the pack this year.

ARKANSAS STATE

2012: 14-20 (6-10 Sun Belt); Lost to North Texas 76-72, Sun Belt semifinals
In-conference offense: 1.02 points per possession (3rd)
In-conference defense: 1.04 points allowed per possession (10th)

Last season, ASU coach John Brady used his bench only 20 percent of the time, more than only 12 coaches in all of D-I. The upside to that now is that four members of his five-man rotation return. Unfortunately, the most efficient player, Malcolm Kirkland, was the one that departed. But senior guard **Trey Finn**, he of the whopping 127.9 offensive rating, returns. Finn shoots from all over and gets to the line but plays in a limited role, never registering more than 17 percent usage and 19 percent of shots taken in his three years on the team. The other three returning contributors were not particularly effective but are key to the team's success. **Marcus Hooten**, a 6-4 senior, will be the leader. He shoots the most and turns the ball over the least among ASU's high-usage guys. If Hooten can improve his accuracy, the Red Wolves will improve. Junior guard **Ed Townsel** led the team in assists and steals but his high turnover rate and poor shooting rendered him relatively inefficient on offense. The final piece, 6-7 senior **Brandon Peterson**, played the most minutes for Arkansas State last year. He didn't shoot much but rebounded very well and blocked shots. The team as a whole didn't foul last year but teams shot fantastically from three against them, a fact that Ken Pomeroy has suggested is largely defense-independent. If that number drops, the defense will improve because it was the 53 effective FG percentage allowed that killed them.

FLORIDA ATLANTIC

2012: 11-19 (7-9 Sun Belt); Lost to Arkansas State 70-55, Sun Belt first round
In-conference offense: 0.99 points per possession (10th)
In-conference defense: 1.00 points allowed per possession (6th)

The Florida Atlantic offense will run through senior guard **Greg Gantt**. Gantt posted a 111 offensive rating on 24 percent of possessions, second only to Sun Belt player of the year favorite Tony Mitchell. In addition to recording an effective FG percentage of 53 on the 31 percent of shots he took during his time on the floor, Gantt turned the ball over an impressively low 10 percent of the time. Though Gantt will likely prove to be one of the best players in the Sun Belt, nobody else returns for Mike Jarvis. Junior **Pablo Bertone** will be called in to offer support at the guard. Senior forward **Jordan McCoy** is the team's best rebounder when on the floor. Overall six of 13 players this year will be freshmen and are expected to compete for playing time. Incoming 5-10 guard **Stefan Moody** was one of just 40 high school basketball players named to the Parade All-American team, a first for the Owls. Also flashing his resume is 6-8 **Chris Bryant**, the Florida 3A state player of the year and someone Jarvis thinks can potentially play multiple positions. Combo guard **Cavon Baker** brings versatility to the backcourt, 6-8 forward **Javier Lacunza** is an intriguing prospect from Spain, and 6-4 **Jackson Trapp** should be a solid shooter for the Owls. If Gantt gets any help from the newcomers, Florida Atlantic could approach .500 again.

LOUISIANA LAFAYETTE

2012: 16-16 (10-6 Sun Belt); Lost to Rice 68-63, CIT first round
In-conference offense: 0.94 points per possession (11th)
In-conference defense: 0.94 points allowed per possession (4th)

The Ragin' Cajuns enter their centennial season having sustained significant roster losses. Their two most efficient offensive players are gone and they keep only three players who've played meaningful minutes. One is sophomore guard **Elfrid Payton**, who turns the ball over more than he assists. If he limits the turnovers, the Cajun offense will improve. Senior guard **Alan-Michael Thompson** is poised to take on a bigger role in the offense; though he was on the floor only 25 percent of the time he took 28 percent of shots when he used the ball. **Bryant Mbamalu**, a junior guard, can shoot accurately from the outside, and 6-9 forward **Shawn Long**, a transfer from Mississippi State, should contribute down low. In the past two years, the Cajuns bowed out early in the Sun Belt conference tournament. This year, if there aren't marked improvements from Bob Marlin's team offensively, it seems like the rest of the Sun Belt will pass them by. It would be surprising if they finish near the top of the conference for a third consecutive year.

TROY

2012: 10-18 (5-11 Sun Belt); Lost to South Alabama 87-81, Sun Belt first round
In-conference offense: 0.99 points per possession (9th)
In-conference defense: 1.09 points allowed per possession (11th)

Troy basketball will be in a new home for the first time in 50 years: pristine Trojan Arena, now complete, holds 5,200 seats for basketball games. The Trojan faithful hope the sense of newness also leads to success for the basketball squad. Last year, Troy had a ghastly defense, allowing conference opponents to put up 1.09 points per trip. Only three times in conference play did Don Maestri's squad hold opponents to less than a point per possession. To exacerbate matters, Maestri returns only four players who logged meaningful minutes. The Trojans lost two of their top three scorers in Will Weathers and Alan Jones. Senior guard **Justin Wright** and junior guard **R.J. Scott** will now lead the way. Wright posted the highest offensive rating on the team while recording usage and shot rates above 21. Scott handled and shot the ball more than anybody on the floor last year but was considerably less efficient as well. **Emil Jones** posted a 107 offensive rating in a shooting role and when 6-6 **Ray Chambers** was on the floor, he grabbed offensive boards at a 14 percent clip, best in the Sun Belt. Last year, Troy was the second-worst team in the league by a comfortable margin and, though there will be a fair amount of starting over, things are unlikely to be as pretty as the new arena they'll be playing in.

FIU

2012: 8-21 (5-11 Sun Belt); Lost to Western Kentucky 67-63, Sun Belt first round
In-conference offense: 1.00 points per possession (4th)
In-conference defense: 1.02 points allowed per possession (8th)

Since joining the Sun Belt 15 years ago, FIU has had one winning season, a 16-14 campaign in 1999-2000. Since then, the team hasn't even approached .500. Isiah Thomas is gone, unable to propel the program forward and so another basketball name, Richard Pitino, inherits a team accustomed to losing. Unfortunately, things don't look like they'll get better soon. The two players with the highest offensive ratings graduated and the other three starters departed for various reasons. The school has become a transfer carousel this offseason, though most of the new arrivals aren't eligible until 2013-14. Senior guard **Gaby Belardo** had high usage and shot percentage rates last year at Canisius but only posted an offensive rating of 89, down from 92 the year before. He's not a game-changer but he'll handle the ball and lead the offense. Freshman **Jerome Frink** is the player with the most accolades coming out of St. Anthony's High School in New Jersey, and junior college transfer junior **Malik Smith** will shoot from the outside immediately. New seven-footer **Ivan Jurkovic** and returning 6-11 center **Joey De La Rosa** give the team big bodies inside, but it's a lot to expect for either of them to excel consistently. Freshman **Dee Lewis**, a combo guard from Ocala, Florida, has the potential to make an impact on the perimeter, and first-year forward **Tymell Murphy** is a slasher. Nothing is expected of Richard Pitino in his first year with the Panthers. This season will be more of an assessment for how to proceed going forward.

LOUISIANA MONROE

2012: 3-26 (2-14 Sun Belt); Did not qualify for Sun Belt tournament
In-conference offense: 0.91 points per possession (12th)
In-conference defense: 1.11 points allowed per possession (12th)

Last season Louisiana Monroe was without question the worst Sun Belt team on both ends of the floor. The Warhawks lost all 13 games they played at home and even dropped a game to Harding, a D-II team. Their top two contributors, Fred Brown and Hugh Mingo graduated and their best rebounder, Steven McClellan, transferred. The good news is Keith Richard used his bench 40 percent of the time, so now he has five returning players that logged between 42 percent and 64 percent of ULM's minutes. Junior guard **Charles Winborne** appears to be the guy who's most likely to break out and lead the team offensively. In his sophomore year, he posted an offensive rating of 108, stemming from excellent shooting and a low turnover rate. Fellow junior guard **Marcelis Hansberry** is the other likely candidate to step up, as he was used second-most among returners and posted a solid assist rate. Three-point shooter **Trent Mackey** is in a position to contribute more on the wings. Richard has high hopes for **Jayon James**, a 6-6 junior college transfer who spent a season at Iona as a freshman. Richard's first two years have been tough ones and his third year with the Warhawks doesn't look to be any better. Clawing their way out of the Sun Belt cellar will be an accomplishment.

SWAC

BY JEFF HALEY

With 5:06 left in the game, Cor-J Cox scored on a layup to give Mississippi Valley State a 16-point lead over Western Kentucky in the NCAA tournament First Four. The Delta Devils had dominated the Southwestern Athletic Conference, going 17-1 during the regular season, and were now on the verge of winning their first NCAA tournament game ever. In the first 35 minutes of the game, WKU scored only 37 points. Overcoming a 16-point lead in five minutes seemed impossible.

Things that seem impossible often are not. Over the final five minutes, the Hilltoppers outscored MVSU 22-5. When the final buzzer sounded, the score was 59-58. Western Kentucky advanced, and the Delta Devils headed home.

Coming off of a high of being minutes away from an NCAA tournament win, the future looks difficult for Mississippi Valley State. Conference player of the year Paul Crosby and all-conference players Cor-J Cox (first team) and Terrence Joyner (second team) have used up their eligibility and departed. Head coach Sean Woods left during the offseason to coach at Moorehead State. Perhaps worst of all, the NCAA hit MVSU with a postseason ban for a low APR score, making the Delta Devils ineligible to play in this season's SWAC tournament. After spending the last several seasons building a conference champion, Mississippi Valley State is now starting from scratch.

This is how it works in the SWAC, at the very fringes of Division I. Junior college transfers and local kids play for coaches starting their careers or starting over. The threat of a postseason ban due to low APR scores always looms. Last season Grambling State and Southern were ineligible for postseason play. This season, Mississippi Valley State and Arkansas-Pine Bluff will be at home during the conference tournament.

In the SWAC, most teams start off the season playing on the road, and serving as cannon fodder for better D-I programs. Collecting guaranteed money in exchange for getting blown out isn't much fun, but it pays the bills. For one example of what a non-conference schedule looks like in the SWAC, take a look Alabama A&M. This season, the Hornets will play at Iowa State, Jacksonville State, Evansville, Mercer, Vanderbilt, Arkansas, and Mississippi State. Of Alabama A&M's four scheduled non-conference home games, only two are against other D-I programs. And this season's schedule is an improvement—last year the Hornets didn't play a single non-conference home game against a D-I school.

With the brutal non-conference schedule out of the way, the teams of the SWAC can get down to the business of playing each other. A defining characteristic of SWAC basketball is that teams have a difficult time scoring. Given the placement of this chapter in this book, you have by now paged through profiles of hundreds of teams that averaged over a point per possession during conference play last season. In the SWAC last year, only one team averaged more than one point per possession: Mississippi Valley State. In each of the last three seasons, the SWAC has averaged fewer points per trip than any other conference in D-I. Over this three-season period, SWAC games featured the lowest effective field goal percentage and the highest turnover rate.

Poor shooting plays a central role in the low offensive output of SWAC teams. Last season, the conference ranked 30th (out of 32) in three-point field goal percentage, last in two-point percentage, and last in free throw accuracy. The average SWAC player makes just under 64 percent of his free throws. And there were a lot of chances to shoot freebies—the free throw rate was higher than in any other conference.

That being said, there are players who can hit a shot in the SWAC. Omar Strong of Texas Southern is one example of a player who can shoot. The tiny guard attempted three fourths of his shots from three-point range last season, and made 39 percent of his those attempts. But Strong is a rare case in the conference.

As turbulent as things are in the SWAC, there aren't traditional powers. The standings are rather different every season. This season, Texas Southern appears to be the favorite. After that, it is anyone's guess.

Teams listed in Jeff's predicted order of finish.

TEXAS SOUTHERN

2012: 15-18 (12-6 SWAC); Lost to Mississippi Valley St. 71-69, SWAC championship game
In-conference offense: 0.99 points per possession (2nd)
In-conference defense: 0.85 points allowed per possession (1st)

It takes a strange set of circumstances for a coach who once had his team playing in the NCAA title game to land in the SWAC. Here are those circumstances: Coming off a second-place finish and a trip to the SWAC championship game, head coach Tony Harvey resigned suddenly in July. Finding a new head coach in the middle of the summer is difficult, as most potential candidates are off the market. Texas Southern announced it would not make a permanent hire until after the 2012-13 season. In August, Mike Davis—former head coach of Indiana and UAB—was named interim coach of the Tigers. Davis inherits what last season was the second-best team in the SWAC, and this season Texas Southern returns many of its key players. The primary sharpshooter is back; at 5-9, second team all-conference guard **Omar Strong** was fourth in the SWAC in three-point accuracy. The weak link on offense was the turnovers. **Dexter Ellington** and **Madarious Gibbs** split time last season as the primary ball handler, and both had horrendous turnover rates. With the exception of his last season at UAB, Davis' teams have historically done fairly well protecting the ball, so some improvement here is likely. The defense will again be anchored by second team all-conference forward **Fred Sturdivant**. Sturdivant was also an important part of the Tiger offense last season, and was active on the glass. There are some holes to fill along the front line due to player departures, so it is not clear that the interior defense will be as good this season as it was last year. Still, Texas Southern looks to be the most talented team in the conference, by far.

PRAIRIE VIEW A&M

2012: 14-18 (10-8 SWAC); Lost to Alcorn State 103-79, SWAC first round
In-conference offense: 0.90 points per possession (9th)
In-conference defense: 0.91 points allowed per possession (3rd)

Although Prairie View struggled on offense, they were one of the better defensive teams in the conference. But those struggles were pronounced. The Panthers were near the bottom of the SWAC on offense. Byron Rimm's team had a hard time putting the ball in the hole, particularly from the free throw line, where they made 54 percent of their attempts. For good or ill, guards **Jourdan DeMuynck** and **Louis Munks** dominated the offense. DeMuynck, Munks, and **Ryan Gesiakowski** give the Panthers three players who can shoot competently from the perimeter. For an offense that only made 41 percent of its twos, more shots from three-point range would probably help. Rimm's history is not that of a coach who is opposed to shooting the three, at least compared with the typical standards of the SWAC, but last year's team only attempted 27 percent of its field goal attempts from three-point range. Several junior college transfers will join **Jules Montgomery** and **Demondre Chapman** inside. Chapman was the only Panther with an effective field goal percentage above 50 last season, but he really struggles at the line. A modest improvement on offense this season would be enough to move coach Rimm's team up the SWAC standings.

ALABAMA A&M

2012: 7-21 (5-13 SWAC); Lost to Texas Southern 75-62, SWAC quarterfinals
In-conference offense: 0.93 points per possession (5th)
In-conference defense: 0.98 points allowed per possession (8th)

Second-year coach Willie Hayes loses leading scorer Casey Cantey, but Cantey was the lone senior on the team last season. Look for **Jeremy Crutcher** and **Brandon Ellis** to let the shots fly on what should be one of the better three-point shooting teams in the conference. On offense, the Panthers' only real problem last season was turnovers (many of these were caused by Cantey). Crutcher was the most turnover-prone of the returning players. On the interior, **Demarquelle Tabb** is good at both ends of the floor. Despite a listed height of 6-5, he's a good shot blocker, and a menace on the offensive glass. Another effective shot blocker is 6-10 **Jerome Hunter**, yet, despite having these two guys available, the Bulldogs' defense against two-point attempts ranked near the bottom of the league. Coach Hayes will have to figure out what happened to what had been a pretty good defense in 2011. Part of the problem was likely foul trouble. Tabb fouled out of two games, and was in foul trouble frequently. Crutcher also struggled at times with fouls, as did Hunter in more limited minutes. If Hayes' team can tighten up a bit on the interior, and not put opponents on the foul line as much, Alabama A&M can expect to see a defensive resurgence.

SOUTHERN

2012: 17-14 (13-5 SWAC); Ineligible for post-season play
In-conference offense: 0.94 points per possession (4th)
In-conference defense: 0.93 points allowed per possession (5th)

Southern was ineligible for the 2012 SWAC tournament, but had a very good regular season, finishing second in the conference. Roman Banks loses his best player from last season, Quinton Doggett, the Jaguars' best shot blocker, rebounder, and a good scorer inside. It is a tough loss for a team that really struggled with rebounding, even with Doggett. Southern's strength will be in the backcourt. **Jameel Grace** is a solid lead guard, one who's a good playmaker and gets to the line. Best of all his turnover rate is not horrendous, given what's typical in the SWAC. **Derick Beltran** is the likely primary option on offense for Banks. The 6-4 senior is another player who knows his way to the line, and is a very good shooter once he gets there. Still, the biggest question for the Jags will be on the interior. Banks doesn't know if he'll have the services of 6-9 senior **Madut Bol** (son of former NBA star Manute Bol), who was sidelined "indefinitely" with a shoulder injury in the preseason.

JACKSON STATE

2012: 7-24 (5-13 SWAC); Lost to Mississippi Valley State 63-60, SWAC quarterfinals
In-conference offense: 0.90 points per possession (10th)
In-conference defense: 0.96 points allowed per possession (7th)

Jackson State suffered through a tough, injury-plagued 2011-12. The Tigers weren't very good on either offense or defense, so what hope does Tevester Anderson have this season? One positive is that Anderson has last season's SWAC freshman of the year, **Kelsey Howard**. The Vicksburg product served notice he could score when he dropped 27 points in a surprising win over SMU prior to the start of the conference season. After the Tigers' best scorer Jenirro Bush tore his ACL in January, Anderson put his offense in the hands of the 6-3 Howard, and the freshman finished the SWAC season with a flurry of points. Outside of Howard's scoring, one of the few strengths Jackson State could claim was their ability to avoid turnovers. Howard was good at protecting the basketball, as was fellow guard **Christian Williams**, at least until his season was ended with a foot injury. Another relative strength of the Tigers this season could be rebounding, and 6-5 sophomore **Derrell Taylor** is a big reason why. Maybe all the injuries last season masked what would have been a good team if they had stayed healthy.

ALCORN STATE

2012: 9-22 (6-12 SWAC); Lost to Texas Southern 60-55, SWAC semifinals
In-conference offense: 0.91 points per possession (8th)
In-conference defense: 0.96 points allowed per possession (6th)

Luther Riley starts his second season as the head coach at Alcorn State, where his predecessor, Larry Smith, once played one of the most extreme up-tempo styles in all of D-I. Riley slowed things down, and the result was a modest improvement on both offense and defense, although the Braves still have a long way to go to catch up with the better teams in the conference. Fortunately, in the topsy-turvy SWAC, it doesn't always take very long to catch up. Alcorn State returns a good outside shooter in **Twann Oakley**, as well as a couple of big men Riley's brought in from junior college, 7-0 **Josh Nicholas** and 6-10 **Stephane Raquil**. This season's recruiting class also includes several freshmen who were prolific scorers in high school. **Clint Nwosuh** out of Houston could push for playing time.

ALABAMA STATE

2012: 12-19 (9-9 SWAC); Lost to Arkansas Pine Bluff 60-56 (OT), SWAC quarterfinals
In-conference offense: 0.93 points per possession (6th)
In-conference defense: 0.92 points allowed per possession (4th)

Alabama State's best returning player is 6-7 senior **Phillip Crawford**, who's notably effective as a scorer by SWAC standards. Crawford is also a very good offensive rebounder, which was one of the strengths of the Hornets' offense last season. Lewis Jackson also returns **Ryan Watts**, but the 6-0 senior will be slowed early in the season as he recovers from a groin injury.. With the departure of so many of the most important offensive players from last season, Jackson's team will have to play well on defense to remain competitive. This was the fourth-best D in the SWAC last season, and the Hornets were good across the board. Jackson's team was particularly good at forcing turnovers and securing rebounds. Steals that lead to transition will give Alabama State one way to score a few points, but the rest of the offense could be a struggle.

GRAMBLING STATE

2012: 4-24 (4-14 SWAC); Not eligible for post-season play
In-conference offense: 0.92 points per possession (7th)
In-conference defense: 1.04 points allowed per possession (10th)

Last season, Grambling State was the worst team in all of college basketball according to the Pomeroy ratings. After the season, coach Bobby Washington was reassigned and replaced by Joseph Price, a career assistant with stops at Morehead State, Ball State, IUPUI, and Lamar. The Tigers' offense relied very heavily last year on St. John's transfer Quincy Roberts, who took 38 percent of the team's shots while on the floor. Perhaps the best player in the conference, Roberts declared for the NBA draft last spring (and went undrafted). That would figure to make Price's job a little harder, but things are actually even worse. Peter Roberson, the Tiger's 7-0 center and second-best player, also declared for the NBA draft (and also went undrafted). That the worst team in D-I would actually have two underclassmen enter their names for the NBA draft is, well, strange. **Xavier Rogers** is the best returning player for Price, and the sophomore is a 29 percent three-point shooter. Joseph Price is in for a very long season.

ARKANSAS PINE BLUFF

2012: 11-22 (9-9 SWAC); Lost to Mississippi Valley State 71-64, SWAC semifinals
In-conference offense: 0.97 points per possession (3rd)
In-conference defense: 0.98 points allowed per possession (9th)

Arkansas Pine Bluff will not be allowed to participate in this season's SWAC tournament, due to a low APR score. Last season, the Golden Lions had one of the better offenses and one of the worst defenses in the conference. Both will be hurt by the loss of Savalace Townsend, who was a senior last season. This raises an interesting question. How did UAPB, a team that led the conference in shot blocking percentage and also had their point guard named conference defensive player of the year, end up having the second worst defense in the SWAC? Part of the answer to this question was opponents shooting 36 percent from three-point range. Another part of the answer was poor rebounding and a tendency to put opponents at the free throw line. The strength of Arkansas Pine Bluff is inside, with big men **Mitchell Anderson** and **Daniel Broughton**. Both are likely to be the primary offensive players for the Golden Lions, as well as the key anchors on defense. Guard **Lazabian Jackson** will be asked to take more responsibility with the loss of Townsend.

MISSISSIPPI VALLEY STATE

2012: 21-13 (17-1 SWAC); Lost to Western Kentucky 59-58, NCAA First Four
In-conference offense: 1.02 points per possession (1st)
In-conference defense: 0.87 points allowed per possession (2nd)

Mississippi Valley State dominated the SWAC last season, overwhelming opponents with an up-tempo offense, physical rebounding, tough defense, and a barrage of threes. Only a late-season loss to Arkansas Pine Bluff prevented the Delta Devils from finishing the conference season undefeated. This season won't be as much fun. MVSU will be sitting out the SWAC tournament, as they were one of this year's recipients of an APR postseason ban by the NCAA. Additionally, the core of last season's senior-heavy team is gone, as is coach Sean Woods. First-year head coach Chico Potts was an assistant on last season's team. Of the seven players who played significant minutes for the Delta Devils, not one returns. Brent Arrington, the lone underclassmen in the rotation from last season, transferred to Morehead State, following coach Woods. The only returning player on the roster is **Blake Ralling**, who averaged less than five minutes per game. In order to be able to field a team, Chico Potts has brought in eight junior college transfers. This incoming class of junior college players includes some size, with 7-0 **Montreal Holley** and 6-11 **Julius Francis**. This year will be an entirely different experience for Mississippi Valley State.

Author Bios

Joey Berlin is a freelance writer and a production editor at a publishing company in Kansas City. He previously spent three years at the Emporia Gazette, where he coaxed Tom Brokaw into a game of tabletop foosball (which Berlin won, 2-0). Before that, Joey worked as a sportswriter and copy editor at the Topeka Capital-Journal. He is a graduate of the University of Kansas, and writes about Kansas City-area and national sports, pop culture and anything else that feels word-worthy at his website, joeyberlin.com.

Drew Cannon is a graduate manager for Butler men's basketball, functioning as the team's de facto statistical analysis department. He graduated from Duke University in May with a degree in statistics and is currently pursuing his MBA at Butler. Drew's work has appeared on ESPN Insider and in the New York Times, and he continues to write for Basketball Prospectus and the KenPom.com blog. He worked under recruiting guru Dave Telep (now of ESPN) beginning in the summer of 2006, and ran the only statistically based NCAA-certified high school scouting service in the summer of 2012 until the impending conflict of interest forced its termination. (@DrewCannon1)

John Ezekowitz is a senior at Harvard where he is studying economics. He is co-president of the Harvard Sports Analysis Collective, a group devoted to the quantitative analysis of sports. John fell in love with the game while watching the Boston College teams led by Troy Bell, Jared Dudley, and Craig Smith. He is an avid golfer who spent one season on the Harvard varsity golf team. John now lives in Princeton, New Jersey, home of the strangest basketball arena in Division I and Hoagie Haven, the best sandwich shop on the East Coast. (@JohnEzekowitz)

Asher Fusco has now contributed to three editions of the College Basketball Prospectus. He covered Kansas basketball for two seasons—along with a smattering of other sports—as a correspondent at the Topeka Capital-Journal, and worked as a web producer and general assignment reporter at the Lawrence Journal-World before leaving the newspaper industry. A graduate of the University of Kansas and first-hand witness of Mario Chalmers' 2008 miracle shot, Asher now lives in New York City, where he works as a copywriter for a digital marketing agency. (@AsherFusco)

John Gasaway became a college basketball fan at the age of five when his parents took him to his first University of Illinois football game. He's written for Basketball Prospectus since the site's inception in 2007, and for ESPN since 2010, all of which constitutes a logical and productive use of his Ph.D. He lives with his wife and two sons in Bergen County, New Jersey. (@JohnGasaway)

Matt Giles is a reporter for New York Magazine and ESPN the Magazine, and contributes to ESPN's College Basketball Insider. He spent countless hours combing through microfiche as a co-author of the ESPN College Basketball Encyclopedia. As an undergrad at Saint Joseph's during the 2004 season, he took an overnight bus to Dayton, Ohio, only to watch the Hawks lose to Xavier in their initial Atlantic 10 tournament game and then promptly board the bus back home. He lives in New York City with his beautiful wife and dog. (@HudsonGiles)

Jeff Haley writes about basketball and Twitter for Burnt Orange Nation, a blog about Texas Longhorns athletics, where he defends Rick Barnes against all takers. He also operates the website Hoop-Math.com, which presents unusual college basketball statistics derived from play-by-play data. Jeff is a Texas alumnus, and received a Ph.D. in chemical engineering from the University of Minnesota. After kicking around as a postdoc in Toronto, he found a real job in research and development in the chemical industry. Jeff currently lives with his wife and two dogs in Cincinnati. (@jeffchaley)

Dan Hanner is a Ph.D. economist in Springfield, Virginia. This is his seventh season writing about college basketball, and his third season as the lead college basketball writer for RealGM.com. His work has appeared in ESPN the Magazine, and various preseason publications. (@DanHanner)

C.J. Moore covers Big 12 basketball and football as well as the Kansas City Chiefs as a blogger for CBSSports.com. He contributes to the Kansas City Star Magazine, Ink Magazine and anywhere else they'll let him write about hoops. You can also find his work at NeedISayMoore.com. Moore is a University of Kansas graduate with a quick crossover and appreciation for proper footwork. (Nick Collison is his hero.) (@cjmoore4)

Jeff Nusser is co-founder of CougCenter.com and author of CougarSportsWeekly.com. When he's not torturing himself by watching Washington State athletics and trying to find some creative way to write about them, he can be found either trying to fake his way through the day as an English teacher or hanging out with his beautiful wife, Sarah, and three charming boys. His 3-year-old, Trystian, is beating leukemia and is his hero. (@NussCoug)

Kevin Pelton has served as an author for Basketball Prospectus since the site's inception in October 2007. His NBA commentary has also appeared on ESPN Insider. Pelton spent four seasons as the beat writer for supersonics.com and has covered the WNBA's Seattle Storm for the team's official site, StormBasketball.com, since 2003. As a 5-9 Pierce Hornung clone, Pelton was unranked by all major scouting services coming out of Mt. Rainier High School. (@kpelton)

Ken Pomeroy has been charting college basketball's advanced statistics at KenPom.com since 2004 when he discovered the existence of the Internet. He lives in Salt Lake City and specializes in the analysis of teams in the western half of the Mountain Time zone. Ken doesn't have a real job anymore so if you have any work for him, let him know. Otherwise, he'll be spending the season advocating that defenses defend the three-point line harder and lamenting the absence of Rick Majerus. (@kenpomeroy)

Mike Portscheller is a freelance basketball writer with an engineering background. In 2008, inspired by the poor "Luck" displayed by his beloved University of Illinois, Mike co-formed Big Ten Geeks, a website tracking the tempo-free goings-on of the Big Ten. In 2009 the Geeks moved their operation to the Big Ten Network's website, where they continue to write and opine. Mike resides in Peoria, Illinois, with his lovely wife and young son. (@bigtengeeks and @mportsch)

Craig Powers is a resident of the great state of Vermont, where he is doing graduate work in statistics, a far cry from his bachelor's in history from Washington State University. His use of tempo-free stats to analyze the WSU basketball team as a managing editor of CougCenter piqued his interest in numbers, and now he is determined to turn that into a real-life job. The two years Craig spent in Nashville cultivated an affinity for mid-major basketball in the South, while growing up in Washington hop country beget his love of craft beer. Craig also gets his writing fix as a contributor to SB Nation and its regional sites. (@TheCraigPowers)

Josh Reed is one half of the blogging duo, Big Ten Geeks, which enters its fourth season at BTN.com this season. When he's not watching and writing about the basketball equivalent to powerwalking, Josh is practicing law in Chicago. He's like Jay Bilas, but shorter and with a much better hairline. He lives with his wife and son on the north side. (@bigtengeeks and @JoshReedBTG)

Nic Reiner began contributing to Basketball Prospectus in the summer of 2011 and has manned the Basketball Prospectus Twitter account since last November. He's been head researcher at KenPom.com since 2010 and counts the day he did reconnaissance work with Gawker's A.J. Daulerio last fall as one of the more educational journalistic experiences of his life. A recent graduate of Stanford University, Nic now works in a communications position at a school in Southern California. (@nicreiner)

Eddie Roach is a junior at Cal State Fullerton studying accounting. He began contributing to Basketball Prospectus this year. Eddie has been a hoops fanatic since he first shot a basketball in the second grade and firmly believes that Michael Jordan will forever remain untouched as the greatest player to ever play the game. Eddie is also a huge fan of the NFL and resides in Irvine, California. (@EddieRoachV)

Corey Schmidt has written for Basketball Prospectus for the last year and most recently ran a league-specific blog about Summit League hoops. He is a graduate of hoops-crazed schools both at the mid-major (Oakland) and high-major (Indiana) level. Corey resides in Cincinnati, where he is employed as a government professional. (@cjschmidt1)

John Templon lives in New York City and is the founder of Big Apple Buckets, which covers all the mid-majors around NYC. He has an undergraduate degree in physics and a masters in journalism from Northwestern. Thus he understands just how out of whack the probability of the Wildcats making the tournament is, compared to how much national reporters will wish for it. When he's not watching or writing about basketball, John works for a technology startup that generates stories from data. (@nybuckets)

Made in the USA
Charleston, SC
19 November 2012